Forex Forever

Forex Forever

The City of London and the Foreign Exchange Market Since 1850

Ranald C. Michie

OXFORD
UNIVERSITY PRESS

OXFORD
UNIVERSITY PRESS

Great Clarendon Street, Oxford, OX2 6DP,
United Kingdom

Oxford University Press is a department of the University of Oxford.
It furthers the University's objective of excellence in research, scholarship,
and education by publishing worldwide. Oxford is a registered trade mark of
Oxford University Press in the UK and in certain other countries

Published in the United States of America by Oxford University Press
198 Madison Avenue, New York, NY 10016, United States of America

British Library Cataloguing in Publication Data

Data available

Library of Congress Control Number: 2023951849

ISBN 9780198903697

DOI: 10.1093/oso/9780198903697.001.0001

Printed and bound in the UK by
Clays Ltd, Elcograf S.p.A.

*I dedicate this book to Francis Pritchard for the support
he has provided over the years*

Preface

I have approached the subject of the City of London and the foreign exchange market in the past. With hindsight, all of the results were flawed. What I had not recognized was the need for a mechanism that adjusted exchange rates on an instant and continuous basis if overall stability was to be maintained. Under the Gold Standard, this stability was attributed to the fixed price of gold in terms of national currencies, the free movement of that metal between countries, and the influence the amount in circulation had upon the money supply in individual countries. However, abundant evidence existed to prove that the movement and use of gold was insufficient to achieve that end. In response, I suggested that it was the movement of stocks and bonds between countries, and the links this had to the money market, that was primarily responsible for the stability of currencies under the Gold Standard. Important as were these global financial flows, I now realize that they were not the mechanism that underpinned the stability of exchange rates under the Gold Standard. That required a market in which currencies could be exchanged for each other quickly and constantly.[1] As no such market appeared to exist in London, where it would most logically be found, it was assumed that the movement of a range of assets, including gold, and the actions of the few central banks in existence, provided the stabilizing mechanism. I have now realized that such a market did exist and that I had already discovered it. It existed through the network of international banking connections centred on the City of London from the mid-nineteenth century onwards and the trading in internationally held stocks and bonds located in and around the London Stock Exchange before the First World War. Having realized that altered my entire approach to the study of the City of London and the foreign exchange market over the last 150 years. That included the years of currency turmoil between the two world wars, the era of fixed exchange rates under the post-war Bretton Woods Agreement, and the development of foreign exchange trading into the world's largest market since 1970. This book is the product of that altered approach.

Chapters 4–6 rely on material which has already appeared in my book *Banks, Exchanges, and Regulators* (OUP 2020). However, it has been reinterpreted to reflect the 2022 survey carried out by the Bank for International Settlements (BIS), the focus

---

[1] See R.C. Michie, 'The Myth of the Gold Standard: An Historian's Approach', *Revue Internationale d'Histoire de la Banque*, (1986), 32–3; R.C. Michie, 'The Performance of the Nineteenth-Century International Gold Standard', in W. Fischer, R.M. McInnis and J. Schneider (eds), 'The Emergence of a World Economy 1500–1914: Papers of the IX International Congress of Economic History', Stuttgart: 1986 (with J. Foreman-Peck); R.C. Michie, 'The Invisible Stabiliser: Asset Arbitrage and the International Monetary System Since 1700', *Financial History Review*, 15 (1998).

on the role played by the City of London, and in light of the analysis and conclusions reached in the earlier chapters of this book.

Making the existence and operation of an active foreign exchange market, involving both spot and forward transactions, central to any attempt to understand the workings of the global monetary system since the mid-nineteenth century provides many of the answers to the questions being asked about its stability and instability both in the past and the present, and a basis for its future direction. As Andrew Bailey, now Governor of the Bank of England, has said, 'I believe understanding financial history is important in thinking about the future of finance.'[2] This is my contribution to that understanding. More specifically, it addresses a lack of research into the practical working of the international financial system that another financial historian, Professor John Turner at Queen's University, Belfast, has identified. In his 2022 introduction to a symposium on the history of banking and currency, Professor John Turner stated that 'We need to know much more about the plumbing of the international financial system.'[3] This book, which is my swansong, is a contribution to making good the existing deficiency. It tries to answer the question of why the centre of the global foreign exchange market is London rather than New York despite the dominance of the US$ and the American economy since the end of the Second World War. As recently as April 2023, the Editorial Board of the *Financial Times* made the following statement, explaining why they considered that the threat to the US$'s dominant role in international finance was greatly exaggerated.

> Since the 1944 Bretton Woods Agreement installed the dollar as the de facto global currency, its dominance has been sustained by America's status as the world's largest economy and geopolitical powerhouse. Just under sixty per cent of official foreign exchange reserves are held in the currency. It is the currency of choice for international trade, accounting for more than four-fifths of trade finance and half of trade invoices. It also dominates foreign exchange and debt markets. ... The greenback's eminence is reinforced by its enormous liquidity, America's openness to trade and investment, and trust in its supporting institutions. ... Global economic activity is still dominated by the US and its allies, which makes it difficult to avoid the dollar.

They concluded, however, with the warning that 'Britain's pound sterling was the dominant currency once.'[4] What they failed to mention was that despite the demise of the UK£ and the eclipse of London by New York as the most important financial centre in the world, the foreign exchange market where the US$ was traded was in London. One reason for that omission is that the answer as to why that is the case has never been established.

[2] A. Bailey, 'The Challenges in Assessing Capital Requirements for Banks', Financial Policy Committee, 6 November 2012, 2.
[3] J.D. Turner, 'Introduction to the Symposium on Banking and Currency', *Economic History Review*, 75 (2022).
[4] Editorial Board, 'Threats to the Dollar's Dominance Are Overblown', *Financial Times*, 19 April 2023.

Contents

Introduction   1

1. Finding Forex, 1850–1914   8

2. Reinventing Forex, 1919–1939   94

3. Forex in Chains, 1945–1970   192

4. Forex Unbound, 1970–1992   226

5. Electronic Forex, 1992–2007   244

6. Forex Today, Post-2007   262

   Conclusion   285

Bibliography   290
Index   325

Introduction

Over the course of the twentieth century, trading foreign exchange emerged from the shadows to become the largest financial market in the world, measured by turnover. This position was confirmed by successive triennial surveys carried out by the Bank for International Settlements (BIS), beginning in 1992, with the latest being conducted in 2022. Between 1992 and 2022, foreign exchange turnover, on a net–gross basis, grew from a daily average of US$1.1 trillion to US$9.8 trillion.[1] The foreign exchange market was totally dominated by banks through trading with their own customers, dealing between each other, or internally matching sales and purchases. It was an over-the-counter market which made no use of a physical trading floor, did not rely on the institutional structure provided by an exchange, or depended upon the services of a clearing house. It also operated largely free from statutory regulation at a national or international level. By its very nature foreign exchange trading was a global market conducted in and between the world's banks, as it involved transactions in the currencies of different states. This placed it beyond the jurisdiction and control of any single government or central bank. It was no accident that it was the Basel-based Bank for International Settlements that took responsibility for collecting the turnover data for the foreign exchange market, for it acted as the coordinating body for the world's central banks.[2] This lack of a physical or institutional structure for the foreign exchange market, its transnational nature, and the absence of supervision or even oversight by national governments and central banks, meant that it has never received the recognition accorded to other financial markets, like stock, and commodity exchanges or the trading in the bonds and bills issued by national authorities.

This lack of recognition given to the foreign exchange market has pervaded the economics profession, whose interest in the working of the monetary system is either focused on the automatic functioning of the Gold Standard and the role of central banks and international agencies or the theoretical and technical aspects of trading which lent themselves to mathematical modelling.[3] Writing in 1962, Jerome Stein

---

[1] Bank for International Settlements, *Triennial Central Bank Survey of Foreign Exchange and Over-the-Counter Derivative Markets in 2022* (Basel: BIS, 2022). There were surveys before 1992, but they were not comprehensive.

[2] See A. Schrimpf and V. Sushko, 'Sizing Up Global Foreign Exchange Markets'; A. Schrimpf and V. Sushko, 'FX Trade Execution, Complex and Highly Fragmented'; M.D.D. Evans and D. Rime, 'Microstructure of Foreign Exchange Markets', *BIS Quarterly Review* (December 2019); H. Goodacre and E. Razak, 'The Foreign Exchange and Over-the-Counter Interest Rate Derivatives Market in the United Kingdom', *BEQB* (20 December 2019); Bank of England, *BIS Triennial Survey* (2022).

[3] For examples of the former, see M.D. Bordo, *Exchange Rate Regime Choice in Historical Perspective* (International Monetary Fund, 2003), and B. Eichengreen, A. Mehl and L. Chitu, *How Global Currencies*

Forex Forever. Ranald C. Michie, Oxford University Press. © Ranald C. Michie (2024).
DOI: 10.1093/oso/9780198903697.003.0001

considered that 'One of the most important and least understood markets is the foreign exchange market. ... Many economists and bankers do not fully understand the nature of the foreign exchange market.'[4] This view was echoed by Chrystal in 1984 when he stated that 'Foreign exchange markets ... are shrouded in mystery.'[5] This lack of interest from economists covers the last 150 years. In 1967, Glahe considered that 'Prior to the 1920s most economists were not concerned with the workings of the foreign exchange market and fewer still were ever aware of the existence of forward exchange.'[6] As foreign exchange grew in importance between the wars, it did attract some interest from economists but only to a limited degree. The expectation was that the Gold Standard would be restored, and so foreign exchange trading would wither and die, being no more than a temporary phenomenon. Brown's long and detailed two-volume work on the international monetary system before and after the First World War, which was published in 1940, largely ignored it.[7] The lack of serious study of the foreign exchange market continued after the Second World War, which was understandable given it hardly existed. That was not to change until the 1960s, when attention began to be turned to it, as it made a tentative reappearance at a time when the Bretton Woods System of fixed exchange rates was breaking down. Despite the growing interest, as the volume of trading expanded exponentially after 1973, it remained a marginal subject among economists.[8] When attempting in 2001 to assess the contribution of the financial system to economic growth and globalization, Rousseau and Sylla ignored the foreign exchange market in favour of the more obvious role attributed to banks and the stock market.[9]

This neglect of the foreign exchange market is surprising as it was an essential part of the global financial system. What explains the neglect is its nature, along with its lack of transparency. The trading of foreign exchange involves the use of one currency to buy another. This takes place through bilateral transactions between parties that were simultaneously buyers and sellers. No change in the ownership of an asset or a commodity, either immediately or at some time in the future, resulted. Instead, what was transferred was nothing more than money either by way of a swap arrangement, a sale and purchase with immediate completion, a forward transaction for a future date, or a combination of all three. Money has three properties as it acts as a unit of account, a store of value, and a means of exchange. All came into play in the foreign exchange market, the central function of which was to allow

Work: Past, Present, and Future (Princeton: Princeton University Press, 2018). For examples of the latter, see C. Osler, 'Market Microstructure and the Profitability of Currency Trading', *Annual Review of Financial Economics*, 4 (2012); N. Doskov and L. Swinkels, 'Empirical Evidence on the Currency Carry Trade, 1900–2012', *Journal of International Money and Finance*, 51 (2015).

[4] J.L. Stein, 'The Nature and Efficiency of the Foreign Exchange Market', *Princeton Studies in International Finance* (1962), 1.

[5] K.A. Chrystal, *A Guide to Foreign Exchange Markets* (Federal Reserve Bank of St Louis, 1984), 1.

[6] F.R. Glahe, 'An Empirical Study of the Foreign Exchange Market: Test of a Theory', *Princeton Studies in International Finance* (1967), 1.

[7] W.A. Brown, *The International Gold Standard Reinterpreted, 1914–1934* (New York: National Bureau of Economic Research, 1940), 2 vols.

[8] J.S. Frankel, G. Gianpaolo and A. Giovannini (eds), *The Microstructure of Foreign Exchange Markets* (Chicago: University of Chicago Press, 1996).

[9] P.L. Rousseau and R. Sylla, 'Financial Systems, Economic Growth and Globalisation', *NBER*, 2001.

banks to match assets and liabilities not only in terms of different currencies but also over time, across locations, and in terms of amount, either to generate a profit or to cover a risk they were exposed to. The outcome of these transactions was the price at which this was done, and it is this which produced the headline rate at which one currency was exchanged for another. With the multiple uses of money, and the involvement of numerous participants at all levels and from different countries and for different purposes, the market was simultaneously decentralized but interconnected, and fragmented and complex but also deep and broad. Whether to generate a profit or hedge a risk, activity in the market thrived on speed and liquidity, as each transaction was linked to what had already happened and led to the next one. The faster the transaction could be completed, the more liquid the market was, and the wider the international connections, the greater was the volume and value of foreign exchange trading. Hence, the explosive growth in turnover from the 1970s onwards as national exchange controls were dismantled and an electronic revolution transformed international communications and the ability to trade financial instruments.[10] However, this was not the first time that the market was transformed in such a way.

One consequence of the absence of the market from the discussion of the working of the global monetary system was the identification of a trilemma in the choice of regime.[11] Most closely associated with the trilemma was Robert Triffin. In his 1964 book on the evolution of the international monetary system, there is no recognition that a functioning foreign exchange market existed before the First World War or acceptance that it had any contribution to make to the restoration of currency stability that followed the collapse of the Gold Standard, either between the wars or after 1945.[12] The trilemma postulates that it is impossible to achieve more than two out of three objectives. In monetary history, the three objectives are a fixed rate of exchange, free movement of capital, and an autonomous monetary policy. Under the Gold Standard the first two were achieved at the expense of the last. Under the Bretton Woods system the first and the third were achieved but not the second. These two periods were seen as golden ages for the global monetary system because of the exchange rate stability they delivered. Since 1973 fixed exchange rates have been sacrificed. However, since then exchange rates have been relatively stable under normal circumstances. Even under the Gold Standard and the Bretton Woods System exchange rates fluctuated and adjustments had to be made. This suggests that there are flaws in the monetary trilemma and that it is possible to have all three at the same time, if it is accepted that none are achieved in their entirety. Exchange rates are stable but

[10] For a succinct account of the foreign exchange market, see A. Nordstrom, *Understanding the Foreign Exchange Market* (Riksbank, 2022). For an explanation of trading, see G.W. Hoffman, *Futures Trading Upon Organized Commodity Markets in the United States* (Philadelphia: 1932), 401, 417, 429, 454.
[11] For a discussion of the trilemma, see M. Obstfeld, J. Shanbaugh and A.M. Taylor, 'The Trilemma in History: Trade-offs among Exchange Rates, Monetary Policies and Capital Mobility', *The Review of Economics and Statistics*, 87 (2005); R. Esteves and B. Eichengreen, 'The Trials of the Trilemma: International Finance, 1870–2017', Centre for Economic Policy Research Discussion Paper DP 12365 (London: 2019).
[12] See R. Triffin, 'The Evolution of the International Monetary System: Historical Reappraisal and Future Perspectives', *Princeton Studies in International Finance* (1964).

not fixed; capital mobility exists but restrictions apply, and governments can pursue independent monetary policies but only within limits.

Instrumental in delivering this compromise since 1973 has been the foreign exchange market, because this is where adjustments are continually made, and equilibrium is restored if warranted by underlying conditions of supply and demand. It is accepted that the foreign exchange market alone cannot deliver a stable exchange rate if the relative value of a currency is not supported by fundamental economic conditions. Governments have come to accept, however reluctantly, this situation. Shorn of its monetary connections the foreign exchange market acts in the same way as those for commodities, stocks, bonds, and derivatives, where compromise is achieved through continuous adjustments involving not only price but also amount, type, location, and time. Markets can only operate within the conditions of supply and demand that exist at any particular time. Periods of relative stability for exchange rates, such as the operation of the Gold Standard between 1890 and 1914 and the Bretton Woods System of fixed exchange rates from 1950 to 1970, generated limited trading in the foreign exchange market. However, that did not mean a market did not exist and that it had no role to play. Conversely, periods of exchange rate volatility such as in the 1920s and at times after 1973 produced heightened levels of trading. That did not mean that the market was responsible for currency volatility but rather it was responding to the underlying instability. What the volume of foreign exchange trading identified by the BIS since 1992 is evidence of is a trading system either responding to or taking advantage of continuous but minor variations in price. The foreign exchange market was the mechanism through which banks from all over the world were constantly adjusting their positions relative to each other, either to cover the current or future currency risks they were exposed to or to take advantage of profitable opportunities to buy and sell or lend and borrow. For that reason a high turnover was only to be expected. Though dismissed as speculation by many, or ignored because it involved only the buying and selling of money, the foreign exchange market has played a vital role in the functioning of the global monetary system since 1973.[13] The intention here is to discover whether it played such a role in the hundred years before 1973, despite the apparent lack of evidence that it existed and the widespread belief that when it did develop after 1919 its contribution since then has been marginal at best, and even harmful.

Aiding this process of discovery is the recognition that the foreign exchange market possessed a central location despite operating round-the-clock on a global basis. Between 1919 and 1939, and again after 1973, that location has been London. In 2022, the BIS acknowledged that 'The United Kingdom remained the most important FX trading location globally.'[14] By the UK they meant London as that was where

---

[13] L. Bartolini and G.M. Bodnar, 'Are Exchange Rates Excessively Volatile? And What Does Excessively Volatile Mean Anyway?', *IMF Staff Papers*, 43 (1996); P. Clark, N. Tamirisia and S.-J. Wei, *Exchange-Rate Volatility and Trade Flows—Some New Evidence* (International Monetary Fund, 2004); E. Ilzetzki, C.M. Reinhart and K.S. Rogoff, 'Will the Secular Decline in Exchange Rate and Inflation Volatility Survive Covid 19?' NBER Working Paper 28108 (2020).
[14] Bank for International Settlements, *Triennial Central Bank Survey* (2022).

all the foreign exchange trading took place. In 1992, the UK's share of global foreign exchange trading was 27 per cent and it stood at 38 per cent in 2022. Evidence also suggests that London was the centre of the foreign exchange market between the two world wars. However, that appeared to not be the case before the First World War. All that was visible then were brief biweekly meetings at the Royal Exchange between the representatives of a few British merchant banks and a small number of foreign banks with branches in London. These meetings ceased in 1919, when the modern foreign exchange market is considered to have begun.[15] The explanation given for the absence of an active foreign exchange market in London before 1919 is twofold. The first is the near-universal use of the £ sterling as the currency used in all Britain's dealing with other countries, whether it was trade or investment. Britain was the world's largest exporter and importer, provider of international services to the world economy, and global investor. These generated a vast volume of payments and receipts, virtually all of which were in sterling. It was other countries that faced the necessity of converting international payments and receipts into their national money, and covering the currency risks that they ran, so the foreign exchange market was located in such centres as Berlin, New York, and Paris. The second reason for the almost complete absence of a market in London was the stability of exchange rates under the Gold Standard. That stability eliminated the need for an active foreign exchange market for any country adhering to the Gold Standard by suppressing volatility. With the price of those national currencies using the Gold Standard fixed by reference to a specified quantity and quality of gold, any significant deviation would prompt a movement of the metal between countries, once a profit could be made, allowing for the cost of transport, insurance, commission fees, and forgone interest. The movement of gold would then automatically restore the exchange rate in terms of the national currency as supply and demand would be rebalanced. Under these conditions there was little profit to be made from foreign exchange trading or any requirement to cover potential falls and rises in the exchange rate as these would be brief. For these two reasons it was regarded as unsurprising that no foreign exchange market existed in London, leaving it for other centres to provide routine money changing facilities.[16]

These arguments have fundamental weaknesses. They fail to take account of the existence of multiple currencies, the profit that could be made trading them, and the need to hedge currency risk because exchange rates, though relatively stable, did fluctuate, even for those currencies fixed to gold. It took time for equilibrium to be restored and this created both opportunities for profitable trading and the necessity to cover exposure to currency fluctuations. The economics of the foreign exchange market were also transformed in the fifty years before the First World War as the cost of international communication fell dramatically and the speed of transmission

[15] See O. Accominotti and D. Chambers, 'If You're So Smart: John Maynard Keynes and Currency Speculation in the Interwar Years', *Journal of Economic History*, 76 (2016).

[16] Based on my reading of the contemporary literature, these were the explanations I put forward in 2007. See R.C. Michie, 'The City of London as a Global Financial Centre, 1880–1939: Finance, Foreign Exchange and the First World War', in P.L. Cottrell, E. Lange and U. Olsson (eds), *Centres and Peripheries in Banking: The Historical Development of Financial Markets* (Aldershot: Ashgate Publishing Company, 2007).

was revolutionized through the introduction and use of the telegraph. All that was required were banks and individuals willing to enter the market and grasp the opportunities that were appearing. This is what happened in London in the 1920s and, again, after 1970, but, apparently, not before the First World War. This was despite London being the largest, most interconnected, completely open financial centre in the world at that time.[17] If any environment could give birth to a foreign exchange market before 1914, it was that one, but it seemed that it did not until after the First World War.

What developed in London in the 1920s was a large and active foreign exchange market through which the world's banks traded currencies amongst themselves. That market was then closed with the outbreak of the Second World War and remained largely dormant until the 1970s, when it exploded into life, attracting banks and talent from around the world. Prior to that foreign exchange trading appeared to be more active outside London, with New York and Zurich being important locations. Again, the reason given for the lack of a foreign exchange market in London before 1973 is the stability of international currencies under the Bretton Woods Regime of fixed exchange rates that was inaugurated after the Second World War. As under the Gold Standard, that was believed to leave little scope or need for an active foreign exchange market as intervention by central banks could be guaranteed to maintain fixed exchange rates. In addition, the UK£ was still extensively used in Britain's own international transactions, as well as by other countries, thus reducing the need for a foreign exchange market in London, leaving it to develop elsewhere in the world. However, the UK£ was quickly displaced by the US$ after 1950 as the international currency of choice, and the growing instability of exchange rates under the Bretton Woods System in the 1960s did create growing opportunities for profitable trading in foreign exchange markets as well as the need to hedge against currency fluctuations. This was the situation long before the final collapse of the Bretton Woods System in 1973, and the ending of fixed exchange rates. When the end came it was, as before, London that became the hub of the global foreign exchange market, though now trading was dominated by transactions involving the US$. On these two occasions London had quickly emerged as the dominant centre of the global foreign exchange market, overtaking those where it had appeared to be based.[18]

What is attempted here is to place the foreign exchange market at the heart of any discussion of international monetary relations and to solve the mystery of why that market was in London. There is already an emerging literature that explores the development of the foreign exchange market since 1973 and the contribution this has

---

[17] See O. Accominotti, D. Lucena-Piquero and S. Ugolini, 'The Origination and Distribution of Money Market Instruments: Sterling Bills of Exchange during the First Globalisation', *Economic History Review*, 74 (2021).

[18] See H. James, 'Rethinking the Legacy of Bretton Woods', *Journal of European Economic History*, 51 (2022); I. Maes and I. Pascotti, 'The Legacy of Bretton Woods', *Journal of European Economic History*, 51 (2022); Subacchi, 'The System That Became a Non-system: The End of Bretton Woods Fifty Years Later', *Journal of European Economic History*, 51 (2022); B. Eichengreen, 'Somnolence to Dominance: A Hundred Years of the Foreign Exchange Market in London', *Journal of European Economic History*, 51 (2022).

made to the free flow of funds around the world and the stability of currencies. This literature recognizes that though fixed exchange rates might deliver both a higher level of international integration and a superior economic performance than flexible exchange rates, their survival depended upon the maintenance of an underlying equilibrium. If that equilibrium was lost, fixed exchange rates could not be maintained. What the foreign exchange market could deliver was a mechanism through which constant adjustments could be made, thus dampening extreme volatility and delivering short-run stability. That was sufficient to provide the environment within which international trade and investment could flourish unhindered by government-imposed barriers and governments could pursue relatively independent economic policies. Can the same be said for the hundred years preceding 1973?[19] There also remains something of a mystery surrounding the dominant position occupied by London in the global foreign exchange market. With the apparent absence of such a market in London both before 1919 and again in the 1950s and 1960s, allied to the demise of the UK£ as a global currency, any explanation related to inertia cannot be sustained. That leaves geography because of London's time zone advantage but that would apply equally well to any European financial centre such as Amsterdam, Paris, or Zurich and fits poorly with the existence of active foreign exchange markets in New York and Singapore.[20] There has to be something that explains London's dominance.

---

[19] See Chrystal, *Guide to Foreign Exchange Markets*; M.D. Bordo and M. Flandreau, 'Core, Periphery, Exchange Rate Regimes and Globalisation' (NBER, 2001); Osler, 'Market Microstructure'.
[20] See Nordstrom, *Understanding the Foreign Exchange Market.*

1
Finding Forex, 1850–1914

Introduction

Part of the problem of identifying the foreign exchange market in London lies with the definition that is applied.[1] Too narrow a definition restricts the market to trading money as a unit of account and omits its role as a store of value and a means of exchange. Though it is the trading of one currency against another that produces the headline figure of the exchange rate, the market is much more than that. The central function of the modern market is to allow banks to match assets and liabilities not only in terms of currencies but also over time, across locations, and in terms of amount. The final element is the price at which this is done, and it is this which produces the headline rate of exchange. Even between countries using the same currency, a market exists. The price that a currency can command varies according to location, because of supply and demand. When sterling was widely used as the currency in different countries, it was quoted at a premium or discount to the price it commanded in London. Under the Gold Standard, which was assumed to deliver a fixed rate of exchange, there was a range around the price at which a specific quantity of gold was bought and sold in terms of the local currency, determined by the point at which it was profitable to either buy in gold from another country or sell it abroad. These multiple uses of money need to be borne in mind when searching for a foreign exchange market in London before 1914. The market was also a complex one, involving the participation of not only banks but also dealers and brokers and the employment of different strategies, including the use of vehicle currencies and asset transfers. This is evident from the position today making it akin to the futures trading that took place on organized exchanges in the past. The absence of a formalized

---

[1] Until recently, I shared the judgement that London lacked a foreign exchange market before 1914. See R.C. Michie, 'The City of London: Functional and Spatial Unity in the Nineteenth Century', in H.A. Diedericks and D. Reeder (eds), *Cities of Finance* (Amsterdam: North-Holland, 1996), 189–206; R.C. Michie, 'Friend or Foe: Information Technology and the London Stock Exchange Since 1700', *Journal of Historical Geography*, 23–3 (1997); Michie, 'Invisible Stabiliser'; R.C. Michie, 'One World or Many Worlds?: Markets, Banks, and Communications, 1850s–1990s', in T. de Graaf, J. Jonker and J.J. Mabron (eds), *European Banking Overseas, 19th–20th Centuries* (Amsterdam: 2002); Michie, 'The City of London as a Global Financial Centre'. I have now changed my mind as a result of the research I have carried out over the years, without realizing the implications it had for an understanding of the foreign exchange market. That research had two strands. One was British with a focus on the LSE, the City of London as a financial centre, and the development of the British banking system. That has made me appreciate the importance of the money market and the role played by banks in providing the mechanism through which the financial system functions. The other strand was international with a strong North American bias. This made me aware of the central role played by London in all financial transactions before the First World War, which made the absence of a foreign exchange market even more of a mystery.

Forex Forever. Ranald C. Michie, Oxford University Press. © Ranald C. Michie (2024).
DOI: 10.1093/oso/9780198903697.003.0002

structure to the foreign exchange market or the lack of official recognition should not be treated as sufficient evidence that it either did not exist or was nothing more than uncontrolled speculation of little or no value.[2]

Nevertheless, as it stands, the search for a foreign exchange market in London before the First World War draws a blank, which is very odd.[3] London had possessed such a market in the eighteenth century and well into the nineteenth, but that had apparently disappeared.[4] Considering the growing depth and diversity of London as a financial centre after 1850, and its increasingly international orientation, the non-existence of an active foreign exchange market is difficult to accept. The absence of the market in London before 1914 is like one of the contemporary Sherlock Holmes mysteries, namely the story which was published in 1892 and featured the mystery of the dog that didn't bark.

GREGORY: Is there any other point to which you would wish to draw my attention?
HOLMES: To the curious incident of the dog in the night-time.
GREGORY: The dog did nothing in the night-time.
HOLMES: That was the curious incident.[5]

To Sherlock Holmes, the solution to the mystery was the fact that the dog did not bark. Is the same true of the foreign exchange market? The market was there, but its silence led contemporaries to assume it was not. It was only when the market became visible after the First World War that its existence was recognized. In 1922, Dudley Ward wrote in *A Description of the Foreign Exchange Market in London* that 'As it exists to-day the London Foreign Exchange Market is very largely an after-war development.'[6] His description was one of a series of articles commissioned by John Maynard Keynes. They appeared in a supplement to the *Manchester Guardian*

[2] See Hoffman, *Futures Trading*, 401, 417, 429, 454.
[3] See O. Accominotti, J. Cen, D. Chambers and I.W. Marsh, 'Currency Regimes and the Carry Trade', *Journal of Financial and Quantitative Analysis*, 54 (2019), 2233–2260; Eichengreen, 'Somnolence to Dominance', 51 (2022).
[4] London Stock Exchange: Committee for General Purposes: 1 October 1822, 6 January 1823, 10 July 1833, 8 June 1834, 9 June 1834, 26 October 1836, 30 January 1837, 29 July 1840, 17 November 1848, 29 December 1847, 12 January 1848, 17 January 1848, 24 January 1848, 28 July 1848; Foreign Funds Market: Committee Minute Book, 9 September 1823, 6 September 1844, 7 September 1824, 1 June 1825, 6 October 1826; S.D. Chapman, 'The Establishment of the Rothschilds as Bankers', *Transactions of the Jewish Historical Society*, 29 (1982–6), 187; L. Neal, *The Rise of Financial Capitalism: International Capital Markets in the Age of Reason* (Cambridge: Cambridge University, 1990), 38, 143, 151, 171, 175–6, 180, 200, 229; L. Neal, 'The Integration and Efficiency of the London and Amsterdam Stock Market in the Eighteenth Century', *Journal of Economic History*, 47 (1987), 97, 115; E.S. Schubert, 'Arbitrage in the Foreign Exchange Markets of London and Amsterdam during the 18th Century', *Explorations in Economic History*, 26 (1989), 6–7, 17; S.R. Cope, 'The Stock Exchange Revisited: A New Look at the Market in Securities in London in the Eighteenth Century', *Economica*, 45 (1978), 8–10, 15, 17; C.F. Smith, 'The Early History of the London Stock Exchange', *American Economic Review*, 19 (1929), 207; P.G.M. Dickson, *The Financial Revolution in England: A Study in the Development of Public Credit, 1688–1756* (London: Macmillan, 1967), 473–5, 507–19; D. Weatherall, *David Ricardo: A Biography* (The Hague: 1976), 3, 12, 14, 16; S.E. Oppers, 'The Interest Rate Effect of Dutch Money in Eighteenth-Century Britain', *Journal of Economic History*, 53 (1993), 40.
[5] A. Conan Doyle, 'The Adventure of Silver Blaze', *Strand Magazine* (December 1892), 645–660.
[6] Dudley Ward, 'A Description of the Foreign Exchange Market in London', in 'Reconstruction in Europe', *Manchester Guardian Commercial*, 20 April 1922, 9.

dealing with post-war reconstruction. This publication was widely circulated both in Britain and abroad, being translated into many languages, and proved to be very influential at the time and subsequently. The extent and endurance of that influence can be attributed to John Maynard Keynes, one of the twentieth century's most famous economists. This helps explain why Dudley Ward's verdict on the pre-First World War foreign exchange market in London has been so widely accepted and remains unchallenged today. Paul Einzig wrote in 1962 that 'Even though sterling was by far the most important international currency and London was by far the most important international financial centre, the turnover of the London foreign exchange market was distinctly smaller than that of a number of less important international financial centres.'[7] Atkin, in his 2005 history of the London foreign exchange market, concluded that it was 'a backwater' before the First World War and 'played second fiddle to more important centres in New York, Paris and Berlin.'[8] In advertising a conference planned for 2019, to celebrate one hundred years of the London foreign exchange market, the claim was made that 'the modern foreign exchange market as we would recognize it today first emerged in London in 1919 when forward contracts in London started to be continuously traded'.[9] Finally, as recently as 2022, one of the world's leading experts on monetary history, Barry Eichengreen, stated that '2020 marked the centennial of the modern foreign exchange market in London. The anniversary serves as a reminder that prior to 1920 there was little in the way of a foreign exchange market in London'.[10]

Contributing to this dismissal of the pre-1914 London foreign exchange market was its identification by contemporaries as the brief, poorly attended, biweekly meeting at the Royal Exchange, at which bills of exchange payable abroad were bought and sold. In 1868, Seyd described what took place at that meeting: 'The foreign bankers and merchants of London meet in the open court of the Royal Exchange every Tuesday and Friday, between the hours of two and three in the afternoon, to transact business in the purchase and sale of foreign bills. The majority of the firms represented are sellers of bills that have come to them as remittances from abroad or from the country. ... A large number of the firms present on "Change are foreign bankers, and exchange dealers, who purchase such made or drawn paper, or who sell to merchants or other drafts on places abroad for such specific amounts as may be required."'[11] When comparing the foreign exchange market that developed in the 1920s with that which had existed before the First World War, it was this meeting at the Royal Exchange that Phillips referred back to in his 1926 book, *Modern Foreign*

---

[7] P. Einzig, *The History of Foreign Exchange* (London: Macmillan 1962), 183. See S. Battilossi, 'Financial Innovation and the Golden Ages of International Banking: 1890–1931 and 1958–81', *Financial History Review*, 7 (2000), 155.

[8] See J. Atkin, *The Foreign Exchange Market of London: Development Since 1900* (London: Routledge, 2005), 5–9, 31.

[9] University of Cambridge Judge Business School, Bank of England and the Centre for Economic Policy Research, *A Hundred Years of the Modern Foreign Exchange Market in London*.

[10] Eichengreen, 'Somnolence to Dominance', 51 (2022), 75.

[11] E. Seyd, *Bullion and Foreign Exchanges* (London: Effingham Wilson, 1868), 434.

Exchange and Foreign Banking, "There were Rothschild and his friends, the German banks would be near one another; and scattered about, although never far separated, further groups would consist of the principals or representatives of banks and houses such as Frederick Huth, Credit Lyonnais, Baring Brothers, Samuel Montagu & Company, Lazard Brothers. These groups rarely mixed, and, on business, did not speak directly to one another. Brokers moved from group to group and ascertained the positions and desires of the dealers. As business resulted, the names were passed and entries made in little note-books."[12] As Phillips' description implies, long before it was finally abandoned after the First World War, very little business was done at this Royal Exchange meeting, being confined to trading in bills of exchange payable in marks and francs.

Neptune Must Exist, 1850–1914

Judging the absence of a foreign exchange market in London before 1914 from the lack of business done at the Royal Exchange, as did many contemporaries, leads to a false conclusion. Many markets operate without the need for a physical location or an institutional structure.[13] One such was the London discount market, through which bills of exchange were traded between banks, and money was borrowed and lent. This market flourished before the First World War and was in the hands of a small number of discount houses and brokers who walked from bank to bank in the City of London, buying bills and borrowing money from some and selling bills and repaying loans from others. They operated out of small offices, had no fixed place of business, belonged to no formal organization, and did not abide by any agreed set of rules and regulations. What they relied upon was the concentration of bank offices in a particular part of London and the trust they commanded from all those with whom they dealt, which included the Bank of England and the major banks. Trading without the need to congregate at a particular place and specific time was becoming easier with the telegraph and the telephone and did eventually make redundant the whole apparatus of the physical space provided by stock and commodity exchanges for transacting sales and purchases. Rather than provide evidence of the lack of an active foreign exchange market in London, the limited business done at the Royal Exchange was an early example of a switch in the way that trading was conducted, which well-informed contemporaries were aware of. In 1893, George Clare reported that trading in foreign exchange in London took place directly between banks using the telegraph.[14] By 1895, he considered that this way of trading foreign exchange in London

---

[12] H.W. Phillips, *Modern Foreign Exchange and Foreign Banking* (London: MacDonald & Evans, 1926), 50–5.

[13] Bank of England, 'The Foreign Exchange Market in London', *BEQB*, 20 (1980).

[14] G. Clare, *A Money-Market Primer and Key to the Exchanges* (London: Effingham Wilson, 1893), 79–82, 92, 104, 131, 136, 138, 148.

had made the business done at the Royal Exchange 'insignificant'.[15] What was happening to foreign exchange trading in London before 1914 became standard practice over the course of the twentieth century but was difficult for less-informed contemporaries to recognize because they identified financial markets with particular places such as stock and commodity exchanges. The market that Phillips described as having displaced the Royal Exchange meetings in the 1920s was one based entirely on office-to-office communication both within London and internationally.[16] A number of those writing about this new foreign exchange market did trace its origins to developments that had taken place before the First World War, emphasizing that the major difference was the scale of activity rather than its novelty.[17] It is this scale which would have impressed contemporaries in the 1920s, and could have made it appear that they were witnessing the birth of a new market rather than the huge expansion of an existing one. Instead of the mystery of the dog that didn't bark, the puzzle may be why nobody heard it, and that may be because it was invisible at the time. This makes the puzzle of the foreign exchange market like that over the existence of the planet Neptune. Long before Neptune was discovered by physical observation through a telescope, mathematical modelling proved to astronomers that it must exist because of the behaviour of other parts of the solar system.[18] Can the same be true for London and the foreign exchange market, considering that the fifty years before the First World War were ones of considerable innovation and development in both banks and financial markets?[19] As early as 1873, Nicholson noted the willingness of those dealing in foreign exchange in London to embrace change.[20] That would include abandoning any reliance on the gathering at the Royal Exchange and its replacement with other ways of conducting a market, including the use of new technology, whether it was the telegraph and the telephone or calculating machines.

Preventing the acceptance that a foreign exchange market existed before 1914, whether in London or anywhere else, is the conviction among many that the operation of the Gold Standard made one unnecessary. When joining the Gold Standard, a government made that metal the basis of the money supply, and specified the price that had to be paid for a precise quantity and quality of gold in terms of the national currency. Having done that, governments left gold to move freely across borders. Under these conditions, any deviation from the fixed price paid for gold in a national currency prompted an inflow or outflow of the metal. A profit could be made by buying where the price was lower and selling where it was higher, once account was taken of transaction charges, expenditure on carriage and insurance, and financing costs. With gold being of such high value relative to its weight and bulk, the price

[15] G. Clare, *The ABC of the Foreign Exchanges: A Practical Guide* (London: Macmillan, 1895), 12–14, 29, 39, 42, 83, 119.
[16] Phillips, *Modern Foreign Exchange*, 50–5.
[17] H.E. Butson, 'The Banking System of the United Kingdom', in H.P. Willis and B.H. Beckhart (eds), *Foreign Banking Systems* (London: Pitman & Sons, 1929), 1187–8; F. Whitmore, *The Money Machine* (London: 1930), 106.
[18] J. Davis, 'Who Discovered Neptune?', *Astronomy*, 9 November 2020.
[19] Battilossi, 'Financial Innovation', 145.
[20] N.A. Nicholson, *The Science of Exchanges* (London: Cassell, Petter and Galpin, 1873), 117.

it commanded differed by only a small margin around the world. As a result, even a small variation in the price of gold between different countries could lead to out-flows and inflows. As gold was the basis of a country's money supply, these flows would equalize the supply of and demand for a national currency, and so bring the exchange rate back to the previous level. Under the Gold Standard, there appeared to be an adjustment mechanism in place that automatically returned exchange rates to a fixed point. In this lay the appeal of the Gold Standard, for it provided a means of maintaining stable prices whether within a country or in the rate at which its cur-rency was exchanged for that of another. Under the circumstances, there was no requirement for a foreign exchange market other than the routine task of swopping one currency for another at a fixed rate of exchange when a payment had to be made or received. That explains why there is no mention of a foreign exchange market in Bordo and Schwarz's collective retrospective on the Gold Standard, which was pub-lished in 1984.[21] The foreign exchange market was considered to be a product of the collapse of the Gold Standard after the First World War, and reflected a nostalgia for the stability and certainty that was associated with that pre-war era.[22]

In a normal market, the interaction of supply and demand generates changing prices. Rising demand or decreasing supply increases prices. Falling demand or increasing supply reduces prices. In turn, rising prices reduce demand and increase supply, while falling prices increase demand and reduce supply. In that way, fluctu-ations in supply and demand are matched by fluctuations in prices to generate an ever-changing equilibrium. A feature of an active market is, therefore, price volatil-ity, which creates opportunities for profit and so draws in those willing to take the risk of buying for a rise or selling for a fall. These fundamentals apply to all markets. What varied were the mechanisms in place to maintain orderly behaviour in each market and reduce or eliminate counterparty risk. Some markets were governed by strict rules controlling participation and behaviour, while others were unregulated, relying on trust. However, when prices were fixed, the conditions that would give rise to a market were absent and this is considered to have been the case under the Gold Standard. Instead of price volatility generating market activity, flows of gold between countries equalized supply and demand and so automatically stabilized exchange rates. The problem with such a thesis is that gold could not, and did not, play the role assigned to it under the Gold Standard, and this has been widely acknowledged. When the Gold Standard was in ascendancy, especially between 1870 and 1914, the stability of the underlying supply of and demand for gold was in a state of flux. At the same time, the world's money supply became a product not of the gold mining industry but the development of banking systems. Banks monetized savings through the circulation of notes, the use of cheques and bills, and the provision of credit. The

---

[21] See M.D. Bordo and A.J. Schwartz (eds), *A Retrospective on the Classical Gold Standard, 1821–1931* (Chicago/London: 1984).

[22] T.E. Gregory, *Foreign Exchange Before, during and after the War* (Oxford: Oxford University Press, 1921), 12–13, 16, 21–4, 28, 46, 52; S.E. Thomas, *The Principles and Arithmetic of Foreign Exchange* (London: MacDonald & Evans, 1925), 8, 169; H.R. Miller, *The Foreign Exchange Market: A Practical Treatise on Post-war Foreign Exchange* (London: Edward Arnold & Co, 1925), 94–7; Battilossi, 'Financial Innovation', 150–3.

more sophisticated the national financial system, the more it dispensed with the use of gold apart from everyday transactions, residual payments, and in crises.[23] In 1908, Easton considered that gold had no significant international role to play.

> As commerce between nations is more or less mutual and the negotiability of well-known instruments of credit is universally recognized, it is very rare for gold to be exported or imported in quantities which bear anything but the slightest ratio to the vastness of the amounts involved in the business transactions out of which the payments or receipts arise.[24]

The assumption that adherence to the Gold Standard removed the need for a foreign exchange market is also undermined by those who have examined in detail its practical working in the years before the First World War. By joining the Gold Standard, countries pledged to exchange a fixed quantity of gold for a specific amount of domestic currency units. The fixed nature of the equivalence between gold and currency is then equated to fixed exchange rates, but that is not correct. What joining the Gold Standard meant was a commitment to stable not fixed exchange rates. Exchange rates fluctuated within a narrow spread but one large enough to support a foreign exchange market which became increasingly active as both transaction costs and the risks involved fell as global communications were transformed, international banking networks were established, and links between stock exchanges facilitated asset arbitrage. A foreign exchange market was also required to cover transactions involving currencies not on the Gold Standard, where volatility in exchange rates was greater. For those countries that stuck to silver rather than gold as the basis of their currency, exchange rate volatility was related to the differential between the prices of the two metals. This could be high as silver was increasingly treated as a commodity and its price allowed to fluctuate. Membership of the Gold Standard system was not universal but piecemeal and grew only slowly and partially before the First World War. Germany joined in 1872, France in 1878, USA in 1879, Russia and Japan in 1897, and Brazil in 1906. Even after joining, it took time for exchange rates to stabilize while some countries dropped out of the regime, for example Portugal. Portugal had joined the Gold Standard in 1854 but left it in 1891 after a financial crisis. Even the commitment of countries that stuck with the Gold Standard to monetize gold inflows or contract money supply in face of an outflow was not guaranteed. Under the circumstances, it is not surprising that in the late nineteenth and early twentieth centuries every national financial centre featured a foreign exchange market where bankers bought and sold foreign currency. In the multi-currency world that existed before 1914, the UK£ occupied the position of first among equals. Its

---

[23] Seyd, *Bullion and Foreign Exchanges*, 423–7; H.K. Brooks, *Foreign Exchange Textbook* (Chicago: H K Brooks, 1906), 1; For examples, see J. Viner, *Canada's Balance of International Indebtedness, 1900–1913* (Cambridge: Harvard University Press, 1924), 148–9; J.H. Williams, *Argentine International Trade under Inconvertible Paper Money, 1880–1900* (Cambridge: Harvard University Press, 1920), 15, 18, 21, 80, 139, 146, 157, 258; T.J.O. Dick and J.E. Floyd, *Canada and the Gold Standard: Balance of Payments Adjustments, 1871–1913* (Cambridge: Cambridge University Press, 1992), 10, 15, 128, 160, 166, 171–3.

[24] H.T. Easton, *Money, Exchange and Banking* (London: Sir I Pittman &Sons, 1908), 51.

share of currencies in central bank reserves was 48 per cent in 1913 compared to the French franc at 31 per cent, and the German mark at 15 per cent. With the extensive use of sterling across the whole range of international financial transactions there would have been a need to exchange it for other currencies, especially as it operated as the most important vehicle currency. In turn, that would have generated a need for an active foreign exchange market in London where banks could cover their current and future exposure to currency risks.[25]

Nevertheless, despite the critique of the practical working of the Gold Standard, there remains a reluctance to abandon the belief that equilibrium was achieved through gold flows, because of the lack of consensus on the mechanism in place to explain the stability of exchange rates. The operation of a foreign exchange market is not one of the alternative explanations put forward, such was the level of conviction that none existed. However, if conditions were suitable, such a market must have existed, driven by the profits speculators could make and the need among banks to cover currency risks through the use of forward contracts. As with Neptune, all the theoretical evidence points to the existence of a functioning foreign exchange market.[26] Under the Gold Standard, exchange rates were not fixed to such a degree

[25] See A.I. Bloomfield, 'The Significance of Outstanding Securities in the International Movement of Capital', *Canadian Journal of Economics and Political Science* 13, November 1940, 495–524; A.I. Bloom-field, *Monetary Policy under the International Gold Standard, 1880–1914* (Bloomfield: Federal Reserve Bank of New York, 1959); A.I. Bloomfield, 'Short-term Capital Movements under the Pre-1914 Gold Standard', *Princeton Studies in International Finance*, 1963; A.I. Bloomfield, 'Patterns of Fluctuation in International Investment before 1914', *Princeton Studies in International Finance*, 1968; P.H. Lindert, 'Key Currencies and Gold, 1900–1913', *Princeton Studies in International Finance* (1969); P. Krugman, 'Vehicle Currencies and the Structure of International Exchange', *Journal of Money, Credit and Banking*, 12 (1980), 513–526; M.D. Bordo and B. Eichengreen, *The Rise and Fall of a Barbarous Relic: The Role of Gold in the International Monetary System* (NBER, 1998); C.M. Meissner, 'A New World Order: Explain-ing the Emergence of the Classical Gold Standard, 1860–1913', *Journal of International Economics*, 66 (2005), 335–406; M. Flandreau and C. Jobst, 'The Ties That Divide: A Network Analysis of the Interna-tional Monetary System, 1890–1910', *Journal of Economic History*, 65 (2005), 977–1007; B. Eichengreen, 'Sterling's Past, Dollar's Future: Historical Perspectives on Reserve Currency Composition', paper deliv-ered Leicester 2005; M. Flandreau and C. Jobst, *The Empirics of International Currencies: Evidence from the 19th Century* (Centre for Economic Policy Research, 2006); M. Flandreau and C. Jobst, 'Describing and Explaining the International Circulation of Currencies, 1890–1910', *EH.Net*; J. Reis, R.P. Esteves and F. Ferramosca, 'Market Integration in the Golden Periphery: The Lisbon/London Exchange 1854–1891', *Explorations in Economic History*, 46 (2009), 324–345; C. Jobst, 'Market Leader: The Austro-Hungarian Bank and the Making of Foreign Exchange Intervention, 1896–1913', *European Review of Economic His-tory* 13 (2009), 287–318; Doskov and Swinkels, 'Empirical Evidence', *How Global Currencies Work 512* (2015), 370–389.
[26] R. Nurse and W.A. Brown, Jr, *International Currency Experience: Lessons of the Interwar Period* (Geneva: League of Nations, 1944), 14–16, 29, 71–2; L.B. Yeager, *International Monetary Relations: The-ory, History and Policy* (New York: 1966), 287; H. Van B. Cleveland, 'The International Monetary System in the Interwar Period', in B.J. Rowland (ed.), *Balance of Power or Hegemony: The Interwar Monetary System* (New York: 1976), 19–21; R. Triffin, *Our International Monetary System: Yesterday, Today and Tomorrow* (New York: 1968), 19–24; B. Eichengreen, *Golden Fetters: The Gold Standard and the Great Depression, 1919–1939* (New York/Oxford: 1992), xi, 3–5, 38–54, 66, 390–8; L.H. Officer, *Between the Dollar-Sterling Gold Points: Exchange Rates, Parity and Market Behaviour* (Cambridge: 1996), 198; C.H. Feinstein, P. Temin and G. Toniolo, 'International Economic Organisation: Banking, Finance and Trade in Europe between the Wars', in C.H. Feinstein (ed.), *Currency and Finance in Europe between the Wars* (Oxford: 1995), 16–17; G.M. Gallarotti, *The Anatomy of an International Monetary Regime: The Classical Gold Standard, 1880–1914* (New York: 1995), 6, 8, 12; Dick and Floyd, *Canada and the Gold Standard*, 10, 170–3; R. Ally, *Gold and Empire: The Bank of England and South Africa's Gold Producers, 1886–1926* (Johannesburg: 1994), 8; B. Eichengreen, 'Central Bank Co-operation and Exchange Rate Commitments:

that no variation took place. What the Gold Standard delivered was a high degree of stability to exchange rates, and this was found generally before the First World War. This reflected the willingness of most governments around the world to adhere to fiscal prudence, and an absence of major military conflicts between 1870 and 1914 that could have disrupted exchange rates. The result was a lack of volatility in exchange rates, which would have done much to suppress the level of speculative activity but not to the extent that all trading was eliminated.[27] As Cornwallis observed in New York in 1879, 'Every change in the Bank of England rate of discount has its effect in raising or lowering the rate of exchange for sterling at short sight here.'[28] The level of currency fluctuations did decline before 1914 as countries joined the Gold Standard and the degree of confidence in the stability of exchange rates grew, and this would have suppressed the level of speculation.[29] Nevertheless, speculative opportunities continued to exist, as in the Argentinian peso, for example, whose exchange rate fluctuated with the seasons.[30] Even the exchange rates of the currencies of the leading economies of the pre-1914 era fluctuated, though they all adhered to the Gold Standard. Over the January–March 1914 period, for example, the exchange rate of the French franc to the UK£ ranged from 25.30 to 25.00; the German mark from 20.52 to 20.43; and the US$ from 4.84 to 4.83, and these were all currencies on the Gold Standard.[31]

Though the fluctuation in exchange rates was very low between 1870 and 1914, reducing the need for a foreign exchange market either for speculation or insurance, the revolution in communications and global financial integration had a reverse effect. As the nineteenth century drew to a close, the *Wall Street Journal* reflected that 'The cable, the telegraph, the railroad and the steamship have so knitted together

The Classical and Interwar Gold Standards Compared', *Financial History Review*, 2 (1995), 99; D.E. Moggridge, *British Monetary Policy, 1924–1931: The Norman Conquest of $4.86* (Cambridge: 1972), 260; P. Einzig, *A Textbook on Foreign Exchange* (London: 1966), 1–13; M. Friedman and A.J. Schwartz, *Monetary Trends in the United States and the United Kingdom: Their Relations to Income, Prices and Interest Rates, 1867–1977* (Chicago: 1982), 161; L. Jonung, 'Swedish Experience under the Classical Gold Standard, 1873–1914', in Bordo and Schwartz (eds), *Retrospective on the Classical Gold Standard*, 368–9; H. James, *International Monetary Co-operation Since Bretton Woods* (Washington: 1996), ch. 17; M. de Cecco, *Money and Empire: The International Gold Standard, 1890–1914* (Oxford: 1974), 138; W.M. Scammell, 'The Working of the Gold Standard', *Economic and Social Research*, 17 (1965), 33–5; A.G. Ford, 'International Financial Policy and the Gold Standard, 1870–1914', *Warwick Research Papers*, 104 (1977), 6, 9, 22; McCloskey and Zecher, 'How the Gold Standard Worked', 187–8; A.J. Schwartz, 'Introduction', in Bordo and Schwartz (eds), *Retrospective on the Classical Gold Standard*, 6; P. Einzig, *A Dynamic Theory of Forward Exchange* (London: 1961), 8–10, 2nd ed. (1967), 2, 25–6; Bordo and Flandreau, 'Core, Periphery', 424–5. See B. Eichengreen and R. Esteves, 'International Finance', in S. Broadberry and K. Fukao (eds), *The Cambridge Economic History of the Modern World*, vol. 2, *1870 to the Present* (Cambridge University Press: 2021).

[27] E.L. Stewart Patterson, *Domestic and Foreign Exchange* (New York: 1917), 41; H.D. White, *The French International Accounts, 1880–1913* (Cambridge: 1933), 157.

[28] K. Cornwallis, *The Gold Room, and the New York Stock Exchange and Clearing House* (New York: 1879), 15.

[29] M. Levy-Leboyer, 'Central Banking and Foreign Trade: The Anglo-American Cycle in the 1830s', in C. Kindleberger and J.-P. Pierre Laffargue (eds), *Financial Crises: Theory, History and Policy* (Paris: 1982), 99; Balogh, *Studies in Financial Organization* (Cambridge: Cambridge University Press, 1947), 234; Gregory, *Foreign Exchange*, 12–13, 16, 21–4, 28, 46, 52.

[30] Officer, *Dollar-Sterling Gold Points*, 61–3, 103, 107–8, 113, 182–4, 191–4, 198, 206, 272–6, 281; Williams, *Argentine International Trade*, 15, 18, 21, 80, 139, 146, 157, 258.

[31] E. Dieson, *Exchange Rates of the World* (Christiana: 1922).

the very ends of the earth that the two hemispheres are really one market for all forms of wealth from grain to credit.'[32] As the twentieth century opened, the *Montreal Gazette* made a similar claim. 'Nowadays the great bankers and financiers can put themselves in instantaneous communication with all parts of the world, and this fact has played the leading part in the growth of the world's financial operations, and certainty of success with which such operations can be carried out.'[33] The fundamental change in communications came with the ability to separate the flow of information from its physical transportation, creating huge opportunities for the development of forward markets and the use of option and future contracts. This is what the telegraph began to deliver from 1840 in Britain and internationally from 1851 with the London–Paris link. By converting information into a series of electrical impulses which could be transmitted along a wire, and then decoded at the other end, it was possible to communicate without requiring any physical movement at all. As these electrical impulses could travel much faster than any known form of transport, the result was revolutionary. With a mail service reliant on physical transport by land and sea, replaced by the near-instant transmission of the telegraph, delays between the sending and receipt of prices were reduced to minutes rather than hours and days from the 1870s. This communications revolution made possible the interaction between geographically separate markets throughout the trading day, facilitating constant adjustments of prices. Even more dramatic than the twenty-mile cross-channel connection which began operation in 1851 was the permanent submarine cable connection which linked London and New York in 1866, a distance of 3,000 miles, under the Atlantic. When the submarine cables reached Australia in 1872, a rapid and reliable global communication network was in place, connecting all major financial centres during the trading day, with only a slight delay in the transmission and receipt of prices. Britain led this revolution with its contribution to international telegraphy, making London the centre of the global communications system between 1850 and 1914.[34]

The effect of the global communications revolution from the 1850s simultaneously increased the opportunities and reduced the costs for profitable trading in financial instruments of all kinds. As the speed of transmission accelerated, the capacity to carry messages grew, and the costs of transmission fell—the outcome was market integration on a global scale. Instead of having to respond to the erratic arrival of out-of-date information, markets had access to reliable prices that were only minutes old when using the telegraph and current with the London-Paris telephone connection established in the 1890s. The outcome was a high correlation of commodity and asset prices between all the world's financial and commercial centres.[35] As was reported to

[32] *Wall Street Journal*, 14 December 1899.

[33] *Montreal Gazette*, 1 January 1901.

[34] See D. Read, *The Power of the News: The History of Reuters* (Oxford: Oxford University Press, 1992), 45.

[35] A.J. Field, 'The Magnetic Telegraph, Price and Quantity Data, and the New Management of Capital', *Journal of Economic History*, 52 (1992), 403–4; R.B. Duboff, 'The Telegraph and the Structure of Markets in the United States, 1845–1890', *Research in Economic History*, 8 (1983), 261; J.L. Kieve, *The Electric Telegraph: A Social and Economic History* (Newton Abbot: 1973), 13, 103, 112–13, 211; H. Barty-King, *Girdle*

the London Stock Exchange (LSE) in November 1906: 'The increased rapidity of communication has made everyone want to deal at the closest possible price.'[36] The result was to transform all global markets as the constant updating of prices allowed buyers and sellers to anticipate future movements, continually adjust their positions and so reduce their exposure to a sudden rise or fall. This was particularly important where transactions were financed on credit whether it involved commodities or securities. Before the telegraph, the delay in the receipt of information in London from abroad made all internationally orientated commercial and financial markets highly speculative. These included the foreign exchange market that was operating at that time. It was only the most experienced operators, who could tap into international trust networks, that were willing to take the risks involved in such speculative transactions, as was the case with the Rothschilds. Sudden variations in commodity, stock and bond prices, foreign exchange rates, and interest rates, which could not be anticipated, had the potential to generate huge gains or losses. Hence, the high failure rate among the merchants, bankers, and brokers who became involved, along with the immense wealth of a few who were sufficiently clever to predict the market, or simply lucky. In the face of the huge risks involved most avoided such markets. That position was transformed with the communications revolution which brought speed and certainty to the flow of information.[37]

It appears to be highly improbable that those trading foreign exchange did not respond to the challenges and opportunities created by the global communications revolution and the economic integration that was transforming global markets between 1850 and 1914. This was what happened elsewhere in the financial system before the First World War, ranging from the insurance market at Lloyds to numerous commodity and stock exchanges. The whole concept of terminal markets rested upon the ability to trade spot and forward contracts simultaneously and so anticipate future prices. It was trading on the London Metal Exchange (LME) before 1914 which established the global reference price for contracts on the future deliveries of copper and tin. Such contracts were used extensively by producers, consumers, merchants, bankers, and brokers to cover their positions as well as speculators hoping to profit by acting as counterparties. The LME was one among the many exchanges that developed from the mid-nineteenth century onwards around the world to provide forward markets for traditional products like copper and tin or wheat and sugar along with new ones such as rubber, as well as for stocks and bonds. The LSE developed as an international market where a large proportion of the world's government and corporate bonds were bought and sold both for either immediate payment and

Round the Earth: The Story of Cable and Wireless and Its Predecessors (London: 1979), 89, 393; LSE: Com. for General Purposes, 15 February 1904; J. Ahvenainen, 'Telegraphy, Trade and Policy: The Role of the International Telegraphs in the Years 1870–1914', in W. Fischer, R.M. McInnis and J. Schneider (eds), The Emergence of a World Economy (Bamberg, 1986), 507–9, 514; S.G. Sturmey, The Economic Development of Radio (London: 1968), 74–5; M. Edelstein, Overseas Investment in the Age of High Imperialism: The United Kingdom 1850–1914 (London: 1982), 82, 178–9, 330.
[36] LSE: Com. for General Purposes, 20 November 1906.
[37] M.L. Muhleman, Monetary Systems of the World (New York: 1896), 177–8; W.S. and E.S. Woytinsky, World Commerce and Governments (New York: 1955), 199–200.

delivery or to be completed at the end of the fortnightly trading period. This created opportunities for dealers, known as jobbers, to buy what they could not pay for or sell what they did not own, confident that they could reverse the bargain before they had to deliver. These markets included ones where the spread between buying and selling prices was very narrow, as was the case with many exchange rates before 1914. The price of the British government's own debt, consols, which were the safest securities in the world at the time, fluctuated within a very narrow range, largely in response to changes in interest rates. Nevertheless, consols commanded an active market with Warren claiming in 1903 that 'during normal times consols can be sold for cash at any moment'.[38]

Despite the currency stability that came with the Gold Standard, the foreign exchange market generated constant fluctuations in foreign exchange rates as it responded to minute fluctuations in supply and demand on a minute-to-minute, hour-by-hour, and day-to-day basis. In the absence of interventionist central banks under the Gold Standard, with few countries having any at all, this required constant fine-tuning if the stability of exchange rates was to be preserved within the narrow band observable before the First World War. As this was not achieved by either the movement of gold or central bank intervention, it must have been the product of the foreign exchange market through a combination of spot and forward transactions and the actions of intermediaries who would buy or sell in expectation of reversing the deal in the future at a profit. Price stability in an open market was achieved not by mandating fixed prices but through constant buying and selling, and mechanisms that anticipated future movements, such as short selling. In that way, liquid markets were established in which buyers and sellers could be confident that prices would remain stable, at least in the short run. This was particularly important in foreign exchange markets as they were highly sensitive to the slightest movement in such variables as interest rates. It is impossible to explain the stability of exchange rates before the First World War without accepting that an active foreign exchange market must have existed, as that was the only way through which adjustments could be made on a continuous basis. The question is why can no such market be found? Neptune must exist but it cannot be observed.

The most detailed account of the working of the international monetary system under the Gold Standard was carried out by the American economist, W.A. Brown, and published in 1940. His mission was to try and explain why the monetary system had worked so well under the Gold Standard, as it operated before 1914, and did not do so subsequently, having to be abandoned in the 1930s after being revived in the 1920s. Despite the depth of research and the massive detail provided, Brown had little to say about the foreign exchange market before 1914, contributing to the widespread belief that it was almost non-existent, especially in London. 'Before the war London was not greatly interested in foreign exchange dealings. The foreign exchange market ... was not an active market before 1900' (p. 637). Though the focus of his research was the Gold Standard, the conclusion he reached was that gold itself played

[38] H. Warren, *The Story of the Bank of England* (London: 1903), 142.

a marginal role. 'Even under the pre-war Gold Standard, the corrective influence of gold movements on price levels was not as vital in forcing international adjustments as has often been asserted' (p. 1335). Instead, his conclusion was that the success of the Gold Standard depended on the environment within which it operated, especially the adherence of governments to policies that delivered economic, monetary, and financial stability. Providing a mechanism for delivering that stability was the central position occupied by the City of London within the global financial system, especially its role as the hub of the international banking network through which money flowed quickly and smoothly around the world from 1870 onwards. 'London, before the war, stood at the apex of a world hierarchy of financial centers ... all countries secured the essential money-market services in part from their own financial center and in part from London' (p. 142). Though dismissive of the pre-war foreign exchange market, Brown does provide useful clues suggestive that it not only existed but also played an increasingly important role after 1900. 'After 1900 the market increased in activity, especially with the beginning of trading in the exchanges by the joint stock banks' (p. 637). In addition, while crediting trading in foreign exchange in centres such as Berlin, New York, and Paris, with helping to keep rates stable, he implies that the City of London played an essential coordinating role. 'The world's foreign exchange markets were interconnected through London' (p. 774). What he had identified was the interbank network which enabled assets and liabilities to be matched not only according to amount, location, and timing but also currency, and that was all done through London.

> London was the principal market for the Continent of dollars, Yen, and the South American and Empire Exchanges. ... In the ordinary course of foreign exchange dealings sterling currently accumulating ... was always redistributed on the books of the London banks to the accounts of individuals and institutions in need of sterling balances to make payments.
>
> (pp. 9–10)

To Brown, it was through the constant adjustment of sterling balances in London that the world's banking system balanced their debits and credits with each other, especially between Europe and the rest of the world.[39] Another American economist, Anderson in 1917, had already stated that 'The foreign exchange of every country in the world was freely dealt in London and could consequently be made the basis of bank credit.'[40]

Despite these references to the existence of an active foreign exchange market before 1914, it continued to be ignored by those examining the operation of the Gold Standard. These included the economist Oskar Morgenstern in his 1959 book *International Financial Transactions and Business Cycles*. What he emphasized was how

---

[39] Brown, *International Gold Standard*, xv, xvii, 9–10, 55, 60, 65, 142–5, 154, 509, 521, 533–7, 550–2, 637–9, 659–66, 774, 1027, 1335.
[40] B.M. Anderson, *The Value of Money* (New York: 1917), 541–2.

integrated the global economy was before 1914 compared to between the wars, especially within Europe. The Gold Standard contributed to this integration by instilling
confidence that exchange rates would remain stable and that international financial
flows would be unhindered. What his measurements revealed was not only the high
degree of integration, as measured by differential interest rates, but also the steady
improvement in the decades before the First World War. The level of integration was
most marked between the financial centres of London, Paris, Berlin, and New York
with even minor variations in interest rates, prompting financial flows to take advantage of the profitable opportunities generated to borrow in one location and lend in
another. These opportunities were not confined to money but extended to securities.
As Morgenstern concluded,

> Internationally traded securities, woefully neglected in studies on international
> finance, are a powerful link between the various national stock markets. ... On
> different national stock markets the prices of the same share are as a rule not a
> variance, owing to perfect arbitrage. ... Bankers specializing in foreign exchange
> operations were particularly active in foreign trading with American securities.

He then added that, unfortunately, 'no adequate statistical data are available to estimate the volume and character of international securities arbitrage operations'.[41]
Morgenstern had turned to the contribution made by securities arbitrage because
his statistical analysis demonstrated that, with variations in exchange rates regularly
deviating from the range dictated by adherence to a fixed price for gold and the
lack of influence exercised by central banks over exchange rates, there was nothing
automatic about the operation of the international monetary system under the Gold
Standard. Instead, it must have relied upon the interaction of markets around the
world, covering the entire spectrum of assets that performed some or all the functions
associated with money. What he concluded was that 'The workings of the international monetary system had improved greatly up to 1914 and were tremendously
upset by World War 1.' However, how that had been achieved was not explained
apart from financial flows being stabilizing before 1914 but destabilizing after 1918.
That change was due to the lack of confidence that governments were committed to
maintaining current exchange rates, or able to do so, between the wars. What was
omitted was any examination of the foreign exchange market and the role it had to
play, whether in an environment of stable or unstable exchange rates.[42] The mystery
was not whether a foreign exchange market existed, as some such mechanism must
have been in place to explain the stability of currencies under the Gold Standard, but
where was it to be found. London was the most logical location as it was the most
important financial centre in the world before 1914.

[41] O. Morgenstern, *International Financial Transactions and Business Cycles* (Princeton: 1959), 27, 508,
524–6.
[42] Morgenstern, *International Financial Transactions*, 17–18, 27, 44–52, 76, 152, 159, 211, 217, 290, 297,
469–73, 361, 508, 524–6, 567–72.

The City of London 1850–1914

The most obvious location for this foreign exchange market was the City of London. This is where it was to be found after the First World War and when it took root again in the 1970s. The City of London was the dominant financial centre in the world before 1914, and the most international, with strong connections to Western Europe, the USA, the British Empire, and independent countries like Argentina and Japan. Financial activity tends to concentrate in a few locations both within countries and internationally, and the foreign exchange market is no exception. A financial centre provided a place where payments were made and received, funds were borrowed and lent, assets and liabilities were matched, and specialist services provided. Each of these placed a potential demand on the foreign exchange market once they involved international transactions, and that was the direction of travel of the City of London before 1914.[43] During the second half of the nineteenth century, the City changed from being a densely populated residential area engaged in industrial and commercial activities to a specialist business district serving the needs of both domestic and international trade and finance.[44] To make way for those specialist services, the resident population was replaced by a growing army of commuters employed on either a daily basis or regularly visiting the offices and markets located there.[45] By 1911, only 19,657 lived in the City but 364,061 worked there. Indicative of the variety of those working in the City in 1911, and picked up in the day census conducted that year, were 14,394 stockbrokers, 13,406 bankers, 10,663 lawyers, 5.447 accountants, and 15,064 in insurance, as well as numerous others spread across a huge variety of different activities.[46] After a tour of the City in 1902, Charles Turner was in no doubt that 'London, in spite of the rivalry of New York and the growing importance of Paris and Berlin as money centres, is still paramount as a headquarters of exchange and banking.'[47] Based on more scientific evidence, Edgar Crammond told a meeting of the Royal Statistical Society in 1914 that 'The predominance of London in the international money markets has probably never been greater than it is at the present time.'[48] These judgements were supported by those looking at the City of London

[43] Committee on the Global Financial System, *Long Term Issues in International Banking* (BIS July 2010), 125. See the collected articles in R. Roberts (ed.), *International Financial Centres: Concepts, Development and Dynamics* (Aldershot: Edward Elgar, 1994); R. Roberts (ed.), *Global Financial Centres: London, New York, Tokyo* (Aldershot: Edward Elgar, 1994); R. Roberts (ed.), *Offshore Financial Centres* (Aldershot: Edward Elgar, 1994).

[44] J. Innes, 'Managing the Metropolis: London's Social Problems and Their Control, c 1660–1830', in P. Clarke and R. Gillespie (eds), *Two Capitals: London and Dublin 1500–1840* (Oxford: Oxford University Press, 2001), 63; D. Barnett, *London, Hub of the Industrial Revolution: A Revisionary History, 1775–1825* (London: I.B. Tauris, 1998), 13.

[45] D.R. Green, *From Artisans to Paupers: Economic Change and Poverty in London: 1790–1870* (Aldershot: 1995), 36, 58, 74–5, 83, 155, 173; D. Keene, 'The Setting of the Royal Exchange: Continuity and Change in the Financial District of the City of London: 1300–1871', in A. Saunders (ed.), *The Royal Exchange* (London: 1997), 254–70; G. Norton, *Commentaries on the History, Constitution and Chartered Franchises of the City of London* (London: 1828), 195.

[46] City of London Day Census, 1911: Report (London: 1911).

[47] C. Turner, 'Money London', in C. Sims (ed.), *Living London* (London: 1902), 1.

[48] E. Crammond, 'The Economic Relations of the British and German Empires', *Journal of the Royal Statistical Society*, lxxvii (1914), 785.

from outside, such as Canadian bankers. L.D. Wilgress wrote in 1912 that 'London is the world's financial centre, and is the clearing house for international payments.'[49] W.W. Swanson said in 1914 that 'Although New York, Berlin and Paris have become great money centres they have never been able, despite the adoption of every expedient they could think of, to seriously threaten the paramount position of London as a world market.'[50] These views of contemporaries have been confirmed by later research, which placed the City of London at the centre of the global financial system before the First World War.[51] Despite the City's successful transition to an international financial centre between 1850 and 1914, it retained its position as the world's leading commercial centre. The City was capable of advancing along a broad front, with no profitable opportunity being missed. As international trade became increasingly complex, it was the City that met its needs for cheap and abundant short-term credit, access to a dense global communication network for the transmission of prices and orders, and a constant supply of ships to move commodities and manufactures around the world. The revolution in communications that had begun with the telegraph in the 1850s, and then extended to the telephone from the 1890s, permitted a growing separation between the physical movement of goods and the arrangements that underpinned international distribution. This allowed the City of London to emerge as an intermediary centre for international commercial transactions. The City was the only location that possessed the range and depth of expertise, connections, and markets necessary to support the functioning of the increasingly integrated world economy that was emerging before the First World War.[52] The City also provided the futures markets where buyers, sellers, merchants, brokers, and bankers could cover the risks they were exposed to. German legislation banning futures trading in 1896 transferred much of the business, previously done in that country, to London.[53] The result was that of the 357,361 people who worked daily in the City

[49] L.D. Wilgress, 'The London Money Market', *Journal of the Canadian Bankers Association*, 20 (1912–13), 210.

[50] W.W. Swanson, 'London and New York as Financial Centres', *Journal of the Canadian Bankers Association*, 20 (1914–15), 198. See Y. Cassis, *City Bankers, 1890–1914* (Cambridge: 1994), 5–7.

[51] See Y. Cassis, *Capitals of Capital: A History of Financial Centres, 1700–2005* (Cambridge: Cambridge University Press, 2006), ch. 3; B. Eichengreen, *The Gold Standard in Theory and History* (New York: 1985), 16. Among the contemporaries who placed the City of London at the top of the hierarchy of financial centres were F.E. Steele, 'On Changes in the Bank Rate of Discount, First, Their Causes; and Secondly, Their Effects on the Money Market, on the Commerce of the Country, and on the Value of All Interest-Bearing Securities', *JIB*, 12 (1891), 477; C. Rozenraad, *The International Money Market* (London: 1893), 27; G. Rozenraad, *The History of the Growth of London as the Financial Centre of the World and the Best Means of Maintaining That Position* (London: 1903), 15; F. Schuster, 'Foreign Trade and the Money Market', *The Monthly Review*, xiv (January 1904), 5. *Report and Proceedings of the Standing Sub-committee of the Committee for Imperial Defence on Trading with the Enemy (1912)*: Evidence of A.C. Cole, Governor of the Bank of England, 108.

[52] Y. Cassis (ed.), *Finance and Financiers in European History, 1880–1960* (Cambridge: 1992), 433–41; H. Withers, *Money-Changing: An Introduction to Foreign Exchange* (London: 1913), 43–6; A.G. Ford, *The Gold Standard, 1880–1914: Britain and Argentina* (Oxford: 1962), 19; Bloomfield, Short-Term Capital Movements, 34–5, 43–4, 92; Cassis, City Bankers, 5, 7, 17–23, 35–7, 57–9, 68–9, 93–4, 110, 144, 181, 208, 272, 315.

[53] F.H. Jackson *et al.*, *Lectures on British Commerce, Including Finance, Insurance, Business and Industry* (London: 1912), 14–17, 90–1, 125, 144. See G.B. Magee and A.S. Thompson, *Empire and Globalisation: Networks of People, Goods and Capital in the British World, c 1850–1914* (Cambridge: Cambridge University Press, 2010), 57–60, 114, 201; D.C.M. Platt, *Latin America and British Trade, 1806–1914* (London:

in 1911, a total of 130,779 were still employed in commercial and related services, or 36.6 per cent. That was almost three times the size of those employed in financial services.[54]

The City of London should have also provided fertile ground for the development of a foreign exchange market before 1914, rather than New York, Paris, and Berlin.[55] Between 1850 and 1914, the City of London was becoming an increasingly cosmopolitan centre as it attracted businesses and individuals from throughout the world because of the markets that were located there and the facilities it possessed. These ranged from bankers and merchants to the numerous clerks they employed. An estimate for 1887 suggested that 35 per cent of the leading firms employed staff from overseas because of their language and technical skills. Most came from Europe, especially Germany, where there had been a very active foreign exchange market before currency unification in the 1870s. When Lionel Fraser gained employment with the City firm of Bonn and Company shortly before the First World War, he found himself working with French and German clerks. Bonn and Company were among those City firms that entered the foreign exchange market in the 1920s. There was no lack of expertise in the City before 1914 that could be tapped by an emerging foreign exchange market.[56] London was also an ideal location for such a market as proved time and again in other international commercial and financial activities. From a City location, merchants, bankers, brokers, dealers, and agents were able to communicate quickly and reliably around the globe using the telegraph, and had access to numerous different markets, permitting them to adjust positions on a continuous basis and so avoid sudden shocks by the anticipation of problems and the sharing of risk. The increasing international orientation of the City was found throughout the commercial, financial, and related activities that took place there. The insurance market, Lloyds, for example, moved from covering the risk of loss of British vessels to insuring ships and their cargoes from every country in the world and against every possible liability. A large amount of business was done on European account, with much of the German merchant fleet obtaining its insurance cover at Lloyds. Lloyds also developed catastrophe insurance, covering the risk of damage occurring from earthquakes and hurricanes anywhere in the world.[57] A similar

1972), 110; R. Perren, *The Meat Trade in Britain, 1840–1914* (London: 1978), 202–8, 211; S. Chapman, *Merchant Enterprise in Britain: From the Industrial Revolution to World War 1* (Cambridge: 1992), 176–83, 202, 248, 289, 299–301, 304, 309, 312; S.B. Saul, *Studies in British Overseas Trade, 1870–1914* (Liverpool: 1960), 60; A.H. Beavan, *Imperial London* (London: 1901), 231; T. Critchell and J. Raymond, *A History of the Frozen Meat Trade* (London: 1912), 102, 105–6, 172, 184; G.L. Rees, *Britain's Commodity Markets* (London: 1972), 133, 138, 171–2, 280, 197, 241, 325, 351, 416–17, 437, 444; W.J. Loftie, *London City: Its History, Streets, Traffic, Buildings, People* (London: 1891), vol. 1: 179–81; J. Schneer, *London 1900: The Imperial Metropolis* (New Haven: 1999), 7, 41–2, 64–5.

[54] *City of London Day Census, 1911: Report* (London: 1911), 41–3.

[55] See Cassis, *City Bankers*, 5–8; Cassis (ed.), *Finance and Financiers*: Burk, 360; H. Bonin, *Société Générale in the United Kingdom, 1871–1996* (Paris: 1996), 11, 16.

[56] M. Ball and D. Sunderland, *Economic History of London* (London/New York: Routledge, 2001), 327; L. Fraser, *All to the Good* (London: 1963), 34–5, 64; See R.C. Michie, 'Insiders, Outsiders and the Dynamics of Change in the City of London Since 1900', *Journal of Contemporary History*, 15 (1998).

[57] Committee for Imperial Defence: Evidence of Sir John H. Luscombe, a Marine Underwriter at Lloyds, and Robert Lewis and Robert Ogilvie from the Insurance Companies.

pattern of product diversification and geographical spread was found on the Baltic Exchange. It was through the Baltic Exchange that a large proportion of the world's shipping fleet found employment, whether it was carrying Argentinian wheat to Europe or Japanese coal to markets in Asia. The City of London proved to be an ideal location from which to handle the distribution of the world's commodities, finance projects to develop mineral deposits, or organize the construction of railways around the world, and it flourished as a result before the First World War.[58]

What was evident in the City before the First World War was the continual turnover of personnel and firms as the new replaced the old, the foreign replaced the British, the public replaced the private, and the balance between enterprising and conservative waxed and waned. Only a financial centre of the size and connections of the City of London could support the degree of specialization evident by the late nineteenth/early twentieth century. Important as was the challenge coming from other financial centres, especially Paris, Berlin, and New York, it appears that London was more than holding its own as a financial centre before the First World War.[59] As Mira Wilkins has concluded, 'There was something very special about London.'[60] What this implies was that London had the potential to become the centre of the foreign exchange market in the same way it was doing across a broad range of markets and services before 1914. As the City of London's success was not achieved through inertia but by change, this makes the absence of an active foreign exchange market even more mysterious. The need for such market in London is evident from an examination of international investment flows involving the UK. In terms of the long-term movement of capital, it has been estimated that between 1865 and 1914 a total of £4 billion, or an average of £82 million a year at current prices, flowed from London to foreign countries in the shape of subscriptions to loans issued there and subsequently paid up. In addition, there was extensive trading in the London market of securities issued elsewhere, especially the USA, but also Canada, Australia, and South Africa. In return there was a constant inflow of interest payments, dividends, and maturing loans to be handled. All this involved a multiplicity of currencies and was processed by the banks on behalf of their customers.[61]

One consequence was that the investment banking community in the City was especially large and cosmopolitan, with numerous specialists in all types of international finance, while the LSE provided markets in all types of securities from around the world. These included ones denominated in foreign currencies, especially US$s, for which special provision was made in terms of a standard sterling equivalent. These

[58] For these points, see R.C. Michie, 'The City of London and International Trade, 1850–1914', in D.C.M. Platt (ed.), *Decline and Recovery in Britain's Overseas Trade, 1873–1914* (London: 1993); C. Harvey and J. Press, 'The City and International Mining, 1870–1914', *Business History*, 32 (1990).
[59] See R. Roberts and D. Kynaston, *City State: How the Markets Came to Rule Our World* (London: 2000), 192; D.W. Elmendorf, M.L. Hircheld and G.D.N. Well, 'The Effect of News on Bond Prices: Evidence from the UK 1900–1920', *Review of Economics and Statistics*, 78 (1996), 341.
[60] Cassis (ed.), *Finance and Financiers*: Wilkins 433–4.
[61] I. Stone, The Global Export of Capital from Great Britain, 1865–1914: A Statistical Survey (London: 1999), 6, 28, Tables 56 and 61; D.C.M. Platt, *Britain's Investment Overseas on the Eve of the First World War: The Use and Abuse of Numbers* (London: 1986), 45–7.

outward flows of funds took in 150 separate countries, including many that had their own currencies, such as those of Europe and the Americas. Among the largest recipients of investment from the UK were Argentina, Brazil, Canada, and Russia, all of which had a national currency, while the USA was the single largest borrower of all, resulting in $ stocks and bonds being widely distributed among investors spread across Western Europe. The money raised in London by the issues made there, or through purchases of foreign securities on the LSE, then had to be remitted abroad as most was not used within Britain. There was no attempt to force those raising funds in Britain to use the money within the country. The money that flowed from Britain to Canada, for example, was mostly spent there or on goods imported from the USA. In turn, these outward flows of capital from the UK produced a return in the form of interest or dividends, unless the borrower defaulted or the company went bankrupt. Again, there was no restriction on what this money could be used for or where it was employed. Though taking place in London the purchases of securities made there were not confined to British-based investors but attracted many from continental Europe, especially the shares of South African gold mining companies and the $ bonds of US corporations. The City of London was acting as a conduit between the affluent investors of Western Europe and the attractive investment opportunities emerging elsewhere in the world. It had the capacity and facilities to handle the borrowing requirements of any government or company, no matter how large or complex, and then provide a deep and broad market on which trading could take place, thus ensuring the liquidity of the resulting stocks and bonds.

   This placed the City of London at the centre of a continuous flow of funds from and to countries located all round the world. It was no accident that the City's investment bankers were a highly cosmopolitan group being sourced from around the world because of their connections and expertise. The firm Dunn Fischer and Company, for example, which prospered in the years before the First World War, was a combination of a Canadian, who knew the investment opportunities, and a Swiss national, who was in touch with potential investors in continental Europe. It largely channelled German funds into Latin American tramway projects through an office in London.[62] That type of business generated a need for foreign exchange facilities, and it was one among the many banks and brokers who had established themselves in London in the half-century prior to the First World War. At the same time, the City of London was well integrated into a network of leading financial centres between which funds flowed in continuous streams. Paris was an especially important financial centre for the Mediterranean and Russia, Brussels was at the centre of the finance of tramway projects around the world, Johannesburg attracted investors in gold mines from around the world, while New York increasingly dominated the North American market, including that of Canada. The City of London had no monopoly position in terms of European capital outflows, for example before the First World War, for other

   [62] Stone, *Global Export of Capital*, 24, 26; Edelstein, *Overseas Investment*, 126, 130; *Britain's Investment Overseas*, 45–7.

European centres were serious rivals in particular regions or in certain activities. In terms of capital flows, the City was simply the largest, most sophisticated, and best connected of the major European financial centres at that time.[63] What was happening before the First World War was that the City was developing along such a wide front as a commercial and financial centre that it could accommodate many different markets. With the degree of change that took place in the City between 1850 and 1914, and the challenges and opportunities it experienced, it was inconceivable that it would have not have possessed an active foreign exchange market.[64]

Nevertheless, most remained convinced that no such market existed, and various ideas put forward explain why that was the case, including by Dudley Ward in 1922.[65] The most widely accepted of these was that the dominance of the UK£ in international trade and finance meant that virtually all transactions in London took place in sterling. There was no need for a foreign exchange market in London, unlike the position in other financial centres like Berlin, Paris, and New York where markets existed to facilitate the transfer of the local currency against sterling.[66] Before 1914, Britain was the largest exporter of manufactures and coal; the largest importer of commodities, the largest provider of international services like shipping, communications, credit, and insurance; and the largest international investor. All these generated a constant stream of payments and receipt, but these were, almost wholly, in sterling. Pownall observed in 1881 that 'Almost all the operations of external trade are settled by payment in London. ... London is the financial centre for bales of cotton shipped to Liverpool, for coal exported from Newcastle, for the consignments of Manchester merchants to India.'[67] Similarly, in 1917, Escher wrote, in his book *Foreign Exchange Explained*, that 'London conducts the vast bulk of its foreign business—both export and import—in its own currency, the pound sterling.'[68] Under these circumstances, there was considered to be no call for a market in London in which the UK£ was traded for other currencies. Both sides to a transaction were willing to use sterling as it was a currency that was in universal demand. As Nurse and Brown stated in their classic account of the *International Currency Experience*, published by the League of Nations in 1944, 'The international gold standard was in effect a sterling standard. London was the commercial and financial heart of the whole system.'[69] It was not until the dominance of the UK£ was lost, beginning with the impact of the First World War, that the need arose for a foreign exchange

[63] R.C. Michie, *The London and New York Stock Exchanges, 1850–1914* (London: 1987), ch. 1–5.
[64] See W. Jansson, *The Finance-Growth Nexus in Britain, 1850–1913* (Cambridge D.Phil., 2018); W. Jansson, 'Stock Markets, Banks and Economic Growth in the UK, 1850–1913', *Financial History Review*, 25 (2019).
[65] Ward, 'Foreign Exchange Market in London'.
[66] Clare, *The ABC of the Foreign Exchanges*, 18; Einzig, *Forward Exchange*, 8–10; Einzig, *History of Foreign Exchange*, 182–5, 198; Atkin, *The Foreign Exchange Market of London*, 5–8, 31.
[67] G.W. Pownall, 'The Proportional Use of Credit Documents and Metallic Money in English Banks', *JIB*, 2 (1881), 642–3.
[68] M. Escher, *Foreign Exchange Explained* (New York: 1917), 11.
[69] Nurse and Brown, *International Currency Experience*. See D. Williams, 'The Evolution of the Sterling System', in C.R. Whittlesey and J.S.G. Wilson (eds), *Essays in Money and Banking* (Oxford: 1968), 267–74.

market in London, in which sterling was traded for other currencies, particularly the US\$.[70] Supporting this thesis is the argument that the leading financial centre was never the location of the foreign exchange market because it conducted all its business in its national currency. According to the Bank for International Settlements, in their triennial survey of the global foreign exchange market, in 2019, 43 per cent of turnover took place in London. This position was achieved at a time when New York was the most important financial centre in the world and the use of the US\$ dominated international transactions. This thesis would explain the position of London before the First World War and New York after the Second World War.[71] However, when London emerged as the principal centre of the global foreign exchange market in the 1920s, the UK£ was still the most important currency in the world, followed by the US\$ and the French franc, and London remained the most important financial centre despite the rivalry of New York.[72] It is also incorrect to state that London had no need for a foreign exchange market of its own, and could rely on the facilities provided by Berlin, Paris, and New York. Important as was the UK£, it was not the only currency extensively used in international commercial and financial transactions before the First World War. Though half world trade was financed in sterling before the First World War, this meant the other half was not.[73] Warren observed in 1903 that London's 'position as the clearing house of the world is now less powerful than formerly, owing to large accumulations of capital in other centres'.[74] The French franc was the currency of the French Empire, second in size only to that of Britain, and stretching from Africa to Asia. The franc was also an important currency elsewhere in Europe and the countries bordering the Mediterranean. Britain's relative economic importance was also in decline from the 1870s, and it was losing out to Germany, Japan, and the USA, each of which had their own currency. The German mark and Japanese yen grew in importance after they joined the Gold Standard in the 1870s and 1890s, respectively, while the US\$ became more widely used in the twenty years before the First World War as the bimetallism controversy died away. Even key members of the British Empire retained their monetary independence with India using the rupee while the Canadian \$ was tied to that of the USA. According to Eckardt, in his 1908 *Manual of Canadian Banking,*

There is no independent market for sterling in this country. We get our quotations from New York. The reason is because the market there is broad and strong. The great bulk of the exports and imports of the whole continent is settled for in New York. There are nearly always plenty of buyers and plenty of sellers. So it happens

---

[70] Atkin, *The Foreign Exchange Market of London*, 5–8, 31. See O. Accominotti and D. Chambers, 'If You're So Smart: John Maynard Keynes and Currency Speculation in the Interwar Years', *Journal of Economic History*, 76 (2016).

[71] This was my original deduction from the evidence.

[72] H. Goodacre, 'The Foreign Exchange and Over-the-Counter Interest Derivatives Market in the United Kingdom', *BEQB*, 20 December 2019; P. Newman, M. Milgate and J. Eatwell (eds), *The New Palgrave Dictionary of Money and Finance* (London: Palgrave Macmillan, 1992), 154–8.

[73] S.E. Thomas, *Banking and Exchange* (London: Gregg Publishing, 1930), 381.

[74] Warren, *Bank of England*, 103.

that the Canadian banks use that market for their sterling exchange. The New York quotations for sterling are fixed each day according to the demand for, and supply of, London remittance.[75]

Britain's commercial and financial relations with other countries also created exchange requirements for Britain's own banks. Britain remained the largest trading nation, and that included extensive imports from and exports to numerous different European countries, all of which had their own currencies. Britain was also the principal market for agricultural commodities like wheat and cotton, and this led to strong seasonal and cyclical fluctuations in the demand for foreign exchange. These had to be accommodated. In addition, Britain's extensive international investment resulted in massive flows of currency as assets were purchased and sold and interest and dividends were received involving countries spread around the world. Though much of this was in sterling, a significant portion was not, including that with the USA, Russia, Canada, Argentina, Brazil, Australia, India, Japan, and China. International travel and migration, which involved the movement of millions of people from diverse countries, also required the conversion of one currency into another as funds were remitted across borders. As most of these financial flows involved banks, and London was the hub of the global banking system, an active foreign exchange market located there was to be expected.[76] With the City of London the most important financial centre before the First World War, it was inconceivable that these financial flows would not pass through it and call forth activity in a conveniently located foreign exchange market. It was through London that most countries engaged with international commercial and financial transactions. London acted as the interface between the countries of Western Europe and the wider world, and these involved numerous different currencies. What this meant was that there was a need for a foreign exchange market where sterling could be traded for other currencies either because of bilateral transactions or when it was being used as a vehicle for third-country transactions.[77]

Nevertheless, the assumption is made that it was foreign exchange markets in other financial centres that provided for both the regular exchange of one currency against another and to cover the risks that exposure to currency fluctuations created when most international trade and finance was conducted on credit.[78] Writing in 1908, Easton took the view that 'The foreign exchanges are of more importance abroad than in England.'[79] Whereas this may be true in the spot market, where the local currency

[75] H.M.P. Eckardt, *Manual of Canadian Banking* (Toronto: 1908), 108.

[76] A. Ellis, *The Rationale of Market Fluctuations* (London: 1876), 72; A.W. Margraff, *International Exchange* (Chicago: 1903), 31; Withers, *Money-Changing*; Clare, *ABC of the Foreign Exchanges*, 29–32; Brooks, *Foreign Exchange Textbook*, 120; Einzig, *History of Foreign Exchange*, 122, 134, 137; McCloskey and Zecher, 'How the Gold Standard Worked', 385.

[77] Clare, *The ABC of the Foreign Exchanges*, 13, 28–35, 39, 42–3, 45, 51, 53, 58, 68, 70, 76, 79, 80–6, 89, 96, 107, 120, 125; J. Braga de Macedo, B. Eichengreen, and J. Reis (eds), *Currency Convertibility: The Gold Standard and Beyond* (London: 1996): chapters by de Cecco, 108 and Eichengreen and Flandreau, 121; Ball and Sunderland, *Economic History of London*, 327.

[78] Phillips, *Modern Foreign Exchange*, 66; Einzig, *History of Foreign Exchange*, 182–5, 198.

[79] Easton, *Money, Exchange and Banking*, 57.

was exchanged for the UK£, it hardly applied to the forward market. Neither Paris nor New York had significant forward markets, despite the importance of the franc and the dollar, respectively, while those which had operated in Berlin and Vienna in the nineteenth century had declined in importance before the First World War. This absence of active forward markets in foreign exchange was in the face of the growing need for banks to cover the exchange risks that their customers were passing on to them, and their own exposure to currency mismatches between assets and liabilities. The lack of a forward market for foreign exchange before the First World War becomes harder and harder to explain once the activities of banks in a multi-currency world is accepted.[80] London would have been the most obvious location for such a market as it was at the centre of the global financial system before the First World War and sterling was the default currency for international trade as well as financial and commodity markets.[81] As Saul concluded in his study of Britain and the world economy between 1870 and 1914, 'It was around Britain that this whole complicated network of multilateral settlements centred itself.'[82] Leslie Pressnell suggested in 1978 that London played a central role in the stabilization of exchange rates before 1914.[83]

The communications revolution also had a transformational effect on London's markets for money, commodities, securities, and money, and it seems inconceivable that foreign exchange trading would not be similarly affected.[84] Writing in 1912 Lord Revelstoke, the chairman of Barings Bank, considered that the conduct of international finance had been revolutionized as a result of the transformation of communications.

> The whole of the commerce and finance of the world is now so intermingled and intertwined by the telephone and the telegraph, and the sympathy between the various countries is so acute and so quick, that any bad feature which occurs anywhere is instantly reflected in almost every other part of the globe.[85]

In 1908, Carson, the London manager of the Anglo-American Telegraph Company, claimed that transatlantic communication was 'practically instantaneous', with the delay between a cable message sent from London to New York, and a reply received, being within one to three minutes.[86] By then, the telegraph was being superseded by the telephone when it came to communication between London and Continental

---

[80]   Escher, *Foreign Exchange Explained*, 12–13; Einzig, *Forward Exchange*, 1st ed., 8–10, 2nd ed., 1967, 2; B. Brown, *The Forward Market in Foreign Exchange: A Study in Market-Making, Arbitrage and Speculation* (London: 1983), 3, 13.

[81]   Yeager, *International Monetary Relations*, 235, 256–9; Eichengreen, *The Gold Standard*, 16.

[82]   Saul, *British Overseas Trade*, 44. See Accominotti *et al.*, 'The Origination and Distribution of Money Market Instruments'.

[83]   L.S. Pressnell, '1925: The Burden of Sterling', *Economic History Review*, 31 (1978), 67–8.

[84]   G.A. Fletcher, *The Discount Houses in London: Principles, Operations and Change* (London: 1976), 16–40.

[85]   *Report and Proceedings of the Standing Sub-committee of the Committee for Imperial Defence on Trading with the Enemy, 1912*: Evidence of Lord Revelstoke from Barings Bank, 96.

[86]   30 May 1908: Evidence of M. Carson, the Manager of the Anglo-American Telegraph Company, London Stock Exchange, Committee for General Purposes: Memorandum on the Daylight Saving Bill, 1908.

Europe, as it delivered instant and continuous contact. As early as 1903, it was reported to the LSE that 'The telephones to Paris and Brussels were used almost exclusively by the Foreign Market that they were rapidly superseding telegrams.'[87] The result for the LSE, in a report produced in 1908, was that

> From its geographical position, aided by other causes, London is the clearing house of the world in stock exchange matters. Business, both for investment and speculation, centres in London from the Continent of Europe, from the United States and Canada, from South Africa, and to a lesser degree from India, Australia and Japan. Investors and speculators in these countries find it convenient to send the bulk of their orders to London where owing to its central position they find a ready market. … The American and colonial operator deals almost exclusively in the securities of his own country, while British and Continental operators deal in all, and there is a free market in all in London. Placed as it is, London attracts business in American and South African securities from all parts of the Continent, and in American securities to a large extent from America itself.[88]

There were hints from a few contemporaries that London's foreign exchange market shared in the transformation taking place, especially from observers in North America. Writing from New York in 1903, Pratt was of the opinion that 'The foreign exchange market is … a vast international clearing house. … As London clears for the world, so New York clears for the United States.'[89] Another was Brooks, whose book, a Foreign Exchange Textbook, was published in Chicago in 1906. In it, he stated that 'London is the exchange centre of the British Empire and partly of the entire world.' He credited the telegraph with having transformed the foreign exchange market. 'The cable has brought about a most marvellous change in the method of operating in foreign exchange. For at least a portion of the day transactions … can be executed simultaneously—an order in one city being executed in the other.'[90] Another who recognized London's importance within the pre-war foreign exchange market was the Canadian banker, Stewart Patterson, in his book *Domestic and Foreign Exchange*, which was published in New York in 1917. 'The quotations in New York for exchange on Berlin or Paris are largely influenced by the price of sterling exchange.' This influence extended to the Far East on the one hand and North America on the other as London 'knows the conditions in eastern markets before they close and is open long enough to operate in New York before her own markets close.' The conclusion that Patterson drew was that 'In foreign exchange the London market is dominant.'[91] What this leaves unanswered is the question of where in London was this foreign exchange market? The most obvious location was the discount market as it already

[87] Committee of Trustees and Managers: Sub-committee on the Enlargement of the House, 22 December 1903.
[88] Committee for General Purposes: Memorandum on the Daylight Saving Bill, 1908.
[89] S.S. Pratt, *The Work of Wall Street* (New York: 1903), 227.
[90] Brooks, *Foreign Exchange Textbook*, 3, 217.
[91] S. Patterson, *Domestic and Foreign Exchange*, 41–3, 126–7, 141–2, 151, 154, 158, 160, 170, 184, 242–4, 249.

possessed the intermediaries and the network that handled the constant borrowing and lending that took place between the world's banks, either directly through the offices and branches they maintained in the City of London or indirectly by those acting on their behalf.

The Money Market, 1850–1914

Central to the microstructure of the City of London as a financial centre was its money market. As Britain was the most advanced economy in the world by the nineteenth century, and London long contained the largest concentration of the wealthiest people; was the centre of trade and a hub for transport and communications; a major location for manufacturing; and housed the seat of government, it possessed a highly developed money market. The money market connected savers, investors, and borrowers, matching their requirements in terms of amount, time, type, location, and degree of risk. From this grew banks and bankers, serving the needs of individuals and businesses for saving and investment opportunities or the supply of credit and capital. Those banks that were heavily reliant on deposits from savers for the funds that were lent out were especially vulnerable to large and sudden withdrawals, which could overwhelm their cash reserves and force them out of business. To ward against that situation, banks of this kind had to maintain a highly liquid position, which meant that they were always in a position to meet withdrawals. As Easton explained in 1908,

> Large sums are left with banks on deposit accounts. In order that the banker may make a profit out of such transactions he must lend the money at a rate of interest considerably in excess of that which he pays to the depositor. ... It is most essential that banks should not lend even their unemployed capital for any considerable length of time, they must be prepared for sudden emergencies.[92]

To Spicer in that same year, 'The very existence of a bank depends upon it being able at all times to meet the demands made upon it.'[93] The dilemma faced by banks of this kind was that the money they kept in reserve to meet such a situation earned no rate of interest while remaining unused most of the time. If that money could be employed, while remaining liquid, then the bank would receive a return while also able to meet sudden withdrawals.

In 1903, Warren spelled out the balance between risk and return that these banks had to maintain.

> Undoubtedly our banking system is exposed to the gravest dangers, but as it brings us cheap money we accept the risks. ... The dangers of our system are very

---

[92] Easton, *Money, Exchange and Banking*, 2nd ed., 51–3, 57, 64, 72, 77, 82, 111, 132, 169, 182, 185.
[93] E.E. Spicer, *An Outline of the Money Market* (London: 1908), 18.

apparent, but so are its advantages; and though we consider it pays us to take the risks, it is evident that we cannot afford to neglect the necessary precautions.[94]

Those precautions required a bank to hold reserves, including assets that could be easily and quickly converted into cash, and that was where the London money market played an essential role. What the London money market could provide were short-term borrowing and lending opportunities that allowed banks to employ their reserves remuneratively while keeping them liquid. In 1904, it was estimated that London bankers kept 15 per cent of their assets in cash or on deposit with other banks, which meant it earned little or no interest but was immediately available to meet withdrawals by depositors and others from whom the bank had borrowed money. A further 15 per cent was lent out at call or short term, and this did earn interest while being easily accessed by requesting repayment. Another 23 per cent was invested in securities, which either paid dividends or on which interest was received, and these could be sold but that could take time though some could be realized quickly. Finally, 47 per cent was lent to customers in one form or another and for periods of varying duration, and none of this was readily available until the loans matured.[95] Faced with growing competition, it became increasingly necessary for each bank to minimize the amount of money on which it received no interest as that would maximize the amount of business it could do and the returns it could generate for its owners and staff. All banks faced seasonal and cyclical imbalances in the amount of money they received on deposits and the requests made upon them for loans. This left them either in surplus or in deficit, which forced them to hold an excess of reserves to equalize supply and demand. This was not a peculiarly British problem but applied to all countries and was also the case internationally, and so required a solution at the national and the global level.[96]

The British solution was provided by the London money market, and it was increasingly made use of not only by banks from London but throughout the UK. It was in the London money market that banks could employ surplus funds remuneratively or raise additional funds when required at short notice.[97] This can be seen in the case of the Irish banks. They found that the Dublin money market lacked sufficient depth to provide them with the liquidity they required and so they turned to London. As early as 1854, the National Bank of Ireland opened a branch in London which both accepted deposits and made loans. By 1914, access to the London money market had become essential for all British banks, as no other British financial centre could match its depth and breadth. From the mid-nineteenth century onwards, the increasing size, scale, and complexity of financial transactions forced all British banks to turn to the London money market as only there could they find the contacts

---

[94] Warren, *Bank of England*, 70, 80.
[95] F. Straker, 'The Daily Money Article', *JIB*, 25 (1904), 5–6; Schuster, 'Foreign Trade', 58; D. Spring-Rice, 'The Financial Machinery of the City of London', *JIB*, 50 (1929), 8–13.
[96] Kemmerer, *Season Variations*, 53, 136.
[97] E. Seyd, *The London Banking and Bankers' Clearing House System* (London: 1872), 21–3, 61; W. Howarth, *The Banks in the Clearing House* (London: 1905), 118–19, 173.

and services they required to make and receive payments, and borrow and lend any amount at all times. British banks were then followed by banks from around the world in making use of the London money market.[98] Writing in 1902, Sykes reflected that the turning point for the London money market was the effect on Paris of war and revolution in 1870–1. 'Paris was for a time London's chief rival, but the suspension of cash payments by the Bank of France, after the Franco-German War, led to the transfer of a great deal of her financial business to London, and she has never recovered this lost ground.'[99] On the eve of the First World War, Edward Holden, the chairman of the Midland Bank, considered that the London money market occupied a central position in the global financial system.[100]

Key to the operation of the London money market in the nineteenth century was the use made of the bill of exchange. In return for a loan from a bank, a borrower signed a banker's bill promising to repay at the end of a specified period. That bill would be issued at a discount to the amount that had to be repaid, and that represented the profit which the bank would make when the loan matured. During the duration of a bill, it could either be held until it matured, usually after ninety days, or be bought and sold many times over. The nearer a bill was to the date when it was redeemed, the closer was its price to the maturity value, as the period between purchase and return was less and the chance of a possible default lower. Whenever a bill was purchased, those buying it paid less than face value and their return was represented by the difference between what they paid and what they received from a subsequent sale or on maturity. Bills were highly liquid assets that allowed banks to either employ the funds at their disposal, by buying and holding them until redemption, or raise additional funds by selling them on. By selling on bills that it had issued, while remaining liable to paying out the face value on maturity, banks could raise additional funds which, in turn, could be lent out generating more bills which could also be sold, and so repeating the process.[101] Spicer in 1908 defined a bill of exchange as 'a note promising payment at a specified date in the future.'[102] This combination of a means of payment, a source of credit, and an interest-paying asset gave bills of exchange a near-universal appeal. As early as 1864, Goschen claimed that 'Most international transactions are settled by a transfer of debts, through the medium of foreign bills of exchange.'[103] In 1904, Schuster observed that 'A bill of exchange on London is the recognised medium of settling international transactions, which is made use of in all parts of the world.'[104] Money's 'Fiscal Dictionary', published in London in

[98] P. Ollerenshaw, *Banking in Nineteenth-Century Ireland: The Belfast Banks*, 1825–1914 (Manchester: 1987), 81, 94, 105, 182–5; C. Munn, 'The Emergence of Central Banking in Ireland', *Irish Economic and Social History*, 10 (1983), 28; C.W. Munn, *Clydesdale Bank: The First 150 Years* (London: 1988), 25, 72–3, 83, 97, 102, 143–5.
[99] E.W. Sykes, 'The Growth of London as the Financial Centre of the World, and the Best Means of Maintaining That Position', *JIB*, 23 (1902), 367.
[100] E.H. Holden, 'The World's Money Markets', *The Statist*, 24 January 1914.
[101] S. Moshenskyi, *History of the Weksel: Bill of Exchange and Promissory Note* (New York: Xlibris Corporation, 2008), 167.
[102] Spicer, *Outline of the Money Market*, 34.
[103] G.J. Goschen, *The Theory of the Foreign Exchanges* (London: 1864), 23.
[104] Schuster, 'Foreign Trade', 58.

1910, defined a bill of exchange as 'a piece of negotiable money if the names upon it are reputable' and claimed that 'the sending of these slips of paper between nations is the only form of payment which usually passes'.[105]

Banks made extensive use of bills of exchange when they employed the originate-and-distribute model of banking, either by issuing bills and selling them on or buying bills using surplus funds. Increasingly, banks all over the world turned to the use of sterling bills as liquid assets which could, at a moment's notice, either absorb surplus funds or be sold to cover a shortfall. Sterling bills underpinned global trade and finance before the First World War, whether as a means of payment, a source of short-term credit, or a temporary investment, smoothing out seasonal and cyclical variations and equalizing supply and demand between banks. Sterling bills constituting a form of international currency and the London money market played a central role in enhancing and maintaining their attractions worldwide.[106] As Spalding explained in 1911,

> When no commercial bills can be bought, the bankers in one country draw on those in another, and subsequently square the liability they have incurred to the acceptors of the bills by buying up and remitting export bills as soon as the goods have been shipped and drafts are available.[107]

The use of the bill of exchange and the development of the London money market went hand-in-hand during the nineteenth century. The former required a market where they could be bought and sold, which made them liquid, while the latter required a financial asset that could be readily traded. Contributing to the appeal of the London money market was the emergence of specialist intermediaries, in the form of bill brokers. Employing a small capital, and operating at margins as low as 0.25 per cent, they made it their business to maintain daily contact with the banks, either to borrow money at interest, promising to repay the following day, or to buy and sell bills of exchange at a discount to their face value. The entry in the daily diary of one firm of bill brokers, Smith St. Aubyn, in January 1914, reveals the routine nature of the business by then. 'We had a big book but found no difficulty in getting the money required at c.2/2¼% for a week. Bills as scarce as ever and rates still falling. It is extraordinary how long the drop has now lasted. 1 and 2 months can be sold at 2½%.'[108] As bill brokers bought bills of exchange at a discount to their face value, they were called discount houses and the money market was also referred to as the discount market.[109] The presence of bill brokers provided banks with the certainty that

---

[105] L.G. Chiozza Money, *Money's Fiscal Dictionary* (London: 1910), 52.

[106] E.W. Kemmerer, *Season Variations in the Relative Demand for Money and Capital in the United States* (Washington: 1910), 140–1.

[107] W.F. Spalding, 'The Establishment and Growth of Foreign Branch Banks in London, and the Effect, Immediate and Ultimate, upon the Banking and Commercial Development of This Country', *JIB*, 32 (1911), 455.

[108] Smith St. Aubyn, Business Diary, 23 January 1914.

[109] For the early development of the London money market, see K.F. Dixon, *The Development of the London Money Market, 1780–1830*, unpublished University of London PhD, 1962, 7–8, 14, 18, 32–3, 37, 92, 98, 156, 160, 190.

they could buy or sell bills and lend or borrow money whenever they wanted. According to Straker in 1904, 'Their business demands great knowledge and discrimination as to the standing of parties, and they are practically bound to buy at the prevailing market price all good bills offered to them, or they lose their connection and business.'[110] Financed by borrowing from banks bill brokers engaged in a continuous business of buying and selling bills and borrowing and repaying money. This could only be done if the bank was confident that it could always lend excess funds, that loans would be repaid on demand, and bills were available to purchase. Helping to provide that confidence was the role played by the Bank of England and the LSE. The Bank of England acted as lender of last resort to the discount houses. Any shortfall between the bills the discount houses bought from the banks and money they borrowed from the banks was made up by the Bank of England on a routine basis and at a profit. The Bank of England lent to the discount houses receiving bills of exchange and other securities as collateral.[111] Secure in the knowledge that the Bank of England would act as lender of last resort on a daily basis, the bill brokers were able to buy all the bills they were offered. Bill brokers were also confident that they could employ whatever money they received from the banks because of the facilities provided by the LSE. It housed the deepest and broadest market for stocks and bonds in the world before the First Word War and this liquidity provided the discount houses with immediate investment opportunities. Funds were borrowed at low rates of interest to buy higher yielding stocks and bonds, and so profit from the differential in yield, confident that they could resell quickly if the loan had to be repaid on maturity and could not be replaced with another.[112] According to A.C. Cole in 1904, 'Money in the City is lent indifferently in the discount market, on the Stock Exchange, and in the produce markets. It is merely a question of which market offers the best rate of interest, taking into account the security and the duration of the loan.'[113] Conversely, the LSE also provided the discount houses with a means of selling their holdings of stocks and bonds for immediate repayment, thus allowing them to repay their loans from banks in full and on time. What this meant was that banks with access to the London money market were guaranteed that they could always borrow and lend short term, which greatly increased its attractions, and left it without rivals in the world before 1914.[114] One contemporary who was impressed was Keynes, writing in 1914 that 'I believe our banking system, and indeed the whole intricate organism of the City, to

[110] Straker, 'Daily Money Article', 6.

[111] Interview between the Governor and Directors of the Bank of England and the National Monetary Commission, 1910, 311–12, 319.

[112] R.C. Michie, 'The City of London and British Banking, 1900–1939', in C. Wrigley (ed.), *A Companion to Early Twentieth Century Britain* (Oxford: 2003). For some examples, see L. Gall, G.D. Feldman, H. James, C.-L. Holtfrerich and H.E. Buschgen, *The Deutsche Bank, 1870–1995* (London: 1995), 17, 131; H. Bauer, *Swiss Bank Corporation 1872–1972* (Basel: 1972), 135–6; Cleveland and Huertas, *Citibank*, 43–4, 73, 80.

[113] A.C. Cole, 'Notes on the London Money Market', *JIB*, 25 (1904), 134.

[114] Straker, 'Daily Money Article', 5–6; Schuster, 'Foreign Trade', 58; D.M. Mason, 'Our Money Market and American Banking and Currency Reform', *JIB*, 30 (1909), 203; Spalding, 'Foreign Branch Banks in London', 435, 437, 455, 461; E. Sykes, 'Some Effects of the War on the London Money Market', *JIB*, 36 (1914), 73, 78; Spring-Rice, 'Financial Machinery of the City', 8–13.

be one of the best and most characteristic creations of that part of the genius and virtue of our nation which has found its outlet in business.'[115]

Bills of exchange were simultaneously instruments of transfer, credit, and investment and the discount houses acted as intermediaries between buyers and sellers, providing banks with ready access to funds or investment opportunities and the ability to balance assets and liabilities on a current and future basis. Such a facility was of immense value to a bank as it was continually engaged in maximizing the use of the funds at its disposal while minimizing its exposure to the risks posed by being in a position of borrowing short and lending long. Banks had to be certain that they could quickly draw on the money market for funds or employ their excess, and the discount houses provided this certainty. They were always ready to either buy bills or borrow money from each bank that they visited, aiming to balance their account by the end of the day. The London money market was, simultaneously, a source of cheap finance, with interest rates lower than in any other major financial centre, and of liquidity, which was essential for every bank.[116] As Warren put it in 1903, 'Our great credit machine, when skilfully managed, can successfully endure considerable strain.'[117] Such a market was relied upon by banks around the world as they drew on London when money was tight at home and then lent in London when it was easy.[118] As Huth Jackson, a director of the Bank of England, observed in 1912, 'Every country recognises that London is still the centre of the international money market.'[119] Though other financial centres possessed large and active money markets before 1914, such as Paris, Berlin, Amsterdam, and New York, none could match London.[120] The annual turnover of bills in London grew from £425 million in 1840 to £2,000 million in 1913.[121] On the eve of the war in 1914, it was estimated by Sykes that London banks held about £200 million in bills and had lent £100 million to bill brokers.[122]

The domestic role played by the London money market, and the use of bills of exchange, was increasingly challenged by the development of large banks with nationwide operations from the mid-nineteenth century onwards. The 1,000

[115] J.M. Keynes, 'The Prospects of Money', *Economic Journal*, 24 (1914), 633.
[116] Warren, *Bank of England*, 70, 80, 103, 142–5, 151, 316–17; A. Andreades, *History of the Bank of England* (London: 1909), 316–20, 385; National Monetary Commission, *Statistics for Great Britain, Germany and France*, 143.
[117] Warren, *Bank of England*, 251.
[118] *Wall Street Journal*, 9 September 1889, 9 May 1891, 20 February 1893, 2 February 1895, 16 September 1895, 25 October 1897, 14 December 1899, 5 December 1907, 8 February 1913.
[119] Jackson *et al.*, *Lectures on British Commerce*, 14–17. See H. Withers, *The English Banking System* (Washington: 1910), 55.
[120] See Accominotti *et al.*, 'The Origination and Distribution of Money Market Instruments'; J.T. Madden and M. Nadler, 'The Paris Money Market', *Bulletin of the Institute of International Finance* (New York: 1 June 1931); G. Tullio and J. Wotters, 'Was London the Conductor of the International Orchestra or Just the Triangle Player? An Empirical Analysis of Asymmetries in Interest Rate Behaviour during the Classical Gold Standard, 1896–1913', *Scottish Journal of Political Economy*, 43 (1996); D.T. Merrett, 'Global Reach by Australian Banks: Correspondent Banking Networks, 1830–1960', *Business History*, 37 (1995).
[121] T.M. Rybczynski, 'The Merchant Banks', *Manchester School of Economic and Social Studies*, 41 (1973), 109; M. Collins and M. Baker, *Commercial Banks and Industrial Finance in England and Wales, 1860–1913* (Oxford: 2003), 74–5, 125.
[122] Sykes, 'Some Effects of the War', 73, 78.

individual banks at the beginning of the nineteenth century, each practising originate-and-distribute banking, were replaced by a small number of very large banks managing nationwide branch networks. By 1913, a few London-based banks were in control of retail banking in England and Wales, with only Scotland and Ireland remaining outside their orbit. Their scale, depth, and spread allowed them to internalize many of the operations once performed by the London money market as they could internally match supply and demand among their customers. One of the leading discount houses was Gilletts, and its banking connections fell from 273 in 1873 to 67 in 1885.[123] These large banks perfected a way of operation that allowed them to employ short-term deposits in longer-term loans that was both safe and remunerative, while their size meant that they recruited and trained staff who could assess risk under the supervision of experienced inspectors and auditors. The result was a constant balancing of assets and liabilities that minimized the liquidity and solvency risks that all banks were exposed to. This was the lend-and-hold model and it largely replaced the originate-and-distribute one, with customers being provided directly with revolving credit that matched their needs, rather than through a bill of exchange for a fixed amount and duration. Such was the successful implementation of the lend-and-hold model after 1866 that British banks became highly resilient, and there was no major crises in British banking until the outbreak of the First World War, though a few individual banks did collapse. The effect was to shrink the reliance previously placed on the London money market by Britain's domestic banks.[124]

Despite the switch from the originate-and-distribute to the lend-and-hold model of banking, the London money market continued to play a very important role within the British banking system. At any one time, an individual bank, even a very large one, could find itself either short of funds or with an excess, depending on the actions of its customers when repaying loans, making deposits, or seeking to borrow. In the past, meeting these challenges meant a bank had to either maintain a large reserve and be forced to turn away business or risk a liquidity crisis. In 1913, 88 per cent of UK bank liabilities consisted of bank deposits. As these could be quickly withdrawn, it forced banks to prioritize liquidity. Maintaining this liquidity restricted the ability of the bank to lend, forced it to prioritize short-term over long-term loans, reduced the interest that it could pay depositors, increased the charges made to borrowers, lowered the profits it could make, and shrunk the level of remuneration received by its employees. Through a mechanism by which banks could lend to and borrow from each other on a continuous basis, the level of the reserve necessary to maintain liquidity could be kept low, and this is what the London money market provided. By selling a bill to a discount house, a bank received money, while giving a loan to a discount

---

[123] R.S. Sayers, *Gilletts in the London Money Market, 1867–1967* (Oxford: 1968), 1–2, 36–7, 45–55, 60, 68, 78, 80, 87, 95, 101–2, 122, 126, 158–9.

[124] Collins and Baker, *Commercial Banks*, 56, 62–9, 74–7, 87, 94, 98, 105, 109, 125, 181, 257–8; F.E. Steele, 'On Changes in the Bank Rate of Discount, First, Their Causes; and Secondly, Their Effects on the Money Market, on the Commerce of the Country, and on the Value of All Interest-Bearing Securities', *JIB*, 12 (1891), 497; J.B. Attfield, 'The Advantages, or Otherwise, of the Establishment of Branches by Bankers, from the Point of View (a) of the Bankers, and (b) of the General Interests of the Community', *JIB*, 13 (1892), 469–73.

house meant they employed otherwise idle money.[125] According to Tritton, in 1902, the business of the bill broker was 'to discover each morning in his rounds which banks are full of money, and therefore lenders. And which are poor and therefore taking money off the market'.[126] He estimated that there was a continuous turnover of up to £2 million a day in the London money market.

What sustained this level of business before the First World War was the increasing international orientation of the London money market as it came to serve the global banking community. It became pivotal in the constant movement of money around the world, and the place where all banks, either directly or indirectly, employed surplus funds or made up any temporary shortfall.[127] Writing in 1922 about the pre-war situation, Furniss explained that

> The ease with which sterling long bills could be sold in all quarters of the world has been … but a reflection of the willingness of bankers to acquire credits in London. … The very fact that sterling long bills have been widely used as financing instruments has, of itself, resulted in a broad and widely diffused demand for sterling sight drafts.[128]

This can be traced through the value of sterling bills in circulation, which rose from an average of £352 million in 1836–40 to £1,317 million in 1876–80, fell back to £1,202 million in 1890–1900, recovered to £1,384 million in 1901–10, before reaching £1,730 million in 1911–13. Beneath these overall numbers, the use to which bills was being put was being transformed by the changing structure of banking not only in Britain but also elsewhere in the world, as the lend-and-hold model replaced the originate-and-distribute one. For Britain, this meant that the domestic issue of bills of exchange peaked at £697 million in 1876–80 and then fell back, running at £614 million in 1911–13. What sustained the recovery in the total value of bills in circulation, after the dip in the 1890s, was their increasing international use. By 1911–13, there were £1,116 million sterling bills in circulation on foreign account compared to £690 million in 1890–1900 and a mere £68 million in 1836–40. Furthermore, there was a major change in the use made of sterling bills. As banks abroad also adopted the lend-and-hold model, rather than the originate-and-distribute one, the use of commercial bills declined. That left banks not only with a commitment to supply borrowers with credit on demand but also accept unlimited deposits and repayments. Any other response would leave them with dissatisfied customers, who could turn to their competitors for a better service. The result was that banks could find themselves with insufficient funds available to lend to customers or with an excess for which they had

[125] W.A. Cole, 'The Relations between Banks and Stock Exchanges', *JIB*, 20 (1899), 409; J.H. Tritton, 'The Short Loan Fund on the London Money Market', *JIB*, 23 (1902), 96–100, 108–9, 114; J.H. Tritton, 'Bills of Exchange and Their Functions', *JIB*, 23 (1902), 213, 216.
[126] Tritton, 'Short Loan Fund', 100.
[127] M. Collins, *Money and Banking in the UK: A History* (London: 1988), 29, 106, 111, 149–54, 221, 245; E. Nevin and E.W. Davis, *The London Clearing Banks* (London: 1970), 105.
[128] E.S. Furniss, *Foreign Exchange: The Financing Mechanism of International Commerce* (New York: 1922), 314–18, 317–18, 324–8, 361.

no immediate demand. What they required was a source of additional funds to supplement their own resources and an investment to absorb the money they had idle. Generating a finance bill and its sale in the London money market would provide a bank with instant access to funds, while either purchasing a finance bill or lending money to a discount house was an instant investment that generated a return. Of the £350 million in prime bills outstanding in London in 1913, £210 million, or sixty per cent, were finance bills, while in the same year an estimated £1.9 billion of foreign money was employed in London. As the lend-and-hold model of banking gradually supplanted the originate-and-distribute one not only in the UK but also around the world, and more countries and a greater variety of economic activity were drawn into international trade and finance, banks turned to the London money market to either supplement the funds they had available or employ those which were excess to requirements.[129]

Sterling bills were increasingly challenged by telegraphic transfers from the 1870s as a quicker and more convenient way of moving money around the world, though only for those countries with relatively sophisticated financial systems and large and well-established banks. Elsewhere, the sterling bill continued to reign supreme. A telegraphic transfer permitted the immediate transfer of funds between banks and so eliminated the risk that existed until a bill of exchange matured. However, a telegraphic transfer depended on the existence of trusted counterparties, with each side of a transaction confident that the other would pay and deliver. That was the case among the largest banks located in the principal financial centres of the world, with those found in London, Paris, Berlin, and New York being the most important. In addition to those, there were tens of thousands of smaller banks scattered around the world and relatively little was known about them. This created a deficit of trust which prevented a universal reliance upon telegraphic transfers. Hence, the continued use of sterling bills as part of the mechanism through which banks lent and borrowed among each other, international payments and receipts were made, and credit was provided for much of the world's trade, especially in agricultural produce. The sterling bill of exchange and the London money market served many different masters by the First World War being reinvented time and again as the growing volume, variety, and complexity of global trade and finance called for solutions.[130] Writing in his *History of the London Discount Market*, which appeared in 1936, King reflected that 'In the few years before the war, London had become in every sense a true international market, in daily, even hourly, contact with foreign centres, which constantly studied its variations, followed its tendency, and took its bills.'[131]

---

[129] A. Crump, *The Key to the London Money Market* (London: 1877), 15; Spalding, *Eastern Exchange Currency*, 2, 106–7, 429; Sayers, *Gilletts*, 2, 36–7; Collins and Baker, *Commercial Banks*, 74–5, 125. See W.M. Scammell, *The London Discount Market* (London: 1968).

[130] W.T.C. King, *History of the London Discount Market* (London: 1936), 30, 39, 42, 47–8, 50, 63, 67, 99, 113, 117, 120–3, 175, 183, 191, 265, 268, 270, 273, 276–82, 288; Fletcher, *Discount Houses*, 6, 11, 13, 16–19, 25, 29–31; Scammell, *London Discount Market*, 123, 160–6, 171; G. Cleaver and P. Cleaver, *The Union Discount: A Centenary Album* (London: 1985), 18–21, 58, 69; Cater Ryder & Co., *Cater Ryder, Discount Bankers, 1816–1966* (London: 1967), 5–13; Levy-Leboyer, 'Central Banking and Foreign Trade', 99–101.

[131] King, *London Discount Market* (London: 1936), 282.

To make use of the London money market, a bank had to establish a connection between itself and those who operated there. That was easy for those British banks with head offices in London or those from elsewhere in the UK that established branches there. In addition, from the mid-nineteenth century a growing number of foreign banks began to open branches in London through which they could participate in the money market. Between 1860 and 1913, the number of foreign banks with London branches rose from three to seventy-one. At the same time, there also came into existence a small group of British overseas banks. These had a London head office but operated elsewhere in the world, especially Asia, Africa, Australasia, and Latin America. There were also numerous small privately owned banks in the City that survived by focusing on specialist niches like trade credit and government and corporate finance, and some of these had strong foreign connections. By 1913, there were 226 banks and quasi-banks with offices in London.[132] This was a tiny proportion of the world's banks, especially as their overall number expanded enormously from the mid-nineteenth century onwards in response to a growing demand for banking services around the world. For most of these banks, it was only when the volume of business was sufficiently large that opening a branch could be justified. A branch cost money for the space, equipment, and staffing and exposed it to risks as it was responsible for what took place there. The solution was to replicate internationally the correspondent network that had served the British banking system before it was replaced by banks operating their own branch networks.[133]

From 1860, the Banking Almanac began to take notice of those foreign and colonial banks with offices in London and, especially, the much greater number that had appointed agents to represent them. Even then, it was not until 1890 that they began to capture the full number. The figure for those with offices or agents in London in 1860 was only 18, rising to 52 in 1880, reaching 237 in 1890, 762 in 1900, and then climbed to 1,356 in 1913.[134] Among the most popular choice as London agent for a foreign bank was one of the large domestic banks as they were trusted counterparties. There was also no conflict of interest or overlap of business as these domestic banks largely confined their activities to the UK. Before 1914, there was a separation between those British banks that operated at home and those with foreign activities. Such was its popularity as a correspondent that the Midland Bank opened a department in 1902 to cater for the needs of those foreign banks for which it had correspondent agreements and for which it acted as their London agent. The number of the Midland's correspondents reached 132 in 1910.[135] These correspondent

---

[132] *The Banking Almanac* (London: 1913), 38–57; A.S.J. Baster, *The International Banks* (London: 1935), 4; A. Teichova, G. Kurgan-Van Hentenryk and D. Ziegler (eds), *Banking, Trade and Industry; Europe, America and Asia from the 13th to the 20th Century* (Cambridge: 1997): Nishimura, 379–92; O. Checkland, S. Nishimura and N. Tamaki (eds), *Pacific Banking, 1859–1959: East Meets West* (London: 1994), 17, 36, 47–8, 175. See also Cassis, *City Bankers*; G. Jones, *British Multinational Banking, 1830–1990* (Oxford: 1993); Cassis (ed.), *Finance and Financiers*: Cottrell.

[133] Merrett, 'Global Reach', 70–3, 75, 80.

[134] The Banking Almanac, *List of Foreign and Colonial Banks with Offices/Agents in London: 1860, 1880, 1890, 1900, 1913.*

[135] *The Banking Almanac* (London: 1913), 38–57; Easton, *Money, Exchange and Banking*, 52, 77, 82; Baster, *International Banks*, 4; Teichova et al., *Banking, Trade and Industry*: Nishimura, 379–92;

agreements placed strict obligations on both parties as Furniss explained. The foreign bank had to maintain a positive balance on its deposit account with the London bank which, in turn, had to provide it with credit up to an agreed amount. This was in addition to both undertaking routine administrative tasks for the other, including making and receiving payments on behalf of each other's customers. According to Furniss in 1922, a correspondent agreement had 'the effect of making the London bank either a partner or an agent of the foreign bank in transactions which involve the two markets.'[136]

The more links London banks had to other banks around the world, the greater was the necessity for other banks to establish a London connection, as that was the easiest, cheapest, and most convenient way of connecting to the global payments network and accessing the facilities of the London money market. In 1895, George Clare referred to London as 'the international clearing house and pay-office', while Rozenraad, who worked for the London branch of the Banque d'Escompte de Paris, observed in 1903 that 'Transactions between countries which have no direct or no sufficient exchange relations, are settled by bills or cheques on London.'[137] As confidence grew on both sides of a correspondent agreement, the amount of business expanded, including the amount kept on deposit and borrowed from the London money market. The American Escher wrote in 1917 that 'London is today, as she has been for centuries, the world's banker ... internationally speaking, everyone carries a balance in London.' He explained that

With the banks all over the world leaving large sums of money on deposit in London at all times, and with the use of all this money in British hands, is there any further explanation needed of the fact that the discount market in London completely overshadows in importance the discount market of every other point? ... This fact that banks all over the world keep balances in London is of the utmost importance. At all times these banks stand ready to sell drafts in sterling on their London balances. At all times they stand ready to buy drafts drawn in sterling on London, for the purpose of replenishing these balances. Practically anywhere in the world and at any time, in other words, you can buy drafts on London if you need one, or, if you have a draft on London to sell, you can find a bank which will take it off your hands. ... That being the case, it has come about that London conducts the vast bulk of its foreign business—both export and import—in its own currency, the pound sterling.[138]

Checkland et al., *Pacific Banking*, 17, 36, 47–8, 175; C.W. Phelps, *The Foreign Expansion of American Banks: American Branch Banking Abroad* (New York: 1927), 7–8, 21, 34, 38, 83, 98–102, 127, 136, 139, 141–2, 147, 151–2. See Jones, *Multinational Banking*; P.L. Cottrell, 'Aspects of Commercial Banking in Northern and Central Europe, 1880–1931', in S. Kinsey and L. Newton (eds), *International Banking in an Age of Transition: Globalisation, Automation, Banks and Their Archives* (Aldershot: 1998), 124–6.

[136] Furniss, *Foreign Exchange*, 314–18, 317–18, 324–8, 361.

[137] Clare, *The ABC of the Foreign Exchanges*, 12–14, 42, 83; Rozenraad, *The History of the Growth of London*, 15.

[138] Escher, *Foreign Exchange Explained*, 10–11, 14, 39, 49, 86, 88–94, 100.

The UK government inquiry into trading with the enemy, which reported in 1912, revealed the intricate nature of the financial flows between countries that were in place by then, with London at their centre because of the depth and breadth of its money market. Such was the depth and breadth of these links that the merchant bankers, Huth Jackson and Lord Revelstoke, warned that a major war, such as with Germany, would have 'extremely grave' financial consequences and could lead to a 'severe financial depression'. Huth Jackson explained that 'Within the last fifty years a gigantic system of credit had grown up and had now become the basis of all international commercial transactions. Any interference with international financial relations could only be attended by disastrous consequences to the credit system.' One example of what had taken place was that 'the greater part of the trade between Germany and the British Empire, and a good deal of the trade between Germany and other countries, is financed in London'. It was calculated that bills valued at £7 million matured in London every day, of which £4 million were foreign, including £1 million on German account. He considered that

> The business of acceptances, by which was meant the financing of movements of produce from one place to another, was so complicated, and the interdependence of old contracts upon new ones so close that it was impossible to conceive what would happen if the business with one particular country came to a stop.

At the very least, it would destroy the delicate equilibrium of international credit. Lord Revelstoke was of the opinion that

> To talk of a panic in Berlin, and to assume a panic non-existent in London, Paris, Amsterdam, New York, and Buenos Aires is, under present conditions, ridiculous. A panic now means a panic everywhere; it is almost impossible to localise it ...

> Should a European war take place, the chaos in the commercial and industrial world would be stupendous, and would result in the ruin of most people engaged in business. It certainly would lead to a disastrous run and to the shutting of the doors of most joint-stock banks.

Only the USA could be expected to benefit from a European war. The banker, Sir Felix Schuster, added further support to the central role played by the London money market by reporting that 'French banks, German banks, Austrian banks, and Italian banks hold large balances here with the various banking institutions.' A.C. Cole, the Governor of the Bank of England, concluded that 'The financial system of every country is partially dependent upon London so far as external trade is concerned.'[139]

This extensive use of the London money market, where all transactions were in sterling, suggests that the currency risk was minimal, as might be expected under

---

[139] *Report and Proceedings of the Standing Sub-committee of the Committee for Imperial Defence on Trading with the Enemy*, 1912, 67, 90–2, 103–4, 108, 111, 134–46, 152, 164.

the Gold Standard. Nevertheless, as long as an exchange-rate risk existed, and the scale of activity was sufficiently large to make it significant, banks would look for ways of minimizing it, which was one of the functions of a foreign exchange market. Using the London money market did leave foreign banks with an exchange-rate risk when their domestic currency was not the UK£. Foreign banks made extensive use of sterling bills, kept money on deposit with London-based banks, employed funds in the London money market, and borrowed extensively there, and this left them with a potential currency mismatch between their assets and liabilities. For those countries on the Gold Standard, the risks could be considered to be outweighed by the benefits because of the low volatility of currency fluctuations. At the same time, the constant stream of payments and receipts, and the ability to both borrow and lend in London, meant that foreign banks were able to cover most of their currency imbalances most of the time. All that remained was a small residual element. The pound sterling was such a widely used international currency and one whose value was tied to gold that banks were willing to hold it as it could be employed remuneratively in London more easily than elsewhere. There was the expectation among all banks that they would need to obtain sterling and so it was an attractive option for them to continue to hold whatever sterling they received in London as they could sell the use of it time and again to their customers when they needed to make payments internationally. In the meantime, that sterling could be placed in the London money market in such a way as to ensure that it was both immediately available if needed and earning a positive rate of return in the meantime. That would also allow them to match their sterling assets and liabilities. Under those circumstances, banks all over the world appeared willing to take the risk of having a small element of their liabilities in one currency and their assets in another because of the low risk being run compared to the profits generated.[140] Under these circumstances, there was no pressure on the London bill brokers to extend their operations into foreign exchange trading. It was only when the transaction involved a non-sterling bill of exchange that a foreign exchange transaction occurred, as Spicer noted in 1908: 'When a Foreign Bill of Exchange is purchased the transaction resolves itself into buying for a sum of money payable in one country, the right to a certain amount of currency in another country, either immediately or at a definite future date.'[141] That was a rare occurrence in London because both parties were willing to use sterling though it was somewhat more common abroad, as Easton observed, also in 1908. 'London has become by degrees a kind of clearing house in which international indebtedness is settled', and this was mainly done through the use of sterling bills. He added that

> The foreign exchanges are of more importance abroad than in England, because there are more dealings in bills, especially as bills on England form a favourite investment in these centres. The value of sterling bills fluctuates in terms of the

---

[140] Warren, *Bank of England*, 70, 80, 103, 142–5, 151, 316–17; Andreades, *History of the Bank of England*, 316–20, 385; National Monetary Commission, *Statistics for Great Britain, Germany and France*, 143; Balogh, *Studies in Financial Organization*, 234.
[141] Spicer, *Outline of the Money Market*, 34.

local currency and this generates business. ... Foreign banks and mercantile firms abroad invest their surplus funds in bills payable in England which mature at various dates.

Sterling bills were an asset that was easily converted into cash at short notice while yielding a return, and as there were few alternatives to them, other than in Paris, Berlin, and New York, banks took the risk of using them, especially where the volatility of exchange rates was low.[142]

In many ways, the London money market incorporated a foreign exchange component but an invisible one because the final element was absent. That final element involved trading one currency for another. Those analysing the foreign exchange market that developed in London after the First World War recognized that there were strong parallels between what they were experiencing and the pre-war money market. Writing an account of the foreign exchange market in 1925, Lever, in association with Wallis of the British Overseas Bank, compared it to what had existed before the First World War. At the core of the pre-war market was the three-month bill of exchange, which he described as 'a cheque with the introduction of the time factor'. 'Before the war, the greater part of foreign Exchange business was transacted in long bills.' After the war, this was replaced by cable transfers and spot deals. What he was reporting was a change of emphasis rather than a completely new market.[143] Thomas in 1925 reached the same conclusion, stressing the central role played by sterling bills before the First World War, and the limited nature of foreign exchange transactions because of the relative stability of the rates of exchange.

> The exchange banker conducted a profitable and non-speculative business by supplying drafts to order drawn on his balances with agents in foreign centres, the balances being replenished from time to time by the purchase of such bankers' and commercial long bills or sight drafts as happened to be available. When rates were fairly stable and there was an absence of marked fluctuation, it was not imperative as it would be under present conditions that the banker should at once cover his sales of exchange by corresponding purchases, but it is clear that if his business of issuing drafts to order was to continue, he had to take steps to maintain his credit balances abroad or to reduce any overdraft which he might have created.

There was a very limited forward market in foreign exchange before 1914, and it was confined to US$s and, to a lesser degree, French francs, while the stability of exchange rates restricted the volume and speed of the transactions that took place. This business was not handled by the large British joint-stock banks because they did not keep accounts with foreign banks, relying instead on dealing with the other banks

---

[142] Easton, *Money, Exchange and Banking*, 2nd ed., 51–3, 57, 64, 72, 77, 82, 111, 132, 169, 182, 185; E.F. Foster, *Seasonal Movements of Exchange Rates and Interest Rates under the Pre–World War 1 Gold Standard* (New York: Garland Publishing, 1994), 23–31, 41.

[143] E.H. Lever, *Foreign Exchange from the Investor's Point of View* (London: 1925) (written in association with S.H. Wallis of the British Overseas Bank), 7, 13–17, 26, 45–9, 73–7, 84–5.

in London. They were not well placed to conduct a foreign exchange business which required banks to have access to money in different locations. In contrast, foreign banks carried considerable balances in their home countries while also maintaining large balances in London, and so it was they that undertook what foreign exchange business there was. To do so required a presence in London, which is why other observers reported that London was at the centre of the global foreign exchange market.[144]

As Spalding pointed out in 1921, 'it is debts which are bought and sold in foreign exchange' and these could include anything that could be used as 'a form of international currency', including 'coupons of the well-known foreign stocks and shares'. This business was conducted by banks as exporters and importers, investors and borrowers, passed the risks on to them, and so they sought ways of covering their exposure.[145] In 1928, Spalding looked back on the pre-war London money market, seeing in it a precursor of the foreign exchange market that developed in the 1920s, but without the actual exchange of currencies. 'The fact that there is no difficulty in converting sterling bills into cash in London when required is an important factor in their worldwide negotiability. There is constantly a flow of funds from foreign centres for investment in London bills, and these constitute important international exchange operations.' The bills in question were finance bills which had a duration of three months and were drawn by one bank on another bank, and the lack of currency volatility meant that banks were willing to hold them until maturity without attempting to hedge the currency risk involved.[146] He was echoing the judgement passed by others who were equally familiar with what had preceded the foreign exchange market of the 1920s. In 1921, Gregory emphasized that the foreign exchange market dealt in credits and debts not in currency, which made it an extension of the pre-war money market.[147] Miller in 1925 also referred back to the pre-war position when finance bills were used extensively as a way of lending and borrowing money short term between banks, and noted that all this was done in sterling because of the stability of exchange rates.[148]

What emerges from a study of the London money market before the First World War was how central it was to the operation of the global financial system under the Gold Standard. It was the London money market that provided the mechanism through which international payments were made and received and banks were able to borrow and lend between themselves, thus equalizing seasonal and cyclical imbalances on a continuous basis. The London money market also contributed to the switch from the originate-and-distribute model of banking to the lend-and-hold one by permitting individual banks to constantly balance their assets and liabilities through tapping the collective reserves of the global banking system. All these

---

[144] Thomas, *Principles and Arithmetic*, 8, 69, 168–73, 180–7, 193, 197.
[145] W.F. Spalding, *Foreign Exchange and Foreign Bills* (London: 1921), 4th ed., 5, 13, 51, 78, 152, 175.
[146] W.F. Spalding, *Dictionary of the World's Currencies and Foreign Exchanges* (London: 1928), 21, 38, 55, 66–7, 82, 89, 125–6.
[147] Gregory, *Foreign Exchange*, 12–13, 16, 21–4, 28, 30, 46, 52, 109.
[148] Miller, *The Foreign Exchange Market*, 9, 65, 94–7, 120, 126, 147.

were major achievements of the London money market in the years before the First World War. What appeared to be absent, however, was a foreign exchange market that would allow banks to exchange one currency for another, both immediately and in terms of future commitments. This meant that banks were left exposed to the risks that they ran when assets and liabilities were in different currencies. Though the level of risk was low for those currencies that had adopted the Gold Standard, it did exist and banks were conscious of it. Evidence for that exists from the choice of New York over London by Canadian banks when conducting money-market operations before the First World War. The financial centre of Canada at that time was Montreal but there was no Canadian money market before 1914. Instead, Canadian banks had the choice between using either New York or London, in order to connect with the global payments network and engage in money-market activity. The Canadian banks made much greater use of New York rather than London, despite the superior depth and breadth of the London money market and the strong imperial and financial connections between Canada and the UK. By the First World War, a total of six Canadian banks had London branches, but these were mainly used when arranging the issue of Canadian securities in London and obtaining trade credit. They were also used to trade bills of exchange where Canadians were involved in the transaction. However, Canadian banks chose to direct money-market activity to New York rather than London once the stability of the US$ became more assured, as happened after the USA joined the Gold Standard in 1879 and the question over monetizing silver died away in the 1890s. The reason was that physically Montreal was much closer to New York than London, which lessened the time and cost involved in correcting any deviation from the exchange rate fixed in terms of gold. The result was that the exchange rate between the Canadian and US$s was more stable than that between the Canadian $ and the UK£. As Canadian banks favoured the use of the New York money market over London, despite its inferior depth, breadth, and volatility, this indicates that they were conscious of their greater exposure to currency imbalances between assets and liabilities in the latter over the former.[149]

In addition to those countries on the Gold Standard, where there was a high degree of currency stability, there were other currencies that were more volatile and so the level of risk was much greater in those cases. Under these circumstances, it remains curious that the London money market did not take steps to provide a means through which these risks could be eliminated. There were no signs that the key players in the London money market before 1914, the bill-brokers, were making any move in the direction of adding a foreign exchange trading strategy to their existing business, which had already been extended to include a wider range of financial instruments such as finance bills, government bonds, and corporate stocks

---

[149] J. Powell, *A History of the Canadian Dollar* (Bank of Canada, 2005), 33–40; R.T. Naylor, *Foreign and Domestic Investment in Canada: Institutions and Policy, 1867–1914*, University of Cambridge PhD, 1979, 130–1, 144–5, 273–4, 277–80; H.M.P. Eckhart, 'Banks and Canada's Foreign Trade', *Industrial Canada*, August 1912, 62–3, H.M.P. Eckhart, 'Banks and Foreign Trade', *Industrial Canada*, October 1912, 342; H.M.P. Eckhart, 'How to Dispose of Foreign Exchange', *Industrial Canada*, March 1912, 934; *Canadian Finance*, 7 January 1914, 9.

and bonds. One explanation for that failure to move into foreign exchange trading could be that it was already being handled by others. The switch from the originate-and-distribute model to the lend-and-hold one did lead banks to extend the type of business that they did, including invading the territory of other financial businesses. From the mid-nineteenth century onwards, the large banks expanded aggressively and this did not stop with the opening of numerous branches and the swallowing of rivals in retail banking. It also included encroaching on the role played by merchant banks and discount houses as their scale and size allowed them to internalize ever more of the activities that had once passed through the money market.

Banks and the Management of Money, 1850–1914

A banker employs money belonging to others when lending to borrowers. The bank obtained this money in three ways. It could accept deposits from savers by promising to pay interest and repay on demand, raise loans from other lenders, or issue its own notes that could be used as a convenient means of payment, backing them with an equivalent in gold or other currencies. Successful banking involved a constant compromise between the opposing needs of those who provided a bank with money and those who borrowed from it. Lenders to a bank wanted to take minimal risks, be able to withdraw their money instantly, and receive a high rate of interest. Borrowers from a bank wanted to provide minimal collateral, be charged a low rate of interest, and only repay when it was convenient for them. A bank had to strike a balance between the two, which generated sufficient income for it to cover its costs, particularly staff remuneration and office space, and make profits for its owners. This required skilful management of a bank's assets, which were the loans and investments it had made, and its liabilities, comprising the deposits it had received, the loans it had accepted, and the notes it had issued. Occupying this middle ground made banking a risky business. Borrowers could default which made a loan potentially worthless, leaving a bank insolvent if its liabilities to depositors, lenders, and note-holders was greater than the assets it possessed. Conversely, savers could withdraw their deposits without notice and note-holders demand to exchange their notes for coin or the notes of another bank, and this could exceed the cash currently available, making the bank illiquid. It was thus vital for a bank to adopt a strategy that left it both solvent and liquid and this required it to maintain the trust of all who used it.

While the principles behind banking remained the same, the structure of British retail banking underwent a transformation during the nineteenth century. Banking moved from being the preserve of the individual banker to become a business undertaken by large companies employing numerous highly trained staff, and spread across an extensive branch network and a diversified range of activities. This transformation was not confined to Britain but was found across the world though it took different forms in other countries. There were banks that combined both retail and wholesale activities, being known as universal banks, and those that adopted a highly specialized approach, such as the investment banks. Whatever the strategy chosen, the result

was the emergence of increasingly resilient banks better able to withstand both solvency and liquidity crises. These resilient banks became trusted counterparties to
their customers, whether depositors, note-holders, or borrowers. They also became
trusted counterparties to other banks as a vast amount of banking business involved
transactions taking place within the banking system. Banks were constantly making and receiving payments, accepting the notes issued by competitors, and lending
and borrowing between themselves as they sought to cover a shortfall or employ
an excess of funds and match assets and liabilities across time, space, and type. The
more banks engaged in transactions with each other, the greater was the necessity
to become trusted counterparties. In the past, that status had relied upon personal
relationships, strengthened by family and religious bonds, but that dependence limited the scale and scope of the business that could be done. With the emergence
of large and resilient banking companies, the depth and extent of trusted networks
expanded greatly, providing the world with a system through which money could
move seamlessly. This is what took place in the fifty years before the First World War
with the result that banks became the dominant force in domestic and international
finance. Whereas the first half on the nineteenth century was associated with individual bankers such as Rothschild and Baring, the second half was the era of the Midland
Bank, Deutsche Bank, Société Générale, National City Bank, Yokohama Specie Bank,
and the Hong Kong and Shanghai Bank, despite the prominence given to people such
as J.P. Morgan.[150]

One effect of this transformation of banking in the fifty years before 1914 was upon
the relationship between banks and financial markets. There was a continuous process of cooperation and rivalry between banks and markets as the balance between
the two was in a constant state of flux. In the decades before the First World War,
both banks and markets were expanding and evolving as they met a growing need
for the services each could provide in an increasingly large and complex global economy. One example of this was that while banks made an extensive use of the London
money market, they also developed ways of bypassing it through internalizing the
routine work of collecting receipts and making payments or gathering deposits from
one group of customers while making loans to another. They did this both through
the advantages that their growing size and scale provided, and the connections they
established with other banks. The development of branch banking in Britain, for
example, greatly reduced the reliance of the domestic banks on the London money
market, as the lend-and-hold model of banking took over from the originate-and-
distribute one from the mid-nineteenth century onwards, facilitated by near-instant
communication using the telegraph and rapid transport by rail. In the originate-and-
distribute model, when a bank made a loan it generated a bill of exchange in return,
which could then be sold on, thus releasing funding for further loans. These bills were
then traded in the London money market, being bought and sold by banks as they

---

[150] R.W. Barnett, 'The History of the Progress and Development of Banking in the United Kingdom
from the Year 1800 to the Present Time', *JIB*, 1 (1880); H. Withers, *International Finance* (London: 1916),
113–14.

either lent out idle balances or sought to access additional funds. With the lend-and-hold model, a bank made a loan to a borrower, which it retained until maturity, by using funds received from customers making deposits. In this way, a bank internalized the process of collecting savings and making loans as it acted as the intermediary connecting the two parts.

Key to the originate-and-distribute model, and the use of the London money market, had been the correspondent link, in which a London bank acted as the hub for a network of independent banks not only handling payments and receipts but also providing them with credit and accepting deposits up to agreed limits. As Bagehot, who had personal experience of the correspondent system, explained in 1873,

> All country bankers keep their reserve in London. They only retain in each county town the minimum of cash necessary in the transaction of the current business in that country town. Long experience has told them to a nicety how much this is, and they do not waste capital and lose profit by keeping more idle. They send the money to London, invest a part in securities, and keep the rest with the London bankers and the bill brokers.[151]

However, as individual banks either combined to form a single unit with multiple branches or expanded by opening branches located further and further away from the head office, the domestic correspondent network gradually disappeared. By 1913, there were only 104 commercial banks in Britain, and they controlled a network of 8,910 branches and held over £1 billion in deposits. The result was a system of banking which internalized the constant ebb and flow of credits, debits, and payments. Confidence in the stability of banks encouraged savers to deposit money on a near-permanent basis and not rush to remove it in a crisis. On the back of that, banks were able to switch to the lend-and-hold model of banking and away from the use of bills as they could rely on the absence of sudden withdrawals. British banks also became trusted worldwide, allowing them to become repositories of short-term funds from around the globe before 1914 through the international extension of correspondent links. To maintain this trust, banks had to ensure that they were highly liquid, and so able to meet all withdrawals. In turn, that meant a continued dependence upon the London money market, as that was where they could employ temporarily surplus funds or cover a shortage. Nevertheless, the displacement of the originate-and-distribute model with the lend-and-hold one greatly reduced the level of dependence of British banks on the London money market when it came to their domestic business. The ratio of bills to total assets for London-based banks more than halved between the 1860s and the early 1890s, for example.[152]

As this internalization of banking in Britain was a feature of what was taking place domestically, the possibility exists that it was also happening internationally, thus masking the existence of a foreign exchange market. Banks were the first point of contact for all who needed to make or receive payments involving a foreign currency

---

[151] See W. Bagehot, *Lombard Street: A Description of the Money Market* (London: 1873).
[152] Dixon, The Development of the London Money Market, 7–8, 14, 18, 32–3, 37, 92, 98, 156, 160; Collins and Baker, *Commercial Banks*, 74–7, 87, 94, 98, 105, 109, 125; Rybczynski, 'Merchant Banks', 109.

and it was through a bank that such transactions were accomplished. Reflecting on the pre-war foreign exchange market in 1926, from a US perspective, the *Wall Street Journal* observed that it was 'largely confined to a few of the leading New York banks. ... These were the foreign exchange giants in those days and the market was influenced according as they were buyers or sellers'.[153] The larger and more diversified the bank, the greater was its ability to match transactions involving foreign currencies, with the payments of one customer being cancelled by the receipts of another. This could be done on both a current and future basis, assisting a bank in covering its exposure to currency mismatches between its assets and liabilities.[154] With the huge expansion in the volume and variety of international trade and investment before 1914, there was a growing demand for foreign exchange facilities, creating opportunities for those banks that were in a position to provide them.[155] Such a bank would be one that could balance its assets and liabilities across different currencies in response to supply and demand, and so minimize the risks it was running. A bank that had operations in different countries was in this position as it could manage its own exposure to exchange risks through internal transfers, as well as provide foreign exchange services to other banks. Conversely, a bank could accept deposits and make loans in different currencies from a single office. It could then cover its exposure to exchange-rate fluctuations by constantly matching its assets and liabilities by currency, either internally by expanding or contracting its borrowing and lending, or externally through a transaction with another bank. Only if there was confidence in the stability of fixed exchange rates could the risk posed by a currency be left uncovered, and then only if the amount involved was low and the duration small.[156]

Nevertheless, in his history of the London foreign exchange market since 1900, Atkin suggests that the contribution of banks was a limited one and the volume of business they did was low because of the stability of currencies against the UK£. To support that claim, Atkin suggests that the switch from bills to telegraphic transfers, which generated the need for active interbank spot and forward foreign exchange markets, did not take place until the 1920s.[157] However, the evidence points to telegraphic transfers replacing bills of exchange in the international transfer of money from the 1880s onwards, which greatly boosted the role played by banks. Telegraphic transfer required banks to hold cash reserves against which payments could be made, and to make allowance for future commitments. Increasingly, the global payments system shifted from merchants and merchant bankers into the hands of deposit banks as a result. Deposit banks had access to large liquid reserves through the deposits they held as well as the means of debiting and crediting payments in different

---

[153] *Wall Street Journal*, 29 December 1926.

[154] Brown, *The Forward Market*, 13; Einzig, *Forward Exchange*, 2nd ed., 23–8.

[155] Spalding, *Eastern Exchange Currency*, 4th ed., 2, 106–7, 429; Sayers, *Gilletts*, 2, 36–7; Collins and Baker, *Commercial Banks*, 74–5, 125; Gall *et al.*, *Deutsche Bank*, 17, 131; Bauer, *Swiss Bank Corporation*, 135–6; H. van B. Cleveland and T.F. Huertas, *Citibank, 1812–1970* (Cambridge: 1985), 43–4, 73, 80; Jackson *et al.*, *Lectures on British Commerce*, 14–17; Withers, *English Banking System*, 55; Madden and Nadler, 'Paris Money Market', 3–4; See Tullio and Wotters, 'Was London the Conductor?'; Merrett, 'Global Reach'.

[156] Gregory, *Foreign Exchange*, 12–13, 16, 21–4, 28, 30, 46, 52, 109; Balogh, *Studies in Financial Organization*, 234.

[157] Atkin, *The Foreign Exchange Market of London*, 7–10, 19, 32, 35, 48.

centres either by way of their branch network or correspondent links. Deposit banks could mobilize and transfer large amounts of money quickly and easily. Those banks that gained most from this shift were those with large London operations as that was where they could most easily employ idle balances profitably and access additional funds when required. The banks with London head offices but branches elsewhere in the world were in a prime position as they could offer their facilities to other banks from around the world. They were not alone in possessing this facility as they were soon followed by those foreign banks that opened London branches. Bills were relegated to being used for trade purposes and the provision of credit, rather than the movement of money internationally through the intrabank and interbank networks.[158]

The USA, for example, had relied on the sterling bill of exchange as its main means of international payment until the introduction of a permanent telegraphic link between London and New York in 1866. Cable transfer then came into increasing use as the principal system of moving money between London and New York. Bankers' bills and bankers' acceptances replaced commercial bills as the chief credit instrument.[159] From the outset, the telegraph was a highly disruptive technology when applied to global financial markets. The cable made possible both the rapid transfer of money between banks in geographically separate locations, and an instant response to variations in rates of exchange. The immediacy of transfer provided by the cable had implications for the foreign exchange market, favouring those banks able to command large amounts of money in multiple currencies rather than the merchant banks with their international trust networks. Writing from a US perspective in 1906, Brooks revealed the practical workings of the foreign exchange market and the central position occupied by London.

> Large banking houses and financial concerns in this country, keeping accounts with banks abroad, are kept advised daily by cable of exchange between cities of the different foreign countries and whenever they see any material advantage to be gained by having their funds or credit transferred from one point to another, they avail themselves of it ... most banks have accounts or balances only at London.[160]

London was the location for numerous banks of all types and sizes and with connections spread around the world.[161] Among these, it would be surprising if they did not engage with the foreign exchange market. In Turkey, for example, before the First World War, it was banks that conducted foreign exchange operations and they relied on their links with London to engage with other banks.[162]

---

[158] Clare, *The ABC of the Foreign Exchanges*, 2; Einzig, *Textbook on Foreign Exchange*, 22–3.
[159] Officer, *Dollar-Sterling Gold Points*, 61–3, 113.
[160] Brooks, *Foreign Exchange Textbook*, 3–5, 75, 114, 117–18, 120–3, 136–7, 150, 157, 166, 189, 193.
[161] Cottrell, 'Aspects of Commercial Banking', 124–6.
[162] Furniss, *Foreign Exchange*, 314–18, 324–8, 361; Lever, *Foreign Exchange from the Investor's Point of View*, 45; Thomas, *Principles and Arithmetic*, 170–83, 180–3, 187, 193, 197; E. Eldem, *A History of the Ottoman Bank* (Istanbul: 1999), 21, 266, 514.

One who understood the connections between banks and the foreign exchange market was George Goschen, whose family was engaged in banking in Leipzig and London. In his 1861 book, *The Theory of the Foreign Exchanges*, the foreign exchange market involved the exchange of debts and claims between countries and relied on the use of bills of exchange. 'The basis of settlement through a bill of exchange is the payment of a sum of money in one place, in order to receive the equivalent in another.' In contrast, though the basis of the foreign exchange market remained the same by 1875, William Stanley Jevons placed banks at its centre, as he explained in his treatise, *Money and the Mechanism of Exchange*. What had changed was that London had become 'the banking centre of the world as regards all large and international transactions'. As a consequence, 'It is found to be advantageous to deposit money in London, or to obtain credit and make bills payable there, rather than anywhere else. By such concentration of banking operations, London tends to be the seat of a world-wide Clearing House.' What Jevons had discovered was that those foreign banks with branches in London engaged in both borrowing and lending there. As payments were received in London on behalf of their customers, these foreign banks had funds available to lend out to others on a short-term basis. Conversely, when payments had to be made on behalf of customers, funds were run down, and additional amounts were borrowed to cover any temporary shortfall. At the end of each accounting period, only a residual item was left to be settled between banks and this could be met 'in the form of a bill upon the holders of the funds in London'. These operations were not confined to the sixty foreign banks that he estimated had opened branches there but extended to a further thousand bankers of all kinds around the world. All these had appointed banks in London to act as their agents when making and receiving payments. 'The agency system leads at once to a clearing of transactions.' He concluded that 'It must almost inevitably follow that transfers of money will be more and more made through London.'[163] A partial survey by the Banking Almanac of foreign and colonial Banks with offices or agents in London produced only 18 banks with London branches or agents in 1860 and 237 in 1890 but they admitted that was a serious undercounting. By 1913, the number had reached 1,356 and even that was accepted as not the full list.[164]

What Jevons has identified was an emerging role in the foreign exchange market for Britain's domestic banks as they were ideally placed to act as London agents for foreign banks. They became some of the largest financial institutions in the world between 1850 and 1914, employing thousands of skilled staff, commanding vast sterling deposits and integrated into the City of London and its money market. At a time when most banks were small, it was difficult to justify the expense involved in terms of the increased business that would be generated from opening an office in London while a branch exposed it to possible liquidity and solvency issues.

---

[163] W.S. Jevons, *Money and the Mechanism of Exchange* (London: 1875), 192, 260, 280, 302–8; G.J. Goschen, *The Theory of the Foreign Exchanges* (London: 1861), 3, 57, 115, 138.

[164] *Banking Almanac*: List of Foreign and Colonial Banks with Offices/Agents in London: 1860, 1880, 1890, 1900, 1913.

Instead, most banks from around the world chose the simpler option of negotiating a correspondent agreement with a bank that already had either its head office in London or a branch there. By 1912, a total of 1,211 banks from around the world had formal correspondent links with London banks, with the large domestic retail banks being among the most favoured for this role.[165] Through these links, foreign banks were able to borrow and lend in London and make and receive payments. They also gained indirect access to the London Clearing House, where banks offset their debits and credits with each other through a single payment.[166] Such was the volume and variety of business being generated by their correspondents that the leading British domestic banks even set up specific branches in the City of London to handle it. Lloyds Bank established its 'foreign' branch in 1898, while the Midland Bank's 'foreign' branch became the centre of a very extensive web of connections totalling over 850 by the First World War. In contrast, Barclays waited until 1914 before forming a foreign department, having rejected many of the requests from foreign banks to act as their London correspondent. Unlike Barclays, a number of the other domestic banks made the foreign branch an independent profit centre, expected to generate revenue from the business that it did.[167] All this business was conducted in sterling whether for the bank itself or its correspondents, and this made sterling into a vehicle currency, which was one used to facilitate a transaction that, ultimately, involved a foreign exchange transfer. The attraction of a vehicle currency was that it possessed a deep and broad market, making a two-step transaction easier, quicker, and cheaper than a direct exchange of currencies.[168] What this meant was that before 1914 there developed in London the microstructure of a foreign exchange market. This market allowed banks from all over the world to settle debits and credits with each other on a near-continuous basis, through the intermediation of a dense correspondence network, with London as its hub. What this reflected was a growing reliance on international money transfers being accomplished through the use of the telegraph rather than bills of exchange.

When it came to the final element, which involved an exchange of currency, the British domestic banks were poorly positioned as they had not expanded internationally by opening branches in foreign financial centres. Branches were an integral

[165] For an excellent description of what a correspondent agreement involved, see Furniss, *Foreign Exchange*, 314–27. For an example, see F.H.H. King, *The History of the Hongkong and Shanghai Banking Corporation*, vol. 1, *The Hongkong Bank in Late Imperial China 1864–1902: On an Even Keel* (Cambridge: Cambridge University Press, 1987), vol. 1: 100–1, 279, 300.

[166] Baster, *International Banks*, 4; Teichova *et al.*, *Banking, Trade and Industry*: Nishimura, 379–92; Checkland *et al.*, *Pacific Banking*, 17, 36, 47–8, 175; S. Kinsey and L. Newton, *International Banking in an Age of Transition: Globalisation, Automation, Banks and Their Archives* (Aldershot: 1998): Newton, 83, Cottrell, 106, 121, 124, 126; S. Muirhead, *Crisis Banking in the East: The History of the Chartered Mercantile Bank of India, London and China, 1853–93* (Aldershot: 1996), 180–4; Sir Compton Mackenzie, *Realms of Silver: One Hundred Years of Banking in the East* (London: 1954), 9–10, 25, 62; G. Tyson, *100 Years of Banking in Asia and Africa: History of National and Grindlays Bank 1863–1963* (London: 1963), 57.

[167] Rozenraad, *The History of the Growth of London*, 31; A.R. Holmes and E. Green, *Midland: 150 Years of Banking Business* (London: 1986), 81–4, 91–2, 100, 132–5, 141, 165, 238, 249; J.R. Winton, *Lloyds Bank, 1918–1919* (Oxford: Oxford University Press, 1982), 33–4, 87–8, 106; D.W. Matthews and A.W. Tuke, *History of Barclays Bank Ltd* (London: 1926), 24.

[168] See Krugman, 'Vehicle Currencies'; Chrystal, *Guide to Foreign Exchange Markets*.

part of a bank's business, putting them in direct touch with their customers, but they also exposed them to liquidity risks, if deposits were suddenly withdrawn, and solvency risks, if borrowers failed to repay loans. Such risks were difficult to control if the branches did a large business and were located far from the head office, which had responsibility for monitoring, supervising, and policing what was done in its name, as well as keeping it supplied with sufficient cash to meet all withdrawals. Foreign branches would also expose the entire bank to exchange risks if different currencies were involved.[169] With no policy of accepting foreign currency deposits in London and no significant branches abroad, Britain's domestic banks lacked the ability to adjust assets and liabilities across different currencies and so balance their exposure to exchange risks. In 1914, Burrell recommended that those British domestic banks that were beginning to engage with the foreign exchange market should open foreign branches.[170] By then, the large British banks had recognized that they were missing out on the profits to be made from trading in currencies, using the huge sterling deposits they had at their disposal and their strategic position at the centre of dense correspondence networks. In 1907, an anonymous writer in the *Journal of the Institute of Bankers* observed that 'For some time past there have been signs that some of the English Joint Stock Banks favoured the idea of getting into their own hands some of the foreign exchange business which has been so largely under the control of the foreign banks and firms.'[171] Martins Bank had started trading in foreign exchange in 1886 and the Midland followed in 1904 after acquiring the City Bank in 1898, which was one of the leading correspondent banks.[172]

Under the leadership of Edward Holden, the Midland Bank expanded into the territory of other banks, and the foreign exchange market was an obvious target according to Van Beek, who was recruited to head their foreign exchange department in 1906.[173] Lacking access to foreign currencies the Midland's attempt to enter the foreign exchange market was made in close association with J.E. Gardin at the National City Bank of New York, which also lacked access to foreign currencies. Acting in concert, the Midland and National City Bank could command a huge sterling deposit base in London and a dollar one in New York. During 1906 good progress was being made but profits were difficult to achieve trading £s against $s using the cable because of the existing competition and the narrowness of the £/$ spread. The Midland had acquired a small firm of foreign exchange dealers, Frederick Burt & Co, as a way of entering the market but discovered that success in the foreign exchange market depended upon making instant decisions on whether to buy and sell and

[169] Warren, *Bank of England*, 70, 80, 103, 142–5, 151, 316–17; Andreades, *History of the Bank of England*, 316–20, 385; National Monetary Commission, *Statistics for Great Britain, Germany and France*, 143; Balogh, *Studies in Financial Organization*, 234. See Accominotti *et al.*, 'The Origination and Distribution of Money Market Instruments'.

[170] H.V. Burrell, 'The Opening of Foreign Branches by English Banks', *JIB*, 35 (1914), 42.

[171] 'Questions on Points of Practical Interest', *JIB*, 27 (1907): Banks and the Foreign Exchange Business, 478–9.

[172] G. Jones, 'Lombard Street on the Riviera: The British Clearing Banks and Europe, 1900–1960', *Business History*, 24 (1982), 186–7, 191, 201.

[173] Midland Bank Letter Book, 1906–1909: Correspondence between Mr Van Beek in London and J.E. Gardin, National City Bank, New York, 24 July 1906.

then trading in volume because the margins were so narrow. It was only by taking a position that they could make any money, and that exposed both banks to a currency risk. Even though this risk was considered to be low, as the £/$ exchange rates fluctuated little, it was not one that the Midland was entirely happy with. Unfortunately for the Midland, Van Beek was run over and killed by a motor bus on his way into the City in November 1907. His death appeared to take the momentum out of the Midland's entry into the foreign exchange market. Before the First World War, the Midland made little impact on the foreign exchange market.[174]

Though the large domestic banks were slow to enter the foreign exchange market before 1914, this did not apply to all British banks, as was recognized at the time and subsequently.[175] The merchant bank, Samuel Montagu & Co, was conducting a large and profitable foreign exchange business before the First World War.[176] There was also a group of British banks that were ideally placed because they had London head offices and branch networks in other countries, giving them a deposit base in two separate locations. These banks had both a need to engage in foreign exchange transactions and the opportunity to make this into a profitable business. The number of these London-based banks with overseas operations rose from 15 in 1860 to 25 in 1913, while their branch network expanded from 132 to 1,387.[177] However, not all these British overseas banks had the same foreign exchange requirements or were exposed to the same risks. A number of these banks operated in areas of recent British settlement, such as Australia and New Zealand, which used the UK£ as the local currency. This meant there was not a difficulty with exchange, but it was still important for banks to ensure that they had adequate supplies of coin to support the circulation of their own notes. In the past, equilibrium between their London and overseas business had been maintained by these banks through the use of ninety-day bills of exchange. By selling or buying bills, and adjusting their lending and borrowing across the entire bank, they could match their assets and liabilities by amount, time, space, and currency. With the coming of the telegraph, which reached Australia in 1872, it was necessary for these banks to maintain sufficient funds in London to meet demand as transfers could take place instantly. As Brett explained in 1882, an Australian

> bank which has funds or securities in London against which it can draw possesses a reserve which, for general purposes, is the best it can hold, seeing that in ordinary times it can always sell exchange at a slight premium, and can thus fortify its position in the colony by withholding remittance for a time.[178]

[174] Van Beek to Gardin, 24 July 1906, 20 October 1906, 15 October 1907, 9 September 1908, 17 October 1908, 12 March 1909; Letter to Mr Holden from the Foreign Exchange Department, 2 May 1907; Midland Bank Overseas Department: Diary and Minute, Book 21 September 1901, 2 October 1908, 17 December 1910.
[175] Clare, *The ABC of the Foreign Exchanges*, 14–15, 39, 76, 119; Interview between the Governor and Directors of the Bank of England and the National Monetary Commission, 1910, 312; Miller, *The Foreign Exchange Market*, 94, 120.
[176] Phillips, *Modern Foreign Exchange*, 52–6.
[177] For an overview of British overseas banking, see Jones, *Multinational Banking*.
[178] E. Brett, 'The History and Development of Banking in Australasia', *JIB*, 3 (1882), 30.

The telegraph gave an advantage to the British overseas banks as they could draw on funds in both London and in Australia or New Zealand, depending on where the demand was, and then make adjustments between the two locations. With operations in both London and Australia and New Zealand, these British overseas banks possessed a mechanism through which money could be moved from one location to another. Banks established locally in Australia and New Zealand replicated the same arrangement by establishing branches in London, blurring the distinction between them and the British overseas banks. Through London, these banks were able to make and receive payments, lend out surplus funds, borrow to cover a shortfall, and provide the mechanism that maintained the equilibrium between the price of sterling in Australia and New Zealand and that in the UK. All this was hidden from view as sterling was the common currency in use.[179] A similar situation arose with South Africa, which also operated on the basis of sterling. In the 1860s and 1870s, bills drawn on London were used to finance South African exports and imports as well as a means of remitting money between the two countries. A difficulty arose when supply and demand did not match as was frequently the case because South African exports were seasonal. The solution was to keep a large balance in London which could be lent out when not required and to borrow in London to make up a deficit. In the 1890s, the mining companies and finance houses began acting as conduits between London and South Africa as they had large funds in both locations. Also, by then telegraphic transfers were increasingly used in the transfer of funds.[180]

In contrast to those British overseas banks that provided banking services in countries where the UK£ was used, there were others that served parts of the world which had their own currency, as was the case for those operating in Europe, Asia, Latin America, and much of Africa. Some of these British overseas banks had been founded by the expatriate community to meet their specific needs, only later transferring their head office to London. Others were formed in Britain by those who had commercial interests in the country in which they were intending to open branches, and who saw profitable opportunities in establishing a bank linked to London. In these parts of the world, these banks faced strong competition from established native bankers who already provided a range of financial services tailored to local conditions. Under these circumstances, these British overseas banks specialized in those activities where

[179] S.J. Butlin, *The Bank of New South Wales in London: 1853–1953* (Sydney: 1953), 4–15; S.J. Butlin, *Australia and New Zealand Bank: The Bank of Australasia and the Union Bank of Australia Limited, 1828–1951* (London: 1961), 6, 121, 192–4, 221, 240–1, 255, 283, 306, 359, 369, 392, 397; R. Wilson, *Capital Imports and the Terms of Trade: Examined in the Light of 60 Years of Australian Borrowing* (Melbourne: 1931), 36; G. Blainey and G. Hutton, *Gold and Paper, 1858–1982: A History of the National Bank of Australia Ltd* (Melbourne: 1983), 45–7, 75, 86, 90, 97–100, 195–7, 206, 214; D.T. Merrett, *ANZ Bank* (London: 1985), 27; R.J. Wood, *The Commercial Bank of Australia Ltd* (Melbourne: 1990), 93–8, 121–4, 137–8, 223; R.F. Holder, *Bank of New South Wales: A History* (Sydney: 1970), 143, 196, 528, 571; N.M. Chappell, *New Zealand Banker's Hundred: A History of the Bank of New Zealand, 1861–1961* (Wellington: 1961), 74; D. Pope, 'Australia's Payments Adjustment and Capital Flows under the International Gold Standard, 1870–1913', in M.D. Bordo and F. Capie, *Monetary Regimes in Transition* (Cambridge: 1994), 209, 215; Merrett, 'Global Reach', 70–5, 80; N. Cork, 'The Late Australian Banking Crisis', *JIB*, 15 (1894), 180–200.
[180] J.A. Henry and H.A. Stepmann, *The First Hundred Years of the Standard Bank* (London: 1863), 17, 43, 101, 110, 116, 133, 141, 225; G.T. Amphlett, *History of the Standard Bank of South Africa, Ltd, 1862–1913* (Glasgow: 1914), 3, 8, 33.

they had specific expertise and connections, which was internationally, with London acting as the hub. Inevitably, this drew them into the foreign exchange market, as they were required to provide the credit required for external trade, and to handle international financial flows and remittances. Included among these British overseas banks were those operating in Latin America, where countries had their own currencies, most of which were linked to silver not gold, leading to foreign exchange volatility. Mexico did not adopt the Gold Standard until 1905. The external trade of many of these countries, such as Argentina, was heavily directed towards the UK, which was also the source of most of the foreign investment that poured in during the half-century before the First World War. The result was a major requirement for foreign exchange facilities not only to permit the conversion of one currency into another but also to cope with fluctuations in exchange rates and the risks that created for banks providing credit. To cover the exchange risks they ran, British banks operating in Latin America matched assets and liabilities simultaneously across the different currencies. Where that could not be done the amount of business was restricted because the level of risk was deemed too high. This indicates the degree to which it was necessary to cover exposure to foreign exchange fluctuations even in the Gold Standard era, creating expanding opportunities for banks to engage in a profitable business. These British overseas banks operating in Latin America were in a position to provide other banks with a means of making and receiving payments involving countries there through their London head offices and local branch networks, as well as arranging the transfer of funds and other financial transactions. This included the ability to bypass official currency restrictions, as was the case with those imposed by the Brazilian government in 1893. The operations of the British overseas banks were copied by Latin American-based banks establishing correspondent links, offices, and branches in London. The result was to internalize the foreign exchange market involving Latin American currencies within those banks with strong London connections.[181]

Among the British overseas banks, the Anglo-Indian ones provide an excellent example of how foreign exchange was managed by the banking system before the First World War and the change caused by the introduction of the telegraph. As India retained its own currency, the rupee, while Britain was on the Gold Standard, there was a need for a mechanism through which payments and receipts between the two countries, which were extensive, could be settled, and exposure to foreign exchange risks, especially among banks, covered by spot and forward transactions. From the mid-nineteenth century, two types of banks were developed to serve India. On the one hand, there were the Presidency banks that confined their operations to within India, meeting the needs of the British expatriate community. On the other hand, there were the Exchange banks, which had an external focus and had strong connections with the City of London. These Exchange banks acted as the interface between the Indian money market, where transactions took place in rupees, and the

---

[181] V.B. Reber, *British Mercantile Houses in Buenos Aires, 1810–1880* (Cambridge: 1979), 100, 138; D. Joslin, *A Century of Banking in Latin America* (London: 1963), 25, 53–4, 110, 194, 200; D. Tiner, *Banking and Economic Development: Brazil 1899–1930* (London: 2000), 25, 77–81; W.F. McCaleb, *Present and Past Banking in Mexico* (New York: 1919), 3, 148.

international money markets, in which business was largely conducted in sterling. By maintaining deposits and making loans in both London and India, these Exchange banks could internalize the foreign exchange market, replacing the East India Company and the merchants and agency houses that had played this role in the past. This functional and spatial divide between the Presidency banks and the Exchange banks was formalized in 1876. It was through links between the Presidency banks and the Exchange banks that money flowed between Bombay (Mumbai) and London. The Presidency banks discounted inland bills and accepted deposits. Depending upon the time of year, because of the seasonality of the crops, they either borrowed from the Exchange banks, by selling them bills, or deposited money with them. In turn, the Exchange banks either sold these bills in the London money market or employed there the funds they received. When money was tight in London, the Exchange banks drew on India, but drew on London when it was tight in India. However, there was a currency risk as the exchange rate between the rupee and sterling fluctuated. This risk was handled by the Exchange banks using the deposits they had in London and Bombay or Calcutta. The Exchange banks tried to maintain a balance of assets and liabilities in each location. Rather than remit money between the two countries, they conducted separate operations and so minimized exchange risks. Increasingly, the firms engaged in exporting and importing left the banks to handle the remit of money between the UK and India and shoulder the exchange risk. The arrangement between the Presidency and the Exchange banks was also extended to other parts of Asia, such as Ceylon. Before 1914, the UK ran a deficit with Ceylon and a surplus with India. The Exchange banks had sterling in London as they financed exports from India and Ceylon through the purchase of sterling bills, but they needed rupees to make payments in India and Ceylon. In contrast, one of the Presidency banks, the Bank of Madras, had surplus rupees in Ceylon as India ran a sizeable export surplus with Ceylon. The Exchange banks provided the Bank of Madras with rupees in India by selling the India Council bills they bought in London, receiving rupees in return which they could use in Ceylon. This meant the exchange market between rupees and sterling and between the UK, India, and Ceylon was internalized within the Exchange/Presidency banking structures, and the relationships they maintained with each other.[182]

There were ongoing exchange problems with India throughout the years before the First World War. India exported agricultural products, which required payment in rupees, but sales were to British consumers, who paid in sterling. Conversely, imports were largely manufactured goods from Britain that had to be paid for in sterling but sold to consumers in India who paid in rupees. These payments and receipts were also unbalanced in time as exports came after the harvest while imports were on a continuous basis. In addition, there were investment flows from Britain to India

[182] A.K. Bagchi, *The Evolution of the State Bank of India*, vol. 1: *The Roots, 1806–1876* (Bombay: 1987), part 1: *The Early Years*, 1806–60, 32, 44–9, 54–5, 353–8, 524, 547–62; part 2: *Diversity and Regrouping*, 1860–76, 64–5, 88–90, 314–16, 348, 455–8; vol. 2: *The Era of the Presidency Banks, 1876–1920* (New Delhi: 1997), 16–17, 30–1, 70–1, 450–4, 519, 535, 549, 562; B. Ramachandra Rau, *Present-Day Banking in India* (Calcutta: 1922), 53–6, 62, 265.

associated with railway finance and investments in mining, manufacturing, agriculture, and commerce. Those then generated reverse flows of interest and dividend payments from India to Britain. Finally, there was a constant stream of remittances from India to Britain generated by business and the government, as well as a much smaller amount in the opposite direction. There were many British people resident in India, such as civil servants, soldiers, merchants, and bankers who had dependants back in the UK. Conversely, there were a small number of wealthy Indians located in Britain, such as maharajas, who had expensive lifestyles to maintain. All these numerous and varied financial transactions created currency risks.[183] These currency risks were serious, especially before the rupee was linked to sterling at a fixed exchange rate in 1898. Prior to that year, the value of the rupee was linked to the price of silver, which depreciated steadily from the early 1870s until 1895, as production increased but demand fell. This led to volatility in the exchange rate between the UK£ and Indian rupee, which exposed the Exchange banks to potential losses. One of the earliest and largest of the Anglo-Indian banks was the Oriental. It had been founded in India in 1842, moved its head office from Bombay to London in 1845 but collapsed in 1884. The response of the Anglo-Indian banks was to accept deposits and make loans in sterling at their head office in London and in rupees at their branches in India, so giving them the ability to match their assets and liabilities in each currency. In turn, this allowed the Exchange banks to act as counterparties to any other bank that wanted to buy and sell £s for rupees, and to cover their exposure, both at the time and in the future, to fluctuations in the £/rupee exchange rate.[184]

Before the telegraph the use of ninety-day bills of exchange, denominated in either sterling or rupees, had given the Exchange banks time to match and adjust their exposure to currency risk. During their life, bills could be bought or sold in either London or Bombay with other banks, including the Presidency banks in India, acting as counterparties. In 1870, a direct telegraph connection between London and Bombay was opened and this was extended to Shanghai, Yokohama, and Singapore the following year. The telegraph facilitated immediate transfers between banks. In response the Exchange banks balanced deposits and loans in India and London rather than move funds between each location, thus covering their currency exposure. However, this still left an exchange risk when the Exchange banks bought bills denominated in either rupees or sterling, due to the fluctuation in the value of sterling against the rupee. This exchange risk was met by the banks through the use of a forward transaction in the appropriate currency. By buying and selling bills, the Exchange banks could match their assets and liabilities not only by maturity dates but also by currency. These bills were generated by merchants through exports and imports—the government of India, as they made and received payments in both the UK and India,

[183] Bagchi, *The Evolution of the State Bank of India*, vol. 1, part 1: 32, 44–5, 54–5, 353–8, 562; part 2: 65, 88, 314–16, 455–8; vol. 2: *The Era of the Presidency Banks, 1876–1920* (Delhi: 1997), 16–17, 30; A. Ray, 'Two Centuries of Apex Banking: The State Bank of India and the Evolution of Modern Banking in India', in Gerald D. Feldman *et al.* (eds), *Finance and Modernization* (Farnham, 2008), 258–60, 262–4, 267.
[184] Tyson, *100 Years of Banking*, 61, 64, 75, 79, 81, 115, 132, 135; Mackenzie, *Realms of Silver*, 9–10, 36–8, 40, 45, 120; R.S. Rungta, *The Rise of Business Corporations in India, 1851–1900* (Cambridge: 1970), 178–80; Sayers, *Gilletts*, 45–55, 60, 68, 78, 80, 87, 95, 101–2, 122, 126, 158–9.

and the banks themselves, as they lent out money in London and abroad, receiving bills in return from the borrowers. This activity became increasingly multilateral, involving not only the UK and India but also bringing in China and other countries in Asia. London acted as the hub for the whole operation.[185]

What this meant was that in exchange transactions between Asia and Europe, the market was already located in London before the First World War, being internalized within the networks of offices and branches maintained by the likes of the Chartered Bank. By accepting deposits and making loans throughout its entire network, it was in a position to balance assets and liabilities across different currencies using London as the central hub. It then established hubs in other locations, opening an agency in New York in 1902 and Hamburg in 1904 to better service its American and German customers in Asia. These exchange operations combined bills of exchange and telegraphic transfers to provide the means through which money was transferred both within their own network and between them and other banks, especially those lacking an Asian presence. It was within this intrabank and interbank network that the foreign exchange market for India and adjoining countries functioned from the 1870s onwards. As a result, the need to actually exchange one currency for another was very limited as so many transactions were netted off either within banks, such as the Chartered, or between them and other banks.[186] As these Anglo-Indian banks acquired a dominant position in the exchange market involving the rupee and related currencies, other banks turned to them when they had any business of that kind. That was done in London as it was where the greatest concentration of bank offices, branches, and agencies existed, providing a high degree of connectivity.[187]

Maynard Keynes studied Indian currency and finance, publishing his analysis in 1913. To him, it was actions of the government of India which not only stabilized the exchange rate between UK£ and Indian rupee but also provided a means of transferring money between the two currency zones. This it did by maintaining large reserves in India in rupees and in sterling in London, as that enabled it to act as counterparty to buyers and sellers and those wishing to move money between the two countries. For that, the government of India was heavily criticized, particularly by Indian nationalists, who believed these reserves could be put to more productive use within India. Keynes endorsed this nationalist view, reflecting his inclination to ignore the importance of maintaining liquidity in all financial transactions.[188] It was not only India that maintained large liquid reserves in London before the First World War but the entire banking system of the world.[189] What Keynes also

---

[185] Tyson, *100 Years of Banking*, 2, 15, 19, 24–5, 32, 44; Mackenzie, *Realms of Silver*, 9–10, 25, 62; Muirhead, *Crisis Banking in the East*, 6–8, 180–4.

[186] Mackenzie, *Realms of Silver*, 7–14, 33–8, 40, 44–51, 57–66, 70–1, 90, 100, 112, 120, 127–8, 133–8, 144–50, 162, 195, 202, 218, 240.

[187] D. Sunderland, *Managing the British Empire: The Crown Agents, 1833–1914* (London: Royal Historical Society, 2004), 224–9.

[188] See J.M. Keynes, *Indian Currency and Finance* (London: Macmillan, 1913). Keynes does not address the subject of the working of foreign exchange market in his 1930 work, *A Treatise on Money* (London: 1930).

[189] De Cecco, *Money and Empire*, 105–10; Scammell, 'The Working of the Gold Standard', 33–5; A. Cairncross and B. Eichengreen, *Sterling in Decline: The Devaluations of 1931, 1949 and 1967* (Oxford:

ignored in his analysis, though acknowledging their existence, was the important role played by the Exchange banks in moving money around the world at an ever-increasing speed through the use of the telegraph.[190] Keynes himself recognized that 'The method of telegraphic transfers enables them to act with great despatch on receiving advices from their Indian agents.'[191] What he appears not to have appreciated were the implications this had for the foreign exchange market and the role played by the Exchange banks. These Exchange banks became the go-to institutions for all banks with business to transact that involved India and neighbouring countries. When the opportunity arose to profit from the sterling-rupee exchange rate, the Exchange banks took it as they could move money around their branch network and the correspondent links they possessed. Conversely, these banks were also able to cover their exchange exposure through the use of the spot and forward market. The profits made by one of the Exchange banks, the Mercantile Bank of India, from exchange operations stood at £39,806 in 1913.[192]

Important as was the involvement of British overseas banks in the foreign exchange market, they only provided partial cover for the diverse currencies of the world. Their coverage was particularly strong in Australia, New Zealand, and South Africa, where sterling was used as the local currency, and India, where it was not. They also had a significant presence in Latin America but were weak in Europe and the Far East, declining in Canada and non-existent in the United States. With British domestic banks ignoring opportunities to expand abroad, and British overseas banks following a cautious policy in opening branches, because of the risks involved, the way was open for foreign banks to open branches in London and engage in foreign exchange transactions. There were no restrictions on foreign banks opening London offices or establishing branches there. As Stewart Patterson reflected in 1917, London 'allows freedom in banking privileges to all comers of good standing.'[193] The main motivation, especially for the largest banks, was to access the London money market and to participate directly in the international payments network.[194] Spalding calculated in 1911 that the number of foreign banks with branches in London doubled from thirteen in 1898 to twenty-six as did the capital they employed, from £50 million to £100 million.[195] These foreign banks were also attracted by the possibility of engaging in the foreign exchange market and generating profits from currency

1983), 10; Cleveland, 'The International Monetary System', 19–21; Williams, 'Sterling System', 280, 286; K.W. Dam, *The Rules of the Game: Reform and Evolution in the International Monetary System* (Chicago: 1982), 18; Pressnell, '1925: The Burden of Sterling', 67–8; I.M. Drummond, *The Floating Pound and the Sterling Area, 1931–1939* (Cambridge: 1981), 4.

[190] L.S. Pressnell, 'The Sterling System and Financial Crises Before 1914', in C.P. Kindleberger and J.-P. Laffargue (eds), *Financial Crises: Theory, History and Policy* (Paris: 1982), 155–6.

[191] Keynes, *Indian Currency and Finance*, 206–21.

[192] Muirhead, *Crisis Banking in the East*, 6–8, 180, 200–1, 215–18, 283; E. Green and S. Kinsey, *The Paradise Bank: The Mercantile Bank of India, 1893–1984* (Aldershot: 1999), 29, 203–4; Ramachandra Rau, *Present-Day Banking in India*, 53–4, 62, 265; H.A. de S. Gunasekera, *From Dependent Currency to Central Banking in Ceylon* (London: 1962), 44, 80, 183; Fletcher, *Discount Houses*, 6, 11, 13, 16–18, 25.

[193] Stewart Patterson, *Domestic and Foreign Exchange*, 249.

[194] F.J. Fuller and H.D. Rowan, 'Foreign Competition in Its Relation to Banking', *JIB*, 21 (1900) and 25 (1904); D.M. Mason, 'Our Money Market and American Banking and Currency Reform', *JIB*, 30 (1909).

[195] W.F. Spalding, 'The Foreign Branch Banks in England, and Their Influence on the London Money Market', *Economic Journal*, 22 (1912), 435–7, 445, 455, 461.

speculation, which Spalding recognized in 1912. 'The foreign banker expects to make a profit on the exchange in the currency of the two countries when remittances are sent here to meet bills maturing.'[196] Opening an office in London was a strategy long followed by individual bankers, especially those from Continental Europe and the USA. It was then taken up by banks from countries with which Britain had strong economic ties as in the case of Australia, Canada, New Zealand, and South Africa, despite the existence of British overseas banks serving many of these countries. What banks based in these countries discovered was that they could compete more effectively with British overseas banks if they had a London branch as that gave them a direct presence there. The largest European banks followed suit finding London a convenient location from which to manage the financial interface between their country and the rest of the world. They were then joined by banks from elsewhere in the world, including Japan. One group of foreign banks that became embedded in the City of London at this time were those from Germany. Deutsche Bank opened a London branch in 1873, followed by Dresdner Bank in 1895, and Discontogellschaft in 1899. By 1913, these three German banks were employing £12–15 million in the London money market and through them flowed a constant stream of debits, credits, and payments from throughout the world. These activities led them to engage in the foreign exchange market both for their own convenience and to cover the risks they were exposed to. As a result, the London branches of these banks became the go-to institutions for all banks with foreign exchange activities involving the German mark.[197]

The London offices of the German and Austrian banks were closed down at the outbreak of the First World War and a leading accountant, Sir William Plender, was appointed to wind up their affairs. His reports provide a revealing snapshot of the volume and nature of the business undertaken by London branches of foreign banks. What impressed him was the 'magnitude' and 'diversity' of the business these banks had been conducting. Between them, the London offices of the three German and two Austrian banks employed a total of 968 staff on 31 July 1914. Their main business was on behalf of their own nationals, including those operating elsewhere in the world, such as Latin America. It was through London that much of Germany's financial and commercial interface with the non-European world took place. The German banks also used their London offices to internalize the foreign exchange market involving the mark. They could act as counterparties to the buying and selling of other banks, whether spot or forward, balancing their exposure through drawing on their assets and liabilities in Germany. The turnover of Deutsche Bank's London branch rose from £7.7 million in 1874 to £1.1 billion in 1913.[198] The activities of these German and Austrian banks was mirrored by those of the other European countries that established branches in London before 1914, like Société Générale from France

---

[196] Spalding, 'Foreign Branch Banks in London', 620–6.

[197] M. Pohl and K. Burk, *Deutsche Bank in London: 1873–1914* (Munich: 1998), 14, 19, 24, 41, 43, 55; P. Barret Whale, *Joint Stock Banking in Germany* (London: 1930), 67–8, 79–91; R. di Quirico, 'The Initial Phases of Italian Banks' Expansion Abroad, 1900–31', *Financial History Review*, 6 (1999), 9, 31.

[198] Enemy Banks (London: Agencies): Report by Sir William Plender, 16 December 1916, 6, 8, 12, 27; Enemy Banks (London: Agencies): Report by Walter Leaf and R.V. Vassar Smith, 12 January 1917), 2; Enemy Banks (London: Agencies): Second Report of Sir William Plender, 13 December 1917), 18.

and Schweizerischer Bankverein (Credit Suisse) from Switzerland. They built up a general banking business involving both bills and securities and had extensive dealings with Germany, Holland, Russia, and the USA as well as their own countries. As a consequence, they had assets and liabilities in sterling which could be balanced with those in other currencies in their home market, making them key conduits in the foreign exchange market.[199]

This use of London by foreign banks was not confined to those from Europe or parts of the British Empire. Though often grouped with the British overseas banks, the Hong Kong and Shanghai Bank (HSBC) retained its head office in Asia and operated in London through a branch. HSBC was established in Hong Kong in 1864 and opened its London branch in 1865. As traditional banking was well established in China, HSBC concentrated on meeting the needs of the expatriate community and the finance of international trade, acting as the interface between the Chinese native bankers and the London money market.[200] One of its key roles was to balance out the marked seasonality of China's external trade, because of the timing of the harvests, by lending and borrowing in London over the course of the year. These operations exposed HSBC to foreign exchange risks as London was on the Gold Standard while China remained on silver, as did the British colony of Hong Kong. To minimize the foreign exchange risk that it ran, HSBC balanced its assets and liabilities in its London branch in sterling by accepting deposits and making loans there. It did the same in China, from its twin head offices in Hong Kong and Shanghai, but on the basis of the local silver currency, by accepting deposits and making loans there. This meant that it could call upon its reserves of different currencies for its own use and those of its customers, including other banks that needed to balance their currency exposure.[201] With a presence in both London and China, HSBC could monitor constantly the exchange rate between sterling, on the Gold Standard, and silver-based currencies in the Far East as these fluctuated with a steady downward trend. These fluctuations caused HSBC difficulties. Merchants demanded fixed exchange rates when arranging contracts, leaving it to the HSBC to cope with the changes that could occur before receipt or payment. HSBC was only able to do this because it had extensive operations in both China and London. With the switch to the use of telegraphic transfers from the 1870s, HSBC was faced with a constant rebalancing of assets and liabilities if it was to minimize the exchange risks it was running. This encouraged HSBC to do an increased business in London as this generated sterling assets and liabilities which could be matched with its obligations in that currency. Through London, sterling

---

[199] See Bonin, *Société Générale*, 164; Swiss Bank Corporation, *Fifty Years of Swiss Banking in London: 1898–1948* (London: 1948), 1–3.

[200] C.-M. Hou, *Foreign Investment and Economic Development in China, 1840–1937* (Cambridge: 1965), 54–7, 130; G.C. Allen and A.G. Donnithorne, *Western Enterprise in Far Eastern Economic Development: China and Japan* (London: 1954), 31, 102–14.

[201] S. Nishimura, 'The Foreign and Native Banks in China: Chop Loans in Shanghai and Hankow before 1914', *Modern Asian Studies*, 39 (2005), 110–15, 122, 125–6, 128, 130–1; J. Zhaojin, *History of Modern Shanghai Banking: The Rise and Decline of China's Finance Capitalism* (New York: 2003), 3, 12, 25, 37–8, 43, 48–552, 65–8, 70–2, 76–8, 90, 99, 107–8; T. Kawamura, 'British Business and Empire in Asia: The Eastern Exchange Banks, 1851–63', in D. Bates and K. Kondo (eds), *Migration and Identity in British History* (Tokyo: 2006), 193–207; M. Collis, *Wayfoong: The Hongkong and Shanghai Banking Corporation* (London: 1965), 21–3: cf. Prospectus, reprinted on p. 255.

was being used as a vehicle currency in HSBC's dealings with other banks, such as those from Germany. Even after the establishment of the Deutsch-Asiatische Bank in 1889, German merchants continued to rely on the facilities provided by HSBC, both for credit and exchange facilities, with sterling acting as the vehicle currency between the German mark and the silver-based Chinese tael. In the late nineteenth century, HSBC even opened a branch in Hamburg in 1889 to cater for this business. As an exchange bank, HSBC constantly juggled its position in and between Hong Kong, a British colony; Shanghai, the commercial and financial centre of China; and London, the international financial centre.[202] Writing in 1928, Spalding, in his *Dictionary of the World's Currencies and Foreign Exchanges*, referred to Sir Charles Addis, who joined HSBC in 1880, as 'probably the foremost foreign exchange banker of his time.[203]

Another foreign bank in a similar position to HSBC was the Japanese bank, the Yokohama Specie Bank (YSB). The YSB was founded in 1880 and one of its first acts was to open an office in London in 1881, converting it into a branch in 1884. That branch acted as the hub through which debits and credits were balanced over space and time with sterling used as the vehicle currency. Until Japan joined the Gold Standard in 1897, the currency fluctuated in value in line with the falling price of silver. This created exchange difficulties which the YSB was designed to alleviate. Until then, it was left to the foreign banks operating in Japan to cope with the volatility of currencies. The YSB maintained funds in London in sterling which could be used for foreign exchange operations. It could accept payments in Japan in yen and make payments in sterling in London, or undertake the reverse transaction, and so meet the needs of customers while maintaining a balance between assets and liabilities in the two currencies. London and Tokyo became the twin hubs for its foreign exchange transactions, competing with HSBC and the British overseas banks.[204] Other Asian banks then followed its lead and opened London offices. Even the Banque de L'Indochine, with a head office in Paris, and the US-based but Asia-focused International Banking Corporation, routed their international business through their London branches, where they operated on the basis of the UK£. Conversely, by 1914, four British overseas banks had branches in Hamburg, namely the Anglo-South American, British Bank of West Africa, the Chartered Bank, and the Standard Bank of South Africa, in addition to HSBC. This tied London to the prime commercial centre in Germany, providing it with an essential exchange link to Asia, Africa, and Latin America.[205]

[202] King, *On an Even Keel*, 98, 151, 199, 202, 262–4, 270–7, 281, 291, 299–300, 307, 320–1, 452–4, 472, 479, 491–3; F.H.H. King, *The History of the Hongkong and Shanghai Banking Corporation*, vol. 2, *The Hong Kong Bank in the Period of Imperialism and War, 1895–1918: Wayfoong, the Focus of Wealth* (Cambridge: 1988), 242, 530–2, 539, 543–6, 577, 619; M. Collis, *Wayfoong*, 21–3: cf. Prospectus, reprinted on p. 255; F.E. Hyde, *Far Eastern Trade, 1860–1914* (London: 1973), 61–2, 201.

[203] Spalding, *Dictionary of the World's Currencies*, 21.

[204] N. Tamaki, *Japanese Banking: A History, 1859–1959* (Cambridge: 1995), 46, 70–2, 82, 109, 118–19, 129, 131, 155–6, 167, 205. See M. Schiltz, *Accounting for the Fall of Silver: Hedging Currency Risk in Long-Distance Trade with Asia, 1870–1913* (Oxford: Oxford University Press, 2020).

[205] Tamaki, *Japanese Banking*, 17, 29, 46, 70–2, 107, 129, 131, 155–6; S. Ogura, *Banking, the State and Industrial Promotion in Developing Japan, 1900–73* (London: 2002), 10, 14, 16, 37–42; *The Mitsui Bank: A History of the First 100 Years* (Mitsui Bank, 1976), 38, 59, 72, 79–80; P. Rudlin, *The History of Mitsubishi Corporation in London: 1915 to Present Day* (London: 2000), 10; Sir Paul Newall, *Japan and the City of London* (London: 1996), 6; G. Fox, *Britain and Japan, 1858–1883* (Oxford: 1969), 335–6, 378–80;

In his account of the Gold Standard, Brown was aware of existence of this global banking network and the central role played by London, and connected them both to the successful working of the monetary system before 1914.[206] With international financial transactions routed via London, and carried out through the banking system, the settling of payments, lending and borrowing, and the matching of debits and credits across time, space and currency, was accomplished by the constant debiting and crediting of bank balances there. He reported that the likes of the Bank of Montreal, the Eastern Exchange banks, and the Anglo-South American banks all had either head offices or branches in London, through which they could internalize foreign exchange operations involving Canada, India, and the Far East, and Latin America, on both a current and forward basis as they were able to make loans, accept deposits, or trade in bills and bonds either in London or in the countries within which they operated. What impressed him was the

> highly integrated world banking structure centered in London and operating on the basis of the strong international creditor position of Great Britain. This system of banking provided for an efficient and rational distribution of long- and short-term credit and of gold on a world-wide scale. It provided a common medium of payment for the financing of world trade. ... It was also the center of a system of international clearance. ... The world's foreign exchange markets were interconnected through London, and in many instances remittance from one market to another was habitually made in sterling, in preference to direct remittance. London was the world center for the clearance of foreign exchange transactions, though smaller patterns centered directly around Paris, Berlin and New York were woven into the main design of the picture. In this pre-war system of foreign exchange markets all countries had a substantial interest in keeping their particular currencies as stable as possible in terms of sterling, and their success in doing so contributed to the stability of their currencies in terms of one another. ... Many of the international transactions of other financial centers, such as the large scale security arbitrage transactions of the French banks, were passed through London. Paris. Amsterdam, and Berlin were vital, but subordinate parts of a system of which London was the leader. ... Highly sensitive movement in the holdings by different countries of an international bill portfolio, and the confident movement of bank balances and of securities between London and other markets.[207]

Those researching the development of the large European universal banks also discovered that they had the ability to internalize foreign exchange transactions but only through a reliance upon London. London had the deepest and broadest commercial and financial links of any financial centre before the First World War and the

G. Odate, *Japan's Financial Relations with the United States* (New York: 1922), 32–6; M. Kasuya (ed.), *Coping with Crisis: International Financial Institutions in the Interwar Period* (Oxford: 2003), 14; Allen and Donnithorne, Western Enterprise, 213–18; H.T. Patrick, 'Japan 1868–1914', in R. Cameron, O. Crisp, H.T. Patrick and R. Tilly (eds), *Banking in the Early Stages of Industrialization* (New York: 1967), 253–4, 267.
[206] Brown, *International Gold Standard*, 666.
[207] Brown, *International Gold Standard*, 774.

UK£ was the most internationally accepted currency in the world. This drew banks to London where they engaged in international transactions even if they possessed branches elsewhere in the world such as Asia and Latin America and their domestic currencies were of growing importance internationally. Despite the growing rivalry of European financial centres, currencies and banks before the First World War, they were dwarfed in importance by London, the UK£ and British banks. British overseas banking, for example, expanded from 400 branches in 1881 to 1,523 in 1913, by which date they were distributed between 63 different countries.[208]

The exception to London's banking connection with the rest of the world was the USA. It was a hostile territory for British overseas banks, as US banking was simultaneously highly competitive and highly restricted by legislation. US legislation prohibited commercial banks from opening branches outside the state within which they were based. This led to intense competition within each state but prevented the development of nationwide banks. The absence of nationwide banking created a gap in the US financial system that was filled by others, such as the Western Union Telegraph Company. In 1885, the president of that company, Norven Green, described to the telegraph pioneer, Cyrus W. Field, how they were in a position to provide a nationwide payments system.

> We have money all over the country more or less at each of 13,600 offices, and have to keep some deposits in the banks of all the principal towns and cities to meet the requirements of our money-order transfer business. It has frequently happened that we were a little short of money in New York on the approach of dividend day, and call loans have been made to eke out the amount but such loans are always paid within thirty to sixty days.[209]

Unlike in the UK, money transfers could not be internalized within the banking system in the USA, leaving it with a unitary banking system and connections through correspondent arrangements. This favoured small local banks that were close to their customers and left no scope for foreign banking companies to establish themselves. Another consequence of legislation was to prevent the international expansion of US banks. Until 1913, US commercial banks were not allowed to open branches abroad. This lack of foreign branches meant that US banks were ill placed to engage in foreign exchange dealing because they could not easily internalize operations by moving funds and matching assets and liabilities across time and space. A number of US banks did attempt to enter the foreign exchange market, such as the Bank of New York from 1893 and Citibank from 1897, but with limited success.[210] This left the business

[208] Brown, *International Gold Standard*, 533, 550, 659, 664–6, 774, 1027. See Jobst, 'Market Leader'; W. Kisling and L. von London, 'A Comparative, Empirical Analysis of German and British Global Foreign Banking and Trade Development, 1881–1913', *Economic History Review*, 75 (2022).

[209] Norven Green, President, Western Union Telegraph Company to Cyrus W. Field, 20 January 1885.

[210] Phelps, *The Foreign Expansion of American Banks*, 3–4, 83, 7–8, 83, 102, 127, 136, 139, 141–2, 147, 151–2; S. Stern, *The United States in International Banking* (New York: 1951), 3–8; Cleveland and Huertas, *Citibank*, 42–3; Easton, *Money, Exchange and Banking*, 132; G. Chandler, *Four Centuries of Banking* (London: 1964), vol. 1: 270, 430, 505.

to others such as the Anglo-American merchant banks. These had long been engaged in foreign exchange transactions, benefitting from a presence in such US financial centres as New York, Boston, or Philadelphia and offices in London or Liverpool. Under the name of Morton, Bliss in New York and Morton, Rose in London this private bank conducted a varied international banking business which included trading foreign exchange whenever a favourable opportunity arose. However, the nature of the business conducted by the Anglo-American merchant banks changed after the opening of the transatlantic cable in 1866. International banking became much more competitive, forcing firms to specialize in order to survive. It was no longer possible to carry out a mixed commercial and financial business profitably unless conducted on a large scale and with a strong focus. Under the circumstances, most of the Anglo-American merchant banks abandoned trading in foreign exchange apart from moments when the high level of profits justified the combination of expense and risk.

The barrier the Anglo-American private banks faced from 1870 onwards was that successful trading of foreign exchange using the telegraph required access to large deposits in different currencies in both London and New York. As private banks, they were not in a position to provide that and so withdrew whenever the margins between buying and selling prices became so fine as to limit the chance of profit. With operations in both the UK and the USA, the Anglo-American merchant bank, Brown Brothers, had been heavily engaged in foreign exchange transactions in the 1860s and 1870s, which was a time of great currency volatility involving the US$. With the return of USA to the Gold Standard in 1879 the exchange rate between the US$ and the UK£ stabilized and with it the opportunity for large profits. Before the USA formally abandoned bimetallism in favour of the Gold Standard, the £/$ exchange rate fluctuated sufficiently to make the exchange business profitable from time to time, as in the 1880s, but once it settled down in the 1890s, the fluctuations were smaller, making it difficult to generate large profits. J.W. Seligman were private bankers with a head office in New York and a branch in London and had previously engaged in foreign exchange transactions. However, in 1912, Henry Seligman in New York wrote to Isaac Seligman in London that 'There is no money in the exchange business.'[211] Nevertheless, one of the long-established Anglo-American merchant banks, Brown Shipley, the London affiliate of Brown Brothers, did decide in 1904 that there was the possibility of a profit to be made from foreign exchange trading. By 1907, they had established a foreign exchange department run by a German, Robert Hecht, and were trying to develop a business trading the UK£ against the US$. To do successfully required a joint operation with the New York partners of the bank, Brown Brothers, but even by 1911 they had not yet managed to establish this. Such were the thin margins and the risks involved that the private banks were reluctant to commit resources to the foreign exchange market, preferring to leave it to the large joint stock banks as they were able to command large liquid deposits. Before the First World War, the Anglo-American private banks, including the likes of J.P. Morgan/Morgan Grenfell,

---

[211] Henry Seligman in New York to Isaac Seligman in London, 11 September 1912.

did not carry sufficiently large balances in London and New York so as to engage in extensive currency trading despite the strength of their London/New York connections. Instead, they preferred to specialize in activities that offered greater profits and fewer risks, such as handling the issue and trading of stocks and bonds, and providing the credit required for international trade and finance.[212]

One group of North American banks that might have taken advantage of the restrictions placed on US deposit banks were those from Canada. A number of Canadian banks had grown into very large businesses, operating nationwide branch networks from head offices in Montreal and Toronto, and holding huge deposits and making extensive loans. They also had strong connections with both London and New York, which they had converted from correspondent links into branches. The impediment these Canadian banks faced was that Canada had chosen to create its own currency, the Canadian $, and so that was the basis of their operations. What this meant was that Canadian banks faced an exchange risk whenever they dealt in US$s or UK£s, which was the case in both London and New York. With the Canadian $ lacking an international presence, they had to conduct their exchange operations through either London or New York. Neither the Montreal nor the Toronto money market was sufficiently deep or broad before 1914 to provide the domestic banks with the liquidity they required, forcing them to maintain reserves in London and New York in order to make and receive payments, borrow to cover temporary shortfalls, and lend when they were in surplus. This was more easily done, and with less risk, in New York because of distance, despite the revolution in communications provided by the telegraph. It was faster to conduct business between Canada and New York than with London, and that mattered when it came to the delicate task of balancing assets and liabilities on a continuous basis. The Bank of Montreal, which had a major presence in both London and New York, conducted its foreign exchange operations through the latter not the former. As the Toronto-based Canadian Bank of Commerce reported in 1898, the balance in New York 'represents money invested by our own agents chiefly in call and short time loans'.[213] In contrast, what the Canadian banks used the London money market for was to even out the seasonal imbalance caused by the country being so heavily dependent on the annual wheat harvest, which was concentrated in July and August. In May 1903, for example, the Canadian Bank of Commerce was running a deficit of $2.5 million in London, whereas in November it

[212] D. Greenberg, *Financiers and Railroads, 1869–1889: A Study of Morton, Bliss and Company* (Newark: 1980), 31–4, 166–9; C. Brown, *A Hundred Years of Merchant Banking* (New York: Brown Brothers & Co., 1909), 281–2; A. Ellis, *Heir to Adventure: The Story of Brown, Shipley & Co., Merchant Bankers, 1810–1960* (London: 1960), 121, 141, 145, 148; J.A. Kouwenhoven, *Partners in Banking: An Historical Portrait of a Great Private Bank—Brown Brothers Harriman & Co., 1818–1868* (New York: 1968), 163–9; V.P. Carosso, *The Morgans: Private International Bankers, 1854–1913* (Cambridge: 1987), 155–8; J. Wake, Kleinwort Benson: The History of Two Families in Banking (Oxford: Oxford University Press, 1997), 136–144, 166, 211–14; S. Diaper, 'Merchant Banking in the Inter-war Period: The Case of Kleinwort, Sons & Co.', *Business History*, 27–8 (1985–6), 61, 73; Easton, *Money, Exchange and Banking*, 132; Letters from Morton, Bliss & Co., New York, to Morton, Rose & Co., London, 1884–1895; Brown Shipley/Brown Brothers Correspondence, 28 November 1903, 11 August 1911, 13 October 1911; Letter Book of J.W. Seligman & Co., Banker, New York, 1885–7, 1912.
[213] Canadian Bank of Commerce, *Annual Report*, 31 May 1898.

was a surplus of $3.4 million. With no independent market for the Canadian $, the Canadian banks looked to New York and that was where they sold their sterling bills. This meant that the Canadian banks conducted almost all their exchange operations via New York.[214] As Breckenridge observed in 1895, Canadian banks used New York for 'the purchase and sale of sterling exchange, and making transfers of money by cable.'[215] Eckardt made the same point in 1908 and 1914.

> There is no independent market for sterling in this country. We get our quotations from New York. The reason is because the market there is broad and strong. The great bulk of the exports and imports of the whole continent is settled for in New York. There are nearly always plenty of buyers and plenty of sellers. So it happens that the Canadian banks use that market for their sterling exchange.[216]

With the US$ being the vehicle currency for North America, and the UK£ for much of the rest of the world, the Canadian banks were in no position to provide a bridge between the two as the basis of their operations was the Canadian $. Though closely allied to the US$, the Canadian $ was an independent currency responsive to its own supply and demand conditions, even with both countries on the Gold Standard. This weakness in the UK/US banking connection was a major problem for the foreign exchange market. There was a growing need for a mechanism that would cope with fluctuations in the UK£/US$ exchange rate because of the absence of branches of US banks in London.

To service those banks doing a foreign exchange business in London before 1914, a small number of specialist brokers began to emerge. They began by copying the discount brokers in going round bank offices looking for business but then adopted the telephone as a means of maintaining regular and continuous contract. Hints of this pre-war telephone market emerged between the wars from those who had been

[214] R.M. Breckenridge, *The Canadian Banking System, 1817–1890* (New York: 1895), 455–7; Viner, *Canada's Balance of International Indebtedness*, 92, 148–9, 153–5, 176–8, 182–3, 257; Dick and Floyd, *Canada and the Gold Standard*, 10, 15, 128, 160, 166, 171–3; B.K. MacLaury, *The Canadian Money Market: Its Development and Its Impact*, Harvard University, PhD, 1961, 9; E.P. Neufeld, *The Financial System of Canada: Its Growth and Development* (New York: 1972), 478, 482–3, 527–8, 555; Naylor, *Foreign and Domestic Investment in Canada*, 144–5, 273–4, 277–80; *Canadian Financial Post*, 23 March 1907, 18 May 1907; F.W. Field, *Capital Investments in Canada* (Toronto: 1911), 147; H.M.P. Eckhart, 'The Growth of Our Foreign Investments', *Journal of the Canadian Bankers' Association*, vii (1900/01), 346; H.M.P. Eckhart, 'Banks and Foreign Loans', *Journal of the Canadian Bankers' Association*, xv, 63–6; H.M.P. Eckhart, 'Modes of Carrying Cash Reserves', *Journal of the Canadian Bankers' Association*, xvi (1908/09), 102; H.M.P. Eckhardt, 'The Stock Exchange Loans', *Journal of the Canadian Bankers' Association*, xxii (1914/15), 63–4; Eckhardt, 'Banks and Canada's Foreign Trade', 62–3; Eckhardt, 'Banks and Foreign Trade', 342; Eckhardt, 'How to Dispose of Foreign Exchange', 934; Eckhardt, *Manual of Canadian Banking*, 108–10; *Canadian Finance*, 7 January 1914, 5 August 1914; *Monetary Times*, 1 December 1876; *Canadian Monetary Times Annual*, January 1914, 50; V. Ross, *A History of the Canadian Bank of Commerce* (Toronto: 1920–34), vol. 1: 14, vol. 2: 25, 61–4, 109, 251, 307, 312, 349, 378; M. Denison, *Canada's First Bank: A History of the Bank of Montreal* (New York: 1966–7), vol. 1: 96, 124–9, vol. 2: 9, 172, 254, 321–2, 330, 354, 369; J.L. Darroch, *Canadian Banks and Global Competitiveness* (Montreal: 1994), 31, 38–44, 88, 126–8, 170–6; N.S. Garland, *Banks, Banking and Financial Directory of Canada* (Ottawa: 1895);
Bank of Montreal, *General Manager's Report*; Canadian Bank of Commerce, Toronto, *Annual Report 1872–1914*; G.R. Stevens, *The Canada Permanent Story, 1855–1955* (Toronto: 1955), 19.
[215] Breckenridge, *Canadian Banking System*, 455.
[216] Eckardt, *Manual of Canadian Banking*, 108.

involved. One was George Bolton, who had started working for a French bank as an exchange dealer in London in 1916.[217] Further evidence is provided by Frederick Dixon in 1939 as he gave an account of his early career as a foreign exchange broker. Dixon had begun as a clerk with an insurance company in 1890 but became a foreign exchange broker in 1907, building up a successful business before the First World War, in association with S.P. Scaramanga.

> In those days one walked or ran between the banks to execute orders. ... Scaramanga and myself conceived the idea of putting in private telephone lines to such of the banks as would permit us to do so and were the first to receive such permission. The arrangement was possible because the Scaramangas and I were not competitors; S.P. Scaramanga being specialist in the dollar exchange and I occupying myself with Continentals. In 1911 he became a partner in an established firm of money, discount and exchange brokers, Edward B. Meyer. However, to take advantage of the private wire installation I still occupied a seat in S.P. Scaramanga's office.'[218]

What his testimony suggested was that there was a growing interbank foreign exchange market in London before the First World War. This was sufficient to attract a small number of brokers who acted as intermediaries between banks in the development of this market, especially when it involved European currencies and the US$. However, this was not picked up on in the directories listing the various trades being pursued in the City of London. The City of London Directory listed only one firm of foreign exchange brokers in 1907, Jourdan and Newton, and that rose to two in 1909 with the addition of Sichel & Co, but they then stopped listing trades. The London Post Office Directory had no category of foreign exchange broker until 1922, but of those listed then five were to be found as exchange brokers in the 1914 edition.[219] It always took time for the directories to recognize newly emerging occupations which contributed to the invisibility of foreign exchange brokers before the First World War. Nevertheless, what appears evident was that an interbank foreign exchange market was established in London before the First World War and that it had many of the features of the one that grew rapidly in the 1920s.

What the City of London housed before the First World War was all the elements of a foreign exchange market with the UK£ acting as a vehicle currency. Central to this market were the banks. Banks provided the infrastructure of the world's payments system. It was their customers who were generating trans-border payments and receipts through exports and imports, travel and remittances, and credit and capital flows. Customers looked to banks for the facilities through which payments and receipts in foreign currencies were converted into the money they used domestically.

---

[217] G. Bolton, *London Foreign Exchange Market* (Bank of England, 7 August 1930); G. Bolton, *The Development of the Foreign Exchange Market* (Bank of England, 8 July 1936).

[218] Bankruptcy of Frederick Timothy Dixon, Foreign Exchange Broker, 9 September 1939 (BT 226/5073): Bankruptcy Proceedings, 20 December 1939; Statement by F.T. Dixon, 21 August 1939.

[219] *City of London Directory (1907–1909); London Post Office Directory (1922).*

This could only be done through banks dealing with each other and matching supply and demand across different currencies. These transactions also left banks exposed to fluctuations in exchange rates as commitments to make payments or accept receipts in foreign currencies would extend into the future. The easiest way of covering the risk posed by exposure to foreign exchange was to match assets and liabilities over time, amount, and currency. Banks with branches in different currency zones were best place to do this by equalizing borrowing and lending in each country. Any influx of funds was matched by an increase in lending while an outflow produced a contraction. The depth and breadth of the London money market allowed them to do that. These banks were in a position to absorb or release funds in response to changing demand. In London, funds could be borrowed or loans made overnight in the discount market, being either repaid or renewed on a daily basis. This meant that a bank could operate in both the spot and forward sterling market. Conversely, in the countries where their head offices were located, or branches in the case of the British overseas banks, they could borrow and lend in the local currency, balancing their sterling commitments on a continuous basis. In this way, they could ensure that assets and liabilities were matched not only in terms of time and space but also currencies. In that way, they acted as counterparties to what other banks were doing but as they did so on the basis of sterling, their contribution to the foreign exchange market passed unnoticed by contemporaries and later commentators.[220]

With the advent of cable transfers from the 1870s, it was those banks that held large reserves in London as well as abroad that were best placed to engage in the foreign exchange transactions, as they could match holdings in London denominated in UK£s with deposits in other countries in national currencies. This was the case with a number of European banks, beginning with those from France, Switzerland, and Germany and then extending to other countries like Italy. It also included banks operating elsewhere in the world whether they were British overseas banks with branches in Africa, Asia, Australia, New Zealand, and Latin America or banks based in those countries but with branches in London. In contrast, British and US domestic banks were placed in a difficult position with regard to the foreign exchange market as they lacked the multi-country branch network required, and thus the facilities to internalize foreign exchange transactions. This left North America without banks to service it as well as smaller European countries.[221] When the activities of banks are included in an examination of the foreign exchange market, and the role played by the UK£ as a vehicle currency is understood, it becomes evident that London was already at its centre before the First World War. This foreign exchange market had developed since the 1870s, being a product of the transformation of banks into large financial institutions and the revolution in communication generated by the telegraph. Most transactions were passed through those banks whose operations covered specific parts of the world, whether internalized within their own structure or an emerging interbank market. London provided the location where banks from all over

---

[220] Spicer, *Outline of the Money Market*, 34.
[221] King, *London Discount Market*, 278–82; Battilossi, 'Financial Innovation', 149.

the world could trade with each other either directly as major players or indirectly through the correspondent network. Omitted from this bank-based foreign exchange market was the trading of the UK£ against the US$. The mystery of where this market was remains because no banks catered for it because of the legislative barriers placed on the expansion of US banks abroad.

The London Stock Exchange and International Arbitrage, 1850–1914

Before the First World War, foreign exchange trading in London was never confined to a specific location, group, or institution and nor was it governed by a single organization or an agreed set of rules and regulations.[222] Instead, it took place in multiple venues such as the Royal Exchange, in and between the London offices of banks, through the intermediation of brokers, and from office to office using the telegraph and the telephone. This made it a very fluid market which could change quickly and radically in the face of both challenges and opportunities. It was unlike most other markets in London in the nineteenth century that gradually acquired an institutional structure such as the Baltic Exchange catering for wheat and shipping, the Metal Exchange for tin and copper, and the Stock Exchange for stocks and bonds. It even lacked the dedicated intermediaries found in the money market in the form of the discount houses and bill brokers, whose role was recognized and supported by the Bank of England. The lack of an institutional form or official support makes it difficult to identify the foreign exchange market. Nevertheless, convincing evidence can be found that considerable foreign exchange trading took place in and between the large number of diverse banks that increasingly populated the City of London in the nineteenth century. What obscured the role that this intrabank and interbank market played was the use of the UK£ as a vehicle currency. Most transactions involved the use of sterling by both counterparties, leaving only a small residual element in which a currency exchange took place.

While the discovery of the role played by banks, and the acceptance of the UK£ as a vehicle currency, brings to the surface the existence of a large and flourishing foreign exchange market in London before 1914, it contains one major omission. That omission is the market in which the UK£ was traded for the US$. This leaves a huge gap in the search for the market in London before 1914. Sterling was, by far, the most important currency in the world before 1914, used not only in Britain's own international financial and commercial transactions, which were the largest in the world, but also as the key vehicle currency. Much of the financial interface between such major economies as Germany, Japan, India, China, Argentina, and South Africa, and the rest of the world involved the use of the UK£. The US$ was also of growing

---

[222] I have written a history of both the LSE and the global securities market. See R.C. Michie, *The London Stock Exchange: A History* (Oxford: Oxford University Press, 1999); R.C. Michie, *The Global Securities Market: A History* (Oxford: Oxford University Press, 2006).

importance, reflecting not only the rise of the USA to become the largest economy in the world by 1914 but also its increasing use as a vehicle currency for North America and expanding into Latin America and across the Pacific. After the First World War it was the trading of the UK£ against the US$ that was central to the rapid emergence of a recognizable foreign exchange market in London. It seems inconceivable that this £/$ market appears to have had no major existence before the First World War. Without it, the importance of a pre-First World War foreign exchange market is considerably reduced, especially one located in London.

As with the discovery of the planet Neptune, it is possible that the search for this key component of the foreign exchange market fails because it omits a possible location associated with a different type of financial activity. One potential candidate is the LSE, which was a relatively open and dynamic institution in the nineteenth century. In the fifty years before the First World War, the LSE expanded greatly in size and membership while providing a market for an increasing diversity of securities, including many that commanded an international following. No longer was trading on the LSE confined to the debt of the UK government and the stocks and bonds issued by British railway companies. The LSE became a market for securities ranging from the speculative shares in mining companies working deposits throughout the world, through the stocks and bonds issued by railways operating in numerous different countries, to the fixed-interest debt of governments from those with a record of serial defaults to others with an impeccable pedigree of meeting payments. Whether these securities appealed to gamblers, as with the shares of mining companies, or were beloved of insurance companies, which was the case with railroad and government bonds, the LSE provided them all with a market and so made them liquid assets. This liquidity meant that the LSE was in a strong position to play a role in the foreign exchange market. The simultaneous sale and purchase of the same asset using different currencies was a foreign exchange transaction. In the same way as the UK£ was used as a vehicle currency before the First World War, particular stocks and bonds could act as vehicle assets.[223]

As a financial institution the LSE was a multipurpose organization, though many viewed it solely in terms of its contribution to the primary capital market. The stocks and bonds quoted on the LSE before the First World War were created to provide business and government with long-term finance, which did make it an integral part of the capital market.[224] However, the contribution of the LSE extended much further than this. Its central function was to provide these stocks and bonds with liquidity through the ability to buy and sell them with minimal delay and little cost at current prices. This attracted investors to quoted securities by guaranteeing the possibility of exit and entry whenever required. In turn, the liquidity that the LSE provided made it an integral part of the money market. In 1848, according to R. Hichens, a stockbroker who did a large business for banking clients, 'The stock exchange is the

---

[223] I have written a history of both the LSE and the global securities market. See Michie, *London Stock Exchange*; Michie, *The Global Securities Market.*

[224] For a recent work that ignores the LSE's money-market functions, see Jansson, *The Finance-Growth Nexus*; Janson, *Stock Markets.*

channel through which all the money business in London flows.'[225] Those investors with temporarily idle funds, such as the banks, could employ them remuneratively by either buying stocks and bonds or lending to those that did, in the certain knowledge that they would be repaid on demand, having generated a profit in the interim. Key to the liquidity provided by the LSE was the role played by a class of members known as jobbers, who comprised half the membership of over 5,000 by the First World War. Whereas brokers mainly bought and sold securities on behalf of their customers, charging commission for the service they performed, the jobbers were independent dealers who traded on their own account in the expectation of making a profit from the difference between the buying and selling price. As Greenwood put it in 1921, the jobber 'sells what he has not got and buys what he does not want, relying on obtaining later what he has sold and selling, before the settlement, what he has bought.'[226] The presence of these jobbers made the LSE the most liquid in the world before 1914, highly responsive to minute changes in interest rates as so much of the trading was done on credit provided by banks.[227]

Trading on the LSE could take place either for payment and delivery on the day or for a date in the future. Most trading was for the fortnightly account which covered a fixed two-week period at the end of which all sales and payments had to be completed. British government debt was covered by a monthly settlement. Transactions could also be extended from account to account through processes known as contango, which delayed payment, or backwardation, which postponed delivery. In addition, options were widely used which further extended the life of a transaction. Writing in 1896, Higgins claimed that 'London is ... the option market of the world.'[228] With these facilities readily available, the LSE was the ideal market for those wanting to either employ money for a short period or raise a temporary loan. Initially, this practice had been confined to the British government's own debt, principally consols, because of the depth of market they commanded, but it was increasingly expanded to include any security that was actively traded. Even speculative mining shares could serve as money-market instruments as long as counterparties could be relied upon to honour their side of the bargain, as these were actively traded.[229]

In the judgement of W.A. Cole in 1899,

Nearly the whole of the "professional" speculation on the Stock Exchange is carried on with bank money, which can be borrowed on negotiable securities with ease and cheapness, and in larger proportion to value than on any other descriptions of security; so that a dealer can, under favourable circumstances, keep on buying and borrowing on his purchase to a remarkable extent.[230]

[225] London Stock Exchange: Committee for General Purposes, Committee Minutes, 16 February 1848.
[226] W.J. Greenwood, American and Foreign Stock Exchange Practice, Stock and Bond Trading and the Business Corporation Laws of All Nations (New York: 1921), 273, 573.
[227] A. Crump, *The Theory of Stock Exchange Speculation* (London: 1874), 8–10, 19, 64–5, 70, 81; Clare, *Money-Market Primer*, 148.
[228] L.R. Higgins, *The Put-and-Call* (London: 1896), 4, 58.
[229] R.G. Hawtrey, *A Century of Bank Rate* (London: 1938), 10–11, 56, 69, 107.
[230] W.A. Cole, 'The Relations between Banks and Stock Exchanges', *JIB*, 20 (1899), 409.

Gellender in 1899 discovered that there were specialist money brokers in the Stock Exchange, who acted as intermediaries between banks and smaller brokers so as to facilitate borrowing and lending. He also identified a group of securities that were regarded by bankers as 'quasi-money' because of their ease of transfer not just domestically but also internationally.[231] As Conant reported in 1904, 'Securities form one of the greatest and most important parts of the modern mechanism of exchange. They are, in many cases, as good as money, and in some cases are better than money.'[232]

It was for that reason that banks lent extensively on liquid stocks as these could be easily and quickly sold and the money repaid.[233] This practice became a huge business on the LSE between 1870 and 1914.[234] It was not only British banks that made use of this facility of employing money either directly or indirectly on the LSE in these ways. With London being the global payments centre, there was, at any one time, a constant circulation of funds from around the world seeking profitable employment, and these found an outlet on the LSE.[235] In turn, the facilities provided by the LSE attracted investors from throughout the world, including bankers with funds to employ on a temporary basis. In 1912, Salmon and Company, who was a member of the LSE, reported that 'A large proportion of the business coming to London from the Continent consists of orders from banks.'[236] Though other financial centres possessed stock exchanges none were as liquid as London, and this made it an indispensable part of the global money market. However, all business on the LSE was conducted in sterling before 1914 and did not involve a foreign exchange transaction. It was another practice that made the LSE a key player in the foreign exchange market before the First World War. This was arbitrage, dismissed by most as a variant of speculation though recognized by some as making a contribution to financial stability.[237] Charles A. Conant tried to explain the role played by arbitrage to the US Senate in 1914, using as his example the connection between New York and London.

> If we had no general market like the stock exchange, and no great mass of listed securities which are known abroad as well as at home, the movements in the international money market would be much more violent and acute than they are

[231] E.E. Gellender, 'The Relations between Banks and Stock Exchanges', *JIB*, 20 (1899), 492, 497.

[232] C.A. Conant, *Wall Street and the Country: A Study of Recent Financial Tendencies* (New York: 1904), 107.

[233] T.F. Woodlock, *The Stock Exchange and the Money Market* (New York 1908), 28–9.

[234] Memorandum by London Bankers on Stock Exchange Commission, 24 January 1914; King, *London Discount Market*, 30, 39, 42, 47–8, 50, 63, 67, 99, 113, 117, 120–3, 175, 183, 191, 265, 268, 270, 273, 280–2, 288; Holmes and Green, *Midland*, 81, 84, 91–2, 100; Ollerenshaw, *Banking in Nineteenth-Century Ireland*, 182–5; Andreades, *History of the Bank of England* (London: 1909), 385.

[235] Baster, *International Banks*, 4; Teichova *et al.*, *Banking, Trade and Industry*: Nishimura, 379–92; Checkland *et al.*, *Pacific Banking*, 17, 36, 47–8, 175; Bonin, *Société Générale*, 28.

[236] London Stock Exchange: Committee of General Purposes, Subcommittee on Commissions, 11 June 1912.

[237] R. Estcourt, 'The Stock Exchange as a Regulator of Currency', *The Annalist*, 14 (1919), 136–8; H.S. Martin, *The New York Stock Exchange* (New York: 1919), 168–71, 190, 212; A. Cragg, *Understanding the Stock Market* (New York: 1929), 160, 178, 192, 196–8, 210–13; Crump, *The Theory of Stock Exchange Speculation*, 8–10, 19, 64–5, 70, 81; T.W. Lawson, *High Cost Living* (Dreamwold: 1913), 76–85; H.J. Howland, 'Gambling Joint or Market Place? An Inquiry into the Workings of the New York Stock Exchange', *The Outlook*, 28 June 1913, 426.

now ... if we had no general securities market by which we could borrow on securities in Europe and sell drafts to meet demands, you would have a more violent and convulsive movement of the foreign exchanges, which would react upon the whole money market. You would have large exports of gold, because there was no other way of meeting obligations or getting credits abroad. ... There is a class of persons who make it a business of seeking a profit of a small fraction of 1% when securities are ... a little lower in London than they are in New York. Their operations tend to keep uniform ... the supply of credit and they influence the foreign exchange market.

The lawyer representing the New York Stock Exchange also justified arbitrage by claiming that it took place in 'considerable volume and is not only legitimate, but has a distinct value, recognized by economists, in assisting the adjustment of international dealings.'[238]

Those securities that were quoted on multiple exchanges commanded an international market and were actively traded between them.[239] As early as 1870, Haupt reported that 'The London stock and share list contains about sixty different stocks and shares suitable for arbitration with foreign Bourses, and forming, indeed, the constant study of many operators.'[240] In 1875, Schmidt also identified a group of securities that London shared with other financial centres, and noted that the prices of these were very responsive to fluctuations in interest rates.[241] To aid the arbitrageur, Maurice Cohn produced in 1874 a manual advising those trading securities between the LSE and foreign bourses on how to calculate equivalent prices. Stocks and bonds were quoted in different ways on each stock exchange, such as whether they included or excluded accumulated interest or dividends. It was also necessary to adjust for fluctuating exchange rates as sales and purchases involved different currencies. Cohn implied that by 1874 trading those securities quoted in both London and foreign stock exchanges had become big business. 'The enormous increase in business on the London Stock Exchange within the last few years is mainly attributable to the development of arbitrage transactions between the London and Continental Bourses.'[242] Arbitrage transactions required the existence of stock exchanges as only they provided the certainty of liquid markets in which counterparty risk had been eliminated.[243] In 1957, the LSE itself defined arbitrage as

the business of buying and selling a security as a principal in one centre, with the intent of reversing such transaction in a centre in a country different from that in

---

[238] Regulation of the Stock Exchange: Hearings before the Committee on Banking and Currency, United States Senate, Washington 1914 Minutes of Evidence, 130–2, 189, 261, 529, 551–3.

[239] LSE: Committee for General Purposes: Memorandum to Chancellor of the Exchequer on Stamp Duty, 1 July 1909, 13 July 1909; H.D. Wynne-Bennett, *Investment and Speculation* (London: 1924), 19–20.

[240] O. Haupt, *The London Arbitrageur: Or, the English Money Market in Connexion with Foreign Bourses* (London: 1870), lv.

[241] H. Schmidt, *Foreign Banking Arbitration: Its Theory and Practice* (London: 1875), 184.

[242] Maurice Cohn, *The London Stock Exchange in Relation with Foreign Bourses: The Stock Exchange Arbitrageur* (London: Effingham Wilson, 1874), Preface.

[243] J.E. Meeker, *The Work of the Stock Exchange* (New York: 1922), 44–5.

which the original transaction has taken place, in order to profit from the price difference between such centres and which business is not casual but contains the element of continuity. It is therefore essential that there is a market in the security in both centres independently.[244]

When that transaction involved two currencies, it became part of the foreign exchange market.

Until the revolution in communications that came with the telegraph, arbitrage as practised in the fifty years before the First World War was not possible. Prior to the simultaneous access to prices on different exchanges, and a means of sending and receiving messages at high speed, the delay between a purchase or sale in one market and its reversal in another was so great that it was only done by the experienced operator with large resources. This made it a risky speculation, resulting in large profits and losses, and not one undertaken as a routine business. Representative of the type of information that was available in London about prices on other stock exchanges before the telegraph is this report to the Foreign Funds Market Committee of the LSE in 1824.

> Mr J.B. Lousada said that soon after the Stock Exchange opened on the 5th of August he sat near Mr De Roure. They were reading their letters. The prices of French stock were quoted to Mr Lousada at 98.35. Mr Benfil came up to them and said Mr Rothschild does not come today to tell the prices, as they are lower. This was between 11 and 1 o'clock. Mr Morgan asked him if he would buy 100,000 French Rentes, which he declined. Mr J. Ricardo ask'd him if he knew the prices were 98.35? He said he knew it as there had been a letter from Mr Waller.[245]

It was only possible to conduct relatively risk-free arbitrage when trading between London and foreign stock exchanges became a continuous, high-volume business based on very recent prices. That began with the opening of the London-Paris submarine cable in 1851, which replaced a twelve-hour delay with one of a matter of minutes, and so eliminated rumour in favour of certainty. It then took time for the telegraphic service to become sufficiently reliable to be trusted by arbitrageurs, for the expenses involved to fall to a level that encouraged constant use, and even longer to perfect methods of operation that eliminated risks and generated profits. A high degree of trust between counterparties in London and Paris was required if instructions to buy or sell were to be acted upon instantly because of the potential losses as well as profits. Even then, there was an obstacle to London-Paris arbitrage as there were few securities that commanded an active market in both exchanges. Most stocks and bonds in the UK and France were held by domestic investors. This meant that the arbitrageurs had to rely on matching sales and purchases of British government consols in London with French government rentes in Paris, relying on both being equally responsive to fluctuations in interest rates and so maintaining a stable relationship.

---

[244] Council of the London Stock Exchange: Minutes, 28 January 1957 (repeated 31 July 1973).
[245] London Stock Exchange: Foreign Funds Market Committee Minutes, 7 September 1824.

The added risk of using different securities limited the activities of the arbitrageurs as the market for each was driven by local as well as international conditions.[246]

Nevertheless, the arbitrage business between London and continental Europe steadily expanded, encompassing more and more securities and financial centres. By 1909, the LSE claimed that 'The magnitude and freedom of our market has attracted here many important foreign banks, who have established branches in our midst and are doing a considerable stock exchange business.' They highlighted the contribution that this international business was making to global financial stability through the ability of banks to sell securities quickly and cheaply and so raise cash when required. 'The international character of the London market forms the safety-valve of financial disturbance.'[247] Reflecting the integration of the LSE into the network of European stock exchanges was the volume of telegraphic messaging. In 1909, the members of the LSE sent to, or received from, Continental Europe a telegram every second of the working day, with the members of the Amsterdam, Berlin, Brussels, Frankfurt, and Paris bourses being the main source or recipients of these. By then, the telegraph was giving way to the telephone, which provided instant and constant two-way contact. A London-Paris service had been established in 1891 and that was extended to Brussels in 1903.[248] It was reported to the LSE in 1903 that 'the telephones to Paris and Brussels were used almost exclusively by the Foreign Market' and 'that they were rapidly superseding telegrams.'[249]

The global transformation of arbitrage came in 1866 with the opening of a permanent telegraphic link between the UK and the USA, joining the London and New York stock exchanges in one transatlantic market. A delay of days or even weeks was now reduced to minutes by means of cables sent between London and New York. The effect of the link to London was transformative for the New York Stock Exchange.[250] In 1886, Statist observed that

> The two markets, London and New York, move together as well as they can, but not so closely that the arbitrageur cannot get his oar in here and there. His business is to detect gaps between the latest New York prices and the corresponding prices in London. ... The game is played simultaneously from both ends.[251]

Eames, in 1894, reported that, on the New York Stock Exchange,

> Instantaneous quotations from the stock exchanges of Europe are continuously received. The endeavour to make a profit when there is a different price for the

---

[246] Crump, *The Theory of Stock Exchange Speculation*, 19, 65, 71, 76.

[247] LSE: Committee for General Purposes: Sub-committees of a Non-permanent Character, 3 June 1909.

[248] LSE: Committee of Trustees and Managers: Minutes, 7 September 1824; LSE: Foreign Funds Market Committee: Minutes, 9 September 1823, 6 September 1824, 7 September 1824; LSE: Committee for General Purposes: Minutes, 9 June 1834, 3 August 1835, 17 November 1847, 17 January 1848, 28 July 1848, 17 November 1851; LSE: Committee for General Purposes: Sub-committee on Commissions, 2 May 1912, 9 May 1912, 16 May 1912, 4 June 1912.

[249] Committee of Trustees and Managers: Sub-committee on the Enlargement of the House, 22 December 1903.

[250] H.G. Hemming, *History of the New York Stock Exchange* (New York: 1905), 31.

[251] *The Statist*, 14 August 1886, 179–80.

same stock in two markets has created what is called the arbitrage business. Competition of the arbitrageurs results in nearly equivalent prices in all markets at the same time.

He calculated that trading in the twenty most active stocks, which were the ones favoured by the arbitrageurs, amounted to 80 per cent of total turnover on the New York Stock Exchange.[252]

Writing in 1903, Pratt expressed a similar view, also highlighting the link to the LSE, where 'the bonds of every country, the stocks of every country, are traded', whereas the New York Stock Exchange 'confines itself to the securities of the United States'. Compared to Eames he calculated that there were about 150 actively traded stocks in New York, which were the ones most favoured by the arbitrageurs.

> Since the introduction of the cable there have been opportunities for what are called arbitrage dealings between the New York and London stock markets. Instantaneous quotations are exchanged between New York and London, but as there is generally a difference in the prices, an active broker may, through his representative abroad, be able to buy in one market and sell in another at the same time and clear a profit.[253]

As Escher observed in 1911, regarding the situation between the London and New York stock exchanges,

> With the wires continually hot between the two markets and a number of experts on the watch for the chance to make a fraction, quotations here and abroad can hardly get very far apart, at least in the active issues, but occasionally it does happen that the arbitrageur is able to take advantage of a substantial difference. Always without risk, the bid in one market being in hand before the stock is bought in the other.[254]

In 1914, William C. Van Antwerp, who was a member of the New York Stock Exchange, provided a detailed description of activity in one of the markets in which the arbitrageurs played a major role, which was that for US Steel common stock.

> The Steel Crowd ... the biggest, most active stock that we have. ... In Steel there are gathered 30 or 40 traders. They are not brokers. They do not accept orders. They are traders who make it a business to stay there all the time and watch these fluctuations in Steel. In any normally active market the group of traders on the floor of the stock exchange in Steel, 30 or 40 of them, will trade in 50,000 shares of Steel in a day. ... A trader is a man who is catching a turn, who buys and sells for himself. ... London is very fond of steel as a speculative and investment security. The orders

[252] F.L. Eames, *The New York Stock Exchange* (New York: 1894), 90, 97.
[253] Pratt, *The Work of Wall Street*, 19, 35, 50–1, 114–16, 142, 185, 214, 227–9.
[254] F.E. Escher, *Elements of Foreign Exchange* (New York: 1911), 13–18.

from London on a good day in Steel certainly equal 40,000 shares. I think that is a very conservative estimate. I have known it to exceed that four or five time over. ... Sometimes they will buy from us in the morning and sell back in the afternoon and vice versa.[255]

It was reported in 1899 that trading between the London and New York stock exchanges was very active as 'shares were largely used as a medium of remittance between the two countries'.[256]

As a result of previous British investment in the USA there already existed a mass of US stocks and bonds traded in both London and New York. Speculative buying and selling in each market, with the deal undone in the other, predated the telegraph connection, though it was highly risky because of the lengthy delay in transmitting prices and orders by steamship. The brokers, Heseltine Powell & Co, who were among the early pioneers of transatlantic arbitrage using the telegraph, had been trading between London and New York, but observed in 1908 how different that was from the arbitrage they were now conducting. By 1908, they employed a staff of 'highly trained and specialised clerks' and relied upon 'expensive administrative machinery which has taken many years to perfect'.[257] Another firm heavily engaged in transatlantic arbitrage by then was P.E. Schweder & Co in London, who traded with Raymond, Pynchon & Co in New York. They explained the basis of their operations.

The modus operandi of our conducting our arbitrage business is the same as that of the other arbitrageurs ... it is conducted by means of cables direct from the floor of the stock exchange here to the floor of the stock exchange in New York, we keeping a special staff for the decoding of the cables received.[258]

The delay between sending and receiving a message between London and New York fell from twenty minutes in 1866, when the Anglo-American Telegraph Company opened a permanent link, to as low as one minute by 1911, with transmission time reduced to thirty seconds. In 1908, it was estimated that the exchange of telegrams averaged one every six seconds.[259] Nelson had reported in 1904 that 'The arbitrageurs' clerks in London have desk accommodation in the London cable offices and they have a constant stream of cable orders transmitted by messenger boy service to the market.'[260]

By then, this London–New York link had become the central element in an international network of submarine cables through which arbitrage connected stock exchanges in all the major financial centres. 'The most important arbitrage accounts

---

[255] Regulation of the Stock Exchange: Hearings before the Committee on Banking and Currency, United States Senate, Washington, 1914 Minutes of Evidence, 130–2, 189, 261, 529, 551–3.
[256] Committee for General Purposes: Memorandum on Stamp Duty, 24 April 1899.
[257] London Stock Exchange: Committee for General Purposes, Committee Minutes, 27 February 1908, 2 July 1908.
[258] LSE: Committee for General Purposes, Minutes, 3 March 1908.
[259] LSE: Committee for General Purposes, Minutes, 30 May 1908.
[260] S.A. Nelson, The A.B.C. of Options and Arbitrage (New York: 1904), 53.

are conducted between New York and London', wrote Nelson in 1904.[261] These arbitrage links were recognized as contributing to the foreign exchange market when they involved transactions in different currencies, as they did between trading in London in £s and $s in New York.[262] Among the most popular arbitrage securities were Canadian stocks and bonds as these were widely held in the UK and Canada as well as the USA and Continental Europe. The $180 million of Canadian Pacific common stock in circulation in 1910 was held by 24,000 investors spread across the UK (65 per cent), Continental Europe (15 per cent), USA (10 per cent), and Canada (10 per cent). This distribution made it an ideal arbitrage stock orchestrated from London, from which the European banks conducted their arbitrage operations, especially those involving $-denominated securities.[263] Deutsche Bank used their London branch as the base for their arbitrage operations between Continental Europe and the USA.[264] These European banks were engaged in a two-stage arbitrage business, linking countries such as France and Germany to the USA and Canada through trading on the LSE. Arbitrage between Canada and Belgium, for example, involved sales and purchases on the Brussels Bourse and either the Montreal or Toronto stock exchanges with an intermediary transaction in London. The $-denominated stocks or bonds of Canadian companies such as Brazilian Traction and Canadian Pacific were used as they were actively traded on all these stock exchanges.[265]

By the First World War, the LSE provided a market for securities with a paid-up value of £11.3 billion (current prices), of which at least half was foreign. These included stocks and bonds that had been issued abroad and so were denominated in foreign currencies. The *Canadian Financial Post* noted in 1909 that

> The London Stock Exchange is the greatest centre for investment and speculation in the world. ... Nearly every stock and share under the sun is dealt in ... and it is a very rare occasion when some sort of a market cannot be found even in the most out-of-the way stocks.[266]

This was a judgement endorsed by the New York broker R.M. Bauer in 1911. 'The London Stock Exchange is the only really international market of the world. Its interests branch over all the parts of our globe. There is no country where British capital is not engaged.'[267] With the depth and breadth of its market, the LSE could provide buyers and sellers of stocks and bonds from around the world with unrivalled liquidity. Over the fifty years before the First World War, a web of arbitrage connections was then built up. As early as 1872, the LSE welcomed the opening of telegraphic

[261] Nelson, *A.B.C. of Options and Arbitrage*, 51.
[262] Fletcher, *Discount Houses*, 40.
[263] *Canadian Financial Post*, 10 August 1907; Field, *Capital Investments*, 9, 17–19, 41–5, 84–8; F.W. Field, 'How Canadian Stocks Are Held', *Monetary Times Annual* (January 1915), 35; LSE: General Purposes: Minutes, 14 April 1914; Viner, *Canada's Balance of International Indebtedness*, 90–1, 148; Neufeld, *The Financial System of Canada*, 482–3, 555; Naylor, *Foreign and Domestic Investment in Canada*, 130–1.
[264] LSE: Committee for General Purposes, Minutes, 1 February 1909.
[265] *Canadian Finance*, 5 August 1914.
[266] *Canadian Financial Post*, 10 April 1909.
[267] LSE: Committee for General Purposes, Committee Minutes, 15 May 1911.

communications between them and the Melbourne Stock Exchange.[268] The partners in the stock exchange firm of Robinson, Clark & Co came to London from Australia and built up a large business trading stocks between there and London.[269] Though Anglo-Australian arbitrage did not involve an exchange of currency, only a shift in location, others did, as in the case of Argentine securities denominated in pesos.[270] The LSE was the hub of this arbitrage activity. In 1912, Walter Landells described it 'as the nerve centre of the world, the hub of the financial universe. ... All the country exchanges, all the continental bourses, all the United States stock exchanges, act and react upon London.'[271]

The LSE itself claimed in 1908 that 'Placed as it is, London attracts business in American and South African securities from all parts of the Continent, and in American securities to a large extent from America itself.'[272] In 1909, there were 357 arbitrage connections maintained by 265 member firms of the LSE with stock exchanges in 53 different financial centres. In fifteen of these, the connection between the LSE and the foreign stock exchange was through a single firm, such as for Zurich, Shanghai, and Buenos Ayres, but for others there was a particularly dense network. In the case of New York thirty-nine members of the LSE were connected to sixty-one members of the New York Stock Exchange. Other dense networks were between London and Paris (twenty-seven members in London), Amsterdam (sixteen), Brussels (sixteen), Berlin (thirteen), Johannesburg (ten), Melbourne (nine), Montreal (nine), Sydney (six), Cairo (five), Boston (three), and Philadelphia (three).[273] Even before the opening of the LSE at 10 a.m., local time, to the end of trading in New York around 8 p.m., local time, or a period of around ten hours, London was the scene of frantic and continuous arbitrage trading that linked it to the major continental European centres of Paris, Brussels, Amsterdam, and Berlin, across the Atlantic to New York, Philadelphia, Boston, and Montreal, and then further afield to the likes of Johannesburg, Bombay, and Sydney. Though the LSE closed at 4 p.m., trading continued at a high level in the courtyard outside, which gave immediate access to the telegraph offices. This outside trading could last unabated until 8 p.m. in London, which was 3 p.m. in New York, when the stock exchange there closed. In this after-hours market there was a high degree of cooperation between firms that were members of the LSE and those that were not.[274]

Despite the importance of the LSE as the centre for international arbitrage, it remained a marginal activity undertaken by a small minority of the members. Most members did not understand what arbitrage involved and considered that it provided

---

[268] LSE: Committee for General Purposes, Minutes, 23 October 1872.
[269] LSE: Committee for General Purposes: Sub-committee on Rules and Regulations, 13 April 1910.
[270] Williams, *Argentine International Trade*, 80, 14.
[271] Walter Landells, 'The London Stock Exchange', *Quarterly Review*, 217 (1912), 106–7.
[272] Committee for General Purposes: Memorandum on the Daylight Saving Bill, 1908.
[273] LSE: Committee for General Purposes, Minutes, 21 December 1908, 28 December 1908, 4 January 1909, 11 January 1909, 18 January 1909, 25 January 1909, 27 January 1909, February 1909, 8 February 1909, 16 August 1909, 30 August 1909, 13 September 1909.
[274] LSE: General Purposes, 14 April 1914. See R. Roberts, *Schroders: Merchants and Bankers* (London: 1992), 370.

a way of escaping the rules and regulations and diverting trading away from the floor of the Stock Exchange. This belief was fuelled by the large outdoor market largely populated by arbitrageurs and the fact that the most successful of these were German Jews. This general animosity towards arbitrage and the arbitrageurs grew as the business became concentrated in the hands of a few members. The *Financial Times* observed in 1908 that

> The average London broker has, as a rule, very few foreign connections. Our international market is almost entirely in the hands of Germans and Frenchmen, who keep in close touch with the great international banks and finance houses. New York arbitraging is also a speciality. Not a dozen firms in our American market cultivate it on a large scale.[275]

As arbitrage became a matter of experience, skill, calculation, and speed, a small number of firms made it a speciality, displacing those that were either unwilling to make the investment of capital and staff or accept the risks involved. This was the case among both members and non-members of the LSE. The established merchant banks, for example, were reluctant to commit to arbitrage because of the risks involved and their unwillingness to drop their other lines of business, which were safer and, also, more profitable at times. The Anglo-American merchant bank, Morton Bliss/Morton Rose, for example, was well placed to conduct a transatlantic arbitrage business but withdrew from it in the late nineteenth century. The investment banker J.W. Seligman & Co was equally well placed, with branches in New York, London, Paris, and Berlin, but it also pulled back.[276]

The experience of E.F. Satterwhaite, who were members of the LSE, is very revealing on the reluctance of bankers to commit to arbitrage in the late nineteenth century and the risks involved. In the 1850s, E.F. Satterwhaite had an arrangement with the New York investment banker, Richard Irwin & Co, which involved the speculative buying and selling of US railroad stocks and bonds in London and New York. This arrangement continued into the 1870s with increasing use made of the telegraph. However, as the level of competition grew and the margins between buying and selling prices in London and New York shrank, they had to take a decision of whether to increase their exposure to arbitrage or withdraw from the business. Joint account arbitrage was conducted at speed and required a high volume of trading to make it profitable, which increased the level of risk which each party shared. Richard Irwin & Co were unwilling to make this commitment as they had a successful investment banking business which they did not want to give up or endanger. In contrast, Satterwhaite was keen to embrace joint account arbitrage and so found another partner, who were members of the New York Stock Exchange. This did not work out and they

---

[275] *Financial Times*, 25 January 1908.
[276] Letters from Morton, Bliss & Co., New York, to Morton, Rose & Co., London, 27 June 1884, 1 July 1884, 22 July 1884, 23 July 1884, 28 July 1884, 23 December 1884, 2 January 1885, 21 January 1885, 21 February 1885, 4 June 1885, 19 August 1885, 31 December 1886, 15 January 1892, 15 December 1892, 3 December 1893; J.W. Seligman & Co., New York, to J.W. Seligman, London, 24 December 1884, 22 July 1885, 11 August 1885, 22 August 1885, 2 July 1885, 2 July 1887.

went bankrupt in 1893 during a US financial crisis.[277] Even a successful arbitrage firm such as Nathan and Rosselli, who were members of the LSE, found it difficult to make arbitrage consistently profitable. They did an extensive arbitrage business between continental Europe and the USA, operating a joint account with E&C Randolph in New York. They were 'well acquainted with the handling of arbitrage orders', occupying in 1912 'two excellent positions at the arbitrage rail of the New York Stock Exchange'. According to E&C Randolph, 'there is good money in properly conducted arbitraging', but found it 'a difficult and trying business'.[278] Successful arbitrage required an immediate and correct response to a single word telegram, and on that depended whether a profit or loss was the result. Writing in 1913, Van Antwerp referred to arbitrage as calling 'for the utmost speed, since it involves taking advantage of fractional differences that arise from time to time in the prices of stocks that are listed on foreign bourses as well as on the New York Stock Exchange'.[279]

Among those firms that dedicated themselves to arbitrage in London and New York, undertaking a joint account business, the most successful were a group headed by German Jews.[280] Writing from a New York perspective in 1904, Nelson noted that

There are less than a dozen firms engaged in the arbitrage trade. They are all wealthy firms, and have invariably been engaged in the stock brokerage and banking business for many years. It may also be remarked that they are invariably "foreign houses," that is to say, they are English or German firms and here the Hebrew financier is in a business environment that appeals to him. Of course arbitraging between New York and London makes necessary a strong financial London connection. ... The English and German financier has a keener appreciation of a volume of small profits, and will spend more money in the form of work to secure the small profit than his New York brother.[281]

German Jewish financiers had become experienced foreign exchange arbitrageurs in Germany when the country was divided into numerous individual states with their own currencies. When currency unification followed political unification in 1871, they applied their skills to securities arbitrage, benefitting from the Jewish diaspora that placed so many of them in different financial centres around the world, especially

[277] Correspondence between E.F. Satterwhaite & Co., Stockbrokers in London, and Richard Irwin & Co., Bankers in New York, 15 April 1879, 22 April 1879, 3 May 1879, 20 May 1879, 17 February 1880, 17 March 1880, 3 December 1880, 15 December 1880, 15 December 1880, 21 December 1880, 18 January 1881, 16 February 1881, 26 February 1881, 11 October 1881, 28 March 1882, 4 August 1882, 9 February 1883, 7 March 1883, 1 May 1883, 17 June 1887, Memorandum, 31 January 1883, W.B. Peat & Co to Richard Irwin & Co., 17 March 1894, 15 December 1894; Edward F. Satterwhwaite: Circular, 10 May 1854.
[278] Nathan and Rosselli: Special Notes Regarding Foreign Clients, January 1911; Nathan and Rosselli, Memorandum on Arbitrage, 1911; Correspondence between Nathan and Rosselli in London and Sternberger, Sinn and Co., Brokers, New York, 27 March 1906, 4 November 1912, 20 January 1913, 5 March 1913, 30 March 1914; Correspondence between Nathan and Rosselli in London and with E. and C. Randolph, Brokers, New York, 7 June 1911, 8 June 1911, 24 April 1911, 1 August 1911, 15 August 1914, 22 August 1911, 24 August 1911, 6 September, 1911, 28 September 1911.
[279] W.C. Van Antwerp, The Stock Exchange from Within (New York: 1913), 104, 283–4, 344, 362.
[280] LSE: Committee for General Purposes, Minutes, 5 September 1908.
[281] Nelson, A.B.C. of Options and Arbitrage, 53.

London, New York, Paris, and Berlin. The outlawing of speculation in Germany in the 1890s encouraged many of them to migrate abroad, with London and New York being favoured destinations. In 1914, there were 153 members of the LSE who had been born in Germany, and among these were numbered those who specialized in arbitrage and had built up a large business in it. One of these was Julius Stamm, who specialized in arbitrage business between London and Continental Europe. As the LSE banned the admission of bankers, many of these continental arbitrageurs did not become members, preferring to continue conducting an integrated money-market business. One firm that remained outside the LSE was the Anglo-German merchant bank, S. Japhet & Co. It claimed to be the leading arbitrageurs in London in 1912, paying net commission of £50,000 per annum to members of the LSE because of the volume of transactions it was generating. Despite the split between members and non-members of the LSE, the outcome was a vibrant trading environment that combined the certainty provided by the rules and regulations of the LSE and the flexibility of an outside market. With telephone links within London, and telegraphic connections to all the major financial centres, the London arbitrageurs were at the centre of a global trading network.[282]

The arbitrageurs responded to the slightest deviation in price buying or selling in London and immediately reversing the deal by an equivalent sale or purchase through a counterparty on another stock exchange. Before having to pay or deliver, the deals were then reversed again.[283] Reflecting the presence of so many bankers this arbitrage activity was heavily integrated with the money market.[284] The LSE explained this to the Chancellor of the Exchequer in 1909.

> Operations in international stocks and shares largely influence the money markets of the world. ... These arbitrage operations, especially as regards American securities, are of great value to the money market and provide at times a very useful set-off to the remittances, which might otherwise have to be made in the shape of gold to pay for the imports of produce. ... A very considerable amount of foreign capital is employed on the London Stock Exchange for carrying-over purposes.[285]

On 1 August 1914, members of the LSE had an uncovered position amounting to £105 million. This meant that they held securities upon which they had borrowed £80 million from banks and bought securities from other members upon which they had to make payments amounting to £25 million. The expectation was that they would

---

[282] LSE: Committee for General Purposes: Sub-committee on Commissions, 2 May 1912, 9 May 1912, 16 May 1912, 4 June 1912; S. Japhet, *Recollections from My Business Life* (London: 1931), 75–8, 112.

[283] Nelson, *A.B.C. of Options and Arbitrage*, 54.

[284] Clare, *Money-Market Primer*, 148; Clare, *ABC of the Foreign Exchanges*, 13, 42; S. Patterson, *Domestic and Foreign Exchange*, 141–9, 249; R.G. Hawtrey, *The Art of Central Banking* (London: 1932), 127, 164; Hawtrey, *Century of Bank Rate*, 10–11, 56, 69, 107; Einzig, *History of Foreign Exchange*, 67, 71, 123.

[285] Committee for General Purposes: Memorandum to Chancellor of the Exchequer on Stamp Duty, 13 May 1909.

be able to either sell the securities and so repay banks and pay other members or borrow to meet their commitments.[286]

One contemporary who recognized the wider role played by arbitrage before the First World War was the US economist, S.S. Huebner. In 1910, he produced an analysis that linked arbitrage to the enormous increase in the volume and distribution of stocks and bonds, the increasing tendency to use such securities as collateral for loans, and the creation of a large number of stock exchanges which provided a guaranteed market. Between these stock exchanges passed a continuous stream of telegraph messages resulting in constant buying and selling, with the London and New York connection being, by far, the most important.

> It happens daily that the quotations for given stocks sold on the New York and London exchanges are not exactly the same, but for various reasons differ slightly. Furthermore, because of organized stock markets in which a market for active stock is always assured, and the use of the cable, it is possible for an arbitrageur to buy a security in the low market and sell the same security in the other market, where it is selling higher, at almost the same time, and thus realize the difference. Hence the moment a security in London is higher than in New York, or vice versa, by a sufficient amount, a foreign exchange dealer in New York with stock exchange affiliations as an arbitrageur, who wishes to remit money to London, may sell that security in London, and at the same time buy that security in New York. Then, instead of sending the money to London, he may use the debt of the London purchaser of the security to settle the account for which he desired to remit the money, while, at the same time, he may pay for the securities bought in New York with the money paid to him by the debtor in New York, who desired him to settle the account in London. Hence, by selling securities in London, and buying them in New York, or vice versa, international debts may be balanced without the transfer of any bullion. Such arbitraging, it is clear, must also tend to bring the prices of securities to a common level in all the leading stock markets of the world, so that an important stock will have a uniform price practically everywhere.

He then related this arbitrage activity to the money market.

> The first blow, when money becomes dear, nearly always falls upon the stock market ... the first loans called are usually those protected with stock and bond collateral, and it frequently happens that a period of forced liquidation in this market sufficiently corrects the money situation so as to leave other business practically unmolested.[287]

---

[286] Committee for General Purposes: Memorandum, 10 September 1914.

[287] S.S. Huebner, 'Scope and Functions of the Stock Market', in S.S. Huebner (ed.), 'Stocks and the Stock Market', *Annals of the American Academy of Political and Social Science*, xxxv, 3 (Philadelphia: May 1910), 5, 17–20.

In a later analysis published in 1922, Huebner connected this pre-war arbitrage between the London and New York stock exchanges directly to the foreign exchange market, and the constant adjustments that banks had to make as they balanced assets and liabilities across all possible variables. He considered arbitrage to have been an essential tool in foreign exchange transactions between London and New York since the introduction of the transatlantic telegraph in 1866. For 1914, he estimated that twenty firms specialized in these arbitrage operations in New York, generating 5,000 cable messages a day each day. In turn, that led to the buying and selling of 100,000 shares a day between the two markets.

> Only a few minutes will suffice, following the opening of the New York market, to make important sales of the leading arbitrage stocks, in that market, to collect the quotations, and to have them transmitted to London by experienced operators. Of fundamental importance to the business is a cable service capable of keeping pace with the fractional differences as they occur in the two markets. It is only through this means that the arbitrager may hope to remain constantly posted as to differences in quotations, and to continue to make transactions almost simultaneously in the two markets.[288]

This trading on and between the London and New York stock exchanges provided the missing £/$ component of the foreign exchange market.[289] It also comprised the central component of arbitrage operations between numerous other stock exchanges that contributed to the functioning of the market before the First World War. Evidence for this has emerged from a number of sources ranging from the study of the widely distributed ownership of US securities through those examining the cross-listing of stocks and bonds on different stock exchanges to the links between the markets for credit and capital. What all of these highlighted was the centrality of the LSE, whether it was within the London money market or the global securities market, and its key role as provider of liquidity to the world's banking system. As the American economist Anderson reflected in 1917, in his treatise on money,

> What comes to London became liquid, and everything came to London. ... The London stock market ... was a wide and dependable stock market, which made readily marketable a greater range of securities than would be marketable in any other center, and which consequently made good collateral of securities which could not serve as collateral safely, on other financial centers.[290]

In his treatise on money, published in 1969, the British economist, Roy Harrod, was more specific when he related the actions of an arbitrageur to the foreign exchange market. 'An arbitrageur may buy dollars for sterling in London and simultaneously sell an equal amount of dollars for sterling in New York. His assets will be the same as

[288] S.S. Huebner, *The Stock Market* (New York: 1922), 20–30, 49, 85–97, 179, 185, 292–5.
[289] Stewart Patterson, *Domestic and Foreign Exchange*, 126, 154, 158.
[290] Anderson, *Value of Money*, 541–2.

they were before these two deals.'[291] This made an asset arbitrage transaction risk-free as long as the two deals were made simultaneously. In the years between Anderson and Harrod, Brown had picked up on the important contribution that securities arbitrage had made to the working of the international monetary system under the Gold Standard. 'The presence of an international securities market contributes to the stability of the exchange of that country in which it is located by broadening the market in that exchange.'[292] To Brown, 'The flow of international securities ... was in the main one of the important elements of adjustment in the gold standard mechanism.'[293] He explained that

> Trading in securities having an international market in a world in which demand and supply were more responsive to changes in yield than in the speculative possibilities of capital appreciation or depreciation provided an almost ideal cushion tending to counteract charges in exchange rates. Since the exchange rise involved in the purchase of securities in one market and their sale in another had to be covered immediately, small movements in the exchange were often quickly counteracted by a transfer of part of the floating supply of these international securities. ... These had a tendency to move as a counterweight to the net balance of other items. In the post-war world, however ... the international movement of securities, far from being a source of strength and stability in the exchanges, had become one of the most disturbing of all the influences in the market.[294]

By reducing time delays in communicating information and prices the telegraph so compressed inter-market price differentials that there emerged unified financial markets within as well as between countries. Included in this was a very narrow range of government securities and railroad bonds before 1914. These commanded the same price on separate exchanges and so were ideal for arbitrage purposes connected to the foreign exchange market. This linked not only London and New York but also London with Amsterdam, Berlin, Brussels, Paris, and Vienna, as well as each other, in the years before the First World War. As the revolution in global communications brought down the cost of trading between geographically separate markets, and lowered the risks involved through reducing the delay between initiating and completing a transaction, so an active foreign exchange market grew in importance serviced by the arbitrageurs located in the world's leading stock exchanges. There was a strong correlation, for example, between the prices of Russian bonds traded in London and Paris between 1907 and 1913, with a bank such as Credit Lyonnais playing an important role as it had a major presence in both cities.[295]

[291] R. Harrod, *Money* (London: Macmillan, 1969), 67.
[292] Brown, *International Gold Standard*, 521.
[293] Brown, *International Gold Standard*, 552.
[294] Brown, *International Gold Standard*, 659.
[295] See Anderson, *Value of Money*; Brown, *International Gold Standard*; Harrod, *Money*; K.D. Garbade and W.L. Silber, 'Dominant and Satellite Markets: A Study of Dually Listed Securities', *Review of Economics and Statistics*, 61 (1979); M.D. Bordo, B. Eichengreen and J. Kim, *Was There Really an Earlier Period of International Financial Integration Comparable to Today?* NBER Working Paper 6738 (1998);

All this ended with the First World War, when arbitrage was suspended. After the First World War, the restrictions imposed by the LSE drove the business away from its members, but, by then, the circumstances had so changed that a new foreign exchange market had to be developed.[296] Even before the war, the transatlantic arbitrage conducted between the London and New York stock exchanges was being threatened by the direct links established between banks in London and New York, including the branches of those from continental Europe.[297] It was this interbank market that was to replace stock exchange arbitrage after the First World War.

The contribution made by arbitrageurs to the working of the foreign exchange market before 1914 went largely unrecognized over the course of the twentieth century.[298] One exception was Alex Chrystal but then only for the period after 1960.

> Just as arbitrage increases the efficiency of markets by keeping prices consistent, so speculation increases the efficiency of forward ... markets by keeping these markets liquid. Those who wish to avoid foreign exchange risk may thereby do so in a well-developed market. Without speculators, risk avoidance in foreign exchange markets would be more difficult and, in many cases, impossible.

He added that

> Markets that permit banks, firms and individuals to hedge foreign-exchange risk are essential in times of fluctuating exchange rates. In the absence of markets that permit foreign exchange risk hedging, the cost and uncertainty of international transactions would be greatly increased, and international specialization and trade would be greatly reduced.[299]

It was only under certain conditions that securities arbitrage could serve the foreign exchange market and they were to be found in the fifty years before the First World War. It came about through the revolution in global communications begun

---

M.D. Bordo, C.M. Meissner and A. Redish, *How Original Sin Was Overcome: The Evolution of External Debt Denominated in Domestic Currencies in the United States and the British Dominions, 1800–2000* (NBER: 2003); M. Baltzer, 'Cross-listed Stocks as an Information Vehicle of Speculation: Evidence from European Cross-listings in the Early 1870s', *European Review of Economic History* (2006); L.Q. Corre, *The Paris Bourse and International Capital Flows before 1914* (Paris: CNRS, 2007); Jobst, 'Market Leader'; G. Campbell and M. Rogers, 'Integration between the London and New York Stock Exchanges, 1825–1925', *Economic History Review*, 70 (2017); O. Accominotti *et al.*, 'The Organisation and Distribution of Money Market Instruments'; Kisling and von London, 'German and British Global Foreign Banking'; R. Stuart, 'Measuring Stock Market Integration during the Gold Standard', *Cliometrica*, 2023.

[296] LSE General Purposes, 23 September 1914, 22 December 1914, 4 January 1915, 22 January 1915, 16 March 1915, 19 April 1915, 19 August 1915, 15 March 1916, 5 May 1916, 24 August 1916, 29 January 1917, 15 March 1918, 19 March 1919, 20 November 1919, 22 December 1919, 26 January 1920, 9 April 1920, 22 April 1920, 20 December 1920, 23 May 1921, 2 November 1921; Sub-Committee of a Non-permanent Character, 29 December 1914; Sub-committee on Rules and Regulations—Minutes, 19 January 1922, 18 October 1922; S. Rainsbury, 'The War and the Arbitrage Dealer: Its Effects on the London and Paris Markets', *JIB*, 36 (1915), 193.

[297] New York Stock Exchange, Special Committee on Foreign Business, Report, 23 February 1911, Report, 8 March 1911.

[298] Eichengreen, *Golden Fetters*, 38–54, 66; Gallarotti, *Anatomy*, 41, 47, 176.

[299] Chrystal, *Guide to Foreign Exchange Markets*.

by the laying of the London-Paris cable in 1851 followed by the London-New York one in 1866. It relied on the huge holdings of British, European, and North American investors in stocks and bonds, which were actively traded in stock exchanges on both sides of the Atlantic. Finally, it was made possible by the relative stability of exchange rates and the absence of restrictions on the movement of funds around the world. These conditions ended with the First World War and were never to reappear in the same form. As arbitrage was associated with the stock exchange, and that institution was treated as part of the capital rather than the money market, its contribution to the foreign exchange market was ignored. It was not that the dog did not bark, but none recognized the noise for what it was. Neptune was discovered but only when the search was directed to the appropriate quadrant of the financial universe.

Conclusion

There were important developments in foreign exchange trading in London before the First World War, necessitated by the growing importance of currencies other than the £ and facilitated by rapid international communications and the development of banking companies. Most of this took place either away from public scrutiny or identified as stock exchange speculation, though clues to the existence of an active foreign exchange market did exist. What was visible was the foreign exchange trading that took place during the short biweekly meetings at the Royal Exchange when banks traded bills of exchange payable abroad rather than in London. This business was largely undertaken by a few merchant banks, especially the Rothschilds and Samuel Montagu, and the London representatives of the major German and French banks. Behind this visible and tiny foreign exchange market, there existed another that was invisible but vast. It had two components. One was the arbitrage that took place in and around the LSE and catered for North America and Europe with outliers to Australia and South Africa. It involved transactions in the $ and the major European currencies like the franc and the mark. The other operated through the global banking network centred in London, and this dealt with the world's other currencies such as those of India, China, Japan, and Latin America. The boundaries between these two segments of the foreign exchange market were not fixed but fluid. Banks were keen to invade the business done by the arbitrageurs through extending direct dealing between themselves. Conversely, the arbitrageurs were always looking to extend the range of securities they traded in and the markets with which they were in constant contact. This was no more than the perennial battle between banks and markets.

The onset of the First World War was to transform that battle and out of it emerged a new foreign exchange market in the 1920s. What remained the same was that this market was also located in London. As the previous foreign exchange market had been located at the LSE and within the banks, it had not been recognized as such. In contrast, the new foreign exchange market brought to the fore a recognizable group of foreign exchange brokers and dealers at a time when currencies were highly volatile, and their activities were widely reported at the time. This created the impression that something entirely new was taking place rather than the metamorphosis of what had already existed. One who reached the conclusion of novelty was the economist, John Maynard Keynes, and his views were very influential both at the time and subsequently, especially as his field of expertise was currency and finance. In his *Tract on Monetary Reform*, which was published in 1924, Keynes claimed that 'the nature of forward dealings in exchange is not generally understood', and then went to state that 'the present situation did not exist before the war ... and did not begin until after the "unpegging" of the leading exchanges in 1919, so that the business world has only begun to adapt itself', though he acknowledged that 'even at that time forward rates for the dollar were regularly quoted'. He was aware of the role played by arbitrage, such as between the spot and forward trading, but did not apply this to securities, which was commonplace before the First World War. Like most contemporaries, he considered such operations as nothing more than speculation. In the absence of an appreciation of the pre-war foreign exchange market, his recommendation was that 'We have reached a stage in the evolution of money when a managed currency is inevitable.'[300] That stage was eventually reached after the Second World War with the Bretton Woods system, which eventually collapsed between 1971 and 1973.

The development of the foreign exchange market in London before 1914 had gone step by step with the emergence of an increasingly integrated global economy. The combination of the telegraph, developments in banking, and the actions of arbitrageurs provided the world with a functioning foreign exchange market before the First World War. Unfortunately, it was one of the casualties of that conflict, but its passing went unnoticed because nobody had recognized that it had existed. Instead, the stability of exchange rates was attributed to the magic of the Gold Standard which governments tried to recreate after the war, with devastating consequences for the world. This failure to recognize the contribution that a functioning foreign exchange market made to the success of the pre-1914 world economy left as legacy the belief that only interventions by governments would restore monetary stability which was the route followed in the 1930s and again after the Second World War. It was not until the 1970s that the futility of pursuing managed currencies was finally accepted.

The Forex market in London before 1914 was invisible not because a dog didn't bark for a number did. However, one barked in private and so nobody heard it while another's barking, which was loud and public, was mistaken for the sound made by another animal. Like the search for Neptune, that for the foreign exchange market was in the wrong direction, misled by what happened after the First World War. The First World War did not create the foreign exchange market in London. Instead, it brought it into the public arena in such a way that it was recognized for what it was. The barking dog was now heard, and the public believed that it signified something entirely new rather than having always been there but having escaped detection. The microstructure of the foreign exchange market in London long pre-dated the 1920s as it was found in the dealings that banks had directly with each other and the actions of the arbitrageurs in and around the Stock Exchange. Neither the role played by gold

---

[300] J.M. Keynes, *A Tract on Monetary Reform* (London: Macmillan, 1924), 111, 138.

nor sterling was sufficient to eliminate the need for a foreign exchange market though both helped to dampen the level of activity, encouraging some to believe that it was unnecessary. What always existed in a world of multiple national currencies was the need for banks to constantly adjust their assets and liabilities so as to balance their exposure to exchange rates as a result of providing the world with not only a global payments system but also the credit that underpinned international trade and investment. The failure to recognize the vital contribution made by the foreign exchange market before 1914 was to have disastrous consequences in the 1920s and 1930s. It was only from the 1970s that there was an acceptance that governments could not impose rigidity on exchange rates and that a functioning foreign exchange market was a necessity if underlying stability was to exist. What was rediscovered after 1970 was the pre-1914 foreign exchange market which had been lost. One reason it had been lost was because nobody realized it had existed.

This stability of exchange rates achieved by the pre-First World War foreign exchange market allowed banks from all over the world to maximize the use of the funds at their disposal, so making credit available to finance the growth of international trade and capital to be employed equipping the world with a modern transport system in the form of railways. Confident in the stability of exchange rates, banks could lend and borrow among themselves in the secure knowledge that funds could always be employed and loans would be repaid on demand. No longer were funds compartmentalized behind national boundaries. The result was one vast pool of liquidity accessible to all banks through a dense network of correspondent links that had London at its hub. As London became the payments centre for the global economy in the nineteenth century, it was a simple step to provide a market in which temporarily idle funds could be remuneratively employed. This had already taken place within Britain and was then extended to the world from the 1850s onwards when the revolution in global communications largely eliminated the barriers of distance. In the fifty years before the First World War, there was a convergence of financial, monetary, and technological forces that transformed the operation of the global economy. Undetected in that was the contribution made by the links between banks the world over and the trading of arbitrageurs on the floor of the LSE and their counterparties spread around the globe.

2
Reinventing Forex, 1919–1939

Introduction

There is a deep divide between monetary history and financial history despite the obvious link between the two, as each deals with money. This divide becomes deeper in the twentieth century as governments and central banks have come to dominate the creation, supply, and use of money. Monetary history has as its focus monetary policy and the role and development of central banks. Financial history deals with the origins and workings of banks and financial markets. The effect of this divide is that those writing monetary history tend to be monetary economists, seeking to use the past as a way of understanding the aims and consequences of government intervention in the monetary system and so predict future trends. In contrast, financial history tends to be undertaken by historians with an interest in the diversity of past experiences, and what lessons that may provide.[1] That divide between monetary historians and financial historians helps to explain why the development and role of the foreign exchange market in the twentieth century has been so little studied. When pursued by monetary economists, their interest is the effects of actions taken by governments and central bankers on exchange rates. When pursued by financial historians, the lack of an institutional or business structure to the foreign exchange market makes it difficult to research, unlike stock exchanges or banks. One consequence has been that the foreign exchange market has been omitted from any account of the global monetary system as it operated under the Gold Standard before the First World War. Though the foreign exchange market does feature in the study of the period between the two world wars, it is only used to help explain the damaging consequences of the failure to return to the Gold Standard. The inability to fully and permanently restore the Gold Standard was held responsible for the volatile exchange rates and monetary turmoil that undermined international trade and finance and destroyed national economies between the wars. With the foreign exchange market dismissed as a speculators' paradise, the only alternative to a return to the Gold Standard was seen to be government intervention, as took place in the 1930s, leading to the emergence of the regime of managed currencies after the Second World War. That regime eventually collapsed in the 1970s.

The discovery of an active and extensive foreign exchange market before the First World War, and the appearance and growth of another from the 1970s, changes this analysis. Rather than being a product of an adherence to the Gold Standard, the

---

[1] For an example, see Eichengreen, Mehl and Chitu, *How Global Currencies Work.*

Forex Forever. Ranald C. Michie, Oxford University Press. © Ranald C. Michie (2024).
DOI: 10.1093/oso/9780198903697.003.0003

stability of exchange rates before the First World War was an outcome of an increasingly integrated world economy, within which the forces of supply and demand were balanced internationally and so equilibrium prevailed. There were no major wars to disturb this global equilibrium and most governments followed fiscally conservative policies, matching income and expenditure and servicing debts. That environment inspired confidence in the stability of exchange rates, regardless of whether or not countries were on the Gold Standard. The additional element required was a functioning foreign exchange market which contributed to the day-to-day stability of exchange rates. That foreign exchange market developed from the 1870s, benefitting from the revolution in world communications, the creation of a global banking network, and links between stock exchanges where internationally mobile assets were traded, aided by an absence of barriers to financial flows. Its hub was in London which emerged as the most important financial centre in the world at that time.

However, that world came to an end with the First World War, forcing the foreign exchange market to respond as it was put under great pressure because of an enormous increase in underlying currency volatility. As Adam Iqbal, the global head of G10 FX options trading at Goldman Sachs, observed in 2022, regarding the financial crisis he was witnessing, 'Until globalising forces re-emerge, the post-pandemic world will remain one of high foreign exchange volatility.'[2] If that was the consequence of a global pandemic, then the impact of a four-year-long intense military conflict that drew in almost the whole world would be far deeper and long-lasting. Though the foreign exchange market that developed after the First World War was not a new creation, for it already existed though hidden from view, it had to be substantially remodelled to cope with the changes caused by the disruptive effects of a military conflict involving the leading economies in the world. These effects did not end with peace in 1918 but continued long into the 1920s as the world economy searched for a new equilibrium that reflected the changed economic relationship between countries that was a legacy of the war. Achieving that new equilibrium was not helped by a widespread belief that currency stability was associated with the Gold Standard and fixed exchange rates. That belief left no role for the foreign exchange market despite the contribution it could make to discovering what rates of exchange would deliver currency equilibrium. To reach that equilibrium would, inevitably, involve a period of volatility as relationships between economies adjusted to the legacy left by the war. That volatility would force the foreign exchange market to devise new ways of working, as it coped with much greater currency fluctuations not only day-to-day but also in the underlying rates, especially as governments intervened to mitigate the continuing disruption caused by the legacy of the war. Complicating the ability of the foreign exchange market to deliver a new equilibrium was the expectation that fixed rates would be reimposed in some form in the near future, including a return to pre-war Gold Standard. As there was no recognition that a foreign exchange market had existed before the war, its appearance in the 1920s was considered a

---

[2] A. Iqbal, 'Deglobalisation Is Boosting Foreign Exchange Volatility', *Financial Times*, 31 May 2022.

novel but temporary response to a set of exceptional circumstances. Once the world economy returned to the conditions that had prevailed before the outbreak of war in 1914, and the Gold Standard had been restored, there would be no need for this foreign exchange market and so it would disappear. Such were the assumptions that underpinned the foreign exchange market that developed between the wars.[3]

Shattered Stability, 1919–1939

It is important to recognize the environment within which the foreign exchange market operated from the outbreak of the First World War in 1914 to the beginning of the Second World War in 1939. These were years of conflict and crises, and they represented a complete change from the fifty years of peace and prosperity that preceded the First World War. They presented the foreign exchange market with enormous challenges and opportunities. Every financial system is vulnerable to disruption caused by events such as wars, regime change, natural catastrophes, and political decisions. Among the events that can disrupt a financial system, wars are the most extreme. The more intense and prolonged a war, the greater and more long-lasting the damage it inflicted. Wars were military conflicts involving human and physical destruction, but they also caused inflation and monetary dislocation as expenditure outran income. Wars also placed huge financial burdens on current and future generations and led to the erection of barriers to trade and financial flows that distorted global patterns of supply and demand. During wars, governments took control of the economy, suppressing or bypassing market mechanisms, and this had both short and long-term consequences. No financial system could anticipate the consequences of wars as they were external shocks against which financial systems could not protect themselves. The financial journalist, E.T. Powell, wrote in 1915 that, 'The German war crisis of 1914 was entirely political. Neither in banking, industry, nor commerce had anything been done which would have created any crisis.'[4] The First World War, which began in 1914 and ended in 1918, was a conflict that was unprecedented and unparalleled in terms of its loss of life, cost, and disruption, and its consequences reverberated throughout the 1920s. The war contributed to the worst financial crisis in history between 1929 and 1932, followed in the 1930s by the greatest ever economic depression, culminating in another world war of unbelievable magnitude from 1939 until 1945.

One of the first to recognize the structural impact made by the First World War on the world economy was the economist, J.M. Keynes. He had been present at the peace negotiations that followed the end of fighting. Observing these negotiations Keynes considered that those taking the decisions that shaped the post-war world failed to appreciate the scale of the disruption caused by the war, and were unwilling to implement the measures required to address them. In 1920, he wrote that

[3] See Brown, *International Gold Standard*; Glahe, 'Empirical Study'.
[4] E.T. Powell, *The Evolution of Money Market, 1385–1915* (London: 1916), 669.

The spokesmen of the French and British people have run the risk of completing the ruin, which Germany began, by a peace which, if it is carried into effect, must impair yet further, when it might have restored the delicate, complicated organization, already shaken and broken by war, through which alone the European peoples can employ themselves and live.[5]

The assumptions made at the time of the peace treaties were that Germany could be made to pay for the war, there would be a swift return to pre-war patterns of international trade and finance, and stable currencies would emerge through a return to the Gold Standard, ideally at the exchange rates prevailing in the past. This is what had happened after the Franco-German War of 1870 and so there was no reason to expect a different result. What was ignored was the massive scale and intensity of the First World War and thus the magnitude and duration of its impact.

With the benefit of hindsight others came to recognize that the First World War destroyed the equilibrium that had underpinned the stability of the global economy before 1914, and that restoring it would be a long and difficult process. One who did was the economist W.S. Woytinsky, who had lived through the entire period. In 1955, he reflected that 'World War One drastically changed the creditor–debtor relations of nations and reshaped their balance of payments.'[6] Representing a later generation of economists, Paul Krugman reached the same conclusion in 2000. 'World War 1 was a watershed dividing the central bank autonomy of the nineteenth century from the more politicized monetary policy environment of the inter-war years.'[7] Such was the impact of the First World War that it required a complete rebalancing of the world economy before stability could be regained, but that would take time and involve massive changes in the volume and direction of international trade to reflect relative competitiveness. This was not achievable in the short run even if governments had been willing to accept the inflation or deflation required, as well as the accompanying structural changes in their economies. In the absence of this restructuring, only the continual recycling of US$s in the 1920s maintained a fiction of equilibrium. When that recycling ceased during a series of financial crises between 1929 and 1932, including the Wall Street Crash, banking failures in Central Europe and the USA, the German debt moratorium, and Britain's departure from the Gold Standard, the absence of fundamental equilibrium was exposed, leading to a collapse of international trade and finance.[8]

The problem with the 1930s was that the world economy failed to recover from the depths of depression reached in 1932. The almost universal response by governments around the world to the depression was to protect their own economies from the avalanche of cheap imports, as exporters tried to generate whatever income they

---

[5] See J.M. Keynes, *The Economic Consequences of the Peace* (London: 1920).
[6] Woytinsky, *World Commerce*, 199–208.
[7] P. Krugman, *Currency Crises* (Chicago: 2000), 18.
[8] L. Neal and M. Weidenmier, 'Crises in the Global Economy from Tulips to Today', in M.D. Bordo, A.M. Taylor and J.G. Williamson (eds), *Globalization in Historical Perspective* (Chicago: NBER, 2003), 502.

could from their products. Numerous barriers were erected to international trade in the early 1930s which largely remained in place for the rest of the decade. The very fabric of the world economy was undermined as consumers were denied access to the cheapest products and the most efficient producers prevented from supplying them. Until the 1930s, international flows of commodities, manufactures, services, people, credit, and capital had been engines of global economic growth, but that process was then reversed. National economies retreated to within their own borders, as with Germany and the USA or, like Britain, converted their imperial possessions into protected zones.[9] The panel of experts assembled by the League of Nations in the 1930s identified the consequences for the world economy of all these barriers to international trade and finance.

> International specialization has been greatly restricted in recent years and this restriction continues, involving a very drastic reorganization of international trade. ... Such restrictions, narrowing the area of international trade and specialization, and breaking essential links in the chain of transactions by which trade was formerly conducted, present a formidable obstacle to the return of worldwide prosperity.[10]

However, nothing was done to reverse what had happened and the world drifted towards war during the 1930s.

Under such conditions, it was unrealistic to expect that the fixed exchange rates dictated by the Gold Standard would be adhered to and exchange-rate stability could be delivered through adjustments to interest rates, even if governments were willing to allow the global money market to operate unimpeded.[11] Nevertheless, the preference among most governments at the end of hostilities was to retain the Gold Standard or to restore it as soon as possible if they were forced to suspend it.[12] The difficulties posed by a continuing adherence to the Gold Standard were examined as early as 1918, in a report commissioned by the British government. The underlying commitment to the Gold Standard was spelled out. 'Nothing can contribute more to a speedy recovery from the effects of the war, and to the rehabilitation of the foreign exchanges, than the re-establishment of the currency upon a sound basis.' The problem lay in achieving that objective. A regime of low interest rates would help manufacturing recover its competitiveness but undermine the value of the £ on international markets. Conversely, a regime of high rates would support the value of the £ but undermine competitiveness. To do both was impossible as it would be impractical 'to prevent people from borrowing at the low home rate and contriving in one

---

[9] N. Forbes, *Doing Business with the Nazis: Britain's Economic and Financial Relations with Germany, 1931–1939* (London: 2000), 5–40, 166; M. Obstfeld and A.M. Taylor, *Global Capital Markets: Integration, Crisis and Growth* (Cambridge: 2004), 222.

[10] See League of Nations, *World Economic Survey* (Geneva: 1935–6).

[11] P. Einzig, 'London as the World's Banking Centre', *The Banker*, xxvii (September 1933), 183; Einzig, *Textbook on Foreign Exchange*, 89; Atkin, *The Foreign Exchange Market of London*, 59–60, 69–72, 81, 86–7.

[12] F. Capie and G. Wood, 'Policy Makers in Crisis: A Study of Two Devaluations', in D.R. Hodgman and G.E. Wood (eds), *Monetary and Exchange Rate Policy* (London: 1987), 169–70.

way or another to re-lend at the high foreign rate'. Even with exchange controls, low interest rates would stimulate domestic demand and suck in imports without making exports more competitive, leading to a balance of payments crisis.[13] During the war, the British government had intervened to support the international value of the UK£, but this could not continue into peacetime because gold shipments resumed once the danger of ships being sunk by enemy action was ended.[14] Due to the contrasting fortune of the UK and the USA during the war, the UK£ was left overvalued and the US$ undervalued, which would produce an immediate transfer of gold from the former to the latter. Britain had no option but to leave the Gold Standard, which it did in 1919.[15] In the free for gold that followed market the UK£ fell in value against the US$.[16]

Britain's departure from the Gold Standard was considered to be a necessary but temporary measure. Only a return to the Gold Standard would deliver the currency stability considered essential for Britain's economy with its high dependence upon exports and imports.[17] That return took place in 1925, at almost the pre-war exchange rate, under the assumption that this was now sustainable.[18] However, this new exchange rate was only sustainable through the maintenance of a higher interest rate in the UK than in the USA, as that encouraged a flow of funds from the latter to the former. The high UK interest rates and the overvalued £ had the effect of making British exports uncompetitive, putting pressure on the balance of payments and thus the value of the £. The converse was true for the USA, where the low interest rates stoked a credit bubble. Eventually, Britain was forced to abandon its commitment to the Gold Standard in 1931 and accept the devaluation of the £ against the $. The USA itself abandoned the Gold Standard in 1933. Though the aspiration for a restoration of the Gold Standard continued to be widely held, there was to be no return with the outbreak of the Second World War ending such hopes.[19] However, nothing was done to reverse what had happened as the world drifted towards war during the 1930s. There was to be no return to the Gold Standard.[20] In 2012, a study commissioned by Deutsche Bank concluded that the attempt to return to the Gold Standard in the 1920s had contributed to the world economic depression of the 1930s. The verdict it passed was that 'Fixed currency regimes in general can be highly destructive if a country is on the wrong exchange rate.'[21] What was misunderstood about the

---

[13] Committee on Currency and Foreign Exchanges after the War: *First Interim Report 1918*, 2, 12–13.

[14] P. Einzig, *Exchange Control* (London: 1934), 24, 32.

[15] Phillips, *Modern Foreign Exchange*, 34, 53, 249; Atkin, *The Foreign Exchange Market of London*, 28, 32.

[16] P. Bareau, 'The London Gold and Silver Markets', in T. Balogh, *Studies in Financial Organization*, 214.

[17] Gregory, *Foreign Exchange*, 55.

[18] L. Waight, *The History and Mechanism of the Exchange Equalisation Account* (Cambridge: 1939), 3–4.

[19] Collins, *Money and Banking*, 278–84; Einzig, *Forward Exchange*, 10; L.T. Conway, *The International Position of the London Money Market, 1931–1937* (Philadelphia: 1946), 20, 27, 33, 39, 48; I.M. Drummond, 'London, Washington and the Management of the Franc, 1936–39', *Princeton Studies in International Finance*, 45 (1979), 6–7.

[20] Conway, *The International Position*, 20, 27, 33, 39, 48; Drummond, 'London, Washington', 6–7.

[21] Deutsche Bank, *LT Asset Return Study: A Journey into the Unknown* (2012), 7–8.

Gold Standard between the wars was the assumption that it would lead to a return to fixed exchange rates. In reality, it was the underlying equilibrium in the world economy that had supported the overall stability of exchange rates before 1914. Trying to force fixed exchange rates onto a world economy that lacked equilibrium destabilized economies, leading to a series of crises that culminated in the Great Depression of the 1930s.[22]

Prior to Britain's return to the Gold Standard in 1925, the global financial system was discovering ways of coping with exchange-rate instability in the form of an active foreign exchange market. However, that market was continually discredited by press reporting throughout the interwar years, which publicized erratic currency movements and attributed these to speculators.[23] Dudley Ward, a close associate of Keynes, and an observer of developments in the foreign exchange market, set the tone for this negative image. In 1922, he claimed that 'The foreign exchange market, in these days of rapid and wide fluctuations, has become the hunting-ground of the speculator.'[24] This became the accepted verdict in the 1920s and 1930s. The foreign exchange market was considered an aberration, and all awaited the restoration of the Gold Standard. Furniss in 1922 referred to current monetary conditions as 'abnormal and temporary', and these would continue until there was a return to the Gold Standard.[25] Lever in 1925 looked forward to Britain rejoining the Gold Standard because that would address the instability that had existed since it had been abandoned in 1919.

> When the unpegging of the exchanges took place in 1919, all the forces which directly or indirectly influence rates of exchange were given practically free play and with conditions fundamentally altered and many factors unknown or difficult to gauge, it is hardly to be wondered at that nobody was in a position to take more than a short view.[26]

To Hawtrey in 1932, 'Monetary conditions have been abnormal since the end of the war. After the chaos of the inflation period, there came a lucid interval of a few years before the crisis and depression which started in 1929. But even the lucid interval was not very lucid.'[27] As there was no recognition that the foreign exchange market had made any contribution to the stability of exchange rates, normality was associated with the Gold Standard, and this view continued into the 1930s. Deutsch's handbook on arbitrage, published in 1933, observed that 'the Great War and depreciation of currencies altered the face of Foreign Exchanges'.[28] Clare's 'Money Market Primer

---

[22] Bordo and Flandreau, 'Core, Periphery', 424–5.
[23] For an example of press reporting, see *Wall Street Journal*, 27 January 1917, 2 February 1918, 21 November 1918, 20 March 1919, 22 March 1919, 11 June 1919, 9 July 1919, 5 January 1920, 27 December 1923, 7 January 1926, 12 January 1927, 17 July 1931, 27 January 1932, 20 February 1933, 27 July 1934, 5 September 1934, 25 October 1935, 4 June 1936, 13 May 1939.
[24] Ward, 'Foreign Exchange Market in London', 10.
[25] Furniss, *Foreign Exchange*, Preface and 365.
[26] Lever, *Foreign Exchange from the Investor's Point of View*, iv, 59.
[27] Hawtrey, *Art of Central Banking*, 229.
[28] H. Deutsch, *Arbitrage*, 3rd ed., revised by O. Webber (London: 1933), 5.

and Key to the Exchanges', which appeared in 1936, acknowledged that 'The war has been responsible for drastic changes in the money and foreign exchange markets.'[29]

Between the wars, most believed that there could be no permanent solution to the volatility of exchange rates until the return of the Gold Standard.[30] As Barry Eichengreen has written, 'The gold standard was viewed as synonymous with financial stability.'[31] The Bank of England was wholly committed to the restoration of the Gold Standard and, according to Sir George Bolton, 'could not respond to the signals and impulses of a chaotic exchange market' that reacted to political events rather than interest rates. Bolton had traded foreign exchange in London in the 1920s and had been recruited by the Bank of England in the 1930s because of his expertise.[32] As the prospects of a return to the Gold Standard faded in the 1930s, those searching for a solution to foreign exchange instability increasingly favoured government intervention with managerial responsibility devolved to central banks. This was the response adopted by the US government in the early 1930s for the stock market because of 'the unduly large volume of uncontrolled speculation, coupled with the frequent interference with the free play of supply and demand by manipulative activity', according to a 1934 report by the Twentieth Century Fund.[33] One who expressed his support for central bank intervention in 1938 was B.G. Catterns, the Deputy Governor of the Bank of England.

> Since 1914, the attitude of the public towards intervention has entirely changed, and there is no field in which the need for some regulation, even in peace-time, is more obvious or more generally accepted than in foreign exchange. Bitter experience has made people exchange-minded, and they would take alarm if, in an emergency, nothing was done to protect sterling and conserve the country's reserves.

The emergency he was anticipating was the declaration of a war with Germany.[34] What his assessment reflected was a major change from the commitment to the Gold Standard as expressed in the 1918 report by the Committee on Currency and Foreign Exchanges after the War. In its place had come a willingness to embrace intervention by governments and central banks. Over the course of the 1920s and 1930s, the volatility of exchange rates and the behaviour of speculators had generated the view that the foreign exchange market could not be trusted to deliver stability, especially as the pre-war precedent had been hidden from the public. One response was

[29] J. Sangway, *Clare's Money Market Primer and Key to the Exchanges* (London: 1936), 177. See L.L.B. Angas, *The Problems of the Foreign Exchanges* (London: 1935), 87; C. Iversen, *Aspects of the Theory of International Capital Movements* (Copenhagen: 1936), 30, 55, 84, 333.

[30] Hawtrey, *Century of Bank Rate*, 10–11, 56, 69, 107. See S.V.O. Clarke, *Central Bank Co-operation, 1924–31* (New York: 1967), 219.

[31] B. Eichengreen, 'International Monetary Instability between the Wars: Structural Flaws or Misguided Policies?', in Y. Suzuki, J. Miyake and M. Okabe (eds), *The Evolution of the International Monetary System: How Can Efficiency and Stability Be Attained* (Tokyo: 1990), 105.

[32] Sir George Bolton, *Memoirs* (13 January 1977), ch. 4, 7.

[33] Twentieth Century Fund, *Stock Market Control* (New York: 1934), 163.

[34] B.G. Catterns, Bank of England, to Sir Richard Hopkins, Treasury, 8 July 1938.

the establishment of the Bank for International Settlements in 1930 as a clearing mechanism for international payments.[35]

The City of London, 1919–1939

The First World War ended currency stability and created an even greater need for a functioning foreign exchange market. It also upset the existing London-based foreign exchange market that operated through a combination of the global banking network and arbitrage between stock exchanges. All the major European financial centres experienced a serious setback during the war, including London, while the role played by New York greatly expanded. The opportunities presented to New York built upon the pre-war advances which included the freedom given to US banks to expand abroad, and the establishment of a US central bank as a lender of last resort in 1913.[36] By the 1920s, New York benefited from the USA being the world's largest and most successful economy; the $ challenging the £ as a widely used vehicle currency; the USA becoming the most important source of international finance; and US banks expanding their global branch network.[37] Though London still retained many advantages as an international financial centre, especially compared to Paris and Berlin, even in Europe it faced competition from those cities located in countries that had remained neutral during the war, especially the Netherlands and Switzerland, while there had also been a shift away from the Eurocentric financial system that had existed before the First World War. Under these circumstances, there was no guarantee that London would retain its position as the hub of the global foreign exchange market after the First World War, particularly after Britain departed from the Gold Standard in 1919. A commitment to the Gold Standard signified a stable exchange rate, and this was considered a vital ingredient for an international financial centre because so many transactions involved the conversion of one currency into another. Also, it was London that continued to possess the microstructure required to support the operation of an international financial centre unlike any of the alternatives, including New York.[38]

On the eve of the First World War, the City of London was the most important financial centre in the world, possessing the largest money, capital, and securities markets, and the only one with a truly international role. It was also the leading commercial centre in the world with numerous commodity markets, merchants, brokers, and agents. Finally, it was the global hub for international communications

---

[35] See Brown, *International Gold Standard*.

[36] Furniss, *Foreign Exchange*, 376–7, 380, 385, 402, 404.

[37] See B. Eichengreen and M. Flandreau, *The Rise and Fall of the Dollar; or When Did the Dollar Replace Sterling as the Leading Reserve Currency?*, Paper presented in Cambridge and Genoa, 2008; L. Chiu, B. Eichengreen and A. Mehl, 'When Did the Dollar Overtake Sterling as the Leading International Currency? Evidence from the Bond Markets', *European Central Bank Working Paper Series*, 1433 (2012); Eichengreen, Mehl and Chitu, *How Global Currencies Work*, 43–4, 56–7, 67, 70–1, 107, 175, 178, 183.

[38] Brown, *International Gold Standard*, 306, 211, 494, 551, 600, 1263.

and shipping and the provision of services such as marine insurance.[39] This position made it highly vulnerable to the inevitable disruption that a period of intense and prolonged military conflict would bring, especially one involving Britain, its Empire, and the other major economic powers. Such a conflict would not only shatter the international payment flows that took place continuously, but also destroy the trust upon which so much paying, receiving, lending, investing, borrowing, buying, selling, and exchanging took place. The City of London had thrived in a world where the financial and commercial barriers between nations had fallen away through the revolution in transport and communications and the removal or reduction of the restrictions imposed by governments on the movement of commodities, manufactures, money, capital, and people in the fifty years before the First World War. That war began a process that reversed most of these gains between 1918 and 1939, creating an environment that was much more hostile for the City of London, undermining its ability to function as an international financial centre.[40]

During the war, there was a reorientation away from the international arena by the City of London, as the British government monopolized the money and capital markets through a combination of appeals to patriotism and official/unofficial controls. One measure of the financial demands made by the government was the huge increase in the national debt. This rose from £706.2 million in 1914 to £7,481.1 million in 1919, or a tenfold increase in five years, whereas it had remained static in the previous hundred. The effect was to crowd out other borrowers, especially from abroad, thus greatly reducing the City's ability to finance international trade and investment. As financial transactions between nations continued during the war, the result was a transfer of business once done in London to other financial and commercial centres around the world. New York in the USA, which did not enter the war until 1917, was one of the major beneficiaries in this process of displacement. Prior to the war, the City of London had provided the credit that underpinned the external trade of the USA, but it lost that role to US banks and the New York money market. The City of London did gain some international business that had previously been routed through continental European centres. However, this was small compensation for what was lost between 1914 and 1918.[41]

Compounding the undermining of the City of London's position as a global financial centre during the First World War was the loss of the huge holdings of US securities built up by British investors over the previous fifty years. These were either sold by their owners to American investors or surrendered to the British government for disposal in New York. Around £850 million, or $4.0 billion, of these securities were sold during and immediately after the war. In addition, the British government

[39] Cassis (ed.), *Finance and Financiers*: Burk, 360.

[40] E.V. Morgan, *Studies in British Financial Policy, 1914–25* (London: 1952), 74–8; Balogh, *Studies in Financial Organization*, 231. See J. Peters, 'The British Government and the City-Industry Divide: The Case of the 1914 Financial Crisis', *Twentieth-Century British History*, 4 (1993).

[41] Butson, 'The Banking System', 1158; D.T. Merrett, 'Capital Markets and Capital Formation in Australia, 1890–1945', *Australian Economic History Review*, 37 (1997), 192–3; A. Turner, 'British Holdings of French War Bonds: An Aspect of Anglo-French Relations during the 1920s', *Financial History Review*, 3 (1996), 154–5; Morgan, *British Financial Policy*, 332.

also borrowed extensively in the USA during the war. Total such borrowing reached £1.4 billion by the end of the war. As the economy of the USA was booming at this time, boosted by the absence of European competition and the demand for war supplies, American investors had the money to buy back those US securities held abroad and purchase those being issued by the British government. The result was to greatly diminish London as an international financial centre, while enhancing that of New York. As New York was already a major financial centre, it possessed the depth and breadth of personnel, banks, brokers, and markets required to replace the services once provided by London, not only within the USA itself but also in Canada and Latin America. It was during the First World War that New York replaced London in providing Latin America with the credit facilities required for its international trade, especially the countries of Central America. Even Argentina, which had particularly close ties to the UK, increasingly entered the US orbit, with the Argentinian peso being linked to the US$ in 1931. Similarly, it was in 1916 that Japanese banks shifted from a reliance on London to an increasing orientation towards New York and the development of a Tokyo-based money market.[42] By the end of the war, New York had emerged as a powerful rival to London as an international financial centre.[43]

In contrast to the strengthening of New York's international links during the war, those of London were weakened, especially those to Europe. Inevitably, the link between the City and Germany, which had been so important before 1914, suffered the severest damage, as commercial and financial ties were cut. In addition, many of the numerous Germans, who had made such a valuable contribution to the City of London as an international financial centre before the war, either returned home or transferred their business to New York. Those Germans who remained in London were ostracized and excluded from membership of City institutions like the London Stock Exchange (LSE) and the Baltic Exchange, making it difficult for them to remain in business. The London branches of German banks were also closed, on the orders of the British government. The result was to undermine London's intermediary role between Europe and the rest of the world, whether it involved credit, capital, or commodities.[44] Nevertheless, it would be a mistake to magnify the damage inflicted on the City of London by the First World War. Britain was neither invaded nor experienced regime change, while its Empire remained intact and even expanded. The effect of the First World War was much more damaging for Berlin, Vienna, and Paris than it was for London. The forced sale and then seizure of German foreign securities during the war, and then the post-war hyper-inflation, destroyed Berlin as an international financial centre, while the wholesale repudiation of Russian debts by the Bolshevik government, and the instability of the franc in the early 1920s, undermined Paris. Though damaged by the war, the City of London remained a leading financial

[42] Odate, *Japan's Financial Relations with the U.S.*, 32–6.

[43] Cassis (ed.), *Finance and Financiers*: Burk, 360–5; C.R. Geisst, *Wall Street: A History* (Oxford: 1997), 152, 161; Morgan, *British Financial Policy*, 332; Joslin, *Banking in Latin America*, 217, 228–30, 251, 270; A.M. Quintero Ramos, *A History of Money and Banking in Argentina* (Puerto Rico: 1965), 127, 156.

[44] Morgan, *British Financial Policy*, 332; C. Lewis, *America's Stake in International Investments* (Washington: 1938), 119, 653; Spalding, *Foreign Exchange*, 119.

centre. While acknowledging that London had lost out to Amsterdam in Europe and New York internationally, neither Escher or Patterson in 1917 nor Whitaker in 1919 believed that it was in any danger of being replaced as the leading financial centre in the world.[45] As the First World War drew to a close in 1918, the *Wall Street Journal* reported that

> In the opinion of a leading British financial authority, London will be back to her old position of financial power within ten years. ... There is a marked feeling of confidence in banking circles in London that the nation will be able to carry on and meet the great problems which may arise without any serious or permanent impairment of financial influence.[46]

While such a judgement was highly optimistic, it did reflect a belief that the City of London's intrinsic strengths were sufficiently powerful for it to withstand the effects of the First World War. In the 1920s, London continued to possess major advantages as a financial centre through the depth and breadth of its money market, the continued use made of the £ as an international currency, the scope and scale of its financial and commercial links, and the role it played as the hub of the world's largest Empire. London remained central to the global payments system, and so it not only retained the offices and branches of banks from around the world but also attracted new ones.[47] By the 1920s, there had been little substantial change in the structure, composition, and orientation of the City compared to pre-war years. London remained both a commercial and financial centre serving the British and world economy. What was taking place was a growing engagement between the City of London and the domestic economy at the expense of provincial centres. The legacy of the war was a great increase in the British government's short- and long-term borrowing requirements, while British business turned to the City in search of additional finance because of the effects of high taxation and low profitability upon internal and informal sources of funds. In many ways, the City of London prospered in the 1920s as the global economy recovered and new areas of domestic business were engaged with. That was in sharp contrast to the economic difficulties that affected the British economy throughout that decade, and it was this which generated the growing criticism of the City of London in the 1920s.[48]

[45] Escher, *Foreign Exchange Explained*, 105; Stewart Patterson, *Domestic and Foreign Exchange*, 255, 269, 273–4; A.C. Whitaker, *Foreign Exchange* (New York: 1919), 624–7.

[46] *Wall Street Journal*, 19 October 1918.

[47] C.C. McLeod and A.W. Kirkaldy, *The Trade, Commerce and Shipping of the Empire* (London: 1924), 131; *International Banking in London: FBSA 50th Anniversary*, Financial Times/Banker Special Supplement (7 November 1997), 30, 39; Newall, *Japan and the City*, 19; Bonin, *Société Générale*, 34; B. Attard, 'The Bank of England and the Origins of the Niemeyer Mission 1921–1930', *Australian Economic History Review*, 32 (1992), 67–8.

[48] Cassis (ed.), *Finance and Financiers*: Burk, 360–5; Whitmore, *Money Machine*, 26; Cleveland and Huertas, *Citibank*, 114; Geisst, *Wall Street*, 161; Y. Cassis, 'Financial Elites in Three European Centres: London, Paris, Berlin, 1880s–1930s', *Business History*, 33 (1991), 56; Roberts, *Schroders*, 154, 174, 213–14; A. Gleeson, *London Enriched: The Development of the Foreign Banking Community in the City Over Five Decades* (London: 1997), 26.

Nevertheless, the position London occupied in the 1920s was a much less secure one than in the years before 1914. In terms of capital exports, the USA emerged as the dominant source of funds. Holdings of foreign securities by US investors rose from $2.3 billion in 1919 to $7.3 billion in 1929, or by $5 billion during the 1920s. The City of London was now in second position. Loans totalling £1.2 billion were made in London between 1920 and 1929 on behalf of overseas borrowers. Countries around the world, including ones in the Empire like Canada and India, no longer turned automatically to London when searching for external funding. The City of London maintained its superiority as an international centre in competition with other major European centres but lost in comparison with those located elsewhere in the world, especially New York.[49] By 1928, according to Kniffin, 'New York is now fast becoming a rival to London in respect of worldwide financial affairs.'[50]

The 1931 monetary crisis represented even more of a turning point for the City of London as an international financial centre. It destroyed much of the confidence that had continued to be placed in London during the 1920s, especially after the return to a new Gold Standard in 1925.[51] Richard Roberts has concluded that, 'Overall, the 1930s were little short of calamitous for most aspects of the City's international activities.'[52] With the value of the UK£ no longer fixed, London became a much less attractive international financial centre, undermining its position as the hub of the global payments system and a location where funds could be employed safely and remuneratively. There was no longer the certainty that the value of money held in sterling-denominated accounts would remain constant in terms of other currencies such as the US$, French franc, or Japanese yen. There was also the possibility that the UK government would impose exchange controls, making it difficult to repatriate funds located in London. The precedent for such a move existed as the German government had applied a moratorium on international payments in 1931. Even for those countries whose currencies were pegged to the UK£, the departure from the Gold Standard imposed currency risks as they had commitments outside the sterling area. This encouraged a switch to New York because of its greater safe-haven status, being far removed from the growing political instability in Europe. This was reflected in the growing status of the US$ as an international currency. However, it was not only London that was damaged as an international financial centre by what happened in the 1930s and the collapse of the attempt to revive the Gold Standard. Meeker considered in 1932 that 'No such international crisis had been faced by the world since

[49] J.M. Atkin, *British Overseas Investment, 1918–1931* (New York: 1977), 129, 134, 147, 278; K. Buckley, *Capital Formation in Canada, 1896–1930* (Toronto: 1955), 101–4, 108; M. Kidron, *Foreign Investments in India* (London: 1965), 10; Geisst, *Wall Street*, 161; Cleveland and Huertas, *Citibank*, 74, 82–3, 123–6; Lewis, *America's Stake*, 653.

[50] W.H. Kniffin, *The Practical Work of a Bank* (New York: 1915), 7th ed. (1928), 548.

[51] 'Fourth Report of Committee on Economic Information: Survey of the Economic Situation in July 1932', in S. Howson and D. Winch (eds), *The Economic Advisory Council, 1930–1939: A Study in Economic Advice during Depression and Recovery* (Cambridge: Cambridge University Press, 1977), 274–80.

[52] R. Roberts, 'The City of London as a Financial Centre in the Era of Depression, the Second World War and Post-war Official Controls', in A. Gorst, L. Johnman and W.S. Lucas (eds), *Contemporary British History, 1931–61* (London: 1991), 68; For a similar judgement, see Sir Cyril Kleinwort, 'The City in Britain's Invisible Earnings', *The Banker*, 121 (1971), 170.

July 31 1914' as was caused by Britain leaving the Gold Standard in 1931.[53] In the face of the exchange controls, trade embargoes, preferential agreements, barter arrangements, and cartels that became standard practice in the international economy in the 1930s, the scope for any city to operate as a global commercial and financial centre was considerably reduced.[54] The restrictions and controls imposed by governments in the 1930s affected all international financial centres not just London. The challenge to London coming from New York had also been badly dented by the Wall Street Crash of October 1929 and the subsequent US banking collapse in the early 1930s. As a consequence of the severity of the domestic financial crisis experienced by the USA, which far outweighed anything in the UK, and the much greater losses made by US investors on foreign investments made in the 1920s, especially as a result of the German moratorium in 1931, New York was undermined as a financial centre in the 1930s. Such was the severity of the financial crisis in the USA that the government intervened to restrict the operations of banks and the financial markets, while continuing turmoil in foreign exchanges forced the $ off the Gold Standard in 1933.[55]

As a result of what took place in the 1930s, the relative position of the City of London as an international financial centre was not further undermined. To well-informed contemporaries like Einzig in 1933 and Truptil in 1936, London remained the leading financial centre in the world, despite the challenge from New York. Writing in 1933, Einzig took the view that 'There is no financial centre which would be in a position to replace London.'[56] Contributing to the continuing importance of London as a financial centre in the 1930s was the development of both imperial preference and the sterling area. Britain found some compensation for the collapse of world trade in the 1930s by retreating to imperial markets, with British manufactures being given preferential access to countries such as Australia, Canada, India, New Zealand, and South Africa as well as numerous smaller economies spread across Africa, Asia, the Caribbean, and the Pacific. London acted as a hub for much of this trade and provided such services as shipping, insurance, and credit. Also, in the wake of Britain's departure from the Gold Standard, many countries pegged their currencies to the UK£, creating the sterling area as a result. Though most of these were members of the British Empire, it also included others with strong commercial and financial ties to the UK. They continued to route their transactions through London and make use of the facilities it provided, including the money, capital, and securities markets. No other financial centre possessed the range and depth of international links found in London in the 1930s. Though the dominance of the City of London as a financial

---

[53] J.E. Meeker, *Short Selling* (New York: 1932), 133.

[54] C. Armstrong, *Blue Skies and Boiler Rooms: Buying and Selling Securities in Canada, 1870–1940* (Toronto: 1997), 172, 211; Roberts, *Schroders*, 249; Balogh, *Financial Organization*, 231; Bonin, *Société Générale*, 34. See D. Williams, 'London and the 1931 Financial Crisis', *Economic History Review*, 15 (1962–3).

[55] Conway, *The International Position*, 157–61; Lewis, *America's Stake*, 653; Cleveland and Huertas, *Citibank*, 161–2, 169; Geisst, *Wall Street*, 230–33. See M. Wilkins, 'Cosmopolitan Finance in the 1920s: New York's Emergence as an International Financial Centre', in R. Sylla, R. Tilly and G. Tortella (eds), *The State, the Financial System, and Economic Modernization* (Cambridge: 1999).

[56] Einzig, 'London', 184. See R.J. Truptil, *British Banks and the Money Market* (London: 1936), 274.

centre in the 1930s was much diminished compared to what it had been before the First World War, it remained without a serious rival, including New York.[57] Nevertheless, all the evidence indicates that the City's money and capital markets turned inwards during the 1930s in line with the collapse of international commercial and financial flows. What underpinned the City as a financial centre during the 1930s was the growth of domestic activities, though that is not what contemporaries believed.[58]

On the eve of the First World War, the City of London was the leading financial centre in the world. By the end of the 1930s, it shared that position with New York. The First World War had been very damaging for the City. Important sectors of the City experienced a considerable collapse of business, as with those handling and financing international trade or issuing and trading foreign securities. There were compensations for some through the vast increase in government borrowing, but the overall result was both a major disruption and a greatly diminished role for the City in the world economy as foreign countries either looked to their own resources or turned to the USA.

Nevertheless, the City was not destroyed by the First World War, having suffered little physical damage, while Britain escaped invasion and emerged victorious. It was battered rather than destroyed by the war, ready to rebuild its position as the foremost financial centre, despite the increased importance of New York. That it proceeded to do in the 1920s despite the weakened state of the British economy. In September 1931, Britain was forced off the Gold Standard as the world economy slipped into depression and economic nationalism. This was also exceedingly damaging for the City of London, which had thrived as the financial and commercial centre of an open world economy. The result of the 1931 financial crisis was an international environment that was positively hostile to the City's international operations through trade barriers and exchange controls. However, the City found salvation in serving the needs of the domestic economy, the Empire, and the British government. The result was that the City remained the most important financial centre in the world even by the end of the 1930s, and the one with the greatest international orientation. As a consequence, the City remained the logical location for the global foreign exchange market despite the challenge coming from New York. What was also apparent throughout the inter-war years, but especially before 1925 and after 1931, was the far greater need for an active foreign exchange market than had been the case before the First World War. In particular, that market had to provide a mechanism for trading the UK£ against the US$ as these were now the twin vehicle currencies of the world economy.[59]

[57] Conway, *The International Position*, 2–3, 7, 19–20, 27, 33, 39, 48, 54, 57–61, 69, 72, 77.

[58] Royal Institute of International Affairs, *The Problem of International Investment* (Oxford: 1937), 11; Cleveland and Huertas, *Citibank*, 161–2, 169; Geist, *Wall Street*, 230–3; M.D. Bordo and R. Sylla (eds), *Anglo-American Financial System: Institutions and Markets in the Twentieth Century* (New York: 1995), 199; M.G. Myers, *Paris as a Financial Centre* (London: 1936), 163, 170–7; Merrett, 'Global Reach', 81–2; Jones, *Multinational Banking*, 414–15; G. Toniolo (ed.), *Central Banks' Independence in Historical Perspective* (Berlin: 1988): Cairncross, 42–6; E. Hennessy, *A Domestic History of the Bank of England, 1930–1960* (Cambridge: 1992), 83; W.R. Garside and J.I. Greaves, 'The Bank of England and Industrial Intervention in Interwar Britain', *Financial History Review*, 3 (1996), 71–3, 75, 79, 81–3; Balogh, *Financial Organization*, 268.

[59] Brown, *International Gold Standard*, 1075, 1289; Glahe, *Empirical Study*, 5.

The Money Market, 1919–1939

Underpinning the success of the City of London as a financial centre before the First World War was the money market. It was the liquidity provided by the money market that attracted banks from around the world, whether through establishing a branch, opening an office, setting up an agency, or operating through a correspondent relationship. From the 1860s onwards, it became essential for a bank, once it reached a significant size, to have a means of accessing the London money market as that was where idle funds could be employed and temporary loans obtained far more easily than anywhere else in the world. Access to that money market was also a critical factor in the expansion of British overseas banks into Africa, Asia, and Australasia. The money market dovetailed with London's role as the clearing centre of the international economy, providing banks with an outlet for money received from receipts but before payments had to be made, or a source of short-term finance to fill a temporary gap between payments made and funds received. In the fifty years before the First World War, the London money market had evolved in numerous different ways as it responded to new supplies of funds, especially from abroad, and new investment opportunities, such as those presented by stocks and bonds traded on the Stock Exchange. These changes had provided the London money market with a depth and breadth unmatched in any other financial centre. It was the needs of this money market that drove developments in the pre-war foreign exchange market as it became increasingly necessary to match commitments across currencies, so as to minimize the risks being run, even at a time of relatively stable exchange rates.

The functioning of the London money market was highly dependent upon trust between counterparties, which was very vulnerable to rumours that either side might default on their commitment to repay. That could lead to a partial freezing of the market with banks refusing to lend to each other. It was here that the discount houses or bill brokers played a crucial role, borrowing from some and buying bills of exchange from others. This made the London money market and the London discount market synonymous. Bill brokers bought bills from banks at a discount to their face value, using funds borrowed from other banks. These bills were either retained until maturity or sold to other banks at slightly less of a discount to their face value. Though many of these bills were of a commercial nature, generated through the credit provided to finance international trade, most were finance bills in the years before the First World War. By creating a finance bill, and then selling it in the discount market, a bank could raise a temporary loan, repaying the sum borrowed. In this way, a bank could always respond to the borrowing needs of its customers. The bill was repaid on maturity but could pass from hand to hand until then, at ever smaller discounts to its face value, through the dealings of the bill brokers. These bills were bought by banks using money they received from customers by way of deposit, for which they had no immediate employment. In that way, banks continually borrowed and lent from each matching assets and liabilities by time and amount, using the discount houses as intermediary. In turn, the discount houses relied on the Bank of England as lender of last resort, ready to supply them with funds to make up any deficiency between their commitment to buy bills and the money they needed to borrow to finance their purchases. The Bank of England would lend the discount houses what they needed at a rate of interest above that in the market, taking only the highest quality bills as collateral. That left the discount houses to assess the quality of the bills they bought, and take the greater risks, but it meant they could always balance their borrowing and lending and so avoid a liquidity crisis. Confident that they would always be able to employ any money they were lent or purchase any bills they were offered, the discount houses acted as constant and reliable counterparties to the banks.

The role played by the discount houses was supplemented by the brokers and jobbers on the Stock Exchange who borrowed from the banks to finance their purchases of stocks and bonds, confident that they could repay the loans on maturity because of the liquidity of the securities that they held. That liquidity came from the market provided by the LSE and its connections to other stock exchanges located around the world. The combination of bill brokers, stockbrokers, and jobbers provided those banks that had access to the London money market with the certainty that they would always be able to employ temporarily idle funds or access short-term funds whenever they needed. It was this certainty that made the London money market so appealing, placing it at the heart of the chain of transactions that connected the world's banking system into a network through which flowed, seamlessly, payments and receipts, debits and credits, loans and investments. Over the fifty years before the First World War, this money market had grown in size, scale, and sophistication to become an essential element in the global financial system. The operation and even existence of this money market was then threatened by the outbreak of the First World War, with serious implications for the working of the global financial system.[60] This threat was widely recognized by bankers around the world. The Japanese banker J. Inouye, who was the president of the Yokohama Specie Bank between 1913 and 1919, reflected in 1926 that 'The outbreak of war in August 1914 ... instantly paralysed the financial vitality of London, the nerve centre on which depended the trading activities of the entire world.'[61]

In the climate of uncertainty that grew up during the days leading up to the declaration of war in 1914, the London discount market broke down. Fearing a rush by their customers to withdraw cash, banks around the world called in loans and refused to lend, destroying the liquidity that was vital for its functioning. The discount house, Smith St. Aubyn, which had been established in 1891, recorded the unfolding situation in brief but stark detail in their daily Business Diary.[62] On 1 August 1914, they reported that 'The Joint Stock banks panicked, and it was only at a quarter to one that we were able to get anything. A truly fearful Saturday. ... The worst day we have ever had since the business began. ... The whole market absolutely broke.' Holding a

---

    [60] W.F. Spalding, *The London Money Market: A Practical Guide to What It Is, Where It Is, and the Operations Conducted in It* (London: Sir Isaac Pitman, 1930), 200.

    [61] J. Inouye, *Problems of the Japanese Exchange, 1914–1926* (Glasgow: 1931) (English translation by E.H. de Bunsen from the Japanese original written in 1926), 4.

    [62] See Smith St. Aubyn: Business Diary, 1 August 1914, 7 August 1914, 2 September 1914, 24 November 1915, 8 January 1917.

portfolio of bills which they could not sell and unable to repay the loans being called in by the banks, the discount houses faced immediate bankruptcy and looked to the Bank of England for support. With all discount houses in the same position, and their demands likely to overwhelm the cash reserves of the Bank of England, it was fearful that a run would develop which would bring down the entire British banking system. Facing a financial crisis of unparalleled magnitude, the British government, intervened. The UK government's response was an act that came into force on 3 August 1914 that suspended payment on bills of exchange.[63] This moratorium prevented banks from calling in their loans, which stabilized the situation. On 7 August, Smith St. Aubyn recorded that 'A moratorium declared for one month, which saved the whole financial situation. We reopened for business but did nothing.'

However, the moratorium only delayed the inevitable as banks remained reluctant to lend to the discount houses because they had no guarantee when they would be repaid. With a continuing liquidity crisis, the Bank of England was forced to intervene again. Backed by the support of the London joint-stock banks, the Bank of England managed to restore confidence, and this led to a limited revival of the discount market, as Smith St. Aubyn reported. On 2 September, they noted 'things getting on to a more workable condition'. Despite the optimism, this was not a return to normal working in the London discount market but the beginning of a transformation. For the duration of the war, it was not bank borrowing and lending that drove the discount market but the British government's funding requirements, as orchestrated by the Governor of the Bank of England (Cunliffe). The issue of treasury bills crowded out most other business. On 24 November 1915, Smith St. Aubyn reported that 'All the clearing banks have been ordered to charge 4½ for call, notice and evening money, with what object is not clear except that Cunliffe hopes to get more money from the Banks at 4½ to lend to the government at 5%.' Such a situation continued to the end of the war, as revealed in this comment from Smith St. Aubyn on 8 January 1917: 'Bank of England (Cunliffe) is up to his old Tricks and is offering to take any money from the Bankers at 5 per cent. Even foreign bankers are lending "through" their bankers.' Over the course of the First World War, the British government's net debt rose from £0.7 billion in 1914 to £7.4 billion in 1919 or from 26 per cent of GDP to 128 per cent. Of this debt, a total of £4.1 billion was long term but a further £1.4 billion was short term, mainly in the form of treasury bills which dominated the discount market.[64]

For those banks willing to hold treasury bills, they provided a means of engaging in short-term lending and borrowing, either directly or through the bill brokers. The value of treasury bills outstanding rose from £15.5 million in July 1914 to £1.1 billion in January 1919. However, not all banks wanted to hold sterling-denominated

---

[63] *Further Papers Relating to the Measures Taken by His Majesty's Government for Sustaining Credit and Facilitating Business*, 1914: Public Statements, 5 September 1914, 3 November 1914; Letter from Treasury to Bank of England, 30 September 1914; Enemy Banks (London Agencies): Report by Sir William Plender, 16 December 1916, 12.

[64] S. Broadberry and P. Howlett, 'The United Kingdom during World War 1: Business as Usual?', in S. Broadberry and M. Harrison (eds), *The Economics of World War 1* (Cambridge: 2005), 218.

debt in London at a time when exchange rates were becoming more volatile and the movement of money around the world made more difficult because of hostilities and government restrictions.[65] This was especially the case with foreign banks located in countries where the UK£ was not the currency in use. It also applied to British overseas banks and those from countries where sterling was the currency in use because of the spatial mismatch between assets and liabilities. The result was to undermine the role played by the London discount market in the global financial system over the duration of the war. Alternatives to the London discount market were encouraged. Within Europe, banks turned to Amsterdam in the Netherlands, which remained neutral throughout the conflict.[66] In Asia, it was Tokyo, Bombay, and Shanghai that gained.[67] The greatest beneficiary was the New York money market, which quickly replaced London in meeting US requirements.[68] Banks in Latin America and Asia were also attracted by the facilities available in New York as that was where they could find ready access to a money market offering cheap credit.[69] By August 1918, the *Wall Street Journal* reported that in New York, 'We have established every facility that should give us a discount market similar in scope to that of London.'[70] This process had begun shortly before the war with the establishment of the Federal Reserve Bank in 1913, as this created a lender of last resort in the USA. However, the need for a domestic discount market in the USA became a necessity during the war as the British government's own short-term funding requirement crowded out other business, including that coming from the USA.[71] It was during the war that the New York money market emerged from beneath the shadow of London and became internationally competitive.[72] The final alternative was for banks to dispense with the discount market altogether. This had already happened within countries like the UK. As banks grew bigger, they could switch from the originate-and-distribute model of banking to the lend-and-hold one. In the originate-and-distribute model, a bank created a bill which it then sold on, though remaining responsible for its redemption on maturity. In the lend-and-hold model, a bank made a loan which it retained until maturity. The operation of the lend-and-hold model was made possible when a bank reached a scale sufficient for it to match deposits from customers with the loans it was

[65] Inouye, *Problems of the Japanese Exchange*, 4. See Morgan, *British Financial Policy* and A.W. Kirkaldy (ed.), *British Finance during and after the War, 1914–21* (London: 1921).

[66] Odate, *Japan's Financial Relations with the U.S.*, 32–6, Tamaki, *Japanese Banking*, 119, 131, 155–6; S. Ogura, 'Mitsui Bank's Lending Policy in Transition', 84, 88, 94; Newall, *Japan and the City*, 16–18; King, *Hongkong Bank*, vol. 2, 569–70; Ji, *Modern Shanghai Banking*, 141, 150.

[67] Odate, *Japan's Financial Relations with the U.S.*, 32–6; A.K. Bagchi, *The Evolution of the State Bank of India*, vol. 2: *The Era of the Presidency Banks, 1876–1920* (New Delhi: 1997), 16–17, 30–1, 70–1, 450–3, 519, 535, 549.

[68] *Wall Street Journal*, 25 September 1914, 31 August 1918; Cleveland and Huertas, *Citibank*, 74.

[69] Whitaker, *Foreign Exchange*, 627; Joslin, *Banking in Latin America*, 217, 228; Newall, *Japan and the City*, 16–18.

[70] *Wall Street Journal*, 31 August 1918.

[71] E.C. Gibson, 'A Critical and Historical Account of the Working of the American Federal Reserve Banking System', *JIB*, 48 (1927), 467.

[72] Whitmore, *Money Machine*, 26, 98; Ellis, *Heir to Adventure*, 149; H. Rockoff, 'Until It's Over, Over There: The US Economy in World War 1', in S. Broadberry and M. Harrison (eds), *Economics of World War 1*, 335.

making and do so consistently. However, few banks were in a position to wholly rely on the lend-and-hold model, leaving a need for an active discount market.

Despite the disruption and losses caused by the war, the London discount market retained much of its pre-war business as banks continued to route payments via London and employ or borrow funds there. Supporting this inertia were the superior facilities available in London, especially the role played by the discount houses. The *Wall Street Journal* had predicted this in October 1918. 'This effort to attract foreign money to London during wartime helps to hold up exchange and also continues London's machinery as an international money market, which may be helpful in the revival after the war.'[73] Scott, who was manager of the London office of the Union Bank of Scotland, explained in 1921 the vital role that the bill broker and the discount market continued to play. Once he had estimated whether he wanted to borrow or lend, and for how long, he was ready when the bill broker called. Money could be lent out in the morning for repayment at the end of the day or overnight with repayment in the morning. If he was short of funds, loans were called in or bills sold.

It is a matter of considerable surprise to the uninitiated to watch how easily these sums, which total huge amounts, are rearranged from day to day. ... If, for any particular reason, the banks as a whole are taking in money from the market, it means that the bill-brokers are unable to place their loans with other banks, and accordingly they have "to go to the Bank", which is the colloquial way of saying that they have to obtain a loan, or to discount bills at the Bank of England. It is in this way that the Bank of England is the last resort of the borrower. The bankers never go there if they can avoid it, as the terms are much more onerous than those of the other banks. ... The advantage of buying from the broker is, that you can get any maturity that you wish, and to whatever extent you wish; whereas, if a bank is only discounting bills for its own customers, it has to take them as and when offered, consequently the bank may have large maturities at one time with considerable blanks in between the dates of maturity of its bills as a whole. ... The great advantage to the banks of doing business with the brokers instead of direct with the sellers of bills ... is derived from the fact that the bill-brokers are specialist in bills; they know better than anyone else the standing and means of the parties on the bills, and they watch closely how much paper of the different firms and houses is current on the market. The banker has the benefit of this expert information, and he also has the guarantee of the discount house for any bills bought from it.[74]

Writing in 1930, Whitmore claimed that 'The skill required in acceptance business is not of the kind which can be acquired in a few years, but is based on long experience and the tact and shrewdness which experience gives.'[75]

---

[73] *Wall Street Journal*, 19 October 1918.
[74] G.J. Scott, 'The Bill-Broker in the Bank Parlour (Manager of the London Office of the Union Bank of Scotland)', *JIB*, 42 (1921), 58–62.
[75] Whitmore, *Money Machine*, 26.

Benefitting from this expertise, the London discount market gradually recovered its international role in the 1920s. In 1925, Miller was of the view that 'London acts to a great extent as the world's financial clearing house, and a large portion of the payments between other nations are settled through London.'[76] Phillips stated in 1926 that London still had 'incomparably the best organised money market in the world, with resources at its command equal to any call, no matter how large that may be made upon it.'[77] A similar view was expressed by Greengrass in 1930: 'Here credit is more freely given and, more important still, more cheaply given than anywhere else abroad.'[78] Nevertheless, banks had now to compete with the British government's constant need to refinance its short-term war debts. To Drummond Fraser in 1925, 'Investments of Government short-dated securities now form for all practical purposes a reservoir of cash which may be tapped day by day for discounting bills and making advances.'[79] It was estimated that two-thirds of the bills circulating in the London money market in the 1920s were treasury bills, with the Bank of England managing the London discount market so as to ensure that there was always adequate demand for any that the government needed to sell. The problem was that treasury bills had limited international appeal because of the risk of holding £-denominated debt at a time of volatile exchange rates. Even before Britain left the Gold Standard in 1919, many banks from outside Britain were unwilling to hold sterling-denominated assets because of fluctuations in exchange rates. This situation was then aggravated when Britain did leave the Gold Standard in 1919.[80] This was the case with India. In 1916, the link between the £ and the rupee was broken, leaving both free to fluctuate against each other. Though Indian banks continued to use the London discount market, they did so less readily than in the past, choosing to adopt the lend-and-hold model and make greater use of Bombay.[81] One reason for the rapid return to the Gold Standard in 1925, at an exchange rate that was too high, was the recognition by the Bank of England that external demand for treasury bills was being suppressed by exchange-rate volatility.[82] It was British domestic banks and those from countries that continued to use the UK£ that generated the greatest demand for treasury bills. Australia still used the UK£ and Australian banks had around £40 million on deposit in London for most of the 1920s, and this was extensively employed in the discount market.[83]

Helping the London discount market retain international business in the early 1920s was the much greater currency instability elsewhere in the world. Such volatility undermined both the appeal of the Berlin and Paris money markets and

---

[76] Miller, *The Foreign Exchange Market*, 9, 65, 96–7, 120, 126, 147.

[77] Phillips, *Modern Foreign Exchange*, 63.

[78] H.W. Greengrass, *The Discount Market in London: Its Organisation and Recent Development* (London: 1930), 4.

[79] Sir D. Drummond Fraser, 'British Home Banking Since 1911', *JIB*, 46 (1925), 439.

[80] *Wall Street Journal*, 9 July 1919; Angas, *Problems of the Foreign Exchanges*.

[81] R. Rau, *Present-day Banking in India*, 53–4, 62, 265; Gunasekera, *From Dependent Currency*, 44, 80, 183.

[82] Whitmore, *Money Machine*, 35, 47.

[83] Gregory, *Foreign Exchange*, 55; Wilson, *Capital Imports*, 36; Blainey and Hutton, *Gold and Paper*, 197, 206, 212.

encouraged the placing of short-term funds in London.[84] Nevertheless, the New York money market emerged as an increasingly strong competitor to London as it could provide an equivalent depth and breadth and offer the US$ as a currency. It became common for banks to establish a secondary link to New York in the 1920s. However, it lacked both the expertise and facilities of the discount houses and the network connections found in London.[85] With the return of the £ to the Gold Standard in 1925, and the stability that was brought as a result, the London discount market regained much of the appeal it had long possessed as a centre where temporarily idle money could be remuneratively and safely employed and where credit could be more easily and cheaply obtained than in any other financial centre.[86] London remained the clearing house for international payments, which meant that there was a constant inflow and outflow of funds from around the world.[87] Countering the appeal of the London discount market in the later 1920s was the revival of the Berlin and Paris money markets on the back of growing currency stability in Europe. The Bank of England estimated in 1930 that £500 million had flowed back to France from abroad after July 1926, when the currency restrictions had been removed and confidence in the stability of the franc grew.[88] There was now a two-way pull affecting the London discount market. The continuing weakness of the £ against the $ led the Bank of England to maintain relatively high interest rates as a way of attracting short-term funds from abroad, especially the USA, where the Federal Reserve maintained a low interest rate regime. Conversely, this high rate of interest made London a less attractive place to borrow, especially as the UK government continued to absorb much of the available funds.[89] Each week the discount market was offered around £40 million treasury bills compared to the £100 million that was made available by banks.[90]

As confidence in the value of sterling began to wane in 1929, undermined by the continuing problems experienced by the British economy, a growing stream of short-term money was diverted to New York, attracted by the high interest paid on call loans there because of the stock market boom. That pressure was relieved temporarily when the speculative bubble burst but returned with the credit contraction that followed the melt down in the US banking system in the early 1930s, along with banking crises in Germany and Austria in 1931. All this contributed to a global liquidity crisis, as banks curtailed their lending and called in maturing loans, in anticipation of a possible bank run or in face of one taking place. Making the position particularly

[84] Roberts, *Schroders*, 174, 213–14.
[85] N. Crump, 'The London and New York Markets in the Autumn of 1925', *JIB*, 47 (1926), 307–16; Cassis, *Capitals of Capital*, 168–74; Roberts, *Schroders*, 174, 213–14; Cassis (ed.), *Finance and Financiers*: Burk, 360–5.
[86] McLeod and Kirkaldy, *The Trade, Commerce and Shipping of the Empire* (London: 1924), 131; Ogura, 'Mitsui Bank', 88, 94, 99–101; Tamaki, *Japanese Banking*, 119; Kasuya, M., 'The Activities of the Yokohama Specie Bank', in M. Kasuya (ed.), *Coping with Crisis: International Financial Institutions in the Interwar Period* (Oxford: 2003), 99–101, 132–7, 139, 141–3.
[87] Greengrass, *Discount Market*, 4; Bonin, *Société Générale*, 34; Gleeson, *London Enriched*, 26; Newell, *Japan and the City*, 19.
[88] Bank of England, *Restrictions on Dealing in Foreign Exchange*, 28 March 1930.
[89] Phelps, *The Foreign Expansion of American Banks*, 98–101.
[90] Bank of England: Siepman Correspondence, 18 July 1928; Spring-Rice, 'Financial Machinery of the City', 8–18; Whitmore, *Money Machine*, 35; Sayers, *Gillets*, 78, 80, 95, 101–2.

acute for the London discount market were growing doubts about the exchange stability of the £. As a precaution foreign banks moved funds from London, in case of
a devaluation, even though they could be employed there at attractive rates of interest. The Bank of England observed in February 1931 that 'people would like to take
advantage of higher rates ruling here but are afraid that when they want to withdraw
it they will lose more in the rate of exchange than they make on the differing rate
of interest'.[91] Banks from around the world ran down their London balances, retaining only the amount required to meet current commitments. Australian banks, for
example, reduced the balances they held in London from £39.2 million in 1929 to
£12.7 million in 1930.[92] As the franc now appeared more stable than the £, much
of the money that stayed in Europe flowed to Paris, though some was recycled back
to London via the Bank of France. Between 3 October 1929 and 31 August 1931,
the Bank of France's deposits with Lloyds Bank in London rose from £2.3 million to
£12.7 million.[93]

Despite the arrival of funds such as these, the London discount market remained
very tight, especially in the wake of the collapse of Germany's largest bank, the Darmstädter und National Bank, in July 1931. Smith St. Aubyn reported in July 1931 that
they 'could not sell bills at all'. This difficulty continued throughout the summer until
Britain left the Gold Standard on 21 September 1931. That did not produce an immediate respite, with Smith St. Aubyn reporting on 25 September that 'The market is
very disturbed and wide prices.' Even by March 1933, the level of business remained
low, as Smith St. Aubyn observed: 'Nothing being done in discounts.'[94] Contributing to the difficulty was the rapid withdrawal of funds from London by the Bank of
France after Britain left the Gold Standard. Its deposits with Lloyds Bank fell from
£12.7 million on 31 August 1931 to £2 million on 5 April 1932.[95] In turn, this forced
banks, such as Lloyds, to restrict the credit they provided to correspondent banks,
after reviewing their creditworthiness.[96] In 1928, lending in the London discount
market had reached £328 million, indicating the gradual revival that had taken place
during that decade. That total then fell sharply to £294 million in 1929 and then
kept dropping until 1932, by which time it stood at £150 million.[97] Confidence in
the discount market had been badly damaged by Britain's departure from the Gold
Standard.[98]

[91] Bank of England, Memorandum, 20 February 1931, cf. 11 March 1931, 21 September 1931.
[92] Wilson, *Capital Imports*, 36; *Wall Street Journal*, 17 July 1931.
[93] Lloyds Bank Colonial and Foreign Department, Correspondence and Memoranda 3 October 1929,
27 January 1932, 1 March 1932, 5 April 1932.
[94] Smith St. Aubyn: Business Diary, 13 July 1931, 19 August 1931, 9 September 1931, 25 September
1931, 27 March 1933.
[95] Lloyds Bank Colonial and Foreign Department, Correspondence and Memoranda, 3 October 1929,
27 January 1932, 1 March 1932, 5 April 1932.
[96] Lloyds Bank: Correspondence between Head Office and Overseas Department, 4 September 1929,
27 September 1929, 3 October 1929, 5 February 1931, 28 August 1931, 12 September 1931, 11 March 1932,
29 September 1931, 27 January 1932, 15 March 1932, 5 October 1932, 28 October 1932.
[97] Conway, *The International Position*, 20, 57–61.
[98] A. Ray, *The Evolution of the State Bank of India*, vol. 3: *The Era of the Imperial Bank of India, 1921–
1955* (New Delhi: 2003).

Banks from outside Britain were now fully aware of the risks they ran by having their assets and liabilities in different currencies, regardless of the attractions found in London of employing idle balances and accessing short-term funds. Even before the events leading up to the outbreak of the Second World War in Europe in 1939, there were sudden flights of money driven by rumours, whether of a political, financial, or monetary nature.[99] The German Standstill Agreement of 19 September 1931, which froze external credit arrangements, acted as a warning to banks that government intervention could leave them facing a liquidity and even solvency crisis of sufficient magnitude to force their closure.[100] The response of banks all over the world was to match assets and liabilities domestically and make less use of the London discount market.[101] This was all part of a growing compartmentalization of the global money market as national governments became much more interventionist, especially those where central banks had been established. These included countries which had made extensive use of the London discount market, like Australia, Canada, and India.[102] As Barclays Bank informed its staff in 1940, though the currency in use in South Africa, Australia, and New Zealand was the UK£, 'it is quoted either at a premium or a discount compared with British sterling', adding that 'the difference in value may be considerable'.[103] There was now much less trust in counterparties which made banks reluctant to lend to and borrow from each other through the medium of finance bills as had been the case in the past, despite the advantages it possessed in terms of access to cheap finance or a way of employing spare cash.

Such a catastrophic collapse in international confidence might have led to the beginning of the end for the London discount market. However, banks still needed a market through which they could lend and borrow internationally, even though at a diminished level, and there was no obvious alternative to London.[104] Germany had withdrawn from international finance, leaving Berlin isolated. Though the Paris money market had developed during the late 1920s, it was still markedly inferior to London, according to an in-depth investigation by Madden and Nadler in 1931.[105] This left the New York money market as the only serious rival, but it had been rocked

---

[99] *Wall Street Journal*, 17 July 1931, 27 January 1932, 27 July 1934, 25 September 1934, 25 October 1935, 4 June 1936.

[100] Forbes, *Doing Business*, 35–40, 166.

[101] Hawtrey, *Century of Bank Rate*, 107; Ogura, *Banking, the State and Industrial Promotion*, 37–9; Ogura, 'Mitsui Bank', 99–101; Tamaki, *Japanese Banking*, 46, 70–2, 82, 109, 118–19, 129, 131, 155–6, 167, 205; Ray, *Era of the Imperial Bank of India*, 190–6, 200–2, 208–10, 244–7, 285–91, 393, 529, 547, 571, 637.

[102] Butlin, *Australia and New Zealand Bank*, 369, 392; Wood, *Commercial Bank of Australia*, 238, 241, 247, 256; MacLaury, *Canadian Money Market*, 9; Ray, *The Evolution of the State Bank of India*, vol. 3, 200–2.

[103] Barclays Bank, *Handbook on Foreign Business* (1940).

[104] Einzig, 'London', 184; H. Clay, 'Finance and the International Market', *The Banker*, xx (October 1931), 30–2; P. Einzig, 'The Future of the London Foreign Exchange Market', *The Banker*, xx (November 1931), 110; P. Einzig, 'Branch Banks v Affiliate Banks', *The Banker*, xxxi (July 1934), 23–5; Conway, *The International Position*, 2–3, 7, 19–20, 27, 33, 39, 48, 54, 57–61, 69, 72, 77; Lloyds Bank: Foreign and Colonial Branch Business, 30 June 1938; *Barclays Bank, Foreign Exchange Control: A Brief Survey of Its Theory and Application: Memorandum by Barclays Bank to Its Staff* (1947), 1–3; Winton, *Lloyds Bank*, 155; Hambros Bank, *Hambros Bank Ltd*, 42; Green and Kinsey, *Paradise Bank*, 75; N. Crump, 'Finance and the Crisis', *JIB*, 59 (1938), 387; Cleveland and Huertas, *Citibank*, 74, 82–3, 123–6; Joslin, *Banking in Latin America*, 217, 228–30, 270.

[105] Madden and Nadler, 'Paris Money Market', 13.

by the domestic banking crisis that followed the Wall Street Crash, and never fully
recovered. Whereas there was a modest revival in the London discount market after
1932, with lending reaching £174 million in 1937, that did not happen in New York.
Lending there had climbed to $1.4 billion in 1929 but sank to $0.5 billion in 1932
and then continued to fall, reaching $0.3 billion in 1937. Increasingly, business in
the New York money market was confined to the finance of US exports and imports
and lending to members of the New York Stock Exchange (NYSE).[106] What New York
did attract were funds from abroad driven there by its safe haven status. As war in
Europe approached in the late 1930s it was to New York that funds flowed, along
with Switzerland.[107] These funds had previously flowed to London. The Bank of England calculated that foreign deposits in London rose from £559 million in December
1931 to £720 million in September 1937. As the Second World War loomed from 1938
onwards, foreign banks then ran down their London balances, either repatriating the
money or sending it to New York or Switzerland. The Bank of England estimated that
foreign deposits in London fell over £100 million in 1938.[108]

What also saved the London discount market in the 1930s was that it had reinvented itself. Since the First World War, and the ballooning of the national debt, the
Bank of England had used the discount market to support the government's funding
requirements, which was its responsibility. In May 1938, treasury bills outstanding
stood at £834 million compared to £10 million in May 1913. The result was to transform the discount market into the mechanism through which the British government
raised short-term funds and managed its monetary policy. In 1913, only 5 per cent of
the bills handled by discount houses had been issued by the British government but
50 per cent by 1918. There was a revival of non-treasury bill business in the 1920s,
but that shrank dramatically during the crisis of 1931 and never recovered. The transformation can be seen in the business done by one of the leading discount houses,
Gilletts. Before the First World War, virtually all Gilletts' business was done directly
with banks in London, acting as an intermediary in their interbank borrowing and
lending and the buying and selling of commercial and finance bills. This business
was badly affected by the war but recovered in the 1920s. It then shrunk again in the
1930s, by which time Gilletts was largely engaged in discounting UK treasury bills
using funds borrowed from banks in London, especially the large domestic ones.[109]

[106] Conway, *The International Position*, 20, 57–61; W.K. Duke, *Bills, Bullion and the London Money Market* (London: 1937), 14, 86.
[107] Crump, 'Finance and the Crisis', 387; Conway, *The International Position*, 2–3, 7, 19–20, 27, 33, 39, 48, 54, 57–61, 69, 72, 77; Cleveland and Huertas, *Citibank*, 74, 82–3, 123–6; Joslin, *Banking in Latin America*, 217, 228–30, 270.
[108] Bank of England, Memoranda on Foreign Exchange, 24 March 1932, Report on the Exchange Equal-isation Account, 13 July 1937, War Measures: Foreign Exchange and Gold. Memorandum by Sir F. Phillips, 24 June 1938, Note of a Telephone Conversation with George Bolton in Ottawa, 14 November 1938, H.C. Note, 16 November 1938, Foreign Exchange Market Reports, 26 January 1939; *Financial News*, 9 August 1939; *Wall Street Journal*, 27 July 1934, 22 October 1934, 25 October 1935.
[109] Spalding, *Foreign Exchange*, 5, 51, 197, 223; Miller, *The Foreign Exchange Market*, 9, 56; Sir Edmund Stockdale, *The Bank of England in 1934* (1967 but actually written between 1934 and 1936), 53, 56, 127, 132; Waight, *Exchange Equalisation Account*, 3–4; Scammell, *London Discount Market*, 31, 48, 161–4, 193–8, 205, 223, 243–4; Fletcher, *Discount Houses*, 36–40, 48–9, 248–9, 253; Nevin and Davis, *London Clearing Banks*, 146; Sayers, *Gilletts*, 45–55, 60, 68, 78, 80, 87, 95, 101–2, 122, 126, 158–9; *The Mitsui*

No longer were bill brokers required to be able to judge the quality of the bills they bought and sold because almost all were treasury bills guaranteed by the British government. The business of Smith St. Aubyn, for example, was reduced to the routine of submitting a regular bid to the Bank of England to buy treasury bills and then borrowing the money to pay for them from banks in London.[110] As the sole supplier of these treasury bills, acting on behalf of the British government, the Bank of England was in the position of a monopoly, giving it the power to dictate the structure of the discount market, which it used to ensure that it was always able to carry out the government's funding requirements.[111] In 1943, the New York-based Institute of International Finance traced the disintegration of the London discount market from a core component of the global banking system, through which banks borrowed and lent among themselves, into a servant of the British government, operating through the Bank of England. Rather than the First World War, it was Britain's departure from the Gold Standard that was the pivotal moment when this change took place.[112]

Before the First World War, the London money market and the London discount market were virtually the same. It was through the discount market that banks from all over the world borrowed and lent among each other through the agency of the discount houses. That was no longer the case in the 1930s, with the First World War and then the Global Financial Crisis of 1931 destroying the confidence upon which the reliance on the London discount market had been based. By then, the London discount market had been converted from a servant of the global banking community to a tool of the Bank of England. It still served the interests of the British domestic banks but not those from elsewhere in the world. That transformation of the discount market eliminated the contribution made by the skills and knowledge of the experienced bill broker, which reduced its competitive advantage over other components of the money market, whether within London or abroad. It also greatly reduced the benefits that banks obtained from using the money market rather than relying upon their ability to manage internally the matching of credits and debits or assets and liabilities. One element which made the London discount market especially vulnerable to competition was its continued reliance on sterling as the sole currency it used to conduct business. Even before the First World War, the activities of the London discount market had to be supplemented by the arbitrageurs on the LSE and the ability of banks to internalize transactions. That need was far greater in the years between 1919 and 1939, especially after 1931, but the discount market failed to respond, secure in the business it did as the intermediary between the Bank of England and the British banking system. Given the international role of sterling,

Bank, 110; Rudlin, *The History of Mitsubishi Corporation in London*, 54, 58; O. Hobson, *How the City Works* (London: 1940), 38; Cleaver, *The Union Discount*, 58, 69.

[110] Smith St. Aubyn: Business Diary, 3 August 1934, 17 August 1934, 28 September 1934, 3 September 1938.

[111] N. Crump, 'The Evolution of the Money Market', *JIB*, 59 (1938), 291–301; N.F. Hall, 'The Control of Credit in the London Money Market', *JIB*, 59 (1938), 64–70.

[112] Institute of International Finance, 'Effects of the War on British Banking' (New York, IIF), 124 (1943), 3–4, 22–5.

and Britain's extensive imperial possessions, it was sufficient to maintain London's money market as the most important in the world, which Brown recognized in 1940.

> The continued use of the sterling-dollar exchange as the trunk-line rate for the Empire and the Continent of Europe and even for certain other countries, notably Japan, China, and Argentina, in their dealings in New York was evidence of the failure of the New York market to develop this characteristic of a central international money market

He added that 'The injury done to London as an international financial centre by the shock of Great Britain's leaving the gold standard was not as great as might have been expected.' The rapid recovery of sterling as an international currency and the lack of competition from Paris and New York helped to sustain the position of the London money market.[113]

The End of Arbitrage, 1919–1939

Before the First World War, asset arbitrage was an important element in the foreign exchange market, though the contribution it made went largely unrecognized. It was trading in and between the floors of the leading stock exchanges in the world, but especially London and New York, that was central to this arbitrage, with German Jewish financiers being at its heart. It was their trading from within the LSE, and then from outside the building when the formal market had closed, that maintained close and constant contact with associates in New York throughout the hours between 10 a.m. and 3 p.m. (Eastern Standard Time) or 3 p.m. to 8 p.m. (Greenwich Mean Time) regardless of the weather and visibility. What they traded on both sides of the Atlantic were $-denominated stocks and bonds issued by US and Canadian corporations, which were held extensively throughout North America and Western Europe. A consequence of that wide dispersal of ownership, and the huge size of the individual issues by companies like the Atchison, Topeka, and Sante Fe Railroad and the US Steel Corporation, was that they possessed deep and broad markets on a number of leading stock exchanges but, principally, London and New York. By buying and selling these securities on one stock exchange and then reversing the deal almost instantly on the other, through the speed of communication provided by the telegraph, an arbitrageur could trade £s for $s and then undo the transaction before either payment or delivery was required. To the public, and even many members of stock exchanges, such a transaction was dismissed as speculation. In reality, it provided the mechanism of adjustment that kept the exchange rate between UK£ and the US$ stable as it provided a constant counterbalance to the ebb and flow of international payments and receipts across the Atlantic and beyond.

[113] Brown, *International Gold Standard*, 602, 1263.

On the eve of the First World War, the LSE was the largest and most important stock exchange in the world. It had established such a position for itself on the back of the huge holdings of foreign stocks and bonds by British investors. Over 40 per cent of internationally held securities were in the hands of British investors in 1914. Its success also owed a great deal to its location within the heart of the City of London, which hosted the dominant money market in the world. The facilities it provided played a key role in these money market operations because the liquidity of many of the stocks and bonds it quoted meant that they could be held using short-term funds, in the knowledge that they could be easily, quickly, and cheaply sold if the loans used to purchase them were called in. Numbered among these securities were a key group that were traded on different exchanges. It took only thirty seconds to telegraph between London and New York, while there was a telephone connection between London and Paris. The constant sale, purchase, and transfer of these stocks and bonds internationally contributed greatly to the equilibrium enjoyed by the world economy at this time. It was this mechanism that was shattered and then destroyed by the First World War. The LSE, along with all others in the world, including those located in neutral countries like the USA, closed shortly before or after the outbreak of hostilities. The uncertainty created by the prospect of war had produced an avalanche of sales, the calling in of loans by the banks, and a steep fall in prices. Without closure and the suspension of business, many members of the LSE would have been financially ruined because they could not complete deals and owed money to banks having used securities as collateral. These securities could only be sold, if at all, at prices that would not cover the loan. In addition, the international nature of the London securities market meant that many members had acted on behalf of foreign clients, especially German, who now could neither pay for their purchases nor deliver securities.

The LSE did not reopen until January 1915 and then only under strict conditions imposed by the government. Trading was on a cash basis, while international business was strictly controlled. Compounding these externally imposed conditions were the restrictions introduced by the LSE itself. During the war, those members who had long wanted a more highly regulated trading system gained the upper hand to the detriment of those doing an international or money market business. Action was also taken to expel members of German nationality even though they made an important contribution to the internationalization of the LSE. Finally, over the course of the war, the British government sold virtually all the US$ securities that were owned by British investors, using the proceeds to purchase war material from the USA. These sales, along with the defaults by Russia on its massive international debts, removed the securities that had formed the main arbitrage securities, leaving a rump of mining stocks and bonds issued by utilities. By the end of the First World War, the LSE was a very different institution from the one that existed at the beginning. The restrictions imposed during the war also made the market provided by the LSE less valuable to those operating internationally and in the money market, while the risks of buying securities using short-term funds, and profiting from the interest rate differential, had been exposed in the crisis that preceded the war.

During the First World War, with stock exchanges closed or operating under strict government controls, the constant ebb and flow of securities between markets was virtually impossible. This destroyed the arbitrage business.[114] According to Kirkcaldy in 1915, 'Arbitrage operations, which in more normal times are used as a level to redress variations from normal exchange rates, ceased altogether, the creation of finance bills stopped abruptly; the Stock Exchanges of the world were closed.'[115] Apart from this interruption during hostilities, the war had also serious long-term consequences for arbitrage, especially the disposal of US$-denominated stocks and bonds. British holdings of American railroad securities fell from c. $3 billion before the war to $0.1 billion, and never recovered. This was part of a general disposal of $ securities by all European investors and their replacement by owners from the USA. Even Canadian Pacific stock suffered the same fate with much being repatriated to Canada or held in the USA rather than spread across the UK and continental Europe. Another blow to the arbitrageurs was the Russian repudiation of all its debts, whether state or corporate, after the revolution of 1917. Russian stocks and bonds had been held extensively across Europe and they commanded active markets in London, Paris, Amsterdam, and Brussels.[116] No longer could Europe support the deep and broad markets that had been the main business of the arbitrageurs.[117] The world was left without the assets whose mobility had contributed to the stability of pre-war exchange rates, especially that of the UK£ versus the US$. It was these securities that were among the most popular form of collateral pledged with banks in London and New York. On the eve of the First World War, members of the LSE owed £80 million ($400 million) to banks and other financial institutions, though that amount had fallen in the financial crisis caused by the anticipation of a war. In New York in 1912, thirty-one financial institutions had $790 million (£160 million) outstanding in loans with securities as collateral.[118]

During the First World War, the closure of stock exchanges, the severing of links with enemy countries, the expulsion of members born in Germany, and, finally, the disposal of virtually all US$-denominated stocks and bonds destroyed arbitrage. Arbitrageurs also had limited access to international communications as priority was given to the military, creating both considerable delays and inadequate capacity.[119] It was not until the early 1920s that the members of the LSE were able to regain the level of service they had before the war.[120] Also, as a condition for allowing the LSE to reopen in 1915, the Bank of England and the Treasury insisted that arbitrage be banned for the duration of the war in order to prevent currency speculation. This

[114] Rainsbury, 'The War and the Arbitrage Dealer', 193.

[115] A.W. Kirkcaldy (ed.), *Credit, Industry and War* (London: 1915), 246. See Kirkcaldy (ed.), *British Finance*, 355.

[116] LSE: General Purposes, 7 April 1919, 18 April 1921.

[117] Royal Institute of International Affairs, *Problem of International Investment*, 130, 155–6; Lewis, *America's Stake*, 117, 544.

[118] H. Withers, *War and Lombard Street* (London: 1915), 85, 118.

[119] *Wall Street Journal*, 13 November 1918.

[120] LSE: Com. for General Purposes, 30 June 1919, 22 December 1919, 26 January 1920, 20 December 1920, 18 April 1921, 26 June 1933, 11 March 1935, 17 April 1939; LSE Subcommittee on Country Jobbing/Country's Business, 4 October 1934.

drove out those members who had specialized in arbitrage. Aggravating the position of the arbitrageurs was the anti-German hostility that took hold during the war, as so many had been born in that country.[121] After the war, economists like J.E. Meeker made the case for a revival of arbitrage conducted from the floor of stock exchanges. In 1922, he stated that 'Many delicate financial operations—such as arbitrage—can be carried on steadily and considerably only in organised security markets.'[122] However, even within stock exchanges, including New York, which employed Meeker, there was little support for any attempt to revive arbitrage. Most members of the LSE considered it a loophole that allowed non-members to trade at official prices while evading commission charges. They had welcomed the demise of arbitrage during the First World War and opposed its reappearance, favouring continuing restrictions and even an outright ban instead. That opposition remained throughout the interwar years.[123]

Between the wars, the LSE remained the premier international market for stocks and bonds, continuing to provide a market that was unrivalled in terms of its combination of depth and breadth, and thus the liquidity it could give to the securities it quoted. In an assessment of stock exchanges carried out by Greenwood in 1921, it was London that emerged as the most international, and superior to that of New York, despite the huge gains the latter had made as a result of the First World War. 'London trades in the securities of all nations and in all kinds of moneys; New York deals chiefly in American stocks and bonds and in foreign security issued in New York and payable in dollars.' Greenwood attributed this superiority to the existence of the jobbing system on the LSE. Jobbers were dealers who made a market in the stocks and bonds quoted, being always ready to buy or sell. A London jobber 'sells what he has not got and buys what he does not want, relying on obtaining later what he has sold and selling, before the settlement, what he has bought.'[124] The LSE retained this superiority throughout the interwar years even though the USA experienced a stock market boom in the 1920s, of which the NYSE was a major beneficiary. This superiority was recognized in 1935 by the New York-based research organization, the Twentieth Century Fund. It described the LSE as 'unique in the vast international scope of its trading' and added that 'only with this system, in which there exist jobbers who specialise in various securities, would it be possible to provide a market for trading in the gigantic numbers of issues found on the London Stock Exchange.'[125]

[121] LSE General Purposes, 23 September 1914, 22 December 1914, 4 January 1915, 22 January 1915, 16 March 1915, 19 April 1915, 19 August 1915, 15 March 1916, 5 May 1916, 14 August 1916, 29 January 1917, 15 March 1918, 19 March 1919, 20 November 1919, 22 December 1919, 26 January 1920, 9 April 1920, 22 April 1920, 20 December 1920, 23 May 1921, 2 November 1921; Sub-committee of a Non-permanent Character, 29 December 1914; Sub-committee on Rules and Regulations—Minutes, 19 January 1922, 18 October 1922.
[122] Meeker, *The Work of the Stock Exchange*, 44–5.
[123] LSE: Com. for General Purposes, 22 December 1914, 22 January 1915, 16 March 1915, 29 February 1916, 6 March 1916, 22 March 1920, 11 November 1920, 8 November 1920, 28 November 1927, 24 June 1929, 12 August 1929, 17 November 1930, 2 February 1931, 17 October 1932, 8 April 1940.
[124] Greenwood, *American and Foreign Stock Exchange Practice*, 264, 273, 573, 584.
[125] Twentieth Century Fund, *The Security Markets* (New York: 1935), 577–8.

That had been the case before the First World War when the LSE dominated the global securities market. However, between the wars, it was in a much less powerful position because not only had a large part of the international holdings of British investors been sold or lost, but it was now much more hemmed in by regulations, partly of its own making. This was especially the case with arbitrage. In the aftermath of the First World War, central banks and governments, especially in Europe, were reluctant to accept the revival of arbitrage, which undermined the degree of control they were able to exert over their national financial systems. Arbitrage was classed as speculation, which contributed to financial instability and undermined their attempt to return to fixed exchange rates.[126] The official attitude towards arbitrage between the wars was best expressed in a report drawn up by the Royal Institute of International Affairs in 1937.

> It is true that a large movement of capital from one stock exchange to another is likely to be followed in due course by a movement in the opposite direction and such movements help to preserve rather than destroy international equilibrium. None the less, the rapidly growing traffic in international securities is fraught with serious dangers.[127]

In April 1921, twenty member firms of the LSE who had been active in arbitrage complained that 'The difficulties surrounding Arbitrage business today are far greater than in the pre-war period.'[128] Nevertheless, despite opposition from inside and outside the LSE, a number of firms like L. Messel & Co, Leon Brothers, and Nathan Rosselli, who were all experienced arbitrageurs, attempted to re-establish the business once they were permitted to do so in 1919. Both the Bank of England and the Treasury attempted to block them and they received little support from the stock exchange authorities. It was not until December 1920 that joint-account arbitrage, which was the most efficient form, was again permitted by the stock exchange.[129]

Nevertheless, the principle of asset arbitrage was so well established that there were always those looking to make a profit from it. In 1924, Wynne-Bennett noted that 'Whenever a stock is quoted on two different exchanges at different prices, it will be found possible for traders in the respective towns or countries to take advantage of such difference in prices in order to settle their liabilities.'[130] However, the increased risks, complexities, and costs involved, along with the restrictions and prohibitions imposed by governments and exchanges, made arbitrage increasingly hazardous, discouraging most from undertaking it. Brown reported in 1940 that 'After the war the

---

[126] R.S. Sayers, *The Bank of England, 1891–1944* (Cambridge: 1976), 2, 5–8, 298; Moggridge, *British Monetary Policy*, 9, 35, 232–3; W.A. Morton, *British Finance 1930–1940* (Madison: 1943), 27; Feinstein et al., 'International Economic Organisation', 14–17.

[127] Royal Institute of International Affairs, *International Investment*, 108, but see also 50, 73.

[128] LSE: General Purposes, 18 April 1921.

[129] LSE: General Purposes, 3 February 1919, 11 October 1920, 8 November 1920, 18 April 1921, 25 April 1921, 29 March 1922, 15 May 1922, 29 May 1922, 15 September 1924; M.C. Reed, *A History of James Capel & Co* (London: 1975); S.D. Chapman, *Raphael Bicentenary, 1787–1987* (London: 1987), 43.

[130] Wynne-Bennett, *Investment and Speculation*, 19–20.

movement of balances and securities from one market to another was both large and erratic, and this had a profound influence upon the effectiveness and the practice of London as an international financial center.'[131] Armstrong acknowledged this in 1934 when he wrote that 'The chaotic state of the exchanges has made arbitrage business extremely difficult to transact of recent years.' He highlighted the virtual collapse of arbitrage between London and New York by then. 'The restrictions imposed during the war, and the conditions laid upon us by peace, have successfully interfered with the once free market between the two centres, until now the value transacted is but a skeleton of what it once was.' He attributed the virtual disappearance of arbitrage to all the barriers imposed. To him, the risks and costs that arbitrage involved no longer justified the effort required to carry it out:

> When it is remembered that there must be taken into account exchange rates, commission charges, interest, cables, insurance, fluctuations in money, settlement days, and the possibility that a commitment entered into in one centre may not be successfully undone or closed in another, it will be seen that arbitrage is a highly-skilled and technical business.

The arbitrage that still took place was largely confined to trading between London and Paris and Amsterdam and Brussels using the telephone, and between London and Johannesburg and Montreal and New York using the cable.[132] Among the few securities actively traded were those issued by the hydroelectric companies promoted by Alfred Loewenstein, a Belgium-born financier operating out of London in the 1920s, as these had international appeal.[133]

What became apparent between the wars was that the arbitrage business that remained was drifting away from the LSE.[134] In the 1920s, a growing number of New York banks and brokerage firms had established branch offices in London. By 1927, there were ten members of the NYSE with offices in London and this rose to twenty-five in 1937, despite the bankruptcy of some firms in the wake of the 1929 crash. These firms traded directly between their New York and London offices using the telegraph, as the sole market for US$ stocks was now in the USA. In a reversal of the pre-war position, these US firms were trading UK£-denominated stocks in London against the same stocks in New York, where they had been repackaged as US$-denominated American depository receipts. That business was killed off by the Wall Street Crash of 1929.[135] A by-product of the hostility towards the NYSE after the Wall Street Crash was the tightening of the rules and regulations governing what members of the NYSE were able to do. Not only did the NYSE itself take action, but it was also subjected to

[131] Brown, *International Gold Standard*, 782.
[132] F.E. Armstrong, *The Book of the Stock Exchange* (London: 1934), 105–6, 130, 163–7.
[133] W. Norris, *The Man Who Fell from the Sky* (New York: 1987), 44–6, 151.
[134] LSE General Purposes, 17 November 1930, 19 November 1930, 2 February 1931, 14 March 1932, 5 September 1932; Sub-committee of a Non-permanent Character, 25 November 1930, 2 December 1930, 4 December 1930, 16 December 1930, 27 January 1931.
[135] LSE General Purposes, 29 March 1922, 15 May 1922, 29 May 1922, 29 October 1923, 15 December 1924, 5 January 1925, 8 June 1925, 28 November 1927, 14 January 1929, 24 June 1929, 12 August 1929.

external scrutiny and control, with the Securities Act of 1933 and the establishment of the Securities and Exchange Commission in 1934. Anything that hinted of speculation, such as short-selling and arbitrage, was subjected to restrictions despite the contribution they made to a smoothly functioning market.[136]

Despite official displeasure and obstruction, there were attempts to revive asset arbitrage after the First World War, but it never regained the size and importance it had once commanded. In the 1920s, the place of North American and Russian securities was taken by the stocks and bonds of a miscellaneous group of companies, among which were those involved in gold mining, tropical plantations, oil production, and urban utilities, together with issues of various indebted governments. Brokers and dealers on different stock exchanges tried hard to generate active markets in a wide range of such securities. Austria's largest bank, the Credit-Anstalt, for example, commanded an international market during the late 1920s, when half its stock was held by foreign investors.[137] Even after the Wall Street Crash of 1929 and the monetary, banking, and financial crises of the early 1930s, there remained some brokers who persisted with the practice of arbitrage in the face of exchange controls, managed currencies, and central bank stabilization funds. Kindersley, writing in 1936, observed that 'Royal Dutch, Unilever, Mexican Eagle, Brazilian Traction, International Nickel, the South African gold mines, are only a few examples of companies whose shares are subject to international trading on a substantial scale whenever currency fears, disturbed political situations and other international complications occur. From a national standpoint, the mobility of these assets and the ease with which they are realizable give them an important advantage over the shares of British companies since in times of national emergency, they may be mobilized to provide a reservoir of foreign exchange.'[138] However, these miscellaneous stocks and bonds never generated the depth and breadth of markets that had made such assets so useful to the arbitrageurs before the First World War.[139] Large and permanent differences appeared in the prices at which internationally held securities were traded in separate markets reflecting the compartmentalization of national financial systems.[140]

The First World War destroyed this delicate mechanism of adjustment provided by the arbitrageurs working from the floor of the LSE and the adjoining courts and streets. Though there were attempts to revive arbitrage between the wars, the loss

[136] Twentieth Century Fund, *Stock Market Control* (New York: 1934), 163; C.H. Meyer, *The Securities Exchange Act of 1934: Analyzed and Explained* (New York: 1934), 23; H.V. Cherrington, *The Investor and the Securities Act* (Washington: 1942), 1–36, 58, 10, 246; P.F. Wendt, *The Classification and Financial Experience of the Customers of a Typical New York Stock Exchange Firm from 1933 to 1938* (Maryville, TN: 1941), 222; Meeker, *Short Selling*, 133; E.T. McCormick, *Understanding the Securities Act and the SEC* (New York: 1948), 298.

[137] R.M. Kindersley, 'British Foreign Investments', *Economic Journal*, 40 (1930), 176–77 and the companion article in 42, 1932, 193; A. Schubert, *The Credit-Anstalt Crisis* (Cambridge: 1991), 11.

[138] Kindersley, 'British Foreign Investments', 654; see companion articles in 47 (1937), 643, 650; 48 (1938), 623; and 49 (1939), 689.

[139] Iversen, *Theory of International Capital Movements*, 30, 55, 84, 333.

[140] B. Eichengreen, *Elusive Stability: Essays in the History of International Finance* (Cambridge: 1990), 152, 243, 271; Drummond, *The Floating Pound*, 13, 18, 257; Feinstein *et al.*, 'International Economic Organisation', 29; Nurse and Brown, *International Currency Experience*, 29, 87, 100, 142; Schubert, *Credit-Anstalt*, 93.

of internationally mobile stocks and bonds, possessed of deep and broad markets on multiple stock exchanges, provided an impossible barrier to bridge. At the same time, the attempts that were made were thwarted by a combination of official intervention from central banks and governments and a lack of support, and even blocking tactics, from the LSE itself. Arbitrage had long been conducted by a small minority, and the most successful arbitrageurs were identified as German and Jewish, provoking anti-foreign and anti-Semitic sentiments among the membership at large. With the failure of arbitrage to revive, a replacement was sought, which came in the form of banks swapping their currency commitments with each other, trusting counterparties not to default as there were no longer assets to back each deal. The penalty for default was exclusion from the foreign exchange market, which was a powerful sanction forcing compliance wherever possible.

In 1928, Spalding even referred to this way of conducting foreign exchange operations as arbitrage.

> Arbitrage is essentially a business for the expert, who, owing to his intimate knowledge of the condition of markets in other countries, and the efficiency of the working arrangements he has with other correspondents, is able to seize the psychological moment for the transfer of funds to places where it can be most profitably employed. ... For its successful operation, arbitrage requires proper equipment and expert knowledge of the exchanges. The equipment comprises the constant supply of free and floating funds in various active exchange centres—free, that is, in the sense that such funds may be readily moved from place to place at the shortest possible notice. A further sine qua non is precise and reliable cable information concerning the rates of exchange existing at any moment in foreign markets. The operator and his correspondents require vision—the ability to look ahead and to judge accurately the factors that may be expected to govern future movements in exchanges. Given a sufficiency of funds, and with the required information immediately available, the exchange dealer is in the position to take advantage of the most favourable rates in two or more centres to transfer his funds at a profit before his competitors get to work.

To Spalding, arbitrage could involve multiple financial centres and currencies so as to produce a profit in the overall transaction, but 'prompt action is the keynote of success, and most of the dealers have tables ready at hand to enable them to judge if rates are propitious.'[141] With even greater restrictions and controls in the 1930s, it was this form of arbitrage that was to triumph. Asset arbitrage as conducted from the floor of the LSE, or outside, was dismissed as speculation, as it had been in the past, with little or no role to play in the stabilization of currencies. By then, that was probably true as it was the wide disparities between the prices of a few internationally held stock and bonds that attracted the speculator, Considering the complexities and expenses involved only a speculator was willing to take the risks.

---

[141] Spalding, *Dictionary of the World's Currencies*, 9–10.

Global Banking, 1919–1939

Banks and money are closely connected, and that extends to foreign exchange. For a bank, engagement with foreign exchange meant much more than buying one currency using another. Instead, it involved the constant matching of assets and liabilities in terms of not only amount and duration but also currency. By expanding or contracting its borrowing and lending in different currencies, and then matching these with reverse actions in terms of amount and maturity, a bank could eliminate its exposure to exchange-rate volatility. That was most easily done by concentrating the entire business in one location where debits and credits could cancel each other out, leaving only a small residual element that required a foreign exchange transaction. Before the First World War, this was done in London, which acted as the clearing house for international interbank transactions and where money could also always be borrowed or lent. Most banks had connections to London, and the UK£ was used as the vehicle currency to settle transactions between them. With the world economy in equilibrium, exchange rates stable, and barriers to international financial flows non-existent, banks could be confident that any funds employed in London and denominated in sterling would remain liquid, be accessible, retain their value, and be largely self-cancelling, with debits matching credits over time. Under these conditions, the level of business generated in the foreign exchange market was low and the opportunities for profit limited. Few banks engaged with it as a result, especially as most confined themselves to operating within one currency zone, which meant that they were not exposed to the risks posed by fluctuations in foreign exchange. This applied to Britain's largest banks that did a largely domestic business.

When a bank did engage in a transaction that had a foreign exchange element, most passed it on to those that made a speciality of the business. There were a few banks whose business forced them to take account of fluctuations in foreign exchange, because their operations extended over diverse countries, and they lent and borrowed across a range of currencies. As they had assets and liabilities in different currencies, they had to take steps to cover their exposure to foreign exchange risks if they were to avoid a catastrophic loss that could destroy the bank. Conversely, they were able to provide other banks with the means of covering their exposure to exchange-rate volatility, charging for the service provided. Any foreign bank that had taken the trouble to establish a branch in London was in this position. Almost all lending, borrowing, and the making and receiving of payments carried out by a bank in London were conducted using the UK£, regardless of the currency employed elsewhere in its business. Among the banks in this position were those from Europe that had established branches in London such as Deutsche Bank from Germany and Société Générale from France, leaving them exposed to fluctuations in the £/mark and £/franc exchange rate. The Yokohama Specie Bank from Japan also had a branch in London, which meant it faced volatility in the £/yen exchange rate. The same applied to the Hong Kong and Shanghai Bank (HSBC), which conducted most of its business in China, where the currency was based on silver, but had a London branch, which used the gold-based UK£. Another group of banks in a similar position was that of the British overseas banks. These had London head offices but a branch network elsewhere in the world, where they collected deposits and made loans. Most of their business was in countries that also used the UK£ as their domestic currency, such as Australia, New Zealand, and South Africa, but a number of them conducted their banking using other currencies, such as those operating in India and across Latin America. That left them exposed to foreign exchange risks. This exposure also made them uniquely positioned to handle foreign exchange transactions both for their own internal purposes and as a profitable business. The British overseas banks operating in India were known as Exchange Banks, for that reason, and any bank handling transactions involving both the £ and the rupee passed it on to them. What this meant was that a number of banks were actively involved in the foreign exchange market before the First World War but not the large domestic ones, though they had begun to explore the possibility of doing so. Conversely, the merchant banks, who had been engaged in foreign exchange transactions in the past, had largely abandoned the business due to competition, the low level of profits because of currency stability, and the better opportunities to be found elsewhere in international finance.

What changed the nature of the foreign exchange market, and banks' involvement with it, was the First World War. The duration, magnitude, and intensity of the conflict upset the equilibrium of the world economy, interfered with the free flow of funds, and increased the volatility of exchange rates. These effects did not disappear once the war ended in 1918 but remained throughout the 1920s. The rupturing of the smooth flow of funds around the world, and the deep structural imbalances created by the conflict, made it more difficult for banks to use sterling as a vehicle currency when balancing credits and debits. This undermined the utility of the London money market where banks, which had gained the trust of their peers, could settle their debits and credits, employ spare funds remuneratively, and borrow short-term funds cheaply. With that mechanism no longer functioning as smoothly and effectively as before the war, banks were forced to supplement its use through alternative arrangements. Additionally, banks were now exposed to greater risks when engaged in international transactions because of the increased frequency and amplitude of fluctuations in exchange rates, and doubts over the value of once stable currencies, including the UK£. Prior to the war, banks had become accustomed to using London not only as a clearing house for interbank transactions but also when following the originate-and-distribute model of banking. This model relied on the ability of a bank to make a loan, repackage it as a bill, and then sell it to other banks. When applied internationally, the originate-and-distribute model made extensive use of the London money market as that was where banks from all over the world increasingly employed idle funds by either lending them out or using them to buy bills. The depth and breadth of the London discount market, supplemented by loans to members of the LSE, meant that this could always be done. As the level of exchange-rate risk was low, and supply and demand were in equilibrium, banks had few concerns about using the London money market, even those whose main business was not in sterling and took place elsewhere in the world.

However, during the war, British exports of goods and services contracted and imports expanded while foreign interest payments and dividends dwindled as overseas assets were sold and foreign borrowers defaulted. The result was a rapid build-up of unspent sterling balances, and this continued into the 1920s because of the UK's structural deficit, inherited from the war, and the lack of competitiveness of British manufacturing. With sterling off the Gold Standard from 1919 and 1925, and again from 1931, along with underlying concerns over its stability throughout the interwar years, banks holding these sterling balances were left exposed to foreign exchange risks. Under these circumstances, they cut back on their use of the London money market and switched to the more nationally focused lend-and-hold model of banking. This undermined those banks that had made a success of transnational banking, either in whole or in part, and thus the contribution they had made to the functioning of the foreign exchange market. The German banks had already lost this role because of the closure of their London branches during the war, as these did not reopen. In response, they were forced to hold large balances abroad to match their exchange commitments.[142] The problems of conducting transnational banking at a time of currency instability also extended to those banks that retained their London branches, such as Société Générale, the Yokohama Specie Bank, and HSBC. They now had difficulty matching assets and liabilities in sterling in London, leaving them with large unspent sterling balances or investments in UK government debt. At the same time, they were under pressure to build up exposure to the US$, which had emerged as a rival vehicle currency to the UK£.[143] The risks these changes posed to banks carrying out a transnational business are revealed by what happened to Japan's Mitsui Bank, which was a relative newcomer and somewhat inexperienced. Mitsui had opened a London office in 1916 to take advantage of the partial withdrawal of foreign banks from transnational banking involving Japan during the war. The Yokohama Specie Bank was already profiting from their absence. This office was then converted into a branch in 1924 from which Mitsui conducted an extensive foreign exchange operation. Using deposits from Japanese exporters, they engaged in currency speculation involving the UK£, the US$, the Indian rupee, and the Japanese yen. This left the bank exposed when the UK left the Gold Standard on 21 September 1931 as the £ fell in value against the US$. The bank was only saved from bankruptcy by the depreciation of the Japanese yen against the UK£. In the wake of that scare, Mitsui, along with other Japanese banks, scaled back their use of the London money market and their foreign exchange transactions.[144] This retreat of foreign banks with London branches from the foreign exchange market, beginning with the First World War, created a void for others to exploit, especially as currency instability in both the 1920s and 1930s generated profitable opportunities for those willing to accept the risks.

[142] Barret Whale, *Joint Stock Banking in Germany*, 219, 252, 278.
[143] Jones, *Multinational Banking*, 414–15; Ray, *Era of the Imperial Bank of India*, 196, 200–2, 208–10, 289, 291, 547; King, *Hongkong Bank*, vol. 2, 242, 530–2, 539, 543–6, 577, 619; F.H.H. King, *The History of the Hongkong and Shanghai Banking Corporation*, vol. 3, *The Hongkong Bank between the Wars and the Bank Interned, 1919–1945: Return from Grandeur* (Cambridge, 1987), 165, 366; Hou, *Foreign Investment*, 54–7, 130; Miller, *The Foreign Exchange Market*, 65, 120, 126.
[144] Tamaki, *Japanese Banking*, 46, 70–2, 82, 109, 118–19, 129, 131, 155–6, 167, 205; Ogura, 'Mitsui Bank', 88, 94, 99–101; Ogura, *Banking, the State and Industrial Promotion*, 10, 14, 16, 37–42.

Among those transnational banks that retreated from the foreign exchange market between the wars were the British overseas banks, including those operating in the parts of the Empire where sterling was used. This was especially between 1919 and 1925 and again after 1931. These banks were indirectly exposed to foreign exchange risks because of a mismatch between assets and liabilities held in sterling in London and their need to make payments or accept receipts in other currencies, especially the US$, which had grown in popularity. Included in this retreat, especially in the 1930s, were those banks based in the Empire that had established London branches to compete with the British overseas banks. The Commercial Bank of Australia, for example, lost heavily when Britain left the Gold Standard in 1931, and so it reduced its exposure to sterling as a result, as was the case with other banks from Australia, New Zealand, and South Africa.[145] Those British overseas banks operating in Latin America faced even greater difficulties, as they had to cope with conducting business in sterling in London and in local currencies in places such as Argentina and Brazil. Before the war, it was these banks that were largely responsible for providing the foreign exchange interface between Latin America and the rest of the world, with the UK£ being used as the vehicle currency. This remained the case for Britain in 1918 as the West Yorkshire Bank made clear:

> Customers transacting business with South and Central America, payable in currency, may protect themselves from adverse fluctuations in exchange rates by requesting the West Yorkshire Bank to arrange in advance with the Anglo-South American Bank at a rate at which their currency bills will be converted into sterling at date of payment or maturity.[146]

Though remaining important, the sterling-based network of payments and receipts shrunk between the wars, especially after 1931, in the face of exchange controls and central bank intervention. In its place emerged a US$-based network centred on New York and using the US$ as the vehicle currency. The result was growing competition from US banks that spelled the end for the separate existence of those British overseas banks operating in Latin America. Eventually, they were all merged into one bank, the Bank of London and South America (Bolsa), under the control of Lloyds Bank.[147]

The Indian Exchange Banks also faced growing problems after the First World War. Though there were profits to be made trading the £ against the rupee, that did not compensate for the lack of cheap credit that had been obtained by using the London money market and the ability to employ idle balances remuneratively. The effect was to undermine the competitiveness of these Exchange Banks, and they faced a growing challenge from banks based in India and the UK. There had long been a divide between the London-based Exchange Banks and the Indian-based Presidency banks, even though the latter were a product of the British expatriate

---

[145] Butlin, *Australia and New Zealand Bank*, 369, 392, 397; Blainey and Hutton, *Gold and Paper*, 195–7, 206, 212; Wood, *Commercial Bank of Australia*, 223, 238, 241, 247, 256; Henry and Stepmann, *First Hundred Years*, 225.

[146] West Yorkshire Bank: Foreign Exchange Department, Regulations and General Information, 1918.

[147] Joslin, *Banking in Latin America*, 217, 228–30, 244, 253, 270.

community. Lacking a London branch meant that the Presidency banks could not manage exchange operations by switching assets and liabilities between the UK and India, and so they left that to the Exchange Banks. However, in response to the threatened invasion of Indian banking by British domestic banks after the First World War, the Imperial Bank of India was formed in 1920 as an amalgamation of the three Presidency banks. The Imperial Bank established a London office allowing it to compete with the Exchange Banks. These Presidency banks had accumulated huge sterling balances in London during the First World War through the funds deposited with them by Indian exporters, as these had not been spent on imports from the UK and remittances to the UK as had been the practice in the past. The result was that the Imperial Bank possessed not only large assets and liabilities in rupees in India, through its business there, but also these sterling balances. By matching assets and liabilities in London and Bombay in terms of sterling and rupees, it was now in the position to cover exchange risks. During the 1930s, it increasingly competed with the Exchange Banks, investing surplus funds in London by purchasing treasury bills or lending to other banks through the discount market. However, it was increasingly conscious of its vulnerability to currency volatility, especially the weakness of sterling. In response, it formed closer links with New York, especially through the Chase National Bank, giving it access to US$s. With access to debits and credits in UK£s, US$s, and Indian rupees, it was able to internalize exchange operations. By expanding or contracting in sterling in London, dollars in New York, and rupees in Bombay, it was able to not only cover the exchange risk it was running but also provide this service to other banks in competition with the Exchange Banks. It was better placed to carry this out because of the much greater volume of business it did in India, and so the Exchange Banks were gradually squeezed out of the foreign exchange business. The Exchange Banks were also being squeezed by competition coming from Britain's domestic banks. Both Lloyds and National Provincial expanded into India in the 1920s, by acquiring banks that did business there, giving them direct access to both sterling and rupees. Lloyds bought Cox & Co, while National Provincial purchased Grindlay & Co. In response, one of the Exchange Banks, the Chartered, expanded into local banking in India and opened branches in Manchester and Liverpool in the UK.[148]

What happened to the British overseas banks operating in India and Latin America reflected the increasing encroachment on their business by domestically focused banks. By the early 1920s, British domestic banks had consolidated their hold on England and Wales with the Midland even venturing into Ireland and Scotland. It took over the Glasgow-based Clydesdale Bank in 1920 followed by the Aberdeen-based North of Scotland in 1924, integrating both into its domestic network.[149] The

---

[148] Spalding, *Eastern Exchange Currency*, 107–9; Green and Kinsey, *Paradise Bank*, 29, 76, 203–4; Ramachandra Rau, *Present-day Banking in India*, 53–4, 265; Gunasekera, *From Dependent Currency*, 44, 80, 44, 110, 183; Bagchi, *The Evolution of the State Bank of India*, vol. 2: 16–17, 30–1, 70–1, 450–4, 519, 535, 549, 562, 574, 582, 586, 603; Ray, *The Evolution of the State Bank of India*, 28, 67–76, 190–6, 200–2, 208–10, 244–7, 285–91, 393, 529, 547, 571, 637; Mackenzie, *Realms of Silver*, 222, 228, 240, 259–61.

[149] Munn, *Clydesdale Bank*, 158, 161, 189, 225.

Midland Bank had also merged with the London Joint Stock Bank in 1918, which gave it a very extensive and well-established international correspondent network. As the centre of a worldwide web, the Midland saw little need to expand internationally by acquiring British overseas banks, conscious of the additional risks a branch network in a foreign country would expose them to. In contrast, other British domestic banks were willing to take those risks, seeing the acquisition of a British overseas bank as a quick route to international expansion. In 1919, Lloyds attempted to take over one of the leading Exchange Banks, the National Bank of India, but this was blocked by the Bank of England. Lloyds then turned its attention to South America, forming the Bank of London and South America (Bolsa) through the merger of the various British overseas banks operating in that region. Barclays focused on Africa and the West Indies, grouping its acquisitions into a subsidiary, Dominion, Colonial and Overseas (DCO). This overseas expansion of Britain's domestic banks was opposed by the Bank of England, being concerned that instability abroad would endanger the entire bank and so precipitate a domestic banking crisis. For those reasons, there continued to be a separation between the British and the overseas banking business, even when both were under the control of a single bank.[150]

Generally, transnational banking experienced growing difficulties between the wars, faced with currency instability and the erection by governments of barriers separating national financial systems and impeding the free flow of funds. Even though the British government, unlike many others, did not introduce formal exchange controls in the 1930s after the abandonment of the Gold Standard, the creation of the Exchange Equalisation Account (EEA) in 1932, which was managed by the Bank of England on its behalf, was an instrument through which intervention could and did take place.[151] The EEA spelled the end of the world that had existed before 1914, in which banks were left free to follow the dictates of the market in choosing where, how, and when to employ their funds. In 1943, the New York-based Institute of International Finance identified 1931 as the year in which banks moved away from relying on the originate-and-distribute model to embrace the lend-and-hold one. That switch had inevitable consequences for the way that the foreign exchange market had operated in the past, especially the reliance on banks that were transnational.[152] As most banks operated within the boundaries of a nation state, there continued to be a need for a mechanism through which they engaged with each other, which Barrett Whale recognized even in the middle of the global monetary crisis of 1931.

At the centre of every developed banking system, there is a highly-concentrated money market, around which the head offices of all the leading banks and financial houses are clustered. In this market the banks are able to employ funds in a manner

---

[150] Jones, *Multinational Banking*, 414–15; Tyson, *100 Years of Banking*, 154; Ray, *Era of the Imperial Bank of India*, 196, 200–2, 208–10, 289, 291, 547; Matthews and Tuke, *History of Barclays Bank*, 365; A.W. Tuke and R.J.H. Gillman, *Barclays Bank Ltd, 1926–1969: Some Recollections* (London: 1972), 12–13; Joslin, *Banking in Latin America*, 217, 228–30, 244, 253, 270.
[151] Collins, *Money and Banking*, 196.
[152] Institute of International Finance, *Effects of the War*, 22–5.

which is both safe and highly liquid. ... On the other side, this market provides the funds required for financing trade—particularly international trade—dealings on the stock exchange, and the temporary deficits of the Government. Finally, these markets provide contacts between the different national banking systems, since balances are readily transferred from one centre to another.[153]

In the international arena, the foreign exchange market lies at the interface of these interbank contacts. With the role being played by banks providing a transnational branch network in decline, a void was created that others could fill.

There was always a fringe of banks in the City of London ready to seize any profitable opportunity, and that including trading in foreign exchange. As Gurney, who managed the National and Provincial Bank's Foreign Department, observed, after Britain abandoned the Gold Standard for the second time in 1931, 'Now that dealing was more profitable, certain counterparties who, during the period of stability had been inactive, were coming into the market again.'[154] The same was true after Britain abandoned the Gold Standard for the first time in 1919 with an immediate response coming from the British merchant banks. They had long been engaged in international finance, and so possessed the connections and expertise required to take advantage of the opportunities emerging in the foreign exchange market. However, most had gradually dropped trading in foreign exchange in favour of the greater and more reliable profits to be made from handling issues of stocks and bonds on behalf of governments and companies or providing finance through bills of exchange. Nevertheless, foreign exchange remained a business that was allied to the global finance they specialized in, and one they continued to dabble with when a profitable opportunity arose. A number of these merchant banks had an incentive to take up dealing in foreign exchange in the early 1920s because their pre-war business had largely disappeared.[155] What they lacked was trained staff and modern equipment, but that was quickly remedied. Unlike securities and commodities, currency trading was not conducted on organized exchanges but between banks and brokers operating as independent agents. That made it easy for the merchant banks, who were already part of established trust networks, to enter the business.[156] According to Lionel Fraser, 'Dealing in foreign exchange is essentially a matter of mutual trust.' The risks being taken made it essential that counterparties could be relied upon when it came to forward transactions.[157]

Lionel Fraser had worked for a small merchant bank, Bonn and Co, before the First World War and rejoined it when his military service ended. Bonn and Co had done a largely German business, which the war had destroyed, and so it moved into foreign exchange trading. Bonn and Co was then taken over by a larger merchant bank,

[153] P. Barrett Whale, 'English and Continental Banking', *JIB*, 52 (1931), 204–9.
[154] Liverpool and Manchester District Bank: Letters from the London Manager to the Head Office in Manchester, 13 October 1931.
[155] B.D. Nash, *Investment Banking in England* (Chicago: 1924), 63.
[156] Diaper, 'Merchant Banking', 61, 73; Balogh, *Studies in Financial Organization*, 248.
[157] Fraser, *All to the Good*, 66. See L.E. Jones, *Georgian Afternoon* (London: 1958), 115.

Helbert Wagg, which was keen to enter the foreign exchange business because of the profits to be made. Fraser described his experience of dealing in foreign exchange in the early 1920s in his autobiography.

> This meant constant telephone communication abroad. … By lightning reference to the calculators in front of us we could immediately ascertain whether a margin existed between the two centres. If so we would act, buy or sell, and undo the transaction in our market here. Our London business was always with foreign exchange brokers, with most of whom we had direct lines. … At this time numerous banking institutions of smaller or greater importance came into the market, and made the position highly competitive. … It cannot be said that our business was of a speculative nature, for we always endeavoured to close the day with our book square. With the violent movements it was dangerous to do otherwise. It was a wild game but for those who were participants it was anything but wild. They had to be ice-cold and bank on the spot all the time. It was easy to get burnt fingers. … Altogether it was killing and frenzied work, and except that the department was able to make a substantial contribution to the profits of the firm, I found it difficult to persuade myself that we were doing anything particularly constructive or helpful in those very disturbed times. Indeed I was not sorry when activity in the world currencies subsided, and we found diminishing scope for our skill.[158]

Among the other merchant banks who took up foreign exchange trading in the 1920s was Kleinwort Sons & Company, which had conducted a large Anglo-German business before the war. Initially, they were very successful, employing a manager, six dealers, and forty support staff. That success ended once the years of hectic trading died away after 1925, and so the foreign exchange department was closed down. They only engaged in currency trading again when the prospects of large speculative profits beckoned, as in the late 1930s.[159] The profits made from exchange dealing at Kleinworts fell from £50,275 in 1926 to £10,730 in 1929, around which level it fluctuated, rising briefly to £19,098 in 1936, when there was much speculation against the franc, before falling to £12,924 in 1937 and rebounding to £18,431 in 1938 as war fears generated volatility.[160] Not only were the profits of the early 1920s never reached again, but the business of foreign exchange trading remained a risky and volatile one.

Another merchant bank that took up and then dropped foreign exchange trading was the Anglo-American firm of Brown Shipley.[161] In alliance with its associated bank in New York, Brown Brothers, Brown Shipley engaged in trading the UK£ against the US$, which they had done in the past. They took up the business in 1918 and were well established by 1920. It involved buying or selling the £ and the $ in London with the deal being immediately reversed in New York. 'These exchange operations frequently assume the aspect of a chain of transactions spread between New York and

[158] Fraser, *All to the Good*, 66–71.
[159] Wake, *Kleinwort Benson*, 211–18, 244, 255, 294–300, 308.
[160] Kleinwort Sons & Company: *Annual Profit and Loss Account* (Guildhall Library, 1926–1938).
[161] Ellis, *Heir to Adventure*, 121, 141, 145–9.

London over several days.' In 1921, Brown Shipley claimed to occupy 'a very leading position in the exchange market. ... Most of our forward purchases of dollars are for Government account. ... All the largest transactions for these purchases go through Morgan's office,[162] and quite probably that Firm knows in advance the considerable amount of dollars we have made ourselves liable'. To try and limit the risks they were exposed to, Brown Shipley engaged in large forward transactions matched to their liabilities. 'Dealing in such large figures, it is very advisable that we should make every effort to match these dates more exactly than in the past. ...Every operation of ours has to be reversed from our viewpoint to yours.' However, it was not always possible to achieve this, leaving them with an exposure that could reach £0.5 million. This was a high-risk business, which both Brown Shipley in London and Brown Brothers in New York constantly monitored.

> Every day and all day he (the foreign exchange dealer) has his exact position in front of him, and his figures are always ready for our inspection at any time of the day, and are brought into the Parlour for investigation at frequent intervals. In addition to this our Partners and the management closely watch the combined weekly cabled totals, and make prompt investigation into any excess.

As the size of foreign exchange dealings grew, so did the profits and the risks, especially when running unmatched forward positions. As a result, Brown Brothers in New York were unwilling to commit staff and capital to foreign exchange trading because of the rising level of risk, especially as they were developing a successful investment banking business. In contrast, Brown Shipley in London was keen to expand in this direction because of the profits to be made despite the risks. They were more confident that every exposure could be covered as soon as possible by matching deals in London and New York, if the two firms worked closely together. Positions were to be matched 'even at a loss as soon as the market gives them an opportunity to do so'. However, as profits shrank, even Brown Shipley decided to scale back their involvement. By 1925, they had become 'distinctly disappointed with our Foreign Exchange profits. ... There were a great many new entrants into the field in this particular business, and as a consequence the spread between the spot and future became much less, and the initiatory business became less profitable. ... The days of big profits for a private firm such as ours, we feel, are past'. They chose to return to the safer business of providing commercial credit and handling stock and bond issues.[163]

[162] Morgan Grenfell in London and J.P. Morgan in New York.

[163] Brown Shipley Correspondence, London to New York 1914–1929 (Guildhall Library), 27 August 1914, 4 September 1914, 24 October 1918, 21 November 1918, 16 July 1920, 22 April 1921, 31 January 1922, 30 August 1922, 5 February 1924, 27 June 1924, 30 July 1924, 8 October 1924, 16 January 1925, 2 April 1925, 1 July 1925, 12 January 1928, 8 January 1929, 30 January 1930, 9 April 1930, 7 January 1931, 22 January 1931, 2 April 1936; Memorandum on Joint Exchange Account, 9 June 1921; James Brown, New York to Edward Clifton Brown, London, 16 May 1921, 17 May 1921, 23 March 1925, 10 January 1927; Louis Curtis, Boston Office, Brown Brothers, to Brown Shipley, London, 27 January 1925, 23 March 1925, 27 January 1927; Telegrams between London and New York, 5 April 1921, 8 April 1921.

It was not only merchant banks that had responded in the early 1920s to the opportunities that the foreign exchange market provided. A number of new businesses were set up, such as the Foreign Exchange Securities Trust in 1920 and Foreign Exchange and Investments Ltd in 1923, but these hardly survived beyond the speculative phase of currency trading.[164] A more permanent entrant was the British Overseas Bank, which was formed in 1919. It was the product of a number of smaller domestic banks that were already involved in foreign exchange trading in a small way. They wanted to expand the business that they did but lacked the resources and were conscious of the risks involved. By acting collectively, and capitalizing on their connections at home and abroad, they hoped to be in a position to become a major force in the foreign exchange market. In 1922, the British Overseas Bank claimed that

> The foreign exchange side of the Bank has been equipped and organised with a view to offering unrivalled facilities for every description of foreign business. By reason of its associations and overseas arrangements, the bank is in an exceptional position to insure clients against loss arising through violent fluctuations in the various rates of exchange.[165]

The British Overseas Bank installed the most modern equipment and recruited those with experience in the London offices of European banks. In 1923, it even purchased what had been the London operations of Deutsche Bank. However, the only success it had was trading Central and Eastern European currencies, which others avoided because of the risks. These countries were newly formed and the value of their currencies had yet to be established. Trading these currencies was a highly speculative business as the British Overseas Bank was forced to leave foreign exchange positions open because of the lack of counterparties, as in Polish zloty. The British Overseas Bank was then badly hit by the German Standstill of 1931, as that froze its funds. It never recovered and was eventually closed down.[166]

By the late 1920s, the speculative era of the foreign exchange market was over and the smaller banks, like the British Overseas Bank and the merchant banks, had largely withdrawn from the business. These banks suffered a further blow in the Global Financial Crisis that took place between 1929 and 1932, when doubts were expressed over their stability, and even survival.[167] What was required was a new way of working that coped with the legacy of the First World War, including the diminished role played by the transnational and merchant banks. That legacy included a huge increase in the demands made on retail banks from their customers

---

[164] Foreign Exchange Securities Trust, 1920; Foreign Exchange and Investments Ltd, 1923, National Archives.

[165] Brochure for the British Overseas Bank (London: 1922–3), 7.

[166] B. Sweet-Escott, *Gallant Failure: The British Overseas Bank Ltd, 1919–1939* (1977) (RBS Archives), 1–3, 6, 19–20, 30, 55, 63–6, 84–6, 91.

[167] Liverpool and Manchester District Bank: Letters from the London Manager to the Head Office in Manchester, 17 September 1931, 21 September 1931, 30 September 1931, 7 October 1931, 13 October 1931, 15 October 1931, 26 October 1931, 28 October 1931, 16 December 1931, 7 January 1932, 11 January 1932, 15 January 1932, 2 February 1932, 9 March 1932, 1 June 1932, 13 June 1932, 2 September 1932, 2 September 1932, 8 March 1933, 12 March 1933.

for foreign exchange cover because of the far greater instability of exchange rates, including the UK£.[168] As Phillips observed in 1926, 'Exporters want their own money in exchange.'[169] In 1925, the Westminster Bank had reflected that 'We were once in a position to force our sterling currency on other nations.' However, due to 'violent fluctuations in exchange', this was no longer possible.[170] A solution had to be found and customers turned to their banks, which all had to respond as they existed in a competitive environment.[171] The volume of foreign exchange trading handled by Glyn Mills, one of these retail banks, grew from £1.3 million in 1919 to £5.5 million in 1925, reached £7.1 million in 1929, despite the return to the Gold Standard, and then averaged around £9 million per annum in the early 1930s before jumping to £20.8 million in 1935 and £46.1 million in 1936.[172] As early as 1917, the Manchester and Liverpool District Bank set up a foreign department to cope with the demands being made upon it. Firms involved in the cotton textile trade turned to it to provide a means of covering forward purchases involving payments in US$ and forward sales resulting in receipts in French francs. In turn, the District Bank looked for ways of covering the currency risks it was exposed to. This led it to open a department in London where it could engage directly with the foreign exchange market. However, as the foreign exchange market settled down into a high-volume/low-risk business in the later 1920s, smaller retail banks gradually withdrew from direct involvement, such as the District Bank and Martins Bank.[173]

Increasingly, the profits to be made from providing foreign exchange services no longer justified the expenses involved in terms of staff and equipment. Instead, these smaller banks passed their foreign exchange business onto those banks that chose to specialize in it by investing in the latest technology and recruiting, training, and retaining the most skilled staff.[174] From the outset, the Edinburgh-based Bank of Scotland had channelled all its foreign exchange business through the Westminster Bank, even though it had a London office of its own. 'The arrangement with the Westminster Bank Ltd to pass Foreign Business arising at this office through them has worked smoothly and satisfactorily during the past sixteen years.' The alternative, which they considered, was to set up their own foreign exchange operation, but that would mean considerable additional expense and expose them to increased risk with no guarantee of profits.[175] It was not just smaller British banks that were in this position but also banks from around the world. One was the Canadian Bank of Commerce whose London manager, Buckerfield, complained in 1928 that 'profits

---

[168] Waight, *Exchange Equalisation Account*, 3–4; Gunasekera, *From Dependent Currency*, 18.

[169] Phillips, *Modern Foreign Exchange*, 150.

[170] Westminster Bank, *The Financial Machinery of the Import and Export Trade* (London: 1925), 5–6, 19.

[171] Spalding, *Eastern Exchange Currency*, 107; Tuke and Gillman, *Barclays Bank*, 81.

[172] Glynn, Mills and Company: Statistics Book, 1919–1936.

[173] The Manchester and Liverpool District Bank: Foreign Department Minute Book (Manchester), 11 April 1919, 5 November 1920, 8 November 1920, 17 December 1920, 25 January 1921, 4 November 1924, 4 March 1925, 1 April 1925, 7 December 1925.

[174] Lloyds Bank, Letter to Chief Inspector, 14 February 1924.

[175] Bank of Scotland: London Branch Procedure Book no.5 Foreign Exchange Business, January 1935.

are difficult to make in the Foreign Department at present'.[176] In 1932, Shaw, who was the assistant manager at the London office of the Bank of New Zealand, admitted that 'they had very few foreign exchange transactions of any sort' and 'they had no one on the staff with any expert knowledge of foreign exchange'.[177] It was the biggest banks that were best able to spread the expenses involved over a large volume of transactions. These costs grew substantially in the 1930s as a result of the complications caused by the intervention of governments and central banks.[178]

What happened after the First World War was that currency instability complicated the business being done by the banks, forcing them to engage with the foreign exchange market. As banks were left with the exposure to the foreign exchange risk that their customers off-loaded, they had to try to cover it. The solution was to develop counterparty relationships between banks. By matching currency exposure over time and amount, but in reverse, banks could, collectively, eliminate the risks that they ran. To achieve that position required the existence of counterparties who could be relied upon to honour their commitments regardless of circumstances, and that was where trust was so important. A forward transaction involved a commitment to make a payment of a precise amount at a specific time in the future. While the transaction was open, the bank was vulnerable to a default, which would leave it exposed. Under the circumstances, a bank needed to be certain that the counterparty to such deals would deliver, especially when no collateral was provided by either side. The only guarantee that a default would not take place was the reputation of the bank. The volatility of currencies after the First World War put a premium on selecting a counterparty that could be trusted never to default on a deal in the foreign exchange market.[179] According to Gregory, by 1920, 'With the telephones and telegraphs in operation, dealings in foreign exchange take place at a furious pace all day long, and they are mainly in cable transfers, which fluctuate every few minutes'.[180]

Only a few banks were in a position to command the trust of their peer group and so become counterparties in this continuous trading of foreign exchange that developed after the First World War. These were found among the small number of very large banks that were coming to dominate national banking systems by the beginning of the twentieth century. In 1920, the level of concentration in banking in

[176] The Manchester and Liverpool District Bank: Foreign Department Minute Book (Manchester), 25 June 1928, 6 July 1928, 6 February 1929, 10 April 1929.
[177] Liverpool and Manchester District Bank: Letters from the London Manager to the Head Office in Manchester, 7 January 1932, 15 January 1932.
[178] Waight, *Exchange Equalisation Account*, 1–4, 12, 15–16, 39–40; H.T. Easton, *The Work of a Bank* (London: 1930, revised and rewritten by H.G. Hodder), 270, 293.
[179] Liverpool and Manchester District Bank: Letters from the London Manager to the Head Office in Manchester, 17 September 1931, 21 September 1931, 30 September 1931, 7 October 1931, 13 October 1931, 15 October 1931, 26 October 1931, 28 October 1931, 16 December 1931, 7 January 1932, 11 January 1932, 15 January 1932, 2 February 1932, 9 March 1932, 1 June 1932, 13 June 1932, 2 September 1932, 2 September 1932, 8 March 1933, 12 March 1933; Liverpool and Manchester District Bank: London Foreign Managers Minute Book, 24 September 1933, 22 January 1937, 19 July 1937; R.C. Crompton, *History of the Foreign Department of the District Bank of Liverpool and Manchester*, RBS Archive.
[180] Gregory, *Foreign Exchange*, 12–13, 16, 21–4, 28, 30, 46, 52, 55, 109.

the UK and Germany was already very similar, for example.[181] There was also a high level of concentration in France and Canada, which had led to their banks becoming major players in the foreign exchange market even before the First World War. This participation then expanded between the wars with Canadian banks, in particular, being considered highly reliable counterparties, especially as they proved resilient during the financial crises of the 1930s.[182] Reflecting from the vantage point of 1940, Brown concluded that the lend-and-hold model of banking was being applied internationally, replacing the use of bills and bonds as the mechanism though which money was borrowed, lent, transferred, or exchanged around the world. He was of the opinion that the 'encroachment of the great joint stock banks upon every field of money market activity' was observable in London since the end of the First World War. Rather than acting as agents, these joint-stock banks were becoming principals: 'They were becoming more interested in the foreign exchange market, and assuming new responsibilities in connection with the capital market. ... The post-war tendency was for the joint stock banks to take care of all the business of their British clients, including their foreign business.' This led them to compete for business with foreign banks, Exchange Banks, and merchant banks.[183] The outlier in this process of concentration and the rise of the giant joint-stock banks was the USA where legislation continued to restrict the size of banks through the prohibition of interstate banking. A further restriction in the USA came in the 1930s with the Glass–Steagall Act, which prevented the combination of deposit and investment banking. These laws made it impossible in the USA to emulate either the UK, with nationwide deposit banks, or Germany, where universal banks developed. Only those US banks located in the financial centre of New York could reach a scale to match their counterparts elsewhere in the world.[184]

[181] R.S. Grossman, *Unsettled Account: The Evolution of Banking in the Industrialized World Since 1800* (Princeton: Princeton U.P., 2010), 33, 63, 72–6.

[182] Darroch, *Canadian Banks*, 31, 38–44, 88, 126–8, 170–6; Denison, *Canada's First Bank*, vol. 2: 9, 172, 321–2, 330, 354, 369; Ross, *History of the Canadian Bank of Commerce*, vol. 2: 349, 378; A. St. L. Tigge, *History of the Canadian Bank of Commerce* (Toronto: 1934), vol. 3: 7, 46, 167.

[183] Brown, *International Gold Standard*, 624–5, 1027.

[184] C. Fohlin, *Finance Capitalism and Germany's Rise to Industrial Power* (Cambridge: Cambridge University Press, 2007), 6, 62, 72, 83, 105, 253, 332–3; F. Capie and G. Wood, *Money Over Two Centuries: Selected Topics in British Monetary History* (Oxford: Oxford University Press, 2012), 3, 49–50, 64; Grossman, *Unsettled Account*, 72, 96, 111–12, 125, 147–8, 178–81; Lucy Newton, 'Change and Continuity: The Development of Joint Stock Banking in the Early Nineteenth Century' (Reading: Henley Business School, 2007), 4, 20; J.H. Wood, *A History of Central Banking in Great Britain and the United States* (Cambridge: Cambridge University Press, 2005), 111–13; Collins and Baker, *Commercial Banks*, 108, 179–81; R. Sylla, 'Comparing the UK and US Financial Systems, 1790–1830', in J. Attack and L. Neal (eds), *The Origin and Development of Financial Markets and Institutions: From the 17th Century to the Present* (Cambridge: Cambridge University Press, 2009), 234–5; Collins, *Money and Banking*, 40; J. Singleton, *Central Banking in the Twentieth Century* (Cambridge: 2011), 37; Y. Cassis, 'Management and Strategy in the English Joint Stock Banks, 1890–1914', *Business History*, 27 (1985), 301; M. Collins and M. Baker, 'Financial Crises and Structural Change in English Commercial Bank Assets, 1860–1914', *Explorations in Economic History*, 36 (1999), 429–30; J. Armstrong, 'Hooley and the Bovril Company', *Business History*, 28 (1986), 24; M. Collins, 'English Bank Lending and the Financial Crisis of the 1870s', *Business History*, 32 (1990), 210; L. Newton, 'The Birth of Joint-Stock Banking: England and New England Compared', *Business History Review*, 84 (2010), 27–52.

Not all these large banks were in a position to become reliable counterparties in the global foreign exchange market, with confidence shaken from time to time by a succession of financial crises and bank failures around the world as well as the consequences of government interventions. The German Standstill of 1931, for example, made it impossible for banks from that country to honour the commitments they had made to other banks. Similarly, the introduction of exchange controls in 1933 by Japan undermined the international role played by the Yokohama Specie Bank.[185] As a result, it was a relatively few large banks that came to dominate the foreign exchange market, principally from the UK and the USA. Like the British banks, those from the USA had also played little role in the foreign exchange market, but both came to the fore in the 1920s and 1930s.[186] Generally, once these large banks began to engage with the foreign exchange market after the First World War, they quickly came to dominate it. In 1927, Phelps observed that 'In all the world financial centers, the various branches of foreign banks engage in exchange operations which run up into considerable figures.'[187] Ten years later, in 1937, George Bolton, the Bank of England's expert on the foreign exchange market, made a similar observation.[188] Trust between these counterparties was crucial in determining which could participate in foreign exchange trading, where there were no rules and regulations imposed and enforced by either institutions or governments, as in other markets. The remedy was to exclude from direct participation all banks considered possible candidates for default, leaving a small inner core. It was exceedingly difficult to gain entry to this inner core because that required a bank to establish that it was reliable counterparty. That could only be done by becoming a member of the inner core.[189]

Among the banks that became the ideal counterparties in the foreign exchange market that developed between the wars were those from the UK as they had already established that position for themselves over the previous fifty years. When British banks were small, local, and reliant upon a limited pool of individual talent, they suffered from regular liquidity and solvency crises. This made them unreliable as counterparties being subject to frequent defaults. It was not only those who deposited their savings in a bank who suffered when it failed but also other banks to which it

---

[185] Lloyd's Bank Ltd: Overseas Department: Correspondence 27 September, 1929, 3 October 1929, 5–6 February 1931, 28 August 1931, 5 October 1931, 12 January 1932, 18 January 1932, 22 January 1932, 27 January 1932, 15 February 1932, 1 March 1932, 11 March 1932, 15 March 1932, 16 March 1932, 22 March 1932, 5 April 1932, 7 April 1932, 29 June 1932, 18 July 1932, 28 October 1932, 13 January 1933, 25 July 1935, 30 July 1935, 30 March 1936, 8 December 1936, 24 December 1936, 10 November 1937. Memorandum on Japanese Banks, 12 September 1932; Memorandum re pre-war Chinese Business 16 July 1943; Kasuya, 'Yokohama Specie Bank', 132–3, 138, 141–3; *The Mitsui Bank*, 110; Rudlin, *The History of Mitsubishi Corporation in London*, 54, 58.

[186] Phelps, *Foreign Expansion of American Banks*, 3–4, 7–8, 21, 38, 83, 98–102, 127, 136, 139, 141–2, 147, 151–2; Stern, *U.S. in International Banking*, 3–8; J. Kelly, *Bankers and Borders: The Case of American Banks in Britain* (Cambridge: 1977), 3, 8, 11–12, 158.

[187] Phelps, *Foreign Expansion of American Banks*, 83.

[188] Bank of England, Memoranda on London Foreign Exchange Market, 17 June 1935, 16 December 1935; Some Aspects of Forward Exchange in Relation to Control, September 1937; George Bolton, Memorandum, 11 January 1937; Report on Direct Dealing, 31 March 1937; Foreign Exchange and Gold: Market Organisation and Technique, 6 April 1937.

[189] Einzig, *Forward Exchange*, 1st ed., 12; 2nd ed., 19–20, 23, 53, 77, 116, 311, 354, 497; Forbes, *Doing Business*, 35–40, 166.

owed money. Banks were frequently creditors and debtors to each other as they made and accepted payments on behalf of customers, lent out spare funds, and borrowed to fill a shortage. For those reasons, the failure of one bank could bring down others as depositors rushed to withdraw money from those banks rumoured to be in difficulty. For those reasons, banks limited the business they did with each other, favouring the few that had gained a reputation for being dependable counterparties. That reputation was increasingly attached to banks that were large and diversified because the scale and spread of their business made them less vulnerable to liquidity crises. Their size also meant that they could employ and train staff with the range and depth of expertise and experience necessary to assess lending risks and so avoid solvency crises. These large banks were the product of the consolidation that had taken place in British banking after the Overend and Gurney crisis of 1866. Between 1870 and 1921, in England, there were 264 mergers, leading to the disappearance of 370 banks. From this emerged a small number of very large banks that dominated the British banking system. In 1870, the ten largest banks controlled 33 per cent of retail deposits in England and this doubled to 65 per cent in 1910 before reaching 97 per cent in 1920. Over that period, very few British banks failed and the frequency and severity of both liquidity and solvency crises faded. The result was that the largest of these banks were viewed as highly resilient and so unlikely to default on any deal they were involved in.[190] As Fraser reflected in 1907, 'The small banks dotted about England in isolated detachment, with no cohesion, confined in space and operations, are replaced by the branches of a homogenous whole, with centralised control of directors and managers, who place all deliberations on a purely business footing.'[191]

By the beginning of the twentieth century, the large British banks had perfected a business model that allowed them to use short-term deposits to make long-term loans in such a way that was both safe and remunerative. They were based in London, which was the hub of the foreign exchange market, but they were little engaged in it. They confined their business to the UK and conducted it in sterling. Nevertheless, they were well integrated into the global banking network through their correspondent links, making them trusted partners to banks from around the world, with a proven reputation for honouring all their commitments. They could also call on the Bank of England as the lender of last resort through the agency of the discount houses and the London money market. The First World War had been a shock for these banks, exposed as they were to panic withdrawals by depositors worried by their stability in the face of a major European conflict. With the support of the UK government and the Bank of England, the large British banks had withstood that crisis and emerged from the First World War with an enhanced reputation for resilience and stability. The close cooperation between the Treasury, the Bank of England, and these large banks, forged during the First World War, was then continued into the 1920s and 1930s, cementing the belief that the British banking system was the most stable

---

[190] F. Capie and G. Rodrik-Bali, 'Concentration in British Banking, 1870–1920', *Business History*, 24 (1982), 281–91.
[191] D. Fraser, 'A Decade of Bank Amalgamations, 1897–1906', *JIB*, 29 (1907), 35.

in the world.[192] The war and its aftermath also led to further concentration among British banks, from which emerged the Big Five, namely the Midland, Lloyds, Barclays, Westminster, and National and Provincial.[193] The assessment of Billings and Capie was that 'The increased concentration arising from the amalgamation process which created the Big Five clearing banks had produced powerful and resilient institutions.'[194]

These large banks proved resilient in the face of the difficulties experienced by the British economy in the 1920s, survived the Global Financial Crisis that took place between 1929 and 1932, and then overcame the challenges of the world depression in the 1930s without requiring any support from the British government. To Evitt, in 1931, 'None other than the British banking system could have withstood so successfully such a financial upheaval as we have recently witnessed, and this undoubtedly has been due to the deeply-rooted belief in the integrity and prudence of our banks.'[195] Taylor reflected in 1935 that 'The strength of the British banks has been amply demonstrated during the last few years of crisis and depression. During that period there has not at any time been any hint of failure or even of real anxiety for their safety.'[196] Such was the reputation for stability that these large British banks had acquired that they were even immune to the effects of rumour and contagion, which brought down numerous other banks, including sound ones, around the world. There were no panic withdrawals, for example, after the collapse of Farrow's Credit Bank in 1920, despite the revelations of fraud and mismanagement that followed, as it was considered an exceptional case.[197] It is thus unsurprising that these large British banks became the most trusted counterparties in global banking and so ideal partners in foreign exchange transactions.

Before the war, these large retail banks had already developed a successful international business by acting as correspondents for those foreign banks needing to make and receive payments in London and access the London money market. According to Furniss, in 1922, a correspondent agreement had 'the effect of making the London bank either a partner or an agent of the foreign bank in transactions which involve the two markets'. In order to operate in London, a foreign bank 'must establish and maintain a foreign balance, and must engage the services of a London banker as agent for the management of the balance, crediting it with certain items, charging it with others'. The obligations of a London correspondent were spelled out ranging from routine administrative tasks to providing its customers with credit. These were itemized in the agreement signed between the two banks. Before the war, the London correspondent was in receipt of a constant stream of sterling bills from around the

[192] Butson, 'The Banking System', 1238–9.

[193] See Kirkaldy (ed.), *British Finance*; R. Roberts, *Saving the City: The Great Financial Crisis of 1914* (Oxford: Oxford University Press, 2013).

[194] M. Billings and F. Capie, 'Financial Crisis, Contagion and the British Banking System between the World Wars', *Business History*, 53 (2011), 211.

[195] H.E. Evitt, 'Exchange Dealings under Current Conditions', *JIB*, 52 (1931), 456.

[196] C.W. Taylor, 'The Case against the Nationalisation of the Banks', *JIB*, 56 (1935), 374, 385–6.

[197] E. Nicholls, *Crime within the Square Mile: The History of Crime in the City of London* (London: 1935), 127–31.

world, which they either held themselves until maturity or discounted. This gave the London money market the depth and breadth that made it so attractive to banks from all over the world, whether they wanted to raise short-term funds or employ temporarily idle balances. To make the market work, there had to be a balance between supply and demand. In Furniss' words,

> The ease with which sterling long bills could be sold in all quarters of the world has been … but a reflection of the willingness of bankers to acquire credits in London. … The favourable buying prices, and the stability of the sterling rates, have been due to the broad, competitive market created by the buying bankers. … The very fact that sterling long bills have been widely used as financing instruments has, of itself, resulted in a broad and widely diffused demand for sterling sight drafts.[198]

What this meant was that even before the war, the large domestic banks were aware of the expanding opportunities presented by foreign exchange trading. However, the level of potential profits was low because of the stability of exchange rates, while the risks to be taken were high as the business had to be conducted in volume and at speed. Also, they were at a competitive disadvantage because they lacked foreign branches doing an extensive business in countries using currencies other than sterling. Nevertheless, the potential was there to develop these correspondent agreements into mutually profitable foreign exchange arrangements. In 1912, 1,211 banks from around the world had London correspondents and that rose to 2,362 in 1938.[199] One of the smaller domestic banks, the National, had in 1925 links with three banks in New York, two in Berlin, and individual ones in Montreal, Paris, Brussels, Zurich, Milan, Rome, and Amsterdam.[200] Allied to the continuing advances in international communications, the conversion of correspondent links into two-way relationships would allow Britain's large domestic banks to take centre stage in the foreign exchange market. The Midland Bank and the National City Bank of New York, for example, had begun to experiment with this way of working before the First World War, as they explored the potential profits that could be derived from the foreign exchange market, making use of the speed of communication provided by the transatlantic telegraph. Further advances in technology between the wars, such as a transatlantic telephone service in 1923, delivered a depth of contact that could cope with more complicated instructions.[201]

It was this conversion of correspondent links into a foreign exchange network that took place as a result of the First World War, as Easton reported in 1924, 'The changes which have occurred from 1910–21 have completely altered the policy of banks with regard to financing overseas trade and undertaking foreign exchange business.'[202]

---

[198] Furniss, *Foreign Exchange*, 314–18, 324–8, 361.
[199] Bankers' Almanac, 1912, 1938.
[200] National Bank, *Foreign Exchange* (1925).
[201] Kieve, *The Electric Telegraph*, 13, 103, 112–13, 211; Barty-King, *Girdle Round the Earth*, 89, 393; Meeker, *The Work of the Stock Exchange*, 504, 507, 516; D. Kynaston, *Cazenove & Co.* (Batsford, 1991), 137–8; Reed, *James Capel & Co.*, 96–7; Chapman, Raphael Bicentenary, 43–4.
[202] H.T. Easton, *History and Principles of Banks and Banking* (London: 1924), 3rd ed., 282–6.

In 1921, Lloyds had sent a member of staff, John Fea, to New York to develop for-eign exchange dealing.[203] The correspondent network was converted from one that brought business to and from London into a set of arrangements in which banks had accounts with each other, which could be in credit or debit depending on current circumstances. These accounts allowed a bank to engage in the foreign exchange market. In 1931–2, the Midland led with 991 of these accounts followed by the Westminster with 570, Barclays with 560, and Lloyds with 397.[204] The Midland ded-icated a London branch to meeting the needs of its foreign banking correspondents. From this branch, in 1929, 773 staff sent and received approximately 1,000 telegrams every working day.[205] The Westminster Bank also devoted a branch to handling its foreign business.[206] Occupying a similar position was the Overseas Department of Lloyds Bank, which employed 350 staff in 1938.[207] Knowing the risks involved in foreign exchange dealing, these banks carefully managed their exposure to both specific currencies and individual correspondent banks. They set limits, constantly assessed their position, and then continuously monitored what was happening.[208] The banks were particularly exposed to risks when engaged in forward contracts. Phillips, who had worked for Barclays as a foreign exchange dealer, explained in 1926 that 'Once a bank had made a foreign exchange transaction with a customer they covered their position with a forward deal in the foreign exchange market. The result was a continuous chain of transactions all dependent upon each bank honour-ing the commitments it had made.' He then added that 'Of recent years dealings in forward exchange have increased so considerably in number and volume that a very large market exists, in which huge amounts are turned over daily.'[209]

The maturing of the relationship between the largest British banks and the for-eign exchange market can be traced through what happened in the case of Lloyds, Midland, and Barclays. To begin with, Lloyds Bank treated its foreign exchange as a service provided to customers and for which they could charge. When the amount of business was low, branches handled it either by directing customers to the appro-priate bank in London or passing it on to the bank's own Foreign and Colonial Department in London. However, as competition for the foreign exchange business grew, branches directed large customers to London where they received a discount. In the early 1920s, Lloyds Bank continued to direct customers to other banks when they had specialist currency requirements, such as the Exchange Banks for India, Bolsa for South America, through the Bank of British West Africa for West Africa, and New Zealand via the Bank of New Zealand. From that, Lloyds then developed a

[203] Winton, *Lloyds Bank*, 33–4, 87–8, 106, 155.
[204] Merrett, 'Global Reach', 75–83.
[205] Midland Bank Overseas: Description of Operations, August 1930; Lloyds Bank Ltd: Foreign Busi-ness Regulations, 1925; District Bank: Foreign Department Minute Book, 8 June 1918; A.R. Holmes and E. Green, *Midland*, 131, 141, 158–9, 165, 249.
[206] Bank of Scotland, Foreign Exchange Business, January 1935.
[207] Lloyds Bank: Foreign and Colonial Branch Business 30 June 1938.
[208] Midland Bank Overseas: Description of Operations, August 1930; Lloyds Bank Ltd: Foreign Business Regulations, 1925; District Bank: Foreign Department Minute Book, 8 June 1918.
[209] Phillips, *Modern Foreign Exchange*, 132–3, 138–41.

foreign exchange business in its own right. That involved providing foreign exchange facilities to other banks, including ones from abroad, such as Germany and the USSR. Trading in German marks, for example, produced profits of £24,214 in 1921 but only £346 in 1924, rose to £20,316 in 1929, and then settled down at around the £6,000 level in the 1930s. What developed between the wars was a two-way correspondent relationship between Lloyds and its foreign correspondents, which was of mutual benefit as it allowed each bank to participate in the foreign exchange market both on behalf of its own customers and as a profitable business. There were risks attached to these arrangements as it exposed Lloyds to defaults by its partner banks. When Germany imposed its standstill agreement in 1931, Lloyds Bank was left with an exposure of £1.1 million, half of which remained outstanding when war broke out in 1939. Careful assessment of potential partners and then constant scrutiny of the accounts made these defaults rare and kept losses low.[210]

The overseas department of the Midland Bank acted as the hub for the foreign exchange operations of the entire group, including the Belfast Bank in Northern Ireland and the Clydesdale Bank in Scotland. In addition, it was at the centre of a dense web of connections to other banks in London through the use of the telephone and messengers, while there were also direct telegraph lines to the cable company offices. In 1929, the Midland received 76,326 telegrams and sent 100,348. To deal with this, it employed a total of 568 men and 215 women to support the work of the dealers.

> The Department consists of the Dealers who make the purchase and sale contracts of foreign exchange, both for spot and forward delivery, and who are responsible for maintaining the Bank's position with each of the foreign banks with which an account in currency is kept. The dealers work by countries. The dealers have direct telephone lines into the offices of the various London Foreign Exchange Brokers and they are also, of course, in constant cable and telephonic communication with overseas foreign correspondents.

The aim was to maintain a level balance by currency and country both current and forward and to ensure that no position became too large. Though this was a risk-adverse strategy, it was reported that 'Large profits are made by this Department and a very considerable sum is taken into the Bank's profits after the naturally very heavy charges for cables, telephone messages and Exchange Brokerage have been paid.' In 1929, £10,992 was spent on cables, £6,397 on telephone calls, and £8,923 on paying commission to brokers, but this generated gross profits of £106,710.

[210] Lloyds Bank: Foreign Business Regulations, 1925, 3, 5, 8, 22, 27; Lloyds Bank Ltd: Overseas Department: Correspondence, 27 September, 1929, 3 October 1929, 5–6 February 1931, 28 August, 5 October 1931, 12 January 1932, 18 January, 1932, 22 January 1932, 27 January 1932, 15 February 1932, 1 March 1932, 11 March 1932, 15 March 1932, 16 March 1932, 22 March 1932, 5 April 1932, 7 April 1932, 29 June 1932, 18 July 1932, 28 October 1932, 13 January 1933, 25 July 1935, 30 July 1935, 30 March 1936, 8 December 1936, 24 December 1936, 10 November 1937. Memorandum on Japanese Banks, 12 September 1932; Memorandum on German Business 14 July 1943; Memorandum re Pre-war Chinese Business, 16 July 1943; Memorandum on State Bank of the USSR, 19 July 1943; Managers' Files: Colonial and Foreign Department, Birmingham, 19 February 1945.

By then, the Midland Bank regarded foreign exchange trading as a source of profit rather than simply a service to its customers, though that remained a consideration.

It is the general rule that all Forward purchases or sales effected should be immediately covered by sale or purchase of a similar amount for the same value date. It may happen that it is not possible to cover a Forward contract by a corresponding purchase or sale at the time, and to meet these occasions an account called Forward Cover account has been opened in Overseas Currency Ledgers for the principal correspondent in each country. ... In the process of covering contracts it may happen that a loss may be made on the spot transaction, and a profit on the forward transaction or vice versa ... 'might, for example, be advantageous to go long of French francs if the Paris interest rate were higher than that being paid in London, as the extra interest earned on the francs in Paris would more than compensate for the loss of interest on the sterling'.

The Midland Bank aimed to cover all its foreign exchange exposure by either lending or borrowing an equivalent amount in that currency or buying and selling the currency at spot and buying forward for delivery. In addition to the business done in London, the bank maintained 300 foreign currency accounts with banks abroad. These included fifty-five in the USA, thirty-eight in France, twenty-seven in Spain, twenty-two in Italy, nineteen in the Netherlands, seventeen in Germany, and seventeen in Switzerland. In addition, there were another 100 foreign currency accounts in the name of customers. 'It is possible for any customer of the Bank to maintain a currency balance in any town abroad by arrangement through Overseas.' Through its connections with foreign banks, the Midland was continuously making and receiving foreign currency payments on their behalf and providing credit to their customers.[211]

Before the First World War, Barclays Bank had been one of the laggards in exploring the potential of foreign exchange business, but they quickly caught up. As early as 1917, it was 'rapidly developing foreign business' in response to demands from its customers.[212] By then, it was evident that the London money market was facing a serious challenge from New York with the US$ displacing the UK£ as the preferred currency in US trade with Latin America and the Far East.[213] If Barclays was to retain the business of those customers engaged in international trade, it had to try and accommodate their demand for credit in currencies other than the UK£. This business was then expanded between the wars, which involved opening and maintaining foreign currency accounts with a number of its correspondents, either on behalf of its customers or for its own benefit. According to the merchant bank, Lazards, by 1925, Barclays had become 'probably the biggest foreign exchange dealers in the

---

[211] Midland Bank Overseas Department: Diary and Minute Book, 25 June 1920; Midland Bank Overseas: Description of Operations, August 1930.

[212] Barclay & Co., *Report of the Annual General Meeting*, 24 January 1917, 8. See Matthews and Tuke, *History of Barclays Bank*, 24.

[213] Whitaker, *Foreign Exchange*, 624–7.

market'.[214] This dealing was coordinated by the Chief Foreign Branch, which was located in the City of London, supplemented by subsidiary branches in the West End of London, Birmingham, Bradford, Liverpool, and Manchester. Barclays Bank would either provide its customers with the currency they required or purchase whatever they received by way of payment, while covering their own exposure to the foreign exchange risk they had taken on. In their 1940 handbook to staff covering foreign business, they explained how it was conducted.

> It is usual when remittances are made in foreign currency to purchase the currency at the time the instructions are sent out and for the Bank to authorise its corre-spondents to debit the Bank's account in their books. This necessitates the Bank carrying accounts in foreign currency in all the leading centres of the world so that each Foreign Branch may be in a position to supply remittances either in sterling or in foreign currency with a minimum of delay.

It was through its correspondents that Barclays operated in sterling and all other currencies, either settling the transactions abroad or making payments and remit-ting proceeds back to London. To the bank, foreign exchange and credit transactions were intertwined. Payment was not made until delivery, but the commitment to do so existed as soon as the bank accepted responsibility, creating an asset or a liability in a foreign currency that had to be matched if it was not to be left exposed.[215]

During the 1920s, it was these large banks that quickly took command of the for-eign exchange market. They were responding to the external needs of their customers and the internal requirements of the bank as exposure to fluctuations in foreign exchange became a major concern.[216] It was these large British domestic banks that possessed the financial resources necessary to invest in the highly skilled staff and telephonic equipment necessary to cope with the risks and complexities of the for-eign exchange market. In 1925, Miller reported that a 'dealer in foreign exchange in a big bank requires speed, accuracy and calmness to a greater extent than almost any other position in the financial world'.[217] By 1930, the Midland Bank maintained a team of

> dealers who make the purchase and sale contracts of foreign exchange, both for maintaining the Bank's position with each of the foreign banks with which an account in currency is kept. The dealers work by countries. The dealers have direct telephone lines into the offices of the various London foreign exchange brokers and they are also, of course, in constant cable and telephone communication with overseas foreign correspondents.[218]

---

[214] The Manchester and Liverpool District Bank: Foreign Department Minute Book (Manchester), 1 April 1925.
[215] Barclays Bank, *Handbook on Foreign Business* (1940), 2–6, 13–14, 16.
[216] Whitmore, *Money Machine*, 106–8.
[217] Miller, *The Foreign Exchange Market*, 58.
[218] Midland Bank Overseas Department: Report on Workings, 1930 (HSBC Archives), 104–5.

These dealers were also fully integrated into the London money market and enjoyed the trust of their peers.[219] The large British banks were also well placed to occupy a central position in the global foreign exchange market because London remained 'the principal exchange market of the world', according to the Bank of England in 1935.[220] As competition between the banks drove down the margin between buying and selling rates, it was these banks that could cover their costs and still generate a profit through the high volume of trading they were responsible for. The smaller banks that had entered the foreign exchange business immediately after the war, attracted by the speculative profits to be made, abandoned it, calculating that the returns were no longer justified by the risks.[221]

In 1925, Thomas compared and contrasted the pre-war and post-war experience of the banks. Before 1914,

> The exchange banker conducted a profitable and non-speculative business by supplying drafts to order drawn on his balances with agents in foreign centres, the balances being replenished from time to time by the purchase of such bankers' and commercial long bills or sight drafts as happened to be available. When rates were fairly stable and there was an absence of marked fluctuation, it was not imperative as it would be under present conditions that the banker should at once cover his sales of exchange by corresponding purchases, but it is clear that if his business of issuing drafts to order was to continue, he had to take steps to maintain his credit balances abroad or to reduce any overdraft which he might have created.

In the years before the First World War, the large British banks did not keep accounts with foreign banks, relying instead on dealing with the other banks in London. This meant that they were not well placed to conduct a foreign exchange business, which required banks to have access to money in different locations. That changed after the war. Thomas explained that 'All the big banks have of late years either inaugurated or expanded their foreign departments so that at the present time there is practically no class of foreign business which cannot be undertaken by these banks directly with agents or branches in all foreign centres of importance.' The Foreign Exchange Department of the bank was in constant communication with the other departments of a bank as it attempted to match currency commitments in terms of amount and timing. Through the use of the forward market in foreign exchange, banks could 'eliminate much of the risk which must necessarily accompany the frequent and sometimes violent movements characteristic of exchange rates in recent years.'[222]

Another witness to the transformation taking place was Dowling. He wrote in 1929 that since the end of the First World War, 'the banks had been gradually developing

---

[219] Jones, *Multinational Banking*, 139, 149, 182, 192–3; Morton, *British Finance*, 270; Collins, *Money and Banking*, 22; Truptil, *British Banks*, 136; Brown, *The Forward Market*, 13.

[220] Bank of England: Memorandum for the Committee of London Clearing bankers, 2 May 1935.

[221] E.E. Evitt, *Practical Banking, Currency and Exchange* (London: 1933), 405–8.

[222] Thomas, *Principles and Arithmetic*, 170, 175–97.

their foreign business, often effecting their transactions through the brokers who called round from bank to bank, and today the large joint-stock banks, and certain important private firms, transact the greater portion of foreign exchange business'. All these banks had dedicated Foreign Exchange Departments to carry out the business. 'Three or four highly-skilled operators sit at a table arranged so that each operator has a switchboard placing him in direct communication with thirty or forty dealers, brokers and any special customer who deals in foreign currencies.' The aim was to balance the banks' credit and debit position in each currency, but 'as orders by wire and phone are pouring in all day long it is not always an easy matter to preserve the ideal level book'. To Dowling,

> The market itself is merely a group of brokers, bankers and other dealers linked by a network of telephones and cables, and with Continental and other foreign centres. Neither are their exclusive membership formalities, nor written code of regulations to control the methods of business as in other exchanges. Anyone can deal in foreign exchange providing he has the substance and credit sufficient to gain the confidence of the other dealers.

However, from the vantage point of 1929, these immediate post-war developments were only a temporary response to the currency chaos that existed at that time. As currency stability returned, with Britain rejoining the Gold Standard, much of what had been set up became redundant. A swap transaction, for example, which combined a spot and forward deal, had allowed a bank to either lend or borrow for a specific period while covering the exchange risk. By 1929, Dowling claimed that

> One result of the general improvement in the stability of foreign currencies is a big fall in the volume of exchange operations. The necessity of covering contracts by the purchase of futures against possible loss by fluctuations of foreign currencies has, to a large effect, been eliminated. ... The amount of business in foreign currencies is, therefore, negligible compared with what it was in 1921.[223]

With currency stability, it was no longer considered necessary to engage in forward transactions to remove the risks associated with fluctuations in exchange rates.[224]

Despite Dowling's optimism, the return to the Gold Standard in 1925 had not eliminated all the risks associated with foreign exchange in the 1920s, and so the measures banks had to take to cover these remained necessary. Banks continued to keep spot balances in other currencies with their agents abroad in reciprocity for balances kept in sterling by those agents. This allowed a bank to sell forward currency that it covered by a spot purchase, which it left on its account in the other centre until the forward contract matured. This all depended on mutual trust among counterparties, not the fixed rate of exchange imposed under the Gold Standard.[225]

---

[223] S.W. Dowling, *The Exchanges of London* (London: Butterworth & Co., 1929), 208–13, 234.
[224] Deutsch, *Arbitrage*, 5, 25, 50.
[225] Evitt, 'Exchange Dealings', 457–60.

Maintaining these accounts in foreign currencies, which domestic banks increasingly did, exposed a bank to a foreign exchange risk. Spalding made this clear in 1928: 'In selling exchange to his client, the banker sells telegraphic transfers or bills of exchange drawn on funds which he had previously laid down with his foreign correspondent.'[226] The bank was committed to repaying a deposit in whichever currency the customer had chosen and so had to be ready to do so. Similarly, when agreeing a foreign currency loan, the bank had to have the money available in the required currency. This exposure was met by the British bank opening accounts with its correspondents around the world through which they could either make deposits or arrange to borrow an amount equivalent to that which they were committed to provide. These transactions were in the currency that was used by the correspondent bank in its everyday business. In opening these accounts using their existing correspondent links, the large British domestic banks placed themselves in the position of being able to not only cover their foreign exchange exposure across the entire spectrum of amount, time, place, and currency but also provide this facility to other banks.[227] It was in this way that the foreign exchange market worked in the 1920s whether before or after the return to the Gold Standard in 1925. As Spring-Rice reported in 1929, 'The market in foreign exchange nowadays is almost wholly between banks, and predominantly based on telegraphic transfers.'[228]

This market relied on trust between counterparty banks, and when that evaporated, as it did in 1931 when Britain left the Gold Standard, it broke down. During the crisis, foreign exchange dealers in London found it impossible to cover their positions as foreign banks were unwilling to deal in £s against their own currency. However, that hiatus lasted only two weeks, after which a normal market gradually returned, but one hampered by government-imposed exchange restrictions. A month after the crisis, a relatively free foreign exchange market was operating again in London across a wide range of currencies but not all. Germany and Italy were major problems, as were many Central European and Latin American countries like Brazil.[229] Nevertheless, the overall resilience in the face of a global crisis was evidence of the strength that the London foreign exchange market had built up by then. That resilience depended on counterparty trust as Duke emphasized in 1937: 'In order to be able to supply any demand for foreign currency, which may be made of it, a bank must hold or have access to deposits in all the important centres of the world.'[230] Even in the world depression of the 1930s, when international trade and finance was greatly reduced and government barriers impeded the free flow of funds around the world, it was these links between banks that provided the world with a means of making and receiving payments, lending surplus funds, borrowing to cover a temporary deficit, and both covering and settling foreign exchange transactions.[231] It even delivered

---

[226] Spalding, *Dictionary of the World's Currencies*, 55, 82, 89, 125–6.
[227] Angas, *Problems of the Foreign Exchanges*; Barclays Bank, *Foreign Exchange Control*, 4, 8.
[228] Spring-Rice, 'Financial Machinery of the City', 15.
[229] Evitt, 'Exchange Dealings', 457–60.
[230] Duke, *Bills, Bullion*, 14, 17, 80, 86–9.
[231] Einzig, 'Branch Banks', 23–5; Einzig, *Textbook on Foreign Exchange*, 147.

relatively stable exchange rates once the turmoil of the early post-war years died down.[232] Key to this bank-based foreign exchange market was the constant ebb and flow through London, as the Bank of England noted in 1935: 'London is the principal exchange market of the world.'[233] That all ended with the outbreak of the Second World War. Reflecting in 1946 on what happened at the Midland Bank, which had invested heavily in specialist equipment and staff, Wadsworth reported that 'When war began, dealings on the foreign exchange market ceased; all rates of exchange for sterling were fixed by the authorities and competitive buying and selling of foreign currencies ended.'[234] What had begun during the First World War, and was then developed during the 1920s and 1930s, came to an abrupt end with the beginning of the Second World War. It was to be many years after that war before the foreign exchange market would eventually re-emerge.

However, what had been achieved up to then was not the result of the banks alone and the dealers they employed. Others stepped into the void created by the demise of stock exchange arbitrage and the active intermediation of transnational banks. What the Big Five banks could contribute was an unrivalled depth and breadth of assets and liabilities, a network of global connections, and the ability to command the confidence of counterparties. In 1937, the Bank of England claimed that

> One reason among many others why London has the largest and most varied forward exchange market in the world and why this market has been retained is the care the Bank of England have taken to prevent banking failures affecting the completion of contracts. ... This factor alone, together with the large variety of strong names, makes intra-market transactions relatively simple and concentrates the world's surplus of forward transactions in London.[235]

The result was that within ten years of the ending of the Gold Standard in 1919, with Britain's departure, a new foreign exchange market had emerged, centred on the activities of dealers located in the Big Five British banks. It was their constant buying and selling that restored stability to global currencies once the chaotic trading of the early post-war years had died away. The contribution that they made continued even after the Gold Standard had been restored in 1925 with Britain's return, and then expanded in the wake of Britain's departure again in 1931. However, the parameters within which this new foreign exchange market operated were heavily influenced by the actions taken by governments and central banks in the 1930s. Nevertheless, it was the dealing rooms of the Big Five banks that facilitated the constant balancing of assets and liabilities across different currencies, without which the routine business of international trade and finance could not be conducted. Though dismissed as speculation, in the same way as stock exchange arbitrage before the First World War had been, it was the continuous trading of one currency against another, for both

[232] Officer, *Dollar-Sterling Gold Points*, 103, 192, 276.
[233] Memorandum from Bank of England to the Committee of London Clearing Banks, 2 May 1935.
[234] J. Wadsworth, *Counter Defensive: The Story of a Bank in Battle* (London: 1946), 9, 11, 18, 30.
[235] Bank of England, *Some Aspects of Forward Exchange in Relation to Control*, September 1937.

immediate and future delivery, that ensured that exchange rates remained relatively stable and so exporters and importers, lenders and borrowers, and investors and issuers could continue to engage in their normal business or, at least, the semblance of it that existed in the 1930s.

However, the dealers located in the Big Five banks were not the only new players in the foreign exchange market that emerged between the wars. The volume and variety of activity in this emerging interbank foreign exchange market also required additional intermediaries in the form of brokers. Banks had long turned to brokers in the discount market, where they acted as intermediaries, borrowing money from some and buying bills from others. Scott, who was the manager of the London office of the Union Bank of Scotland, explained in 1921 the part that these bill brokers continued to play:

> The advantage of buying from the broker is, that you can get any maturity that you wish, and to whatever extent you wish; whereas, if a bank is only discounting bills for its own customers, it has to take them as and when offered, consequently the bank may have large maturities at one time with considerable blanks in between the dates of maturity of its bills as a whole.

Conversely, banks could sell bills to put themselves in funds. He then added that

> The great advantage to the banks of doing business with the brokers instead of direct with the sellers of bills ... is derived from the fact that the bill-brokers are specialist in bills; they know better than anyone else the standing and means of the parties on the bills, and they watch closely how much paper of the different firms and houses is current on the market. The banker has the benefit of this expert information, and he also has the guarantee of the discount house for any bills bought from it.[236]

What was now required were brokers performing a similar role to those in the discount market, where all transactions were in sterling, but covering different currencies, as this could not all be done by direct dealing between the banks.[237]

There were numerous banks in London that did not do sufficient foreign exchange business to justify the expenses involved in setting up a dealing team or persuade the dealers in the big banks to do business directly with them. Nor could many of them qualify as trusted counterparties when trading with each other or with the dealers. Under these circumstances, they employed brokers who acted as intermediaries between the banks using their trusted counterparty status.[238] There was even a need for brokers to act between the Big Five banks when they wished to keep their identity hidden so as not to reveal the position they had taken. Brokers were also able to construct matches on behalf of dealers as it was not always possible for them to

---

[236] Scott, 'The Bill-Broker', 61–2.
[237] Bank of England: *The Times Foreign Exchange Quotations*, 21 May 1928.
[238] National Bank, *Foreign Exchange* (1923), 9.

complete deals by trading directly with each other. The importance of brokers to the foreign exchange market was emphasized in 1928 by Fraenkel, who worked for the Anglo-International Bank. He divided the foreign exchange market in two. One half comprised banks dealing directly with each other in large amounts, but that was confined to the few that could command the trust of their peers. Direct dealing avoided brokerage charges, which was an important consideration in what was a fiercely competitive market. 'The English joint-stock banks were certainly the chief dealers in the market as far as dollars were concerned but ... the foreign banks were foremost dealers in the market when transactions in Continental currencies were taken into account.' Some transactions could take the entire day to complete, or even longer, if the amount involved was large.

> Business could not be attracted to the London Foreign Exchange market unless the principals in the market were prepared to deal in large amounts and to deal at once or almost at once. Under present conditions this could not possibly be done through a broker and therefore direct deals with other banks were necessary. ... Telephone calls are expensive and from the Continent in particular. If rates and amount could not be quoted almost at once, the Continent would stop phoning and the London market lose good customers.

He estimated that half the trading was done directly between banks, but that left the rest to be handled by brokers. Brokers were in contact with numerous dealers, both on the telephone and 'informally each day, say at lunch', and were aware of all that was going on in the market, and so they were essential sources of information. 'The broker has a very definite position on the Exchange market and is far too useful to the dealer for the latter to allow him ever to go out of business.'[239]

Foreign exchange brokers had operated in London before the First World War, but their numbers were few and the amount of business done was low. In 1907, the City of London Directory listed only one firm of foreign exchange brokers, Jourdan and Newton, who had begun as stockbrokers. In 1909, they were joined by Sichel & Co before the directory ceased to list trades.[240] The London Post Office Directory did not begin listing firms of foreign exchange brokers until 1922. Of those listed in 1922, five appeared in 1914 as Exchange Brokers, who undertook all type of financial activities. In 1922, seventeen foreign exchange broking firms were listed, rising to thirty-one in 1923 before reaching forty in 1924, which was the highest number ever achieved. The number for 1925 was thirty-eight, dropping to thirty-four in 1926, which was the year Britain rejoined the Gold Standard, but then recovered to thirty-eight in 1927 and fell back to thirty-five in 1928, thirty-three in 1929, and thirty-two in 1930 before stabilizing at around thirty for the rest of the decade. There were twenty-eight firms of foreign exchange brokers in 1939 and thirty in 1940 before collapsing to fourteen

---

[239] Notes of Conversations with Mr Fraenkel at the Anglo-International Bank, 30 May 1928, 15 August 1928, 20 August 1928, 1 September 1928, 13 November 1928, 28 November 1928.
[240] *City of London Directory*, Foreign Exchange Brokers, 1907–9.

in 1941 and nine by 1945. At that stage, the foreign exchange market no longer existed being under the control of the Bank of England.[241]

What changed the demand for foreign exchange brokers was the transformation of trading in currencies, which grew exponentially in volume and variety after the First World War.[242] Though attempts were made to capture the volume of trading, writing in 1930, Mr Speed, from the Westminster Bank, considered that 'There is no means of accurately estimating the turnover of the market.' Nevertheless, he was of the view that between eight and ten currencies were actively traded on a daily business.[243] In addition to the extensive trading in currencies such as the US$, the French franc, and the German mark after the First World War, there were transactions in many others in London. In 1926, daily turnover of the Spanish currency was equivalent to £200,000, Denmark £30,000, Czechoslovakia £10,000, Austria £7,000, Finland and Romania £5,000, Greece £3,000, Yugoslavia £2,000, Poland and Portugal £1,000, Hungary £300, and Bulgaria £100.[244] Where turnover was as low as this, the roles of dealer and broker were combined, as it was necessary to act as an agent and make a market. 'Competition is absent and there is therefore no incentive to quote fine rates' was the verdict of the Bank of England in 1928.[245] In contrast, there was high-volume trading in the US$ in London. In January 1928, the Bank of England estimated that the daily turnover in the London foreign exchange market was £5.2 million of which £4.1 million (77 per cent) was in the US$ and $1.2 million (23 per cent) was other currencies, mainly the German mark and the French franc. The London foreign exchange market traded in fifteen different currencies that year, including the Indian rupee and the Canadian $ as well as a wide range from Europe, such as the Roumanian lei and the Yugoslavian dinar. It was reported that 'considerable business is transacted with the Continental centres and transactions take place with every part of the world' and that 'there are dealings in most classes of foreign exchange business'. Nevertheless, it was pointed out that 'spot and forward telegraphic transfers predominate', which implies that it was the market where UK£s and US$s were bought and sold that lay at the heart of the London foreign exchange market in the 1920s.[246]

This high-volume trading was the product of money market activity as banks took advantage of differential interest rates in London and New York.[247] Increasingly, in the 1920s, activity in the foreign exchange market was generated by banks borrowing and lending amongst each other as already took place in the discount market. By

---

[241] *London Post Office Directory*, Number of Foreign Exchange Brokers 1922–45. This lists firms and thus does not capture the number of individual brokers or those who engaged in foreign exchange broking as a subsidiary activity. However, it does provide a measure of the number of foreign exchange brokers.

[242] *Wall Street Journal*, 20 March 1919, 22 March 1919, 11 June 1919, 9 July 1919, 18 July 1919, 22 July 1919, 5 January 1919, 12 January 1927; Bank of England Memorandum: London Foreign Exchange Market, 17 June 1935.

[243] Bank of England: London Foreign Exchange Market, 7 August 1930.

[244] M.W. Marshall & Co to Chief Cashier, Bank of England, 3 September 1926.

[245] Bank of England: Confidential Memorandum, 4 December 1928.

[246] Bank of England, Approximate Amounts of Foreign Currency Changing Hands on the London Market Daily, 28 January 1928.

[247] Bank of England: Memorandum, 9 March 1929.

buying 'forward' and selling 'spot', a bank obtained the use of the money for the intervening period. Conversely, by selling 'forward' and buying 'spot', the bank employed money for that period. The difference in price between the forward and the spot price represented the interest paid or received. This made the foreign exchange market an integral component of the London money market but one that used different currencies rather than restricting itself to sterling.[248]

Through a foreign exchange deal, a banker could either employ surplus cash or obtain additional funds on a temporary basis. That made it an extension of its existing business of borrowing and lending whether directly with retail customers or with other banks.[249] However, unlike the discount market, the foreign exchange market never made a complete transition to an accepted component of the London money market. It lacked the official recognition afforded to the discount market by the Bank of England or the status that went with being a regulated market, such as the LSE for stocks and bonds, or the likes of the Baltic Exchange or the London Metal Exchange for commodities. It also suffered by comparison with the stability of currencies under the Gold Standard. The foreign exchange market was where currencies were bought and sold, with the wider the price difference, the higher the profit, as was the case in the immediate post-war years. According to Dudley Ward in 1922, 'The foreign exchange market, in these days of rapid and wide fluctuations, has become the hunting-ground of the speculator.'[250] As a director of the British Overseas Bank, he spoke with some authority because it was heavily involved in foreign exchange dealing in the 1920s. His views resonated with the public and left a lasting legacy, not least because they were endorsed by Maynard Keynes, the leading economist of the interwar years. Dudley Ward had been chosen by Keynes to contribute to the publication he was editing on reconstruction in Europe, on behalf of the *Manchester Guardian*. That meant his comments received wide publicity, and his description of the chaotic state of the foreign exchange market influenced Keynes, who favoured a managed currency.[251] However, one of Dudley Ward's colleagues at the British Overseas Bank, Bickham Sweet-Escott, who joined it in 1930, described Dudley Ward as 'far from being a City man. He was much more like a Treasury mandarin or a don'.[252] What Sweet-Escott's comments reveal is that Dudley Ward had a limited knowledge of banking, let alone the foreign exchange market, and he was expressing his views at a time when currency trading was at its most volatile. Britain had only left the Gold Standard in 1919, and both the German mark and French franc, especially the former, were under extreme pressure, as all currencies had yet to establish new relative values in the aftermath of the First World War. The foreign exchange market

---

[248] Forward Exchange: Views of Sir Henry Strakosch, 7 February 1924; Bank of England: Memoranda on London Foreign Exchange Market, 27 April 1928, 9 March 1929; Bank of England, Sterling Dollar Exchange, 18 July 1928; Spalding, *Dictionary of the World's Currencies*, 55, 89, 125; Deutsch, *Arbitrage*, 50.

[249] Spring-Rice, 'Financial Machinery of the City', 15; Deutsch, *Arbitrage*, 50.

[250] Ward, 'Foreign Exchange Market in London', 9–10.

[251] See P. Clarke, 'Keynes and the Manchester Guardian's Reconstruction Supplements', *Annals of the Fondazione Luigi Einaudi*, LI (2017); Keynes, *A Tract on Monetary Reform*.

[252] Sweet-Escott, *Gallant Failure*, 1–3, 6, 19–20, 30, 55, 63–6, 84–6, 91.

then evolved over the course of the 1920s and 1930s, before being closed down on the outbreak of the Second World War. By then, the speculative activity of the early 1920s was a distant memory but one that continued to influence attitudes towards the foreign exchange market.

Regulation and Control, 1919–1939

The assumption is usually made that once trading begins, a market appears and there the story ends.[253] However, that is only the beginning because such a market needs to be organized and policed and this takes time and money. Rules and regulations need to be devised that cope with the diverse interests of participants, deal with the complexities of trading, cover counterparty risk, and overcome attempts at fraud and manipulation. These must be generally accepted and ways to ensure compliance must be introduced. Overcoming all these obstacles took time and ingenuity with numerous examples of delays and even failures to achieve an acceptable outcome. Moves to regulate the London stock market began in the eighteenth century, but it took until 1801 before an acceptable formula was agreed upon.[254] It took even longer in the case of the Amsterdam stock market, where trading dated from the seventeenth century, but a formal stock exchange was not established until 1876.[255] Even with multiple models to choose from, it took years before formal stock exchanges were established in China in the early twentieth century though active markets existed in the late nineteenth.[256] Considering the chaotic conditions that surrounded foreign exchange trading in the wake of the First World War, it should not be surprising that placing the market on a regulated basis was no easy matter, and so it proved. Even by the time the foreign exchange market was closed on the outbreak of the Second World War, it had failed to establish itself as either a regulated exchange or receive the official recognition and guaranteed support of the Bank of England.

This was not because of any lack of effort from those involved with the foreign exchange market. There were attempts to agree a regulatory structure for it in the early 1920s. W.H. Taylor, Chief Manager of the Colonial and Foreign Department at Lloyds Bank, was the main person behind these moves. In 1924, he complained that 'the market is devoid of any organisation existing for its governance, or that is able to speak with any kind of authority', and referred to certain aspects of the market as being in 'chaos'.[257] He was keen to introduce regulations, establish a foreign exchange

---

[253] This section makes extensive use of material from the Bank of England archives—see Bibliography.

[254] H.V. Bowen, '"The Pests of Human Society": Stockbrokers, Jobbers and Speculators in Mid-Eighteenth-Century Britain', *History*, 78 (1993), 38–40, 45–7, 52–3.

[255] L. Petram, *The World's First Stock Exchange* (New York: Columbia University Business School Publishing, 2014), 31, 61, 81–2, 98, 125, 140, 154, 163–76, 181, 196–211.

[256] Niv Horesh, 'Gerschenkron Redux? Analysing New Evidence on Joint-Stock Enterprise in Pre-war Shanghai', *Asian-Pacific Economic Literature*, (2015), 27–30, 42.

[257] Foreign Exchange Market Memorandum by W.H. Taylor, Chief Manager of the Colonial and Foreign Department, Lloyds Bank, 21 March 1924 (Foreign Exchange Committee Minutes, London Metropolitan Archives).

clearing house, and get the Bank of England involved.[258] All these came to nothing. With Britain's return to the Gold Standard in 1925, the assumption was made that the foreign exchange market would fade away as exchange rates stabilized. However, even without the belief that the foreign exchange market was only temporary, there were fundamental difficulties to be overcome before it could emerge as either a version of the LSE or the London discount market, which were two of the possible models that it could copy. It was never obvious which of these models best fitted the foreign exchange market, or neither, especially as the increasing use made of the telephone was undermining traditional face-to-face trading whether on the floor of an exchange or visiting individual offices. The *Financial News* reported in 1936 that 'Today it is almost as easy to transact foreign exchange business with Paris, New York, or even with more distant centres, as it is to do business with the bank situated across the road.'[259] Though long-distance calls were expensive, the combination of national and international telephony transformed the ability of foreign exchange dealers to communicate directly with each other, regardless of where they were located as long as a connection existed.[260] Similarly, brokers stopped visiting bank offices looking for business, relying on the telephone instead.[261]

The huge increase in the volume and variety of foreign exchange business in the immediate post-war years attracted many to take up the business, whether as dealers, brokers, agents, or any combination that would generate profits. They included merchant banks like Brown Shipley or lone operators such as Leopold Joseph, who had managed Swiss Bankverein's city office from 1906 until 1917.[262] One of the established brokers, Edward B. Meyer, wrote in 1930 that

> Since the war we have maintained a well-organised Foreign Exchange Department with private line connections to all the important London banks, and as the result of specialising we are unquestionably the only London broker who has a constant market in Dutch Guilders. We are also regarded as being the leading broker in Italian lire, and as ranking among the largest dealers in German marks.[263]

In the 1920s, the distinction between brokers and dealers was fluid as Mr Frankau of the Anglo-International Bank explained in 1928: 'A dealer acted as an agent as far as his customers were concerned but he certainly did not act as an agent but a principal when employing the funds of the Bank in one centre or another.' As brokerage charges in London were 'very high in some cases', dealers in banks were always tempted to avoid them by trading directly with each other. 'Brokers were necessary to an extent

---

[258] Memorandum on Establishing a Foreign Exchange Clearing House, by W.H. Taylornager, Colonial and Foreign Department, Lloyds Bank, 21 March 1924, Revision 3 April 1924; Letter to Each of the London Clearing Banks, 27 June 1924.

[259] *Financial News*, 3 September 1936; 4 September 1936.

[260] Memorandum of Conversation with Mr Ogg at the Anglo-International Bank, 8 January 1929.

[261] Memorandum: London Foreign Exchange Market, 17 June 1935.

[262] Correspondence between Brown Shipley and Brown Brothers, 30 August 1922, 5 February 1924, 30 July 1924; M. Anson and T. Gourvish, *Leopold Joseph: A History, 1919–2000* (London: 2002), 5–6.

[263] Edward B. Meyer to Bank of England, 26 June 1930.

and deals were occasionally given to them.' However, the preference among dealers was to trade among themselves as this reduced counterparty risk and avoided the payment of commission. 'Dealers naturally dealt with friends.' Frankau then provided an example of the type of business conducted between banks. 'If the Anglo-International Bank were approached for, say 10 million marks, they would telephone to one of their friends and obtain the necessary currency at the middle rate ruling at the time the customer would obtain a good rate and the Anglo-International Bank and their friend would make reasonable profit.' Banks would regularly deal directly with each other when the amounts were large, while passing smaller amounts through brokers.

> Business could not be attracted to the London Foreign Exchange market unless the principals in the market were prepared to deal in large amounts and to deal at once or almost at once. Under present conditions this could not possibly be done through a broker and therefore direct deals with other banks were necessary. Telephone calls from the Continent in particular are expensive. If a dealer in London could not offer a reasonably large amount of currency at a good rate at once or almost at once, such calls would stop and the London market lose good business.[264]

During the speculative frenzy that followed Britain's departure from the Gold Standard in 1919, movements in exchange rates were so rapid, and turnover so great, that dealers and brokers had to quote firm buying and selling prices or risk losing the sale or purchase.[265] It was estimated in 1928 that 'The normal interval during which an offer is held good in the London market is three minutes.'[266] As the market settled down, especially after Britain rejoined the Gold Standard in 1925, profitable opportunities in the foreign exchange market quickly declined. The Bank of England reported in 1928 that whereas in the early 1920s, 'The Big Banks were connected by private telephone lines to perhaps as many as twenty different brokers but they now seldom used more than five or six, according to the currencies in which these specialised.'[267] By then, a clear division had emerged between the dealers and brokers. The dealers were employed by the banks, and they made their profit from the spread between the bid and asking prices that they quoted. In 1928, there were at least 120 of these. In contrast, the brokers operated on their own buying and selling on commission. They did not take a position but acted either for their retail clients or as inter-dealer brokers. They numbered over forty in 1928.[268] There continued to be those who combined dealing and broking, specializing in those currencies in which the volume of trading was low.[269]

[264] Interview with Mr Frankau of the Anglo-International Bank, 30 May 1928.
[265] Memorandum: London Foreign Exchange Market, 16 December 1935.
[266] Bank of England: Memorandum on Foreign Exchanges, 10 December 1928.
[267] Bank of England: Memorandum on Foreign Exchanges, 17 May 1928.
[268] Bank of England, London Foreign Exchange Market, 1 May 1928, Addendum 17 May 1928; Committee of London Foreign Exchange Managers: Report by George Bolton, 9 June 1936.
[269] Bank of England: Names to be Accepted in Connection with Foreign Exchange Dealings, 3 November 1930.

One broker, Frederick Dixon, provided a personal account in 1939 of the way his career as a foreign exchange broker had been transformed. On 1 April 1914, he became a partner of S.P. Scaramanga. 'During the war restrictions were imposed but fortunately in the early days there was an extraordinary activity in dollars.' Dixon then joined the RAF and was not demobilized until December 1919. 'Business in exchanges again became active in March 1919', but 90 per cent of the profits he made were taken by the Excess Profits Tax and Income Tax.

> The boom had attracted a large number of competitors. Moreover, the majority of the brokers engaged a number of young assistants—a course to which our senior partner—Christo—would not consent—and generally speaking, gave a better service than we did as they kept in closer contact with the banks. These two factors had their natural effect, and we did less and less of the bank-to-bank business. The nature of the business had changed. Brokers were quoting firm (dealing) prices to the banks and therefore taking risks, which it was not the business of the broker to assume. The bankers naturally gave the business to those who quoted firm. Moreover, the exchange business between banks is perhaps the most exacting of all broking and requires young men. It became necessary for us to cultivate other businesses with our customers such as the short term (3 months) investment of surplus sterling or dollars (swap and deposit, the granting of acceptance credits and other credits to banks abroad and the like; also we were reappointed agents of a New York house—Passeri, brokers—which cabled us orders in banking and exchange for execution on the London market.

A swap transaction involved buying currency spot and selling forward. With the currency acquired, they either bought foreign short-dated treasuries or deposited it with a well-known institution at interest. In 1922–3, he became involved in arranging credits with British and American banks for banks in Italy, Czechoslovakia, Austria, and Hungary. These contacts led him to relocate to Berlin in 1925 where he operated as a broker, arranging German borrowing in London.

After the failure of the German banks in 1931, and the restrictions imposed, Dixon's business dried up and he returned to Britain via Paris, but with very depleted funds. In London, he tried to revive the business of S.P. Scaramanga: 'During my absence in Germany the foreign exchange business in London had fallen to nothing. ... The foreign exchange business of the firm was carried on with moderate success by the older Scaramanga and his son, my partners.' Dixon 'again obtained permission to put private lines into the banks, and engaged six dealers. But the foreign exchange business was not successful, owing to international difficulties, and losses were made'. He conducted few foreign exchange transactions after 1936 and only acted as a broker. 'We never carried any currencies.' The foreign exchange business was finally abandoned in 1939, after he had moved into other financial activities, including the finance of a wolfram mine in Czechoslovakia. 'From 1922 the foreign exchange business definitely declined mainly owing to increased competition in the market and to the elder Scaramanga's conservative and old-fashioned business methods—he refused to make firm prices, to act as a dealer as others in the market did—he was a broker and remained one.' The Scaramangas and Dixon were squeezed out by those brokers willing to take greater risks and adopt new ways of working. To Dixon, who had experience of both the pre- and post-war foreign exchange markets, the scale and ways of working was fundamentally different. In the 1920s, it was the new entrants who succeeded, because they were willing to adapt to those changes, while the established brokers stuck to what they had always done and so were bypassed. By the 1930s, the foreign exchange business had changed yet again, making life difficult for all brokers, which is why Dixon gave it up. What was common throughout, as Dixon explained, was trading in the foreign exchange market depended on counterparty trust, which was not only confined to that between the dealers working for the Big Five banks but also extended to all those involved, including the brokers. 'Everyone in the foreign exchange business expects and deserves to be trusted.'[270]

It was relatively easy to establish trust between the dealers employed by the Big Five banks. The size and scale of these banks meant that they could stand behind every deal and police the behaviour of those who worked for them. They had a proven record of doing so across all areas of banking. The problem arose when transactions extended beyond the dealers employed by those banks. With more transactions bringing in more participants involving more currencies and more complex deals, the issue of counterparty risk became a serious one in the 1920s and remained so in the 1930s. The point was made in 1930 that 'Dealers in Foreign Exchange who employ brokers usually supply such brokers with a list of names they are prepared to accept without reference and the amounts to which they can go.'[271] It was in that way the dealers dealt with counterparty risk when it extended beyond those working for other large banks in Britain or abroad. One who was conscious of this issue was George Bolton. In 1936, he produced a report for the Bank of England that detailed the development of the foreign exchange market in London since the First World War and highlighted the steps that needed to be taken for it to achieve the acceptance and respectability it now deserved. Underlying that was the reduction or removal of counterparty risk. He began by referring to the pre-First World War foreign exchange market, which was dominated by a group of German, French, and Swiss universal banks along with a few established British merchant banks. The reputation of this restricted circle of participants meant that counterparty risk was not an issue. A telephone market was developing, but this was a limited affair and largely brought in the large British joint-stock banks, and so counterparty risk could also be discounted there.

---

[270] Bankruptcy of Frederick Timothy Dixon, Foreign Exchange Broker, 9 September 1939 (BT 226/5073): Statement by F.T. Dixon, 21 August 1939; Bankruptcy Proceedings, 20 December 1939.

[271] Names to be Accepted in Connection with Foreign Exchange Dealings, 3 November 1930.

It was the war that caused a fundamental change. Bolton went on to describe this post-war market.

> Profits were large, risks appeared negligible and practically every financial insti-
> tution in London blossomed out either with a new or a greatly enlarged foreign
> exchange department. In no branch of finance had practice and technique
> advanced so rapidly to an apparent fundamental simplification of such an order
> that an operator needed only the minimum of intelligence together with a facil-
> ity for mental arithmetic to make profits. Thus a completely new type of market
> developed in London without tradition, practically without personality and a com-
> plete lack of any supervision or control except that imposed on individual firms by
> experience or fearful ignorance.

In his opinion, this market was rife with corruption and counterparty risk though it improved, especially after 1928, 'due to more capable management and a large reduction in profits'. With the abandonment of the Gold Standard in 1931, trading in foreign exchange expanded and what was now required was to put that on a sounder basis. What he advocated was the establishment of an organization for the foreign exchange market that had the authority to impose rules and regulations while leaving trading to be as free as possible: 'If we wish to keep our national tradition and incli-nation towards free markets and individualism the foreign exchange market needs to impose on itself a condition of controlled freedom and to accept some degree of direction from the authorities.'[272]

George Bolton was well qualified to make these observations and the recommen-dations he drew from them, as he explained in his memoirs. He had started in the City of London in 1917, working for the French bank, Société Générale, whose foreign exchange business expanded rapidly after the Armistice of November 1918.

> It should be remembered that no-one knew anything about foreign exchange mar-
> kets, and techniques were invented as we went along. Bankers brought up on
> the Gold Standard methods—occasional shipments of gold bars and coin to help
> maintain fixed rates of exchange plus Bank Rate—regarded the Bill on London the
> only means of financing foreign trade and were quite at sea and paid little or no
> attention to the daily operation of the exchange market, and in most cases had no
> capacity or desire to formulate a policy.

He left Société Générale in 1921 to work as a foreign exchange dealer for the stock-broker turned investment bank, Helbert Wagg. From there, he was recruited by the Bank of England to assist in their foreign exchange department, which was being rapidly expanded after Britain left the Gold Standard in 1931. He joined the Bank of England on 1 January 1933 as an assistant to Robert Kay, head of the foreign exchange department. When Kay died in 1935, Bolton replaced him, leaving his

---

[272] The Development of the Foreign Exchange Market: A Report by George Bolton, 8 July 1936.

deputy, Cyril Hawker, to handle day-to-day foreign exchange operations. What he faced at the Bank of England was an institution that was 'wholly adapted to the automatic operation of the gold standard' and

> had no knowledge or experience of, nor access to, the Exchange markets, and was still trying to control fluctuating sterling exchange and money rates by gold standard methods. Its operations in gold went through Rothschilds and it dealt in foreign exchange through a single broker. As a result it was necessary to build up both a network and expertise.

Over the course of the 1930s, the staff at the foreign exchange department at the Bank of England rose from 20 to 1,500.

Bolton claimed to be instrumental in the organization of a Foreign Exchange Brokers Association 'for the purpose of making the foreign exchange market more respectable'. What Bolton, like Dixon, had identified was the importance of counter-party trust in the foreign exchange market, especially as trading expanded beyond a few large banks.

> Banks dealt directly with each other in foreign exchange, spot and forward, payment being effected simultaneously in two markets. As a great deal of trust was, and is, involved in such transactions, in the early stages (developed after 1919) only banks of international reputation could deal. But as other markets developed, particularly Paris and Zurich, brokers began to establish themselves as channels of communication and makers of rates.

Bolton considered many of these brokers to be 'undesirables'. Most came from Central Europe and, initially, the banks lacked the knowledge, expertise, and systems to control what they were doing because of its volume and novelty. It was only by the late 1920s that the banks were able to exercise some discipline over this emerging foreign exchange market. A more disciplined market emerged after 1931, which Bolton attributed to the influence that the Bank of England exerted in eliminating the fringe element. 'The dominant position that the Bank of England had attained in the exchange markets meant a great loss of earnings and reputation to brokers who were outside the charmed circle.' By acting in concert with the Big Five banks, the Bank of England could refuse to conduct any business with those brokers who refused to obey the rules and regulations that the others had agreed to. The outcome was a close working relationship between the brokers, the banks, and the Bank of England in the 1930s. This was reflected in the promise that Bolton made to Jones, the Chairman of the Brokers Association, that 'in the event of war, the market would be closed but that alternative employment would be available to all brokers and their employees.'[273]

---

[273] Sir George Bolton, *Memoirs* (Bank of England Archives, 13 January 1977).

Over the course of the 1920s and 1930s, the London foreign exchange market experienced a complete transformation, which can be traced from various contemporary accounts. These began by noting the demise of the pre-war foreign exchange market, which was closely identified with the meetings held at the Royal Exchange, ignoring all its other components such as the role played by the transnational banks and stock exchange arbitrage. *The Times* reported in 1920 that

> An institution that has existed in the City for a generation is about to come to an end, owing to the altered conditions existing at the present day. We refer to the meetings of merchants, bankers, and brokers which take place in the Royal Exchange, each Tuesday and Thursday (post days as they are called), for dealings in foreign exchange. Originally these dealings were chiefly in the form of bills; nowadays, with the telephones and telegraphs in operation, dealings in foreign exchange take place at a furious pace all day long, and they are mainly in cable transfers, which fluctuate every few minutes. The necessity for the old post-day meetings has therefore largely disappeared; hence it has been decided for the present to discontinue these bi-weekly meetings after Thursday next week.

The last meeting was scheduled for 30 December 1920. With the end to such meetings, the London foreign exchange market ceased to have any kind of membership criteria, formal organization, or recognized meeting place, leading to descriptions that concentrated upon its lack of discipline and speculative trading.[274]

One of the first to produce a detailed account of the new foreign exchange market that emerged after the First World War was Gregory in 1921. What impressed him was the scale and pace of activity. 'With the telephones and telegraphs in operation, dealings in foreign exchange take place at a furious pace all day long, and they are mainly in cable transfers, which fluctuate every few minutes.' Due to exchange-rate volatility, banks matched the currency of their assets and liabilities on a continuous basis by trading with each other either directly or via brokers. This was done over the telephone or the telegraph, which provided instant or near instant methods of communication.[275] It was the foreign exchange market's lack of a trading floor or even meeting place, along with the absence of a formal organization and agreed rules and regulations, that impressed Dudley Ward in 1922:

> The London market has no central meeting place and dealers, in the course of business, never see each other in the flesh. The market is nothing more than a close network of telephones connecting up dealers and brokers, and spreading out further by telephone to the provinces and to nearer continental centres and by cable to all the rest of the world. The acceleration of business by this means are enormous. ... Just as there is no essential institution, so also there is no formal membership of the exchange market. Anyone who wishes may deal in exchange

---

[274] 'The End of On "Change"', *The Times*, 24 December 1920.
[275] Gregory, *Foreign Exchange*, 21–2.

if he can find others to deal with him. In practice, however, what may be called the wholesale dealing is confined to the joint stock banks and the larger banking houses, many of whom, especially in the former group, have only taken up the business since the war.[276]

By 1925, more detailed descriptions of the newly emerging foreign exchange market appeared, possibly motivated by its anticipated decline as Britain returned to the presumed stability of the Gold Standard that year. These accounts covered the volume of trading being conducted, the nature of the participants, the speed of the transactions, and its international dimension. The work by Miller focused on the work of the dealers and the brokers. 'The broker is an intermediary ... the dealer is a principal.' The dealers were employed by the big banks and required

> speed, accuracy and calmness to a greater extent than almost any other position in the financial world ... allowing for the payment of brokerage, it is very seldom that a dealer can make a profit by buying a currency spot through one broker and selling it simultaneously through another broker. ... It is often only a matter of seconds before knowledge of any pronounced change in a rate becomes disseminated among all the brokers.

In contrast, the brokers worked for themselves, specialized in particular currencies, and were paid commission by their clients. They required little capital, operated in small teams of around five with the same number of backup staff, and their main expense was the private lines they maintained to the offices of banks and finance houses. What Miller emphasized was the importance of trust between brokers and dealers in the absence of any formal organization to the market.[277] Lever's 1925 book, for which he received assistance from S.H. Wallis at the British Overseas Bank, was designed as more a general guide to the foreign exchange market for those whose curiosity had been whetted by the speculative outbursts of the early 1920s. 'The London Foreign Exchange Market, in fact, consists of nothing more than a close network of telephones connecting up the dealers and brokers and spreading out further to the provinces and to the nearer continental centres, and by cable to the rest of the world.' What impressed him was the technology of the foreign exchange market with its 'sound-proof cabins for trunk calls, mechanical slide-rule parity machines for calculations and private lines to cable companies for ensuring facilities for the despatch of orders to New York'. It took only eight minutes to complete a London/New York transaction. With no central exchange, no formal rules, and no control of membership, 'anyone can do foreign exchange who can persuade other people to deal with him. ... There is a market all day long'. Nevertheless, the business was confined to a small number of brokers and dealers because the need for speed, and the degree of counterparty risk necessitated a high level of mutual trust.[278]

[276] Ward, 'Foreign Exchange Market in London', 9–10.
[277] Miller, *The Foreign Exchange Market*, 54–8.
[278] Lever, *Foreign Exchange from the Investor's Point of View*, 85–7.

Thomas' 1925 book took as its theme the mechanics of the foreign exchange market, which was driven by 'colossal' turnover conducted at speed due to the frequent and violent fluctuations in exchange rates. There were around 150 dealers who were located 'in the foreign exchange departments of the British and foreign banks and of the various financial houses in the City, and are engaged throughout the day in the purchase and sale of foreign currencies on behalf of their respective institutions'. In addition, there were around fifty brokers. 'Most of these brokers can lay claim to long years of experience as actual exchange brokers, chiefly in connection with the purchase and sale of foreign coupons, bonds, and notes, or as bill brokers in connection with the purchase and sales of bills of exchange.' However, there were others who lacked this experience and had been attracted by the potential profits to be made because of the volume of speculative trading. As speculation died away, these fringe elements were disappearing. A broker was required to possess

> considerable ability ... to bargain accurately and profitably in a room where possibly a dozen telephone conversations are being conducted simultaneously, and especially in view of the fact that the broker must listen to his colleagues with one ear, so also to catch at once any change in the rate in which he is operating, and at the same time carry on a conversation with his client.

As with the others, he emphasized the importance of trust between counterparties as any reneging on a deal would lead to a refusal to do business next time. Foreign exchange trading was a high-risk/high-reward business conducted by specialists where one of the problems was enforcing discipline in a market without formal regulation, with separate organizations representing brokers and dealers.[279]

Appearing in 1926 was Phillips' account of the foreign exchange market. He had been a dealer with Barclays and a broker for S.P. Scaramanaga. In his book, he emphasized that foreign exchange trading was a telephone market involving around 7,000 people in London. At its core were 120 banks and finance houses and 30 brokers with about 600 people involved. They were assisted by over 6,000 clerical staff. The broker specialized in particular currencies and maintained close contact with particular banks and finance houses, acting as intermediary between the dealers. They provided dealers with information, which helped to establish current exchange rates, but did not take a position themselves. The brokers confined their business to London, leaving the dealers to make their own arrangements with banks located in other financial centres.[280] Dowling's 1929 account of the foreign exchange market paints it as the poor relation to London's other markets, as it lacked a physical location or a regulatory organization.

> There is no actual building known as the Foreign Exchange which is a recognised and definite centre, in the sense that other Exchanges are the head-quarters of their

---

[279] Thomas, *Principles and Arithmetic*, 170–80.
[280] Phillips, *Modern Foreign Exchange*, 69–74.

respective industries. ... The market itself is merely a group of brokers, bankers and other dealers linked by a network of telephones and cables, and with Continental and other foreign centres. Neither are there exclusive membership formalities, nor written code of regulations to control the methods of business as in other Exchanges. Anyone can deal in foreign exchange providing he has the substance and credit sufficient to gain the confidence of the other dealers.

All he could add was that 'The brokers have formed an association amongst themselves, and their representatives have occasionally met an informal committee of the bankers, in order to discuss small details of mutual interest, such as rates of brokerage.' He gave the impression that the foreign exchange market was in decline since the restoration of the Gold Standard in 1925 and that it had a rather limited future.[281]

Nevertheless, though lacking the physical presence and institutional structure of an exchange, trading in currencies in London did develop into a relatively well-organized market by the late 1920s. A meeting of bankers held in 1930 concluded that the foreign exchange market worked with 'precision, rapidity, and economy', and the problems it encountered were caused by those central banks that tried to manipulate it.[282] In Whitmore's 1930 account of the foreign exchange market, what was emphasized was the expertise and professionalism of those involved.

It will be obvious that operating in the foreign exchange market, whether as broker or dealer, is a highly-skilled job. During rush periods, when quotations may be fluctuating wildly from minute to minute, though the business is naturally less exciting (and less harassing) than in the war and early post-war years, operators need unusual nervous strength combined with business acumen to keep their own position straight and their tempers at the same time. If, nowadays, those engaged in foreign exchange business are apt to complain of dull times, they are always quick to admit that they are living more comfortable, if less profitable, times.[283]

What this reflected was the far greater appreciation of the complexity and importance of the foreign exchange market among those in finance. No longer was the foreign exchange market dismissed as a temporary phenomenon or the haunt of speculators. After ten years of development, the foreign exchange market had matured, settling down into a routine activity conducted by dealers and brokers who had become expert in the business they conducted, and commanded the confidence of each other and those for whom they quoted prices and bought and sold. Foreign exchange trading had become one of the many markets located in the City of London, relied upon by banks and others at home and abroad. In March 1931, the Bank of England appreciated the international role played by London's foreign exchange market when it reported that 'A Frenchman wishing to place money in Berlin therefore first buys £

---

[281] S.W. Dowling, *The Exchanges of London* (London: Butterworth & Co., 1929), 206, 213.
[282] Bank of England: Summary of the Meetings of the Committee for Transactions in Foreign Exchange and Gold with Representatives from Continental Europe, 24 and 25 November 1930.
[283] Whitmore, *Money Machine*, 108–10.

sterling spot and simultaneously sells £ sterling forward. He then buys marks spot in London and sells marks forward in London.'[284]

In Evitt's 1933 book, banking, currency, and exchange were combined, with foreign exchange described as an interbank market operating through a network of brokers and dealers. The forty brokers were at the centre of a dense telephone network linking them to one hundred banks. However, direct dealing between the dealers was growing, involving Britain's Big 5 and a number of French and American banks. The American banks were in direct touch with the main dealers in London and kept in constant touch with their New York offices. The French banks were in direct telephone contact with Paris. Compared to the early 1920s, the profit margins in foreign exchange trading had become very low, putting immense pressure on the dealers employed by the banks, which is why they were cutting out the brokers.

> An exchange dealer is born, not made, and there are not many men who can stand the strain of working at such high pressure day after day indefinitely. ... The exchange dealer ... must make a certain profit out of his operations merely to cover the expenses of his department, and as the margins of profit are so narrow, he must endeavour to make his turnover of business as large as possible in order that he may show a net profit after paying expenses.

Though there had been attempts to regulate the market, none had succeeded, leaving it without a physical trading floor or a formal organization.[285] This lack of a formal organization seemed to matter less and less by then because the foreign exchange market appeared to be operating without problems. Basil Cattern at the Bank of England noted in 1935 that forward transactions in foreign exchange were routed through London because of the existence of a free and active market there and the standing of the joint-stock banks as reliable counterparties.[286] In that year, the Bank of England was in no doubt that 'London is the principal exchange market of the world', and used that fact to explain why it was reluctant to intervene in order to curb speculation in case that would undermine it.[287]

By then, the foreign exchange market had become an important source of profits for the Big Five British banks, though one that was subject to considerable fluctuation. The profits made by foreign exchange dealers in London was estimated at £2.86 million for 1933, with half coming from overseas customers. The Bank of England reported in 1934 that 'Dealers, in particular, made large sums in speculative operations in US$ owing to the wide fluctuations in the exchange rate, and, at times, to its predictable future trend'. Profits were also made dealing in French francs, while 'unofficial dealings in blocked currencies constituted an additional and lucrative source of revenue'. Profits then fell substantially in 1934 and 1935 but recovered in 1936. The Bank of England verdict in 1937 was that 'A number of UK firms, if not exchange

---

[284] Bank of England: Memorandum, 11 March 1931.
[285] Evitt, *Practical Banking*, 405–16.
[286] Basil Cattern to Sir Frederick Phillips, 29 April 1935.
[287] Bank of England: Memorandum for the Committee of London Clearing Bankers, 2 May 1935.

dealers, must have made considerable profits out of the devaluation of the gold-bloc currencies.' For 1937 and 1938, it was reported that 'considerable earnings must have been made out of forward exchange transactions'.[288] These profits cemented the commitment of the Big Five British banks to the foreign exchange market in the 1930s. Judging from the extensive dealing in both US$s and French francs that took place in the 1930s, the foreign exchange market had become an integral component of the operation of the City of London as an international financial centre. Turnover in US$s, for example, reached as high as $1,502 million in September 1938, driven by its safe haven appeal as a European war approached.[289]

The *Bankers Magazine* in 1938 had no doubt about the position achieved by the London foreign exchange market, as it reflected on the progress made since 1919. It had taken until 1923 for the new foreign exchange market to settle down into a regular business. 'The success of the business depended in the main upon the freedom with which currencies were allowed to fluctuate, and the absence of limits to such movements.' That ended with Britain's return to the Gold Standard in 1925 and did not reappear until it was abandoned in 1931. By then, the foreign exchange market was well established and able to cope with the currency volatility of the 1930s despite the lack of a formal organization. What existed was a Foreign Exchange Committee of Bankers representing the dealers and a matching Foreign Exchange Brokers Association. The conclusion reached by the *Bankers Magazine* was that 'The development of the market from its early muddle to the present high standard of efficiency and orderliness is the result of its own efforts at self-betterment; which is just as it should be.'[290] That same year, the Treasury civil servant Sir Frederick Phillips praised 'the delicate mechanism of the foreign exchange market' when expressing his concern that 'it would immediately break down' on the outbreak of war, requiring the Bank of England to be given complete control over the market. To Phillips, the foreign exchange market had changed out of all recognition compared to the pre-First World War years, as had Britain's own financial resilience.

> Experience in the Great War affords no useful precedents, if only because the scope and structure of the exchange market, here and abroad, have been completely changed since then, and the pre-war international monetary system has ceased to be. In present conditions, this country is far more vulnerable than it was, from the exchange point of view, in 1914. … The world has become exchange-minded and will be prompt to anticipate the effects of war upon currencies. London is vulnerable, because it now holds more fugitive balances than ever before, while its short-term foreign assets are smaller and illiquid.[291]

[288] Bank of England: Balance of Payments, 8 February 1934; Bank of England: Memoranda on Foreign Exchange Market Profits, 1934–9 for 1938.

[289] Exchange Equalisation Account: Quarterly Report, November 1936–June 1939.

[290] 'The Changing Character of the London Foreign Exchange Market', *Bankers Magazine*, July 1938, 406–9.

[291] UK Treasury, War Measures: Foreign Exchange and Gold. Memorandum by Sir F. Phillips, 24 June 1938.

What all who were familiar with the London foreign exchange market acknowledged by the late 1930s was how much progress it had made over the previous fifteen years, with the development of a forward market being one of its most noteworthy features, generating large profits for those banks that dominated trading.[292] The assessment made of foreign exchange markets around the world in the late 1930s pointed to London's continuing superiority. London dominated trading in forward contracts, regardless of the currency, and these comprised the bulk of turnover in the foreign exchange market. London also dominated trading in the UK£, which remained the most important vehicle currency and was the 'home of refugee and speculative capital'. London operated as the hub of the global foreign exchange market, whereas trading in other financial centres revolved around the national currency as with Paris for the French franc, Amsterdam for the Dutch guilder, Zurich for the Swiss franc, and New York for the US$. Some major financial centres had no forward exchange markets because of government intervention, such as Berlin for the German mark and Milan for the Italian lira.[293] Compared to London, all the other foreign exchange markets either lacked breadth, depth, or both. That of Brussels was dominated by the Société Générale de Belgique, while Amsterdam was 'badly organised in that on the one hand the banks deal direct with one another to a large extent and on the other the brokers pinch the banks' business by having direct relations with a number of commercial concerns'. There was only an interbank market in Zurich and 'the Swiss banks are glutted with money and lack sufficient means of employing it suitably'. The only rival to London in Europe was Paris, but it was

> completely sterling-minded and all currencies are now quoted against sterling and not in terms of francs, unless the Bank of France should be intervening in dollars against francs. A certain amount of deals are done on a franc basis direct, but far the greater part are done first against sterling and the sterling subsequently covered against francs if necessary.

There were sixty to seventy dealers and ten brokers in Paris with trading dominated by the banks, especially Credit Lyonnais, Société Générale, Comptoir Nationale, and Credit Commerciale de France. The only other competitor that London faced as a foreign exchange market was New York, but it was 'small and specialised'.[294]

Despite foreign exchange trading developing into an efficient marketplace, and becoming an integral part of the City of London between the wars, it never gained the widespread acceptance its achievement deserved. One reason was because it was, throughout, compared unfavourably with the Gold Standard, which was widely believed to have delivered currency stability before the First World War. There was an underlying belief that there would be a return to the Gold Standard, once conditions

---

[292] Exchange Equalisation Account: Report, January–February 1938, January–March 1939; Bank of England Memoranda, 27 January 1939, 2 February 1939.
[293] Bank of England, *Some Aspects of Forward Exchange*; Bank of England, 'New Banking Statistics', *Bank of England Quarterly Bulletin*, 15 (1975), 355–367.
[294] Foreign Exchange Market Reports, 26 January 1939.

permitted it, and that would lead to the demise of the foreign exchange market. Britain did return to the Gold Standard in 1925, but even after it had been forced to abandon it in 1931, that did not end the commitment to its restoration in the future. In 1933, Harold Siepmann, at the Bank of England, wrote, 'Eventually, we hope to return to the Gold Standard.'[295] To many bankers, the foreign exchange market was a temporary expedient to be used until the Gold Standard was restored. A.W. Gurney, of the National Provincial Bank, told the foreign exchange broker, F.C. Souch, in 1937 that 'The business of foreign exchange brokers as at present constituted is a direct result of the war and of quite ephemeral character; if it has lasted longer than some of us expected it is due to the long delay in the restoration of confidence and the resultant flights of capital from one centre to another. It is unlikely that business will ever justify and give a reasonable living to about thirty brokerage firms, and as soon as exchanges are stabilized, it is probable that considerably fewer firms will amply serve the requirements of the market. It is consequently essential that brokers take steps to reduce their number, and to reduce all unnecessary expenses.'[296] The expectation was that the foreign exchange market would eventually wither and die, and, thus, there was no incentive to put it on a permanent footing by organizing it as an exchange.

The other reason for the failure of the foreign exchange market to gain acceptance was that it never made the transition to becoming organized as an exchange, as had happened with trading in stocks, bonds, derivatives, and commodities. The foreign exchange market was populated by dealers and brokers conducting an important international business without a physical trading floor, a set of rules and regulations to govern behaviour, or an institutional organization that controlled entry, enforced discipline, and acted as its collective voice when negotiating with the Bank of England or the UK Treasury. This lack of an institutional structure robbed foreign exchange of a body that could represent it in the corridors of power and give it the status in the eyes of the public accorded to the likes of the LSE. The foreign exchange market remained tainted with the aura of speculation with only a few finance professionals understanding the role that it played. The Bank of England described the foreign exchange market in 1935 as 'a free market, there being no official control or supervision, no official list of quotations and no stamp or other duties imposed on dealings.'[297] The conclusion to be drawn was that it lacked the safeguards that went with an organized market and an alternative was required. In 1937, Harold Siepmann painted an unfavourable picture of those whose business was the buying and selling of a foreign exchange:

Foreign exchange dealers have never enjoyed the status which the increasing importance and value of their work deserved; and the result is that the men who have remained dealers are for the most part those who failed to become anything

---

[295] Siepmann Correspondence to Soames Branco, 6 November 1933.
[296] A.W. Gurney (banker) to F.C. Souch (broker), 8 April 1937.
[297] Bank of England Memorandum: London Foreign Exchange Market, 17 June 1935.

else. Practically without exception, they are not men of the moral and intellectual fibre which the Bank requires.[298]

George Bolton, also of the Bank of England, had an equally negative opinion of a number of foreign exchange brokers. He recalled in his memoirs that among the foreign exchange brokers were those 'who had served or should have served prison sentences'.[299] Without the status of an exchange, and widely regarded as temporary, the foreign exchange market never received either the official or public recognition it deserved between the wars.

The explanation for the failure to make the transition to an exchange was that the foreign exchange market was fundamentally unsuited to such a model, because of the absence of a physical trading floor. Exchanges like the LSE, the London Metal Exchange, and the Baltic Exchange all included a space in which members negotiated deals face-to-face in full confidence that they would be honoured. In contrast, 'in London the foreign exchange market is really nowhere, and knows no hours', in the words of George Bolton in 1937.[300] Though the telephone was replacing face-to-face contact, most of London's markets continued to rely on a physical trading floor where buyers, sellers, and their agents congregated. By controlling who could use the physical trading floor, an exchange could levy a fee for access. That levy met the costs of providing not only the facilities but also the organization that supervised the market. Market discipline was enforced by the sanction of denying access to the trading floor to all who could not conform to the rules, and so were not admitted to membership, or broke them when members. The outcome was a regulated market that delivered confidence to every member that counterparties to a sale or purchase could be trusted. It might be expected that the LSE would provide a model that the foreign exchange market could follow. Practices used on the stock exchange, such as arbitrage, were copied in the foreign exchange market. The LSE also contained both dealers and brokers. The brokers connected the market to investors and bought and sold stocks and bonds on their behalf, being paid commission for doing so. The dealers, known as jobbers, quoted to brokers the prices at which they would buy and sell specific securities and were always ready to do one or the other. The difference between the buying and selling price generated a profit for the dealers, and that was where their income came from as they were not paid commission. This was similar to the situation in the foreign exchange market. There was also some direct dealing on the stock exchange between jobbers and investors, when the latter were sufficiently large to justify it, as with banks, insurance companies, and fund managers. As direct contact between dealers and large investors became easier, especially with the telephone, the LSE acted to prevent it, using its rules and regulations to confine the practice to the margins of trading. This concentrated trading on the floor of the LSE and so generated prices in which all could have confidence. One of the major

---

[298] Bank of England: The Staffing of Exchange Management by Harold Siepmann, 2 December 1937.
[299] Sir George Bolton, *Memoirs* (Bank of England, 13 January 1977), ch.11, Epilogue, Appendix 2: Foreign Exchange Markets between Munich and 3 September 1939.
[300] Foreign Exchange and Gold: Market Organisation and Technique, George Bolton, 6 April 1937.

criticisms of arbitrageurs, by other members of the LSE, was that they dealt directly with non-members and so bypassed them when completing a deal.

The explanation for this failure of the foreign exchange market to make the transition to an exchange lies with the relationship between the dealers and the brokers. The big banks dominated trading in foreign exchange with most taking place by either internal matching of sales and purchases or office-to-office transactions between trusted counterparties. The banks were very familiar with internal matching, through operating the lend-and-hold model of banking, while advances in communications and computational technology made it increasingly easy for foreign exchange dealers in different banks to be in direct contact and quote rates to each other. As conducted between the wars, foreign exchange was a high-volume/low-margin business engaged in by very few banks, reducing the need to go through specialist intermediaries.[301] As counterparties, these banks could be trusted to stand by any deal made in their name, whether it was for themselves or on behalf of their customers. Any failure to do so would destroy the reputation of the bank and lose it the status of trusted counterparty, meaning that it would be cut out of future deals. The dealers employed by these large banks were also subject to constant monitoring designed to detect and prevent fraudulent activity, and market manipulation, while restraints were imposed on their behaviour, which curtailed their risk-taking. Foreign exchange dealing exposed banks to large losses, which had to be kept under control if they were not to threaten the survival of the whole bank. As the responsibility for that supervision lay with the bank itself, and self-interest dictated that it be taken seriously, no external regulation was required. The Big Five banks were the most trusted financial institutions in the UK, ranking just below the Bank of England.[302] Furthermore, the dealers would only do business with a select circle of counterparties. Even the brokers had to restrict their clients to those on the dealer's approved list.[303] The result was that foreign exchange trading was largely confined to trusted counterparties, took place using the telephone and the telegraph, and involved both dealer–dealer and dealer–broker transactions. It was also a relatively small circle of participants. In 1928, there were only around 150 dealers and 45 brokers involved. Under the circumstances, there was not the demand for an exchange from those involved, as there was no requirement for a physical trading floor and an unwillingness to agree to binding rules and regulations or fixed charges. The dealers insisted on the freedom to trade with whomsoever they chose, while brokers were unwilling to accept any restraints on their ability to compete for business.[304]

Nevertheless, beginning in the early 1920s, there were attempts to introduce a regulatory structure to the foreign exchange market. These were begun by the dealers forming an association in 1920, but it never took off, failing to agree a constitution.

[301] *Financial News*, 14 January 1937.
[302] Bank of England, Memorandum on Proposed Foreign Exchange Department, 1 November 1926; London Foreign Exchange Market, 27 April 1928; Memorandum on Foreign Exchanges, 17 May 1928.
[303] Names to be Accepted in Connection with Foreign Exchange Dealings, 3 November 1930.
[304] Memorandum of Conversation with Mr Ogg at the Anglo-International Bank, 8 January 1929; Committee of London Foreign Exchange Managers: Report by George Bolton, 9 June 1936.

It had only twelve members in 1928, of which half came from the Big Five banks. According to Speed, in 1928, 'The Dealers' Association was so little in evidence that it was almost doubtful whether it was still alive.'[305] A brokers' association was established in 1922, but it only included a subsection of the total number. Writing in 1929, Mr Sampson, of the brokers M.W. Marshall & Co, explained that it had been formed

> with a view to protecting the brokers from a certain type of undesirable who was attracted to the market by the big profits which were to be made at that time. During the last year or so, however, direct telephonic communication with the Continent on the part of the dealers has become so regular and competition has become so keen that the smaller brokers have been hard put to it to obtain a living. Accordingly, they have been working for half brokerage and have been encouraged in this by the dealers at certain banks who are always prepared to deal in the cheapest market.

The brokers' association was disbanded in 1929 despite agreeing a proper constitution, and it had some success in persuading the banks to favour its members when doing business.[306] In 1928, Mr Speed, assistant to the manager of the Westminster Bank's Foreign Branch Office, reported that

> A broker would stand no chance of getting enough business if he were not a member of that Association, especially nowadays when most of the business comes from the Big Five. ... The big banks were connected by private telephone lines to perhaps as many as twenty different brokers but the Westminster Bank now seldom used more than five or six, according to the currencies in which these specialised.

Persuading banks to confine their dealings to association members, and sticking to the fixed scale of charges, became much more difficult in the late 1920s as the profits to be made in the foreign exchange market declined. As the banks reduced their dealing staff, they also cut back on the number of brokers with whom they did business. At the same time, they also increased the amount of direct dealing, cutting out brokers, as that saved on commission fees. 'Foreign dealers are expected to deal direct with the London banks and not through a broker.'[307]

It was not until Britain left the Gold Standard in 1931, and with some support from the Bank of England, that there was a renewed attempt to introduce rules and regulations covering the foreign exchange market. That year, the banks formed the Foreign Exchange Committee and this was given a more formal structure in 1936,

---

[305] Interview with Mr Speed, the Manager's Assistant, Foreign Branch Office, Westminster Bank, 17 May 1928.
    [306] Bank of England: Memorandum of Conversation with Mr Sampson of M. W. Marshall & Co, 29 May 1929.
    [307] Interview with Mr Speed, the Manager's Assistant, Foreign Branch Office, Westminster Bank, 17 May 1928.

with enhanced powers.[308] A new association for brokers was formed in 1932, with a membership limit set at thirty.[309] Generally, from 1931 onwards, the Bank of England was trying to impose rules and regulations on the foreign exchange market through the pressure it could exert on the British banks and brokers. This pressure covered areas such as restricting direct dealing between the banks, imposing a uniform scale of commission for the foreign exchange business the banks handled for their customers, forcing banks to route trading through brokers who were members of the official association and also to pay brokers according to a fixed scale of charges. The banks resisted these moves because it would damage the way they did business and undermine their ability to compete with foreign banks and foreign exchange markets elsewhere in the world.[310] In 1936, A.W. Gurney, on behalf of the Committee of London Foreign Exchange Managers, pointed out to J.K. Jones of the Foreign Exchange Brokers Association, that as the market was very competitive, 'profits are cut to shreds and direct dealing encouraged.'[311]

Nevertheless, the Bank of England applied pressure on the banks, forcing them to concede some of the brokers' demands.[312] An informal agreement emerged that direct exchange dealing between London banks should not be done, but this was not always adhered to because of high brokerage charges. The British banks were aware that 'The American banks were in the habit of direct dealing because margins were extremely narrow.' This made the large British banks 'unwilling to agree to any form of restriction in the manner of their dealing in foreign exchange' as they would lose business if they did. The outcome in 1937 was that fixed brokerage rates were recommended but not made mandatory, despite continuing pressure from the brokers, and there was no prohibition on direct dealing.[313] What the issues of direct dealing and minimum fixed charges revealed was the fundamental divide that prevented the foreign exchange market taking on the structure of an exchange, even under pressure from the Bank of England. In the absence of a physical trading floor to which

[308] Committee of Foreign Exchange Managers, 13 July 1936, 29 September 1936, 18 October 1936; Bank of England: Report on Organisation of the Foreign Exchange Market, 29 September 1936, 18 October 1936; London Foreign Exchange Brokers Association: Report of Sub-committee, 3 December 1936; Bank of England Memorandum, 16 June 1937, 15 October 1937; Bank of England Memorandum, 16 June 1937, 15 October 1937.

[309] Memorandum: Exchange Control during the War, 12 January 1932; Memorandum: London Foreign Exchange Market, 17 June 1935; C. Souch, Secretary of the London Foreign Exchange Brokers Association, to A.W. Gurney, Committee of London Foreign Exchange Managers, 7 April 1936; Reply from A.W. Gurney, 9 April 1936.

[310] District Bank: Letter from the London Manager to the Head Office in Manchester, 28 October 1931; Bank of England Notice: Commission on Foreign Exchange Transactions, Bank of England, 1939.

[311] A.W. Gurney to J.K. Jones, 9 April 1936.

[312] Committee of Foreign Exchange Managers, 13 July 1936, 29 September 1936, 18 October 1936; Bank of England: Report on Organisation of the Foreign Exchange Market, 29 September 1936, 18 October 1936; London Foreign Exchange Brokers Association: Report of Sub-committee, 3 December 1936; Bank of England Memorandum, 16 June 1937, 15 October 1937; Bank of England Memorandum, 16 June 1937, 15 October 1937.

[313] Minutes of the Foreign Exchange Committee (Guildhall Library), 27 August 1936, 28 October 1936, 11 December 1936, 20 January 1937, 27 January 1937, 3 February 1937; Report of Sub-committee on Direct Dealing, 13 May 1937, 28 May 1937, 19 October 1937, 3 January 1939; Letter from Montagu Norman to the Chairman of the Committee.

access could be granted or denied, there were no sanctions that could be applied to dealers and brokers that would force them all to obey rules and regulations agreed to. That left the foreign exchange market dependent upon the discipline imposed by the banks and their need to safeguard their own reputations. This proved to be effective in eliminating counterparty risk and creating a market that was both efficient and resilient. This position had been achieved largely through a process of change driven from within, as George Bolton recognized in 1937.[314]

Not all markets in London were organized as exchanges whether before 1914 or between the wars. The most notable example of one that was not structured in that way was the discount market, through which banks bought and sold bills of exchange and borrowed and lent amongst each other. This market had evolved over the centuries and had reached a high level of sophistication in the fifty years before the First World War. Lying at its heart in those years were the bill brokers or discount houses and their special relationship with the Bank of England. It was through the discount houses that the Bank of England acted as lender of last resort to the London money market and thus to the British banking system. A discount house knew that it could always balance its assets and liabilities on a daily basis by selling bills to the Bank of England at the end of every working day. This gave them the confidence to buy bills from banks in anticipation of being able to finance their purchases using funds borrowed from other banks. In turn, that gave banks the confidence that they could always raise short-term funds by selling bills or employ idle funds on a temporary basis by buying bills with discount houses acting as counterparties in such transactions. It was the discount market that provided an alternative model for the foreign exchange market between the wars especially as banks increasingly used it in a similar way. However, it was not until Britain left the Gold Standard for a second time in 1931 that the Bank of England began to build a similar relationship to the foreign exchange market to that which it had with the discount market.[315]

Though banks were already using the foreign exchange market as a way of borrowing and lending amongst each other in the 1920s, the Bank of England made no attempt to develop a relationship with it at that time, though recognizing the changes taking place. From 1919 onwards, the forward exchange market for the US$ quickly replaced the facility that had once been provided by the arbitrageurs connected to the LSE. The Bank of England acknowledged this in 1926.

> Although the foreign exchange dealer tries to marry all his transactions, to deal forward and avoid an open position he must be able to employ funds in the country in whose currency he deals. The rate at which he can deal forward will depend on the facilities for the employment of funds and the rate of interest obtainable. In the case of a country with a stable currency but a poorly developed money market the rates at which a banker can deal profitably will not attract the trader. He

---

[314] Foreign Exchange and Gold: Market Organisation and Technique, George Bolton, 6 April 1937.
[315] Bank of England: Exchange Control during the War, 12 January 1932.

will prefer to take the small exchange risk. Spot transactions and the practice of arranging payments in sterling are other factors against an active market in foreign exchange.[316]

The importance of the London foreign exchange market even grew after the return to the Gold Standard as that provided a guarantee of stability that attracted banks from around the world to return to the London discount market, where the currency in use was limited to sterling. That encouraged greater use of the foreign exchange market in order to cover exposure to fluctuations in the value of the UK£, especially in terms of the US$.[317] As Smith St. Aubyn observed in February 1927, the discount houses 'have not been offered so much money for a long time. Telephone rang all afternoon and a large amount must have been unlent. All daily was put up to 4% and not worth it'.[318]

Nevertheless, the Bank of England remained aloof from the foreign exchange market in the 1920s, and stated as such in 1928. 'The Bank does not intervene on the exchange market.'[319] It did act as an agent of foreign central banks when they wanted to buy and sell currencies in the London foreign exchange market. This made some of its staff aware that much money market activity was taking place, of which the Bank was unaware, and was thus unable to influence even though it had a bearing on areas that were its responsibilities, such as the stability of the banking system and the government's finances.[320] One of those at the Bank of England who pressed for greater involvement with the foreign exchange market in the years before Britain left the Gold Standard was the Treasury civil servant turned central banker, Harold Siepmann. He had observed that activity in the foreign exchange market was displacing that in the discount market, which was that part of the London money market that the Bank of England was closely involved with. The problem he identified in 1928 was that the Bank of England had 'no direct contact with the exchange market in London'. 'Being entirely outside the foreign exchange market ... such orders as we receive are carried out not by us but through us, and the only part which we can play is to act as intermediary between our foreign client and the London market.' In that year, the Bank of England judged that 'the market in sterling is such a broad market that it can safely be left to take care of itself'. The London foreign exchange market was 'an absolutely free market untrammelled by any supervision on the part of the Central Bank'. That was not the case elsewhere where government intervention did take place. 'It is natural and right that Central Banks should try to concentrate in their home market the dealings in their own currency, and this has visibly been happening since the war, so that Brussels is the market for Belgas, Vienna for Schillings, Budapest for Pengo.' That attitude towards non-intervention in the market for sterling began to change as volatility grew in the years before Britain finally departed

[316] Bank of England: Memorandum on Proposed Foreign Exchange Department, 1 November 1926.
[317] Sangway, *Clare's Money Market Primer*, 212.
[318] Smith St. Aubyn: Business Diary, 28 February 1927.
[319] Bank of England: Memorandum, 4 December 1928.
[320] Bank of England: Memorandum on Forward Exchange Market, 8 October 1931.

from the Gold Standard in 1931. However, Siepmann admitted in 1931 that a lack of familiarity with the foreign exchange market left the Bank of England at a disadvantage: 'I see so much of the trees that I cannot give you a fair description of the wood.' One of the vital pieces of information the Bank of England continued to lack in 1931 was how much foreign exchange the Big Five banks had at their disposal, and whether it was held at home or abroad.[321]

After Britain left the Gold Standard in September 1931, the Bank of England took steps to engage with the foreign exchange market because it was given responsibility for managing the sterling exchange rate against the US$. In October 1931, Siepmann took the opportunity at a meeting of the newly convened Foreign Exchange Committee to ask

> the opinion of the dealers, of whom there were 5 or 6 present, about the reasons for which sterling stands where it does. None of them mentioned speculation. None of them spoke about an evasion of the exchange regulations. They all seemed to agree that on the one side there is an accumulation of German balances (and) a heavy repatriation of money which has hitherto been invested in dollar securities. And on the other side (the) continued withdrawals of French and Swiss Bank balances, for liquidity's sake (and) unusually heavy payments for commodity stocks delivered in this country during the past weeks or months in anticipation of our putting on a tariff ... all our warehouses are absolutely chock-a-block and even a small space is difficult to obtain. It is for these large accumulated stocks that current commodity payments are being made.

What became clear to the Bank of England staff was that the international value of the UK£ was a combination of what Britain did and the actions of other countries, in terms of not only the intervention in the foreign exchange market but also the policies applied to exports and imports.

Once the shock of leaving the Gold Standard had passed, the Bank of England was left with the task of trying to stabilize the international value of the UK£. They were conscious in December 1932 that 'A currency which fluctuates beyond narrow limits is not a suitable currency to hold reserves.' If they could not hold the UK£ steady, then foreign banks would no longer be willing to hold it, and that would affect the attractiveness of the City of London as a financial centre. It would also undermine foreign demand for UK government debt, as that was denominated in sterling and was popular with banks because of its liquidity. The long-term solution in 1933 remained a return to the Gold Standard, 'if only for lack of any workable alternative', but, in the meantime, a temporary fix had to be found through working with the foreign exchange market. The Bank had long engaged with the discount market and that provided an obvious model. Having distanced itself from the foreign exchange market

---

[321] Siepmann Correspondence: 2 February 1928 to Dr F. Mlynarski, Warsaw, 7 March 1928 to Dr Bosch, 24 October 1928 to Herr Direcktor Tabalovits, Budapest, 1 November 1928 to E. Weber, 8 November 1929 to Gairdner at BOB, 2 January 1931 to R. Auboin, 2 June 1931 to Paul van Zeeland, 11 June 1931 to R. Auboin at Bank for International Settlements.

in the 1920s, after 1931 the Bank began to engage closely with it. It employed two mechanisms through which it could make its influence felt. The first was to convert the informal committee of bankers that oversaw the foreign exchange market from 1932 into a body that would manage it. The Bank had a close relationship with the Big Five banks and it was they that dominated the foreign exchange market. In 1936, Siepmann wrote that

> We want to make it really representative of the market as a whole and we want its rulings to have binding force. ... For good market reorganisation and orderly dealing I am quite certain that a committee of this sort is essential. It has already done great work in settling knotty problems and preventing or suppressing abuses. We shall encourage it to grow and develop and do more.

The Bank wanted to influence the shape and direction of the London foreign exchange market without taking control of it. 'We are in the market but not of it.' By then, the Bank realized that, through cooperation with it and other central banks, the foreign exchange market was able to cope with currency volatility. This was considered preferable to 'a mass of regulations' imposed by governments.[322]

The other mechanism the Bank of England chose to handle its relationship with the foreign exchange market was similar to that already used for the discount market. In the discount market, the Bank operated through a small group of bill brokers or discount houses with whom it developed an especially close relationship in the 1930s. In a matching development in the foreign exchange market, it selected five brokers, establishing direct telephone lines to them. These were the most established firms who had developed expertise in particular currencies and had strong connections to particular banks, such as E.B. Meyer, Harlow & Jones, and M.W. Marshall.[323] Through this small group of brokers, and the pressure it could exert on the Big Five banks, the Bank of England was able to influence the way that the foreign exchange market worked, especially from 1936 onwards.[324] In the belief that it would contribute to a more orderly market, the Bank of England pressed for an end to direct dealing between the banks and the introduction of a fixed scale of charges for all business routed through brokers. These were the demands of the foreign exchange brokers, copied from what already happened on the LSE. As before, the banks resisted these demands because they would damage the way they did business and undermine their

---

[322] Siepmann Correspondence: 6 October 1931 to Professor Clay, 20 October 1931 to Dr Fuchs, 26 October 1931 to Sir Frederick Leith-Ross, 5 November 1931 to Dr Fuchs, 26 August 1932 to J. Postmus, 19 December 1932 to Soames Branco, 10 March 1933 to H.C.F. Finlayson, 6 November 1933 to Soames Branco, 27 October 1936 to Allan Sproul, Vice President Federal Reserve, 31 March 1936 to Sproul, 17 April 1936 to F.F. Powell, 2 May 1936 to Sproul, 27 November 1936 to Lady Blackett, 9 January 1937 to Munakata, 13 August 1937 to C. Rogers, 29 July 1938 to O. Hobson, 23 December 1938 to Per Jacobson, 20 December 1939 to Soames Branco.

[323] Bank of England: Memorandum, 4 February 1931.

[324] Committee of Foreign Exchange Managers, 13 July 1936, 29 September 1936, 18 October 1936; Bank of England: Report on Organisation of the Foreign Exchange Market, 29 September 1936, 18 October 1936; London Foreign Exchange Brokers Association: Report of Sub-committee, 3 December 1936; Bank of England Memorandum, 16 June 1937, 15 October 1937; Bank of England Memorandum, 16 June 1937, 15 October 1937.

ability to compete with foreign banks and foreign exchange markets elsewhere in the world.[325] What the banks did agree to was an informal agreement that limited the amount of direct dealing, but this was widely ignored. The British banks were aware that 'the American banks were in the habit of direct dealing because margins were extremely narrow'. This made the large British banks 'unwilling to agree to any form of restriction in the manner of their dealing in foreign exchange' as they would lose business if they did. The banks also agreed in 1937 to introduce fixed brokerage rates but refused to make them mandatory.[326]

In 1937, the Bank of England claimed that 'Real progress was made with foreign exchange market organisation.' The Bank had 'acted as informal consultants to the different parties in the market, without taking any direct hand in the reorganisation which is now progressing'.[327] However, the Bank was unable to exercise the same degree of control over the foreign exchange market as it did over the discount market. Unlike the latter, which had become a largely domestic affair in the 1930s, and confined to sterling, the foreign exchange market was international and used multiple currencies, especially the US$. In the foreign exchange market, the British banks faced strong competition from US and French banks while there was always the option of shifting trading to Paris or New York. This is what happened to an extent in 1937 after the intervention of the Bank of England in 1936, which George Bolton acknowledged. 'London is becoming a dear market to deal in.'[328] There were ten foreign banks with offices in London that engaged extensively in the foreign exchange market, but it was those from the USA that benefited most from the increased costs and wider spreads forced on the British banks by the Bank of England. These foreign banks undercut the fixed scale of charges when using brokers and continued to deal directly with each other, passing business between their offices in London, New York, and Paris. That allowed them to compete aggressively with the British banks.[329] During January 1937, Bolton concluded that 'If we in London are to retain any semblance of a foreign exchange market we shall be forced to abandon fixed marginal quotes.'[330] That same month, the *Financial News* warned that London was being bypassed as foreign exchange trading was taking place directly between New York and continental centres. 'If the existing trend is allowed to continue, the relative importance of the London foreign exchange market will decline before very long to the level where it stood before the war.'[331]

---

[325] District Bank: Letter from the London Manager to the Head Office in Manchester, 28 October 1931; Bank of England Notice: Commission on Foreign Exchange Transactions, Bank of England, 1939.

[326] Minutes of the Foreign Exchange Committee (Guildhall Library), 27 August 1936, 28 October 1936, 11 December 1936, 20 January 1937, 27 January 1937, 3 February 1937; Report of Sub-committee on Direct Dealing, 13 May 1937, 28 May 1937, 19 October 1937, 3 January 1939; Letter from Montagu Norman to the Chairman of the Committee.

[327] Exchange Equalisation Account: Quarterly Report, 1 October–31 December 1937.

[328] Bank of England: Memorandum by George Bolton, 11 January 1937.

[329] Bank of England: Report by George Bolton on Direct Dealing, 31 March 1937, 5 April 1937; Bank of England: Foreign Exchange and Gold: Market Organisation and Technique, George Bolton, 6 April 1937.

[330] Bank of England: Memorandum by George Bolton, 18 January 1937.

[331] *Financial News*, 22 January 1937.

Outside observers blamed the problems being experienced by London's foreign exchange market on the Bank of England. One of those was the highly influential journalist and expert on financial markets, Oscar Hobson.

> The foreign exchange business of the small trader still comes automatically to the London market. But the same is not true of the big business conducted, for example, by large scale arbitrage operators in gold or securities. One of these told me this week that less than 10 per cent of his foreign exchange business is put through this market. He finds it cheaper to do his business in Paris or Amsterdam or Brussels, as the case may be, even though this involves having to incur the expense of a trunk call. ... Unlike the commodity markets, the foreign exchange markets are not trammelled by tariffs and quotas. There is nothing to prevent the dealer from going to the cheapest centre. Margins and brokerages in London will have to come down if we are to maintain our position as an international exchange market.[332]

The Statist magazine reached a similar conclusion and it also placed responsibility for what was happening on Bank of England intervention.[333] The response in 1937 was to relax the restrictions placed on the British banks with the result that trading returned to the London foreign exchange market.[334]

However, there was a reluctance by the Bank of England to accept any responsibility for the damage it had inflicted. While acknowledging that the London foreign exchange market had lost out to foreign competitors, in 1936, Siepmann sought to blame it on the lack of commitment by the Big Five banks and their failure to recruit and retain expert staff. They

> had got into the habit of regarding their Foreign Exchange Department as a more or less gratuitous service which in some cases they may even have been prepared to run at a small loss. But this had not prevented their losing business to the market—principally the foreign Banks and Private Banks, who are on the whole decidedly more efficient.[335]

Nevertheless, the Bank of England had learnt an important lesson from its attempt to refashion the foreign exchange market in the image of the discount market. This was the limitation of its power when faced with an international market in which trading was dominated by a small group of banks who swapped assets and liabilities amongst themselves. This type of market was best left to regulate itself and adopt their own practices as otherwise intervention by the Bank of England could easily and quickly drive trading into the hands of foreign banks or abroad. This was the advice of George Bolton in 1937, reflecting his experience of the foreign exchange market: 'Markets

---

[332] *News Chronicle*, 23 January 1937.
[333] *Statist*, 6 February 1937.
[334] *Financial News*, 24 February 1937, 25 February 1937; *Financial Times*, 25 February 1937; EEA Quarterly Report, 1 April–30 June 1937.
[335] Bank of England: Memorandum by H.A. Siepmann, 17 November 1937.

have to organise themselves if they are to avoid being organised, sooner or later, despite themselves, by so-called "authorities" who may have the disadvantage of not knowing the business.'[336]

It was not only the limitation of its power with regard to regulation that the Bank of England learnt through its engagement with the foreign exchange market in the 1930s. The Bank also recognized the limitation of its power when intervening in the foreign exchange market itself. Though it had assisted foreign central banks in the 1920s, when they had intervened in the London foreign exchange market to stabilize the exchange rate of their national currency, it only provided them with limited support.[337] At the time, the Bank lacked both the resources and the expertise to intervene in the foreign exchange market either on its own account or on behalf of others. In December 1928, the Bank admitted that they had 'no foreign exchange department and are therefore not only out of touch with the London market but completely cut off from the Continent'. They were reluctant to set up such a department as it

> would be fraught with very great difficulties and disadvantages. If dealings were confined to the execution of orders given by customers, the dealers would be entirely out of touch with the market and lack practice. Continuous and intimate touch with the market here and abroad would be essential. To obtain this the Bank must be prepared to deal with all and sundry. Considerable balances would have to be maintained in foreign centres and it would hardly be practicable or useful to confine dealings with the Continent to the Central Banks.[338]

Under the circumstances, the Bank was forced to rely for advice on those banks and brokers involved in the foreign exchange market.[339] Even before Britain left the Gold Standard in 1931, this situation was becoming unsatisfactory as the Bank tried to stabilize the international value of the UK£ because of the damage being inflicted by speculation. In February 1931, the Bank observed that 'People would like to take advantage of higher interest rates ruling here but are afraid that when they want to withdraw it they will lose more in the rate of exchange than they make on the difference of interest.'[340] It was only when Britain left the Gold Standard in September 1931 that the international value of the UK£ stabilized and speculation died away.[341]

With Britain's departure from the Gold Standard in 1931, the Bank of England was given the task by the British government of managing the sterling exchange rate, and the financial resources to do so.[342] The EEA was set up in 1932 by the UK Treasury,

---

[336] Foreign Exchange and Gold: Market Organisation and Technique, George Bolton, 6 April 1937.

[337] Bank of England, Memorandum on Proposed Foreign Exchange Department, 1 November 1926; Memorandum on London Foreign Exchange Market, 27 April 1928; Memorandum on Foreign Exchanges, 17 May 1928, Memorandum on Foreign Exchanges, 10 December 1928.

[338] Bank of England: Confidential Memorandum, 4 December 1928.

[339] Bank of England, Memorandum on Proposed Foreign Exchange Department, 1 November 1926; London Foreign Exchange Market, 27 April 1928; Memorandum on Foreign Exchanges, 17 May 1928.

[340] Bank of England: Memorandum, 20 February 1931.

[341] Letter Issued by Honorary Secretary of the London Clearing Bankers, 20 September 1931; Bank of England: Memorandum by H.A.S., 24 March 1932 [H.A.S. is Harry Arthur Siepmann].

[342] Einzig, *Exchange Control*, 117.

and the Bank of England was given responsibility for managing it in such a way as to stabilize the sterling exchange rate, especially against the US$.[343] It was not only the British government that looked to the Bank of England for assistance in the stabilization of currencies in the wake of the collapse of the Gold Standard and the absence of a replacement other than a foreign exchange market.[344] The centre of this market was in London as restrictions imposed by the French government constrained Paris, and New York only traded the US$ against the UK£.[345] This meant that the Bank of England was left with the responsibility of trying to manage the foreign exchange market on behalf of central banks from outside the sterling area. George Bolton recalled that there was cooperation between the central banks of the UK, France, Belgium, Holland, and Switzerland to dampen speculation in the foreign exchange market after the Czechoslovakian crisis of 1938.[346] This required the Bank of England to actively engage with the foreign exchange market.[347] To do so, the Bank of England recruited staff from the foreign exchange market, such as George Bolton, and so provided itself with the required expertise.[348] In 1938, Siepmann explained this evolving relationship between the Bank of England and the foreign exchange market. Whereas in 1928–9 the Bank of England was dealing with the market through the Anglo-International Bank, this was widened in 1931, during the crisis over sterling, to include the British Overseas Bank and the Big Five. The circle of banks used was then expanded further in 1933–4 with the addition of Hambros, Glynn's, and the District Bank. The Bank of England also developed a closer working relationship with the foreign exchange brokers. 'By this time also we had begun to train a cadre of efficient dealers and with our increasing exchange business with other Central Banks began to deal direct with the market through the brokers and occasionally for special transactions directly with the more active and responsible institutions.' When the Tripartite Monetary Agreement between Britain, France, and the USA was signed in September 1936, the Bank of England became more interventionist in the foreign exchange market, successfully reducing volatility to a level that made it difficult for the banks and the brokers to generate profits. 'Quite recently the foreign managers of two of the clearing banks have told us that they do much of their customers' exchange business at a loss and regarded their exchange departments as purely service departments.' As the Bank of England intervention grew, some banks retreated and others complained. 'Two of the clearers are inefficient and losing contact with the market, one is a mediocrity ... remainder while still being active and intelligent one is definitely anti-Bank and openly resentful of the existence of the Exchange Fund.' Judging from

[343] Waight, *Exchange Equalisation Account*, 1, 12, 15–16, 39–40.

[344] Sangway, *Clare's Money Market Primer*, 212; Board of Trade, Conference on Exchange Restrictions, 24 November 1932.

[345] Sterling/Dollar Turnover, H.A. Siepman, 26 October 1938; Report on the EEA, 20 February 1939; *EEA Quarterly Report*, 1 January 1938–31 March 1939.

[346] Sir George Bolton, *Memoirs* (Bank of England, 13 January 1977), ch.11, Epilogue, Appendix 2: Foreign Exchange Markets between Munich and 3 September 1939.

[347] Basil Cattern to Sir Frederick Phillips, 29 April 1935, 4 June 1935; Basil Cattern to Signor L. Capodanno.

[348] Bank of England Memorandum on Restrictions on Dealing in Foreign Exchange: France, 28 March 1930.

the commission paid by the Bank of England when trading foreign exchange, this relationship with the foreign exchange market waxed and waned during the 1930s.[349] At times, the Bank of England acted as agent of the UK Treasury and the British government as they sought to stabilize the value of the UK£ in the foreign exchange market.[350] An example of this intervention by the Bank of England had come in 1936 when, at its request, the London foreign exchange market had closed for one day after the collapse of the Gold Bloc on 26 September, and then all dealings in French francs were suspended for five days and Swiss francs for two days.[351] Another was the request to the Bank of England in January 1939, from John Simon, Chancellor of the Exchequer, for it to intervene in order to curb speculation.[352]

In 1938, B.G. Catterns, at the Bank of England, told Sir Richard Hopkins, at the UK Treasury, that intervention in the foreign exchange market had now become publicly accepted.

> Since 1914, the attitude of the public towards intervention has entirely changed, and there is no field in which the need for some regulation, even in peace-time, is more obvious or more generally accepted than in foreign exchange. Bitter experience has made people exchange-minded, and they would take alarm if, in an emergency, nothing was done to protect sterling and conserve the country's reserves.[353]

From July 1937 onwards, the Bank of England stood ready to take full control of the foreign exchange market on behalf of the UK Treasury in the event of a war.[354] During 1938, there was active planning on what to do if a European war should break out, with the Bank of England acting in concert with the Treasury and the government.[355] These plans were then rapidly rolled out when war with Germany was declared on 1 September 1939. George Bolton recalled that 2 September 1939 was the last day of a free foreign exchange market in the UK. 'Before the day ended I had closed down the foreign exchange market from 4th September and offered employment in the Exchange Control as temporary clerks to all the staff and principals of the Brokers. ... It was agreed that New York would maintain a free foreign exchange market with the rate set at $4 to the £1.'[356] The Bank of England was left to handle the numerous complications arising from the ending of the foreign exchange market and the imposition of exchange controls.[357] This included working with the US authorities, as an

[349] Exchange Equalisation Account: Relations with Agents, H.A. Siepman, 13 May 1938.
[350] Bank of England: The Staffing of Exchange Management by Harold Siepmann, 2 December 1937.
[351] Bank of England: Foreign Exchange Market Organisation: A Review, 29 January 1937.
[352] Letter from John Simon, at the Treasury, to Montagu Norman, Governor of the Bank of England, 2 January 1939.
[353] B.G. Catterns, Bank of England, to Sir Richard Hopkins, Treasury, 8 July 1938.
[354] Bank of England: War Measures, 8 July 1937.
[355] B.G. Catterns, Bank of England, to Sir Richard Hopkins, Treasury, 8 July 1938.
[356] Sir George Bolton, *Memoirs* (Bank of England, 13 January 1977), ch.11, Epilogue, Appendix 2: Foreign Exchange Markets between Munich and 3 September 1939.
[357] Bankers' Clearing House: Foreign Exchange Committee, 21 September 1939, 28 September 1939, 9 October 1939, 11 October 1939, 18 October 1939, 23 October 1939, 28 February 1940.

unofficial market in sterling continued to operate in New York.[358] In December 1939, Siepmann wrote that 'We can count upon the loyal observance by the London market of any regulations that may be imposed.' He then added that 'London depends mainly upon the sterling area, and the sterling area remains. It has even been extended, in effect, to include the whole of the French Empire.'[359]

Having been many years in the planning, the Bank of England was confident that it could manage its foreign exchange responsibilities once war broke out and it was given full control. George Bolton claimed that by the late 1930s, he 'had slowly realised that "floating exchanges" do not float like flotsam in an open sea, but are guided, cossetted, coached and generally interfered with not only for domestic political reasons but more importantly because of the international frictions arising through the trade and other consequences of fluctuating rates of exchange.'[360]

In contrast, engagement with the foreign exchange market had left the Bank of England sceptical of the value of intervention during peacetime. In 1928, it considered intervention ineffective, bordering on being counterproductive, based on French experience.[361] Ten years later, it held the same opinion if the intention was to maintain a fixed exchange rate.[362] The more the Bank of England reflected on what had happened in 1931, when Britain had left the Gold Standard, the greater was its conviction that fixed exchange rates could not be defended. This can be seen in the following comment made in 1938: 'In 1931 it was a relief from strain to let sterling fail, because it rendered unnecessary the deflationary pressure on the domestic market which the defence of sterling then involved, and because our chief competitors in export markets did not follow suit.'[363] Another example of the Bank of England's lack of commitment to fixed exchange rates is revealed in its attitude towards 'Hot Money'. This was money that moved in and out of financial centres at speed in search of immediate speculative gains. In the opinion of the Bank in 1937,

Hot money should be discouraged in every way possible. So long as it enjoys its present facilities in England and America, it will be impossible for other countries to remove exchange controls. The freedom of the London market has been illusory since we left the Gold Standard; foreigners are free to put their money here and receive interest, but this country is not free to employ that money in any way that would earn the interest it pays to foreigners.

[358] *Wall Street Journal*, 26 August 1939, 29 August 1939, 10 April 1940, 7 June 1940. An Unofficial Market in Sterling Continued to Operate.
[359] Siepmann Correspondence: 6 October 1931 to Professor Clay, 20 October 1931 to Dr Fuchs, 26 October 1931 to Sir Frederick Leith-Ross, 5 November 1931 to Dr Fuchs, 26 August 1932 to J. Postmus, 19 December 1932 to Soames Branco, 10 March 1933 to H.C.F. Finlayson, 6 November 1933 to Soames Branco, 27 October 1936 to Allan Sproul, Vice President of Federal Reserve, 31 March 1936 to Sproul, 17 April 1936 to F.F. Powell, 2 May 1936 to Sproul, 27 November 1936 to Lady Blackett, 9 January 1937 to Munakata, 13 August 1937 to C. Rogers, 29 July 1938 to O. Hobson, 23 December 1938 to Per Jacobson, 20 December 1939 to Soames Branco.
[360] Sir George Bolton, *Memoirs* (Bank of England, 13 January 1977), ch.11, Epilogue, Appendix 2: Foreign Exchange Markets between Munich and 3 September 1939.
[361] Bank of England, *London Foreign Exchange Market*.
[362] Exchange Equalisation Account Quarterly Report, January–February 1938, 31 March–30 June 1938.
[363] Bank of England: Memorandum on Exchange Policy, 14 October 1938.

The solution it proposed was more flexible exchange rates, but this was resisted by governments, including that of the UK, as they remained wedded to fixed exchange rates because of the certainty they delivered. What the Bank of England pointed out was that 'Exchange stability is defended as being necessary for trade. In fact traders can protect themselves against exchange movements by using the forward market. What really restricts trade is the exchange controls, which hot money perpetuates.'[364]

As war approached, the Bank of England pointed out the impossibility of defending the current exchange rate between the UK£ and the US$. Sterling was already weak against the US$ as 'the dollar is the refugee currency'.[365] The Bank of England felt it was powerless in the face of the worsening political situation in 1938 because the UK£ kept falling against the US$ despite intervention. There was genuine concern that there would be a collapse of confidence 'in the international markets centred in London', leading to an even greater flight from the £.[366] By November 1938, the funds available to the EEA were approaching exhaustion as it was being used to support the £ against the $. If that support was to continue, Siepmann demanded greater power and more resources, with the intention of squeezing the short-sellers, but the Treasury was not willing to provide these. The EEA was only designed to be used as a buffer to absorb the shocks to the £/$ exchange rate, not to support a fixed exchange rate.[367] By the late 1930s, the Bank of England was convinced that in peacetime, the foreign exchange market should be left to cope with exchange-rate volatility rather than rely on central bank intervention.[368] This reflected an awareness of the progress the foreign exchange market had made despite its failure to become like either the LSE or the London discount market. As George Bolton said in 1937, 'Ever since the war, it has been changing out of all recognition.'[369] That evolution of the London foreign exchange market was all to end with the outbreak of the Second World War. Any resurrection of London's foreign exchange market would have to await the end of that conflict, which did not come until 1945. By then, the world was a radically different place.

After the First World War, the London foreign exchange market emerged from the shadows, attracting the public's attention for the first time. The novelist C.S. Forester was one of those who suddenly became aware of what was happening in the foreign exchange market. In his 1926 crime novel, *Payment Deferred*, he featured the bank clerk, Mr Marble, who was a dealer in foreign exchange.

The department of the National County Bank, of which Mr. Henderson was executive chief, with Mr. Marble as his chief assistant, dealt solely with foreign exchange, buying and selling money all day, dollars for cotton spinners, francs for costumiers,

---

[364] Report on the Exchange Equalisation Account, 13 July 1937.
[365] Bank of England: Memorandum on Exchange Policy, 14 October 1938.
[366] Notes of Telephone Conversations with Ottawa Conducted by George Bolton, 14 November 1938, 16 November 1938.
[367] The Depreciation of Sterling, H.A. Siepmann, 22 November 1938; Report on the EEA, 20 February 1939; *EEA Quarterly Report*, 1 January 1938–31 March 1939.
[368] Bank of England: Memorandum, 14 January 1938.
[369] Foreign Exchange and Gold: Market Organisation and Technique, George Bolton, 6 April 1937.

pesetas for wine merchants, and dollars, pesetas, and, above all, marks, for speculators of every trade or none. Gambling in foreign exchange was becoming a national habit by which the National County Bank profited largely.

Acting in a personal capacity, Mr. Marble decided to speculate in French francs, using inside information about government intervention obtained from the bank's Paris agent. By continuously buying and selling as the franc fluctuated in value, he converted an initial investment of £600 into £51,000. When the bank discovered what he had been doing, they dismissed him, as employees were forbidden to speculate on their own account. He was then employed by a firm of foreign exchange brokers because of his expertise.[370]

It was the publicity given to the foreign exchange market in the 1920s, which C.S. Forester had picked up on, that fostered the belief that it was an entirely new development. This perception of novelty was aided by the appearance of specialist foreign exchange brokers and dealers, and the market's reliance on technology for trading rather than the face-to-face transactions found on the floor of the stock exchange or the daily negotiations conducted by the bill brokers as they called in at bank offices in the City on behalf of discount houses. To cope with the huge volume and variety of foreign exchange trading being conducted at speed in the 1920s, the foreign exchange dealers and brokers made extensive use of the telephone to maintain contacts between their offices in London, relied on the telephone and the telegraph to communicate with Paris and New York, and employed the latest model of calculating machine to convert the value of one currency into another as exchange rates fluctuated wildly.[371] While the pre-war currency trading by banks had been hidden from view, and the actions of the arbitrageurs dismissed as stock exchange speculation, the developments of the 1920s were conducted in the full glare of publicity.

Between the wars, foreign exchange trading in London remained a market without a central place of business or an institutional structure despite the precedent in the shape of the LSE. This made it more akin to the discount market but without the discipline imposed on that by the Bank of England. Foreign exchange remained the poor relation to London's other markets. The assumption was always there that its existence was temporary. Once the Gold Standard was restored, there would be no need for an exchange, a clearing house, a lender of last resort, or a set of rules and regulations because there would be no market. As there was no recognition that a market had existed before the First World War, there was also no acceptance that permanent trading arrangements needed to be put in place to cope with foreign exchange trading. That absence of identity contributed to the failure of contemporaries to recognize that it was a market whose form anticipated those that were to develop at the end of the twentieth century. It took the form of an over-the-counter

---

[370] C.S. Forester, *Payment Deferred* (London: The Bodley Head, 1926), 43–7, 62–6, 82.

[371] B. Batiz-Laso and T. Boyns, 'The Business and Financial History of Mechanization and Technological Change in Twentieth-Century Banking', *Accounting, Business and Financial History*, 14 (2004), 226; P. Wardley, *Women, Mechanization, and Cost-Savings in Twentieth Century British Banks and Other Financial Institutions* (Helsinki: WEHC, 2006), 4–5, 15–18.

market in which banks were the main players. As an interbank market, it relied on the reputation of banks as reliable counterparties. Without that reputation, other banks would not deal with them because of the risk of a default. As an interbank market, the foreign exchange market attracted the interest of the Bank of England, but that never extended to direct involvement or the provision of facilities such as acting as a lender of last resort or providing a clearing house. The Bank initially stood aloof from the foreign exchange market as it developed in the early 1920s and marked time between 1925 and 1931, when there was an attempted return to the Gold Standard. Britain's departure from the Gold Standard in 1931 marked a turning point in the Bank's relationship with the foreign exchange market as it increasingly engaged with it at a number of levels. Foreign exchange trading evolved into a successful market in the 1930s, which was appreciated by the banks that used it and recognized by the Bank as a solution to the currency instability that followed the failure to restore the Gold Standard. That position ended with the outbreak of the Second World War when the foreign exchange market was abruptly closed down. As a result, the legacy of what had been achieved before the wars was lost. What remained was the lack of understanding of the foreign exchange market among not only the public but also professional economists.

Conclusion

At the end of the First World War, the Gold Standard collapsed. It became impossible to maintain the fixed exchange rates between national currencies dictated by the relationship to the price of a specified quantity and quality of gold, once governments relaxed the rigid controls imposed during the war. The Gold Standard was followed by a period of highly volatile exchange rates in the early 1920s. In response to this volatility, there was extensive foreign exchange trading. However, the ability of the foreign exchange market to function as normal had been seriously damaged by the First World War. Before the war, banks had developed ways of coping with seasonal and cyclical imbalances by recycling funds. This was done either within branch networks or through interbank borrowing and lending. In both cases, the London money market played a crucial balancing role, reducing the need to exchange one currency for another. However, the war had greatly disrupted the international flow of funds and even reversed some. Banks could no longer rely on matching payments and receipts, and so they needed to cover their exposure to currency risks to a much greater degree than before the war. Another area of the foreign exchange market that had been badly damaged by the First World War was that which relied on asset arbitrage. Through redemptions and defaults, the stock of internationally held stocks and bonds, which were actively traded on different stock exchanges, had shrunk to a small fraction of what it had been. The $ securities held outside the USA had been bought back by US investors during the war while the Russian authorities had defaulted on the foreign debts after the revolution of 1917. There no longer existed a mass of securities that commanded multiple markets whose buying and selling acted as a counterweight to fluctuations in foreign exchange rates. Under these circumstances, the foreign exchange market had to devise new ways of operating that took account of much greater uncertainty and volatility while deprived of internationally mobile assets.

These completely changed monetary conditions that followed the First World War drove a transformation of the foreign exchange market in London. Within a year of the end of hostilities in 1918, and the removal of government controls, a much larger and more active foreign exchange market developed to cope with currency volatility. Though Britain's return to the Gold Standard in 1925 reduced the risks of holding sterling, they still remained and then grew as confidence in the UK£ ebbed from the late 1920s. Britain left the Gold Standard on 21 September 1931. The foreign exchange market then became an established feature of the City of London's financial markets, though there was always the expectation that the Gold Standard would be restored. That was not to be the case. With the outbreak of the Second World War on 1 September 1939, the foreign exchange market was closed down and did not reopen until 1951. By then, the precedents set before the First World War were ignored because it was widely believed that there had been no foreign exchange market due to the stability generated by the Gold Standard. The precedents set between the wars were also ignored because they were associated with a disorganized market characterized by instability and speculation. Instead, the decision was taken after the Second World War to opt for a managed currency that delivered the fixed exchange rates of the Gold Standard and the control that came with central bank intervention. That regime was abandoned in the 1970s.

As with any market, whether for stocks, shares, derivatives, commodities, or currencies, volatility attracted speculators who gambled on the rise and fall of prices. In the case of the foreign exchange market, this was the rate at which one currency was exchanged for another. It was this currency speculation with which the foreign exchange market became identified with between the wars, compared to the stability of the pre-war years. There was little understanding that the volatility was a product of the underlying conditions of monetary instability between the wars and that the foreign exchange market played an essential role as an adjustment mechanism. The market was extensively used by banks between the wars as they attempted to protect themselves from the currency risks they were exposed to. Through the loans they made and the deposits they accepted, banks were exposed, directly or indirectly, to foreign exchange fluctuations unless they matched their assets and liabilities by currency. This is what the market allowed them to do both on behalf of their customers and their own interbank operations. Activity in the market was also driven by banks searching for better rates of return. By selling a claim on the spot market and buying an equal claim on the forward market, a bank lent money with the return being the difference between the amount received and paid. Conversely, by buying in the spot market and selling in the forward market, a bank borrowed money with the cost being the difference between the amounts paid and received. The difference in price between the forward and the spot prices represented the interest paid or received and was thus equivalent to the discount at which bills had been sold at in the past.

While currency volatility made an active foreign exchange market essential, if banks were to cover the greater risks they were exposed to, a London location was no longer a certainty given the enhanced position of New York as a financial centre, and the importance of the US$ as an international currency. By the end of the First World War, the position of the City of London as a global financial centre had been considerably weakened while that of New York had been greatly strengthened, and this was evident throughout the interwar years. However, London continued to hold a major attraction to banks from around the world as it remained the centre of the international payments system, as well as providing a deep and broad money market where funds could easily be employed or obtained. London was still the unrivalled nucleus of the most extensive network of banking connections in the world. That gave it a continuing competitive advantage over New York. The foreign exchange market contributed to that by providing a facility through which banks could limit the greatly increased currency risks they were exposed to after the First World War, as well as another means through which they could either borrow or lend on a short-term basis. Nevertheless, the development of the market in London was not simply a product of the position that the City had established for itself before 1914 and had retained despite the effects of the war and the competition from New York. It also required a response from those in the City of London to the new requirements of the market. This came immediately as banks recruited dealers in foreign exchange and the number of foreign exchange brokers rapidly expanded. Such brokers were needed to handle the volume and variety of foreign exchange transactions taking place between a growing number of banks, though much took place through direct trading. The London foreign exchange market was the most important in the world between the wars, in terms of both volume and variety. The UK£ remained the world's vehicle currency and its main market was London.

Trading in this new foreign exchange market relied on the telephone or the telegraph, lacked a physical trading floor and an institutional structure, and never received the support and recognition accorded to the discount market by the Bank of England. That led to the market being dismissed by many contemporaries as chaotic and open to abuse, leaving governments, businesses, and the public yearning for the certainty of the fixed exchange rates of the pre-war years, which was attributed to the Gold Standard. The combination of nostalgia for the Gold Standard and the volatility of exchange rates between the wars convinced most observers that the market could not provide monetary stability. At best, it was seen as a temporary solution until there could be a return to fixed exchange rates. In the meantime, it was the market that provided the world between the wars with a mechanism through which debits and credits could be cleared internationally. Banks also continued to have a need for a market in which they could borrow from and lend to each other on a continuous basis in order to match their assets and liabilities and employ their funds remuneratively, and the market provided them with a means of doing so without the attached currency risks. That market was located in London between the wars not only because that was where it had been before but also because the depth and breadth of the people, businesses, and facilities located there made it able to respond to the need to fashion a new way of trading. London played a central role in the global foreign exchange market with the connections to Paris, for the French franc, and to New York, for the US\$, being key to its operations. There were some who recognized this even though their overriding desire was a return to the Gold Standard. That included Brown writing in 1940 though he recognized that it was no longer as dominant as it had been before 1914.

> The world's foreign exchange markets were still characterised after the war by the general triangular pattern of the pre-war days. London was still the great market for dollars for all Continental and Empire countries and for Japan. Paris was still the great foreign exchange trading market for the continent, and New York for the Canadian exchange. But London had become more active as a trading market in all exchanges. Sterling had not lost its character as a great international currency, but it had lost its unchallenged primacy. London was no longer in the same degree the place where the debits and credits resulting from foreign exchange trading in other centers were offset by transfers in the books of banks. ... The writ of London no longer ran throughout the world.[372]

[372] Brown, *International Gold Standard*, 602, 642, 782.

3
Forex in Chains, 1945–1970

Introduction

To a financial journalist like Paul Bareau, the future of the City of London as a global financial centre was inextricably linked to sterling as an international currency and that was in decline from 1945 onwards. In its place rose the US$ and that meant the replacement of London by New York.[1] All that stood between London and decline as a global financial centre was inertia, but that did not apply to the foreign exchange market. London's foreign exchange market had been closed down in 1939, on the outbreak of the Second World War, and was not given formal permission to reopen until 1951. Even then, it was subjected to controls and restrictions that suppressed its ability to operate until after 1958. Over these twenty years, both New York and Zurich had been free to trade and so had established themselves at the twin centres of the global foreign exchange market, serving North America and Western Europe, respectively. However, until after 1970, activity on the foreign exchange markets in New York, Zurich, and London remained subdued until the collapse of fixed exchange rates. Under fixed exchange rates, the price at which one currency was exchangeable for another did not vary, being maintained by active central bank intervention. Only when it was necessary to physically convert one currency for another was an exchange facility required. There was no necessity for banks to continually match assets and liabilities across different currencies, to cover current or future exposure, as exchange rates were fixed. There was also no opportunity to profit from exchange-rate volatility by active currency trading. As long as fixed exchange rates were in place, the role of the foreign exchange market was very limited.

At a meeting in Bretton Woods, New Hampshire, USA, in 1944, the representatives of forty-four countries, led by the USA and the UK, committed themselves to introduce and manage fixed exchange rates. The International Monetary Fund was established to oversee the system. Central banks were expected to intervene to maintain fixed exchange rates by buying and selling currencies. This commitment to fixed rates of exchange, and coordinated central bank intervention to preserve them, was an attempt to restore currency stability to the global monetary system. Currency stability would remove the need for governments to intervene with measures to restrict imports and promote exports that had done so much to damage the

---

[1] P. Bareau, 'The International Money and Capital Markets', in E.V. Morgan, R.A. Brealey, B.S. Yamey and G.P. Bareau (eds), *City Lights: Essays on Financial Institutions and Markets in the City of London* (London: Institute of Economic Affairs, 1979), 57–68.

Forex Forever. Ranald C. Michie, Oxford University Press. © Ranald C. Michie (2024).
DOI: 10.1093/oso/9780198903697.003.0004

smooth functioning of the world economy in the 1930s, and fuelled global political tensions that eventually broke out into military conflict. The regime of fixed exchange rates appeared a price worth paying in 1944 to avoid another conflict like the Second World War. With currency stability maintained by central bank intervention, and the discipline that was imposed on governments, it would be possible to restore the open world economy that had existed before the First World War, and so contribute to a revival of world prosperity. One causality was an active foreign exchange market. Under the Bretton Woods system, there would be no need for a foreign exchange market as the relationship of one currency to another was fixed. Central banks were mandated to intervene in order to maintain the agreed exchange rate by either increasing supply or reducing demand. That system eventually collapsed between 1971 and 1973 after a series of crises. What the Bretton Woods system had provided was not a permanent solution to currency instability but a temporary fix as the world economy adjusted to the new international order that emerged after the end of the Second World War. Even before the demise of the Bretton Woods system, a foreign exchange market had gradually developed to meet the need of banks with assets in one currency and liabilities in another. As central bank intervention suppressed currency volatility, the level of activity in this nascent foreign exchange market was very low. Confidence in the ability of central banks to maintain fixed exchange rates removed the need to cover exposure to currency fluctuations, while the lack of volatility made it difficult to generate profits from speculation.[2]

Background

There appear to be two Golden Ages for the global monetary system in modern times if exchange-rate stability is taken as the criteria for measurement. The first is that of the Gold Standard, especially between 1890 and 1914, or a period of twenty-four years. The second is a period of twenty years, from 1950 to 1970, when the Bretton Woods system of fixed exchange rates was in place. These are very different from each other. The first was a period when economies were open, government intervention was very limited, and only a few countries had central banks. The second was one in which economies were closed, government intervention was at a high level, and most countries had central banks. This highlights the issue of the trilemma. It is generally accepted that of the three objectives of monetary policy, it is only possible to combine two at any one time. The three objectives are fixed exchange rates, free financial flows, and autonomy of national monetary policy. In achieving fixed exchange rates under the first Golden Age, it was the autonomy of monetary policy that was sacrificed and free financial flows were preserved. In achieving fixed exchange rates in the second Golden Age, the autonomy of monetary policy was preserved and free financial flows sacrificed. Prior to the Gold Standard, exchange rates fluctuated and that

[2] For these years, see A. Naef, *An Exchange Rate History of the United Kingdom, 1945–1992* (Cambridge: Cambridge University Press, 2022).

was again the case after the collapse of the Bretton Woods system. What is missing in the discussion of the trilemma is any place for an active foreign exchange market and the contribution it could make to achieving a balance between fixed exchange rates, free financial flows, and the autonomy of monetary policy. The existence of a market delivers flexibility to financial instruments, and so meets the diverse and even opposing requirements of all participants. The issuer of a transferable bond obtains a fixed amount of money for a fixed period at a fixed price, while the purchaser acquires an asset that can be sold at any time and price because a market exists. The absence of the role played by the market for currencies is a major omission.[3]

In the periods when foreign exchange rates were fixed, the underlying assumption is that no active foreign exchange market existed. The fixing of exchange rates was sufficient to deliver either free financial flows, as under the Gold Standard, or the autonomy of national monetary policies, which was the case under the Bretton Woods system. In contrast, when foreign exchange rates were not fixed, such as at times between the world wars, an active foreign exchange market operated. That market was associated with currency volatility and economic instability, which is what made fixed exchange rates the preferred option as they delivered certainty and stability.[4] After the experience of currency instability between the wars, governments turned again to fixed exchange rates after the Second World War (1939–1945). During the Second World War, governments had imposed numerous controls over the financial system, both domestically and internationally. International financial flows were blocked, most markets were closed, and banks became agents of the state when collecting deposits and making loans. After the end of the Second World War, many of these controls were retained or even reinforced, as trust in the operation of banks and markets had largely evaporated after the experience of the interwar years. There was a widespread preference for governments to manage financial and monetary systems. International financial flows were regarded as destructive and thus had to be controlled when permitted at all. The result was to seal national financial markets behind national borders.[5] Despite a gradual relaxation of controls between 1950 and 1970, most governments continued to intervene in the working of banks and markets and the operation of the international financial system. Conditions such as these provided the environment within which it was possible to maintain fixed exchange rates through the intervention of central banks. Nevertheless, regular adjustments to exchange rates were required to reflect changes in the relative economic standing of individual countries. The UK£ was devalued against the US$ in both 1949 and 1967 as it proved impossible to defend indefinitely its exchange rate because of the relatively poor performance of the British economy. Conversely, currencies like the German mark and Japanese yen were revalued upwards as their economies

---

[3] R.M. Stulz, 'The Limits of Financial Globalization', *Journal of Finance*, 60 (2005), 1595–9; C.M. Reinhart and K.S. Rogoff, *This Time is Different: Eight Centuries of Financial Folly* (Princeton: Princeton University Press, 2009), 111, 205.

[4] For a discussion of the trilemma, see Obstfeld *et al.*, 'The Trilemma in History'; Esteves and Eichengreen, 'Trials of the Trilemma'.

[5] B.M. Smith, *The Equity Culture: The Story of the Global Stock Market*, Farrar, Straus and Giroux (New York: 2003), 147, 153, 168.

performed well. Central bank intervention to maintain a fixed exchange rate proved powerless in the face of fundamental changes in the value of one currency against another, when governments were unwilling or unable to take the remedial action that would restore equilibrium. Fixed exchange rates were not sustainable unless national governments followed the same policies. As that did not happen, the Bretton Woods system of fixed exchange rates eventually collapsed. In contrast, fixed exchange rates had survived under the Gold Standard because governments intervened little in their economies. The foreign exchange market did contain mechanisms that maintained exchange-rate stability but not permanently if governments followed policies that led to wide structural divergence in their economic performance.[6]

Throughout the 1950s and 1960s, there was a continuous battle to maintain the controls and compartmentalization that contributed to the ability of governments to maintain fixed exchange rates, while countenancing an increase in free financial flows and preserving the autonomy of national monetary policies. The effect of government intervention was to encourage financial activity to seek to evade the controls and compartmentalization imposed both domestically and internationally. It was from 1950 onwards that offshore financial centres flourished. Offshore centres were located in countries like Switzerland and Hong Kong, where they were able to escape not only onerous taxes and regulations but also the controls imposed by national governments on free financial flows. Their rise was accompanied by the growth of international financial markets that provided an alternative to those subject to government control. This happened first with those controls imposed by the British government in its attempt to preserve the value of the UK£ and the existence of the sterling area. It then happened with the US$, which was quickly replacing the UK£ as the preferred international currency, because of the controls and restrictions imposed by the US government. Whereas the route chosen to evade British controls was the use of places such as Hong Kong, Kuwait, the Channel Islands, and the Bahamas, in the case of the US$, it was London that benefited the most. Financial activity that took place in London was not governed by the jurisdiction of the US authorities even when it involved transactions by US banks in US$s for US clients. Within the US money market, funds also developed in order to evade the interest-rate caps placed on banks while ways were devised to bypass the legal prohibitions placed on both interstate banking and the combination of investment and commercial banking. The result in the 1960s was a gradual fraying of the controls and compartmentalization that were imposed by governments on their national financial systems, while internationally the rise of offshore financial centres and markets exposed the dilemmas of the trilemma. What had appeared a permanent solution to exchange-rate volatility at the end of the Second World War eventually proved unworkable in practice, dependent as it was on a degree of international cooperation that was impossible to achieve. The outcome after 1970 was a return to markets,

---

[6] E.M. Bernstein, 'The Search for Exchange Rate Stability: Before and After Bretton Woods', in O.F. Hamauda, R. Rowley and B.M. Wolf (eds), *The Future of the International Monetary System* (New York: 1989), 27–33.

including that for foreign exchange. At Bretton Woods, the search had been made for a system that would solve the impossible trilemma of combining fixed exchange rates, capital mobility, and independent monetary policies. The solution devised was one that relied upon government intervention. The desire was for a managed international monetary system but one that also delivered an open international economy. Even after the system put in place failed in 1971, due to growing fragility throughout the 1950s and 1960s, there remained a belief that a replacement could be found.[7]

The City of London

When the Second World War broke out in 1939, the banks and markets in the City of London were quickly brought under either direct government control or that of the Bank of England. During the war, the City was subjected to large-scale aerial bombing during which around one-third of the buildings were destroyed. These attacks made it impossible for the banks and markets located there to function as normal, even within the constraints imposed by the government and Bank of England.[8] This physical destruction was only the most visible evidence of the severe effects that the Second World War had upon the City. The government imposed from the outset a comprehensive and authoritarian regime of control. Under this regime, the role of the banks and the market was confined to providing the finance required by the government and those areas of economic activity deemed necessary for the war effort. The national debt, for example, tripled from £7.9 billion in 1939 to £21.4 billion in 1945 as the government monopolized the savings of the British people in its quest for the means necessary to achieve a military victory. At the same time, foreign assets with an estimated value of £4 billion were sold and the British government amassed large foreign debts. The inevitable result of these controls, and the diversion of bank and market staff into military and administrative posts, was to prevent the City from fulfilling its traditional functions as an international commercial and financial centre. Countries that had once turned to the City for all manners of financial and commercial services were forced to rely upon their own resources, reversing the relationship that had long existed.[9]

The Second World War also altered the relationship between the City of London and the British government. When the war ended in 1945, the apparatus of state control was not immediately dismantled.[10] In the years immediately following, the government consolidated the power over the City that it had already acquired.[11] One

---

[7] See James, 'Rethinking the Legacy of Bretton Woods'; Maes and Pascotti, 'Legacy of Bretton Woods'; Subacchi, 'System That Became a Non-system'.

[8] See C.H. Holden and W.G. Holford, *The City of London: A Record of Destruction and Survival* (London: 1951).

[9] L.G. Pearce, 'British Exchange Control: The System and Its Effects', in *Banking and Foreign Trade* (London: Institute of Bankers, 1952), 122.

[10] For these years, see S. Howson, *Domestic Monetary Management in Britain, 1919–38* (Cambridge University Press, 1975); S. Howson, *British Monetary Policy 1945–51* (Oxford University Press, 1993); Roberts, 'City of London'.

[11] See D. Sachs, 'Survey of the Financial Institutions of the City of London', in *Current Financial Problems of the City of London* (London: Institute of Bankers, 1949).

of the first acts of the incoming Labour government elected in 1945 was to take the Bank of England into public ownership, which it did in 1946. The Bank of England was turned into an official central bank, answerable to the UK Treasury. Though state ownership was not extended to other parts of the financial system, such as the banks and the London Stock Exchange, they had become accustomed to working closely with the government and the Bank of England during the war years, and that continued in peacetime. The discount market, for example, became exclusively focused on dealing in UK government debt and acting as the Bank of England's agent in the London money market. It had already moved in this direction in the 1930s. Given the perilous state of the balance of payments and the fragility of the UK£ as an international currency, the government retained exchange controls and restricted the movement of funds between the sterling area and the US$ zone. This cut off the City from much of the international business it had traditionally carried out. What remained were the British Empire and the sterling area, though even in these the City played a diminished role.[12]

Nevertheless, the City of London remained an important international financial centre in the 1950s because of the continued importance of the British economy and the existence of both the British Empire and the sterling area, though all were of declining significance. Helping to sustain that position was the lack of rivals. European financial centres had all been badly damaged by the war, including Paris, Brussels, Amsterdam, and Vienna, and they took time to recover. Berlin had been eliminated as a financial centre, isolated in the communist east, forcing West Germany to find an alternative. Frankfurt emerged only slowly as a replacement, with Hamburg being a more obvious choice, but it was not located in the American zone. Those European financial centres undamaged by the war, being located in neutral countries, lacked the depth, breadth, and connections of London, as with Zurich in Switzerland and Stockholm in Sweden. Elsewhere in the world, Tokyo and Shanghai had also been badly damaged by the war, while the likes of Sydney in Australia or Johannesburg in South Africa were too marginal. That left New York as the only serious rival to London as a global financial centre in the 1950s. New York was in the USA, the world's largest and richest economy, and benefited from the growing strength of the US$ as an international currency, and the foreign expansion of American multinational companies and banks. By the end of the Second World War, New York was already the most important financial centre in the world and it built on that position in the 1950s while London faded.[13]

Despite the ascendancy of New York, the rapid recovery of the world economy from the effects of the Second World War and then the enormous expansion in

[12] Bordo and Sylla, *Anglo-American Financial System*, 45; Toniolo (ed.), *Central Banks*: Cairncross, 42–6; Fforde, *The Bank of England and Public Policy, 1941–1958* (Cambridge: 1992), 695–7; Roberts, *Schroders*, 313; Roberts, 'The City of London', 69–72; *Wolff's Guide*, 16–17, 53–63; J. Tomlinson, 'Attlee's Inheritance and the Financial System: Whatever Happened to the National Investment Board', *Financial History Review*, 1 (1994), 143–54; D.M. Ross, 'The Clearing Banks and the Finance of British Industry, 1930–1959', *Business and Economic History*, 20 (1991), 24–5; Pearce, 'British Exchange Control', 101, 121.
[13] R. Middleton, *Government Versus the Market: The Growth of the Public Sector, Economic Management and British Economic Performance, c. 1890–1979* (Aldershot: Edward Elgar, 1997), 91; S. Bell and B. Kettle, *Foreign Exchange Handbook* (London: 1983), 75; G. Dosoo, *The Eurobond Market* (London: 1992), 1–10.

international trade and finance during the 1950s did present great opportunities for the City of London.[14] It retained much of the infrastructure and connections that had made it the leading international financial centre in the past. No other European centre could match the depth and breadth of London's markets for money, securities, and commodities and the network connections of the banks located there.[15] Though New York was now the centre of the global capital market, London retained a lead over it as a centre for banking. Even in 1960, London hosted more offices of foreign banks than New York. In addition, London continued to be home to a group of British overseas banks with extensive international connections, especially to Asia and Africa, while Britain's domestic banks all had numerous correspondent links with banks spread around the world.[16] Holding back the ability of the City of London's banks and markets from responding to the opportunities presented by the rapidly expanding world economy in the 1950s were the controls exercised by the government either directly or via the Bank of England.[17] British banks remained closely supervised by the Bank of England, while the government only gradually allowed the markets for money, capital, currencies, securities, and commodities the freedom they required to operate.[18] What helped preserve the importance of the City of London were the controls other governments applied to most other European financial centres, including Paris. This segmented financial markets and the business of banks along national boundaries. International financial flows were channelled through governments or took place by means of internal transfers within multinational corporations. The use of offshore centres also provided an alternative to the facilities provided by established financial centres. Zurich became an increasingly important European financial centre in the 1950s as it faced fewer restrictions.[19] The controls and complexities of international finance in the 1950s favoured the largest banks as they possessed the management and staff necessary to comply with regulations, the size and spread to internalize transactions, and the reputation to act as trusted counterparties with other banks at home and abroad.[20]

[14] See Central Office of Information, *UK Financial Institutions* (London: 1957); P. Bareau, 'The Financial Institutions of the City of London', in *The City of London as a Centre of International Trade and Finance* (London: Institute of Bankers, 1961).

[15] C.R. Schenk, *Hong Kong as an International Financial Centre: Emergence and Development, 1945–65* (London: 2001), 125.

[16] H.H. Thackstone, 'Work of the Foreign Branch of a Commercial Bank', in *Current Financial Problems and the City of London* (London: Institute of Bankers, 1949), 122, 129; *International Banking in London*, 30; Newall, *Japan and the City*, 21–2; Jones, *Multinational Banking*, 414–15; Winton, *Lloyds Bank*, 155.

[17] Einzig, *Textbook on Foreign Exchange*, 17; Ellis, *Heir to Adventure*, 148–54; Bonin, *Société Générale*, 29–30.

[18] See J.H. Dunning and E.V. Morgan, *An Economic Study of the City of London* (London: 1971); F.W. Paish, 'The London New Issue Market', *Economica*, 18 (1951), 1–17.

[19] Y. Cassis, G. Feldman and U. Olson, *The Evolution of Financial Institutions and Markets in Twentieth-Century Europe* (Scolar Press, 1995), 67–71; M. Ikle, *Switzerland: An International Banking and Finance Center* (Stroudsburg: 1972), 30; Cassis (ed.), *Finance and Financiers*, 364–5; Cleveland and Huertas, *Citibank*, 224–5; Geisst, *Wall Street*, 276.

[20] N. Ferguson, *The Cash Nexus: Money and Power in the Modern World, 1700–2000* (London: 2001), 166; M. Feldstein (ed.), *International Capital Flows* (Chicago: 1999); G. Krozewski, *Money and the End of Empire: British International Economic Policy and the Colonies, 1947–58* (Basingstoke: 2001), 160–5; Schenk, *Hong Kong as an International Financial Centre*, 46, 49–50, 53, 72–3, 85, 115.

Though rival financial centres were also hampered by government controls, the City of London faced an increasingly bleak future by the end of the 1950s because it was tied to the UK economy, the British Empire, and the sterling area. All these were in decline in the face of the economic revival of the likes of Germany and Japan, the pursuit of independent policies by the countries within the British Commonwealth, and the growing ascendancy of the US$ as a reserve currency and for international transactions. What saved the City of London from participating in a similar decline in the 1960s was the switch from the UK£ to the US$ as a basis of its operations. The popularity of the US$ over the UK£ accelerated after the 1957 monetary crisis, when the British government intervened to restrict the international use of sterling. Sterling was then made fully convertible in 1958, making it easier for holders to transfer their allegiance to the US$.[21] All this should have contributed to the ascendancy of New York as the dominant financial centre in the world, the rise of Tokyo as an Asian financial centre, and the displacement of London by either Frankfurt or Paris as the financial centre of Europe. Both Germany and France were members of the European Union, whereas the UK was not until 1973. None of this happened. Neither Paris nor Frankfurt was able to take advantage of an increasingly integrated European economy in the 1960s as it remained deeply divided along national lines when it came to the provision of financial services. Restrictions in Japan held back developments in the financial sector there, such as a version of the Glass–Steagall Act, which hampered the banks. The continuing divisions in Asia along national boundaries also prevented the emergence of Tokyo as a dominant financial centre for that continent. Finally, and most importantly, the long-standing restrictions placed on US banks and financial markets, along with the measures introduced by the US government in the 1960s to support the value of the $, all undermined the importance of New York as a financial centre. In contrast, by ditching the UK£ and substituting the US$, the City of London was able to capture the business that would have flowed to New York if it had not been for the actions of the US authorities on imposing a tax on the interest paid on deposits, curtailing short-term lending to foreigners, and the forcing of US multinational corporations to raise new funds abroad.[22] As the British merchant banker, Sir Cyril Kleinwort, noted in 1971, 'The whole structure of London's financial system and its techniques floated up on a surge of new money and new ideas.'[23]

Helping the recovery of the City of London as an international financial centre in the 1960s was the benign attitude of the British government. The British government saw no problem with this switch to the US$ in London in the 1960s because it involved foreign banks conducting business for foreign clients. The focus of the Bank of England, acting on behalf of the British government, was the supervision and

---

[21] R.M. Levich, *International Financial Markets: Prices and Policies* (New York: 1998), 278–9; Krozewski, *Money and the End of Empire*, 165; C.R. Schenk, *Britain and the Sterling Area: From Devaluation to Convertibility in the 1950s* (London: 1994), 8–9, 15–16, 33, 128.

[22] P. Jorion, 'Risk and Turnover in the Foreign Exchange Market', in J.A. Frankel, G. Galli and A. Giovannini (eds), *The Microstructure of Foreign Exchange Markets* (Chicago: 1996), 21; P. Hartmann, *Currency Competition and Foreign Exchange Markets: The Dollar, the Yen and the Euro* (Cambridge: 1998), 32.

[23] Kleinwort, 'The City', 171.

policing of the domestic financial system and the use of sterling. It made no attempt to control business conducted in US$s by American banks acting on behalf of foreign companies though it took place in their London offices.[24] This business thrived, according to Burn, in 'a non-regulatory vacuum in the City'.[25] The result was that London attracted not only US banks seeking the freedom to operate in ways denied to them at home but also an increasing number of other banks from around the world needing to conduct an international business using US$s but unwilling to do so in New York because of the taxes and restrictions they would face there. Whereas only sixty-nine foreign banks had a direct presence in the City of London in 1957, the number had more than doubled to 159 by 1970.[26] Among these was a large influx of US banks of all kinds who could escape in London the US laws dating from the 1930s that prevented them from combining commercial and investment banking.[27]

It was these new arrivals, especially from the USA, that were responsible for many of the innovations that took place in the City of London in the 1960s, whether it involved products or markets. Between 1962 and 1968, the number of overseas and foreign banks with branches in London grew from 82 to 108 and they increasingly traded among themselves, bypassing the established markets. The result was the emergence of parallel markets, including an interbank one that operated at very narrow margins between interest paid and received. According to the Bank of England, in 1968, 'The market serves to absorb or supply funds when an individual bank is unable from its own resources to match available funds with requirements; interest rate margins between banks are, naturally, narrower than those between bank and customer.' This market was fulfilling the same function that the London discount market had traditionally done but with all transactions being in US$s. In May 1966, the US bank, First National City Bank, introduced to London the negotiable certificate of deposit, which was already in use in New York. These had been developed in New York because Regulation Q prevented interest being paid on deposits of under thirty days while there were also caps on the amount of interest that could be paid on time deposits. 'The merit of the certificate of deposit is that the holder can earn rates very little below those offered for a fixed term deposit, but can still, if necessary, draw on the funds before the deposit matures, by negotiating the certificate in the

[24] For these years, see S. Battilosssi and Y. Cassis (eds), *European Banks and the American Challenge: European Banking under Bretton Woods* (Oxford: 2002). Also, R.C. Michie, *The City of London: Continuity and Change, 1850–1990* (London: Palgrave Macmillan, 1992), 138–9.
[25] G. Burn, 'The State, the City and the Euromarkets', *Review of International Political Economy*, 6 (1999), 236.
[26] Bell and Kettell, *Foreign Exchange Handbook*, 75–6; P. Einzig, *The Euro-Bond Market* (London: 1969), 65, 147, 195; E.W. Clendenning, *The Euro-Dollar Market* (Oxford: 1970), 7, 22–3, 186; Einzig, *History of Foreign Exchange*, 241; *International Banking*, 53; Newall, *Japan and the City*, 24–5, 32, 50; Cleveland and Huertas, *Citibank*, 253–5; Geisst, *Wall Street*, 311, 331, 356–7; Roberts, *Schroders*, 418; L. Gall et al., *Deutsche Bank*, 754; Bonin, *Société Générale*, 60. See C.R. Schenk, 'The Origins of the Eurodollar Market in London: 1955–1963', *Explorations in Economic History*, 35 (1998); W.M. Clarke, *The City and the World Economy* (London: 1965); R. Fry (ed.), *A Banker's World: The Revival of the City, 1957–1970* (London: 1970); Inter-bank Research Organisation, *The Future Of London as an International Financial Centre* (London: 1973); S.F. Frowen (ed.), *A Framework of International Banking* (London: 1979): chapters by Shaw.
[27] R. Shaw, 'London as a Financial Centre'. Reprinted in R.C. Michie (ed.), *The Development of London as a Financial Centre* (London: 2000), 131–2.

secondary market.' These certificates of deposit were denominated in US$s, widely accepted as good collateral, and their negotiability allowed them to be bought and sold until maturity. They, thus, supplemented the discount market where sterling bills of exchange and treasury bills had long been bought and sold between banks, with the discount houses acting as intermediaries and the Bank of England as the lender of last resort.[28]

In contrast to the dynamism exhibited by the new arrivals in the City of London in the 1960s, especially from the USA, the established British banks and institutions were much slower to embrace the opportunities and meet the challenges that the evolving post-war global financial system posed. After the experience of wartime cooperation, those running Britain's banks and markets were willing to work closely with post-war governments of all political persuasions in supporting the operation of its monetary policies. Without the need for active intervention and control, the UK government was able to reshape the UK financial system, benefiting from its insulation from external forces through the rigid policing of exchange controls. In return for this cooperation, the UK financial sector gained the support of government, acting through the Bank of England, in maintaining a regime of anti-competitive practices whether it involved the banks, the discount houses, or the members of the Stock Exchange.[29] One consequence of these anti-competitive practices was the encouragement given to alternative financial institutions as they could expand by either offering higher rates of interest to savers or more generous terms to borrowers. The UK financial system had always included a variety of businesses ranging from the risk-averse savings banks to the risk-orientated investment banks as well as mutual organizations such as the building societies. It was this fluid mixture that had ensured that the financial system maintained a balance between conservative and dynamic behaviour as each participant could choose their own field of operation while competing at the margin with each other. The actions taken by the government after the Second World War introduced a much more rigid compartmentalization, leaving each type of financial institution with a near monopoly over a particular branch of the financial services industry, and thus relatively immune from competition, especially as the business conducted was concentrated in the hands of fewer and fewer participants. Within this segmented system, the large banks monopolized the payments system and lending to business; the investment banks provided access to the capital market; members of the London Stock Exchange had exclusive control over the securities market; the discount houses acted as the interface between government and the money market; and the building societies dominated the collection of retail savings and the provision of mortgage finance to home buyers. There was little incentive to compete or innovate, especially at times when government-imposed controls restricted access to credit and denied savers higher rates of interest.[30] It was not until after 1970 that the

[28] Bank of England, 'Overseas and Foreign Banks in London', *BEQB*, 8 (1968), 156–64.
[29] B. Griffiths, 'The Development of Restrictive Practices in the UK Monetary System', *Economic and Social Studies*, 41 (1973), 8, 12, 15.
[30] C.J. Montgomery, 'The Clearing Banks, 1952–77: An Age of Progress', *JIB*, 98 (1977), 89–91; Rybczynski, 'Merchant Banks', 117–20.

Bank of England attempted to encourage greater competition.[31] As long as the financial system was compartmentalized, the Bank of England could exercise a measure of control that maintained monetary stability, especially when its remit was confined to the largest retail banks and operations involving the £ sterling.[32]

In 1991, the Bank of England provided its own assessment of the years between 1950 and 1970.

> From the war until the 1960s the British banking sector was remarkably stable. It operated within a highly-structured financial system, with clear demarcations from other types of institution. This was reinforced both by its oligopolistic behaviour and by various forms of official controls, such as lending constraints imposed for monetary purposes and exchange controls. Both had the effect of restricting competition.[33]

It was this limited competition that became a pronounced feature of the entire British financial system in the 1950s and 1960s through the extensive use of restrictive practices.[34] These practices were condoned and even encouraged by the Bank of England and the UK government. Government monetary policy, for example, was based on controlling the ability of the largest banks to make loans.[35] What saved the City of London as a global financial centre after 1945 was that the post-war era of control and compartmentalization applied to all countries and was not conducive to the development of alternative financial centres because of the barriers to the free movement of funds around the world and the operation of global markets. Intergovernment transfers, managed currencies, and state regulation of banks and markets, along with national financial systems under the direction of central banks, were characteristics of the twenty-five years that followed the end of the Second World War. Those financial centres that did flourish in this era were those that could provide banks, businesses, and individuals with a means of escaping the controls in place, as well as evading or avoiding high taxes and oppressive regulations. Known as offshore financial centres, they could attract businesses by providing them with an environment of low taxes, minimal regulations, and few controls. Among them were included the likes of

---

[31] Bank of England, 'The Secondary Banking Crisis and the Bank of England's Support Operations', *BEQB*, 18 (1978), 232–3; Bank of England, 'The Performance of Major British Banks, 1970–90', *BEQB*, 31 (1991), 508–15; D. Vander Weyer, 'The Threats and Opportunities Facing British Banks: A 10 Year View', *JIB*, 101 (1980), 72; L.S. Dyer, 'The Secondary Banking Crisis', *JIB*, 104 (1983), 46–8. See J. Grady and M. Weale, *British Banking, 1960–85* (London: 1986).

[32] Singleton, *Central Banking*, 4–9, 18, 83, 127–32, 135–8, 146, 177, 216, 225–6, 229, 236–7; Grady and Weale, *British Banking*, 36–9, 51–7, 60; C.R. Schenk, *The Decline of Sterling: Managing the Retreat of an International Currency, 1945–1992* (Cambridge: 2010), 88–9, 99, 110, 114, 117, 125, 133–4, 212, 216–23, 225–9, 320; R.J. Clark, 'British Banking: Changes and Challenges', *JIB*, 89 (1968), 468–78; R. O'Brien, 'The Euro-Currency Market', *JIB*, 92 (1971), 245–9 (O'Brien was Chairman of Charles Fulton and Company, one of the largest of the inter-dealer brokers); Montgomery, 'Clearing Banks, 1952–77', 89–91; Grossman, *Unsettled Account*, 96, 168, 285, 286–9.

[33] Bank of England, 'Performance of Major British Banks', 508.

[34] Montgomery, 'Clearing Banks, 1952–77', 89–91; Rybczynski, 'Merchant Banks', 117–20.

[35] Griffiths, 'The Development of Restrictive Practices', 8, 12, 15.

Zurich, Geneva, and Luxembourg in Europe; Hong Kong in the Far East; Kuwait in the Middle East; and a growing band of small states such as those in the Caribbean.

Banks and Money

The Second World War had a serious effect on the global network of banking connections through which payments were made and received, money was borrowed and lent, and assets and liabilities were matched by amount, time, location, and currency. The City of London was the hub of this network through the branches, agents, and representatives that banks maintained there. Aerial bombing destroyed many of the offices located in the City, while those of enemy countries were closed, and staff from others were withdrawn for their own safety. No longer could the branches of British overseas banks, for example, rely on London for financial services but were forced to either turn to the resources available locally or use New York as a replacement. With the disruption and uncertainty that remained after the ending of hostilities, there was no rapid recovery of these international connections, especially as exchange and capital controls remained in place and Britain was no longer a source of cheap and plentiful credit. As a country, Britain was bankrupt at the end of the war, with outstanding international liabilities outweighing assets, and had to rely on the forbearance of its creditors and financial assistance from the USA and Canada. These circumstances dictated a continuance of wartime controls and practices into peacetime.[36] The discount market, which had once served the global financial system, became little more than a device through which the Bank of England raised short-term loans from the London banks and managed the government's monetary policy.[37] Banks had already turned to New York and Zurich in the 1940s for financial services.[38] Nevertheless, the City of London remained an important centre for international banking and an important money market in the 1950s, aided by its position within the Empire and sterling area.[39] Sterling was still used extensively for the finance of international trade, only slowly losing out to the US$.[40] The need for an interface between the world's banks had never disappeared during the Second World War and it then grew strongly during the 1950s as the world economy expanded rapidly. Without this interface, it would have been impossible for international trade to recover, with serious consequences for the world economy.[41]

---

[36] Einzig, *Forward Exchange*, 2nd ed., 13.

[37] J. Fforde, *The Bank of England*, 222–3, 727, 756–7; Sayers, *Gilletts*, 124–6, 138.

[38] Einzig, *Forward Exchange*, 41, 303; Einzig, *Textbook on Foreign Exchange*, 17; Ellis, *Heir to Adventure*, 148–54; Ikle, *Switzerland*, 30; *The Times*, 13 October 1952, 19 October 1953, 13 September 1954, 29 December 1958, 31 December 1958, 2 February 1959, 14 March 1960.

[39] F.H.H. King, *The History of the Hongkong and Shanghai Banking Corporation*, vol. 4, *The Hongkong Bank in the Period of Development and Nationalism, 1941–1984: From Regional Bank to Multinational Group* (Cambridge, 1991), 439; Newall, *Japan and the City*, 21–3.

[40] C.R. Schenk, *Britain and the Sterling Area*, 8–9, 15–16, 33, 128.

[41] Scammell, *London Discount Market*, 243–4; Fletcher, *Discount Houses*, 57, 62, 117, 124, 163–4, 253–6; Nevin and Davis, *London Clearing Banks*, 161, 172–5, 181–4, 198–9; D.K. Shephard, *The Growth and*

The City of London continued to provide this interface with foreign banks operating branches there to replace long-standing correspondent arrangements. As banks grew in size and scale after the Second World War, making them better able to serve their business customers and cope with government-imposed regulations, they could support a branch located in a major financial centre like London. A presence in London was becoming essential as the world economy became more integrated, as that was where a bank could conduct business with other banks more easily and quickly than anywhere else. London contained the densest concentration of bank offices in the world as well as indirect connections through correspondent links. By opening a branch in London, a bank could internalize many of the transactions that it outsourced to other banks through a correspondent link, such as to a British domestic bank like the Midland. In that way, the foreign bank could capture for itself the profits to be made from such business as handling payments and receipts as well as manage directly its participation in the interbank money market. US banks, in particular, opened branches in London to engage in an international business with banks already there as well as escape domestic controls on the nature of business they could do. The Glass–Steagall Act of 1933 had forced the separation of deposit and investment banking in the USA, but the combination of the two was becoming essential for any bank that wanted to serve its largest corporate clients. These clients required not only credit facilities but also the ability to raise finance through the issue of stocks and bonds. A US bank could handle both activities in London but not in New York. In the wake of the arrival of a growing number of US banks came others from around the world, such as those from continental Europe who were either reopening closed offices or expanding those that had long existed. Japanese banks were also attracted for the same reason as US ones, because they were subject to an equivalent of the Glass–Steagall Act introduced by the US administration after the Second World War. In 1960, London hosted the offices and branches of 139 foreign banks compared to the 77 in New York.[42]

Contributing to continuing attractions of the City of London as a location for banks from around the world was its money market. This allowed banks to employ idle funds remuneratively and to supplement their own resources by borrowing from other banks to meet a temporary shortfall. The central element in this money market at the end of the Second World War was the discount market. In the discount market, banks could borrow from and lend to each other using bills of exchange as collateral, with discount houses acting as intermediaries. A discount house selling a bill to a bank was borrowing money, whereas the purchase of a bill meant the bank was borrowing money. In each case, the discount house was taking a position as it expected to match its borrowing and lending on a daily basis. If the discount house could not

---

Role of UK Financial Institutions, 1880–1962 (London: 1971), 15–16; Collins, Money and Banking, 268, 272, 293, 317–21, 424, 440, 449, 450, 476; Shaw, London Money Market, 20, 57, 162, 171; Committee on the Working of the Monetary System, Report, 121, 139, 162–6, 197–8; Principal Memoranda of Evidence, vol. 2, 4, 24–5, 49; Sayers, Bank of England, 578–9; Institute of Bankers, The Pattern and Finance of Foreign Trade (London: 1949); Institute of Bankers, The London Discount Market Today (London: 1962); The Institute of Bankers, The Bank of England Today (London: 1964).

[42] Burn, 'The State, the City', 236.

finance the loans it had made through borrowing, it was able to cover the deficit by borrowing from the Bank of England but only at a high rate of interest and providing good quality bills as collateral.[43] It was through the discount houses that the Bank of England acted as the lender of last resort rather than directly to individual banks facing liquidity difficulties. In turn, the discount houses kept the Bank fully informed of the position of every bank they did business with, as they were aware of those that needed to borrow and those able to lend during their twice daily walks around the City. The Bank of England was also in a position to monitor the position of every British bank as they all kept deposits with it and drew on these to make payments to other banks in settlement of their differences in the clearing house. Before 1914, these bills were largely generated through international financial and commercial transactions, but by the late 1930s, they largely comprised the treasury bills issued by the UK government to finance its short-term borrowing, and this was the position after 1945.[44] As Oscar Hobson noted in 1946, 'The Discount Market has during the war become a cog in the machine for the issuing, redemption and replacement of Government loans, under conditions of falling interest rates.'[45]

Apart from that change, the discount market in London operated in much the same way after 1945 as it had in the past. The use made by banks of the discount market was not confined to Britain. Banks with either head offices or branches in London were at the centre of a global banking network through the correspondent links they maintained with other banks located throughout the world. These links largely survived that conflict.[46] It was through this correspondent network centred in London that banks from around the world not only made and received payments but also borrowed and lent to each other, using the sale and purchase of UK Treasury bills as the means of doing so. Though the UK£ was in steady decline as a reserve currency after the Second World War, it long continued to be favoured by banks because of the continuing appeal of the London money market as both a payments centre and a location in which they could borrow from and lend to each other. The problem was that the British government simultaneously exploited its ability to borrow easily and cheaply in its own currency and restricted the use of sterling as an international currency. In 1957, the use of sterling to finance trade between third countries was withdrawn by the UK government because of the strain it was putting on UK foreign exchange reserves. This ban was not lifted until 1963 and then reimposed in 1968. The response by banks was to continue to use London as a location for both payments and lending and borrowing but to switch to the use of the US$ rather than the UK£, leading to the emergence of the Eurodollar market from 1955 onwards.[47]

One consequence of that shift was to undermine the importance of the discount market as alternative money markets emerged during the 1960s that operated either

[43] 'Commercial Bills', *BEQB*, 1 (1960–1), 27.
[44] W.T.C. King, 'War and the Money Market', *JIB*, 58 (1947), 47–61.
[45] O. Hobson, 'Future of the City', *JIB*, 57 (1946), 91–9, cf. 95.
[46] B.B. Boreham, 'The London Information Market', *The Banker*, 19 (August 1945), 90.
[47] Schenk, *Decline of Sterling*, 88–9, 99, 110, 114, 117, 125, 133–4, 212, 216–23, 225–9, 320.

through direct lending and borrowing between banks or the use of inter-dealer brokers.[48] The discount market continued to be used extensively by the British deposit banks, because of their largely domestic business and focus on sterling area transactions. It was other banks that used these alternative money markets to employ deposits that they had no immediate use for and to supplement internally generated funds when demand for loans exceeded what they could supply. As a result, the discount market quickly declined in importance among both the British overseas banks and the foreign banks with branches in London. British overseas banks had long used London as a hub through which to balance their inter-branch business and as a centre where they could lend and borrow for a short term as required.[49] In terms of interbank lending versus the discount market, these banks split their business 75%/25% in favour of the discount market in 1951, but by 1960, they had switched to a 53%/47% split in favour of the interbank market, followed by a rapid decline from then on. In 1970 the ratio was 92%/8% in favour of the interbank market. Over that period, the total value of lending between the British overseas banks and foreign banks with head offices or branches in London had risen from £239 million in 1951 to £4,728 million in 1970.[50] This reflected the increasing international appeal of London as a location for interbank borrowing and lending through a combination of restrictions in other centres and the facilities available there, especially the presence of so many other banks and the operations of the inter-dealer brokers.[51] The same data is not available for UK-based banks until 1971 though what is available for the period from 1951 onwards for the Scottish and Northern Irish banks does not indicate a similar switch to the interbank market away from the discount market over that period.[52]

The Bank of England was well aware of the changes taking place in the London money market with the arrival of foreign banks as they replaced correspondent links with UK banks with branches of their own. The Bank was also well aware of the growth of alternative money markets through which these banks borrowed and lent among each other.[53] Following on from the convertibility of the UK£ in December 1958, they noted a significant increase in the volume of deposits from abroad placed with the British overseas banks and the London branches of foreign banks, with US banks being especially prominent. Of this, approximately 40 per cent was held

---

[48] O'Brien, 'Euro-Currency Market', 245–9 (O'Brien was Chairman of Charles Fulton and Company, one of the largest of the inter-dealer brokers); Montgomery, 'Clearing Banks', 1952–77, 89–91.

[49] G.O. Nwanko, 'British Overseas Banks in the Developing Countries', *JIB*, 93 (1972), 152; F. Bostock, 'The British Overseas Banks and Development Finance in Africa after 1945', in G. Jones (ed.), *Banks and Money: International and Comparative Finance in History* (London: Frank Cass, 1991), 159.

[50] Source: *Bank of England Quarterly Bulletin Statistical Supplement, 1960–1980*. The data used is for 31 December of each year and excludes UK domestic banks. It only includes British overseas banks and those foreign banks with branches in London. These banks were permitted to accept deposits in London, whereas those banks with only representative offices in London were not. What is included are the balances these banks had with other banks and their lending to the London money market.

[51] A.A. Weismuller, 'London Consortium Banks', *JIB*, 95 (1974), 201; B. Mitchell, 'An American Banker's View of the City', *JIB*, 95 (1974), 186; R. Pringle, 'The Foreign Banks in London', *JIB*, 99 (1978), 48.

[52] Source: *Bank of England Quarterly Bulletin Statistical Supplement, 1960–1973*. The data used is for 31 December of each year. It is compiled from the separate data produced for each category of UK domestic banks. It was not until 1971 that a return was produced for London banks' balances with other banks.

[53] Bank of England, 'Overseas and Foreign Banks in London', 18–20.

as foreign currency rather than sterling, and so was not employed in the discount market. The report observed that

> Most of the steep rise shown since 1958 has occurred in foreign currency deposits, predominantly in US dollars or 'Eurodollars'. These deposits are mostly made by banks in Western Europe, and are part of the greatly increased volume of short-term funds which now move readily from one international financial centre to another.

The reason given for this inflow in 1962 was that 'There is available in London an exceptionally broad range of opportunities for the employment of funds overnight or for any longer period, and frequently offering yields that are higher than those readily obtainable in financial markets abroad.' When these opportunities involved the use of foreign currencies, they were all matched between banks. Though recognizing that these foreign currency deposits could be very volatile, and thus pose a threat to the stability of banks, the Bank of England was not unduly concerned because UK deposit banks were little involved.[54] Nevertheless, it steadily increased its coverage of foreign banks in London from December 1962 onwards, in order to monitor what they were doing.[55]

By 1964, the Bank of England was acutely aware that there had been a large increase in foreign currency deposits in London and that the UK banks, who were becoming involved as their correspondents, did not want to hold sterling because of the risks of devaluation. They also knew that much of this money was flowing from the USA because of the restrictions imposed there on the rate of interest paid on deposits.

> Banks in London have been able to attract large sums in dollars by quoting better rates for deposits, including interest on money at call and very short notice—categories which earn nothing at all with New York banks—and have employed them at less than the US lending rate and still made a worthwhile return.[56]

Welcome as this business was in reviving the fortunes of the City of London as an international financial centre, the Bank of England had growing concerns for its ability to act as the lender of last resort to the London money market if a crisis should occur.[57] An unintended consequence of London remaining the centre of the international money market rather than it relocating to New York was that the central bank it looked to in an emergency was not the Federal Reserve but the Bank of England and that institution was no longer able to fulfil that role for a number of reasons.

[54] 'Inflows and Outflows of Foreign Funds', *BEQB*, 2 (1962), 93–9; Bank of England, 'Bank Liquidity in the United Kingdom', *BEQB*, 2 (1962), 248.

[55] See Bank of England, 'New Banking Statistics', 162–5; Bank of England, 'Developments in UK Banking and Monetary Statistics since the Radcliffe Report', *BEQB*, 25 (1985), 392–7.

[56] Bank of England, 'UK Banks' External Liabilities and Claims in Foreign Currencies', *BEQB*, 4 (1964), 100–6.

[57] Bank of England, 'UK and US Treasury Bill Market', 327; Bank of England, 'The London Discount Market: Some Historical Notes', *BEQB*, 7 (1967), 146; 'Overseas and Foreign Banks in London', 156–64.

Firstly, the Bank of England's involvement in the London money market was driven by the needs of UK monetary policy and not the needs of the market itself as had been the case in the past. Secondly, the London money market had grown in both scale and reach to become the central money market for the world's banks.[58] Thirdly, the Bank of England was not in touch with this market because it was now out of the loop as transactions took place directly between banks or via money market brokers whose role it was to arrange interbank business. Finally, the Bank of England lacked the ability to increase the supply of US$s to meet a liquidity crisis in the interbank market, as only the Federal Reserve Bank could do that.

There was always a counterparty risk as banks borrowed from and lent to each other. That risk had been traditionally minimized in two ways. The first was the use of collateral in the shape of bills of exchange, whether commercial or treasury. These were short-dated financial instruments that could be traded until maturity. The other was the existence of a lender of last resort that provided a reservoir of liquidity to the money market, and so balanced supply and demand. What emerged from the late 1950s onwards was an interbank market that operated without collateral and without a lender of last resort, and as it grew, so did the counterparty risk run by each bank.[59] By 1971, the size of the London Interbank Market had grown to £9.1 billion. Of this, only £2 billion or 22 per cent was in the hands of British banks, while £7.1 billion (78 per cent) was with non-UK banks.[60] London hosted this market because the restrictions on international business maintained by governments and central banks around the world drove interbank activity in its direction. The exchange controls imposed by the British government in 1947 only covered the use of the £, and ignored other currencies, including the $. As the US government imposed restrictions on the use of the $, banks discovered they could evade these by operating out of London. London banks had long operated non-sterling accounts on behalf of correspondent banks, having started to do so in the 1920s. Thus, it was both a logical and necessary step for them to move in the direction of the $ if they wished to retain the business they undertook for foreign banks through their correspondent links.[61] Access to $-denominated deposits and loans in London allowed banks to obtain the facilities that they wanted without the restrictions applied by the US government.[62] One estimate suggests that the deposits held by foreign banks in London jumped from £0.3 billion in 1955 to £12.5 billion in 1969, and these were increasingly denominated in

---

[58] Bank of England, 'The Eurocurrency Business of Banks in London', *BEQB*, 10 (1970), 31–7; 'Reserve Ratios: Further Definitions', *BEQB*, 11 (1971), 483; Bank of England, 'The London Dollar Certificate of Deposit', *BEQB*, 13 (1973), 446–9.

[59] Grady and Weale, *British Banking*, 28–31, 43, 64–5, 85–6, 92, 98, 110, 119, 121, 130, 196.

[60] Source: *Bank of England Quarterly Bulletin Statistical Supplement, 1972–1989*. Note: This data is for 31 December.

[61] G. Burn, *The Re-emergence of Global Finance* (London: 2006), 6–7, 17, 23; C.R. Schenk, *Hong Kong*, 82, 72–3, 82–7, 125–6, 135; G. Jones, *Banking and Oil*, vol. 2: *The History of the British Bank of the Middle East* (Cambridge: Cambridge University Press, 1986), 31, 56–9, 93–4, 225, 244–5, 292–9; Einzig, *Forward Exchange*, 116.

[62] Developments in these years have received an authoritative treatment by a number of authors in Battilosssi and Cassis (eds), *European Banks and the American Challenge*. See also Schenk, 'Origins of the Eurodollar Market'; Clarke, *The City and the World Economy*; Fry (ed.), *Banker's World*; Inter-bank Research Organisation, *The Future of London*; Frowen (ed.), *Framework*: Chapters by Shaw.

$s. By 1969, they comprised over 40 per cent of all bank deposits in London. Between December 1958 and June 1961 alone, dollar deposits in London almost doubled from £0.9 billion to £1.6 billion. During the 1960s, further restrictions placed by the US government on the use of New York as an international market drove business to London where the US dollar continued to be used freely.[63] In turn, these deposits were actively traded between banks, creating in the process an interbank market in London that soon rivalled the sterling-based discount market.[64] The more attractive London's interbank money market became in the 1960s, the more foreign banks were inclined to open branches there so that they could directly participate in it. A survey in 1968 revealed the scale of the commitment of these foreign banks to London. In that year, a total of 119 foreign banks operated full branches in London and these employed 9,076 staff. These banks were predominantly from Europe, North America, and the Far East, with the USA being especially important. The US banks alone employed a staff of 2,078, or 30 per cent of the total.[65]

Foreign Exchange at the Margin

As with the era of the Gold Standard, the assumption is made that the foreign exchange market did not operate under the Bretton Woods system, other than to meet basic currency transfers. The market then sprang from nowhere in the 1970s when fixed exchange rates collapsed, and has flourished ever since, achieving a turnover of almost $10 trillion a day in 2022, measured as gross transactions.[66] This is inaccurate. At all times, there was a need for a foreign exchange market not only as a mechanism through which currencies could be exchanged for immediate use but also to limit exposure to future risks. Those banks doing an international business, either directly or through their customers, were especially vulnerable to currency fluctuations as they extended and received credit. Unless they could be guaranteed that there would be no alteration in exchange rates, banks would seek to cover their exposure if it was large, unless they expected to profit from currency movements. For those reasons, banks always engaged in the foreign exchange market to a lesser or greater degree depending on the transactions they were involved in and the level of currency volatility. The greater the confidence in the stability of exchange rates, the less engagement there was with the foreign exchange market, whether from those seeking to minimize their exposure or exploit profitable opportunities. As confidence in the ability of the Bretton Woods system to maintain fixed exchange rates

[63] Bell and Kettell, *Foreign Exchange Handbook*, 75–6; Einzig, *Euro-Bond Market*, 65, 147, 195; Clendenning, *Euro-Dollar Market*, 7, 22–3, 186; Einzig, *History of Foreign Exchange*, 241; Gall et al., *Deutsche Bank*, 754.

[64] P. Einzig, 'Dollar Deposits in London', *The Banker*, 110 (January 1960), 23–4; J.R. Colville, 'London: Europe's Financial Centre', *The Banker*, 116 (July 1966), 467; 'Foreign Banks in London', *The Banker*, 119 (October 1969), 943–5, 945; Kleinwort, 'The City', 171, 175.

[65] Clark, 'British Banking', 468–78.

[66] Bank for International Settlements, *Triennial Central Bank Survey* (2022).

faded, so activity in the foreign exchange market grew. That confidence was relatively strong in the early 1950s, fell during the 1960s, and finally evaporated in the early 1970s, never to return. In contrast, turnover in the foreign exchange market was low in the early 1950s and then gradually picked up, before exploding from the 1970s onwards.

However, that foreign exchange market need not have been in London. According to Wadsworth, writing in 1946, the London foreign exchange market was closed in 1939 and remained so for the duration of the Second World War. 'When war began dealings on the foreign exchange market ceased; all rates of exchange for sterling were fixed by the authorities and competitive buying and selling of foreign currencies ended.'[67] As the formal reopening of London's foreign exchange market did not take place until 1951, the assumption is made that trading ceased until then.[68] However, that was not the case. The pre-war London foreign exchange market had two components. One was the direct trading in foreign exchange that took place between banks. This involved the use of the telephone within London and to continental Europe and the telegraph for long distance communication, especially to New York. This internalized the buying and selling of foreign exchange within the global banking network, restricting transactions to those considered reliable counterparties by their peers. Among these, the major British banks played a central role as they were ranked among the most trustworthy in the world, having passed through the crises of the 1930s without experiencing any doubts about their solvency and liquidity. In addition to this interbank market, there was one operated by a group of brokers in London who not only traded between the major banks but also serviced the wider banking and business community. They were on hand to pick up any business considered too marginal or time-consuming for the dealers located in the banks as well as maintaining contact with customers, such as the large companies, who justified more direct access to the foreign exchange market than provided by the banks. It was this broker-intermediated market that met an abrupt end with the outbreak of the Second World War. Those brokers who had worked closely with the Bank of England in the 1930s were given official positions and the open market in foreign exchange was closed. Despite the official closure of the foreign exchange market in 1939, what was left intact was the mechanism within banks for dealing in currencies and the connections at home and abroad that underpinned it, though it was subjected to official oversight. Even during the war, there was a continuing need to make and receive payments in different currencies and cover exposure to foreign exchange risks. Most of that activity was internalized within banks, and their network of correspondents around the world, and did not rely on the services provided by brokers, who were absorbed into the Bank of England. What the banks were subjected to was supervision by the Bank of England, with the staff involved being greatly expanded. Most of these staff were recruited from the banks and the brokers as that was where those with foreign exchange experience were employed.[69]

[67] Wadsworth, *Counter Defensive*, 9–11, 18, 30
[68] Einzig, *Forward Exchange*, 13–14.
[69] Wadsworth, *Counter Defensive*, 9–10, 30, 31, 100–1; Mackenzie, *Realms of Silver*, 285.

The existence and operation of this wartime foreign exchange market emerges from the shadows in the account of the work undertaken by the foreign department of Barclays Bank during the 1940s. It was this department that was responsible for foreign exchange trading. In 1939, the department experienced 'frenzied activity on the international telephones and the dealers' switchboard in the office'. During the war, the level of trading fell away because 'the margin of profit ... dropped considerably as a result of war restrictions'. The foreign department lost half its staff during the war, and they were difficult to replace as they were 'expert and specialized'. Nevertheless, the remaining staff carried on the foreign exchange business. When the war ended, the number of staff was quickly built up though it took time to train the new recruits because of the complicated nature of the work. Staff numbers fell from 500 in 1939 to 200 in 1945 and then climbed to 800 by 1959. Throughout the 1940s, Barclays foreign department continued to provide for not only the routine transfers of currency, generated by the international buying and selling conducted by their customers, but also the transactions necessary to cover the bank's own foreign exchange exposure. The foreign department was 'able to make a payment in any part of the world, and in any currency' through the contacts it continued to maintain with other banks around the world. What did change was the degree of supervision conducted by the Bank of England, which continued from wartime into peacetime with the Exchange Control Act of 1947. This external supervision led to an enormous increase in the work of the staff as there was a huge amount of form filling associated with every foreign exchange transaction. Despite these onerous restrictions, the foreign department of Barclays Bank had continued to function during the war, leaving it well positioned to expand once hostilities ended.[70] The experience of the other British domestic banks appears similar, judging from their staff numbers. The staff of the foreign branch of the Midland Bank dropped from 750 in 1939 to 260 in 1945 but reached 1,000 by 1948. By 1950, Lloyds Bank had 380 staff engaged in foreign business.[71]

In 1947, Barclays produced a memorandum for its staff detailing the nature of Foreign Exchange Control and what compliance was required. This provides an insight into what changed in London's foreign exchange market during the war and the legacy that it had.

> Up to 1939 movements of goods and balances were, as far as this country was concerned, entirely free and one could buy, sell or invest capital or savings in any currency, vary such currencies and dispose freely over the whole or any part of one's assets in such manner as was thought fit, without let or hindrance.

That changed with the war. The Defence (Finance) Regulations Act of 1939 gave the government control over foreign assets held by British residents as well as the

---

[70] Barclays Bank, *Handbook on Foreign Business*, 1940; 'The Other Man's Job: Chief Foreign Branch', *The Spread Eagle*, xxv (August 1950), 295–6, xxv (September 1950), 351, xxv (October 1950), 392–3.
[71] Cairncross and Eichengreen, *Sterling in Decline*, 10; Holmes and Green, *Midland*, 249–51, 256; Winton, *Lloyds Bank*, 155; Thackstone, 'Work of the Foreign Branch', 122–3; Lloyd's Bank Ltd: Overseas Department Memoranda, 16 July 1943, 16 February 1945, 2 April 1946; Lloyds Bank archives, Report on Foreign Exchange, 1962.

use of foreign currency. Before the war, 'most of the big banks and many customers had foreign currency balances with banks abroad, either directly or through English banks'. These were then placed at the disposal of the government at the outbreak of the war for use by the Bank of England. Foreign securities held by UK residents were also made available to the UK government 'with the owner receiving sterling if sold'. It was also noted that on the outbreak of war, 'all transfers to non-residents became subject to the permission of the authorities' and that 'no foreign account may be opened for an entirely new customer without first obtaining the permission of the Bank of England'. The Exchange Control Act of 1947 carried into peacetime the measures already in practice during the war. One consequence of the control exercised by the Bank of England was to suppress the level of foreign exchange trading in London. Barclays was forced to conduct foreign exchange transactions abroad using its close connections with banks in other countries. The telephone provided a means of instant communication with continental European centres, while the delay on the transatlantic telegraph fell to twenty-five seconds, while the teleprinter constantly updated exchange rates.[72] As a means of bypassing the restrictions imposed by the Bank of England, Barclays also opened branches abroad after the Second World War, beginning with New York, allowing it to internalize foreign exchange transactions. These foreign branches meant Barclays could simplify currency transactions, allowing them to be completed more quickly and at lower cost. Throughout the 1940s, including the war years, London remained attractive for foreign depositors and investors because of the trust placed in British banks and the security offered by an investment in treasury bills and the national debt. These customers had to be provided with an easy means of transferring their funds into and out of sterling, as well as covering the risks of any potential devaluation, if they were to be retained as customers. This meant banks like Barclays engaging with the foreign exchange market through deals with other banks both in London and abroad.[73]

On 17 December 1951, the foreign exchange market in London was formally allowed to reopen. In practice, this meant that the foreign exchange brokers were free to operate on their own account rather than act as agents of the Bank of England. It did not mean that the foreign exchange market in London could revert to the practices it enjoyed before the outbreak of the Second World War. The dealers and brokers remained subject to the numerous capital and exchange controls introduced during and after the Second World War, and rigorously policed by the staff of the Bank of England with a decade of experience behind them. There was a reluctance at the Bank to relax the supervision they had long exercised. The foreign exchange market had long been considered by many as little more than a casino and the control exercised by the Bank was generally welcomed as part of a trend towards greater government involvement in the working of markets and business. The Bank had

[72] Barclays Bank, *Foreign Exchange Control*, 1–18.
[73] Barclays Bank, *A Bank in Battledress: Barclays Bank (DCO) during the Second World War, 1939–45* (1948), 8, 121, 156; Tuke and Gillman, *Barclays Bank*, 82–3.

been taken into government ownership in 1946, making its employees civil servants with the authority that went that position.[74] The determination to exercise strict control over the re-established foreign exchange market was made clear in 1952 by the Assistant Chief Cashier at the Bank, L.G. Pearce, and he was in charge.[75]

Though these controls were gradually relaxed during the 1950s, many remained in place, making it difficult for the foreign exchange market to engage in such activities as forward dealing and arbitrage with the same freedom as before the war. Exchange and capital controls also restricted the access that UK residents had to the foreign exchange market.[76] To escape these controls, active markets in sterling existed in New York and Zurich, as these were not covered by the British regulations. The result was to suppress foreign exchange trading in London during the 1950s and switch activity to centres abroad.[77] Japan's Mitsui Bank directed its foreign exchange dealing to New York instead of London.[78] Indicative of the lack of growth in the foreign exchange market in London was the absence of any expansion in the number of brokers after the reopening in 1951. The number of firms had fallen from thirty in 1939 to nine in 1945 at which level it remained until 1956 when it rose to thirteen but then fell away.[79] What business there was in foreign exchange in London was largely in the hands of the large domestic banks as they were able to cope with the regulatory requirements and command the trust of the Bank of England. That left a residual role for brokers to act as intermediaries either between the dealers in less-traded currencies or between the banks and their major customers.[80]

Under these circumstances, both New York and Zurich were given the opportunity in the 1950s to consolidate the position they had acquired in the foreign exchange market, during the 1940s. New York's foreign exchange market had continued to function during the Second World War, leaving it in a dominant position at the end of hostilities in 1945.[81] That advantage was reinforced in the 1950s when New York replaced London as the most important financial centre in the world and the US$ increasingly supplanted the UK£ as the international currency of choice. At the end of the Second World War, 80 per cent of internationally held foreign exchange reserves were in sterling due to the existence of the sterling area and the accumulated deposits

[74] Hennessy, *Domestic History*, 83–9, 118–19; Sir George Bolton, *Memoirs* (Bank of England, 13 January 1977), ch.10, 5; J.F.A. Pullinger, 'The Bank and the Commodity Markets', in Fforde, *Bank of England*, 785–7.

[75] Pearce, 'British Exchange Control', 101–23. See Roberts, 'The City of London', 65–71.

[76] Einzig, *History of Foreign Exchange*, 302–3; Einzig, *Textbook on Foreign Exchange*, 1, 21–2, 69, 71, 89, 147, 201, 213.

[77] J.Q. Hollom, 'The Methods and Objectives of the Bank's Market Operations', in *The Bank of England Today* (London: The Institute of Bankers, 1964), 20–2 (The author was Chief Cashier at the Bank of England); Bank of England, 'The London Gold Market', *BEQB*, 4 (1964), 16.

[78] Ogura, *Banking, the State and Industrial Promotion*, 65.

[79] *Post Office London Directory*, 1919–77.

[80] Einzig, *Forward Exchange*, 41, 303, Einzig, *Textbook on Foreign Exchange*, 17; Ellis, *Heir to Adventure*, 148–54; Ikle, *Switzerland*, 30.

[81] Institute of International Finance, 'Effects of the War', 4, 13; 'New York: A Center of World Finance', *New York University Institute of International Finance Bulletin*, 147 (30 December 1946), 5, 18; O. Hobson, 'Financial Control after the War', *JIB*, 63 (1942), 9; O. Hobson, 'Future of the City', 91–9; King, 'War and the Money Market', 47–61; Stern, *U.S. in International Banking*, 32.

of Empire and Commonwealth countries in London. The use of sterling then quickly fell to be replaced by the US$. By 1973, the UK£ comprised only 6 per cent of foreign reserves held by central banks compared to 85 per cent for the US$. The UK£s long reign as an important international currency came to an end in the 1970s, but other countries were reluctant to allow their currencies to replace it because of the lack of control it would mean for their ability to control their domestic money market and put pressure on the exchange rate. This was the case with Germany and the mark, Switzerland and the franc, and Japan and the yen. The restrictions imposed by their national governments on the international use of the mark, franc, and yen stifled the development of their foreign exchange markets. In contrast, the restrictions imposed by the UK authorities on the external use of the UK£ from 1957 encouraged the development of a foreign exchange market in London for otherwise the banks located there would lose the extensive business they did on behalf of their international customers. These included the foreign banks with branches in London, the British overseas banks with branches elsewhere in the world, and British domestic banks, both commercial and merchant, who served as correspondents for numerous banks from around the world.[82]

What restrained the ascendancy of the New York foreign exchange market was the lack of freedom granted to domestic and foreign banks there because of the long history of legislative intervention. The system of fixed exchange rates maintained by central bank intervention also encouraged foreign exchange trading to gravitate to offshore financial centres, in order to escape the controls in place.[83] One of the centres that benefited was Zurich, which emerged in the 1950s as the leading European foreign exchange market.[84] As a consequence, London failed to regain its position as the primary foreign exchange market in the world even after its formal reopening in 1951. Almost a year after the reopening, in October 1952, the *Times* reported that there had been no large expansion of trading. It attributed this to the intense training required to make staff ready to resume operations. A year later, in 1953, little had changed, which was again blamed on continuing technical and administrative difficulties and the lack of trained staff. Though some growth had taken place by the end of 1954, it was now recognized that the real barrier to the recovery of London's foreign exchange market were the many restrictions put in place by the government and rigorously policed by the Bank of England. That was not to change until the end of the 1950s, leaving the way open for New York and Zurich to dominate.[85]

It was not until 31 December 1958 that *The Times* reported that instead of exchange rates being determined in New York and Zurich: 'The London foreign exchange market is now making the rates for all the currencies of the world.' It claimed

---

[82] See Bank of England, 'The UK Exchange Control: A Short History', *BEQB*, 1 September 1967; Eichengreen, 'Sterling's Past'; B. Eichengreen, A. Mehl and L. Chitu, *How Global Currencies Work: Past, Present, and Future* (Princeton: Princeton University Press, 2018), 43–4, 56–7, 67, 70–1, 107, 118–19, 124, 129, 145, 152–75, 178, 183.

[83] C.R. Schenk, *Britain and the Sterling Area*, 10–11; Schenk, *Hong Kong*, 72–3, 82–7, 125–6, 135.

[84] Stern, *U.S. in International Banking*, 3, 6, 8, 32, 39.

[85] *The Times*, 13 October 1952, 19 October 1953, 13 September 1954, 29 December 1958, 31 December 1958, 2 February 1959, 14 March 1960.

that the City of London had been restored to 'its traditional place as the foreign exchange centre of the financial world'. Neither New York nor Zurich relinquished without a fight the superior position they had established over London in the 1950s. In February 1959, *The Times* reported that

> The Swiss commercial banks are confident that because of their foreign exchange holdings and the strength of the Swiss franc they will be able to safeguard their position in international foreign exchange arbitrage. Before sterling was made convertible the Zurich foreign exchange market served to turn formally inconvertible currencies into hard currencies.

It was estimated that more than half the turnover in trading the UK£ against the US$ had taken place in Zurich, but that was now returning to London. London was also picking up trading in other currencies as they also became convertible into US$s. The result was that Zurich was declining as a centre for foreign exchange trading. 'Arbitrage transactions between dollars and transferable sterling—once mainly centred on Zurich and New York—are now being done in London'. According to *The Times*, what underpinned the City of London's ability to take back control of the foreign exchange market after 1959 was the dense concentration of banks located there. In 1960, there were 'over one hundred banks authorised to deal in foreign exchange' in London.[86] However, that cluster had existed throughout the 1950s when London's position in the global foreign exchange market remained weak in comparison to both New York and Zurich. The explanation for the transformation in the fortunes of London's foreign exchange market lies in two decisions made by the UK government in 1957–8.

Throughout the 1950s, the London foreign exchange market had remained a pale shadow of what it had been before the Second World War because of the controls and restrictions imposed by the British government and enforced by the Bank of England. It was then transformed by the unintended consequence of two acts by the British government in the late 1950s. Both were driven by the need to protect the fixed exchange rate of the UK£ as agreed to under the Bretton Woods system. The first, in 1957, were the controls placed on the use of sterling by non-UK residents whether to finance trade or investment. This gave the Bank of England greater control over sterling when it intervened in the foreign exchange market to support its fixed exchange rate. The Bank was finding it increasingly difficult to maintain this exchange rate because of the relatively poor performance of the British economy by the late 1950s. It was through intervention in the foreign exchange market that the Bank attempted to bring the supply of and demand for sterling into equilibrium, and so stabilize the exchange rate. This could be done more easily if external access to sterling was restricted as the Bank had less control of that element of the market. This lack of control had come to the fore during the Suez Crisis of 1956.[87] To circumvent these

---

[86] *The Times*, 13 October 1952, 19 October 1953, 13 September 1954, 29 December 1958, 31 December 1958, 2 February 1959, 14 March 1960.

[87] See J.M. Boughton, 'Northwest of Suez: The 1956 Crisis and the IMF', IMF Working Paper 00/192 (Washington: International Monetary Fund, 2000).

new restrictions, the London money market increasingly switched to the use of the US$, which was already replacing the UK£ as the preferred international currency. The result was to place the London money market on a multi-currency basis. No longer did each side of a transaction use sterling though that continued to be the case in the discount market. Instead, transactions between banks in London increasingly involved the use of the US$ especially when a foreign bank was one of the participants. Though the Bretton Woods system mandated fixed exchange rates, there were growing doubts that these could be maintained, especially in the case of the UK£. The effect was to increase the demand for an active exchange market in London through which foreign banks could match their currency liabilities and assets. The carry trade, for example, involved borrowing in a currency with a low rate of interest and lending in one with a high rate of interest, but that could only be done with an acceptable level of risk if the exchange rate was fixed. In the face of the growing instability of sterling, that required the existence of an active foreign exchange market if use was to be made of the London money market. That was only achieved when the restrictions on foreign exchange trading in London, in place since the outbreak of the Second World War in September 1939, were relaxed. The carry trade was only made possible by the simultaneous use of spot and forward contracts as these were required to cover the currency risks involved. Otherwise, the transaction was highly speculative and so avoided by most banks. From 1955 onwards, there was a gradual return to sterling convertibility before it was fully restored in December 1958. In response to the lack of convertibility of sterling within the UK and the existence of alternative foreign exchange markets abroad, banks in London developed internal mechanisms for the transfer of currency using their extensive connections both at home and abroad.[88]

The action by the UK government that took place in 1958 was even more significant for London's foreign exchange market. That was the decision to make the UK£ a fully convertible currency. Convertibility allowed holders of sterling to exchange it for other currencies at the prevailing rate and so reduced pressure on the Bank of England to intervene in the market. The Bank of England's ability to intervene was constrained by the limited reserves of foreign currency it had access to, but the need to do so grew with Britain running balance of payment deficits. The excess supply of £s over demand put pressure on the prevailing rate of exchange. Under the Bretton Woods system, the Bank of England was expected to stabilize the rate of exchange by buying up this excess using its reserves of foreign currency. With convertibility, holders of sterling were free to sell in the open market, which they could do in New York and Zurich. What convertibility did was end the need for these alternative markets as the buying and selling could now take place in London as well.

The effect of convertibility was to greatly increase activity in the London foreign exchange market as banks made increasing use of London for multi-currency transactions. Between 31 December 1958 and 30 June 1961, the total deposits in London held by British overseas banks and foreign banks with London branches doubled

---

[88] Glahe, *Empirical Study*, 45; Harrod, *Money*, 86–8, 131–2. For the carry trade, see Doskov and Swinkels, 'Empirical Evidence'; Accominotti *et al.*, 'Currency Regimes and the Carry Trade'.

from £622 million to £1,162 million. Of the 1961 total, an estimated £500 million was held in foreign currency, or approximately 40 per cent of the total. The Bank of England reported in 1961 that 'Most of the steep rise shown since 1958 has occurred in foreign currency deposits, predominantly in US dollars.' It was through the foreign exchange market that foreign and overseas banks operating in London could match their currency liabilities and assets. With the switch from the UK£ to the US$ for international transactions, and the business being conducted in London, the demands upon London's foreign exchange market grew as it was no longer necessary to direct such business to either New York or Zurich.[89] Through a close working relationship with the principal British banks, developed during the two world wars, the Bank of England was able to exert a high degree of control over the foreign exchange market in London. This had the effect of driving trading abroad in the 1950s. It was not until the late 1950s that decisions taken by the British government freed London's foreign exchange market from these onerous controls. In the wake of these decisions, an active foreign exchange market developed in London during the 1960s. That trading then provided the basis for the foreign exchange market that developed after the central-bank-maintained regime of fixed exchange rates broke down between 1971 and 1973.[90]

Foreign Exchange Re-emerges

In the 1960s, a foreign exchange market was developed in London to meet the needs of the international banking community. With growing financial flows within the global economy, driven by expanding international trade and investment, banks had to handle a greater volume and variety of payments and receipts while also lending and borrowing among themselves as they sought to maximize the funds at their disposal while remaining liquid. These activities exposed banks to currency risks when operating internationally, and the foreign exchange market provided a means through which these could be covered. The need for such a service had never disappeared, even during the Second World War and the era of managed currencies and central bank control that followed. Nevertheless, it had been marginalized and, in the case of London, driven abroad, despite the City of London remaining the centre of global banking. The facilities provided by a foreign exchange market then became of increasing importance in the 1960s as confidence in the ability of central banks to maintain fixed exchange rates faded. After the actions taken by the British government in 1957 and 1958, that market was hosted in London though that was not the intention of the intervention. London was the chosen location for the emerging foreign exchange market because that was where banks from all over the world had long conducted business with each other. That had remained the case in the 1950s

[89] Bank of England, 'Overseas and Foreign Banks in London', 18–20. See Bank of England, 'The Exchange Equalisation Account: Its Origins and Development', *BEQB*, 8 (1968), 385–6.
[90] See Naef, *An Exchange Rate History of the United Kingdom*.

because New York had failed fully to replace London as the world's financial centre. The City of London remained one of the leading financial service clusters in the world, though held back by exchange and capital control and destined to decline in importance along with the British economy, the British Empire, and the sterling area.[91]

What the actions of the British government in 1957 and 1958 did was detach the fortunes of the City of London from the downward trajectory of sterling. Sterling was increasingly abandoned as a reserve currency, because of doubts over its ability to hold its value, while the proportion of international trade financed in £s fell from around 50 per cent in the late 1940s to only 20 per cent in 1970. With the restriction placed on the use of the UK£ by non-residents in 1957, banks in the City were encouraged to switch to using the US$ instead, or lose the international business they had built up over the past hundred years. The introduction of sterling convertibility in 1958 made this switch to the US$ easier while ending the controls that had driven trading in the UK£ to Zurich and New York. The outcome was the development of the City of London as a dollar-based financial centre in the 1960s, which offered banks a rival location to New York. This was attractive to banks as US legislation imposed restrictions on the business that a bank could do there. These included the ability to combine commercial and investment banking and offer competitive rates of interest on deposits. The ability to escape these restrictions even encouraged US banks to open branches in London where they enjoyed greater flexibility in servicing their domestic customers, let alone engaging more closely with the wider banking community. The incentive to open a branch in London was further stimulated in 1963 when the US government introduced restrictions on the external use of the US$. By routing transactions through London banks could provide their customers with a way of continuing to use US$s. What happened in the 1960s was a revival in the City of London's traditional international business and the addition of an expanding offshore element because of the desire by US banks to escape domestic constraints and restrictions. Both these developments lay behind the creation of the Eurodollar and Eurobond markets in the City of London in the late 1950s. These markets allowed lenders and borrowers to conduct their business in US$s while evading US regulations. Reflecting the growing attractions of the City of London was the number of branches of foreign banks it hosted. Whereas 82 foreign banks had branches in the City in 1961, the number had almost doubled to 159 by 1970. Even more impressive was the fact that between 1957 and 1969, the funds handled by foreign banks in London grew from £263 million to £12.5 billion, by which time they comprised over 40 per cent of all bank deposits in London.[92]

[91] Burn, 'The State, the City', 236.
[92] Bell and Kettell, *Foreign Exchange Handbook*, 75–6; Einzig, *Euro-Bond Market*, 65, 147, 195; Clendenning, *Euro-Dollar Market*, 7, 22–3, 186; Einzig, *History of Foreign Exchange*, 241; *International Banking*, 53; Newall, *Japan and the City*, 24–5, 32, 50; Cleveland and Huertas, *Citibank*, 253–5; Geisst, *Wall Street*, 311, 331, 356–7; Roberts, *Schroders*, 418; Gall et al., *Deutsche Bank*, 754; Bonin, *Société Générale*, 60; Michie, *City of London*, 90, 92, 94. For these years, see Schenk, 'Origins of the Eurodollar Market'; Clarke, *The City and the World Economy*; Fry (ed.), *Banker's World*; Inter-bank Research Organisation, *The Future of London*; Frowen (ed.), *Framework*: Chapters by Shaw.

The result was that in the 1960s, there came into existence two almost separate components in the City of London. One was developing in response to the growing international Eurodollar and Eurobond markets for money and capital. This part of the City was heavily dominated by foreign banks, with those from the USA being added to by others from Japan and continental Europe.[93] All this part of the City required in order to flourish was minimal controls and regulations, and, to a large extent, it was given this.[94] The other part of the City of London provided the British government and British business with finance and was conducted in sterling. Though there was an overlap between the two parts of the City of London in the 1960s, they also remained distinct and separate. The continuance of exchange controls created a barrier between the business conducted in sterling and that conducted in other currencies, especially the US$, with the Bank of England acting as a vigilant guardian of the former while leaving the latter alone.[95] In the 1960s, it was this non-sterling element of the City of London that prospered with the foreign exchange market making an important contribution, as it allowed banks to cover their exposure when engaging in multi-currency transactions.[96] This can be seen in the volume of business done between non-UK banks in London. This grew only modestly in the 1950s rising from £239 million in 1950 to £308 million in 1959, with no adjustment for inflation. In contrast, it rose from £356 million in 1960, reflecting the impact of convertibility, to £4,267 million in 1969, with, again, no adjustment for inflation. By then, most of the business was conducted in US$s rather than UK£s as was the case in the 1950s. The sterling-based discount market was being abandoned for the dollar-based interbank market.[97] Much of this activity was closely associated with the growth of the Eurodollar and Eurobond markets, neither of which was sterling-based.[98]

Once freed from the restrictions imposed by the British government and policed by the Bank of England, London's foreign exchange market was able to expand, taking advantage of the City of London's strategic position within the international banking system. Indicative of the strength of London as the centre of global banking was the situation in 1968 when a total of 126 banks from 41 different countries had branches in London and they employed over 10,000 staff. It was trading in and between these banks, along with those from Britain itself, that constituted the foreign exchange market in London. Banks that had opened branches in the City of London, or had their head office there, were able to accept deposits and make loans, and that gave them entry to the foreign exchange market. Trading in the foreign exchange market was an interbank affair, accomplished through the exchange of

---

[93] For this, see Schenk, 'Origins of the Eurodollar Market'; Fry (ed.), *Banker's World*.

[94] Kleinwort, 'The City', 175.

[95] R. Stones, 'Government–Finance Relations in Britain, 1964–7: A Tale of Three Cities', *Economy and Society*, 19 (1990), 50.

[96] See Naef, *An Exchange Rate History of the United Kingdom*, ch. 3, 4, and 6; Bank of England, 'UK Exchange Control'.

[97] *Bank of England Quarterly Bulletin Statistical Supplement, 1960–1980*. The data is for 31 December of each year. It excludes UK domestic banks. What is included are the balances these banks had with other banks and their lending to the London money market.

[98] Einzig, *Euro-Bond Market*, 17; Clendenning, *Euro-Dollar Market*, 2, 7; Kleinwort, 'The City', 170.

bank deposits, whether the transaction was for immediate completion or a date in the future. By swapping assets and liabilities, banks could cover their foreign exchange exposure acquired through their customers as well as take a position in the market that could generate a profit for themselves. There were a select few banks whose depth and breadth of assets and liabilities, and the trust they commanded among their peers, made them the preferred counterparties in the foreign exchange market. Among these, there were an even smaller number who made a business out of currency dealing.[99]

It was the activities of these banks that allowed London to wrest back control of the foreign exchange market from New York and Zurich. Among them were the large British domestic banks who had long conducted a foreign exchange business through their extensive international connections and status as the most trusted counterparties in the global banking community. The problem was that until the restoration of sterling convertibility in 1958, much of their foreign exchange business had to be conducted abroad in places such as New York and Zurich or various offshore centres around the world. With sterling convertibility, the banks could bring this business back to London and engage with the growing number of foreign banks that opened branches there and were actively engaged in US$ transactions.[100] In 1968, Lloyds Bank advertised the fact that its 'Overseas Department maintains currency accounts with its correspondents in all of the principal centres in the world.' Using these connections and accounts, Lloyds was one of the largest dealers in foreign exchange in the London market, employing 767 highly skilled staff for the purpose. They had £1.8 billion in foreign currency contracts outstanding on 31 December 1967.[101] It was from 1960 onwards that British banks began to enjoy the freedom of accepting foreign currency deposits and actively engaging in the foreign exchange market rather than acting as agents of the Bank of England and providing a routine service to their customers.[102] The British merchant bank, Kleinworts, slowly re-engaged with the foreign exchange market as a result, employing three dealers and fourteen back-office staff by 1964.[103] The presence of these British banks, and the foreign exchange business they did, attracted other banks from around the world. In London, banks could most easily connect to other banks, recruit the skilled staff they required, and invest in the dedicated office space and specialist equipment needed to trade foreign exchange. It was only in London that the volume of foreign exchange trading generated could justify the expense involved. The more banks that chose to make London the centre of their foreign exchange operations, the greater the attractions it had for other banks to do the same, which increased its gravitational pull.[104]

[99] *The Banker: Annual Review of Foreign Banks in London*, October 1968.

[100] Joslin, *Banking in Latin America*, 290; Collins, *Money and Banking*, 424–5, 504, 538; Nevin and Davis, *London Clearing Banks*, 284–5; Ross, 'Clearing Banks', 24–5.

[101] Lloyds Bank: Overseas Business, 16 February 1968, 16 December 1968; Winton, *Lloyds Bank*, 155, 160, 180.

[102] Bank of England, 'Foreign Exchange Market in London', 438–44; 'Eurobanks and the Inter-bank Market', *BEQB*, 21 (1981), 351–4; Einzig, *Forward Exchange*, 2nd ed., 31, 41, 303–9.

[103] Wake, *Kleinwort Benson*, 320, 328, 343–5, 384–7.

[104] Swiss Bank Corporation, *Foreign Exchange and Money Market Operations* (1992), 7–9.

Even in the 1960s, London's foreign exchange market remained hindered by Britain's obligations under the Bretton Woods Agreement.[105] International financial flows continued to be regarded as destabilizing and thus to be prevented or controlled.[106] As Paul Einzig stated in his 1966 textbook on foreign exchange, 'Exchange stability is now maintained ... by means of systematic official intervention in the foreign exchange market.'[107] Nevertheless, it was in the 1960s that London's foreign exchange market began its post-war revival, and it had to thank the decisions made in 1957 and 1958 for the opportunity to do so, rather than awaiting the collapse of the Bretton Woods system after 1970.[108] *The Times* claimed in 1967 that the London foreign exchange market was the largest in the world in terms of the quantity traded, the diversity of currencies, and the number and spread of customers being served. By 1968, *The Times* reported that London was experiencing an invasion of foreign banks, predominantly American, who were attracted by the ability to recruit specialist staff experienced in

the more sophisticated departments of foreign-exchange dealing and interest arbitrage ... a good foreign exchange man is worth his weight in gold to a bank and the financial reward can be rich. A competent dealer will pick up £3,000 without much trouble, while for those in top positions the sky is often the limit.

By 1968, there were around 400 foreign exchange dealers in London employed by the 150 banks authorized to deal in foreign exchange. One hundred of these banks actively participated in the foreign exchange market, but most trading was in the hands of twenty-five of them. Within that group of twenty-five, there was an inner core of ten who dominated the market.[109]

Providing an insight into the development of London's foreign exchange market in the 1960s was the Bank of England, as it expanded its coverage of the activities of foreign banks compared to the 1950s.[110] The Bank of England drew a distinction between banks with head offices or branches in London and those with only a representative office or agent, of which there were many. Those with a head office or branch did a full banking business, while the others did not. It was the former group that could accept deposits and make loans, doing so in both £s and foreign currencies after the introduction of convertibility in 1958. Between 31 December 1958 and 30 June 1961, the total deposits in London held by British overseas banks and foreign banks with London branches doubled from £622 million to £1,162 million. Of

[105] Gleeson, *London Enriched*, 28–32, 147–62.

[106] Bank of England, *United Kingdom Overseas Investments, 1938 to 1948* (London: 1950), 4, 6, 9; S. Cassese, 'The Long Life of the Financial Institutions Set Up in the Thirties', special issue, *Journal of European Economic History*, 13 (1984), 276; Yeager, *International Monetary Relations*, 331; Einzig, *History of Foreign Exchange*, 303; James, *International Monetary Co-operation*, 23, 27, 179–80.

[107] Einzig, *Textbook on Foreign Exchange*, 1.

[108] Atkin, *The Foreign Exchange Market of London*, 99, 109, 112–17, 128–34, 137, 148–51, 160–2, 175–80, 191, 194–6.

[109] *The Times*, 29 June 1967, 11 September 1967, 29 May 1968.

[110] Bank of England, 'New Banking Statistics', 162–5; Bank of England, 'Developments in UK Banking', 392–7.

the 1961 total, an estimated £500 million was held in foreign currency, or approximately 40 per cent of the total. The Bank of England reported in 1961 that 'Most of the steep rise shown since 1958 has occurred in foreign currency deposits, predominantly in US dollars.'[111] As the Bank observed in 1962, 'There is available in London an exceptionally broad range of opportunities for the employment of funds overnight or for any longer period, and frequently offering yields that are higher than those readily obtainable in financial markets abroad.' These investment opportunities were in £s and foreign currencies, mainly US$s, as were the deposits being made, which could be quickly withdrawn, being highly sensitive to fluctuations in interest rates. Despite the fixed exchange rates under the Bretton Woods system, there were fears in the banking community that these exchange rates would not be maintained.[112] As it was not possible for an individual bank to match the deposits being accepted and the loans being made by currency, across time and amount, a means of covering that exposure was required. It was that which the interbank foreign exchange market provided.[113]

As foreign currency lending and borrowing became established in London during the 1960s, UK domestic banks were increasingly drawn in as, otherwise, they risked losing the profits generated by the services they provided to other banks through their extensive correspondent networks. By December 1963, UK bank liabilities in foreign currencies had reached £1,166 million and they were matched by assets of £1,094 million. The Bank of England commented in 1964 that

> Banks in London have been able to attract large sums in dollars by quoting better rates for deposits, including interest on money at call and very short notice—categories which earn nothing at all with New York banks—and have employed them at less than the US lending rate and still made a worthwhile return.[114]

All this put extra pressure on the foreign exchange market to respond as did the switch to the use of the US$ for the pricing of commodities. London hosted a number of important international commodity markets such as the London Metal Exchange.[115] What was developing rapidly in London during the 1960s were transactions in multiple currencies as even UK banks abandoned their traditional reliance on the discount market.[116] Over the course of the 1960s, it was estimated by the Bank of England that the number of banks transacting foreign currency business in the UK grew from 132 in 1963 to 193 in 1969. Measured by gross foreign currency claims and

---

[111] Bank of England, 'The Overseas and Foreign Banks in London', 18–20. See Bank of England, 'Exchange Equalisation Account', 385–6.

[112] Bank of England, 'Bank Liquidity', 248.

[113] Bank of England, 'Inflows and Outflows of Foreign Funds', *BEQB*, 2 (1962), 93–9.

[114] Bank of England, 'UK Banks' External Liabilities and Claims in Foreign Currencies', *BEQB*, 4 (1964), 100–3.

[115] Bank of England, 'UK Commodity Markets', *BEQB*, 4 (1964), 194–200; 'Overseas Balances 1963–1973', *BEQB*, 14 (1974), 162.

[116] Bank of England, 'The UK and US Treasury Bill Market', *BEQB*, 5 (1965), 327; Bank of England, 'London Discount Market', 146.

liabilities, the interbank market expanded from £1.3 billion to £12.5 billion over the same period.[117]

Providing an assessment of the state of London's foreign exchange market by the end of the 1960s was a survey carried out by *The Times* in 1970. It asked a number of City of London bankers to take a reflective view of a decade during which the foreign exchange market had been transformed. *The Times* was keen to provide their readers with an explanation of why the global foreign exchange market was centred in London when the transactions largely involved US$s and US banks as that made New York the obvious location. J.R.H. Cooper, a British investment banker, stressed that 'One of the most remarkable factors of the past five or six years in international finance has been the City of London's survival as an international centre in the face of a dramatic and sustained reduction in the international role of sterling.' He attributed that not only to the failure of New York to emerge as a major rival but also the existence in London of 'a genuinely international short-term money market, providing a source of, and employment for, short- and medium-term funds which are permitted to flow across national boundaries. The London foreign exchange market provides just such a market in short-term money'. Another to emphasize the contribution made by the close connection between the foreign exchange market and London's other money markets was the American investment banker, S.M. Yassukovich. To him, London's foreign exchange market both benefited from and played a central role in assisting the development of both the Eurodollar and Eurobond markets as each involved the use of multiple currencies. 'The two markets make use of many common financial structures and the overlap of technique and institutional participation is considerable'. L.C. Mather, the general manager of the Midland Bank, emphasized the key role played by the UK's commercial banks as they were the principal dealers in London's foreign exchange market, trading both for themselves and their worldwide web of correspondent banks. His claim was supported by Lord Aldington, the chairman of one of the remaining British overseas banks, National and Grindlays. What he acknowledged above all, however, was that 'Each of the component parts of the City of London banking system plays its role in maintaining London as the world's major financial centre.'[118] The conclusion that emerges from the comments made by these bankers was that London's ability to command the global foreign exchange market once again in the 1960s was a product of the continuing role it played as the hub of the international banking system. That role had survived the Second World War and the restrictions imposed in the 1950s, leaving it well positioned to recapture the foreign exchange market when the opportunity arose after the UK£ was made convertible in 1958 and the regulatory intervention of the Bank of England ceased to drive trading abroad. It was the combination of the enduring microstructure of the City of London, the removal of the obstacles to it playing an international role, and

---

[117] Bank of England, 'Eurocurrency Business', 31–7; Bank of England, 'Reserve Ratios: Further definitions', *BEQB*, 11 (1971), 483; 'The London Dollar Certificate of Deposit', *BEQB*, 13 (1973), 446–9.
[118] *The Times*, 13 April 1970, 26 October 1970.

the failure of New York to provide an attractive alternative that explained the revival of London's foreign exchange market in the 1960s.[119]

Conclusion

Towards the end of the Second World War in 1944, governments meeting in Bretton Woods took the decision that the Gold Standard could not be restored. The attempt to do so between the wars had all been failures and had damaging consequences. The alternative was to leave exchange rates to be determined by the market, but that was not considered desirable. The legacy of the 1920s and 1930s was that foreign exchange markets were vulnerable to the actions of speculators and generated a high degree of exchange-rate volatility. The solution was to create a managed monetary system with responsibility placed in the hands of central banks. Such a solution met the approval of governments involved in managing their way through a world war since 1939. The problem with the post-war regime introduced to achieve international monetary stability was both its rigidity and its exposure to abuse by the governments and central banks given responsibility for managing it. The stability of the post-war years relied on intervention and cooperation carried out by or on behalf of governments. However, governments were also exposed to pressures other than the need to maintain monetary stability and so were reluctant to take the necessary policy decisions when needed and to the degree required. This was especially so for Britain and the USA, which possessed the currencies that were the foundation of the post-war monetary system. Consequently, even before the system of managed currencies finally collapsed during the early 1970s, there was a revival in international interbank money markets, whether for purposes of lending and borrowing, or matching assets and liabilities over time and space. Included in this revival was the foreign exchange market. Though unrecognized under the Gold Standard, as long as national currencies existed, there was a need for a foreign exchange market to provide the mechanism through which constant adjustments were made and banks were able to balance their exposure both instantly and in the future.

When it is recognized that such a market had always existed in some form or other, then the attempt to fix exchange rates for perpetuity under the Bretton Woods system, and then maintain them through central bank intervention, appears to mark out the years between 1950 and 1970 as a flawed attempt to impose a rigid price regime in the face of changes in supply and demand that dictated flexibility. Though there was an absence of major financial crises in the 1950s, aided by the high degree of control exercised by governments, both internally and externally, as early as the 1960s, it was becoming evident that the Bretton Woods system was breaking down. The global monetary system associated with central bank intervention gradually fell

[119] Einzig, *Textbook of Foreign Exchange*, 22; Clendenning, *Euro-Dollar Market*, v, 1–2, 6–11, 14, 40; The City Research Project, *The Competitive Position of London's Financial Services* (London: 1995), 10, 18–19, A-9; James, *International Monetary Co-operation*, 447.

apart, leaving governments and central banks with little alternative but to accept that the market had a role to play in determining exchange rates. All this was taking place against a background of a growing liberalization of international financial flows and the beginning of a revolution in global communications and the processing power of computers. Distance was no longer a barrier to the integration of financial markets while it was becoming possible to create and operate global banks. The result was not simply to be a return to the pre-1914 world of open economies and limited government intervention. Instead, it led to a new world after 1970 populated by global markets and megabanks. Within that world, the foreign exchange market reinvented itself yet again and flourished.

4
Forex Unbound, 1970–1992

Introduction

Between 1970 and 1992, the global financial system experienced a revolution. Out went the controls and compartmentalization that had characterized the early post-war years as they were exposed to increasing pressure from offshore centres, parallel markets, and shadow banks. In the face of these multiple challenges, governments gave way and accepted that they could not make the world economy operate according to their rules and regulations, either internally or externally. Contributing to the inability of national governments to force the financial system to conform to their requirements was the revolution in global communications as distance no longer provided protection from competition. Accompanying the transformation of communications was another in the organization of business as it became possible to manage companies that not only spanned the world but were also multi-divisional. When applied to banks, the result was highly disruptive. It made possible the creation and expansion of banks that were simultaneously global and universal, and so transcended national boundaries. These banks had the power to internalize within a single organization all those financial activities carried out separately in the past. In 1986, Alan Cane referred to 'the unholy trinity of increased competition, deregulation and technology' that was transforming the operation of the global financial system.[1] This was to have a profound effect on the City of London and the foreign exchange market.

One of the fundamental trends driving change after 1970 was the rapid rise in international connectivity through advances in technology. Fibre optics revolutionized telecommunications, providing cheaper and faster connections as well as increased capacity. Combined with this revolution in the speed, capacity, and cost of global communications was a similar one taking place in the processing and transmission of financial information. In 1973, the Society for Worldwide Interbank Financial Telecommunications (SWIFT) was set up as an interbank cooperative, and in 1977, it introduced a messaging service that provided banks with a standardized, reliable, and secure way of quickly transferring money around the world. By 1991, SWIFT was processing 1.5 million messages daily between 1,885 banks in 73 countries, underpinning the finance of international trade, the cross-border trading in securities, and all transactions involving money. Another fundamental trend was the growing scale of business and its increasingly global nature. As companies became

---

[1] A. Cane, 'Systems Tailored to Market-Makers', *Financial Times*, 16 October 1986.

Forex Forever. Ranald C. Michie, Oxford University Press. © Ranald C. Michie (2024).
DOI: 10.1093/oso/9780198903697.003.0005

larger and more international, they were able to bypass banks and markets through the internal movement of funds. Conversely, they also relied on banks and financial markets to cover the risks they were exposed to and provide the level of funds they required, especially in the more volatile conditions that prevailed from 1970 onwards. Markets devised new products to cover these risks, leading to the proliferation of derivative contracts designed to reduce the risks associated with currency fluctuations, the volatility of stock and bond prices, and the variability of interest rates. Banks were forced to take measures that addressed the increased risks they ran through their mismatch of assets and liabilities across time, space, currency, and interest rates as well as their exposure to default of a single customer that was large enough to cause their collapse.

As important as these fundamental trends were, events also played their part in influencing what took place between 1970 and 1992. There were major financial crises that exposed the growing interdependency in an increasingly integrated global economy. One of these was the monetary crisis of the early 1970s, which spelled the end of the Bretton Woods system of fixed exchange rates. Another was the international debt crisis of 1982. Each of these crises had consequences not least through the response of governments in their attempt to make the financial system more stable and resilient. Out of the collapse of the Bretton Woods system came a growing reliance on the foreign exchange market to provide an adjustment mechanism for the relative value of currencies. Out of the international debt crisis came the encouragement given to a switch from the lend-and-hold model of financing, widely employed by banks, to the originate-and-distribute one. This appeared to offer a safer option by reducing the exposure of banks to a liquidity crisis. Loans made under the lend-and-hold model were non-transferable, or only with difficulty and delay, leaving a bank exposed to a liquidity crisis even if it was solvent. In contrast, in the originate-and-distribute model, loans were converted into bonds that could be sold even at a loss, releasing funds that could be used to meet withdrawals and redemptions. In turn, the switch from lend-and-hold to originate-and-distribute made banks more reliant on the interbank money market to either employ funds that were surplus to immediate needs or supplement a shortage of cash required to meet outflows. This allowed banks to operate with much lower capital and reserves as they could top up supplies by borrowing from those banks with a surplus, as long as confidence was maintained that loans would be repaid. The effect was to return the global financial system to a riskier way of operating but one that generated better returns for savers and borrowers and expanded the supply and lowered the cost of finance. Few at the time recognized that this was happening. One who glimpsed what it all meant was Peter Montagnon in 1984 when he reported that in this interbank market, 'Hundreds of millions of dollars change hands by the minute on the basis of simple telephone calls between dealers. It only works because each participating bank has an inherent trust in other banks' ability and willingness to repay.'[2] It was to be many years in the future before that trust broke down, with devastating consequences for the global

---

[2] P. Montagnon, 'International Powerhouse', *Financial Times*, 21 May 1984.

financial system. In between, the world had enjoyed decades of rising prosperity that were shared by all, and that was a product of the transformation begun after 1970.

It was this combination of fundamental trends and the reaction to crises that underpinned the growth and development of the foreign exchange market in the 1970s and 1980s. This market had to cope with the growing scale, scope and reach of banks, the disappearance of national boundaries as parameters for financial activity, and the increased volatility of prices, interest rates, and exchange rates. The result was to make the foreign exchange market into the largest market in the world. With exchange rates no longer fixed, after the collapse of the Bretton Woods system between 1971 and 1973, the world entered a period of currency instability. This drove up turnover in the foreign exchange market as banks sought to either cover the currency risks they were exposed to or profit from the opportunities that price volatility provided. As the volume of activity in the foreign exchange market expanded exponentially, it also provided banks with a facility where they could easily lend out surplus funds and borrow to meet a shortage, becoming an essential element in their constant management of their liquidity position. Nevertheless, this new foreign exchange market was widely regarded with suspicion, being seen as little more than a casino, and considered to be a temporary solution while the world awaited a return to fixed exchange rates. There remained a nostalgia for a more managed international economic system in which governments, not markets, played a central role, as the Bretton Woods system was meant to deliver. That remained fifty years after its demise.[3] However, over the course of the 1970s and 1980s, the foreign exchange market became a permanent feature of the global financial system. There was no general return to fixed exchange rates managed by central banks, though individual governments continued to use intervention to achieve a particular policy objective. Most governments sacrificed fixed exchange rates in favour of free financial flows and independent monetary policies. The foreign exchange market was unbound as governments retreated from the control and compartmentalization agenda they had pursued since the end of the Second World War. Only when the final objective was political and economic unification, as with the European Union (EU), was the attempt to fix exchange rates pursued and then only when accompanied by monetary unification.[4]

The City of London

Among financial centres, the main development in the 1970s and 1980s was the emergence of a tripolar grouping with New York serving the Americas, Tokyo representing Asia, and London catering for Europe. Whereas the position of the first

---

[3] For an example of that nostalgia, see *Journal of European Economic History*, 51 (2022), 9–111. There are papers by James, 'Rethinking the Legacy of Bretton Woods'; I. Maes and I. Pascotti, 'The Legacy of Bretton Woods'; Subacchi, 'The System That Became a Non-system'; Eichengreen, 'Somnolence to Dominance'.

[4] See H. James, *Making the European Monetary Union* (Cambridge: 2012).

two was largely secured by the relative standing of their domestic economies, that of London owed much to the role it already played internationally. That position was then bolstered by Britain joining the EU in 1973. Though the EU was a long way from achieving a single market in financial services, by joining, London could more easily serve customers across the continent. Europe was ideally placed in the world's time zones, straddling Asia to the east and the Americas to the west, while London already possessed the continent's densest, broadest, and most connected cluster of banks and markets of international importance. These were well placed to benefit from the growing integration taking place within the world economy as barriers to international financial flows were lowered and even removed. That ability of London to serve the global financial community was further strengthened in 1979 when the UK abandoned exchange controls. By 1993, 514 foreign banks were operating in London, which was far more than any other financial centre, including New York. In 1992, Robin Leigh-Pemberton, the governor of the Bank of England, confidently stated that 'London is one of the three major world financial centres, perhaps the only truly international centre and certainly the pre-eminent international centre in Europe, with a depth, variety and liquidity in its money and capital markets.'[5]

As a financial centre, London was subject to a two-way pull after 1970. On the one hand, the removal of barriers to the free flow of money around the world, and London's key location as a banking and telecommunications hub, attracted business to the deep and broad markets it could provide in money, derivatives, Eurobonds, and international equities. Those conditions also favoured the centralization of specialist services in London, where so many banks already had offices and could benefit from the convenient time zone and support facilities it provided. As Richard Lambert observed in 1989, 'Firms come to London because so many other firms are already there, and once they have gone to the expense of setting up shop they will not lightly switch their location.'[6] Conversely, the ending of punitive taxes and the decline of restrictive practices abroad removed a number of the causes that had driven business to London in the 1950s and 1960s. London also suffered from increased regulations imposed by the EU, which harmed its ability to handle cross-border transactions and attract banks from around the world. London was also an expensive location due to the high level of office rents and staff salaries. The result in the 1970s and 1980s was that London gained in those activities where it had a competitive advantage while shedding others. Trading in money and currencies, in particular, gravitated to those locations that could provide the deepest pools of liquidity and greatest breadth of connections. That was found in London, which attracted banks from around the world that wanted to engage in these activities.

What London specialized in was the provision of those high-level financial activities in which it possessed permanent advantages and so could justify the expense incurred by banks when setting up and then maintaining operations there. It continued to be the mecca for banks and brokers because of its cosmopolitan environment

[5] E. Tucker, 'The Square Mile Stays Out in Front', *Financial Times*, 29 May 1992.
[6] R. Lambert, 'Finance Grows into a Threat to the City', *Financial Times*, 1 June 1989.

and international outlook. London's strength had long been in the wholesale markets, which transcended national borders and this applied especially to the foreign exchange market. 'A financial market which never closes, knows no national boundaries and is beyond the control of governments' was how Jim McCallum described it in 1991.[7] The foreign exchange market was dominated by trading in the US$ against other currencies and was conducted between a small number of global banks. That trading was clustered in London, New York, and Tokyo, in that order, because that was where the liquidity was the greatest. Together, these three centres accounted for two-thirds of the total foreign exchange turnover in 1991. To contemporaries, London's premier position after 1970 was a puzzle. By 1971, sterling comprised only 7 per cent of global foreign exchange reserves and that fell even further to 1.8 per cent by 1979. In 1971, sterling was still used in the finance of 20 per cent of international trade, but that also fell, dropping to 7 per cent in 1979.[8] The UK£ had ceased to be a significant international currency greatly diminishing the appeal of the City of London as a financial centre, especially when it came to trading foreign exchange. Shorn of the link to sterling, the explanations suggested for the primacy of London in the global foreign exchange market focused on geography and the restrictions imposed by the US government, as these crippled New York. However, those only suffice to explain why New York, which was the obvious location, had not fulfilled its post-war destiny and why a European centre had advantages within the global time zone. What was not considered was the prehistory of London's foreign exchange market, which had survived the impact of two world wars and the controls and restrictions imposed by the British government and policed by the Bank of England in the 1950s.[9]

When the need to develop an active foreign exchange market appeared after 1970, the most logical location for such a market was London, despite the far greater importance of New York as a financial centre. It was in London that banks already carried out much of their international borrowing and lending, and dealing in foreign exchange had been a natural add-on to that business in the 1960s. What was central to the development of the foreign exchange market in London after 1970 were the presence of so many of the very financial institutions, namely banks, that were potential users and the existence of a foreign exchange market with the microstructure already in place. As the Inter-bank Research Organisation concluded in 1973, after a survey of financial centres, London 'attracts business because of the range of markets and services that it offers and develops new markets and services because of the scale of business it can attract'.[10] One of these was a revitalized foreign exchange market, where the daily turnover rose from $4–5 billion a day in 1973 to $25 billion a day in 1979, by which time it was accepted that the centre of trading was now in

---

[7] J. McCallum, 'Big Three Battle It Out', *Financial Times*, 29 April 1991.

[8] See Schenk, *Decline of Sterling*, 13, 84, 152–3, 206–40, 241, 277, 310, 380, 394–5, 397, 417, 423–5.

[9] Kelly, *Bankers and Borders*, xvii, xxi; Bell and Kettell, *Foreign Exchange Handbook*, 6, 75–6; R.M. Levich, 'Financial Innovations in International Financial Markets', in M. Feldstein (ed.), *The United States in the World Economy* (Chicago: 1988), 219–20; *The New Palgrave Dictionary of Money and Finance*, 154–8.

[10] Inter-bank Research Organisation, *The Future of London*, 1, 8.

the City of London.[11] A last restraint on the further growth of the City of London as a centre for the foreign exchange market disappeared in 1979 with the removal of exchange controls.[12] That allowed banks to fully integrate their London operations into their global business, not only their interbank activities, whether they involved foreign exchange, employing idle balances, or borrowing to supplement a temporary shortfall, as well as the mundane tasks of making and receiving payments on behalf of customers.[13]

Banks and Money

It was after 1970 that global banking became firmly established. Though there had long existed banks with offices and even branches located around the world, most international banking was conducted through correspondent links. Under this system, a bank in one country had a formal arrangement with others elsewhere in the world, through which it and its customers could make and receive payments, borrow and lend money, and exchange currencies. However, the huge advances made in both international communications and the organization and management of multinational businesses created the possibility of global banking. In a global bank, correspondent relationships were internalized within the branch network with the full range of activities being managed centrally. Such banks were in increasing demand from multinational companies who looked to a single organization to provide them with the full range of services rather than rely on a multiplicity of different banks. Similar pressures were coming from large institutional investors who managed complex portfolios spread across different financial instruments and countries. Their needs were best met by banks with proven experience, a depth of resources, a range of expertise, and extensive branch networks. It was these banks that were trusted by their customers and fellow banks to act as counterparties in all manner of transactions. In a global bank, national boundaries were subsumed within a pan-national organization rather than being a bank that specialized in international finance.

Best placed to emerge as global banks after 1970 were those from the USA as they commanded the largest domestic market and conducted their business in US$s, which had become the world's international currency, displacing the UK£. What had held back US banks from supplanting the European banks that had long conducted an international business, especially those from Britain, were the domestic restrictions they had long faced. These ranged from the prohibition on interstate banking dating from the 1860s to the laws introduced in the 1930s that prevented the combination of deposit and investment banking. These were not to be formally repealed until the end of the twentieth century. What had already been removed were those

---

[11] Atkin, *Foreign Exchange Market*, 162.

[12] See Bank of England, 'London as an International Financial Centre', *Bank of England Quarterly Review*, 29 (1989), 516–528.

[13] For this period, see R. Roberts, *The London Financial Services Cluster since the 1970s: Expansion, Development and Internationalisation* (Paris, 2008).

laws that had prevented US banks from opening branches abroad. Nevertheless, those laws that remained hindered US banks from serving their largest corporate customers and fully engaging in an international business. The solution found by a small number of the largest from the 1960s was to open a branch in London where they could conduct any business they chose as they were not subject to US law there. In London, a US commercial bank could expand into investment banking while an investment bank could follow the opposite direction. That meant they could provide their largest US corporate customers with a full range of banking services from a London office. Having opened a London branch, it was then a short step to use it to extend the service offered to US corporate customers to those from other countries, including ones from Britain. Using London as a base but with additional branches strategically placed around the world, US banks could exploit the advantages they derived from their huge domestic market, direct access to the world's currency, the US$, and the capital market facilities found in New York.

What was happening in the 1970s and 1980s was the emergence of a small number of megabanks that were able to offer both a universal and a global service. These comprised an elite group from the USA, Western Europe, and the UK, and all operated out of London regardless of where their head offices were. They invested heavily in staff and equipment and commanded large reserves of capital and liquid assets, which inspired confidence in all those with whom they traded. The increasing adoption of the originate-and-distribute model of banking among these banks also generated trust among their peer group, and the world's central banks, as it was believed to deliver superior resilience in the face of a liquidity crisis, while their spread and depth of activities and the training and expertise of their staff warded against a solvency crisis. Despite the increasing adoption of the originate-and-distribute model of banking, which encouraged greater use made of financial markets, these megabanks had also a greater capacity to internalize financial flows. The result was the simultaneous growth of internal matching of lending and borrowing and a flourishing interbank market. Such was the confidence placed in these megabanks that they were trusted counterparties in all financial transactions whether it was trading in stocks and bonds, commodities and derivatives, or money and currencies. This allowed them to bypass organized markets like the regulated exchanges or dispense with any reliance on central banks as lenders of last resort.

Whereas in the 1950s borrowing and lending between banks in London largely took place through the discount market, and under the supervision of the Bank of England, that was largely displaced in the 1960s by direct lending and the use of inter-dealer brokers. That was especially the case for non-UK banks as they were the ones most exposed to currency risks. In 1951, interbank borrowing and lending by non-UK banks in London totalled £239 million. Of this, 25 per cent was composed of balances held directly with other banks, while 75 per cent was loans to the discount houses. By 1959, the total had only risen to £308 million indicating the diminished appeal of the London money market to foreign banks at a time of rapidly rising bank deposits. The proportion placed directly with other banks had now risen to 38 per cent, while that lent to the discount houses had fallen to 62 per cent. It was in the

1960s that a complete reversal took place. The total lent out and borrowed in the London money market by foreign banks rose more than tenfold, from £356 million in 1960 to £4,267 million in 1969, and by then, 97 per cent was in the form of balances with other banks. Ten years later, in 1979, the total reached £32,175 million and all was placed directly with other banks. Long before Britain had abandoned exchange controls in 1979, sterling had been abandoned as an international currency. It was only by switching to the US$ as a basis of operation from 1960 onwards and replacing the use of the discount market with alternative money market operations that London retained its attractions for the global banking community.[14]

The use of the London discount market also declined sharply as a share of inter-bank borrowing and lending by British banks after 1970. In 1971, total borrowing and lending in London among British banks amounted to £1,960 million, of which 74 per cent was placed through the discount market and 26 per cent directly with other banks. By 1979, the total had risen to £13,014 million, of which only 16 per cent went to the discount market, leaving 84 per cent placed directly with other banks.[15] From 1971 to 1988, data is available for borrowing and lending by all banks in the London interbank market. The total for 1971 was £9,006 million, of which 22 per cent was done by UK banks and 78 per cent by foreign banks. That total reached £154,522 million in 1988, by which time British banks were responsible for 43 per cent of the total compared to the 57 per cent of the foreign banks. What this indicated was that the British banks had abandoned the sterling-based discount market and embraced its replacement, which involved either direct interbank borrowing and lending or the use of the new breed of inter-dealer brokers. This had already happened before Britain dropped exchange controls in 1979. Whereas in 1971 UK banks had balances with other banks of £519 million (26 per cent of the total) and £1,441 million in the money market (74 per cent of the total), the position by 1979 was the reverse with £10,962 million with other banks (84 per cent) and £2,052 million (16 per cent) in the money market.[16]

One market that flourished in this new era of interbank borrowing and lending in London was that for Eurobonds. A Eurobond was a debt security issued outside the country of the currency in which it is denominated. The most common

---

[14] Source: *Bank of England Quarterly Bulletin Statistical Supplement, 1960–1989.*
Note: This data is for 31 December of each year and excludes UK domestic banks. It only includes British overseas banks and those foreign banks with branches in London, which were permitted to accept deposits in London, whereas banks with only representative offices in London were not. What is included are the balances these banks had with other banks and their lending to the London money market. In 1975, lending to the money market ceased to be separately reported having become a very small proportion of the total.

[15] Source: *Bank of England Quarterly Bulletin Statistical Supplement, 1972–1980.* Note: This data is for 31 December for each year. For the period 1971–9, the data was compiled from the separate entries for each type of bank. From 1980 to 1988, the categories used were UK/non-UK banks. After 1989, this data was not included. The data includes both balances with other banks and lending to the money market. There is no comparable data for before 1971.

[16] Source: *Bank of England Quarterly Bulletin Statistical Supplement, 1972–1989.*
Note: This data is for 31 December for each year. For the period 1971–9, the data was compiled from the separate entries for each type of bank. From 1980 to 1988, the categories used were UK/non-UK banks. After 1989, this data was not included. The data includes both balances with other banks and lending to the money market. There is no comparable data for before 1971.

Eurobonds were denominated in US$s and were issued in London, where they were not subject to the controls and taxes imposed by the US government. What these Eurobonds initially lacked was a market in which they could be bought and sold, as the London Stock Exchange refused to amend its rules to cater to their requirements. Without such a market, Eurobonds were less attractive to investors, as they had to be held until redemption, and possessed no mechanism for generating current prices, which was essential if they were to be used as collateral. That market developed after 1970 through direct dealing between the megabanks and the activities of a group of inter-dealer brokers, who acted as intermediaries. The establishment of Euroclear in Brussels in 1968 and Cedel in Luxembourg in 1970 provided the Eurobond market with a mechanism for handling transfers and dealing with counterparty risk. The result was a market that grew in volume and sophistication and so met the needs of the banks for certainty and liquidity. One indication of the growth of the Eurobond market was that turnover on Cedel alone rose to $1,720 billion in 1988. What this generated was a vastly increased demand for the facilities provided by a foreign exchange market as so much business took place in London in currencies other than the UK£.

Foreign Exchange

Closely related to these developments in banking and the money and bond markets were developments in the foreign exchange market, which boomed after 1970.[17] According to the Bank for International Settlements (BIS), which began its survey in 1986, daily foreign exchange turnover was $206 billion in 1986, grew to $744 billion in 1989, and reached $1,115 billion in 1992. The amount of trading conducted in London stood at $90 billion in 1986, $187 billion in 1989, and $297 billion in 1992, but that meant its share fell from 44 per cent to 27 per cent. This relative decline is

[17] See the following pieces from the *Financial Times*: P. Stephens, 'Living with Turbulence', 3 June 1987; D. Lascelles, 'Earnings Continue to Increase', 3 June 1987; J. Bush, 'Pressure Grows for Freer Markets', 3 June 1987; J. Bush, 'Calm Follows Squeezed Margins', 3 June 1987; L. Martineau, 'Hedging Helps the Boom', 3 June 1987; R. Oram, 'Volatility Spurs Cross-trading', 3 June 1987; H. Simonian, 'Banking Growth Bolsters Demand', 3 June 1987; A. Cane, 'Advantage from the Third Phase', 3 June 1987; P. Coggan, 'Lobbying Clout Grows', 3 June 1987; P. Coggan, 'Corporations are Chary', 3 June 1987; S. Fidler, 'A Broader and Safer Market in a Storm', 18 May 1988; D. Lascelles, 'Trusting in Local Judgement', 15 July 1988; P. Daniel, 'B&C Cliff-hanger Still Runs', 15 July 1988; R. Atkins, 'More Join the Risk Business', 15 July 1988; A. Cane, 'Deals System Wins Praise', 15 July 1988; S. Holberton, 'Return of the Large Private Player', 15 July 1988; J. Bush, 'Low Post-crash volumes the Major Problem', 15 July 1988; J. Andrews, 'Trading Likely to Rise by a Quarter This Year', 15 July 1988; H. Simonian, 'Dealers Welcome Rise in Volatility', 15 July 1988; R. Atkins, 'A Sterling Drama at the Money Theatre', 15 July 1988; R. Johnson, 'Reuters Triumphs in the Derivatives Jungle', 21 December 1989; P. Elstob, 'Anxious to Become the ECU Centre', 29 November 1990; J. McCallum, 'Big Three Battle It Out', 29 April 1991; C. Goodhart and A. Demos, 'The Asian Surprise in the Forex Markets', 2 September 1991; J. McCallum, 'End of Controls Provides a Lift', 11 November 1991; J. Blitz, 'Forex Dealers Can Buy Time', 12 August 1992; J. Blitz, 'New Anxieties for the Banks', 26 May 1993; P. Gawith, 'Forex Surge Masks Maturing Market', 24 October 1995; P. Coggan, 'It's Just a Small Problem', 8 February 1996; G. Graham, 'BIS Outlines Forex Settlement Risk Strategy', 28 March 1996; G. Graham, 'Forex Dealers Move to Limit Settlement Risk', 5 June 1996; R. Adams, 'Brokers Alter Shape of Things to Come', 25 June 1999; J. Hughes, 'Where Money Talks Very Loudly', 27 May 2004; J. Hughes, 'A Veteran With a Proud Record of Service', 27 May 2004.

accounted for by the limited coverage of the BIS's first survey. The number of central banks participating rose from four in 1986 to twenty in 1989 and twenty-six in 1992. More indicative of London's relative position is that New York also fell, dropping to 16 per cent in 1992. As New York was London's nearest rival, this suggests that London was tightening its grip on the global market during the 1980s.[18] This position was the product of a steady advance dating from the end of the 1950s.[19] Driving this expansion was the use made of the foreign exchange market by banks whether to cover their currency exposure, manage their liquidity position, or profit from currency volatility. By swapping commitments with each other, banks could continuously cover their positions generated by the constant ebb and flow of payments and receipts, deposits and withdrawals, and loans and borrowings. Such business lies at the heart of banking, and the foreign exchange market provided them with an essential tool through which they managed their affairs, enabling them to remain liquid and solvent and able to generate a profit after meeting all expenses. Those banks with extensive international connections were the main players in this foreign exchange market, trading huge volumes of currency spot and forward in large individual amounts both for themselves and on behalf of smaller banks. As the US$ was the world's dominant currency, US banks were the key players in the foreign exchange market, but the centre of trading was London, which was not only where more banks had offices than anywhere else but also enjoyed a favourable location between Asia and the Americas. Trading in both New York and Tokyo was most active when each overlapped with London. What London was able to do in the 1970s, long before Britain abandoned exchange controls in 1979, was built on the position it had already established in the 1960s, as a centre where banks could trade US$ deposits between each other, with none of the restrictions they faced if the business was done in New York. According to R.S. O'Brien in 1971, there were already 170 banks and 11 brokers actively involved in London. He was in a position to know as he was the chairman of one of the interdealer brokers, Charles Fulton and Company, that were playing an important role in the market by then. The number of banks involved grew further during the 1970s as ever more from Britain and around the world turned to the foreign exchange market not only to cover their exposure to currency volatility after the ending of fixed exchange rates but also to employ idle funds and borrow to meet a shortfall.[20]

It was in the foreign exchange market in London that banks traded time deposits with each other, profiting from the differential between the interest they paid and that which they received. These transactions were largely in US$s and were conducted

[18] Bank for International Settlements, *Triennial Central Bank Survey* (2019); Bank for International Settlements, *Guide to the International Locational Banking Statistics, Monetary and Economic Department* (BIS, 2011). The collection of this data by BIS began in the 1970s. The UK was among the first to report in 1977 with other countries being added over time. This means that the data for any single centre is consistent over time, but the total is not and neither is a particular centre's proportion of that total.
[19] Collins, *Money and Banking*, 504, 538; Atkin, *The Foreign Exchange Market of London*, 137, 148–51, 160–2, 175–80, 191.
[20] O'Brien, 'Euro-Currency Market', 245–9; Mitchell, 'American Banker's View of the City', 186–8; Pringle, 'Foreign Banks in London', 48; M.G. Wilcox, 'Capital in Banking: An Historical Survey', *JIB*, 100 (1979), 99; J. Thirlwell, 'A Look at American Banking', *JIB*, 103 (1982), 3–5.

236   Forex Forever

free from regulations and exchange controls. The Bank of England estimated that the number of banks that engaged with the foreign exchange market had grown from 132 in 1963 to 193 in 1969 and, measured by gross foreign currency claims and liabilities, this interbank market had expanded from £1.3 billion to £12.5 billion over the same period. By July 1970, the Bank of England estimated the total Eurocurrency business to be £19.4 billion, with much consisting of the inter-branch transfer of funds within the same bank. Greatly contributing to this expansion of the non-sterling business being conducted in London was the introduction of the Dollar Certificate of Deposit in 1966. It was a receipt for a US dollar deposit with a London bank in bearer form, making it easily negotiable, and it facilitated the movement of funds between banks as they could be bought and resold repeatedly until maturity. By 1974, a total of 130 banks were engaged in issuing them and 17 brokers were involved in their trading. What this meant is that funds could be transferred between banks without the need for collateral in the form of commercial or treasury bills. Between 1968 and 1973, the dollar certificates outstanding rose from $1.4 billion to $9.6 billion. As the use of sterling as an international currency fell, so the trading in US$ deposits in London grew with most of this business being done either directly between banks or through the twelve firms of foreign exchange brokers operating in 1980. In the most actively traded currencies, especially the US$, it was possible to cover forward transactions for up to a year, and even longer, through the exchange of bank deposits between banks. This market provided banks with a mechanism through which they could lend and borrow among themselves and so constantly adjust their position both in terms of liquidity and currency as well as generate profits. As Chrystal concluded in 1984, 'Given the variability of exchange rates, it is important for banks and firms operating in foreign currencies to be able to reduce exchange rate risk whenever possible.'[21] This was done through the use of forward contracts, swaps, and arbitrage. The banks that participated in this foreign exchange market were pleased with the results, concluding in 1985 that it was 'a system that has expanded tremendously and works well'.[22]

In 1985, the Bank of England calculated that there were 490 foreign banks with an office, branch, or subsidiary in London, either of their own or as part of a consortium. Of these, 472 conducted an international business from London and 315 had either a branch or a subsidiary, thus allowing them to participate directly in the various interbank markets, including that for foreign exchange. Collectively, those foreign banks represented in London did 32 per cent of their entire international business there ranging from 38 per cent for those from Japan to 25 per cent for those from the USA. However, a mere 12 (2.5 per cent) of them were responsible for half the business done in the international interbank market and 37 (7.8 per cent) for three-quarters. Over the 1975–85 period, the size of the international interbank market had grown from $130 billion to $554 billion as it became increasingly diversified.

[21] Chrystal, *Guide to Foreign Exchange Markets*, 17.
[22] Group of Thirty, *Foreign Exchange Markets under Floating Rates* (New York: 1980); P.B. Kenen, *The Role of the Dollar as an International Currency* (New York: Group of Thirty, 1983); Group of Thirty, *The Foreign Exchange Market in the 1980s: The View of Market Participants* (New York: 1985).

The share undertaken by US and British banks fell from 59 per cent to 35 per cent with the rest of the world rising from 41 per cent to 65 per cent. A key element of this interbank market was the daily trading in foreign exchange with 57 per cent done directly and 43 per cent arranged by inter-dealer brokers, operating from a global network of offices connecting London, New York, and Tokyo. By 1992, it was acknowledged that the Foreign Exchange Market in London was much larger and more diversified than that of any centre and was beginning to embrace electronic trading. Though 34 per cent of the business was still done by brokers and 42 per cent directly between banks, 24 per cent relied on automated dealing systems.[23]

Such was the depth and breadth of this London-centred foreign exchange market that it survived an early shock in 1974 with the collapse of the small German bank, Bankhaus Herstatt. That bank had been paid for currency that it had not yet delivered by the time it suspended operations. This exposed the risks being run in a 24-hour market in which payments and receipts were not instantly matched because of time-zone differences. In response, banks themselves quickly devised ways of coping with counterparty risk, encouraging even greater concentration of trading in the hands of a small number of the most active and trusted players clustered in London. Daily turnover in the foreign exchange market in London rose from around $5 billion a day in 1973 to $25 billion in 1979. In the face of continuing currency volatility in the 1980s, combined with increasing trade and international investment, activity in London's foreign exchange market expanded rapidly again but remained concentrated in the hands of a few banks trading out of their London offices, as they were the trusted counterparties of the global banking community. By 1992, foreign exchange turnover in London was $297 billion a day, or 27 per cent of the global total, compared to $182 billion in New York (16 per cent) and $126 billion in Tokyo (11 per cent).[24]

London remained the centre of trading, dominating the European time zone and attracting the business of US banks, which conducted much of their international trading out of London, where they had established international dealing rooms. New York was next in importance, dominating the Americas' time zone. Though Tokyo was the most important Asian centre, it was losing out to Singapore and Hong Kong; the development of the foreign exchange market in Tokyo was hampered by restrictions imposed by the Japanese government encouraging the migration of trading to Hong Kong and Singapore. Supporting the growth of a global 24-hour/7-day a week

[23] See the following pieces from the *Bank of England Quarterly Bulletin*: Bank of England, 'Eurocurrency Business', 31–7, 448; 'Reserve Ratios: Further Definitions', 11 (1971), 483; 'The London Dollar Certificate of Deposit', 13 (1973), 446–9; 'Overseas Balances 1963–1973', 14 (1974), 162; Bank of England, 'UK Commodity Markets', 15 (1975), 245; Bank of England, 'Foreign Exchange Market in London', 20 (1980), 438–44; 'Eurobanks and the Inter-bank Market', 21 (1981), 351–4; Bank of England, 'The Commodity Futures Market', 26 (1986), 217–22; Bank of England, 'Foreign Banks in London', 26 (1986), 368–73; Bank of England, 'The Market for Foreign Exchange in London', 26 (1986), 380; Bank of England, 'Japanese Banks in London', 27 (1987), 518, 521; Bank of England, 'The Role of Brokers in the London Money Markets', 30 (1990), 221–5; Bank of England, 'The International Bond Market', 31 (1991), 521–7; Bank of England, 'Major International Banks' Performance, 1980–1991', 32 (1992), 290–1; Bank of England, 'The Foreign Exchange Market in London', 32 (1992), 409–13.
[24] Bank for International Settlements, *Triennial Central Bank Survey* (2022); Schrimpf and Sushko, 'Sizing Up Global Foreign Exchange Markets'; Schrimpf and Sushko, 'FX Trade Execution', *BIS Quarterly Review* (December 2019), 1–13; Bordo and Flandreau, 'Core, Periphery'.

market centred in London were developments in both dealing technology and communications systems. In 1989, a submarine fibre-optic cable was completed linking London and New York. It provided a cheap, high capacity virtually instantaneous communications conduit between the world's leading financial centres, contributing to the clustering of trading there, especially London which already possessed the market microstructure with its dense concentration of bank offices.[25] Predating the laying of the fibre-optic cables was the other major breakthrough, which came in 1973. That was when the news and information provider, Reuters, introduced its monitor terminals with screens displaying foreign exchange rates but with transactions taking place via the telephone. By 1986, Reuters hosted a network of 17,000 subscribers worldwide connected through 54,000 screens. Competing with Reuters in the provision of real-time foreign exchange rates from 1990 was Electronic Broking Services. Alan Cane observed in 1986 that in the foreign exchange market, 'There is no central, physical market floor and dealing is carried out over the telephone. The calculations required are complex and the risks substantial. So quality of telecommunications and speed of connection between dealers or dealers and brokers are critically important.'[26] In the same year, David Lascelles reported that 'Today's dealing rooms are high-technology nerve centres, bulging with the latest telecommunications equipment to girdle the globe, and packed with computers programmed to spot opportunity in a dozen currencies and in foreign exchange-based instruments like options and futures.'[27] This dependence upon technology for communications and trading also extended to the settlement of transactions, with positions between the major dealer-banks in the leading currencies being netted off at the end of each day.

The result of all these developments was to make foreign exchange trading a global market with buying and selling conducted on a continuous basis. According to Peter Montagnon, in 1984, 'Foreign-exchange dealing is a 24-hour-a-day business, with major centres in the Far East dealing through the European night and European traders staying up late to catch the market in New York.'[28] This judgement was echoed in 1988 by Richard Huber, head of capital markets and foreign exchange at Chase Manhattan Bank. In his judgement, foreign exchange trading had become 'the most global market' where trading took place 'seamlessly across national borders and time zones.'[29] This trading was increasingly driven by international financial flows and the need to cover the risks involved at a time of volatile exchange rates, as Janet Bush explained in 1987: 'The development of ever more sophisticated markets, backed up by hedging mechanisms and a myriad of financial instruments, has meant that a large proportion of the flow of funds through the foreign exchange market can be traced to investment shifts rather than genuine trade transactions.'[30] For most banks,

[25] B. Eichengreen, R. Lafarguette and A. Mehl, 'Cables, Sharks and Servers: Technology and the Foreign Exchange Market', *NBER Working Paper*, 21, 884 (2016).

[26] A. Cane, 'Increasing Quality and Speed in Dealing Rooms', *Financial Times*, 27 May 1986.

[27] D. Lascelles, 'An Established Profit Centre', *Financial Times*, 27 May 1986.

[28] P. Montagnon, 'Novel Offerings Bring Fresh Edge to Competition', *Financial Times*, 14 February 1984.

[29] J. Bush, 'Low Post-crash Volumes the Major Problem', *Financial Times*, 15 July 1988.

[30] J. Bush, 'Pressure Grows for Freer Markets', *Financial Times*, 3 June 1987.

dealing in foreign exchange remained a service they provided for their customers, covering their risks through the spot and forward markets. However, for the emerging megabanks, foreign exchange was becoming a core business where large profits could be generated from taking a position in the market and acting as counterparties to the buying and selling of others. The effect was to drive up volume, making the foreign exchange market into one where liquidity was available virtually 24 hours a day, 7 days a week. As David Lascelles observed in 1988, 'The trading action moves with the clock from one centre to the next, and each centre is responsible for the positions it takes. As the Far East hands over to London, and London to New York, and New York back to Sydney, dealers brief each other about their sensitivities.'[31] This made the use of the foreign exchange market essential for every bank, either directly or indirectly, in the management of its liquidity position.

To maintain their central role in the foreign exchange market required the megabanks to invest heavily in technology and staff and be able to offer a range of currency facilities to their customers. This had the effect of concentrating the business in their hands. According to Phillip Stephens, in 1987, 'Turbulent markets, of course, are more often than not good news for the banks and brokers who dominate the 24-hour-a-day business of foreign exchange trading.'[32] Also encouraging concentration were the enormous risks being run and so banks confined their trading to those counterparties that could be trusted to meet their commitments. This requirement for a high level of trust also limited the switch to electronic trading that automatically matched buyers and sellers, though these systems were being developed by a number of information providers. By April 1992, Reuter's Dealing 2000–2 system was operational, developed at over $75 million, but the thirty banks that took the service made limited use of it because they could not control for counterparty risk. Instead, the banks largely stuck to current practice. When trading foreign exchange, a dealer in a bank contacted his equivalent in another bank directly, either by computer or telephone, and negotiated a bilateral deal. Alternatively, the business was placed in the hands of inter-dealer brokers who used their personal network to complete the transaction. In contrast, the electronic systems matched sales and purchases anonymously with no regard for the reliability of the counterparties involved. Despite the technical superiority of Reuter's dealing system, it had failed to gain immediate acceptability in 1992, and many doubted that it ever would.

Contributing to the development of the foreign exchange market after 1970 was a species of intermediary that became known as inter-dealer brokers. They did not take a position in the market but operated between the banks, which did, hence the term inter-dealer brokers as they arranged sales and purchases between the banks. In many deals, the banks did not want to trade directly with competitors as it revealed whether they were buying or selling, borrowing or lending, and going short or long. Inter-dealer brokers could also handle the deals where the bank lacked the staff, expertise, or connections and so was happy to pay commission to those who possessed all three.

---

[31] D. Lascelles, 'Trusting in Local Judgement', *Financial Times*, 15 July 1988.
[32] P. Stephens, 'Living with Turbulence', *Financial Times*, 3 June 1987.

The explosion in foreign exchange trading generated a need for intermediation to supplement the trading that took place directly between the banks. The inter-dealer brokers were at the centre of a large web of connections, allowing them to aggregate deals before passing them on to the small number of banks that were at the core of the market. As a growing number of banks engaged with the foreign exchange market, the demand for the services of inter-dealer brokers expanded. The result was the appearance and growth in the number of inter-dealer brokers ready to seize the opportunity to make a profit by matching supply and demand between banks and acting as the retailers of the wholesale services provided by the megabanks.

These inter-dealer brokers became established as major players in the foreign exchange market that grew up in London after 1970. At first, they were few in number and all very small firms. Tullett and Riley was set up in London by four men in 1971 to make and maintain a market in Eurodollar deposits and foreign exchange. From these beginnings, these inter-dealer brokers established a network of offices during the 1970s that linked London, Tokyo, and New York into a single global market. They relied on real-time information supplied by the likes of Reuters to constantly monitor current prices and then used telephone links to banks to provide a trading forum. It was the combination of screens displaying current rates and the telephone providing a means of communication that constituted the foreign exchange market in the 1970s, with inter-dealer brokers acting as the intermediaries between the banks supplementing direct dealing. These inter-dealer brokers replaced or absorbed those who had previously acted as intermediaries between the banks, such as London's discount houses, who had confined themselves to dealings in UK government debt and in UK£s. The Bank of England had tried to protect the discount houses from competition because of the role they played in its management of UK monetary policy but eventually abandoned them as it recognized that the London money market was becoming ever more diverse and international. In 1986, Derek Tullett, the then chairman of Tullett and Tokyo Forex International and representative of the Foreign Exchange and Currency Deposit Brokers' Association, observed that 'It is up to the markets to decide which companies it wants to deal with. Why should we have this restriction on us when it is the principals who should be taking the decision.'[33] The inter-dealer brokers acted as intermediaries across all the markets, including foreign exchange, bills and bonds, and interbank borrowing and lending, using the US$ in their transactions wherever they took place.[34]

By the early 1980s, a small group of influential inter-dealer brokers had emerged, trading across the whole range of financial instruments, linking activity in foreign exchange to that in bills, bonds, stocks, swaps, futures, and options. What they

---

[33] G. Graham, 'Hopes of an End to O'Brien Rules', *Financial Times*, 27 May 1986.
[34] *Financial Times*: T. Garrett, 'Giants Head the Broking League', 14 February 1984; J. Burke, 'Tensions Beneath the Surface', 14 February 1984; P.M. Elstob, 'UK Links with Tokyo Houses', 14 February 1984; J. Moore, 'Ultimate Target Is Broad Band of Financial Services', 14 February 1984; A. Rawsthorn, 'Intermediaries' Buy Out', 27 May 1986; G. Graham, 'Hopes of an End to O'Brien Rules', 27 May 1986; D. Lascelles, 'When the Walls Come Down', 23 July 1986; D. Lascelles, 'The Competition Will Get Tougher', 2 October 1986; S. Wagstyl, 'Glint of Change in the Gold Market', 5 December 1986; J. Blitz, 'A Top-Hat Tradition in the Balance', 22 June 1992; R. Peston, 'Silent Launch of the Lifeboat', 19 October 1993.

provided was a service connecting banks together in a closely integrated global network as they continuously bought from one and sold to another on commission while never taking a position on their own. These inter-dealer brokers competed aggressively for the business of the banks both against each other and the banks' own staff. In 1984, Tullett and Riley had a staff of over 1,000, by which time there were significant barriers to entry as banks confined their dealings to a small number of brokers in whom they had confidence because they possessed the expertise, connections, and technology to deliver the service they required. These inter-dealer brokers were responsible for around half of all trading in foreign exchange in the mid-1980s, for example, creating and maintaining liquidity through the depth and breadth they brought to the market. David Lascelles claimed in 1984 that

> Even the world's largest banks have nothing like the intelligence networks built up by the biggest money brokers: thousands of contacts all over the world, dozens of offices, highly-sophisticated and costly communications systems. At the height of trading a large firm like Astley and Pearce has twenty telephone lines permanently open between London and New York.[35]

There was a core group of ten inter-dealer brokers running a global business spanning Tokyo, London, and New York and they were able to provide the 24-hour market that banks now required. These inter-dealer brokers operated as all-purpose money brokers, facilitating the constant borrowing and lending that took place between banks as they sought to maximize the use of the funds they had available and minimize the risks they ran. Though inter-dealer brokers were members of certain exchanges, as with Chicago Mercantile Exchange (CME) and Chicago Board of Trade (CBOT) in Chicago and Liffe (London International Financial Futures Exchange) and the London Commodity Exchange in London, they were also rivals to these institutions, able to provide access to global markets on a 24-hour basis. A liquid 24-hour market enabled banks and their customers to complete transactions at the timing and price of their choice, without having to take risks on currency or interest-rate movements.

Threatening the position achieved by the inter-dealer brokers in the 1980s was the ability of the megabanks to internalize transactions and to trade directly with each other through computerized networks. These megabanks were in a position to hold positions for long periods, accepting the risk of large losses in volatile markets because of the possibility of equally commensurate gains. However, there remained numerous other banks with an increasing need to access the money markets, including that for foreign exchange, and they were reluctant to pass all this business on to a rival. For that reason, there continued to be a role for the inter-dealer brokers, let alone the expertise and connections they could provide. Unless a bank was willing to invest extensively in the staff and technology already possessed by an inter-dealer broker, it had little choice but to continue using the services they provided. The result

---

[35] D. Lascelles, 'Big Business But Competition Keen', *Financial Times*, 14 February 1984.

was a sharing of the market between the inter-dealer brokers and an emerging group of global banks. The inter-dealer brokers fed the banks with current information and acted for them when their dealers wanted to buy and sell. As Robin Packshaw, chairman of International City Holdings and owner of the inter-dealer broker Charles Fulton, explained in 1987, 'A busy dealer simply can't look at too many screens. One, two, three or even four at a pinch is as much as one man can cope with.'[36] By the early 1990s, an exclusive group of inter-dealer brokers complemented the megabanks and together they provided a market across a widening range of financial products, including foreign exchange. Through these markets, banks could be connected to each other and provided with a deep and broad pool of liquidity through which they could constantly balance assets and liabilities and so either take or avoid risk, depending on the strategy to be pursued at any moment in time.[37]

Conclusion

Over the 1950s and 1960s, the ability of regulators to employ a policy of divide and rule to control financial markets was slowly eroded. Faced with the growing liberalization of international trade and finance, the need grew to put in place mechanisms that allowed payments to be made and received, and funds to flow from areas of surplus to those with shortages. As governments continued to impose controls on international financial flows, including investment beyond a country's borders, these arrangements encouraged the development of offshore financial centres and alternative financial markets. A similar erosion of regulatory control took place within those countries operating a market economy as governments gave up attempts to impose interest rates and direct the supply of credit and capital. Technological change contributed to the undermining of government control by rendering boundaries between countries and activities increasingly porous. Physical space no longer dictated the location of a market because transactions took place over the telephone with prices simultaneously displayed on screens in offices around the world. Payments and receipts flowed seamlessly through interbank networks that grew steadily in breadth and depth. In the face of these developments, governments increasingly abandoned exchange controls and other attempts to contain or channel international financial

[36] J. Bush, 'Calm Follows Squeezed Margins', *Financial Times*, 3 June 1987.
[37] For inter-dealer brokers, see the following: *Financial Times* pieces: D. Lascelles, 'Big Business But Competition Keen', 14 February 1984; T. Garrett, 'Giants Head the Broking League', 14 February 1984; C. Batchelor, 'Wider Range of Contracts Urged', 14 February 1984; J. Burke, 'Tensions Beneath the Surface', 14 February 1984; P.M. Elstob, 'UK Links with Tokyo Houses', 14 February 1984; J. Moore, 'Ultimate Target Is Broad Band of Financial Services', 14 February 1984; G. Graham, 'Mercurial Times in the Market', 27 May 1986; A. Rawsthorn, 'Intermediaries' Buy Out', 27 May 1986; G. Graham, 'Hopes of an End to O'Brien Rules', 27 May 1986; J. Brown, 'Major Players in Their Own Right', 27 May 1986; R. Lambert, 'More Products Now Need Round-The-Clock Trading', 27 October 1986; D. Lascelles and R. Oram, 'Key Link Added to a Global Chain', 3 March 1987; J. Bush, 'Calm Follows Squeezed Margins', 3 June 1987; S. Fidler, 'Where British Brokers Rule World', 7 July 1987; D. Lascelles, 'Another Flurry in Money Brokers' World', 19 August 1987; B. Riley, 'More Interdealer Brokers to Open', 28 March 1988; P. Daniel, 'B&C Cliff-Hanger Still Runs', 15 July 1988; S. Fidler, 'Money Brokers Step into the Financial Limelight', 22 November 1990.

flows. Making use of the new technology, financial innovation blurred distinctions between banks and financial markets, as well as between different types of banks as new products were invented, such as financial derivatives and money market funds.

The market that grew exponentially after 1970, as a result of this transformation, was that in foreign exchange, where banks were engaged continuously in balancing their assets and liabilities not only across different currencies but also over time. As with the interbank money market, the foreign exchange market was also one dominated by a small number of very large banks with extensive international connections. The volume of trading and the speed of transaction made it vital that every participant could be relied on not only to complete the deal but also exactly as agreed, as they were all linked. Much of the activity in these interbank markets was located in London, though it operated on the basis of the US$. What was emerging in the 1980s was an integrated global market that revolved round the activities of a small number of banks. It involved not only direct trading between banks but also the activities of a small group of inter-dealer brokers that developed after 1970. These inter-dealer brokers built up close contacts with banks and established a global network that linked the world's financial centres into a continuous market. Increasingly, it was either direct dealing between banks or the links between inter-dealer brokers and their customers that became the market for a variety of financial products ranging from currencies and bonds through to bank deposits and derivatives. These markets had no physical location as trading was conducted between the offices of the banks and inter-dealer brokers through the use of the telephone with screens displaying financial information that was constantly updated. Such was the success of these inter-dealer brokers that they displaced other long-established intermediaries, such as London's discount houses, despite the support the latter were given by the Bank of England. What these megabanks and inter-dealer brokers had done was tap into the simultaneous phenomena of the dematerialization of trading, the globalization of the market, and the use of the US$ as the world currency, making the City of London as its global hub. To many, the role played by the City of London appeared inevitable and permanent. However, the failure of Tokyo to become the hub for Asia in the 1970s and 1980s, and then its subsequent loss of trading to Hong Kong and Singapore, contradicts both these assumptions.[38] What the foreign exchange market in London had achieved was due to its response to the opportunities presented since the end of the 1950s as the UK government relaxed its controls and the US government increased its. That response, combined with the prehistory of the foreign exchange market in London, provided the City of London with the basis from which it could become the centre for the world's largest market, by turnover. However, by the beginning of the 1990s, it was facing a new challenge as the development of electronic markets threatened to make location irrelevant, providing great opportunities for those that could offer cheaper space and employees along with less regulation and lower taxes.

---

[38] Bank for International Settlements, *Triennial Central Bank Survey* (2022).

5
Electronic Forex, 1992–2007

Introduction

By the beginning of the 1990s, it was recognized by central banks that the era of control was over. As Eddie George, the governor of the Bank of England, admitted in 1993, 'we simply could not, even if we wanted them, reimpose the exchange controls that would be needed to isolate our banking system from the rest of the world'.[1] That lack of desire to return to the controls of the past included an acceptance that the foreign exchange market was now a permanent feature of the world's financial architecture. There would be no attempt to impose fixed exchange rates and maintain them through active intervention by central banks. That being the case, there was no need for governments to impose barriers on the free flow of manufactures, commodities, services, money, and capital. What this represented was a greater reliance upon market forces to restore internal equilibrium. This was a partial return to the international financial system that had existed before the First World War. At the same time, a measure of competitiveness could then be restored to national financial systems.[2] In the place of control and compartmentalization the world was moving inexorably towards global twenty-four-hour financial markets and an elite grouping of megabanks. These developments were supported by global economic integration, developments in technology, the retreat of government from direct intervention, and the introduction of policies that promoted competition. Nevertheless, the outcome was not a seamless global market, as major differences in language, culture, laws, and taxes remained. These all contributed to the segregation of markets and banks being constrained by national boundaries.

What was apparent from the early 1990s onwards was the dramatic effects that the electronic revolution was having on global financial markets. As Allen and Hawkins reflected in 2002,

> Electronic trading is transforming financial markets. It can reduce costs, extend participation and remove many physical limitations on trading arrangements. It allows much greater volumes of trades to be handled, and permits customisation of processes that until recently would have been technically impossible or

---

[1] E. George, 'Recent Banking Difficulties: An Address by the Governor of the Bank of England', *BEQB*, 33 (18 January 1993), 103–105.
[2] 'Risk Measurement and Capital Requirements for Banks', *BEQB*, 35 (1995), 177–185; Bank of England, 'Foreign Exchange Market in London', *BEQB*, 25 (1995), 361–369.

Forex Forever. Ranald C. Michie, Oxford University Press. © Ranald C. Michie (2024).
DOI: 10.1093/oso/9780198903697.003.0006

prohibitively expensive. It is a major force for changes in 'market architecture'—the key features of market structure such as participation arrangements, venues and trading protocols.[3]

One example was the electronic payments system supplied by the interbank agency, SWIFT (Society for Worldwide Interbank Financial Telecommunication). This enabled all banks to participate in global markets wherever they were located. The revolution in communications was a two-edged weapon. On the one hand, it made it possible to disperse financial activity to cheaper locations or ones closer to the customer. On the other hand, it encouraged clustering of financial activity where any delay, or latency, of communication mattered. In fast-moving wholesale markets, especially one such as foreign exchange trading, the revolution in technology favoured clustering, while in many other areas it led to dispersion, such as those serving retail customers.

The revolution in technology was not confined to communications but extended to processing. Electronic systems allowed more to be done at faster speeds and lower costs, which encouraged the application of more complex trading strategies and repeated interconnected transactions. Where the new technology of trading was gaining traction, throughout the 1990s and into the twenty-first century, was in those markets dominated by megabanks and global fund managers, as they could be trusted to stand behind the deals made. Despite the high cost of electronic systems, and the rapid rate of obsolescence, those willing to make the investment had the opportunity of breaking into markets long regarded as monopolies. Contributing to the impact made by the electronic revolution in finance was the removal of internal and external barriers by governments. No matter the degree and pace of change in the technology applied to finance, its impact would have been limited if it had been blocked by governments. By the early twenty-first century, it became generally accepted that under the guidance of the Bank for International Settlements, banks had learnt the lessons of past crises and devised strategies that allowed them to cope with the increased risks posed by a more volatile global financial system. The combination of internal risk controls within banks, and the ability to distribute the risks each was exposed to, appeared to have produced a global financial system that was resilient in the face of successive crises. Under the circumstances, the megabanks could be allowed to operate under regimes of lightweight regulation whether applied by institutions or the state. This sidelined the regulated exchanges, for example, and encouraged the over-the-counter (OTC) markets to flourish, such as that for foreign exchange.[4]

---

[3] H. Allen and J. Hawkins, 'Electronic Trading in Wholesale Financial Markets: Its Wider Implications', *BEQB*, 42 (2002), 50.

[4] For an early advocate of the death of distance debate, see R. O'Brien, *Global Financial Integration: The End of Geography* (London, 1992); R. O'Brien and Alasdair Keith, 'The Geography of Finance: After the Storm', *Cambridge Journal of Regions, Economy and Society*, 2 (2009), 245–65.

Financial Centres

Though many prophesied that the revolution in communications taking place spelled the death of distance or the end of geography when it came to the location of financial markets, they ignored the fact that time was not absolute but relative. Even when information travelled at the speed of light through fibre-optic cables, those closest to the source had an advantage, which was vital in fast-moving markets. The effect was to generate a continued clustering of financial markets. Global markets had to have a core, which was where contact was instant and liquidity greatest. Increasingly favoured were those financial centres that could provide global banks and fund managers with the markets and facilities they required. London and New York emerged as joint leaders among global financial centres, each possessing distinctive strengths and weaknesses. This competition between London and New York took place at the wholesale level, involving the markets for money, derivatives, internationally held stocks and bonds, and currency. A comparative study of financial services in London and New York, undertaken in 2000, concluded that 'While both London and New York are global financial centres it would be fair to characterise London's business as being primarily international, whereas New York's business is predicated on its vast domestic market.'[5] Pushing the comparison further, Chrystia Freeland pointed out in 2006 that 'While the City of London does dominate some types of international financial business, such as cross-border bank lending and foreign-exchange trading, New York retains its overall lead in important areas such as equity market turnover and investment-banking revenue, thanks to its huge domestic market.'[6] In 2006, a trio of FT journalists, Fred Thal Larsen, Charles Pretzlik, and Chris Hughes, claimed that London was 'the dominant financial centre of Europe, and a serious rival to New York on the global stage.'[7] It was located in the ideal time zone; used English, which was the language of international finance; and possessed the legal, regulatory, and market infrastructure most familiar to the global business community. Within Europe, London was the only financial centre that was of sufficient size to challenge New York and so business gravitated in its direction from across the continent. In turn, that European base allowed London to mount an increasingly successful challenge to New York for those activities that were truly international in character. To Martin Dickson in 2006, 'The more outstanding the international talent in the City, the more it increases London's competitive advantage, and the greater the advantage, the more it attracts fresh talent from around the world.'[8]

Important as talent was, the key to London's success as a global financial centre was the liquidity of the international markets it hosted. This was recognized in 1994

---

[5] Corporation of London, *London and New York Study: The Economics of Two Great Cities at the Millennium*, Final Report, Section 2: Financial Services (London: 2000), 28, cf. 34.

[6] C. Freeland, 'Capitalism's Capital Fears Being Caught Out as London Booms', *Financial Times*, 4 November 2006.

[7] P.T. Larsen, C. Pretzlik and C. Hughes, 'Big Bang Celebrants Find Party Has Moved On', *Financial Times*, 28 October 2006.

[8] M. Dickson, 'Capital Gain: How London Is Thriving and Taking on the Global Competition', *Financial Times*, 27 March 2006.

by Christopher Taylor, at Barclays: 'There's a tendency for money dealing to gravitate towards London, to pool liquidity in one centre. The powerhouse is here.'[9] It was also the point emphasized in 2006 by Clara Furse, chief executive of the London Stock Exchange: 'London's competitive advantage is clear: it has the world's deepest pool of international liquidity.'[10] By shedding peripheral financial activity to cheaper locations in the UK and abroad, and developing the Docklands as an adjunct financial centre, London was able to create the space for more internationally focussed business in the 1990s. Pen Kent, a director of the Bank of England, observed in 1996 that 'London has learned to make its living by using other people's money.'[11] Ten years later, Jeremy Isaacs, chief executive of Lehman Brothers in Europe and Asia, wrote that 'London is an operating platform that connects to the rest of the world. That is its distinct advantage when compared to other financial centres.'[12] The result by 2006 was that London was the preferred centre in the world for those banks wanting to conduct an international business. In 1999, there were 288 foreign banks with a branch in London compared to 265 in New York.[13] As Simon Wells had concluded in 2004, 'Consistent with London's role as an international financial centre, the UK interbank market is large and banks operating within the United Kingdom lend sizable amounts to banks located elsewhere.'[14]

Banks and Brokers

Between 1992 and 2007, the compartmentalization of banking behind national boundaries and within separate activities was increasingly challenged by the megabanks. This did not apply to all banking as the provision of retail services continued to take place on a largely local basis, because of the difficulty of managing such a business at a distance and across national borders. Where the trend towards both globalization and universality did manifest itself was in wholesale banking, which involved providing a small number of corporate borrowers and institutional investors with the full range of services they required. The demand for such services became a major influence on banks in the 1990s as many of the barriers between countries and different financial activities largely disappeared. Global fund managers required a bank to handle large and complex transactions while multinational companies looked to banks that could provide them with sophisticated ways of managing their demands for credit and capital and employing temporarily idle funds. The result was

---

[9] D. Marsh, 'Powerhouse Holds Its Ground', *Financial Times*, 4 March 1994.

[10] C. Furse, 'Sox Is Not to Blame—London Is Just Better as a Market', *Financial Times*, 18 September 2006.

[11] R. Lapper, 'A Tale of Two Cities', *Financial Times*, 12 June 1996.

[12] P.T. Larsen, 'Action May Be Needed to Maintain Competitive Advantage', *Financial Times*, 26 March 2006.

[13] This table only counts those banks that maintained their own branch or office. It excludes indirect or shared representation. Source: *The Banker*, March 1999 (for New York) and November 1999 (for London).

[14] S. Wells, 'Financial Interlinkages in the United Kingdom's Interbank Market and the Risk of Contagion', Bank of England Working Paper 230 (2004), 16.

the concentration of wholesale financial activity in the hands of a decreasing number of global banks. These were regarded as the most trusted counterparties by fund managers when acquiring or disposing of assets; by corporate treasurers when seeking finance or employing short-term balances; and by each other when conducting deals in the money market and across different currencies and financial products. In 1994, over half the payments handled by SWIFT were generated by only 35 banks out of the 4,300 that used the service. These banks had reached a size and scale that allowed them to absorb huge losses, support sophisticated internal controls, and control the behaviour of staff, making them immune to liquidity and solvency crises, or so was widely believed before 2008. The megabanks became the trusted gatekeepers of the financial system under the overall supervision of statutory regulatory authorities.

The growing importance of these megabanks was associated with their embrace of the originate-and-distribute model of banking. In the 1990s, the structure and practice of global banking increasingly tilted in favour of those banks that possessed the scale and scope to afford the overheads associated with a high-volume/low-margin business and could utilize the advantages provided by a strong balance sheet whether to supply funds to corporate borrowers or assets to institutional investors. The successful global banks were generating more and more of their profits from sophisticated trading systems which were expensive to develop and maintain and so also required a high volume of activity. It was only those banks with a strong capital base that could survive the fluctuations in the volume of business and the volatility in markets. The resilience exhibited by the megabanks also led central banks to rely upon them when searching for ways to regulate the financial system as their own ability to exercise control waned. These megabanks became masters of the financial universe dealing directly with each other and serving the needs of the rest of the banking community. These interbank markets lacked a physical location, such as that provided by a stock or commodity exchange, and operated from a few major hubs where bank offices clustered. London was the most important of these. It was in London that banks maintained the staff and equipment necessary to trade across the entire range of financial instruments that comprised the lifeblood of a modern money market, and where the speed of communication was fastest. In the face of the huge volume of transactions taking place in this interbank market, governments left both surveillance and policing to the banks themselves rather than empowering any regulatory authority whether self or statutory. As so much of the activity of the megabanks was transnational, no central bank or national regulatory agency had either complete oversight or exclusive authority.

Supplementing the direct dealing of the megabanks were the inter-dealer brokers.[15] It might have been expected that the emergence of the megabanks would have

[15] For these, see the following pieces from the *Financial Times*: B. Riley, 'A New Asset Class Created', 7 February 1994; H. Barnes, 'Drift of Trade to London Causes Concern', 7 April 1994; S. Webb, 'Dutch Win Back State Debt Trade', 16 May 1994; A. Sharpe, 'Amsterdam Prepares to Fight Back', 16 June 1994; S. Davis, 'Taking a Position in the Market', 28 June 1994; P. Gawith, 'Brokers Lose Their Voices on the Small Screen', 15 December 1995; N. Denton, 'Banks Plan Clearing House for Trade in Emerging Market Debt', 10 June 1996; R. Adams, 'An Artificial and Antiquated Straightjacket', 5 December 1996; G. Bowley,

eliminated the need for inter-dealer brokers as they acted as intermediaries between banks, conducting deals over the telephone through networks that connected them to the largest banks, with prices and other information displayed on screens provided by the likes of Reuters, Bloomberg, and Thomson. As the megabanks grew into global institutions, whose trading spanned all products, they possessed the ability to either internalize transactions or deal directly with each other, thus cutting out the need for intermediation. The development of interactive electronic platforms that both displayed prices and matched sales and purchases also threatened the inter-dealer brokers. What ensured the survival of the inter-dealer brokers was their response as they not only embraced the electronic technology themselves but also grew in scale and reach, so could provide banks with greatly improved intermediation services. As the volume and variety of trading in the OTC markets expanded exponentially, the inter-dealer brokers were able to support a global network of offices, the use of sophisticated and expensive computing and communications equipment, and the employment of highly trained staff who were very well remunerated.

Driving investment and innovation by the inter-dealer brokers was the competition they faced both from each other and from the megabanks, especially as banks confined their trading to a small number of trusted intermediaries. As Garry Jones, chief executive of Intercapital (ICAP) Electronic Broking Europe, put it bluntly in 2004, 'If you are not number one or number two in your space, it is going to be very hard to break in.'[16] The 1990s was a decade when inter-dealer brokers either expanded aggressively or abandoned the business. There was a spate of mergers and acquisitions that left a small number of dominant firms by the beginning of the twenty-first century. The merger of Prebon Yamane and M.W. Marshall in 1999 resulted in a business with more than 2,000 staff located in offices around the world. A subsequent merger with Tullett and Tokyo, in 2004, pushed the numbers employed to more than 3,000. The resulting business, Tullet Prebon, was run out of London by Terry Smith. Even larger was another London firm, ICAP, run by Michael Spencer. In 1998, ICAP took over one of its main rivals, Exco, followed by another, Garban, in 1999, to create the world's largest inter-dealer broker. By then, the inter-dealer

'Historic Day for Way Bank Goes to Work', 3 March 1997; J. Mackintosh, 'Brokers Reach Merger Agreement', 12 October 1997; J. Guthrie, 'Sighs of Relief as Exco Takeover Get Nod of Approval', 27 October 1998; C. Harris, 'Brokers Agree Merger Terms', 16 February 1999; C. Harris, 'Bid to Set Up Biggest Wholesale Money Broker', 10 June 1999; C. Harris, 'Garban and Intercapital in £300m Merger, 3 July 1999; A. Beattie, 'Tullett and Bloomberg Plan New Broking System', 5 July 1999; A. Mandel-Campbell, 'Not Just a Traditional Market for Shares', 19 March 2001; A. van Duyn, 'Only the Best Will Survive', 28 March 2001; M. Dickson, 'The Market Is Another Country for City's Go-Between', 7 April 2001; D. Cameron, 'Ways to Enhance Voice-Broking Services', 3 April 2002; D. Cameron and J. Hughes, 'Citigroup to Join Online Currency Platform', 8 April 2002; A. Skorecki, 'Voice-Broked Bond Trading Holds Its Own', 19 March 2003; R. Orr, 'Founder of Icap Is New Chairman of Numis', 30 April 2003; A. Skorecki, 'Icap Forms Bond Trading Alliance with MarketAxess', 22 March 2004; E. Rigby, 'Collins Stewart Eyes Prebon', 27 May 2004; A. Skorecki, 'Icap Says Phone Broking Rules Market', 4 June 2004; A. Skorecki, 'Cantor Split Off Bucks the Trend', 18 August 2004; A. Skorecki, 'Bold Vision Demands a Response', 14 December 2004; A. Skorecki, 'Cantor Wrestles to Stay Treasury Heavyweight', 8 February 2005; S. Spikes, 'Icap Chief Caps a 20-Year Rise to the Stars', 22 April 2006; S. Spikes, 'Icap Snaps Up EBS for £464m', 22 April 2006; S. Scholtes, 'Electronic Battle Heats Up', 28 July 2006; T. Buck and G. Tett, 'Battle Heats Up Over Europe's Bond Markets', 30 November 2006; S. Spikes and P.T. Larsen, 'Inter-Dealer Broking Behind Rapid Growth', 19 December 2006.
[16] A. Skorecki, 'Icap Says Phone Broking Rules Market', *Financial Times*, 4 June 2004.

brokers were developing their own electronic platforms, though they continued to use voice broking and electronic price display systems. By 2006, the world of inter-dealer brokers had been reduced to a small group of global businesses dominated by ICAP and Tullet Prebon in London and Cantor Fitzgerald in New York. Oper-ating from hubs in London; New York; and the Asian financial centres of Tokyo, Singapore, and Hong Kong, and directly connected to the dealing floors of the mega-banks and other financial institutions, they were especially good at matching sales and purchases across a wide range of financial instruments.

Foreign Exchange Market

In the years after 1992, the foreign exchange market established itself as the world's largest when measured by turnover.[17] Jennifer Hughes referred to the for-eign exchange market in 2004 as 'the largest, most dynamic market in the world. ... Centred in Tokyo, London and New York, traders deal smoothly across borders and time-zones, often in multiples of $1bn, in transactions that take less than a second.'[18] In 1992, total turnover averaged $1.1 trillion a day and this had grown to $4.3 tril-lion by 2007, according to the Bank for International Settlements, which conducted a survey every three years. Those surveys conducted between 1992 and 2007 were

[17] See the following pieces from the *Financial Times*: T. Corrigan, 'Traditional Split in Derivatives Is Less Clear-Cut', 25 January 1993; L. Boulton, 'Birth of a Hundred Markets', 23 February 1993; A. Gow-ers, 'Island of Integrity', 29 March 1993; J. Blitz, 'All Change in Foreign Exchanges', 2 April 1993; J. Blitz, 'New Anxieties for the Banks', 26 May 1993; D. Marsh, 'Powerhouse Holds Its Ground', 4 March 1994; A. Sharpe, 'Cash Haven Lures Investors', 26 May 1994; K. Cooke, 'Rising Hub of Global Trading', 6 June 1995; P. Gawith, 'Forex Market Growth Startles Exchanges', 20 September 1995; P. Gawith, 'Forex Surge Masks Maturing Market', 24 October 1995; P. Gawith and R. Lapper, 'A Step Away from City Tradition', 2 January 1996; P. Gawith, 'Service Central to Paribas Forex Move', 2 February 1996; P. Coggan, 'It's Just a Small Problem', 8 February 1996; C. Middelmann, 'Domestic Market Is Struggling', 1 March 1996; P. Gawith, 'Exotic But Not for Faint Hearts', 15 May 1996; R. Lapper and P. Gawith, 'Forex Market Growth Slowing, Says BIS', 31 May 1996; R. Khalaf, 'Private Sector Is Quick to Adjust', 8 November 1996; G. Bow-ley, 'Forex Houses Sanguine Despite Possibility of Single Currency', 6 December 1996; S. Kuper, 'Dealers on the Spot as Margins Narrow', 18 April 1997; J. Kynge, 'Exotics Reach the Major League', 9 May 1997; A. Beattie, 'Fighting Spirit Seeps into Dried-Up Markets', 25 June 1999; K. Merchant, 'Market for ECP Opens Up Via Trax', 7 September 1999; G. Graham, 'Forex Trading System Planned', 15 September 1999; C. Swann and D. Cameron, 'FXall Set to Intensify Battle in Online Currency Trading', 10 May 2001; J. Chaffin, 'Recovery from Rare Default Is Taking Time', 21 June 2001; D. Cameron, 'Currenex to Form Exchange', 26 November 2001; A. Skorecki, 'Forex System That Takes the Waiting Out of Wanting', 4 Jan-uary 2002; E. Wine, 'Sidelined Cash May Stay Out of Stocks', 4 January 2002; S. Pritchard, 'A Race to Stay Ahead of Fraudsters', 5 June 2002; D. Ibison, 'Banks Lose Hope Sun Will Rise on Japan's Big Bang', 14 February 2003; C. Pretzlik, 'Benefits to City Would Be Only Marginal at Best, Report Concludes', 10 June 2003; B. Benoit, 'Long-Held Dream Has Proved to Be Unrealistic', 10 June 2003; C. Batchelor, 'Euromts Launches European T-Bill Platform', 16 March 2004; J. Hughes, 'Where Money Talks Very Loudly', 27 May 2004; C. Batchelor, 'Long Pedigree of the Clearing House for Short-Term Funds', 23 July 2004; C. Batchelor, 'London Leads in Trading Volumes', 23 September 2004; J. Hughes and Krishna Guha, 'World Foreign Exchange Trading Soars to a Peak of $1,900bn a Day', 29 September 2004; A. Skorecki, 'Bank of England Lights a Fuse', 30 November 2004; S. Daneshkhu and C. Giles, 'City Becomes Undeniable Engine of Growth', 27 March 2006; A. Hill, 'Financial Inventors Underpin Success', 27 March 2006; S. Johnson, 'London Rules New Wave of FX Deals', 18 July 2006; J. Hughes, 'Bankers Divided on Need for Backstop', 4 May 2006; J. Hughes, 'FX Firebrand Dream of Revolution', 9 May 2006; M. Mackenzie and S. Scholtes, 'Regulators Issue a Warning at Bond Trading's Wild Frontier', 13 November 2006.
[18] J. Hughes, 'Where Money Talks Very Loudly', *Financial Times*, 27 May 2004.

consistent and comprehensive.[19] Driving this turnover was the constant buying and selling by banks as they matched their currency assets and liabilities by amount and timing, covered temporary shortfalls in funding, and employed idle balances. As the volume and variety of financial flows around the world grew, generated by payments and receipts for all manner of transactions, banks faced a continuous struggle to adjust their currency positions so as not to face a catastrophic loss due to any sudden change and to make the fullest use of the funds at their disposal. The simplest way of doing that was to swap assets and liabilities among themselves as for every debit there was a credit and for every deficit there was a surplus.

In the foreign exchange spot market, current commitments across currencies were matched, while in the forward market it was those arising in the future, with a constant interplay between the two as banks sought to either cover their exposure or profit from it. London was the hub of the global foreign exchange market followed by New York. In 1992, daily turnover in London was $297 billion (26.6 per cent of the total) compared to $182 billion (16.3 per cent) in New York. By 1995, that had increased to $479 billion (29.3 per cent) in London and $266 billion (16.3 per cent) in New York. That growth was sustained over the next three years, reaching $685 billion (32.6 per cent) for London and $383 billion (18.2 per cent) for New York. Currency unification in Europe reduced global foreign exchange trading by 2001 as there were no longer transactions involving the mark, franc, lira, and peseta. The amount of trading taking place in London fell as a result to $542 billion but its share of the total was stable at 31.8 per cent. Trading in New York had also fallen to $273 billion and its share to 16.0 per cent. There was then a rebound in the volume of trading after 2001, with London reaching $835 billion (32.0 per cent) in 2004. The rebound was slightly greater for New York, which rose to $499 billion, leaving it with an increased share of 19.1 per cent. The growth in the volume of trading then continued, with London being responsible for $1,483 billion in 2007 and its share increased to 34.6 per cent. Though the amount of trading in New York did rise to $745 billion, its share fell back to 17.4 per cent. Rather than a single European currency, of which the UK was not a member, leading to trading migrating from London to either Frankfurt or Paris, the reverse had taken place. Exploiting its position as the established hub of the foreign exchange market and the global centre of international banking, London was the location with the deepest and broadest pool of liquidity and so it attracted trading in the euro to its market.[20]

Though banks continued to dominate foreign exchange trading, the liquidity of the market increasingly attracted other financial institutions that sought to profit from the constant buying and selling and minor price changes. Their presence added further liquidity, making the market even more attractive to banks and other financial institutions as a place where funds could be employed or borrowed on a short-term basis or a source of profits by speculating on price movements. From the early 1990s, multinational companies and hedge funds participated in the foreign

[19] Bank for International Settlements, *Triennial Central Bank Survey* (2022).
[20] Bank for International Settlements, *Triennial Central Bank Survey* (2019).

exchange market for purposes of their own, driving up turnover, and so compensat-
ing for the loss of business because of greater monetary stability and fewer currency
pairs to be traded. This expansion in the size of the global foreign exchange market was not accompanied by a parallel trend in the number of banks that dominated
trading. Instead of ever more banks being drawn into the foreign exchange market, as
a product of global financial integration, the business of trading currencies became
concentrated in the hands of the megabanks. Foreign exchange transactions were
conducted between or with banks that could be relied upon to honour their commitments. Only the megabanks could convince each other and their customers that
they had the financial resources to provide the required service and carry the risks
that came with large-scale trading. By 1998, there was a core of thirteen banks that
dominated the global foreign exchange market, trading with each other and a few
large customers, and acting on behalf of a host of smaller client banks. The banks that
dominated the global foreign exchange market by then were led by a group from the
USA—Citibank, Chase Manhattan, JP Morgan, Goldman Sachs, Merrill Lynch, and
Bank of America—and from Europe—HSBC, Deutsche, UBS, Credit Suisse, ABN-
Amro, NatWest, and Barclays. Mergers between these and smaller banks had the
effect of concentrating activity in those that remained. These megabanks provided a
liquid twenty-four-hour market in the world's main currencies, which was used by
smaller or regional banks, both for themselves and their customers, as they possessed
neither the capacity nor expertise nor connections to compete. The foreign exchange
market also provided the megabanks with a means through which they could lend
and borrow among themselves in complete confidence that loans would be repaid in
full and on time. Any failure to repay loans in full would destroy the mutual confidence that existed and end the participation of the offending bank, with disastrous
consequences for the business that it could do.

Mirroring the dominance of the foreign exchange market by a handful of global
banks was the increasing concentration of trading in a few locations around the
world, as it was only there that the required depth of liquidity could be found. Here
London continued to exert its pull resulting from its convenient time-zone location combined with the presence there of so many offices belonging to the world's
banks. In 1994, David Marsh referred to London as the 'hub of the world-wide foreign exchange market'.[21] In 2002, Alex Skorecki credited London with 'the lion's share
of forex trade'.[22] Banks were choosing to centralize foreign exchange trading in those
locations where they could simultaneously access liquidity and diversity. By 1996,
Deutsche Bank was conducting its foreign exchange trading from only four financial centres compared to thirty-seven in 1990. As Guy Whitaker observed in 1997,
'Business is gravitating to where the markets are most liquid'.[23] He was head of foreign exchange trading at Citibank, the leading bank in the business at that time. The
concentration of trading in London was at the expense of the other centres in Europe,

[21] D. Marsh, 'Powerhouse Holds Its Ground', *Financial Times*, 4 March 1994.
[22] A. Skorecki, 'Forex System That Takes the Waiting Out of Wanting', *Financial Times*, 4 January 2002.
[23] S. Kuper, 'Dealers on the Spot as Margins Narrow', *Financial Times*, 18 April 1997.

notably Frankfurt, Paris, Amsterdam, and Zurich. Globally, the other casualty was Tokyo, which faded in importance despite the size of its economy and the international role played by the yen. Though Tokyo was the leading centre for foreign exchange trading in Asia in 1992, its volume ($126 billion) was already less than the combined total for Singapore ($76 billion) and Hong Kong ($61 billion). In contrast, London's total ($300 billion) for the same year was almost twice the combined total of its three nearest European rivals, namely Zurich ($68 billion), Frankfurt ($57 billion), and Paris ($36 billion), each of which had the advantage of hosting trading in their domestic currencies, which were used internationally. Accounting for the failure of Tokyo to dominate foreign exchange trading in Asia was the lack of innovation and the regulatory restrictions placed on Japanese markets and banks. Seizing this opportunity was Singapore as it emerged as a serious rival to Tokyo as the Asian centre for the global foreign exchange market. By 2007, Tokyo's share of foreign exchange trading was down to 6 per cent, which was half the level it had been ten years before, and that was now matched by Singapore. What this comparison with Tokyo reveals is that London's success as the hub of the global foreign exchange market was not simply a product of location or inertia, especially with the declining importance of the UK£, but was also the product of the freedom given to its markets and banks and the continuing innovation that took place between 1992 and 2007.

Electronic Revolution

Throughout the years between 1992 and 2007, global financial markets experienced an electronic revolution that totally transformed the way trading was conducted.[24] By 2007, 30 per cent of total UK foreign exchange turnover was executed through electronic systems, made possible by the use of automated high-volume strategies

---

[24] See the following pieces from the *Financial Times*: J. Blitz, 'Foreign Exchange Dealers Enter the 21st Century', 13 September 1993; P. Gawith, 'Technology on the March', 2 June 1994; P. Harverson, 'Exco Staff Suffer as World Markets Slow', 24 November 1995; P. Gawith, 'Brokers Lose Their Voices on the Small Screen', 15 December 1995; P. Gawith, 'Exotic But Not for Faint Hearts', 15 May 1996; S. Kuper, 'Bleak Days Ahead for Forex Traders', 24 December 1996; R. Adams, 'Voice-Brokers Are Lapsing into Silence', 18 April 1997; S. Kuper, 'Reuters Falls Behind EBS in Electronic Broking', 30 June 1997; S. Kuper, 'Old Order Gives Way to the New', 5 June 1998; S. Kuper, 'Information on the Button', 5 June 1998; J. Gapper, 'What Price Information', 20 July 1998; A. Beattie, 'Floor Presence Thins Out', 25 June 1999; R. Adams, 'Brokers Alter Shape of Things to Come', 25 June 1999; A. Beattie, 'Tullett and Bloomberg Plan New Broking System', 5 July 1999; A. Beattie, '"Barrow Boys" at Risk as the Currency Markets Switch On', 6 July 1999; C. Swann and D. Cameron, 'FXall Set to Intensify Battle in Online Currency Trading', 10 May 2001; D. Cameron, 'Currenex to Form Exchange', 26 November 2001; G. Nairn, 'Internet Fails to Transform the Foreign Exchange World', 5 June 2002; T. Burt, 'Bloomberg in Forex Challenge to Reuters', 21 May 2003; J. Hughes, 'Traders Set to Take the Forex Challenge', 22 May 2003; T. Burt, 'A New Vision of Finance Beckons as Rivals Prepare for Court Battle', 12 July 2003; J. Hughes, 'Where Money Talks Very Loudly', 27 May 2004; J. Hughes, 'History Goes Full Circle as Volume Is King', 27 May 2004; J. Hughes, 'The Mouse Takes Over the Floor', 27 May 2004; J. Hughes, 'A Veteran with a Proud Record of Service', 27 May 2004; J. Hughes, 'Interbank Online Action Set to Soar', 25 February 2005; J. Hughes, 'Eurex Issues a Challenge to CME', 17 June 2005; J. Hughes, 'Lava Platform to Challenge Duopoly', 25 April 2006; Hughes, 'FX Firebrand'; S. Johnson, 'London Rules New Wave of FX Deals', 18 July 2006. See also G. Christodoulou and P. O'Connor, 'The Foreign Exchange and Over-the-Counter Derivatives Markets in the United Kingdom', *BEQB*, 47 (2007), 448–555.

known as algorithmic trading. One consequence of the increased speed and capacity of the foreign exchange market and the lowered cost, delivered by electronic trading, combined with the reduction of exchange-rate volatility, was to encourage the carry trade. This involved borrowing in the currency of a country with low interest rates and lending in a country with a higher interest rate with the profit generated through the interest rate differential and not eliminated by exchange rate movement. The popularity of the carry trade greatly boosted turnover in the foreign exchange market. Electronic trading platforms had begun to emerge in the late 1980s. Prior to then, trading in foreign exchange was dependent upon the telephone, and took place through direct voice communication. This was conducted either between banks or through the intermediation of inter-dealer brokers. The electronic revolution began in 1992 when Reuters 2000 was launched. This transformed the price display service Reuters already provided into an interactive trading network for foreign exchange. There was a delay in switching to automated dealing. In the automated system, a foreign exchange dealer posted buy and sell prices on the screen to which another dealer responded by typing instructions onto the terminal. Only when the deal was done were the identities of both parties revealed. That exposed dealers to counterparty risk unlike the use of either a trusted broker or trading directly with another bank. This delay in adopting electronic trading deprived the new system of liquidity. Liquidity was essential in what was a high-risk, high-volume, low-margin business as it allowed deals to be made quickly at current prices. In a bid to improve liquidity and build up a global network, two of the providers of electronic systems, Electronic Broking Services (EBS) and Minex, merged in 1995. Despite the initial hesitancy in using these automated systems, both Reuters and EBS succeeded in gaining traction among banks as the service they provided was both faster and cheaper than voice brokers. The more trading that took place on the automated systems, the greater was the liquidity of the market they could provide, which attracted further users, and so their appeal grew.

Reuters and EBS served different segments of the foreign exchange market. EBS was used extensively in the wholesale or interbank market, which was dominated by the megabanks. The wholesale market was where a small number of global banks traded with each other either for profit or to offset the risks they were taking through exposure to currency volatility, and to employ or borrow money for a short term. During the 1990s, the electronic systems became established for the interbank market, gradually displacing the trading that took place by telephone. The next stage introduced by the megabanks was to build proprietary trading platforms, which allowed them to trade electronically with their customers, often acting as counterparties when providing them with their currency requirements. For this retail market they developed internal networks linking customers with the bank. These customers included smaller banks, who could not afford a dedicated team of highly paid foreign exchange staff with the expensive space and technology they required. What followed was the integration of these trading systems to provide multi-bank platforms. What the banks were addressing was the issue of latency, which was the time taken to complete a deal. Customers of banks were exposed until the deal was completed. The megabanks were exposed for the period their offered prices were displayed. It was important to reduce latency in order to reduce the trading risks being run by all participants. This was one reason for the clustering of foreign exchange traders in London, whether they were human beings or the computers that served the electronic markets. By 2003, EBS had 2,000 terminals in dealing rooms around the world and had captured the high-volume end of the foreign exchange market conducted by the megabanks, handling trading in the most liquid currencies such as the euro, yen, and the US$. In contrast, Reuters serviced the needs of the smaller banks, providing them with access to current prices and the ability to have their buy and sell orders automatically matched, thus reducing their dependence upon the megabanks. Reuters controlled an extensive retail network, with 24,000 connections in 1998. These included many who traded in smaller amounts and in less-liquid currencies. Bloomberg attempted to break the duopoly established by EBS and Reuters. In 1996, it began offering a similar service, but it found it difficult to dislodge Reuters and EBS. Each had established control over key sections of the market.

The success of Reuters and EBS did not mean that electronic trading systems displaced the voice brokers totally. In 1999, Alan Beattie reported that

> the currency markets have a reputation as one of the last outposts of barrow-boy raucousness, where deals are shouted down phones and prices relayed by the constant burble of the 'squawk box'—the two-way loudspeakers that sit on top of every trader's screen, providing perpetual communication with the voice brokers who traditionally bring buyers and sellers together.[25]

For many companies, fund managers, and smaller banks, foreign exchange was a by-product of another transaction, whether it was a financial one or a sale or purchase of goods and services. They were content to give the business directly to one of the megabanks or place it in the hands of an inter-dealer broker, and pass the cost on to their client or absorb it within the business. There were also numerous currency pairings or transactions for small amounts that took time to arrange and involved negotiation and here the inter-dealer brokers remained essential. Even the megabanks made use of their services as none could justify the expense of maintaining a team sufficient to cover all currencies and deals. Despite the continued role played by these voice brokers, the foreign exchange market moved inexorably towards an electronic future. The whole process of dealing in foreign exchange, from initial inquiry through to trade and settlement, increasingly took place without a single human involvement, whether it involved internal bank networks, those provided by EBS and Reuters, or the growing proliferation of alternative systems. One was FXall that catered for the foreign exchange requirements of institutional investors, such as hedge funds, who were trading foreign exchange not as an adjunct to an existing business but as an asset which offered the prospect of substantial gain through frequent buying and selling. What they wanted was a dealing service that was both

---

[25] A. Beattie, '"Barrow Boys" at Risk as the Currency Markets Switch On', *Financial Times*, 6 July 1999.

cheap and fast and could handle the volume of buying and selling that they produced. By 2005, high-volume standardized transactions in the foreign exchange market were largely automated, whether wholesale or retail. One outcome was the merger in 2006 of the largest inter-dealer broker, ICAP, with the biggest inter-dealer platform, EBS, thus combining telephone and electronic trading.

The Herstatt Legacy

An important consequence of London dominating the global foreign exchange market between 1992 and 2007, but most trading taking place in US$s and handled by US banks, was that it was not located in the same country as the one central bank capable of providing it with support, the Federal Reserve.[26] The Bank of England could not act as lender of last resort in US$s. It could only do so in the case of banks operating in the sterling money market, which coexisted in London with the US$-based markets, including that for foreign exchange. This division of the London money market between sterling and non-sterling activity was becoming increasingly anachronistic as British banks made extensive use of the facilities to lend and borrow in US$s both between each other and with foreign banks. There had been a rapid expansion in the volume and value of international financial transactions which were conducted in US$s from 1970, and UK banks had been forced to embrace these because of the international business that they did. That exposed them to liquidity and credit risks in currencies other than sterling. However, it suited the Bank of England to ignore these as its focus was on implementing the UK government's monetary policy

---

[26] See the following pieces from the *Bank of England Quarterly Bulletin*: Bank of England, 'The Over-the-Counter Derivatives Market in the United Kingdom', 36 (1996), 35; Bank of England, 'The Bank of England's Operations in the Sterling Money Markets', 37 (1997), 204–5; Governor of the Bank of England, 'Reforms to the UK Monetary Policy Framework and Financial Services Regulation', 37 (1997), 316; Governor of the Bank of England, 'Prospects for the City: In or Out of EMU', 37 (1997), 431; Bank of England, 'The Bank of England Act', 38 (1998), 93–9; E. George (Governor of the Bank of England), 'The New Lady of Threadneedle Street', 38 (1998), 173–6; Bank of England, 'The Foreign Exchange and Over-the-Counter Derivatives Markets in the United Kingdom', 38 (1998), 349–52; Bank of England, 'Sterling Wholesale Markets: Developments in 1998', 39 (1999), 34–7; Bank of England, 'Risk, Cost and Liquidity in Alternative Payment Systems', 39 (1999), 78; S. Senior and R. Westwood, 'The External Balance Sheet of the United Kingdom: Implications for Financial Stability?', 40 (2000), 351–8; P.J.N. Sinclair, 'Central Banks and Financial Stability', 40 (2000), 383–9; Sam Wharmby, 'The Foreign Exchange and Over-the-Counter Derivatives Markets in the United Kingdom', 41 (2001), 419–21; Bank of England, 'The Bank's Contacts with the Money, Repo and Stock Lending Markets', 41 (2001), 431; Bank of England, 'The Bank of England's Operations in the Sterling Money Markets', 42 (2002), 152–6; A.V. Wetherilt, 'Money Market Operations and Volatility in UK Money Market Rates', 42 (2002), 420–3; M. Burnett and M. Manning, 'Financial Stability and the United Kingdom's External Balance Sheet', 43 (2003), 663–78; S. Millard and M. Polenghi, 'The Relationship between the Overnight Interbank Unsecured Loan Market and the CHAPS Sterling System', 44 (2004), 42–5; Bank of England, 'Reform of the Bank of England's Operations in the Sterling Money Markets: A Consultative Paper by the Bank of England', 44 (2004), 217–22; P. Williams, 'The Foreign Exchange and Over-the-Counter Derivatives Markets in the United Kingdom', 44 (2004), 471–6; A.G. Haldane and E. Latter, 'The Role of Central Banks in Payment Systems Oversight', 45 (2005), 66–70; Sir John Gieve, 'Practical Issues in Preparing for Cross-border Financial Crises', 46 (2006), 452–4; A. Clark, 'Prudential Regulation, Risk Management and Systemic Stability', 47 (2007), 464–7; Christodoulou and O'Connor, 'The Foreign Exchange and Over-the-Counter Derivatives Markets', 448–555.

and that involved operations in sterling. The Bank of England was also less and less interested in the smooth running of the City of London's money markets as they switched from UK£s to US$s. That was the case though financial stability remained the Bank of England's responsibility even after the establishment of the Financial Services Authority in 1998. In a speech in 2000, the governor of the Bank of England, Eddie George, made clear that though the Bank was in subservient position regarding policymaking, it did enjoy a high degree of operational independence. The problem was that the tools it had available to it were emasculated after 1997 by the creation of the Financial Services Authority though it retained continuing responsibility for the stability of the entire financial system, with a focus on systemic risk and acting as lender of last resort.[27]

By 2001, the Bank of England was aware of the consequences these changes had for its ability to maintain stability in London's money markets.[28] In 2006, both the current governor of the Bank, Mervyn King, and his deputy governor, Sir John Gieve, acknowledged the limited power they had to influence London's money markets because of the status of the City of London as an international financial centre.[29] By 1997, the City of London was home to more overseas-incorporated banks than domestic ones and more than one-half of the total deposits of the UK banking system was denominated in foreign currencies, especially the US$. However, it was the British banks and that part of the money market operating in sterling that was the priority for the Bank. Its high exposure to the ebb and flow of international financial flows made London unlike New York, which was much more domestically focussed and so susceptible to far greater influence from the US Treasury and the Federal Reserve Bank than the UK Treasury and the Bank of England. The Bank of England had arranged foreign exchange swaps in 1998 as a means of providing liquidity in a currency other than sterling. The Bank would sell sterling for foreign currency on the spot market, matching that with forward purchases of sterling for foreign currency. This enabled the Bank to provide liquidity in foreign currencies but only to the extent that there were foreign buyers of sterling. The Bank was well aware that the diminishing use of sterling for international transactions, including those undertaken by British banks, exposed them to a liquidity crisis which it could not solve by acting as lender of last resort, as it could only supply UK£s without limit. The position the UK was in was made clear by Stephen Senior and Robert Westwood at the Bank in 2000. 'A comparatively small percentage of UK external banking is carried out in sterling. ... This could potentially expose the banking system to liquidity risk. ... These risks will be mitigated to the extent that the banks manage their liquidity prudently.'[30] What this meant was that the Bank expected the banks to avoid a liquidity crisis as there were doubts that it could act as lender of last resort. In this respect,

[27] 'Central Bank Independence', *BEQB*, 40 (2000), 404–7.
[28] D. Clementi (Deputy Governor, Bank of England), 'Maintaining Financial Stability in a Rapidly Changing World: Some Threats and Opportunities', *BEQB*, 41 (2001), 475–8.
[29] Bank of England, 'The Governor's Speech at the Mansion House', *BEQB*, 46 (2006), 330; Sir John Gieve, 'Financial System Risks in the United Kingdom: Issues and Challenges', *BEQB*, 46 (2006), 337–41.
[30] Senior and Westwood, 'External Balance Sheet of the U.K.', 362.

the UK was in no different position than any other country apart from the USA as the global money market used the US\$ as its vehicle currency and the supply of that currency was the prerogative of the Federal Reserve. The centre of the market was London, where turnover rose from \$716 billion in 1992 to \$3,722 billion in 2007.[31]

When applied to the foreign exchange market it meant that it operated without a lender of last resort. This put the entire burden of avoiding a crisis on the banks themselves. Despite the centre of the foreign market being in London, the Bank of England was content to leave it to look after itself, relying on the structural and operational resilience of the megabanks. In the words of Paul Tucker, executive director for Markets at the Bank of England in December 2006: 'There are, to be clear, a lot of reasons for confidence in monetary and financial stability being sustained. Monetary regimes are much improved. Banks are generally regarded as well capitalised. Innovation has enabled risk to be dispersed more widely, including outside the banking sector. And capital markets are deeper.'[32] To the Bank of England the foreign exchange market was central to its focus on managing monetary policy on behalf of the UK government. Most of the turnover in London was in cross-border transactions involving the US\$ and conducted by foreign banks, especially from the USA. In 2001, the US\$ was used in 92 per cent of deals in London, while foreign-owned, mainly US, institutions were responsible for 81 per cent of turnover. This continued to be the case according to the next triennial surveys in 2004 and 2007.[33]

The main issue in the foreign exchange market was counterparty risk as virtually all trading was done by banks with each other either directly, through inter-dealer brokers, or, more recently, using electronic platforms. In every case the bank stood as guarantor to the deal made, whether it was acting for itself or for its own customers, which extended to the global banking community. What this meant was that trading in the foreign exchange market was underpinned by mutual trust and nothing more. There was no institutional structure, as in the case of an exchange. The foreign exchange market was not served by a clearing house which guaranteed the completion of transactions in many commodity markets. No central bank, individually or collectively, stood ready to act as lender of last resort to the foreign exchange market. As Jennifer Hughes explained in 2004: 'The trading of currencies across borders with no centralised exchanges, and the lack of any regulatory body with a global reach, means the foreign exchange market falls under several national jurisdictions, no one of which can claim overall control.'[34] Instead, the foreign exchange market relied on the confidence among the core participants that each would honour its commitments. George Graham reported in 1996 that 'banks reckon the probability one of their main foreign exchange trading partners will default is small'. However,

---

[31] Bank for International Settlements, *Locational Banking Statistics* (2011). The interbank data was calculated by subtracting bank lending to the non-bank sector from total bank lending. Cf. *Guide to the International Locational Banking Statistics*, Monetary and Economic Department, BIS, 2011.

[32] P. Tucker (Executive Director for Markets), 'Macro, Asset Price, and Financial System Uncertainties', *BEQB*, 47 (2007), 122–30.

[33] Ni. Jenkinson and M. Manning, 'Promoting Financial System Resilience in Modern Global Capital Markets: Some Issues', *BEQB*, 47 (2007), 453–60.

[34] J. Hughes, 'Taking Their Law into Their Own Hands', *Financial Times*, 27 May 2004.

banks were under pressure from central banks to address the issue of counterparty risk because the 'sums involved are so huge that if a default were to occur, the entire banking system could be shaken.'[35] What long worried central banks was the risk that a miscalculation by one bank in the foreign exchange market could lead to its failure and, because of the size of the losses, this would have major consequences for the global financial system. In the foreign exchange market, transactions took place between participants in private and not public and without the use of a centralized trading floor. This exposed participants to a high degree of counterparty risk because of the absence of transparency, regulation, and supervision as in an exchange.[36]

The issue of counterparty risk in the foreign exchange market had arisen as early as 1974, with the collapse of Bankhaus Herstatt, a small Cologne bank. This was followed by subsequent failures as with Drexel Burnham Lambert in 1990, the Bank of Credit and Commerce International in 1991, and Barings Bank in 1995. However, all these involved minor players and each crisis encouraged the further concentration of foreign exchange activity in the hands of the megabanks, as they commanded complete and universal trust. Nevertheless, various plans were put forward to address the issue of counterparty risk. The eventual outcome was the creation by twenty of the world's largest banks of Continuous Linked Settlement (CLS) Services in 1998. This operated as a bank, accepting and making payments, but only completing transactions when they matched, thus eliminating settlement risk for those who used the service. The formation of CLS met the concerns of central banks while leaving a core of global banks to handle the normal routine of trading and be willing to accept the risks involved. Larry Rechnagel, chief executive of CLS services, explained in 1998 what it delivered: 'We haven't taken all risk out of the system. There is still replacement risk, forward risk, liquidity risk. What we have protected against is catastrophic failure, and that is what the central banks are concerned about.'[37] It took until 2000 for the CLS Bank to become fully operational, and 2002 before all technical and administrative hurdles had been overcome. By then what was in place was a payment netting system that virtually eliminated settlement risk by, in effect, the CLS Bank acting as a trusted third party between the two counterparties to a trade. To reflect the use of the US$ as the key currency used in the foreign exchange market, and the central role played by US banks, it was decided that CLS be domiciled in New York and regulated by the Federal Reserve, even though most trading took place in London. In response to prodding by central banks, the foreign exchange market had produced its own solution to the major hazard it faced, which was counterparty risk as revealed by the Herstatt crisis of 1974. That solution was to be fully tested in the Global Financial Crisis of 2008.[38]

[35] G. Graham, 'Foreign Exchange Groups Plan Merger', *Financial Times*, 9 December 1996.
[36] For a discussion of counterparty risk, see L. Sarno and M.P. Taylor, 'The Microstructure of the Foreign Exchange Market: A Selective Survey of the Literature', *Princeton Studies in International Economics* (2001).
[37] G. Graham, 'Banks Settle Down to Action', *Financial Times*, 5 June 1998.
[38] See the following articles in the *Financial Times*: T. Corrigan, 'Traditional Split in Derivatives Is Less Clear-Cut', 25 January 1993; J. Blitz, 'All Change in Foreign Exchanges', 2 April 1993; J. Blitz, 'New Anxieties for the Banks', 26 May 1993; T. Corrigan, 'Divisions Hazy in OTC Derivatives Clearing Battle Debate',

Conclusion

Between 1992 and 2007, the global foreign exchange market expanded and changed, but in one respect it remained the same, which was that the City of London remained its prime location. Approximately one-third of total turnover took place in the City of London, despite the currency in use being mainly the US$ and the principal participants being foreign banks. That dominance of the foreign exchange market by London was a product of inertia, freedom from restrictions, and a willingness to embrace change. The inertia was a product of the City of London's long-standing position as an international financial centre favoured by the world's banks and the reinvention of the foreign exchange market from the late 1950s. This meant that the City was well positioned to provide a home to a reinvigorated foreign exchange market when the era of fixed exchange rates collapsed in the early 1970s. It then built on that position for the rest of the twentieth century, with each arrival of another bank in London enhancing its attractions as a centre of trading foreign exchange. That inertia was sufficient to allow London to capture trading in the euro against competition from within the Eurozone. Success did indeed breed success. However, as the example of Tokyo showed, inertia was not sufficient to ensure that London continued to dominate the global foreign exchange market. That also required a willingness to allow banks the freedom to operate. That had come with the embrace of the US$ as the vehicle currency of the foreign exchange market and the willingness to allow foreign banks to open branches in London and not burden them with regulations. The embrace of the US$ began in the late 1950s and grew as the UK£ declined as an international currency. As the currency in use was not that of Britain, the Bank of England could afford to ignore the business that was being done in it. That was especially the case as so much of that business was being done by foreign banks on behalf of foreign customers. Thus, even before Britain abandoned exchange controls in 1979, the foreign exchange market had taken root in London. Further freedoms granted in the 1980s and into the 1990s meant that the world's banks found in London a convenient location in which to conduct all matters of financial activity without the restraints they had experienced domestically. Finally, the willingness to embrace the technological advances taking place in communications and processing placed London at the centre of the electronic revolution transforming financial markets.

13 September 1993; J. Blitz, 'ERM Crisis Quicken Activity', 20 October 1993; Graham, 'BIS Outlines Forex Risk'; G. Graham, 'Foreign Exchange Groups Plan Merger', 9 December 1996; G. Graham, 'Chase Plans New Forex Derivative', 29 April 1997; G. Graham, 'New Forex Bank to Cut Risk', 9 June 1997; S. Kuper, 'Merrill Makes Up for Lost Time on Forex', 14 July 1997; G. Graham, 'Global Payments Bodies to Merge', 1 October 1997; S. Kuper, 'Old Order Gives Way to the New', 5 June 1998; G. Graham, 'Banks Settle Down to Action', 5 June 1998; A. Beattie, 'Fighting Spirit Seeps into Dried-Up Markets', 25 June 1999; C. Swann, 'Big Banks Play Game of Brinkmanship', 25 June 1999; A. Beattie, 'Floor Presence Thins Out', 25 June 1999; G. Graham, 'Forex Trading System Planned', 15 September 1999; A. Skorecki, 'Forex System That Takes the Waiting Out of Wanting', 4 January 2002; A. Skorecki, 'Web Power Helps Smaller Customers', 27 May 2004; J. Hughes, 'Taking Their Law into Their Own Hands', 27 May 2004; J. Grant and P. Garnham, 'LCH.Clearnet Looks at Forex Markets', 16 October 2008; J. Hughes, 'A Lesson in How to Run a Smooth Global Settlement System', 21 August 2009; C. Flood, 'Regulators Stalk Secretive Financial Giants', 24 February 2014.

From a London base, an inter-dealer broker could trade around the globe and on a continuous basis, providing banks with a market that never closed. This was ideal for the emerging megabanks that were conducting a global business that spanned ever more diverse financial activities. On the eve of the Global Financial Crisis of 2008, there appeared nothing that could hinder the progress of the foreign exchange market or its London location.

6
Forex Today, Post-2007

Introduction

To many, the Global Financial Crisis that engulfed the world in 2008 was an event that could not happen because of the trends that had preceded it. The emergence of the megabanks, the switch to the originate-and-distribute banking model, the introduction of the Basel rules under the guidance of the Bank for International Settlements (BIS), and the use of derivative contracts were all meant to make the global financial system much more resilient. Under the collective management of central banks, the world appeared to have discovered the secret of how to deliver a financial system that met the needs of all users and was simultaneously competitive and stable. Unlike the previous attempt under the Bretton Woods system, which required active intervention to maintain fixed exchange rates, this new financial system successfully balanced the desire of governments to pursue independent economic, monetary, and financial policies with the free movement of funds around the world and relatively stable exchange rates. A solution to the trilemma has been found and the megabanks were the big winners in a world where the barriers to market integration had been removed, both nationally and internationally. These megabanks were the trusted counterparties to all transactions so that payments and receipts could move seamlessly around the world; assets and liabilities continuously matched across all variables; and savers and investors linked to borrowers for the benefit of all. These megabanks were too big and diversified to fail not because of any implied support from a central bank backed by a national government but because of their depth and breadth, their internal controls and supervision, and the way they structured their business. Their existence reassured governments and central banks that the stability of the global financial system could be safely left in their hands, absolving them of responsibility. The operation of an active foreign exchange market centred in London was a key component of this new world as through it, the megabanks could not only cover their currency risks but also lend and borrow for a short term among themselves.

Underlying this new world of finance was the ongoing revolution in the technology of finance. The ability to process and transmit vast amounts of information, and to buy and sell at the speed of light, was transforming the way markets functioned and the actions of banks and fund managers. Writing in 2010, Jeremy Grant and Michael Mackenzie reported that 'Advances in technology have been so great in the past five years that markets are now overwhelmingly driven by machines rather

Forex Forever. Ranald C. Michie, Oxford University Press. © Ranald C. Michie (2024).
DOI: 10.1093/oso/9780198903697.003.0007

than humans punching orders into a keyboard.'[1] By 2017, the interbank communications system, the Society for Worldwide Interbank Financial Telecommunications (SWIFT), was handling 7 billion messages a year, connecting more than 11,000 banks into a single network spanning the world. Within this network, international transactions flowed seamlessly whether they involved the continuous making and receiving of payments; matching assets and liabilities over time, place, amount, and currency; or providing the credit and capital without which economic activity would cease. It was not only the revolution in communications that continued unabated, for the same was true of the investment in the computer-driven processing and analysing of data by banks, and the employment of sophisticated trading strategies based upon the results. These underlying trends favoured the megabanks. They possessed depth and breadth across a wide range of financial activities, and that was what global fund managers and multinational corporations wanted. It was the megabanks that could afford the costs associated with the latest advances in the technology of communication and computing as well as pay the high salaries commanded by the staff with the required expertise, as these could be spread over a huge organization. It was also the megabanks that were in the best position to cope with the supervision being exercised by central banks and regulatory agencies as they had the scale necessary to spread the costs that compliance generated. Even after the confidence placed in megabanks received a major blow with the collapse of Lehman Brothers in 2008, triggering the Global Financial Crisis, they quickly regained their position as trusted counterparties, both to each other and their customers. They also regained the trust of regulators and central banks who could see no other way of exercising supervision over a most complex global financial system. Lacking a global regulator with the power of national agencies, such as the Securities and Exchange Commission of the USA, or a global central bank with the capacity of the US Federal Reserve to provide liquidity, only the megabanks could provide the mechanism for supervising and safeguarding the working of the global financial system. The role that they played can be seen in the operation of the global foreign exchange market throughout the Global Financial Crisis and subsequently.

Financial Centres

Prior to the Global Financial Crisis, London vied with New York as the premier financial centre in the world. Despite predictions to the contrary, London then escaped relatively unscathed from the worst effects of the Global Financial Crisis. Over ten years after the crisis, London remained the biggest player in a number of international markets, including foreign exchange.[2] The power of London's embedded infrastructure, ranging from networks of fibre-optic cables through a dense pool

---

[1] J. Grant and M. Mackenzie, 'Ghost in the Machine', *Financial Times*, 18 February 2010.
[2] C. Binham and P. Jenkins, 'Bailey Signals Need for Brexit Talks Focus on Financial Services', *Financial Times*, 8 May 2019.

of skilled labour to access to specialist support services, along with its favourable location in the world's time zones, continued to give London a competitive edge in attracting and retaining financial business. Omar Ali, of Ernst and Young, concluded in 2017 that 'the UK's financial ecosystem is unique and very hard to replicate.'[3] No cities in the world other than New York could match London in the depth, breadth, and international appeal of what it could provide, especially in such areas as the interbank money and currency markets. New York was poorly located to serve global markets because of its time zone. Eva Szalay emphasized this point in 2019 when she observed that 'London's location, straddling time zones between Asia and the US, gave it a key advantage.'[4] As a consequence, the Global Financial Crisis made little impact on the standing of London as a global financial centre due to the fundamentals attached to the co-location of financial activity. Nevertheless, across the entire range of financial activities, New York remained the leading financial centre in the world. Christian Meissner, global head of corporate and investment banking at Bank of America Merrill Lynch, emphasized this in 2014: 'As much as London might think it's the financial centre, I think New York is still ultimately the centre of the financial system. It's the dollar, it's the Fed—it's because US capital markets and the US economy are the deepest, it has the largest number of big companies.'[5] New York was much more a domestic and retail-orientated financial centre than London, as it relied on the size of the US economy for its continuing prominence. In contrast, London served the international financial community. Philip Stafford reported in 2016 that 'Scores of banks, exchanges and trading venues have based their operations in the UK in recent years, attracted by a mix of the favourable time zone, language, expertise and regulatory approach.'[6]

Britain's decision in 2016 to leave the European Union (EU) did undermine the City of London as Europe's dominant financial centre. Once the UK was no longer a member of the EU, the European Commission (EC) was able to introduce discriminatory policies aimed at forcing the relocation of financial activity out of London and to such continental centres as Amsterdam, Frankfurt, and Paris. The EC put pressure on all users of the City to move all transactions to a financial centre within the EU, on the grounds that this would contribute to better supervision and greater financial stability. In contrast, the preference of banks was to concentrate their trading where the market was deepest and broadest, and that was London. With trading taking place using multiple currencies, among which the $ not the euro was dominant, there remained a strong case for a central trading venue served by a single clearing house, and London was the obvious location. In 2016, Gregory Meyer had observed that 'markets have become increasingly placeless' and 'open in any time zone.'[7] Trading foreign exchange, whether it was the US$, euro, or yen, was drawn to London

[3] O. Ali, 'Dublin is Top Destination for Financial Groups Post-Brexit', *Financial Times*, 9 May 2017.

[4] E. Szalay, 'Jump in London Rupee Trades Rings Alarms', *Financial Times*, 18 September 2019.

[5] M. Pooler, 'New York and London Vie for Financial Crown', *Financial Times*, 2 October 2014.

[6] P. Stafford, 'Brexit Brings Headache to Industry Weary of Regulation', *Financial Times*, 11 October 2016.

[7] G. Meyer, 'Trading', *Financial Times*, 7 July 2016.

because it was the hub of a dense network of fibre-optic cables through which trans-actions took place on a near-instantaneous basis between the participants. As Philip Stafford and Roger Blitz stated in 2017, 'The majority of Europe's critical infrastruc-ture for trading forex, as well as shares and derivatives, is clustered in a 30-mile radius around the City.'[8]

The strength of London's embedded infrastructure, and the liquidity that came from its deep and broad markets, was sufficient to withstand the attempts by the EU to undermine it in the wake of Brexit. In the face of intense rivalry between national financial centres, the EU was unable to emulate the unity and integration that pro-vided the USA with the largest market for financial services in the world, leaving it with no financial centre that could rival London. As Axel Weber, the chairman of the Swiss megabank, Union Bank of Switzerland (UBS), observed in December 2020, 'The division of Europe is a massive benefit to the City of London. ... Europe is a fragmented market of 27 regulators, 27 financial markets, with a 28th regulator on top. You would not invent a system like that if you were to design a functioning sys-tem.'[9] The conclusion drawn in 2020 was that 'Brexit has failed to deliver a big hit to financial services employment in London.'[10] Over 400,000 were employed in finan-cial services in London and only New York could match that number. That was the reason why, in December 2020, the ex-governor of the Bank of England, Mervyn King, concluded that 'the biggest threat to the City comes from New York' rather than any financial centre in Europe or elsewhere in the world.[11] Since Britain's deci-sion to leave the EU in 2016, the megabanks had maintained their level of staffing in London, while the megafunds had increased theirs. The fragmentation of business between Paris, Frankfurt, Dublin, Amsterdam, Luxembourg, and other centres made it hard for any European city to rival the cluster of services and skills to be found in London. With London sitting at the heart of the global financial network, catching the end of the Asian trading day and morning on Wall Street, no large major bank or financial institution could afford to be absent as that would put it at a competitive disadvantage. Once having invested in the space, technology, and staff required to maintain a London presence, it was a simple matter to add on any additional finan-cial activities, when required. The economy of scale and the synergy of operations achieved in London could not be matched anywhere else in the world across a wide range of financial services and markets. The only consequence of the EU's action was to strengthen the position of New York by weakening that of London, and that was only at the margins. The City then remained unaffected by the pandemic of 2020, despite the disruptive effect that had on working patterns.[12]

[8] P. Stafford and R. Blitz, 'Undersea Cables Boost Euro Trading', *Financial Times*, 6 July 2017.

[9] S. Morris and Owen Walker, 'UBS Chairman Backs London to Remain Europe's Top Financial Centre', *Financial Times*, 3 December 2020.

[10] L. Noonan, O. Walker, A. Mooney, S. Morris and S. Riding, 'Finance Jobs Stayed in London after Brexit Vote', *Financial Times*, 12 December 2020.

[11] S. Morris, K. Wiggins, L. Fletcher and L. Noonan, 'Dublin-on-Thames? City Leaders Debate the Post-Brexit Future', *Financial Times*, 21 December 2020.

[12] See the following pieces from the *Financial Times*: C. Binham and P. Jenkins, 'Bailey Signals Need for Brexit Talks Focus on Financial Services', 8 May 2019; E. Szalay, 'Jump in London Rupee Trades Rings

Banks, Brokers, and Money

The Global Financial Crisis of 2008 was a product of the way the financial system was refashioning itself as it moved from an era of control and compartmentalization to freedom and fusion. That refashioning had left the global financial system exposed to the shocks experienced by every market-based financial system but had yet to build in the resilience required to moderate these. That resilience could only come through trial and error because the nature of the shocks changed over time as the global financial system evolved. The trends in the technology of communications and processing, the development of megabanks, the invention of financial derivatives, and the role played by governments and regulators all combined to create a crisis in 2008 that was unparalleled in magnitude and scope. This lack of precedence conditioned the response among governments and central banks as they sought to navigate a course between intervention to prevent the crisis spiralling out of control, leading to a global economic depression and the avoidance of either moral hazard that would encourage excessive risk-taking in the future or the reimposition of strict controls that would stifle innovation. Though many recommended some variation of the return to control and compartmentalization of the past, that was hardly an option considering the degree of change that had not only undermined that regime but had continued since at an accelerating pace. Only the British government persevered with some version of the Glass–Steagall Act in its policy of forcing banks to identify and then ring-fence their activities so as to prevent cross-contamination. However, under guidance from the BIS, all governments sought to impose greater controls and restrictions on banks and markets, to a greater or lesser degree.

For banking, the Global Financial Crisis of 2008 appeared to mark a major change in direction. Before the crisis, a small number of banks had established themselves at the centre of the world's financial system. These banks transcended national boundaries and time zones as they extended their operations around the globe. Their activities also blurred the distinctions between different types of financial institutions, and between banks and markets, through their ability to diversify the businesses they were engaged in and internalize transactions carried out for themselves and others. Located in all the leading financial centres, but with London playing a key role, these banks managed global empires through an ever-expanding

Alarms', 18 September 2019; S. Fleming, J. Brunsden and P. Stafford, 'Brexit and the City: Brussels' New Battle to Rival London in Finance', 22 September 2020; S. Morris and O. Walker, 'UBS Chairman Backs London to Remain Europe's Top Financial Centre', 3 December 2020; M. Sandhu, 'Brexit and Covid Harden the Case for a Proper EU Financial Market', 7 December 2020; J. Ford, 'Future of the City: How London's Reach Will Shrink after Brexit', 9 December 2020; L. Noonan, O. Walker, A. Mooney, S. Morris and S. Riding, 'Finance Jobs Stayed in London after Brexit Vote', 12 December 2020; L. Noonan, J. Guthrie, S. Bernard, L. Faunce and A. Smith, 'How London Grew into a Financial Powerhouse', 15 December 2020; P. Stafford, 'Future of the City: London's Markets Rivalry with EU Intensifies', 16 December 2020; S. Morris, K. Wiggins, L. Fletcher and L. Noonan, 'Dublin-on-Thames? City Leaders Debate the Post-Brexit Future', 21 December 2020; S. Morris and O. Walker, 'HSBC Chief Warns Post-Brexit Fragmentation Could Raise Costs', 2 December 2021; D. Thomas, 'US Overtakes EU as Biggest Financial Services Export Market for Britain', 8 December 2021; S. Fleming, P. Stafford and L. Noonan, 'The EU vs the City of London: A Slow Puncture', 15 January 2022; A. Iqbal, 'Deglobalisation is Boosting Foreign Exchange Volatility', 31 May 2022.

international network and a growing range of activities that destroyed the compartmentalized structures of the past. What was most marked in banking before the crisis
was the increasing replacement of the lend-and-hold model by the originate-and-
distribute one. The use of the originate-and-distribute model increased the use made
of the interbank money market to raise funds, as this maximized the use of short-term
funds for investment. The expectation was that the risk of a liquidity crisis was low
as money borrowed in the interbank market would be immediately repaid while the
securitization and resale of loans reduced the threat of a solvency crisis. The banking
system appeared to have discovered the magic formula that balanced risk and return,
providing borrowers with cheap loans, savers with high yields, and banks and their
employees with ample rewards, and delivered a stable and resilient financial system.
The Global Financial Crisis temporarily shattered that illusion as confidence collapsed in the megabanks, the originate-and-distribute model, and the resilience of
markets. Securitized assets were impossible to sell or even price while doubts existed
that interbank loans would ever be repaid. What began as a liquidity crisis had meta-
morphosed into a solvency one. The inevitable reaction from governments, central
banks, and regulators was to consider breaking up the megabanks, as they were held
primarily responsible for the crisis because of their risk-taking behaviour. That did
not happen, but action was taken to force the megabanks to hold more capital, maintain greater reserves of liquid assets, and withdraw from those activities perceived to
involve the greatest risks.

This response to the crisis by national authorities had consequences for the megabanks, especially those located outside the USA. Prior to the crisis, US$s had been in
plentiful supply as the US megabanks were active lenders in the interbank markets.
That ended with the freeze in the interbank market during the crisis. What then followed were regulations that encouraged US banks to prioritize liquidity over profits,
and so they pulled back from the interbank markets, depriving banks located outside the USA of abundant and cheap supplies of $s. Despite the domestic restrictions
imposed on the US banks, they remained in a powerful position as they had a huge
and captive domestic market and direct access to the currency upon which international trade and finance operated, namely the US$. They could also rely on support
from the Federal Reserve Bank, which was the only central bank in a position to
create US$ in response to demand, as in a liquidity crisis. Access to dollar funding
was crucial for all banks attempting to develop and maintain an international business, as the US$ acted as the global currency, and this meant that US banks were best
placed to obtain it. Also, the crisis had removed the last vestiges of the Glass–Steagall
Act in the USA as it led to the mergers between two of the largest investment banks
and two of the largest commercial banks, in the case of Bear Stearns/J.P. Morgan and
Merrill Lynch/Bank of America. J.P. Morgan also acquired the extensive retail operations of Washington Mutual, after it went bankrupt during the crisis. The two other
leading investment banks, namely Goldman Sachs and Morgan Stanley, converted
into commercial banks while retaining their investment banking operations. Along
with Citigroup, which had already moved in the direction of combining commercial and investment banking, this gave the USA five megabanks with domestic and

global operations. Even though regulations forced them to scale back their commitments, they were in a position to dominate world markets, from a secure base in the USA, with access to unlimited supplies of $s and support from the Federal Reserve as a lender of last resort. This gave them a strong competitive advantage over foreign competitors with even the UK bank, Barclays, which had acquired the US base of Lehman Brothers, struggling to compete. The continental European challenge of Deutsche Bank, BNP Paribas, Société Generale, UBS, and Credit Suisse faded away after the Global Financial Crisis. In 2009, the five leading US megabanks accounted for 48 per cent of global wholesale market activity and that had climbed to 59 per cent by 2014.

Nevertheless, the curbing of the megabanks had implications for the inter-dealer brokers who serviced their needs. The inter-dealer brokers had become essential players in the global markets for a wide variety of financial instruments. On the eve of the Global Financial Crisis in 2007, Michael Mackenzie claimed that 'The inter-dealer market is the bulwark of the global financial system, as it allows banks and other financial institutions to trade bonds, currencies and derivatives across all time zones and from every major financial centre.'[13] Inter-dealer brokers acted as intermediaries between banks and their dealings with each other and with other financial institutions, facilitating trading in bills, bonds, currencies, commodities, and derivatives either on the telephone or electronically on screens. By 2007, the London-based Intercapital (ICAP) was the largest of the inter-dealer brokers, handling transactions of $1,500 billion a day from a network of offices stretching from Sydney to Tokyo and London to New York. By investing heavily in expert staff and advanced technology, developing extensive international networks, and covering an ever-expanding range of financial instruments, these inter-dealer brokers provided the megabanks with continuous access to markets. They did not take positions, as that was the responsibility of the banks. This made them central players in the pre-crisis global financial markets.

The Global Financial Crisis then threatened the business of the inter-dealer brokers. The megabanks retreated from the riskier assets traded on the over-the-counter (OTC) market, where inter-dealer brokers had thrived. In addition, regulators intervened to curb OTC trading, blaming their lack of transparency for the build-up of the risks that had contributed to the crisis. The remedy was to force trading through exchanges and clearing houses, as that would provide better supervision and regulation as well as guarantees that deals would be completed. Robin Wigglesworth observed in 2019 that 'Since the financial crisis, stricter regulations and commercial pressures have forced many banks to pare back or close their once-vast proprietary and market-making desks.'[14] Tougher capital standards weighed on the ability of banks to warehouse corporate bonds and facilitate transactions for investors such as asset managers, hedge funds, and insurers. This forced them to withdraw from

---

[13] M. Mackenzie, 'Global Trade Facilitators Behind a 24-Hour Market', *Financial Times*, 20 April 2007.
[14] R. Wigglesworth, 'IMF Warns of "Tip of the Iceberg" Threat Over Volatility', *Financial Times*, 12 April 2019.

market making, and so they generated much less trading for the inter-dealer brokers. Furthermore, both to reduce costs and in response to regulatory pressure to prevent market manipulation, banks increasingly turned away from the use of inter-dealer brokers and towards electronic platforms. By 2013, 74 per cent of the trading in fixed-income products, currencies, and commodities was conducted on electronic platforms that automatically matched buyers and sellers. In addition, a growing share of the trading was conducted by specialist high-frequency traders rather than the megabanks. To Michael Spencer of ICAP, the future was now electronic, stating in 2016 that 'My dream is to create the world-leading, multi-product global electronic network for over-the-counter products.'[15] As a consequence, he sold ICAP's voice broking division to the other major British inter-dealer broker, Tullet Prebon. ICAP then renamed itself as NEX and focused on the development and operation of electronic markets, where it proved very successful. In 2017, NEX's BrokerTec electronic platform, for example, had captured 80 per cent of the US Treasury bond market. NEX was then bought by the Chicago Mercantile Exchange (CME) in 2018 as part of the growing convergence between the exchange-regulated and OTC markets, as statutory regulatory agencies made no distinction between them. The trading in financial products largely gravitated to electronic platforms whether they were controlled by exchanges, technology companies, or banks. That left the inter-dealers occupying a niche role as voice brokers, where they conducted complex negotiations between banks and acted as gatekeepers filtering out those counterparties over which the megabanks had doubts regarding reliability. Writing in 2018, Philip Stafford judged that Tullet Prebon's acquisition of ICAP's voice broking business, to form TP ICAP, gave it 'the scale to compete in swaps and fixed-income trading as the market was being transformed by the advance of electronic trading, and tougher regulations that squeezed the investment banks that are its main customers and piled on the broker's own compliance costs'.[16] By then, TP ICAP employed 3,300 brokers globally, being the world's largest inter-dealer broker with a 45 per cent share of the business. With the exception of the few remaining inter-dealer brokers, and direct dealing between and within banks, financial markets had become increasingly reliant on electronic platforms that automatically matched buyers and sellers. These were used extensively by the megabanks, which appeared to have survived the Global Financial Crisis and emerged even stronger as a result.[17]

---

[15] P. Stafford, 'ICAP Chief Prepares for Radical Change of Direction', *Financial Times*, 26 February 2016.

[16] P. Stafford, 'Departure of TP ICAP Chief Exposes Tensions at Top', *Financial Times*, 11 July 2018.

[17] See the following pieces from the *Financial Times*: M. Mackenzie, 'Global Trade Facilitators Behind a 24-Hour Market', 20 April 2007; S. Spikes and N. Cohen, 'It's Still Good to Talk on the Cutting Edge', 10 May 2007; N. Cohen and G. Tett, 'Icap Sets Sights on MTS Platform', 25 June 2007; D. Oakley, 'Austria Gives Nod to MTS Eurozone Rival', 1 July 2008; B. Masters, 'Set Apart by Englishness', 14 August 2008; J. Grant, 'Planned Merger Comes at Crucial Time for Industry', 14 August 2008; J. Grant, 'Interdealer Brokers Join Forces on OTC Issues', 9 March 2009; J. Grant and B. Masters, 'Brokers Set Out to Fight Backlash Against OTC Trade', 28 April 2009; J. Grant, 'Tullett Predicts Rebound for OTC Derivatives', 5 August 2009; J. Wheatley, 'São Paulo Adopts a More International Approach', 21 October 2009; A. Gray, 'Tullett Hangs on to Phone Trading', 9 March 2010; P. Stafford, 'High-Speed Electronic Trading Leaves Regulator Far Behind', 3 November 2010; J. Grant, 'D Börse-NYSE Merger "Bad For Markets,"' 5 July 2011; J. Grant, 'Industry in the Midst of a Maelstrom', 10 October 2011; M. Mackenzie, 'Libor Probe Shines Light on Voice Brokers', 17 February 2012; P. Stafford and S. Mundy, 'Icap Nets Exchange Licence in Deal for Plus

Within the megabanks, there had been some reordering among the hierarchy since the Global Financial Crisis, with those from the USA becoming ever more ascendant. Even among the US banks, there had been some changes with a gap opening up between Citibank and a top four of Goldman Sachs, Morgan Stanley, J.P. Morgan Chase, and Bank of America. Whereas the Bank of America had joined the investment banking elite by buying Merrill Lynch in 2008, Citigroup had sold its Wall Street brokerage house, Smith Barney, to Morgan Stanley in 2009. However, the major gap was between these US megabanks and their nearest challengers from Europe, including Barclays which had made the jump to the major league by buying the US operations of Lehman Brothers. Reflecting the apparent dominance of the megabanks was the central position they occupied within SWIFT, the cross-border money transfer network. By 2022, this handled 42 million financial messages a day, connecting more than 11,000 institutions and 4 billion account holders in at least 200 countries, but most transactions went through correspondent banks among which the megabanks were the most important. However, even by 2022, there had been no full return to the level of confidence in these megabanks as had existed before the collapse of Lehman Brothers in 2008. This was reflected in a greater demand for collateral to support interbank borrowing and lending.

Despite the apparent resilience of the megabanks, especially those from the USA, they were in an inferior position by 2022 compared to the one they had occupied in

Unit', 19 May 2012; P. Stafford and M. Mackenzie, 'Interdealer Brokers Braced for Shake-Up', 22 November 2012; FT Reporters, 'Daily Fix That Spiralled Out of Control', 20 December 2012; P. Stafford, A. Massoudi and M. Mackenzie, 'Nasdaq Sets Stage for HFT in Treasuries', 5 April 2013; P. Stafford, 'Settlement a Blow to Spencer', 26 September 2013; D. Schäfer and D. Strauss, 'Moves into Forex E-trading Speed Up', 4 March 2014; P. Stafford, 'Colourful World of Interdealers Faces Deep Structural Changes', 3 June 2014; P. Stafford, 'Sense of Urgency Underpins Fresh Scrutiny of Markets', 16 September 2014; M. Mackenzie, 'Swap Traders Resist Moves to Increase Use of Platforms', 16 September 2014; M. Mackenzie, 'Search for Liquidity Tests Firms' Talent for Innovation', 5 November 2014; J. Grant, 'SGX in Talks on Asian Trading Platform for Corporate Bonds', 17 November 2014; P. Stafford, 'Swiss Broker to Set Up London Repo Venue', 19 May 2015; P. Stafford, 'ICAP Chief Prepares for Radical Change of Direction', 26 February 2016; P. Stafford, 'Voice Brokers Answer Call for Liquidity', 12 August 2016; J. Rennison, 'Bond Trading Platform Muscles in as Banks Retreat', 29 September 2016; P. Stafford, 'ICAP's New Direction Reflects Changing Future of Derivatives', 6 October 2016; J. Rennison, 'Lutnick Makes Treasury Trading Comeback', 16 May 2017; P. Stafford, 'Personal Touch Critical as Banks Trim Brokers', 29 June 2017; P. Stafford, 'Amsterdam Chosen as Tradeweb's EU Base', 4 August 2017; P. Stafford, 'Voice Brokers Fight to Survive Europe's Shake-Up', 10 October 2017; G. Meyer, 'From Ranchers to Fund Managers, Algos Cause a Stir', 10 October 2017; J. Rennison and A. Scaggs, 'US Treasury Dealers Accused of Collusion', 17 November 2017; P. Stafford, 'Spencer Considers a Financial Future without Nex', 17 March 2018; P. Stafford, 'CME Eyes Pole Position in Treasury Trades with Audacious Bid for Nex', 28 March 2018; P. Stafford, 'CME Clinches Spencer's Nex in Deal Set to Shake Up $500bn Treasuries Market', 29 March 2018; P. Stafford, 'Fintech Alley Cat Gets the Cream with £670bn CME Deal', 31 March 2018; P. Stafford, 'CME Expects No Asset Sales after Nex Purchase', 3 April 2018; P. Stafford, 'Electronic Trading Pioneer Throws Down Gauntlet to Brokertec on Treasuries', 8 June 2018; R. Wigglesworth and J. Rennison, 'Algos Blaze Trail in Odd Lots Segment of US Corporate Bonds', 15 June 2018; P. Stafford, 'Departure of TP ICAP Chief Exposes Tensions at Top', 11 July 2018; J. Rennison, 'Bloomberg Snatches Corporate Bond Trade Data Partner from Rival Thomson Reuters', 26 July 2018; H. Murphy, 'TP Icap Names Paris as Its EU Base after Brexit', 8 August 2018; R. Wigglesworth and J. Rennison, 'New Credit Ecosystem Blossoms as Portfolio Trades Surge', 11 October 2018; R. Wigglesworth, 'Markets: Volatile Times', 10 January 2019; R. Wigglesworth, 'IMF Warns of "Tip of the Iceberg" Threat Over Volatility', 12 April 2019; P. Stafford, 'Mifid 2 Rules Tighten Wall Street's Grip on Europe', 27 June 2019; P. Stafford, 'BGC Signs Trio of High-Frequency Trading Firms to Boost European Equity Options', 25 July 2019; J. Rennison and P. Stafford, 'Rise of MarketAxess Mirrors Demise of Traders on Wall Street', 30 August 2019.

2007 because of the growth of the shadow banking sector and the vastly increased power of the central banks. After the financial crisis, the megabanks had been forced to adopt a high liquidity coverage ratio. This was the portion of high-quality assets that they held, such as cash reserves and US Treasury bonds that could be sold quickly in a crisis. The capital and liquidity requirements placed on the megabanks led them to withdraw from certain markets or made them less competitive compared to those financial institutions that were not similarly burdened, such as hedge funds and high-frequency traders. Whereas the assets of banks and non-banks were almost equal, at $58 trillion for the former and $51 trillion for the latter before the crisis of 2008, the balance had shifted towards non-banks by 2021. By then, the assets of banks had grown to $180 trillion, but those of non-banks had reached $227 trillion. These non-banks had thrived by exploiting the gaps left by the megabanks especially as borrowers and investors turned to bonds in the low-yield climate generated by central bank intervention. The quantitative easing programmes introduced by central banks to avoid a financial and economic crisis after the crisis had encouraged businesses to turn to bonds and investors to seek higher returns than those obtainable from bank deposits. In 2008, the total outstanding debt in the world stood at $150 trillion, and this had almost doubled to $280 trillion by 2020. Before the crisis, it was the megabanks that had thrived on the issue of this debt by operating the originate-and-distribute model of banking. Since then, it was the shadow banking sector, including the largest fund managers, that had become increasingly involved as they could purchase this debt and hold it for the yield it delivered either directly or in exchange-traded funds. The restrictions placed on banks limited their ability to absorb all the bonds being issued as well as maintain an active secondary market.

The diminished role of the megabanks left central banks, primarily the Federal Reserve, in a greatly enhanced position, as they were now responsible for providing the liquidity that kept money markets operational as the crisis that occurred in March 2020, due to the pandemic, revealed. Most interbank borrowing and lending involved the US$, making the Federal Reserve the only central bank with the ability to respond to a liquidity crisis when one did occur. The March 2020 crisis had exposed a fundamental weakness in the global financial system erected by central banks after the 2008 crisis, as Mark Sobel noted at the time.

Regulatory reforms after the global financial crisis (GFC) were supposed to have created a more robust and more resilient financial system. ... The post-GFC reform agenda strengthened systemically-important banks. Capital levels were raised, improving the banks' ability to absorb losses, and liquidity coverage was strengthened, and resolution regimes fortified. And so far, banks have weathered the coronavirus storm, although there is no room for complacency. But the real problem is that the post-GFC agenda did not focus with similar intensity on non-banks. Many of the current stresses emanate from these players, which have grown significantly over the past decade. ... The GFC was a self-inflicted banking crisis. Banks were the villains and reforms were readily pursued. The coronavirus crisis is an exogenous shock, not caused by non-banks. But that makes it no less disruptive for the global financial system.[18]

With the US$ featuring in almost 90 per cent of currency transactions, neither the euro, nor the yen, nor the renminbi provided an alternative source of liquidity. This made the resilience of the US money market crucial for the health of the global financial system as Justin Muzinch, the US Deputy Treasury Secretary, acknowledged in December 2020: 'During March, money markets experienced significant outflows, forcing Treasury and the Federal Reserve to step in to prevent a destabilising run. We must now consider reforms to ensure this vulnerability does not threaten financial stability in the future.'[19]

Banks around the world looked to the market for US government treasury bonds as a source of liquidity. When it froze in March 2020, the Federal Reserve was forced to intervene or face a global banking crisis of the magnitude of the one that took place in 2008. Stricter regulations had forced banks to curtail their own trading and act more as brokers intermediating trades between clients. This contributed to more high-speed electronic trading and opened up opportunities for less-regulated hedge funds. When Covid-19 triggered a global scramble for cash, including ditching treasuries, these hedge funds and high-frequency traders engaged in panic sales. This drove down the price of treasury bonds, triggering margin calls for hedge funds that had borrowed hundreds of billions of dollars in the short-term 'repo' market to bet on the difference narrowing, exacerbating the dislocation. The Federal Reserve was then forced to act because it feared that a mass unwinding of these trades would cause even more treasuries to be dumped, worsening the chaos. There was a similar occurrence in the UK in 2022 when the Bank of England was forced to support the market in UK government debt during the liability-driven investment crisis. The twin effects of the restrictions and requirements placed on the megabanks, allied to the quantitative easing programmes carried out by central banks, were to make the money markets dependent on central banks for liquidity, both in normal times and in a crisis.

By the middle of 2021, the global financial system appeared to have weathered the storm caused by the pandemic though there remained serious liquidity issues that could only be met by central bank intervention, especially from the Federal Reserve. Nevertheless, John Plender was one of those who continued to warn in 2021 that the global financial system was unstable.

The banks emerged relatively safe from last year's crisis. But their role as providers of liquidity has increasingly been filled by less-regulated non-banks or shadow banks, such as hedge funds. These borrow heavily, often to maximise the return from trades that arbitrage tiny differences between the prices of closely-related

---

[18] M. Sobel, 'The Clean-Up of the Non-bank Sector Needs to Begin Now Financial System is Failing Its First Real Stress Test after the 2008–09 Crisis', *Financial Times*, 20 April 2020.

[19] C. Smith, 'Money Market Funds Need Reform to Prevent Runs, US Regulators Say', *Financial Times*, 23 December 2020.

assets. With the onset of heightened volatility and market stress last March these non-banks faced margin calls and funding difficulties. They went from being market stabilisers to amplifiers of market stress.[20]

The result was a moral hazard issue as it led to the expectation that the Federal Reserve would intervene in future. By the end of 2021, the Editorial Board of the *Financial Times* was expressing its concern.

Tougher rules on banks, introduced after the 2008 financial crisis, helped make the banking system more resilient—showing its worth during the turmoil in March 2020—but it has also pushed some risk-taking into the shadow banks, such as bond funds and private lenders. These non-banks can, however, exacerbate an economic downturn just like their more traditional cousins. Last year, open-ended bond funds faced a rush of redemptions, similar to a bank run. The funds offer complete liquidity for investors, allowing them to instantly receive the value of their investment back, but the funds themselves own more illiquid assets. With investors spooked by the pandemic, the funds were forced to sell their most liquid assets, often US Treasuries, at steep discounts to meet the redemptions. The fire sale of assets and the disorder in the world's most important asset market was only halted when the US central bank, the Federal Reserve, stepped in as the dealer of last resort.[21]

What this meant, in the words of Michael Howell, Managing Director of Crossborder Capital in December 2021, was that the US Federal Reserve was 'the linchpin of the global monetary system'.[22]

Quantitative easing programmes had made world liquidity dependent upon central banks, forcing them to intervene whenever a liquidity crisis loomed. By March 2022, the Federal Reserve owned 25 per cent of all outstanding treasury debt, the European Central Bank and the Bank of England each owned 40 per cent of their government bonds, and the Bank of Japan had 50 per cent of that country's outstanding government debt. Among those central banks, the one with all the power was the Federal Reserve as the US$ was the most widely used currency in trade, financial transactions, and central bank reserves. Though the importance of the US$ as a reserve currency had fallen after 1999, with the launch of the euro, it still stood at 59 per cent of the total in 2021 compared to 71 per cent in 1999. As Brian O'Toole, a former senior official at the US Treasury, observed in 2022, 'There is no place else that has anything approaching the level of liquidity and access that the US market has. It doesn't exist anywhere.'[23] Indicating the importance of the USA for the stability of the global financial system was this comment made by Robin Wigglesworth in 2022:

[20] J. Plender, 'Stress Test Looms for Financial System in 2021', *Financial Times*, 4 January 2021.

[21] Editorial Board, 'Shadow Banks Must Come Out of the Shadows', *Financial Times*, 7 December 2021.

[22] M. Howell, 'The Liquidity Threat Looming Over Markets in 2022', *Financial Times*, 17 December 2021.

[23] R. Wigglesworth, P. Ivanova and C. Smith, 'Financial Warfare: Will There be a Backlash against the Dollar?', *Financial Times*, 7 April 2022.

'A well-functioning US Treasury market is critical for global financial markets.'[24] Any drying up of liquidity in the US money markets would make an immediate and direct impact upon the health of the global financial system. Whereas before the Global Financial Crisis, this liquidity was provided by the megabanks, that was no longer the case. They had pulled back from the market with their activity replaced by proprietary trading firms and hedge funds. These did not have the capacity to act as buyers or sellers of last resort, ready to reverse a deal when the opportunity arose. This left that task to the central banks, especially the Federal Reserve, but they were much less willing to intervene after 2020 as their focus switched to combatting rising inflation rather than maintaining financial and economic stability.[25]

Foreign Exchange Market

In its 2022 triennial survey of the foreign exchange market, the BIS, which acted as the central banks' central bank, documented the global foreign exchange market since 2007. On a net–gross basis, it estimated that the daily average, for the amount of foreign exchange traded, rose from $4.3 trillion in 2007 to $9.8 trillion in 2022. This made the foreign exchange market the largest and most active in the world.

---

[24] R. Wigglesworth, 'How to Save the Treasury Market', *Financial Times*, 13 September 2022.
[25] See the following pieces from the *Financial Times*: A. Vismara, 'Mifid 2 Drags Down an Ecosystem Along with Europe's Banks', 15 May 2019; P. Stafford, 'Mifid 2 Rules Tighten Wall Street's Grip on Europe', 27 June 2019; FT Reporters, 'Fed Analyses Regulation's Role in Sudden Rates Jump', 2 October 2019; J. Thompson, 'QE Sows Seeds of Next Crisis, Funds Warn', 2 December 2019; M. Howell, 'Rising Tide of Liquidity Lifts Many Boats, But Keep an Eye on the Horizon', 17 January 2020; C. Binham, 'Shadow Banking Sector Shifts into Decline', 20 January 2020; M. Howell, 'Knee-Jerk Rate Cuts Only Make Matters Worse in This Crisis', 19 March 2020; J. Rennison, P. Stafford, C. Smith and R. Wigglesworth, 'Great Liquidity Crisis Strikes System as Banks Step Back', 24 March 2020; Editorial Board, 'Non-bank Lenders Will Bear Brunt of Credit Crisis: Financial Risk has been Pushed from Banks into the Shadows', 24 March 2020; W. Du, 'What Makes This Global Dollar Crunch Different?', 26 March 2020; B. Greeley and C. Smith, 'Federal Reserve Eases Capital Rule to Encourage Bank Lending', 2 April 2020; M. Sobel, 'The Clean-Up of the Non-bank Sector Needs to Begin Now Financial System is Failing Its First Real Stress Test after the 2008–09 Crisis', 20 April 2020; C. Smith, E. Szalay and K. Martin, 'Dollar Blues: Why the Pandemic Is Testing Confidence in the US Currency', 1 August 2020; R. Wigglesworth, 'US Treasury Market's Brush with Disaster Must Never be Repeated', 21 September 2020; C. Smith, 'Money Market Funds Need Reform to Prevent Runs, US Regulators Say', 23 December 2020; J. Plender, 'Stress Test Looms for Financial System in 2021', 4 January 2021; J. Dizzard, 'The Horror Scenario Lurking in the Plumbing of Finance', 24 July 2021; K. Duguid and T. Stubbington, 'Central Bank Sync Puts Foreign Exchange Market to Sleep', 21 September 2021; Editorial Board, 'Shadow Banks Must Come Out of the Shadows', 7 December 2021; I. Kamininska, 'Daylight Overdrafts Must Lose Their Stigma', 13 December 2021; M. Howell (Managing Director), 'The Liquidity Threat Looming Over Markets in 2022', *Financial Times*, 17 December 2021; I. Morse and S. Morris, 'Citi's Jane Fraser Ditches Ambition to Break Into Wall Street's Big League', 18 February 2022; R. Wigglesworth, P. Ivanova and C. Smith, 'Financial Warfare: Will There Be a Backlash against the Dollar?', 7 April 2022; M. Singh, 'We Need New Financial Pipes', 3 June 2022; E. Platt, J. Rennison and K. Duguid, 'Liquidity Is Terrible: Poor Trading Conditions Fuel Wall Street Tumult', 7 June 2022; B. Elder, 'No, Russia Won't Replace Swift with the Blockchain', 20 June 2022; E. Pan, 'Liquidity Strains in Markets Need Structural Fixes', 5 July 2022; K. Martin and C. Smith, 'The Mystery of How Quantitative Tightening Will Affect Markets', 10 July 2022; R. Wigglesworth, 'How to Save the Treasury Market', 13 September 2022; K. Duguid and S. Palma, 'SEC Backs Fresh Push to Shore Up $24tn Treasury Market', 14 September 2022; C. Jones, 'A Global Backlash is Brewing Against the Fed', 22 September 3022; H. Agnew and J. Cumbo, 'Amundi Warns on Hidden Leverage in the Financial System', 25 October 2022.

The BIS also estimated that 35 per cent of this trading took place in London in 2007 and 38 per cent in 2022, which matched the combined total for the next four foreign exchange markets, namely those located in New York, Tokyo, Hong Kong, and Singapore, throughout. The conclusion it reached in 2022 was that 'FX trading continues to be concentrated in major financial centres. The United Kingdom remained the most important FX trading location globally, with 38% of global turnover.'[26] It reported that this trading took place through a mixture of direct contact between buyers and sellers, the intermediation of inter-dealer brokers, and, increasingly, the use of electronic platforms that matched sales and purchases automatically. The foreign exchange market remained an essential tool used by banks in their constant adjustment of assets and liabilities across time, space, quantity, and type; the lending and borrowing they did between each other; and the profitable employment of the resources at their command. Apart from a small dip in trading between 2013 and 2016, which had largely technical causes, the total turnover rose inexorably and London's share climbed from 35 per cent in 2007 to 43 per cent in 2019 before falling back to 38 per cent in 2022. As the Bank of England Report for 2007 stated, 'Foreign Exchange is one of the largest financial markets in London by turnover and, in turn, London is currently the largest centre of foreign exchange activity worldwide.'[27] The Bank of England drew the same conclusion from each subsequent BIS triennial survey, covering 2010, 2013, 2016, 2019, and 2022.

What was traded in the foreign exchange market was money. Money was simultaneously a unit of account, a store of value, and a means of payment, and the transactions that banks made in the foreign exchange market reflected all these features. Much of this trading could be handled by direct dealing between banks, especially the megabanks, operating from strategically placed offices located around the world, where expert staff and advanced technology were employed for the purpose. Key locations included Singapore, Hong Kong, and Tokyo in Asia, London in Europe, and New York in the Americas. The foreign exchange market was always active, creating the opportunity for banks to constantly make and unwind their positions as circumstances changed. In 2007, Peter Garnham observed that 'The foreign exchange market is the world's most liquid and widely-traded financial market. Open 24 hours a day, seven days a week.'[28] Writing later that year, he claimed that

foreign exchange is the market that never sleeps—but it really springs to life when London's traders reach their desks. London dominates the world's largest financial market, accounting for more than a third of the daily volumes in foreign exchange. Unlike other financial markets, there is no centrally-cleared market for foreign exchange. Instead, the market stays open 24 hours a day.[29]

---

[26] Bank for International Settlements, *Triennial Central Bank Survey* (2022).
[27] Christodoulou and O'Connor, 'The Foreign Exchange and Over-the-Counter Derivatives Markets', 553.
[28] P. Garnham, 'Currencies Establish Themselves as Asset Class', *Financial Times*, 5 March 2007.
[29] P. Garnham, 'Quant Techniques Drive Volumes Ever Higher', *Financial Times*, 19 November 2007.

He continued that eulogy to the foreign exchange market in 2009 when he reported that 'From Monday morning in New Zealand, currency prices are changing 24 hours a day, moving continuously across the globe for five days until trading shuts down on Friday after the US close.'[30] The activity generated by banks created openings for others, like hedge funds, to profit from tiny and momentary price differences that appeared, which contributed to overall liquidity.

To support their trading in the foreign exchange market, banks, brokers, and hedge funds invested heavily in the staff, accommodation, and technology required to handle the huge volume of transactions that took place. By 2007, most trading already took place electronically through the use of automated, complex mathematical strategies using dedicated online platforms. The growing ascendancy of electronic trading, whether it involved the banks dealing with each other or with their customers, reinforced London's dominance because of the heavy investment required. It was only those banks that dominated trading in foreign exchange that could afford this investment, and this was concentrated on their London dealing desks because that was where the greatest volume of business took place. As Goodacre and Razak observed in 2019, 'The shift to electronic relative to voice tends to favour London as a financial centre because many major firms run their global e-trading from London.'[31] By then, the foreign exchange market had developed a clearly demarcated two-tier structure with banks dominating trading in both tiers. The top tier was trading between banks, while the lower tier was trading between banks and their customers, including other banks. A growing proportion of these trades were completed within the same bank because of the size and scale reached by the megabanks. It was not only the trading conducted on electronic platforms that took place in London, but those still voice-reliant, because the size and complexity of the deal made them difficult to price other than through negotiation, also clustered in London. It was much less costly to establish and maintain counterparty relationships with dealers and clients in one financial centre than in each country separately.[32]

At the heart of the foreign exchange market in London were ten banks that provided foreign exchange services to the global banking system. These ten banks accounted for 70 per cent of the turnover in 2007, and this rose to 77 per cent in 2010. The crisis contributed to their dominance, as they were considered the most trusted counterparties at a time of great uncertainty. These ten banks enjoyed economies of scale and network advantages, which continued to grow through heavy investment in human expertise, electronic technology, and modern trading floors. The dealers they employed constituted a small group of trusted counterparties who traded continuously with each other without the need for collateral. As Eva Szalay reported in 2019, 'The world's foreign exchange markets do not open or close through the working days

[30] P. Garnham, 'Net Brings Power to the People', *Financial Times*, 29 September 2009.

[31] Goodacre and Razak, 'Foreign Exchange'.

[32] See Schrimpf and Sushko, 'Sizing Up Global Foreign Exchange Markets'; Schrimpf and Sushko, 'FX Trade Execution'; Evans and Rime, 'Microstructure'; Bank for International Settlements, *Triennial Central Bank Survey* (2022); Bank of England, *BIS Triennial Survey* (2022).

of the week. Instead, they operate continuously from Monday to Friday.'[33] Liquidity was normally plentiful in the currency market apart from the period between the New York market closing and the Asian markets opening, creating opportunities for greater volatility, and so little trading took place over the period. Richard Anthony, head of European cash currency trading at Hong Kong and Shanghai Bank (HSBC), explained in 2019 that 'During the transition from New York to Asia, there are many fewer human traders at their desks and the ratio of electronic participation to voice is higher than at other times of the day.'[34] In contrast, the greatest liquidity was found during the London trading hours and so this attracted the bulk of trading. In 2019, Eva Szalay explained that London's success in attracting trading in both the Chinese renminbi and Indian rupee was that 'London's location, straddling time zones between Asia and the US, gave it a key advantage.'[35] Regardless of the participants or the currencies being traded, the location of foreign exchange trading continued to be London because it possessed the greatest pool of liquidity. Despite the foreign exchange market operating continuously from Monday to Friday, liquidity was concentrated when trading took place during the working hours of the London market and in the leading currencies, especially the US$. As Jon Vollemaere, chief executive of trading platform R5FX, observed in 2019, 'In line with the fact that there are more dollars traded in London than in New York and more euros than in the EU, it makes sense that rupee trades here as well.'[36] What this meant was that the London foreign exchange market attracted business in emerging currencies and by additional banks and financial institutions because it already had the infrastructure and connections to support currency trading.

The investment in the foreign exchange market increased the speed at which transactions were conducted and completed, expanded its capacity so that a greater volume of trading could take place, extended participation beyond the core of megabanks, and encouraged new entrants by lowering the barriers to entry, such as cost. The effect was visible through the great reduction in latency. Latency was the time it took for a trade to be completed, so reducing the exposure to sudden price changes. By 2018, latency was down to 37 milliseconds, almost eliminating the risks associated with exposure to currency fluctuations. The reduction in latency stimulated the carry trade. This involved borrowing in the currency of a country with a low interest rate, such as Japan or Switzerland, and lending in a country with a higher interest rate, such as the UK or Australia. As well as participating in the carry trade, the megabanks were able to capture the profit from the bid-ask spread themselves, by internalizing transactions. In addition to the huge reduction in latency lowering the currency risk in the foreign exchange market, the risk of counterparty default had also been eliminated for many through the establishment of the Continuous Linked Settlement (CLS) Bank by a consortium of leading global financial institutions. CLS operated

[33] E. Szalay, 'Fears Over Forex Trading Going Bump in the Night', *Financial Times*, 6 March 2019.
[34] E. Szalay, 'Fears Over Forex Trading Going Bump in the Night', *Financial Times*, 6 March 2019.
[35] E. Szalay, 'Jump in London Rupee Trades Rings Alarms', *Financial Times*, 18 September 2019.
[36] E. Szalay, 'Jump in London Rupee Trades Rings Alarms', *Financial Times*, 18 September 2019.

a payment netting system that acted as a trusted third party between the two counterparties to a deal. The success of this CLS system proved itself during the Global Financial Crisis when foreign exchange transactions were unaffected by the turbulence and illiquidity that temporarily destroyed other markets. More banks turned to the CLS system as a result of the crisis, because of the guarantees it provided. As it was, foreign exchange trading continued as normal during the crisis, especially that which took place between the megabanks. The overall level did drop to $3 trillion a day in 2009, but this was due to a severe contraction in hedge-fund activity. Trading then recovered to $4 trillion a day in 2010. This resilience of the foreign exchange market during the crisis led Jas Singh, global head of Treasury at Thomson Reuters, to claim in 2009 that it was 'a poster child for how over-the-counter financial markets should work.'[37] The foreign exchange market's resilience even led to its increasing use by fund managers as a way of hedging valuation and liquidity risk.[38]

Though the foreign exchange market had functioned normally during the crisis, it was threatened with disruption afterwards by the actions taken by regulators. In the wake of the crisis, regulators, especially in the USA, attempted to push all trading either through exchanges or make the use of clearing houses compulsory. That agenda included ending the position occupied by the foreign exchange market as the 'mostly unregulated, largest financial market in the world.'[39] Policymakers, regulators, and central banks identified the commitments made between banks in the foreign exchange market as a threat to the stability of the global financial system, even though observers such as Jennifer Hughes in 2010 referred to it as 'the world's biggest trading operation, operating smoothly across borders around the clock.'[40] The crisis had destroyed trust in self-regulated markets, including those that had functioned trouble-free, leading to demands for public oversight and legally enforceable safeguards. This attempt to force foreign exchange trading to take place either on exchanges or through clearing houses was strongly resisted by all the major participants, including the largest US banks. The risks that concerned the regulators had already been addressed either through the internal mechanisms put in place by the megabanks or the establishment of the CLS Bank. In 2010, 30 per cent of the daily value of foreign exchange trades was transacted directly between the client and bank,

[37] P. Garnham, 'Keeping Its Head as Others Lost Theirs', *Financial Times*, 29 September 2009.
[38] See the following pieces from the *Financial Times*: P. Garnham, 'Currencies Establish Themselves as Asset Class', 5 March 2007; J. Authers, 'London Blows Its Trumpet Too Loudly', 19 November 2007; S. Tucker, 'Rivals to HK and Singapore Emerge', 19 November 2007; P. Garnham, 'Quant Techniques Drive Volumes Ever Higher', 19 November 2007; P. Garnham, 'Forex Market Soars With Little Sign of Change in Trading System', 15 October 2008; S. Johnson, 'A Little Oasis of Calm for Currencies', 2 February 2009; J. Hughes, 'A Lesson in How to Run a Smooth Global Settlement System', 21 August 2009; J. Hughes, 'FX Faces Prospect of Two-Tier Pricing', 21 August 2009; P. Garnham, 'Keeping Its Head as Others Lost Theirs', 29 September 2009; J. Hughes, 'Concern Over Scope of Initiatives', 29 September 2009; H. Smith, 'Reverberations from Volatility in the Real Economy', 6 October 2009; S. Grene, 'Taking the Sting Out of Fluctuation', 6 October 2009; K. Brown, 'SGX to Offer OTC Derivatives Clearing', 21 September 2010; G. Lambe, 'FX Markets Ride Wave of Widening Appeal', 4 October 2010; J. Noble, 'UK's Share of Renminbi Trade Leaps', 9 October 2013; K. Martin and P. Stafford, 'Banter Banned as Forex Traders Clean Up Act', 23 May 2015.
[39] D. Schäfer and D. Strauss, 'Moves into Forex Etrading Speed Up', *Financial Times*, 4 March 2014.
[40] J. Hughes, 'Worries Over Threat of "Heavy Touch"', *Financial Times*, 30 March 2010.

while the remaining 70 per cent were largely interbank transactions and CLS settled 70 per cent of these, using a combination of payment-versus-payment in central bank funds and multilateral payment netting. This eliminated settlement risk. With these procedures already in place, and backing from the world's central banks, the foreign exchange market was able to withstand the post-crisis challenge from the regulators to force more of the trading through exchanges and clearing houses.

With the centre of the global foreign exchange market being London, the Bank of England was the central bank in closest contact with it during the Global Financial Crisis of 2008, but it had little direct involvement. The foreign exchange market fitted perfectly the term 'Wimbledonization' applied to the City of London collectively. According to Eddie George, in a speech he made in 1999, when governor of the Bank of England,

> A few years ago Japanese bankers used to tease me by asking what I thought of the 'Wimbledonisation' of the City—meaning that this country organised the best competition in the world but the visitors carried off the prizes. I used to explain to them that it was activity—rather than nationality of ownership or even control— that mattered in terms of the City's contribution to the wider economy, and in terms of its direct contribution to growth or employment, or of income or tax base in this country.[41]

In London's foreign exchange market, foreign banks traded foreign currencies on behalf of foreign customers. One consequence of that was to make the involvement of the Bank of England rather marginal as it had no authority to supervise most of the banks involved, the expertise to manage the operation of the market, or the capacity to act as the lender of last resort in a crisis. That did not mean that the Bank of England ignored London's foreign exchange market. It was responsible for collecting the data used by the BIS for its triennial surveys as well as monitoring the composition and behaviour of the market from a British perspective. However, it appeared to have been unaware of the collusion that had taken place among those trading foreign exchange in London, until that was exposed by others in 2013. It then intervened only in association with other central banks and regulators to impose fines on the banks involved.[42]

What emerges from the operation of London's foreign exchange market between 2007 and 2022 was how little it relied on national governments, central banks, or

[41] E. George, *Before the Millennium: From the Bank of England* (Bank of England, 7 December 1999).

[42] See the following pieces from the *Bank of England Quarterly Bulletin*: Christodoulou and O'Connor, 'The Foreign Exchange and Over-the-Counter Derivatives Markets'; T. Broderick and C. Cox, 'The Foreign Exchange and Over-the-Counter Interest Rate Derivatives Markets in the United Kingdom', 50 (2010); J. O'Connor, J. Wackett and R. Zammit, 'The Use of Foreign Exchange Markets by Non-banks', 51 (2011); S. John, M. Roberts and O. Weeken, 'The Bank of England's Special Liquidity Scheme', 52 (2012); J. Lowes and Tsvetelina Nenova, 'The Foreign Exchange and Over-the-Counter Interest Rate Derivatives Market in the United Kingdom', 53 (2013); A.G. Haldane, 'Managing Global Finance as a System', 54 (2014); A. Hutton and E. Kent, 'The Foreign Exchange and Over-the-Counter Interest Rate Derivatives Market in the United Kingdom', 53 (2016); Goodacre and Razak, 'Foreign Exchange'; Bank of England, *BIS Triennial Survey* (2022).

regulators and went relatively untouched by an event such as the Global Financial Crisis of 2008. In 2010, Broderick and Cox concluded that 'The UK FX market provided a liquid and resilient alternative during the financial crisis.'[43] This was a market that operated without the supervision of regulatory authorities, did not use a clearing house, and received no direct support from a lender of last resort. What the Global Financial Crisis did expose was the need for bilateral foreign currency swap lines between the most important central banks. This reflected the fact that most interbank financial activity was conducted in US$s through London, including the foreign exchange market, but only the Federal Reserve Bank could provide liquidity in $s. However, the foreign exchange market was affected indirectly by the actions taken to curb the megabanks after the Global Financial Crisis. Olaf Storbeck and Philip Stafford wrote in 2019 that 'The foreign exchange market is changing rapidly as the banks that have long dominated the market pare back their operations in response to tougher regulations and competitive pressures.'[44] By then, regulators were introducing tougher rules for those deals privately negotiated between banks that did not pass through a clearing house, which curbed the foreign exchange trading between the megabanks and with their customers. The regulators were further motivated to intervene in the foreign exchange market in response to the revelations of market manipulation. The dominance of the foreign exchange market by a small number of banks, engaged in direct trading between each other or operating through interdealer brokers, made collusion relatively easy, despite the vast volume of transactions. This market manipulation was exposed in 2013, leading to various regulatory authorities imposing large fines. By 2019, the fines paid by fifteen banks over currency manipulation had reached $12 billion.

Sensing an opportunity, exchanges tried to move into the foreign exchange market, taking advantage of the regulatory push aimed at the banks. In 2015, both the US-based exchange operators, BATS and Deutsche Börse in Europe, attempted to establish a presence in the foreign exchange market. However, trading remained dominated by the megabanks, as they moved quickly to address the weaknesses in the foreign exchange market that the manipulation scandal had exposed. A Global Foreign Exchange Committee was established comprising the world's central banks and the biggest currency trading banks. By 2017, this committee had introduced, and took responsibility for supervising, a code of conduct for the market, which was also made answerable to the BIS. Though turnover had slipped to $5.1 trillion a day by 2017, it thus remained firmly in the hands of the banks. According to Philip Stafford, 'Most currency trading is conducted between banks, away from exchanges, creating a fragmented market that regulators have found difficult to police.'[45] The only way that exchanges could gain a foothold in the foreign exchange market was by buying existing electronic trading platforms, notably Electronic Broking Services (EBS), owned

[43] Broderick and Cox, 'The Foreign Exchange and Over-the-Counter Interest Rate Derivatives Markets', 361.

[44] O. Storbeck and P. Stafford, 'Deutsche Börse in Talks to Acquire Refinitiv Foreign Exchange Assets', *Financial Times*, 12 April 2019.

[45] P. Stafford, 'Fears Over "Last Look" Spur Tighter FX Code', *Financial Times*, 20 December 2017.

by NEX, the renamed inter-dealer broker, ICAP. EBS had originally been launched by a consortium of banks in 1990 but later bought by ICAP. The other major foreign exchange platform was Matching, owned by the information provider Refinitiv, which had been Thomson Reuters. In 2012, Thomson Reuters had purchased FXall, which provided an electronic trading platform connecting the banks that dealt in foreign exchange with potential users from more than 2,300 asset managers and corporate treasurers. The CME bought NEX 2018, while the London Stock Exchange (LSE) bought Refinitiv in 2019, continuing to operate them as OTC platforms. The provision of electronic platforms for trading foreign exchange was an increasingly crowded field. When the Chicago-based Chicago Board Oprions Exchange (CBOE) launched a currency trading platform in 2020, it joined at least fifty others. Despite the competition, the platforms owned by the CME and the LSE continued to form the backbone of the electronic currency market, hosting trades between the largest dealers. All wanted to trade on the most liquid markets, and so those provided by the CME and LSE were favoured by the banks that continued to dominate the buying and selling of foreign exchange, either acting for themselves or their customers, which included the rest of the world's banks.[46]

The foreign exchange market remained an anomaly after 2008, having escaped regulatory intervention because of the trust placed in the megabanks, the measures taken

---

[46] See the following pieces from the *Financial Times*: J. Hughes, 'Concern Over Scope of Initiatives', 29 September 2009; J. Grant, 'First Steps Towards Clearing for FX', 6 October 2009; J. Grant, R. Milne and A. Van Duyn, 'Collateral Damage', 7 October 2009; J. Hughes, 'Worries Over Threat of "Heavy Touch"', 30 March 2010; G. Lambe, 'Settlement Model Aids FX Market Success', 12 April 2010; G. Lambe, 'FX Markets Ride Wave of Widening Appeal', 4 October 2010; J. Grant, 'Industry Pleads Its Case Against Rules Forged in Heat of Crisis', 29 March 2011; J. Hughes, 'So Where Do They Make Their Money?', 29 March 2011; D. Schäfer and D. Strauss, 'Moves into Forex Etrading Speed Up', 4 March 2014; D. Schäfer and S. Fleming, 'Scandal Puts City's Reputation on the Line', 6 March 2014; D. Schäfer and S. Fleming, 'Forex Probe Poised to Eclipse Libor Cases', 10 March 2014; D. Strauss, 'Five Big Banks Extend Their Domination of Forex Trading', 9 May 2014; D. Schäfer, 'Shrinking Margins and Higher Costs Drive Down Returns', 5 November 2014; R. Blitz and P. Stafford, 'BATS Plans to Open UK Forex Platform', 25 March 2015; M. Arnold, 'Barclays Admits Rigging the Market', 21 May 2015; K. Martin and P. Stafford, 'Banter Banned as Forex Traders Clean Up Act', 23 May 2015; P. Stafford, 'Exchanges Seek Slice of $5tn Forex Pie', 7 August 2015; P. Stafford, 'US Eyes Prize if Swaps Shift from London', 20 October 2016; J. Wild, 'Central Banks Eye Digital Money', 2 November 2016; M. Marriage, 'Scandalous Past Still Haunts Forex Industry', 12 December 2016; P. Stafford, 'Brexit Poses Threat to London's Role as Global Hub', 10 October 2017; P. Stafford, 'Fears Over "Last Look" Spur Tighter FX Code', 20 December 2017; K. Martin, 'Trading Data Show Tougher Rule Book Improves Banks' Forex Behaviour', 4 September 2018; E. Szalay, 'Yen Traders Wrongfooted as Flash Crash Strikes During Asia's Witching Hour', 4 January 2019; E. Szalay, 'London Charm Offensive Pays Off in Race for Renminbi', 9 February 2019; K. Martin, 'Swiss Franc Hit by Mini-Flash Crash during Asian Session', 12 February 2019; E. Szalay, 'Fears Over Forex Trading Going Bump in the Night', 6 March 2019; E. Szalay, 'Offshore Currency Trade Poses Challenge for India's Central Bank', 6 March 2019; O. Storbeck and P. Stafford, 'Deutsche Börse in Talks to Acquire Refinitiv Foreign Exchange Assets', 12 April 2019; E. Szalay and P. Stafford, 'Citigroup Calls for Burden of Managing Risky Trades to be Shared More Widely', 17 April 2019; E. Szalay, 'Asset Managers Scramble to Cut Banks Out of Forex Dealing', 18 April 2019; E. Szalay and R. Toplensky, 'Banks Look for Closure in EU Benchmark Probe', 11 May 2019; E. Szalay, 'Banks Resist Demand to Shed More Daylight on Forex Charges', 16 May 2019; P. Stafford, 'Singapore Exchange Plans to Tighten Grip as Asia's Largest Forex Trading Hub', 11 June 2019; E. Szalay, 'UK Watchdog Lends Teeth to Currency Trading Code', 28 June 2019; E. Szalay and J. Croft, 'Five Banks Face Forex-Rigging Lawsuits in London', 30 July 2019; P. Stafford and E. Szalay, 'London Pulls Away from New York in Forex and Swaps as It Shrugs Off Brexit', 17 September 2019; E. Szalay, 'Jump in London Rupee Trades Rings Alarms', 18 September 2019.

by participants to reduce risks, and the global nature of foreign exchange trading. In the words of Eva Szalay in 2020,

> Spot foreign exchange markets have never been directly regulated because currencies trade 24 hours a day around the world, with more dollars traded in London than in the US. Unlike equity markets, cash currency trading is privately negotiated among a mix of international participants. Deals are settled instantly and central banks are also active in the market. ... Following the global currency-rigging scandal that led to $12bn in fines, major central banks endorsed a set of voluntary standards that sit within a broader and sanctionable regulatory framework, the Global Code of Conduct, rather than push for more detailed and specific regulation in the field.[47]

The foreign exchange market had developed its own mechanisms for coping with the risks being run by participants, such as the CLS bank, thus setting itself apart from other financial markets that made much greater use of exchanges and clearing houses. Nevertheless, by 2020, cracks were appearing in the resilience of this self-regulated structure. This was apparent in the falling share of turnover that used CLS. It had been set up in 2002 to act as a middleman in trades, authenticating and matching instructions to ensure that correct payments were made. The system came through a big test in the Global Financial Crisis, helping to safeguard the smooth functioning of the foreign exchange market. However, by 2020, CLS only handled one-third of the deals that were eligible for settlement. CLS did not handle trading in the renminbi and rouble, for example, as well as a host of other currencies. Instead, it confined itself to the trades carried out in the major international currencies, especially the US$, and by the megabanks, particularly those from the USA. This left part of the foreign exchange market unprotected in the case of defaults by counterparties, which was of growing concern to the BIS. In addition to the barriers to entry operated by CLS, many participants in the foreign exchange market did not use its service because they relied on their counterparties. As these counterparties were mainly the world's megabanks, especially those from the USA, it was considered a sufficient guarantee. By 2021, Citigroup and Standard Chartered had made bilateral arrangements and they were followed by HSBC and Wells Fargo. A number of megabanks had launched their own electronic foreign exchange platforms to cater for trading with their customers and these were being extended to include other major banks, leading to a degree of fragmentation, but not enough to disrupt its operation. Similarly, though programmes such as quantitative easing dampened exchange-rate volatility, and thus turnover, events like the pandemic of 2020 or the Russian invasion of Ukraine in 2022 increased it, stimulating trading. On a net–gross basis, turnover in the global foreign exchange market rose from $8.3 trillion a day in 2019 to $9.8 trillion in 2022.[48]

---

[47] E. Szalay, 'Dispute Brews between EU and Currency Traders on Mifid Reform', *Financial Times*, 1 December 2020.

[48] See the following pieces from the *Financial Times*: E. Szalay, 'Fears Over Forex Trading Going Bump in the Night', 6 March 2019; O. Storbeck and P. Stafford, 'Deutsche Börse in Talks to Acquire Refinitiv

By the beginning of the twenty-first century, the foreign exchange market had become a permanent feature of the global financial system. Turnover had risen from $1.1 trillion a day in 1992 to $98 trillion a day thirty years later in 2022, and it had maintained its position as the largest market in the world by volume, however measured. The centre of the market was London, where the world's banks clustered as they had in the past. That was almost the only element of continuity about the foreign exchange market as virtually all else had changed over time ranging from the relative importance of the participants, the currencies being traded, the means of communication, the technology used, and the strategies employed. The degree of change continued apace as, for example, the traditional distinction between interbank trading and that conducted between banks and their customers was becoming blurred with the increasing importance of hedge funds and high-frequency traders. Nevertheless, the foreign exchange dealers working at major banks had long been central intermediaries. They played the role of liquidity suppliers within their own bank, to dealers in other banks, and to counterparties such as multinational companies, fund managers, and high-frequency traders. Through the use of spot transactions, swap arrangements, and forward contracts, they were able to cover currency exposure as well as engage in borrowing and lending operations to cover a temporary deficit or engage in a profitable carry trade with little or no risk. Though done in the interests of the banks that employed them, this foreign exchange trading contributed to the combination of short-term currency stability and long-run stability required in the complex and integrated global economy of the twenty-first century in the same way as it had in the past, though it was either unrecognized under the Gold Standard or dismissed as speculation between the wars and on occasions since the Second World War.[49]

Foreign Exchange Assets', 12 April 2019; E. Szalay, 'Banks Resist Demand to Shed More Daylight on Forex Charges', 16 May 2019; P. Stafford, 'Singapore Exchange Plans to Tighten Grip as Asia's Largest Forex Trading Hub', 11 June 2019; E. Szalay, 'UK Watchdog Lends Teeth to Currency Trading Code', 28 June 2019; FT Reporters, 'LSE in Talks on $20bn Refinitiv Link-Up with Scale to Rival Bloomberg Empire', 27 July 2019; E. Szalay and J. Croft, 'Five Banks Face Forex-Rigging Lawsuits in London', 30 July 2019; J. Rennison and P. Stafford, 'Rise of MarketAxess Mirrors Demise of Traders on Wall Street', 30 August 2019; P. Stafford and E. Szalay, 'London Pulls Away from New York in Forex and Swaps as It Shrugs Off Brexit', 17 September 2019; E. Szalay, 'Jump in London Rupee Trades Rings Alarms', 18 September 2019; E. Szalay, 'Peer-to-Peer Forex Services Aim to Bypass Wall St Banks', 16 October 2019; E. Szalay, 'Ultra Low Interest Rates Spur Euro to Become World's New Carry Trade', 6 December 2019; E. Szalay, 'Languid Forex Trading Due a Wake-Up Call', 2 January 2020; E. Szalay, 'India Seeks to Lure Rupee Trading Back Onshore', 22 January 2020; E. Szalay, 'CBOE to Challenge CME and Refinitiv with New FX Platform', 25 June 2020; E. Szalay, 'Risks of Failure in $6.6tn Forex Market at Record High', 24 July 2020; P. Stafford, 'TP Icap to Buy Trading Venue Liquidnet for up to $700m', 9 October 2020; E. Szalay, 'Foreign Exchange Data Wars Heat Up as Rivals Take on Big Two', 1 December 2020; E. Szalay, 'Dispute Brews between EU and Currency Traders on Mifid Reform', 1 December 2020; E. Szalay and P. Stafford, 'HSBC and Wells Fargo to Settle Currency Trades with Blockchain', 13 December 2021; R. Wigglesworth, 'Mysterious $11bn Swiss Swapsies', 21 October 2022; N. Asgari, 'London's Hold on Global Currency Market Weakens, BIS Survey Shows', 28 October 2022; A. Faglia, 'The Rise and Rise of Currency Hedging Raises a Financial System Risk', 3 November 2022; N. Asgari, K. Wiggins and R. Waters, 'Why has Big Tech Fallen in Love with Exchanges?', 16 December 2022.

[49] Bank for International Settlements, *Triennial Central Bank Survey* (2022); Bank of England, *BIS Triennial Survey* (2022); Osler, 'Market Microstructure'; Schrimpf and Sushko, 'Sizing Up Global Foreign Exchange Markets'; Schrimpf and Sushko, 'FX Trade Execution', *BIS Quarterly Review*, (December 2019); Evans and Rime, 'Microstructure'; Goodacre and Razak, 'Foreign Exchange'; Nordstrom, *Understanding the Foreign Exchange Market*.

Conclusion

What the foreign exchange market delivered throughout the period between 2007 and 2022 was a mechanism through which banks could receive and make payments across all the different currencies of the world. It also allowed banks to continually adjust their present and future exposure to risks posed by currency volatility. In turn the foreign exchange market created opportunities for banks and others to generate profits both on their own account and through the services they provided to others such as multinational companies, global fund managers, and any who were exposed to currency risks. Central banks, both individually and collectively, were aware of the vital role played by the foreign exchange market in both facilitating international financial flows and maintaining equilibrium. For that reason, those banks that dominated the foreign exchange market were acknowledged as the most systemically important in the world, and so able to look to central banks for support in a crisis and also subjected to careful monitoring. In contrast, regulators were more aware of the risks being run by those banks and so were keen to limit their exposure and subject the foreign exchange market to greater control. As it was, the central banks won the day, and the foreign exchange market was not subjected to the regulations imposed on the other activities of the global banks or the operation of other financial markets. The foreign exchange market was a firmly established element of the global financial system and was largely left to develop according to its own requirements between 2007 and 2022. This was despite events such as the Global Financial Crisis of 2008, the massive quantitative easing programmes carried out by central banks in the years that followed, the global pandemic of 2020, and a major threat to world peace in 2022 with Russia's invasion of Ukraine. There was no attempt by governments to either depart from a reliance on the foreign exchange market to set exchange rates or interfere in its working. The foreign exchange market even transcended an internal scandal in which the manipulation of rates by dealers was exposed.

Conclusion

By the twenty-first century, it was generally accepted that flexible exchange rates provided an essential adjustment mechanism within an integrated global economy. Their use avoided exposure to monetary crises, because of a divergence of domestic and international prices, and removed the need to make fundamental internal adjustments in order to restore equilibrium. Conversely, fixed exchange rates made it easier to control inflation and increased the degree of integration with the global economy. However, any attempt to maintain a fixed exchange rate, without a willingness to make and accept fundamental economic adjustments, was doomed to failure. What was also accepted by the twenty-first century was that a successful flexible exchange rate required a currency market that was liquid, efficient, and responsive to market forces. Without such a market, foreign exchange rates were exposed to excessive volatility on a recurring basis. This market had to have both a wholesale and retail element. In the wholesale market, the principal dealers in currency traded with each other both spot and forward, while in the retail market, they traded with final users. Actions taken by governments and central banks could make this market shallow and inefficient, which encouraged further intervention with the same consequences. Unless given the freedom to operate and develop, the market could not deliver exchange rate stability, leading to a continued reliance on a combination of government and central bank intervention. However, creating this market, and accepting the role that it played, was a complicated and prolonged process, partly because the necessity for its existence was disputed by those who associated currency stability with fixed rates of exchange rather than a mechanism that allowed constant adjustments to be made.[1]

It is only by placing foreign exchange within the context of market creation and evolution over the last 150 years that it can be fully understood. What was needed was a mechanism that allowed exchange rates to be adjusted on an immediate and continuous basis if stability was to be maintained. Under the Gold Standard, this stability was attributed to the fixed price of gold in terms of national currencies, the free movement of that metal between countries, and the influence supplies had upon money supply in individual countries. However, abundant evidence existed to prove that

---

[1] See R. Duttagupta, G. Fernandez and C. Karacadag, 'Moving to a Flexible Exchange Rate: How, When and How Fast?', *International Monetary Fund, Economic Issues*, 38 (2005), 1–25; A.R. Ghosh and J.D. Ostry, 'Choosing an Exchange Rate Regime', *Finance and Development*, 46 (2009), 38–40; E. Elzetzki, C. Teinhart and K. Rogoff, 'Exchange Arrangements Entering the Twenty-First Century: Which Anchor will Hold?', *Quarterly Journal of Economics*, 124 (2019), 599–646; B. Hofman, A. Mehrata and D. Sandri, 'Global Exchange Rate Adjustments: Drivers, Impacts and Policy Implications', *BIS Bulletin*, 62 (2022), 1–8.

Forex Forever. Ranald C. Michie, Oxford University Press. © Ranald C. Michie (2024).
DOI: 10.1093/oso/9780198903697.003.0008

the movement and use of gold was insufficient to achieve that end. Increasingly, gold was supplemented with movement of stocks and bonds between countries, and the links this had to the money market. Important as were these global financial flows, they were not sufficient to provide the constant stability of exchange rates associated with the Gold Standard. That required a market in which currencies could be exchanged for each other quickly and on a continuous basis.[2] As no such market appeared to exist in London, where it would most logically be found under the Gold Standard, it was assumed not to be required. London was the most important financial centre in the world before 1914, possessed of the broadest and deepest money market and the most international connections. Nevertheless, that market did exist but in two locations in London, which hid it from view. One was the trading in internationally held stocks and bonds that took place on the floor of the London Stock Exchange and other stock exchanges located around the world. The other was to be found within banks and the web of connections they maintained around the world through branches and correspondent links. Both the trading in securities and the interbank foreign exchange market were made possible by the revolution in global communications and the emergence of banking companies that took place between 1850 and 1914. With these missing links in place, it was possible to piece together the existence of an increasingly active and sophisticated foreign exchange market in London before the First World War.

That foreign exchange market was then largely suspended during the First World War and had to be rebuilt and refashioned in the years that followed, though it remained located in London. This new foreign exchange market was highly visible as it included groups of dealers and brokers, working for or with banks, who traded currencies at rates that fluctuated widely. This made the foreign exchange market resemble a casino, attracting widespread criticism and a desire to return to the Gold Standard, and the stability it had apparently delivered unaided. That impression of the foreign exchange market as a speculator's paradise, and a determination to restore fixed exchange rates, remained throughout the interwar years. This was despite the return to the Gold Standard proving a disaster and foreign exchange trading settling down into a self-regulated routine that delivered an orderly market that was relied upon by banks. The nostalgia for the past existed because of the belief that it was the Gold Standard that had delivered the monetary and financial stability of the pre-First World War era, not the general commitment of national governments to open and flexible markets, including that for foreign exchange. Confident in the stability of exchange rates, funds could flow around the world seeking the best returns, to the benefit of savers, investors, and borrowers worldwide. The failure to fully restore the Gold Standard was held responsible for the volatile exchange rates and monetary instability that undermined international trade and destroyed national economies between the wars.

---

[2] I took a long time to recognize this. See the following publications: Michie, 'Myth of the Gold Standard'; Michie, 'Nineteenth-Century International Gold Standard'; Michie, 'Invisible Stabiliser'; Michie, 'The City of London as a Global Financial Centre'.

The only alternative to the Gold Standard was seen to be government intervention, as took place in many countries in the 1930s. During the Second World War, the foreign exchange market in London was closed down. When hostilities ended in 1945, the decision had already been taken to introduce a managed currency that delivered the fixed exchange rates of the Gold Standard and the control that came with central bank intervention. Despite the controls and interventions of governments and central banks, a foreign exchange market gradually revived in the 1950s and 1960s being required by banks to protect themselves from the currency risks they were exposed to, either on behalf of their customers or their own interbank operations. Restrictions in the UK led to this market developing more rapidly elsewhere than London in the 1950s, but, once these were relaxed, it quickly returned. Even though New York was now the most important financial centre in the world, London retained its appeal to banks because that was where so many were already clustered, where the international connections were best, and where they could operate with minimal government controls.

After 1970, the trading of foreign exchange developed into the largest market in the world with a turnover exceeding many trillion dollars per day. This market was centred in the City of London where over one-third by value of all trading took place, despite most transactions being in US$s and handled by US banks. Despite the revolution in global communications and processing capacity from the 1970s, also required was for participants to be in immediate contact with each other so as to eliminate any delay in completing a deal in fast moving markets. Only a few of the world's financial centres could provide that combination and London already hosted more of the world's banks than any other and provided them with the facilities, markets, and environment that they wanted.

After 1970, the global financial system experienced a revolution. Out went the controls and compartmentalization that had characterized the early post-war years and in came markets and global banks. Accompanying the revolution was a transformation of communications and computing. Though there was a rapid rise in international connectivity, the effect was not a dispersal of financial activity from London but a clustering of trading there, especially in the foreign exchange market. This market had to cope with the growing scale, scope, and reach of banks, the disappearance of national boundaries as parameters for financial activity, and the increased volatility of prices, interest rates, and exchange rates. The result was to make the foreign exchange market the largest market in the world. With exchange rates no longer fixed, the world entered a period of currency instability. This drove up turnover in the foreign exchange market as banks sought to cover the currency risks they were exposed to, profit from the opportunities that price volatility provided, or use the facility it provided to borrow at low rates of interest and lend out at higher ones internationally. The foreign exchange market became a permanent feature of the global financial system.

This new foreign exchange market was also one increasingly dominated by a small number of very large banks with extensive international connections. The volume of trading and the speed of transaction made trust in counterparties vital. These banks located their principal foreign exchange trading desks in London, which was the hub of the global market. As well as direct dealing between these banks, there were a small group of inter-dealer brokers that developed after 1970. These inter-dealer brokers built up close contacts with banks and established an international network that linked the world's financial centres into a continuous market. This market was located in and between the offices of the banks and the inter-dealer brokers through the use of the telephone, with screens displaying current exchange rates that were constantly updated by companies that specialized in the supply of financial information. What these megabanks and inter-dealer brokers had done was tap into the simultaneous phenomena of the dematerialization of trading, the globalization of the market, and the use of the US$ as the world currency, making the City of London its global hub. The next development from the 1990s was that of electronic markets through which foreign exchange was trading. In these electronic markets, sales and purchase were automatically matched and priced by computer according to preset programmes. The result was to dramatically increase capacity, reduce the time taken to complete a transaction, and greatly lower the cost involved. This further increased clustering of foreign exchange trading in London as that was where banks concentrated their investment in the equipment required. This increasingly electronic trading of foreign exchange was a largely self-regulated one as it was the participating banks that took responsibility for eliminating counterparty risk and delivering an orderly market. This market then proved resilient during the Global Financial Crisis of 2008, the subsequent revelations in 2014 of price manipulation, the pandemic of 2020, and the international tension caused by the Russian invasion of Ukraine in 2022. Each of these events destabilized other markets but not that for foreign exchange.

What the foreign exchange market delivered throughout the period after 1970 was an increasingly robust mechanism through which banks could receive and make payments across all the different currencies of the world, to continually adjust their present and future exposure to risks posed by currency volatility, and to borrow and employ funds instantly and remuneratively when required. Central banks, both individually and collectively, recognized the vital role played by the foreign exchange market in both facilitating international financial flows and maintaining equilibrium. Those banks that dominated the foreign exchange market were acknowledged as the most systemically important in the world, and so able to look to central banks for support in a crisis and also subjected to careful monitoring. The foreign exchange market was a firmly established element of the global financial system and was largely left to develop according to its own requirements. Though governments and central banks could not refrain from intervening in the setting of exchange rates, there was no attempt to return to either some form of the Gold Standard or the internationally managed currency regime in place between 1950 and 1970 unless accompanied by some form of currency union that imposed discipline on all participants. There was no belief that linking the value of currency to the fixed price of a metal such as gold would produce stable exchange rates by itself. That had been tried between the wars and shown to be a failure. Similarly, there was no conviction that governments would abide by internationally agreed rules that would maintain fixed exchange rates unless accompanied by sanctions that could be enforced. That had been tried after the Second World War and was found wanting. There was also no willingness to invest supranational agencies such as the Bank for International Settlements or the International Monetary Fund with additional powers as that would undermine the sovereignty of national governments. The individual states of the USA resisted the centralization of financial authority with the Federal Reserve Bank in Washington while the members of European Union were unwilling to place too much power in the hands of the European Central Bank in Frankfurt. Under the circumstances, the existence and operation of a foreign exchange market appeared the best and only option available, as it had been since the mid-nineteenth century. Throughout that time, that market was located in London apart from a brief interval in the 1940s and 1950s.

Bibliography

'Foreign Banks in London', *The Banker*, 119 (October 1969).

'Fourth Report of Committee on Economic Information: Survey of the Economic Situation in July 1932', in S. Howson and D. Winch (eds), *The Economic Advisory Council, 1930–1939: A Study in Economic Advice during Depression and Recovery* (Cambridge: Cambridge University Press, 1977).

'New York: A Center of World Finance', *New York University Institute of International Finance Bulletin*, 147 (30 December 1946).

'Questions on Points of Practical Interest', *JIB*, 27 (1907).

'The Changing Character of the London Foreign Exchange Market', *Bankers Magazine*, July 1938.

'The End of on "Change"', *The Times*, 24 December 1920.

'The Other Man's Job: Chief Foreign Branch', *The Spread Eagle*, xxv (August 1950), xxv (September 1950), xxv (October 1950).

Accominotti, O. and Chambers, D., 'If You're So Smart: John Maynard Keynes and Currency Speculation in the Inter-war Years', *Journal of Economic History*, 76 (2016).

Accominotti, O., Cen, J., Chambers, D. and Marsh, I.W., 'Currency Regimes and the Carry Trade', *Journal of Financial and Quantitative Analysis*, 54 (2019).

Accominotti, O., Lucena-Piquero, D. and Ugolini, S., 'The Origination and Distribution of Money Market Instruments: Sterling Bills of Exchange during the First Globalisation', *Economic History Review*, 74 (2021).

Adams, R., 'An Artificial and Antiquated Straightjacket', *Financial Times*, 5 December 1996.

Adams, R., 'Brokers Alter Shape of Things to Come', *Financial Times*, 25 June 1999.

Adams, R., 'Voice-brokers are Lapsing into Silence', *Financial Times*, 18 April 1997.

Agnew, H. and Cumbo, J., 'Amundi Warns on Hidden Leverage in the Financial System', *Financial Times*, 25 October 2022.

Ahvenainen, J., 'Telegraphy, Trade and Policy: The Role of the International Telegraphs in the Years 1870–1914', in W. Fischer, R.M. McInnis and J. Schneider (eds), *The Emergence of a World Economy* (Bamberg, 1986).

Ali, O., 'Dublin is Top Destination for Financial Groups Post-Brexit', *Financial Times*, 9 May 2017.

Allen, G.C. and Donnithorne, A.G., *Western Enterprise in Far Eastern Economic Development: China and Japan* (London: 1954).

Allen, H. and Hawkins, J., 'Electronic Trading in Wholesale Financial Markets: Its Wider Implications', *Bank of England Quarterly Bulletin*, 42 (2002).

Ally, R., *Gold and Empire: The Bank of England and South Africa's Gold Producers, 1886–1926* (Johannesburg: 1994).

Amphlett, G.T., *History of the Standard Bank of South Africa, Ltd, 1862–1913* (Glasgow: 1914).

Anderson, B.M., *The Value of Money* (New York: 1917).

Andreades, A., *History of the Bank of England* (London: 1909).

Andrews, J., 'Trading Likely to Rise by a Quarter This Year', *Financial Times*, 15 July 1988.

Angas, L.L.B., *The Problems of the Foreign Exchanges* (London: 1935).

Anson, M. and Gourvish, T., *Leopold Joseph: A History, 1919–2000* (London: 2002).

Armstrong, C., *Blue Skies and Boiler Rooms: Buying and Selling Securities in Canada, 1870–1940* (Toronto: 1997).

Armstrong, F.E., *The Book of the Stock Exchange* (London: 1934).

Armstrong, J., 'Hooley and the Bovril Company', *Business History*, 28 (1986).

Arnold, M., 'Barclays Admits Rigging the Market', *Financial Times*, 21 May 2015.

Asgari, N., 'London's Hold on Global Currency Market Weakens, BIS Survey Shows', *Financial Times*, 28 October 2022.

Asgari, N., Wiggins, K. and Waters, R., 'Why has Big Tech Fallen in Love with Exchanges?', *Financial Times*, 16 December 2022.

Atkin, J., *The Foreign Exchange Market of London: Development since 1900* (London: 2005).

Atkin, J.M., *British Overseas Investment, 1918–1931* (New York: 1977).

Atkins, R., 'A Sterling Drama at the Money Theatre', *Financial Times*, 15 July 1988

Atkins, R., 'More Join the Risk Business', *Financial Times*, 15 July 1988

Attard, B., 'The Bank of England and the Origins of the Niemeyer Mission 1921–1930', *Australian Economic History Review*, 32 (1992)

Attfield, J.B., 'The Advantages, or Otherwise, of the Establishment of Branches by Bankers, from the Point of View (a) of the Bankers, and (b) of the General Interests of the Community', *JIB*, 13 (1892).

Authers, J., 'London Blows Its Trumpet Too Loudly', *Financial Times*, 19 November 2007

Bagchi, A.K., *The Evolution of the State Bank of India*, vol. 1: *The Roots, 1806–1876* (Bombay: 1987)

Bagchi, A.K., *The Evolution of the State Bank of India*, vol. 2: *The Era of the Presidency Banks, 1876–1920* (New Delhi: 1997)

Bagehot, W., *Lombard Street: a description of the money market* (London: 1873)

Bailey, A., 'The Challenges in Assessing Capital Requirements for Banks', Financial Policy Committee, 6 November 2012.

Ball, M. and Sunderland, D., *Economic History of London* (London and New York: Routledge, 2001)

Balogh, T., *Studies in Financial Organization* (Cambridge: Cambridge University Press, 1947)

Baltzer, M., 'Cross-listed Stocks as an Information Vehicle of Speculation: Evidence from European cross-listings in the early 1870s', *European Review of Economic History*, (2006)

Bank for International Settlements, *Guide to the International Locational Banking Statistics, Monetary and Economic Department* (BIS, 2011)

Bank for International Settlements, *Triennial Central Bank Survey of Foreign Exchange and Over-The Counter Derivative Markets in 2022* (Basel: BIS, 2022)

Bank for International Settlements, *Triennial Central Bank Survey of Foreign Exchange and Derivatives Market Activity* (September 2019)

Bank of England Notice: Commission on Foreign Exchange Transactions, Bank of England, 1939

Bank of England Quarterly Bulletin Statistical Supplement (1960–1989)

Bank of England, 'Bank Liquidity in the United Kingdom', *Bank of England Quarterly Bulletin*, 2 (1962)

Bank of England, 'Central Bank Independence', *Bank of England Quarterly Bulletin*, 40 (2000)

Bank of England, 'Commercial Bills', *Bank of England Quarterly Bulletin*, 1 (1960–1)

Bank of England, 'Developments in UK Banking and Monetary Statistics Since the Radcliffe Report', *Bank of England Quarterly Bulletin*, 25 (1985).

Bank of England, 'Eurobanks and the Inter-bank Market', *Bank of England Quarterly I cannoBulletin*, 21 (1981).

Bank of England, 'Foreign Banks in London', *Bank of England Quarterly Bulletin*, 26 (1986).

Bank of England, 'Inflows and Outflows of Foreign Funds', *Bank of England Quarterly Bulletin*, 2 (1962).

Bank of England, 'Japanese Banks in London', *Bank of England Quarterly Bulletin*, 27 (1987).

Bank of England, 'London as an International Financial Centre', *Bank of England Quarterly Review*, 29 (1989).

Bank of England, 'Major International Banks' Performance, 1980–1991', *Bank of England Quarterly Bulletin*, 32 (1992).

Bank of England, 'New Banking Statistics', *Bank of England Quarterly Bulletin*, 15 (1975).

Bank of England, 'Overseas and Foreign Banks in London', *Bank of England Quarterly Bulletin*, 8 (1968).

Bank of England, 'Overseas Balances 1963–1973', *Bank of England Quarterly Bulletin*, 14 (1974).

Bank of England, 'Reform of the Bank of England's Operations in the Sterling Money Markets: A Consultative Paper by the Bank of England', *Bank of England Quarterly Bulletin*, 44 (2004).

Bank of England, 'Reserve Ratios: Further Definitions', *Bank of England Quarterly Bulletin*, 11 (1971).

Bank of England, 'Risk Measurement and Capital Requirements for Banks', *Bank of England Quarterly Bulletin*, 35 (1995).

Bank of England, 'Risk, Cost and Liquidity in Alternative Payment Systems', *Bank of England Quarterly Bulletin*, 39 (1999).

Bank of England, 'Sterling Wholesale Markets: Developments in 1998', *Bank of England Quarterly Bulletin*, 39 (1999).

Bank of England, 'The Bank of England Act', *Bank of England Quarterly Bulletin*, 38 (1998).

Bank of England, 'The Bank of England's Operations in the Sterling Money Markets', *Bank of England Quarterly Bulletin*, 37 (1997).

Bank of England, 'The Bank of England's Operations in the Sterling Money Markets', *Bank of England Quarterly Bulletin*, 42 (2002).

Bank of England, 'The Bank's Contacts with the Money, Repo and Stock Lending Markets', *Bank of England Quarterly Bulletin*, 41 (2001).

Bank of England, 'The Commodity Futures Market', *Bank of England Quarterly Bulletin*, 26 (1986).

Bank of England, 'The Eurocurrency Business of Banks in London', *Bank of England Quarterly Bulletin*, 10 (1970).

Bank of England, 'The Exchange Equalisation Account: Its Origins and Development', *Bank of England Quarterly Bulletin*, 8 (1968).

Bank of England, 'The Foreign Exchange and Over-the-Counter Derivatives Markets in the United Kingdom', *Bank of England Quarterly Bulletin*, 38 (1998).

Bank of England, 'The Foreign Exchange Market in London', *Bank of England Quarterly Bulletin*, 32 (1992).

Bank of England, 'The Foreign Exchange Market in London', *Bank of England Quarterly Bulletin*, 35 (1995).

Bank of England, 'The Foreign Exchange Market in London', *Bank of England Quarterly Bulletin*, 20 (1980).

Bank of England, 'The Governor's Speech at the Mansion House', *Bank of England Quarterly Bulletin*, 46 (2006).

Bank of England, 'The International Bond Market', *Bank of England Quarterly Bulletin*, 31 (1991).

Bank of England, 'The London Discount Market: Some Historical Notes', *Bank of England Quarterly Bulletin*, 7 (1967).

Bank of England, 'The London Dollar Certificate of Deposit', *Bank of England Quarterly Bulletin*, 13 (1973).

Bank of England, 'The London Gold Market', *Bank of England Quarterly Bulletin*, 4 (1964).

Bank of England, 'The Market for Foreign Exchange in London', *Bank of England Quarterly Bulletin*, 26 (1986).

Bank of England, 'The Overseas and Foreign Banks in London', *Bank of England Quarterly Bulletin*, 1 (1961).

Bank of England, 'The Over-the-Counter Derivatives Market in the United Kingdom', *Bank of England Quarterly Bulletin*, 36 (1996).

Bank of England, 'The Performance of Major British Banks, 1970–90', *Bank of England Quarterly Bulletin*, 31 (1991).

Bank of England, 'The Role of Brokers in the London Money Markets', *Bank of England Quarterly Bulletin*, 30 (1990).

Bank of England, 'The Secondary Banking Crisis and the Bank of England's Support Operations', *Bank of England Quarterly Bulletin*, 18 (1978).

Bank of England, 'The UK and US Treasury Bill Market', *Bank of England Quarterly Bulletin*, 5 (1965).

Bank of England, 'The UK Exchange Control: A Short History', *Bank of England Quarterly Bulletin*, 1 September 1967.

Bank of England, 'UK Banks' External Liabilities and Claims in Foreign Currencies', *Bank of England Quarterly Bulletin*, 4 (1964).

Bank of England, 'UK Commodity Markets', *Bank of England Quarterly Bulletin*, 15 (1975).

Bank of England, 'UK Commodity Markets', *Bank of England Quarterly Bulletin*, 4 (1964).

Bank of England, *Approximate Amounts of Foreign Currency Changing Hands on the London Market Daily*, 28 January 1928.

Bank of England, *BIS Triennial Survey of Foreign Exchange and Over-the-Counter Interest Rate Derivatives Markets in April 2022*, UK Data Results Summary, 27 October 2022.

Bank of England, *London Foreign Exchange Market*, 1 May 1928, Addendum, 17 May 1928.

Bank of England, *Restrictions on Dealing in Foreign Exchange*, 28 March 1930.

Bank of England, *Some Aspects of Forward Exchange in Relation to Control*, September 1937.

Banking Almanac: List of Foreign and Colonial Banks with Offices/Agents in London: 1860, 1880, 1890, 1900, 1913.

Barclay & Co., *Report of the Annual General Meeting*, 24 January 1917.

Barclays Bank, *A Bank in Battledress: Barclays Bank (DCO) during the Second World War, 1939–45* (1948).

Barclays Bank, *Foreign Exchange Control: A Brief Survey of Its Theory and Application*: Memorandum by Barclays Bank to Its Staff (1947).

Barclays Bank, *Handbook on Foreign Business* (1940).

Bareau, P., 'The Financial Institutions of the City of London', in *The City of London as a Centre of International Trade and Finance* (London: Institute of Bankers, 1961).

Bareau, P., 'The International Money and Capital Markets', in E.V. Morgan, R.A. Brealey, B.S. Yamey and G.P. Bareau (eds), *City Lights: Essays on Financial Institutions and Markets in the City of London* (London: Institute of Economic Affairs, 1979).

Bareau, P., 'The London Gold and Silver Markets', in T. Balogh (ed.), *Studies in Financial Organization* (Cambridge: Cambridge University Press, 1947).

Barnes, H., 'Drift of Trade to London Causes Concern', *Financial Times*, 7 April 1994.

Barnett, D., *London, Hub of the Industrial Revolution: A Revisionary History, 1775–1825* (London: I.B. Tauris, 1998).

Barnett, R.W., 'The History of the Progress and Development of Banking in the United Kingdom from the Year 1800 to the Present Time', *JIB*, 1 (1880).

Barret Whale, P., 'English and Continental Banking', *JIB*, 52 (1931).

Barret Whale, P., *Joint Stock Banking in Germany* (London: 1930).

Bartolini, L. and Bodnar, G.M., 'Are Exchange Rates Excessively Volatile? And What Does Excessively Volatile Mean Anyway?', *IMF Staff Papers*, 43 (1996).

Barty-King, H., *Girdle Round the Earth: The Story of Cable and Wireless and Its Predecessors* (London: 1979).

Baster, A.S.J., *The International Banks* (London: 1935).

Batchelor, C., 'EuroMTS Launches European T-Bill Platform', *Financial Times*, 16 March 2004.

Batchelor, C., 'London Leads in Trading Volumes', *Financial Times*, 23 September 2004.

Batchelor, C., 'Long Pedigree of the Clearing House for Short-Term Funds', *Financial Times*, 23 July 2004.

Batchelor, C., 'Wider Range of Contracts Urged', *Financial Times*, 14 February 1984.

Batiz-Laso, B. and Boyns, T., 'The Business and Financial History of Mechanization and Technological Change in Twentieth Century Banking', *Accounting, Business and Financial History*, 14 (2004).

Battilossi, S., 'Financial Innovation and the Golden Ages of International Banking: 1890–1931 and 1958–81', *Financial History Review*, 7 (2000).

Battilosssi, S. and Cassis, Y. (eds), *European Banks and the American Challenge: European Banking under Bretton Woods* (Oxford: 2002).

Bauer, H., *Swiss Bank Corporation 1872–1972* (Basel: 1972).

Beattie, A., '"Barrow Boys" at Risk as the Currency Markets Switch On', *Financial Times*, 6 July 1999.

Beattie, A., 'Fighting Spirit Seeps into Dried-Up Markets', *Financial Times*, 25 June 1999.

Beattie, A., 'Floor Presence Thins Out', *Financial Times*, 25 June 1999.

Beattie, A., 'Tullett and Bloomberg Plan New Broking System', *Financial Times*, 5 July 1999.

Beavan, A.H., *Imperial London* (London: 1901).

Bell, S. and Kettell, B., *Foreign Exchange Handbook* (London: 1983).

Benoit, B., 'Long-Held Dream has Proved to be Unrealistic', *Financial Times*, 10 June 2003.

Bernstein, E.M., 'The Search for Exchange Rate Stability: Before and after Bretton Woods', in O.F. Hamauda, R. Rowley and B.M. Wolf (eds), *The Future of the International Monetary System* (New York: 1989).

Billings, M. and Capie, F., 'Financial Crisis, Contagion and the British Banking System between the World Wars', *Business History*, 53 (2011).

Binham, C. and Jenkins, P., 'Bailey Signals Need for Brexit Talks Focus on Financial Services', *Financial Times*, 8 May 2019.

Binham, C., 'Shadow Banking Sector Shifts into Decline', *Financial Times*, 20 January 2020.

Blainey, G. and Hutton, G., *Gold and Paper, 1858–1982: A History of the National Bank of Australia Ltd* (Melbourne: 1983).

Blitz, J., 'A Top-Hat Tradition in the Balance', *Financial Times*, 22 June 1992.

Blitz, J., 'All Change in Foreign Exchanges', *Financial Times*, 2 April 1993.

Blitz, J., 'ERM Crisis Quicken Activity', *Financial Times*, 20 October 1993.

Blitz, J., 'Foreign Exchange Dealers Enter the 21st Century', *Financial Times*, 13 September 1993.

Blitz, J., 'Forex Dealers Can Buy Time', *Financial Times*, 12 August 1992.

Blitz, J., 'New Anxieties for the Banks', *Financial Times*, 26 May 1993.

Blitz, R. and Stafford, P., 'BATS Plans to Open UK Forex Platform', *Financial Times*, 25 March 2015.

Bloomfield, A.I., 'Patterns of Fluctuation in International Investment before 1914', *Princeton Studies in International Finance*, 1968.

Bloomfield, A.I., 'Short-Term Capital Movements under the Pre-1914 Gold Standard', *Princeton Studies in International Finance*, 1963.

Bloomfield, A.I., 'The Significance of Outstanding Securities in the International Movement of Capital', *Canadian Journal of Economics and Political Science* (November 1940).

Bloomfield, A.I., *Monetary Policy under the International Gold Standard, 1880–1914* (Federal Reserve Bank of New York, 1959).

Bolton, Sir George, *London Foreign Exchange Market* (Bank of England, 7 August 1930).

Bolton, Sir George, *The Development of the Foreign Exchange Market* (Bank of England, 8 July 1936).

Bolton, Sir George, *Memoirs* (Bank of England, 13 January 1977).

Bonin, H., *Société Générale in the United Kingdom, 1871–1996* (Paris: 1996).

Bordo, M.D. and Sylla, R. (eds), *Anglo-American Financial System: Institutions and Markets in the Twentieth Century* (New York: 1995).

Bordo, M.D. and Eichengreen, B., *The Rise and Fall of a Barbarous Relic: The Role of Gold in the International Monetary System* (NBER, 1998).

Bordo, M.D., *Exchange Rate Regime Choice in Historical Perspective* (International Monetary Fund, 2003).

Bordo, M.D., Meissner, C.M. and Redish, A., *How Original Sin Was Overcome: The Evolution of External Debt Denominated in Domestic Currencies in the United States and the British Dominions, 1800–2000* (NBER: 2003)

Bordo, M.D. and Flandreau, M., 'Core, Periphery, Exchange Rate Regimes, and Globalization', in M.D. Bordo, A.M. Taylor and J.G. Williamson (eds), *Globalization in Historical Perspective* (Chicago: NBER, 2003).

Bordo, M.D. and Schwartz, A.J. (eds), *A Retrospective on the Classical Gold Standard, 1821–1931* (Chicago/London: 1984).

Bordo, M.D., Eichengreen, B. and Kim, J., *Was There Really an Earlier Period of International Financial Integration Comparable to Today?* NBER Working Paper 6738 (1998).

Bordo, M.D., Taylor, A.M. and Williamson, J.G. (eds), *Globalization in Historical Perspective* (Chicago, NBER, 2003).

Boreham, B.B., 'The London Information Market', *The Banker* (August 1945).

Bostock, F., 'The British Overseas Banks and Development Finance in Africa after 1945', in G. Jones (ed.), *Banks and Money: International and Comparative Finance in History* (London: Frank Cass, 1991).

Boughton, J. M., 'Northwest of Suez: The 1956 Crisis and the IMF', NBER Working Paper 00/192 (Washington: International Monetary Fund, 2000).

Boulton, L., 'Birth of a Hundred Markets', *Financial Times*, 23 February 1993.

Bowen, H.V., '"The Pests of Human Society": Stockbrokers, Jobbers and Speculators in Mid-Eighteenth Century Britain', *History*, 78 (1993).

Bowley, G., 'Forex Houses Sanguine Despite Possibility of Single Currency', *Financial Times*, 6 December 1996.

Bowley, G., 'Historic Day for Way Bank Goes to Work', *Financial Times*, 3 March 1997.

Braga de Macedo, J., Eichengreen, B. and Reis, J. (eds), *Currency Convertibility: The Gold Standard and Beyond* (London: 1996).

Breckenridge, R.M., *The Canadian Banking System, 1817–1890* (New York: 1895).

Brett, E., 'The History and Development of Banking in Australasia', *JIB*, 3 (1882).

Broadberry, S. and Howlett, P., 'The United Kingdom during World War 1: Business as Usual?', in S. Broadberry and M. Harrison (eds), *The Economics of World War 1* (Cambridge: 2005).

Broderick, T. and Cox, C., 'The Foreign Exchange and Over-the-Counter Interest Rate Derivatives Markets in the United Kingdom', *Bank of England Quarterly Bulletin*, 50 (2010).

Brooks, H.K., *Foreign Exchange Textbook* (Chicago: 1906).

Brown, B., *The Forward Market in Foreign Exchange: A Study in Market-Making, Arbitrage and Speculation* (London: 1983).

Brown, C., *A Hundred Years of Merchant Banking* (New York: Brown Brothers & Co., 1909).

Brown, J., 'Major Players in Their Own Right', *Financial Times*, 27 May 1986.

Brown, K., 'SGX to Offer OTC Derivatives Clearing', *Financial Times*, 21 September 2010.

Brown, W.A., *The International Gold Standard Reinterpreted, 1914–1934* (New York: National Bureau of Economic Research, 1940).

Buck, T. and Tett, G., 'Battle Heats Up Over Europe's Bond Markets', *Financial Times*, 30 November 2006.

Buckley, K., *Capital Formation in Canada, 1896–1930* (Toronto: 1955).

Burke, J., 'Tensions Beneath the Surface', *Financial Times*, 14 February 1984.

Burn, G., 'The State, the City and the Euromarkets', *Review of International Political Economy*, 6 (1999).

Burn, G., *The Re-emergence of Global Finance* (London: 2006).

Burnett, M. and Manning, M., 'Financial Stability and the United Kingdom's External Balance Sheet', *Bank of England Quarterly Bulletin*, 43 (2003).

Burrell, H.V., 'The Opening of Foreign Branches by English Banks', *JIB*, 35 (1914).

Burt, T., 'A New Vision of Finance Beckons as Rivals Prepare for Court Battle', *Financial Times*, 12 July 2003.

Burt, T., 'Bloomberg in Forex Challenge to Reuters', *Financial Times*, 21 May 2003.

Bush, J., 'Calm Follows Squeezed Margins', *Financial Times*, 3 June 1987.

Bush, J., 'Low Post-Crash Volumes the Major Problem', *Financial Times*, 15 July 1988.

Bush, J., 'Pressure Grows for Freer Markets', *Financial Times*, 3 June 1987.

Butlin, S.J., *Australia and New Zealand Bank: The Bank of Australasia and the Union Bank of Australia Limited, 1828–1951* (London: 1961).

Butlin, S.J., *The Bank of New South Wales in London: 1853–1953* (Sydney: 1953).

Butson, H.E., 'The Banking System of the United Kingdom', in H.P. Willis and B.H. Beckhart (eds), *Foreign Banking Systems* (London: Pitman & Sons, 1929).

Cairncross, A. and Eichengreen, B., *Sterling in Decline: The Devaluations of 1931, 1949 and 1967* (Oxford: 1983).

Cameron, D. and Hughes, J., 'Citigroup to Join Online Currency Platform', *Financial Times*, 8 April 2002.

Cameron, D., 'Currenex to Form Exchange', *Financial Times*, 26 November 2001.

Cameron, D., 'Ways to Enhance Voice-Broking Services', *Financial Times*, 3 April 2002.

Campbell, G. and Rogers, M., 'Integration between the London and New York Stock Exchanges, 1825–1925', *Economic History Review*, 70 (2017).

Cane, A., 'Advantage from the Third Phase', *Financial Times*, 3 June 1987.

Cane, A., 'Deals System Wins Praise', *Financial Times*, 15 July 1988.

Cane, A., 'Increasing Quality and Speed in Dealing Rooms', *Financial Times*, 27 May 1986.

Cane, A., 'Systems Tailored to Market-Makers', *Financial Times*, 16 October 1986.

Capie, F. and Rodrik-Bali, G., 'Concentration in British Banking, 1870–1920', *Business History*, 24 (1982).

Capie, F. and Wood, G., 'Policy Makers in Crisis: A Study of Two Devaluations', in D.R. Hodgman and G.E. Wood (eds), *Monetary and Exchange Rate Policy* (London: 1987).

Capie, F. and Wood, G., *Money Over Two Centuries: Selected Topics in British Monetary History* (Oxford: OUP, 2012).

Carosso, V.P., *The Morgans: Private International Bankers, 1854–1913* (Cambridge: 1987).

Cassese, S., 'The Long Life of the Financial Institutions Set Up in the Thirties', *Journal of European Economic History*, 13 (1984).

Cassis, Y., Feldman, G. and Olson, U., *The Evolution of Financial Institutions and Markets in Twentieth-Century Europe* (Scolar Press, 1995).

Cassis, Y. (ed.), *Finance and Financiers in European History, 1880–1960* (Cambridge: 1992).

Cassis, Y., 'Financial Elites in Three European Centres: London, Paris, Berlin, 1880s–1930s', *Business History*, 33 (1991).

Cassis, Y., 'Management and Strategy in the English Joint Stock Banks, 1890–1914', *Business History*, 27 (1985), 301.

Cassis, Y., *Capitals of Capital: A History of Financial Centres, 1700–2005* (Cambridge: Cambridge University Press, 2006).

Cassis, Y., *City Bankers, 1890–1914* (Cambridge: Cambridge University Press, 1994).

Cater Ryder & Co., *Cater Ryder, Discount Bankers, 1816–1966* (London: 1967).

Cecco, M. de, *Money and Empire: The International Gold Standard, 1890–1914* (Oxford: 1974).

Central Office of Information, *UK Financial Institutions* (London: 1957).

Chaffin, J., 'Recovery from Rare Default is Taking Time', *Financial Times*, 21 June 2001.

Chandler, G., *Four Centuries of Banking* (London: 1964).

Chapman, S., *Merchant Enterprise in Britain: From the Industrial Revolution to World War 1* (Cambridge: 1992).

Chapman, S.D., 'The Establishment of the Rothschilds as Bankers', *Transactions of the Jewish Historical Society*, 29 (1982–6).

Chapman, S.D., *Raphael Bicentenary, 1787–1987* (London: 1987).

Chappell, N.M., *New Zealand Banker's Hundred: A History of the Bank of New Zealand, 1861–1961* (Wellington: 1961).

Checkland, O., Nishimura, S. and Tamaki, N. (eds), *Pacific Banking, 1859–1959: East Meets West* (London: 1994).

Cherrington, H.V., *The Investor and the Securities Act* (Washington: 1942).

Chiozza Money, L.G., *Money's Fiscal Dictionary* (London: 1910).

Chiu, L., Eichengreen, B. and Mehl, A., 'When Did the Dollar Overtake Sterling as the Leading International Currency? Evidence from the Bond Markets', *European Central Bank Working Paper Series*, 1433 (2012).

Christodoulou, G. and O'Connor, P., 'The Foreign Exchange and Over-the-Counter Derivatives Markets in the United Kingdom', *Bank of England Quarterly Bulletin*, 47 (2007).

Chrystal, K.A., *A Guide to Foreign Exchange Markets* (Federal Reserve Bank of St. Louis, March 1984).

City of London Day Census, 1911: Report (London: 1911).

City of London Directory (1907–9).

Clare, G., *A Money-Market Primer and Key to the Exchanges* (London: 1893).

Clare, G., *The ABC of the Foreign Exchanges: A Practical Guide* (London: 1895).

Clark, A., 'Prudential Regulation, Risk Management and Systemic Stability', *Bank of England Quarterly Bulletin*, 47 (2007).

Clark, P., Tamirisia, N. and Wei, S.-J., *Exchange-Rate Volatility and Trade Flows—Some New Evidence* (International Monetary Fund, 2004).

Clark, R.J., 'British Banking: Changes and challenges', *JIB*, 89 (1968).

Clarke, P., 'Keynes and the Manchester Guardian's Reconstruction Supplements', *Annals of the Fondazione Luigi Einaudi*, LI (2017).

Clarke, S.V.O., *Central Bank Co-operation, 1924–1931* (New York: 1967).

Clarke, W.M., *The City and the World Economy* (London: 1965).

Clay, H., 'Finance and the International Market', *The Banker*, xx (October 1931).

Cleaver, G. and Cleaver, P., *The Union Discount: A Centenary Album* (London: 1985).

Clementi, D., 'Maintaining Financial Stability in a Rapidly Changing World: Some Threats and Opportunities', *Bank of England Quarterly Bulletin*, 41 (2001).

Clendenning, E.W., *The Euro-Dollar Market* (Oxford, 1970).

Cleveland, H. van B. and Huertas, T.F., *Citibank, 1812–1970* (Cambridge: 1985).

Cleveland, H. van B., 'The International Monetary System in the Interwar Period', in B.J. Rowland (ed.), *Balance of Power or Hegemony: The Interwar Monetary System* (New York: 1976).

Coggan, P., 'Corporations are Chary', *Financial Times*, 3 June 1987.

Coggan, P., 'It's Just a Small Problem', *Financial Times*, 8 February 1996.

Coggan, P., 'Lobbying Clout Grows', *Financial Times*, 3 June 1987.

Cohen, N. and Tett, G., 'Icap Sets Sights on MTS Platform', *Financial Times*, 25 June 2007.

Cohn, M., *The London Stock Exchange in Relation with Foreign Bourses: The Stock Exchange Arbitrageur* (London: Effingham Wilson, 1874).

Cole, A.C., 'Notes on the London Money Market', *JIB*, 25 (1904).

Cole, W.A., 'The Relations between Banks and Stock Exchanges', *JIB*, 20 (1899).

Collins, M. and Baker, M., 'Financial Crises and Structural Change in English Commercial Bank Assets, 1860–1914', *Explorations in Economic History*, 36 (1999).

Collins, M. and Baker, M., *Commercial Banks and Industrial Finance in England and Wales, 1860–1913* (Oxford: OUP, 2003).

Collins, M., 'English Bank Lending and the Financial Crisis of the 1870s', *Business History*, 32 (1990).

Collins, M., *Money and Banking in the UK: A History* (London: 1988).

Collis, M., *Wayfoong: The Hongkong and Shanghai Banking Corporation* (London: 1965).

Colville, J.R., 'London: Europe's Financial Centre', *The Banker*, 116 (July 1966).

Conan Doyle, A., 'The Adventure of Silver Blaze', *Strand Magazine* (December 1892).

Conant, C.A., *Wall Street and the Country: A Study of Recent Financial Tendencies* (New York: 1904).

Conway, L.T., *The International Position of the London Money Market, 1931–1937* (Philadelphia: 1946).

Cooke, K., 'Rising Hub of Global Trading', *Financial Times*, 6 June 1995.

Cope, S.R., 'The Stock Exchange Revisited: A New Look at the Market in Securities in London in the Eighteenth Century', *Economica*, 45 (1978).

Cork, N., 'The Late Australian Banking Crisis', *JIB*, 15 (1894).

Cornwallis, K., *The Gold Room, and the New York Stock Exchange and Clearing House* (New York: 1879).

Corporation of London, *London and New York Study: The Economics of Two Great Cities at the Millennium, Final Report, Section 2: Financial Services* (London: 2000).

Corre, L.Q., *The Paris Bourse and International Capital Flows before 1914* (Paris: CNRS, 2007).

Corrigan, T., 'Divisions Hazy in OTC Derivatives Clearing Battle Debate', *Financial Times*, 13 September 1993.

Corrigan, T., 'Traditional Split in Derivatives is Less Clear-Cut', *Financial Times*, 25 January 1993.

Cottrell, P.L., 'Aspects of Commercial Banking in Northern and Central Europe, 1880–1931', in S. Kinsey and L. Newton (eds), *International Banking in an Age of Transition: Globalisation, Automation, Banks and Their Archives* (Aldershot: 1998).

Cragg, A., *Understanding the Stock Market* (New York: 1929).

Crammond, E., 'The Economic Relations of the British and German Empires', *Journal of the Royal Statistical Society*, lxxvii (1914).

Critchell, T. and Raymond, J., *A History of the Frozen Meat Trade* (London: 1912).

Crompton, R.C., *History of the Foreign Department of the District Bank of Liverpool and Manchester*, RBS Archive.

Crump, A., *The Key to the London Money Market* (London: 1877).

Crump, A., *The Theory of Stock Exchange Speculation* (London: 1874).

Crump, N., 'Finance and the Crisis', *JIB*, 59 (1938).

Crump, N., 'The Evolution of the Money Market', *JIB*, 59 (1938).

Crump, N., 'The London and New York Markets in the Autumn of 1925', *JIB*, 47 (1926).

Dam, K.W., *The Rules of the Game: Reform and Evolution in the International Monetary System* (Chicago: 1982).

Daneshkhu, S. and Giles, C., 'City Becomes Undeniable Engine of Growth', *Financial Times*, 27 March 2006.

Daniel, P., 'B&C Cliff-Hanger Still Runs', *Financial Times*, 15 July 1988.

Darroch, J.L., *Canadian Banks and Global Competitiveness* (Montreal: 1994).

Davis, J., 'Who Discovered Neptune?', *Astronomy*, 9 November 2020.

Davis, S., 'Taking a Position in the Market', *Financial Times*, 28 June 1994.

Denison, M., *Canada's First Bank: A History of the Bank of Montreal* (New York: 1966–7).

Denton, N., 'Banks Plan Clearing House for Trade in Emerging Market Debt', *Financial Times*, 10 June 1996.

Deutsch, H., *Arbitrage*, 3rd ed., Revised and Re-written by O. Weber (London: 1933).

Deutsche Bank, *LT Asset Return Study: A Journey into the Unknown* (2012).

Di Quirico, R., 'The Initial Phases of Italian Banks' Expansion Abroad, 1900–31', *Financial History Review*, 6 (1999).

Diaper, S., 'Merchant Banking in the Inter-war Period: The Case of Kleinwort, Sons & Co.', *Business History*, 27/8 (1985/6).

Dick, T.J.O. and Floyd, J.E., *Canada and the Gold Standard: Balance of Payments Adjustments, 1871–1913* (Cambridge: 1992).

Dickson, M., 'Capital Gain: How London is Thriving and Taking on the Global Competition', *Financial Times*, 27 March 2006.

Dickson, M., 'The Market is Another Country for City's Go-Between', *Financial Times*, 7 April 2001.

Dickson, P.G.M., *The Financial Revolution in England: A Study in the Development of Public Credit, 1688–1756* (London: 1967).

Dieson, E., *Exchange Rates of the World* (Christiana: 1922).

Dixon, K.F., *The Development of the London Money Market, 1780–1830*, unpublished University of London PhD, 1962.

Dizzard, J., 'The Horror Scenario Lurking in the Plumbing of Finance', *Financial Times*, 24 July 2021.

Doskov, N. and Swinkels, L., 'Empirical Evidence on the Currency Carry Trade, 1900–2012', *Journal of International Money and Finance*, 51 (2015).

Dosoo, G., *The Eurobond Market* (London: 1992).

Dowling, S.W., *The Exchanges of London* (London: Butterworth & Co., 1929).

Drummond Fraser, Sir D., 'British Home Banking Since 1911', *JIB*, 46 (1925).

Drummond, I.M., *The Floating Pound and the Sterling Area 1931–1939* (Cambridge: 1981).

Drummond, I.M., 'London, Washington and the Management of the Franc, 1936–39', *Princeton Studies in International Finance*, 45 (1979).

Du, W., 'What Makes This Global Dollar Crunch Different?', *Financial Times*, 26 March 2020.

Duboff, R.B., 'The Telegraph and the Structure of Markets in the United States, 1845–1890', *Research in Economic History*, 8 (1983).

Duguid, K. and Palma, S., 'SEC Backs Fresh Push to Shore Up $24tn Treasury Market', *Financial Times*, 14 September 2022.

Duguid, K. and Stubbington, T., 'Central Bank Sync Puts Foreign Exchange Market to Sleep', *Financial Times*, 21 September 2021.

Duke, W.K., *Bills, Bullion and the London Money Market* (London: 1937).

Dunning, J.H. and Morgan, E.V., *An Economic Study of the City of London* (London: 1971).

Duttagupta, R., Fernandez, G. and Karacadag, C., 'Moving to a Flexible Exchange Rate: How, When and How Fast?', *International Monetary Fund, Economic Issues*, 38 (2005).

Dyer, L.S., 'The Secondary Banking Crisis', *JIB*, 104 (1983).

Eames, F.L., *The New York Stock Exchange* (New York: 1894).

Easton, H.T., *History and Principles of Banks and Banking*, 3rd ed. (London: 1924).

Easton, H.T., *Money, Exchange and Banking* (London: 1908).

Easton, H.T., *The Work of a Bank* (London: 1930, revised and rewritten by H.G. Hodder).

Eckardt, H.M.P., 'Banks and Canada's Foreign Trade', *Industrial Canada*, August 1912.

Eckardt, H.M.P., 'Banks and Foreign Loans', *Journal of the Canadian Bankers' Association*, 14 (1912).

Eckardt, H.M.P., 'Banks and Foreign Trade', *Industrial Canada*, October 1912.

Eckardt, H.M.P., 'How to Dispose of Foreign Exchange', *Industrial Canada*, March 1912.

Eckardt, H.M.P., 'Modes of Carrying Cash Reserves', *Journal of the Canadian Bankers' Association*, xvi (1908/09).

Eckardt, H.M.P., 'The Growth of Our Foreign Investments', *Journal of the Canadian Bankers' Association*, vii (1900/01).

Eckardt, H.M.P., 'The Stock Exchange Loans', *Journal of the Canadian Bankers' Association*, xxii (1914/15).

Eckardt, H.M.P., *Manual of Canadian Banking* (Toronto: 1908/1914).

Edelstein, M., *Overseas Investment in the Age of High Imperialism: The United Kingdom 1850–1914* (London: 1982).

EEA Quarterly Report, 1 April–30 June 1937, 1 January 1938–31, March 1939.

Eichengreen, B. and Esteves, R., 'International Finance', in S. Broadberry and K. Fukao (eds), *The Cambridge Economic History of the Modern World*, vol. 2, *1870 to the Present* (Cambridge University Press: 2021).

Eichengreen, B. and Flandreau, M., *The Rise and Fall of the Dollar; Or When Did the Dollar Replace Sterling as the Leading Reserve Currency?*, Paper presented in Cambridge and Genoa, 2008.

Eichengreen, B., 'Central Bank Co-operation and Exchange Rate Commitments: The Classical and Interwar Gold Standards Compared', *Financial History Review*, 2 (1995).

Eichengreen, B., 'International Monetary Instability between the Wars: Structural flaws or Misguided Policies?', in Y. Suzuki, J. Miyake and M. Okabe (eds), *The Evolution of the International Monetary System: How Can Efficiency and Stability Be Attained* (Tokyo: 1990).

Eichengreen, B., 'Somnolence to Dominance: A Hundred Years of the Foreign Exchange Market in London', *Journal of European Economic History*, 51 (2022).

Eichengreen, B., 'Sterling's Past, Dollar's Future: Historical Perspectives on Reserve Currency Composition', Paper Delivered Leicester 2005.

Eichengreen, B., *Elusive Stability: Essays in the History of International Finance* (Cambridge: 1990).

Eichengreen, B., *Golden Fetters: The Gold Standard and the Great Depression, 1919–1939* (New York/Oxford: 1992).

Eichengreen, B., Lafarguette, R. and Mehl, A., 'Cables, Sharks and Servers: Technology and the Foreign Exchange Market', NBER Working Paper 21884 (2016).

Eichengreen, B., Mehl, A. and Chitu, L., *How Global Currencies Work: Past, Present, and Future* (Princeton: Princeton University Press, 2018).

Eichengreen, B., *The Gold Standard in Theory and History* (New York: 1985).

Einzig, P., 'Branch Banks v Affiliate Banks', *The Banker*, xxxi (July 1934).

Einzig, P., 'Dollar Deposits in London', *The Banker*, 110 (Jan 1960).

Einzig, P., 'London as the World's Banking Centre', *The Banker*, xxvii (September 1933).

Einzig, P., 'The Future of the London Foreign Exchange Market', *The Banker*, xx (November 1931).

Einzig, P., *A Dynamic Theory of Forward Exchange* (London: 1961), 2nd ed., 1967.

Einzig, P., *A Textbook of Foreign Exchange* (London: 1966).

Einzig, P., *Exchange Control* (London: 1934).

Einzig, P., *The Euro-Bond Market* (London: 1969).

Einzig, P., *The History of Foreign Exchange* (London: 1962).

Eldem, E., *A History of the Ottoman Bank* (Istanbul: 1999).

Elder, B., 'No, Russia Won't Replace Swift with the Blockchain', *Financial Times*, 20 June 2022.

Ellis, A., *Heir to Adventure: The Story of Brown, Shipley & Co., Merchant Bankers, 1810–1960* (London: 1960).

Ellis, A., *The Rationale of Market Fluctuations* (London: 1876).

Elmendorf, D.W., Hircheld, M.L. and Well, G.D.N., 'The Effect of News on Bond Prices: Evidence from the UK 1900–1920', *Review of Economics and Statistics*, 78 (1996).

Elstob, P., 'Anxious to Become the ECU Centre', *Financial Times*, 29 November 1990.

Elstob, P.M., 'UK Links with Tokyo Houses', *Financial Times*, 14 February 1984.

Elzetzki, E., Teinhart, C. and Rogoff, K., 'Exchange Arrangements Entering the Twenty-First Century: Which Anchor Will Hold?', *Quarterly Journal of Economics*, 124 (2019).

Escher, F.E., *Elements of Foreign Exchange* (New York: 1911).

Escher, M., *Foreign Exchange Explained* (New York: 1917).

Estcourt, R., 'The Stock Exchange as a Regulator of Currency', *The Annalist*, 14 (1919).

Esteves, R. and Eichengreen, B., 'The Trials of the Trilemma: International Finance, 1870–2017', Centre for Economic Policy Research Discussion Paper DP 12365 (London: 2019).

Evans, M.D.D. and Rime, D., 'Microstructure of Foreign Exchange Markets', *BIS Quarterly Review*, (December 2019).

Evitt, H.E., *Practical Banking, Currency and Exchange* (London: 1933).

Evitt, H.E., 'Exchange Dealings under Current Conditions', *JIB*, 52 (1931).

Faglia, A., 'The Rise and Rise of Currency Hedging Raises a Financial System Risk', *Financial Times*, 3 November 2022.

Feinstein, C.H., Temin, P. and Toniolo, G., 'International Economic Organisation: Banking, Finance and Trade in Europe between the Wars', in C.H. Feinstein (ed.), *Currency and Finance in Europe between the Wars* (Oxford: 1995).

Feldstein, M. (ed.), *International Capital Flows* (Chicago 1999).

Ferguson, N., *The Cash Nexus: Money and Power in the Modern World, 1700–2000* (London: 2001).

Fforde, J., *The Bank of England and Public Policy, 1941–1958* (Cambridge: 1992).

Fidler, S., 'A Broader and Safer Market in a Storm', *Financial Times*, 18 May 1988.

Fidler, S., 'Money Brokers Step into the Financial Limelight', *Financial Times*, 22 November 1990.

Fidler, S., 'Where British Brokers Rule World', *Financial Times*, 7 July 1987.

Field, A.J., 'The Magnetic Telegraph, Price and Quantity Data, and the New Management of Capital', *Journal of Economic History*, 52 (1992).

Field, F.W., 'How Canadian Stocks are Held', *Monetary Times Annual* (January 1915).

Field, F.W., *Capital Investments in Canada* (Toronto: 1911).

Flandreau, M. and Jobst, C., 'Describing and Explaining the International Circulation of Currencies, 1890–1910', *EH.Net*.

Flandreau, M. and Jobst, C., 'The Ties That Divide: A Network Analysis of the International Monetary System, 1890–1910', *Journal of Economic History*, 65 (2005).

Flandreau, M. and Jobst, C., *The Empirics of International Currencies: Evidence from the 19th Century* (Centre for Economic Policy Research, 2006).

Fleming, S., Brunsden, J. and Stafford, P., 'Brexit and the City: Brussels' New Battle to Rival London in Finance', *Financial Times*, 22 September 2020.

Fleming, S., Stafford, P. and Noonan, L., 'The EU vs the City of London: A Slow Puncture', *Financial Times*, 15 January 2022.

Fletcher, G.A., *The Discount Houses in London: Principles, Operations and Change* (London: 1976).

Flood, C., 'Regulators Stalk Secretive Financial Giants', *Financial Times*, 24 February 2014.

Fohlin, C., *Finance Capitalism and Germany's Rise to Industrial Power* (Cambridge: Cambridge University Press, 2007).

Forbes, N., *Doing Business with the Nazis: Britain's Economic and Financial Relations with Germany, 1931–1939* (London: 2000).

Ford, A.G., 'International Financial Policy and the Gold Standard, 1870–1914', *Warwick Research, Papers*, 104 (1977).

Ford, A.G., *The Gold Standard, 1880–1914: Britain and Argentina* (Oxford: 1962).

Ford, J., 'Future of the City: How London's Reach Will Shrink after Brexit', *Financial Times*, 9 December 2020.

Forester, C.S., *Payment Deferred* (London: The Bodley Head, 1926).

Foster, E.F., *Seasonal Movements of Exchange Rates and Interest Rates under the Pre-World War 1 Gold Standard* (New York: Garland Publishing, 1994).

Fox, G., *Britain and Japan, 1858–1883* (Oxford: 1969).

Frankel, J.S., Gianpaolo, G. and Giovannini, A. (eds), *The Microstructure of Foreign Exchange Markets* (Chicago: University of Chicago Press, 1996).

Fraser, D., 'A Decade of Bank Amalgamations, 1897–1906', *JIB*, 29 (1907).

Fraser, L., *All to the Good* (London: 1963).

Freeland, C., 'Capitalism's Capital Fears Being Caught Out as London Booms', *Financial Times*, 4 November 2006.

Friedman, M. and Schwartz, J.A., *Monetary Trends in the United States and the United Kingdom: Their Relations to Income, Prices and Interest Rates, 1867–1977* (Chicago: 1982).

Frowen, S.F. (ed.), *A Framework of International Banking* (London: 1979).

Fry, R. (ed.), *A Banker's World: The Revival of the City, 1957–1970* (London: 1970).

FT Reporters, 'Daily Fix That Spiralled Out of Control', *Financial Times*, 20 December 2012.

FT Reporters, 'Fed Analyses Regulation's Role in Sudden Rates Jump', *Financial Times*, 2 October 2019.

FT Reporters, 'LSE in Talks on $20bn Refinitiv Link-Up with Scale to Rival Bloomberg Empire', *Financial Times*, 27 July 2019.

Fuller, F.J. and Rowan, H.D., 'Foreign Competition in Its Relation to Banking', *JIB*, 21 (1900) and 25 (1904).

Furniss, E.S., *Foreign Exchange: The Financing Mechanism of International Commerce* (New York: 1922).

Furse, C., 'Sox is Not to Blame—London Is Just Better as a Market', *Financial Times*, 18 September 2006.

Gall, L., Feldman, G.D., James, H., Holtfrerich, C.-L. and Buschgen, H.E., *The Deutsche Bank, 1870–1995* (London: 1995).

Gallarotti, G.M., *The Anatomy of an International Monetary Regime: The Classical Gold Standard, 1880–1914* (New York: 1995).

Gapper, J., 'What Price Information', *Financial Times*, 20 July 1998.

Garbade, K.D. and Silber, W.L., 'Dominant and Satellite Markets: A Study of Dually Listed Securities', *Review of Economics and Statistics*, 61 (1979).

Garland, N.S., *Banks, Banking and Financial Directory of Canada* (Ottawa: 1895).

Garnham, P., 'Currencies Establish Themselves as Asset Class', *Financial Times*, 5 March 2007.

Garnham, P., 'Forex Market Soars with Little Sign of Change in Trading System', *Financial Times*, 15 October 2008.

Garnham, P., 'Keeping Its Head as Others Lost Theirs', *Financial Times*, 29 September 2009.

Garnham, P., 'Net Brings Power to the People', *Financial Times*, 29 September 2009.

Garnham, P., 'Quant Techniques Drive Volumes Ever Higher', *Financial Times*, 19 November 2007.

Garrett, T., 'Giants Head the Broking League', *Financial Times*, 14 February 1984.

Garside, W.R. and Greaves, J.I., 'The Bank of England and Industrial Intervention in Interwar Britain', *Financial History Review*, 3 (1996).

Gawith, P. and Lapper, R., 'A Step Away from City Tradition', *Financial Times*, 2 January 1996.

Gawith, P., 'Brokers Lose Their Voices on the Small Screen', *Financial Times*, 15 December 1995.

Gawith, P., 'Exotic But Not for Faint Hearts', *Financial Times*, 15 May 1996.

Gawith, P., 'Forex Market Growth Startles Exchanges', *Financial Times*, 20 September 1995.

Gawith, P., 'Forex Surge Masks Maturing Market', *Financial Times*, 24 October 1995.

Gawith, P., 'Service Central to Paribas Forex Move', *Financial Times*, 2 February 1996.

Gawith, P., 'Technology on the March', *Financial Times*, 2 June 1994.

Geisst, C.R., *Wall Street: A History* (Oxford: 1997).

Gellender, E.E., 'The Relations between Banks and Stock Exchanges', *JIB*, 20 (1899).

George, E., 'Recent Banking Difficulties: An Address by the Governor of the Bank of England', *Bank of England Quarterly Bulletin*, 33 (1993).

George, E., 'The New Lady of Threadneedle Street', *Bank of England Quarterly Bulletin*, 38 (1998).

George, E., *Before the Millennium: From the Bank of England* (Bank of England, 7 December 1999).

Ghosh, A.R. and Ostry, J.D., 'Choosing an Exchange Rate Regime', *Finance and Development*, 46 (2009).

Gibson, E.C., 'A Critical and Historical Account of the Working of the American Federal Reserve Banking System', *JIB*, 48 (1927).

Gieve, Sir John, 'Financial System Risks in the United Kingdom: Issues and Challenges', *Bank of England Quarterly Bulletin*, 46 (2006).

Gieve, Sir John, 'Practical Issues in Preparing for Cross-border Financial Crises', *Bank of England Quarterly Bulletin*, 46 (2006).

Glahe, F.R., 'An Empirical Study of the Foreign Exchange Market: Test of a Theory', in *Princeton Studies in International Finance* (1967).

Gleeson, A., *London Enriched: The Development of the Foreign Banking Community in the City Over Five Decades* (London: 1997).

Goodacre, H. and Razak, E., 'The Foreign Exchange and Over-the-Counter Interest Rate Derivatives Market in the United Kingdom', *Bank of England Quarterly Bulletin* (20 December 2019).

Goodhart, C. and Demos, A., 'The Asian Surprise in the Forex Markets', *Financial Times*, 2 September 1991.

Goschen, G.J., *The Theory of the Foreign Exchanges* (London: 1861 and 1864).

Governor of the Bank of England, 'Prospects for the City: In or Out of EMU', *Bank of England Quarterly Bulletin*, 37 (1997).

Governor of the Bank of England, 'Reforms to the UK Monetary Policy Framework and Financial Services Regulation', *Bank of England Quarterly Bulletin*, 37 (1997).

Gowers, A., 'Island of Integrity', *Financial Times*, 29 March 1993.

Grady, J. and Weale, M., *British Banking, 1960–85* (London: 1986).

Graham, G., 'Banks Settle Down to Action', *Financial Times*, 5 June 1998.

Graham, G., 'BIS Outlines Forex Settlement Risk Strategy', *Financial Times*, 28 March 1996.

Graham, G., 'Chase Plans New Forex Derivative', *Financial Times*, 29 April 1997.

Graham, G., 'Foreign Exchange Groups Plan Merger', *Financial Times*, 9 December 1996.

Graham, G., 'Forex Dealers Move to Limit Settlement Risk', *Financial Times*, 5 June 1996.

Graham, G., 'Forex Trading System Planned', *Financial Times*, 15 September 1999.

Graham, G., 'Global Payments Bodies to Merge', *Financial Times*, 1 October 1997.

Graham, G., 'Hopes of an End to O'Brien Rules', *Financial Times*, 27 May 1986.

Graham, G., 'Mercurial Times in the Market', *Financial Times*, 27 May 1986.

Graham, G., 'New Forex Bank to Cut Risk', *Financial Times*, 9 June 1997.

Grant, J. and Garnham, P., 'LCH.Clearnet Looks at Forex Markets', *Financial Times*, 16 October 2008.

Grant, J. and Mackenzie, M., 'Ghost in the Machine', *Financial Times*, 18 February 2010.

Grant, J. and Masters, B., 'Brokers Set Out to Fight Backlash against OTC Trade', *Financial Times*, 28 April 2009.

Grant, J., 'D Börse-NYSE Merger "Bad For Markets"', *Financial Times*, 5 July 2011.

Grant, J., 'First Steps Towards Clearing for FX', *Financial Times*, 6 October 2009.

Grant, J., 'Industry in the Midst of a Maelstrom', *Financial Times*, 10 October 2011.

Grant, J., 'Industry Pleads Its Case against Rules Forged in Heat of Crisis', *Financial Times*, 29 March 2011.

Grant, J., 'Interdealer Brokers Join Forces on OTC Issues', *Financial Times*, 9 March 2009.

Grant, J., 'Planned Merger Comes at Crucial Time for Industry', *Financial Times*, 14 August 2008.

Grant, J., 'SGX in Talks on Asian Trading Platform for Corporate Bonds', *Financial Times*, 17 November 2014.

Grant, J., 'Tullett Predicts Rebound for OTC Derivatives', *Financial Times*, 5 August 2009.

Grant, J., Milne, R. and Van Duyn, A., 'Collateral Damage', *Financial Times*, 7 October 2009.

Gray, A., 'Tullett Hangs on to Phone Trading', *Financial Times*, 9 March 2010.

Greeley, B. and Smith, C., 'Federal Reserve Eases Capital Rule to Encourage Bank Lending', *Financial Times*, 2 April 2020.

Green, D.R., *From Artisans to Paupers: Economic Change and Poverty in London: 1790–1870* (Aldershot: 1995).

Green, E. and Kinsey, S., *The Paradise Bank: The Mercantile Bank of India, 1893–1984* (Aldershot: 1999).

Greenberg, D., *Financiers and Railroads, 1869–1889: A Study of Morton, Bliss and Company* (Newark: 1980).

Greengrass, H.W., *The Discount Market in London: Its Organisation and Recent Development* (London: 1930).

Greenwood, W.J., *American and Foreign Stock Exchange Practice, Stock and Bond Trading and the Business Corporation Laws of All Nations* (New York: 1921).

Gregory, T.E., *Foreign Exchange Before, during and after the War* (Oxford: Oxford University Press, 1921).

Grene, S., 'Taking the Sting Out of Fluctuation', *Financial Times*, 6 October 2009.

Griffiths, B., 'The Development of Restrictive Practices in the UK Monetary System', *Economic and Social Studies*, 41 (1973).

Grossman, R.S., *Unsettled Account: The Evolution of Banking in the Industrialized World Since 1800* (Princeton: Princeton University Press, 2010).

Group of Thirty, *Foreign Exchange Markets under Floating Rates* (New York: 1980).

Group of Thirty, *The Foreign Exchange Market in the 1980s: The View of Market Participants* (New York: 1985).

Guide to the International Locational Banking Statistics, Monetary and Economic Department, BIS, 2011.

Gunasekera, H.A. de S., *From Dependent Currency to Central Banking in Ceylon* (London: 1962).

Guthrie, J., 'Sighs of Relief as Exco Takeover Get Nod of Approval', *Financial Times*, 27 October 1998.

Haldane, A.G., 'Managing Global Finance as a System', *Bank of England Quarterly Bulletin*, 54 (2014).

Haldane, A.G. and Latter, E., 'The Role of Central Banks in Payment Systems Oversight', *Bank of England Quarterly Bulletin*, 45 (2005).

Hall, N.F., 'The Control of Credit in the London Money Market', *JIB*, 59 (1938).

Hambros Bank, *Hambros Bank Ltd, London: 1839–1939* (London: 1939).

Harris, C., 'Bid to Set Up Biggest Wholesale Money Broker', *Financial Times*, 10 June 1999.

Harris, C., 'Brokers Agree Merger Terms', *Financial Times*, 16 February 1999.

Harris, C., 'Garban and Intercapital in £300m Merger', *Financial Times*, 3 July 1999.

Harrod, R., *Money* (London: Macmillan, 1969).

Hartmann, P., *Currency Competition and Foreign Exchange Markets: The Dollar, the Yen and the Euro* (Cambridge: 1998).

Harverson, P., 'Exco Staff Suffer as World Markets Slow', *Financial Times*, 24 November 1995.

Harvey, C. and Press, J., 'The City and International Mining, 1870-1914', *Business History*, 32 (1990).

Haupt, O., *The London Arbitrageur: Or, the English Money Market in Connexion with Foreign Bourses* (London: 1870).

Hawtrey, R.G., *A Century of Bank Rate* (London: 1938).

Hawtrey, R.G., *The Art of Central Banking* (London: 1932).

Hemming, H.G., *History of the New York Stock Exchange* (New York: 1905).

Hennessy, E., *A Domestic History of the Bank of England, 1930–1960* (Cambridge: 1992).

Henry, J.A. and Stepmann, H.A., *The First Hundred Years of the Standard Bank* (London: 1863).

Higgins, L.R., *The Put-and-Call* (London: 1896).

Hill, A., 'Financial Inventors Underpin Success', *Financial Times*, 27 March 2006.

Hobson, O., 'Financial Control after the War', *JIB*, 63 (1942).

Hobson, O., 'Future of the City', *JIB*, 57 (1946).

Hobson, O., *How the City Works* (London: 1940).

Hoffman, G.W., *Futures Trading Upon Organized Commodity Markets in the United States* (Philadelphia: 1932).

Hofman, B., Mehrata A. and Sandri, D., 'Global Exchange Rate Adjustments: Drivers, Impacts and Policy Implications', *BIS Bulletin*, 62 (2022).

Holberton, S., 'Return of the Large Private Player', *Financial Times*, 15 July 1988.

Holden, C.H. and Holford, W.G., *The City of London: A Record of Destruction and Survival* (London: 1951).

Holden, E.H., 'The World's Money Markets', *The Statist*, 24 January 1914.

Holder, R.F., *Bank of New South Wales: A History* (Sydney: 1970).

Hollom, J.Q., 'The Methods and Objectives of the Bank's Market Operations', in *The Bank of England Today* (London: The Institute of Bankers, 1964).

Holmes, A.R. and Green, E., *Midland: 150 Years of Banking Business* (London: 1986).

Horesh, N., 'Gerschenkron Redux? Analysing New Evidence on Joint-Stock Enterprise in Pre-war Shanghai', *Asian-Pacific Economic Literature* (2015).

Hou, C.-M., *Foreign Investment and Economic Development in China, 1840–1937* (Cambridge: 1965).

Howarth, W., *The Banks in the Clearing House* (London: 1905).

Howell, M., 'Knee-Jerk Rate Cuts Only Make Matters Worse in This Crisis', *Financial Times*, 19 March 2020.

Howell, M., 'Rising Tide of Liquidity Lifts Many Boats, But Keep an Eye on the Horizon', *Financial Times*, 17 January 2020.

Howell, M., 'The Liquidity Threat Looming Over Markets in 2022', *Financial Times*, 17 December 2021.

Howland, H.J., 'Gambling Joint or Market Place? An Inquiry into the Workings of the New York Stock Exchange', *The Outlook* (28 June 1913).

Howson, S., *British Monetary Policy 1945–51* (Oxford University Press, 1993).

Howson, S., *Domestic Monetary Management in Britain, 1919–38* (Cambridge University Press, 1975).

Huebner, S.S., 'Scope and Functions of the Stock Market', in S.S. Huebner (ed.), 'Stocks and the Stock Market', *Annals of the American Academy of Political and Social Science*, xxxv, 3 (Philadelphia: May 1910).

Huebner, S.S., *The Stock Market* (New York: 1922).

Hughes, J. and Guha, K., 'World Foreign Exchange Trading Soars to a Peak of $1,900bn a Day', *Financial Times*, 29 September 2004.

Hughes, J., 'A Lesson in How to Run a Smooth Global Settlement System', *Financial Times*, 21 August 2009.

Hughes, J., 'A Veteran with a Proud Record of Service', *Financial Times*, 27 May 2004.

Hughes, J., 'Bankers Divided on Need for Backstop', *Financial Times*, 4 May 2006.

Hughes, J., 'Concern Over Scope of Initiatives', *Financial Times*, 29 September 2009.

Hughes, J., 'Eurex Issues a Challenge to CME', *Financial Times*, 17 June 2005.

Hughes, J., 'FX Faces Prospect of Two-Tier Pricing', *Financial Times*, 21 August 2009.

Hughes, J., 'FX Firebrand Dream of Revolution', *Financial Times*, 9 May 2006.

Hughes, J., 'History Goes Full Circle as Volume Is King', *Financial Times*, 27 May 2004.

Hughes, J., 'Interbank Online Action Set to Soar', *Financial Times*, 25 February 2005.

Hughes, J., 'Lava Platform to Challenge Duopoly', *Financial Times*, 25 April 2006.

Hughes, J., 'So Where Do They Make Their Money?', *Financial Times*, 29 March 2011.

Hughes, J., 'Taking Their Law into Their Own Hands', *Financial Times*, 27 May 2004.

Hughes, J., 'The Mouse Takes Over the Floor', *Financial Times*, 27 May 2004.

Hughes, J., 'Traders Set to Take the Forex Challenge', *Financial Times*, 22 May 2003.

Hughes, J., 'Where Money Talks Very Loudly', *Financial Times*, 27 May 2004.

Hughes, J., 'Worries Over Threat of "Heavy Touch"', *Financial Times*, 30 March 2010.

Hutton, A. and Kent, E., 'The Foreign Exchange and Over-the-Counter Interest Rate Derivatives Market in the United Kingdom', *Bank of England Quarterly Bulletin*, 53 (2016).

Hyde, F.E., *Far Eastern Trade, 1860–1914* (London: 1973).

Ibison, D., 'Banks Lose Hope Sun Will Rise on Japan's Big Bang', *Financial Times*, 14 February 2003.

Ikle, M., *Switzerland: An International Banking and Finance Center* (Stroudsburg: 1972).

Ilzetzki, E., Reinhart, C.M. and Rogoff, K.S., 'Will the Secular Decline in Exchange Rate and Inflation Volatility Survive Covid 19?' NBER Working Paper 28108 (2020).

Innes, J., 'Managing the Metropolis: London's Social Problems and Their Control, c 1660–1830', in P. Clarke and R. Gillespie (eds), *Two Capitals: London and Dublin 1500–1840* (Oxford: Oxford University Press, 2001).

Inouye, J., *Problems of the Japanese Exchange, 1914–1926* (Glasgow: 1931).

Institute of Bankers, *The London Discount Market Today* (London: 1962).

Institute of Bankers, *The Pattern and Finance of Foreign Trade* (London: 1949).

Institute of International Finance, 'Effects of the War on British Banking', Institute of International Finance [New York Based], 124, 15 March 1943.

Inter-bank Research Organisation, *The Future of London as an International Financial Centre* (London: 1973).

International Banking in London: FBSA 50th Anniversary, Financial Times/Banker Special Supplement (7 November 1997).

Iqbal, A., 'Deglobalisation is Boosting Foreign Exchange Volatility', *Financial Times*, 31 May 2022.

Iversen, C., *Aspects of the Theory of International Capital Movements* (Copenhagen: 1936).

James, H., 'Rethinking the Legacy of Bretton Woods', *Journal of European Economic History*, 51 (2022).

James, H., *International Monetary Co-operation Since Bretton Woods* (Washington: 1996).

James, H., *Making the European Monetary Union* (Cambridge: 2012).

Jansson, W., 'Stock Markets, Banks and Economic Growth in the UK, 1850–1913', *Financial History Review*, 25 (2019).

Jansson, W., *The Finance-Growth Nexus in Britain, 1850–1913* (Cambridge DPhil, 2018).

Japhet, S., *Recollections from My Business Life* (London: 1931).

Jenkinson, N. and Manning, M., 'Promoting Financial System Resilience in Modern Global Capital Markets: Some Issues', *Bank of England Quarterly Bulletin*, 47 (2007).

Jevons, W.S., *Money and the Mechanism of Exchange* (London: 1875).

Jobst, C., 'Market Leader: The Austro-Hungarian Bank and the Making of Foreign Exchange Intervention, 1896–1913', *European Review of Economic History*, 13 (2009).

John, S., Roberts, M. and Weeken, O., 'The Bank of England's Special Liquidity Scheme', *Bank of England Quarterly Bulletin*, 52 (2012).

Johnson, R., 'Reuters Triumphs in the Derivatives Jungle', *Financial Times*, 21 December 1989.

Johnson, S., 'A Little Oasis of Calm for Currencies', *Financial Times*, 2 February 2009.

Johnson, S., 'London Rules New Wave of FX Deals', *Financial Times*, 18 July 2006.

Jones, C., 'A Global Backlash is Brewing against the Fed', *Financial Times*, 22 September 2022.

Jones, G., *Banking and Oil*, vol. 2, *The History of the British Bank of the Middle East* (Cambridge: Cambridge University Press, 1986).

Jones, G., *British Multinational Banking, 1830–1990* (Oxford: 1993).

Jones, G., 'Lombard Street on the Riviera: The British Clearing Banks and Europe, 1900–1960', *Business History*, 24 (1982).

Jones, L.E., *Georgian Afternoon* (London: 1958).

Jonung, L., 'Swedish Experience under the Classical Gold Standard, 1873–1914', in M.D. Bordo and A.J. Schwartz (eds), *A Retrospective on the Classical Gold Standard, 1821–1931* (Chicago/London: 1984).

Jorion, P., 'Risk and Turnover in the Foreign Exchange Market', in J.A. Frankel, G. Galli and A. Giovannini (eds), *The Microstructure of Foreign Exchange Markets* (Chicago: 1996).

Joslin, D., *A Century of Banking in Latin America* (London: 1963).

Kamininska, I., 'Daylight Overdrafts Must Lose Their Stigma', *Financial Times*, 13 December 2021.

Kasuya, M. (ed.), *Coping with Crisis: International Financial Institutions in the Interwar Period* (Oxford: 2003).

Kasuya, M., 'The Activities of the Yokohama Specie Bank', in M. Kasuya (ed.), *Coping with Crisis: International Financial Institutions in the Interwar Period* (Oxford: 2003).

Kawamura, T., 'British Business and Empire in Asia: The Eastern Exchange Banks, 1851–63', in D. Bates and K. Kondo (eds), *Migration and Identity in British History* (Tokyo: 2006).

Keene, D., 'The Setting of the Royal Exchange: Continuity and Change in the Financial District of the City of London: 1300–1871', in A. Saunders (ed.), *The Royal Exchange* (London: 1997).

Kelly, J., *Bankers and Borders: The Case of American Banks in Britain* (Cambridge: 1977).

Kemmerer, E.W., *Season Variations in the Relative Demand for Money and Capital in the United States* (Washington: 1910).

Kenen, P.B., *The Role of the Dollar as an International Currency* (New York: Group of Thirty, 1983).

Keynes, J.M., 'The Prospects of Money', *Economic Journal*, 24 (1914).

Keynes, J.M., *A Tract on Monetary Reform* (London: Macmillan, 1924).

Keynes, J.M., *Indian Currency and Finance* (London: Macmillan, 1913).

Keynes, J.M., *The Economic Consequences of the Peace* (London: 1920).

Khalaf, R., 'Private Sector Is Quick to Adjust', *Financial Times*, 8 November 1996.

Kidron, M., *Foreign Investments in India* (London: 1965).

Kieve, J.L., *The Electric Telegraph: A Social and Economic History* (Newton Abbot: 1973).

Kindersley, R.M., 'British Foreign Investments', *Economic Journal*, 40–9 (1930–39).

King, F.H.H., *The History of the Hongkong and Shanghai Banking Corporation*, vol. 1, *The Hongkong Bank in Late Imperial China 1864–1902: On an Even Keel* (Cambridge: Cambridge University Press, 1987).

King, F.H.H., *The History of the Hongkong and Shanghai Banking Corporation*, vol. 2, *The Hong Kong Bank in the Period of Imperialism and War, 1895–1918: Wayfoong, the Focus of Wealth* (Cambridge: 1988).

King, F.H.H., *The History of the Hongkong and Shanghai Banking Corporation*, vol. 3, *The Hongkong Bank between the Wars and the Bank Interned, 1919–1945: Return from Grandeur* (Cambridge, 1987).

King, F.H.H., *The History of the Hongkong and Shanghai Banking Corporation*, vol. 4, *The Hongkong Bank in the Period of Development and Nationalism, 1941–1984: From Regional Bank to Multinational Group* (Cambridge, 1991).

King, W.T.C., 'War and the Money Market', *JIB*, 58 (1947).

King, W.T.C., *History of the London Discount Market* (London: 1936).

Kinsey, S. and Newton, L., *International Banking in an Age of Transition: Globalisation, Automation, Banks and Their Archives* (Aldershot: 1998).

Kirkaldy, A.W. (ed.), *British Finance during and after the War, 1914–21* (London: 1921).

Kirkaldy, A.W. (ed.), *Credit, Industry and War* (London: 1915).

Kisling, W. and London, L. von, 'A Comparative, Empirical Analysis of German and British Global Foreign Banking and Trade Development, 1881–1913', *Economic History Review*, 75 (2022).

Kleinwort Sons & Company, *Annual Profit and Loss Account* (Guildhall Library, 1926–38).

Kleinwort, Sir Cyril, 'The City in Britain's Invisible Earnings', *The Banker*, 121 (1971).

Kniffin, W.H., *The Practical Work of a Bank* (New York: 1915), 7th ed. (1928).

Kouwenhoven, J.A., *Partners in Banking: An Historical Portrait of a Great Private Bank—Brown Brothers Harriman & Co., 1818–1868* (New York: 1968).

Krozewski, G., *Money and the End of Empire: British International Economic Policy and the Colonies, 1947–58* (Basingstoke: 2001).

Krugman, P., 'Vehicle Currencies and the Structure of International Exchange', *Journal of Money, Credit and Banking*, 12 (1980).

Krugman, P., *Currency Crises* (Chicago: 2000).

Kuper, S., 'Bleak Days Ahead for Forex Traders', *Financial Times*, 24 December 1996.

Kuper, S., 'Dealers on the Spot as Margins Narrow', *Financial Times*, 18 April 1997.

Kuper, S., 'Information on the Button', *Financial Times*, 5 June 1998.

Kuper, S., 'Merrill Makes Up for Lost Time on Forex', *Financial Times*, 14 July 1997.

Kuper, S., 'Old Order Gives Way to the New', *Financial Times*, 5 June 1998.

Kuper, S., 'Reuters Falls Behind EBS in Electronic Broking', *Financial Times*, 30 June 1997.

Kynaston, D., *Cazenove & Co.* (Batsford, 1991).

Kynge, J., 'Exotics Reach the Major League', *Financial Times*, 9 May 1997.

Lambe, G., 'FX Markets Ride Wave of Widening Appeal', *Financial Times*, 4 October 2010.

Lambe, G., 'Settlement Model Aids FX Market Success', *Financial Times*, 12 April 2010.

Lambert, R., 'Finance Grows into a Threat to the City', *Financial Times*, 1 June 1989.

Lambert, R., 'More Products Now Need Round-the-Clock Trading', *Financial Times*, 27 October 1986.

Landells, W., 'The London Stock Exchange', *Quarterly Review*, 217 (1912).

Lapper, R. and Gawith, P., 'Forex Market Growth Slowing, Says BIS', *Financial Times*, 31 May 1996.

Larsen, P.T., 'Action May Be Needed to Maintain Competitive Advantage', *Financial Times*, 26 March 2006.

Larsen, P.T., Pretzlik, C. and Hughes, C., 'Big Bang Celebrants Find Party Has Moved On', *Financial Times*, 28 October 2006.

Lascelles, D. and Oram, R., 'Key Link Added to a Global Chain', *Financial Times*, 3 March 1987.

Lascelles, D., 'An Established Profit Centre', *Financial Times*, 27 May 1986.

Lascelles, D., 'Another Flurry in Money Brokers' World', *Financial Times*, 19 August 1987.

Lascelles, D., 'Big Business But Competition Keen', *Financial Times*, 14 February 1984.

Lascelles, D., 'Earnings Continue to Increase', *Financial Times*, 3 June 1987.

Lascelles, D., 'The Competition Will Get Tougher', *Financial Times*, 2 October 1986.

Lascelles, D., 'Trusting in Local Judgement', *Financial Times*, 15 July 1988.

Lascelles, D., 'When the Walls Come Down', *Financial Times*, 23 July 1986.

Lawson, T.W., *High Cost Living* (Dreamwold: 1913).

League of Nations, *World Economic Survey* (Geneva, 1935–6).

Jackson, F.H. *et al.*, *Lectures on British Commerce, Including Finance, Insurance, Business and Industry* (London: 1912).

Lever, E.H., *Foreign Exchange from the Investor's Point of View* (London: 1925).

Levich, R.M., 'Financial Innovations in International Financial Markets', in M. Feldstein (ed.), *The United States in the World Economy* (Chicago: 1988).

Levich, R.M., *International Financial Markets: Prices and Policies* (New York: 1998).

Levy-Leboyer, M., 'Central Banking and Foreign Trade: The Anglo-American Cycle in the 1830s', in C. Kindleberger and J.-P. Laffargue, *Financial Crises: Theory, History and Policy* (Paris: 1982).

Lewis, C., *America's Stake in International Investments* (Washington: 1938).

Lindert, P.H., 'Key Currencies and Gold, 1900–1913', *Princeton Studies in International Finance* (1969).

Loftie, W.J., *London City: Its History, Streets, Traffic, Buildings, People* (London: 1891).

London Post Office Directory (1922–1940).

Lowes, J. and Nenova, T., 'The Foreign Exchange and Over-the-Counter Interest Rate Derivatives Market in the United Kingdom', *Bank of England Quarterly Bulletin*, 53 (2013).

Mackenzie, M. and Scholtes, S., 'Regulators Issue a Warning at Bond Trading's Wild Frontier', *Financial Times*, 13 November 2006.

Mackenzie, M., 'Global Trade Facilitators Behind a 24-Hour Market', *Financial Times*, 20 April 2007.

Mackenzie, M., 'Libor Probe Shines Light on Voice Brokers', *Financial Times*, 17 February 2012.

Mackenzie, M., 'Search for Liquidity Tests Firms' Talent for Innovation', *Financial Times*, 5 November 2014.

Mackenzie, M., 'Swap Traders Resist Moves to Increase Use of Platforms', *Financial Times*, 16 September 2014.

Mackenzie, Sir Compton, *Realms of Silver: One Hundred Years of Banking in the East* (London: 1954) (Assisted by J. Leighton-Boyce and H.E. Faulkner from the Chartered Bank).

Mackintosh, J., 'Brokers Reach Merger Agreement', *Financial Times*, 12 October 1997.

MacLaury, B.K., *The Canadian Money Market: Its Development and Its Impact*, Harvard University, PhD, 1961.

Madden, J.T. and Nadler, M., 'The Paris Money Market', *Bulletin of the Institute of International Finance* (New York: 1 June 1931).

Maes, I. and Pascotti, I., 'The Legacy of Bretton Woods', *Journal of European Economic History*, 51 (2022).

Magee, G.B. and Thompson, A.S., *Empire and Globalisation: Networks of People, Goods and Capital in the British World, c 1850–1914* (Cambridge: Cambridge University Press, 2010).

Mandel-Campbell, A., 'Not Just a Traditional Market for Shares', *Financial Times*, 19 March 2001.

Margraff, A.W., *International Exchange* (Chicago: 1903).

Marriage, M., 'Scandalous Past Still Haunts Forex Industry', *Financial Times*, 12 December 2016.

Marsh, D., 'Powerhouse Holds Its Ground', *Financial Times*, 4 March 1994.

Martin, H.S., *The New York Stock Exchange* (New York: 1919).

Martin, K. and Smith, C., 'The Mystery of How Quantitative Tightening Will Affect Markets', *Financial Times*, 10 July 2022.

Martin, K. and Stafford, P., 'Banter Banned as Forex Traders Clean Up Act', *Financial Times*, 23 May 2015.

Martin, K., 'Swiss Franc Hit by Mini-Flash Crash during Asian Session', *Financial Times*, 12 February 2019.

Martin, K., 'Trading Data Show Tougher Rule Book Improves Banks' Forex Behaviour', *Financial Times*, 4 September 2018.

Martineau, L., 'Hedging Helps the Boom', *Financial Times*, 3 June 1987.

Mason, D.M., 'Our Money Market and American Banking and Currency Reform', *JIB*, 30 (1909).

Masters, B., 'Set Apart by Englishness', *Financial Times*, 14 August 2008.

Matthews, D.W. and Tuke, A.W., *History of Barclays Bank Ltd* (London: 1926).

McCaleb, W.F., *Present and Past Banking in Mexico* (New York: 1919).

McCallum, J., 'Big Three Battle It Out', *Financial Times*, 29 April 1991.

McCallum, J., 'End of Controls Provides a Lift', *Financial Times*, 11 November 1991.

McCloskey, D.N. and Zecher, J.R., 'How the Gold Standard Worked 1880–1913', in J.A. Frenkel and H.G. Johnson (eds), *The Monetary Approach to the Balance of Payments* (London: 1976), republished in D.N. McCloskey (ed.), *Enterprise and Trade in Victorian Britain: Essays in Historical Economics* (London: 1981).

McCormick, E.T., *Understanding the Securities Act and the SEC* (New York: 1948).

McLeod, C.C. and Kirkaldy, A.W., *The Trade, Commerce and Shipping of the Empire* (London: 1924).

Meeker, J.E., *Short Selling* (New York: 1932).

Meeker, J.E., *The Work of the Stock Exchange* (New York: 1922).

Meissner, C.M., 'A New World Order: Explaining the Emergence of the Classical Gold Standard, 1860–1913', *Journal of International Economics*, 66 (2005).

Merchant, K., 'Market for ECP Opens Up Via Trax', *Financial Times*, 7 September 1999.

Merrett, D.T., 'Capital Markets and Capital Formation in Australia, 1890–1945', *Australian Economic History Review*, 37 (1997).

Merrett, D.T., 'Global Reach by Australian Banks: Correspondent Banking Networks, 1830–1960', *Business History*, 37 (1995).

Merrett, D.T., *ANZ Bank* (London: 1985).

Meyer, C.H., *The Securities Exchange Act of 1934: Analyzed and Explained* (New York: 1934).

Meyer, G., 'From Ranchers to Fund Managers, Algos Cause a Stir', *Financial Times*, 10 October 2017.

Meyer, G., 'Trading', *Financial Times*, 7 July 2016.

Michie, R.C., 'The Invisible Stabiliser: Asset Arbitrage and the International Monetary System Since 1700', *Financial History Review*, 15 (1998).

Michie, R.C., 'Friend or Foe: Information Technology and the London Stock Exchange Since 1700', *Journal of Historical Geography*, 23–3 (1997).

Michie, R.C., 'Insiders, Outsiders and the Dynamics of Change in the City of London Since 1900', *Journal of Contemporary History*, 15 (1998).

Michie, R.C., 'One World or Many Worlds?: Markets, Banks, and Communications, 1850s–1990s', in T. de Graaf, J. Jonker and J.J. Mabron (eds.), *European Banking Overseas, 19th–20th Centuries* (Amsterdam: 2002).

Michie, R.C., 'The City of London and British Banking, 1900–1939', in C. Wrigley (ed.), *A Companion to Early Twentieth Century Britain* (Oxford: 2003).

Michie, R.C., 'The City of London and International Trade, 1850–1914', in D.C.M. Platt (ed.), *Decline and Recovery in Britain's Overseas Trade, 1873–1914* (London: 1993).

Michie, R.C., 'The City of London as a Global Financial Centre, 1880–1939: Finance, Foreign Exchange and the First World War', in P.L. Cottrell, E. Lange and U. Olsson (eds.), *Centres and Peripheries in Banking: The Historical Development of Financial Markets* (Aldershot: Ashgate Publishing Company, 2007).

Michie, R.C., 'The City of London: Functional and Spatial Unity in the Nineteenth Century', in H.A. Diedericks and D. Reeder (eds.), *Cities of Finance* (Amsterdam: North-Holland, 1996).

Michie, R.C., 'The Invisible Stabiliser: Asset Arbitrage and the International Monetary System Since 1700', *Financial History Review*, 15 (1998).

Michie, R.C., 'The Myth of the Gold Standard: An Historian's Approach', *Revue Internationale d'Histoire de la Banque*, (1986).

Michie, R.C., 'The Performance of the Nineteenth-Century International Gold Standard', in W. Fischer, R. Marvin McInnis and J. Schneider (eds.), *The Emergence of a World Economy 1500–1914: Papers of the IX International Congress of Economic History*, (Stuttgart: 1986) (with J. Foreman-Peck).

Michie, R.C., *The City of London: Continuity and Change, 1850–1990* (London: Palgrave Macmillan, 1992).

Michie, R.C., *The Global Securities Market: A History* (Oxford: Oxford University Press, 2006).

Michie, R.C., *The London and New York Stock Exchanges, 1850–1914* (London: 1987).

Michie, R.C., *The London Stock Exchange: A History* (Oxford: Oxford University Press, 1999).

Middelmann, C., 'Domestic Market is Struggling', *Financial Times*, 1 March 1996.

Middleton, R., *Government Versus the Market: The Growth of the Public Sector, Economic Management and British Economic Performance, c. 1890–1979* (Aldershot: Edward Elgar, 1997).

Millard, S. and Polenghi, M., 'The Relationship between the Overnight Interbank Unsecured Loan Market and the CHAPS Sterling System', *Bank of England Quarterly Bulletin*, 44 (2004).

Miller, H.F.R., *The Foreign Exchange Market: A Practical Treatise on Post-war Foreign Exchange* (London: 1925).

Mitchell, B., 'An American Banker's View of the City', *JIB*, 98 (1977).

Moggridge, D.E., *British Monetary Policy, 1924–1931: The Norman Conquest of $4.86* (Cambridge: 1972).

Montagnon, P., 'International Powerhouse', *Financial Times*, 21 May 1984.

Montagnon, P., 'Novel Offerings Bring Fresh Edge to Competition', *Financial Times*, 14 February 1984.

Montgomery, C.J., 'The Clearing Banks, 1952–77: An Age of Progress', *JIB*, 98 (1977).

Moore, J., 'Ultimate Target Is Broad Band of Financial Services', *Financial Times*, 14 February 1984.

Morgan, E.V., *Studies in British Financial Policy 1914–25* (London: 1952).

Morgenstern, O., *International Financial Transactions and Business Cycles* (Princeton: 1959).

Morris, S. and Walker, O., 'HSBC Chief Warns Post-Brexit Fragmentation Could Raise Costs', *Financial Times*, 2 December 2021.

Morris, S. and Walker, O., 'UBS Chairman Backs London to Remain Europe's Top Financial Centre', *Financial Times*, 3 December 2020.

Morris, S., Wiggins, K., Fletcher, L. and Noonan, L., 'Dublin-on-Thames? City Leaders Debate the Post-Brexit Future', *Financial Times*, 21 December 2020.

Morse, I. and Morris, S., 'Citi's Jane Fraser Ditches Ambition to Break into Wall Street's Big League', *Financial Times*, 18 February 2022.

Morton, W.A., *British Finance 1930–1940* (Madison: 1943).

Moshenskyi, S., *History of the Weksel: Bill of Exchange and Promissory Note* (New York: Xlibris Corporation, 2008).

Muhleman, M.L., *Monetary Systems of the World* (New York: 1896).

Muirhead, S., *Crisis Banking in the East: The History of the Chartered Mercantile Bank of India, London and China, 1853–93* (Aldershot: 1996).

Munn, C., 'The Emergence of Central Banking in Ireland', *Irish Economic and Social History*, 10 (1983).

Munn, C.W., *Clydesdale Bank: The First 150 Years* (London: 1988).

Murphy, H., 'TP Icap Names Paris as its EU Base after Brexit', *Financial Times*, 8 August 2018.

Myers, M.G., *Paris as a Financial Centre* (London: 1936).

Naef, A., *An Exchange Rate History of the United Kingdom, 1945–1992* (Cambridge: Cambridge University Press, 2022).

Nairn, G., 'Internet Fails to Transform the Foreign Exchange World', *Financial Times*, 5 June 2002.

Nash, B.D., *Investment Banking in England* (Chicago & New York: 1924).

National Bank, *Foreign Exchange* (1923).

National Bank, *Foreign Exchange* (1925).

National Monetary Commission, *Statistics for Great Britain, Germany and France, 1867–1909* (Washington: 1910).

Naylor, R.T., *Foreign and Domestic Investment in Canada: Institutions and Policy, 1867–1914*, University of Cambridge PhD, 1979.

Neal, L. and Weidenmier, M., 'Crises in the Global Economy from Tulips to Today', in M.D. Bordo, A.M. Taylor and J.G. Williamson (eds), *Globalization in Historical Perspective* (Chicago: NBER, 2003).

Neal, L., 'The Integration and Efficiency of the London and Amsterdam Stock Market in the Eighteenth Century', *Journal of Economic History*, 47 (1987).

Neal, L., *The Rise of Financial Capitalism: International Capital Markets in the Age of Reason* (Cambridge: 1990).

Nelson, S.A., *The A.B.C. of Options and Arbitrage* (New York: 1904).

Neufeld, E.P., *The Financial System of Canada: Its Growth and Development* (New York: 1972).

Nevin, E. and Davis, E.W., *The London Clearing Banks* (London: 1970).

Newton, L., *Change and Continuity: The Development of Joint Stock Banking in the Early Nineteenth Century* (Reading: Henley Business School, 2007).

Newton, L., 'The Birth of Joint-Stock Banking: England and New England Compared', *Business History Review*, 84 (2010).

Nicholls, E., *Crime within the Square Mile: The History of Crime in the City of London* (London: 1935).

Nicholson, N.A., *The Science of Exchanges* (London: 1873).

Nishimura, S., 'The Foreign and Native Banks in China: Chop Loans in Shanghai and Hankow before 1914', *Modern Asian Studies*, 39 (2005).

Noble, J., 'UK's Share of Renminbi Trade Leaps', *Financial Times*, 9 October 2013.

Noonan, L., Guthrie, J., Bernard, S., Faunce, L. and Smith, A., 'How London Grew into a Financial Powerhouse', *Financial Times*, 15 December 2020.

Noonan, L., Walker, O., Mooney, A., Morris, S. and Riding, S., 'Finance Jobs Stayed in London after Brexit Vote', *Financial Times*, 12 December 2020.

Nordstrom, A., *Understanding the Foreign Exchange Market* (Riksbank: 2022).

Norris, W., *The Man Who Fell from the Sky* (New York: 1987).

Norton, G., *Commentaries on the History, Constitution and Chartered Franchises of the City of London* (London: 1828).

Nurse, R. and Brown, W.A., Jr, *International Currency Experience: Lessons of the Inter-war Period* (Geneva: League of Nations, 1944).

Nwanko, G.O., 'British Overseas Banks in the Developing Countries', *JIB*, 93 (1972).

O'Brien, R. and Keith, A., 'The Geography of Finance: After the Storm', *Cambridge Journal of Regions, Economy and Society*, 2 (2009).

O'Brien, R., *Global Financial Integration: The End of Geography* (London: 1992).

O'Brien, R., 'The Euro-Currency Market', *JIB*, 92 (1971).

O'Connor, J., Wackett, J. and Zammit, R., 'The Use of Foreign Exchange Markets by Non-banks', *Bank of England Quarterly Bulletin*, 51 (2011).

Oakley, D., 'Austria Gives Nod to MTS Eurozone Rival', *Financial Times*, 1 July 2008.

Obstfeld, M. and Taylor, A.M., *Global Capital Markets: Integration, Crisis and Growth* (Cambridge: 2004).

Obstfeld, M., Shanbaugh, J. and Taylor, A.M., 'The Trilemma in History: Trade Offs among Exchange Rates, Monetary Policies and Capital Mobility', *The Review of Economics and Statistics*, 87 (2005).

Odate, G., *Japan's Financial Relations with the United States* (New York: 1922).

Officer, L.H., *Between the Dollar-Sterling Gold Points: Exchange Rates, Parity and Market Behaviour* (Cambridge: 1996).

Ogura, S., 'Mitsui Bank's Lending Policy in Transition in the Interwar Years', in M. Kasuya (ed.), *Coping with Crisis: International Financial Institutions in the Interwar Period* (Oxford: 2003).

Ogura, S., *Banking, the State and Industrial Promotion in Developing Japan, 1900–73* (London: 2002).

Ollerenshaw, P., *Banking in Nineteenth-Century Ireland: The Belfast Banks*, 1825–1914 (Manchester: 1987).

Oppers, S.E., 'The Interest Rate Effect of Dutch Money in Eighteenth-Century Britain', *Journal of Economic History*, 53 (1993).

Orr, R., 'Founder of Icap Is New Chairman of Numis', *Financial Times*, 30 April 2003.

Osler, C., 'Market Microstructure and the Profitability of Currency Trading', *Annual Review of Financial Economics*, 4 (2012).

Paish, F.W., 'The London New Issue Market', *Economica*, 18 (1951).

Pan, E., 'Liquidity Strains in Markets Need Structural Fixes', *Financial Times*, 5 July 2022.

Patrick, H.T., 'Japan 1868–1914', in R. Cameron, O. Crisp, H.T. Patrick and R. Tilly (eds), *Banking in the Early Stages of Industrialization* (New York: 1967).

Pearce, L.G., 'British Exchange Control: The System and Its Effects', in *Banking and Foreign Trade* (London: Institute of Bankers, 1952).

Perren, R., *The Meat Trade in Britain, 1840–1914* (London: 1978).

Peston, R., 'Silent Launch of the Lifeboat', *Financial Times*, 19 October 1993.

Peters, J., 'The British Government and the City-Industry Divide: The Case of the 1914 Financial Crisis', *Twentieth Century British History*, 4 (1993).

Petram, L., *The World's First Stock Exchange* (New York: Columbia University Business School Publishing, 2014).

Phelps, C.W., *The Foreign Expansion of American Banks: American Branch Banking Abroad* (New York: 1927).

Phillips, H.W., *Modern Foreign Exchange and Foreign Banking* (London: 1926).

Platt, D.C.M., *Britain's Investment Overseas on the Eve of the First World War: The Use and Abuse of Numbers* (London: 1986).

Platt, D.C.M., *Latin America and British Trade, 1806–1914* (London: 1972).

Platt, E., Rennison, J. and Duguid, K., 'Liquidity Is Terrible: Poor Trading Conditions Fuel Wall Street Tumult', *Financial Times*, 7 June 2022.

Plender, J., 'Stress Test Looms for Financial System in 2021', *Financial Times*, 4 January 2021.

Pohl, M. and Burk, K., *Deutsche Bank in London: 1873–1914* (Munich: 1998).

Pooler, M., 'New York and London Vie for Financial Crown', *Financial Times*, 2 October 2014.

Pope, D., 'Australia's Payments Adjustment and Capital Flows under the International Gold Standard, 1870–1913', in M. Bordo and F. Capie (eds), *Monetary Regimes in Transition* (Cambridge: 1994).

Powell, E.T., *The Evolution of Money Market, 1385–1915* (London: 1916).

Powell, J., *A History of the Canadian Dollar* (Bank of Canada, 2005).

Pownall, G.W., 'The Proportional Use of Credit Documents and Metallic Money in English Banks', *JIB*, 2 (1881).

Pratt, S.S., *The Work of Wall Street* (New York: 1903).

Pressnell, L.S., '1925: The Burden of Sterling', *Economic History Review*, 31 (1978).

Pressnell, L.S., 'The Sterling System and Financial Crises Before 1914', in C.P. Kindleberger and J.-P. Laffargue (eds), *Financial Crises: Theory, History and Policy* (Paris: 1982).

Pretzlik, C., 'Benefits to City Would Be Only Marginal at Best, Report Concludes', *Financial Times*, 10 June 2003.

Pringle, R., 'The Foreign Banks in London', *JIB*, 99 (1978).

Pritchard, S., 'A Race to Stay Ahead of Fraudsters', *Financial Times*, 5 June 2002.

Pullinger, J.F.A., 'The Bank and the Commodity Markets', in J. Fforde (ed.), *The Bank of England and Public Policy, 1944–1958* (Cambridge: Cambridge University Press, 1992).

Quintero Ramos, A.M., *A History of Money and Banking in Argentina* (Puerto Rico: 1965).

Lapper, R., 'A Tale of Two Cities', *Financial Times*, 12 June 1996.

Oram, R., 'Volatility Spurs Cross-trading', *Financial Times*, 3 June 1987.

Wigglesworth, R. and Rennison, J., 'Algos Blaze Trail in Odd Lots Segment of US Corporate Bonds', *Financial Times*, 15 June 2018.

Rainsbury, S., 'The War and the Arbitrage Dealer: Its Effects on the London and Paris Markets', *JIB*, 36 (1915).

Ramachandra Rau R., *Present-Day Banking in India* (Calcutta: 1922).

Rawsthorn, A., 'Intermediaries' Buy Out', *Financial Times*, 27 May 1986.

Ray, A., 'Two Centuries of Apex Banking: The State Bank of India and the Evolution of Modern Banking in India', in Gerald D. Feldman *et al.*, (eds), *Finance and Modernization* (Farnham, 2008).

Ray, A., *The Evolution of the State Bank of India*, vol. 3: *The Era of the Imperial Bank of India, 1921–1955* (New Delhi: 2003).

Read, D., *The Power of the News: The History of Reuters* (Oxford: OUP, 1992).

Reber, V.B., *British Mercantile Houses in Buenos Aires, 1810–1880* (Cambridge: 1979).

Reed, M.C., *A History of James Capel & Co* (London: 1975).

Rees, G.L., *Britain's Commodity Markets* (London: 1972).

Reinhart, C.M. and Rogoff, K.S., *This Time Is Different: Eight Centuries of Financial Folly* (Princeton: Princeton University Press, 2009).

Reis, J., Esteves, R.P. and Ferramosca, F., 'Market Integration in the Golden Periphery: The Lisbon/ London Exchange 1854–1891', *Explorations in Economic History*, 46 (2009).

Rennison, J. and Scaggs, A., 'US Treasury Dealers Accused of Collusion', *Financial Times*, 17 November 2017.

Rennison, J. and Stafford, P., 'Rise of MarketAxess Mirrors Demise of Traders on Wall Street', *Financial Times*, 30 August 2019.

Rennison, J., 'Bloomberg Snatches Corporate Bond Trade Data Partner from Rival Thomson Reuters', *Financial Times*, 26 July 2018.

Rennison, J., 'Bond Trading Platform Muscles in as Banks Retreat', *Financial Times*, 29 September 2016.

Rennison, J., 'Lutnick Makes Treasury Trading Comeback', *Financial Times*, 16 May 2017.

Rennison, J., Stafford, P., Smith, C. and Wigglesworth, R., 'Great Liquidity Crisis Strikes System as Banks Step Back', *Financial Times*, 24 March 2020.

Report and Proceedings of the Standing Sub-committee of the Committee for Imperial Defence on Trading with the Enemy (1912).

Rigby, E., 'Collins Stewart Eyes Prebon', *Financial Times*, 27 May 2004.

Riley, B., 'A New Asset Class Created', *Financial Times*, 7 February 1994.

Riley, B., 'More Interdealer Brokers to Open', *Financial Times*, 28 March 1988.

Roberts, R. (ed.), *Global Financial Centres: London, New York, Tokyo* (Aldershot: Edward Elgar, 1994).

Roberts, R. (ed.), *Offshore Financial Centres* (Aldershot: Edward Elgar, 1994).

Roberts, R. and Kynaston, D., *City State: How the Markets Came to Rule Our World* (London: 2000).

Roberts, R., (ed.), *International Financial Centres: Concepts, Development and Dynamics* (Aldershot: Edward Elgar, 1994).

Roberts, R., 'The City of London as a Financial Centre in the Era of the Depression, the Second World War and Post-war Official Controls', in A. Gorst, L. Johnman and W.S. Lucas (eds), *Contemporary British History, 1931–61* (London: 1991).

Roberts, R., *Saving the City: The Great Financial Crisis of 1914* (Oxford: Oxford University Press, 2013).

Roberts, R., *Schroders: Merchants and Bankers* (London: 1992).

Roberts, R., *The London Financial Services Cluster Since the 1970s: Expansion, Development and Internationalisation* (Paris, 2008).

Rockoff, H., 'Until It's Over, Over There: The US Economy in World War 1', in S. Broadberry and M. Harrison (eds), *The Economics of World War 1* (Cambridge: 2005).

Ross, D.M., 'The Clearing Banks and the Finance of British Industry, 1930–1959', *Business and Economic History*, 20 (1991).

Ross, V., *A History of the Canadian Bank of Commerce* (Toronto: 1920–34).

Rousseau, P.L. and Sylla, R., 'Financial Systems, Economic Growth and Globalisation', in M. D. Bordo, A. M. Taylor and J. G. Williamson (eds), *Globalization in Historical Perspective* (Chicago: 2003).

Royal Institute of International Affairs, *The Problem of International Investment* (Oxford: 1937).

Rozenraad, C., *The History of the Growth of London as the Financial Centre of the World and the Best Means of Maintaining That Position* (London: 1903).

Rozenraad, C., *The International Money Market* (London: 1893).

Rudlin, P., *The History of Mitsubishi Corporation in London: 1915 to Present Day* (London: 2000).

Rungta, R.S., *The Rise of Business Corporations in India, 1851–1900* (Cambridge: 1970).

Rybczynski, T.M., 'The Merchant Banks', *Economic and Social Studies*, 41 (1973).

Sachs, D., 'Survey of the Financial Institutions of the City of London', in *Current Financial Problems of the City of London* (London: Institute of Bankers, 1949).

Sandhu, M., 'Brexit and Covid Harden the Case for a Proper EU Financial Market', *Financial Times*, 7 December 2020.

Sangway, J., *Clare's Money Market Primer and Key to the Exchanges* (London: 1936).

Sarno, L. and Taylor, M.P., 'The Microstructure of the Foreign Exchange Market: A Selective Survey of the Literature', *Princeton Studies in International Economics* (2001).

Saul, S.B., *Studies in British Overseas Trade, 1870–1914* (Liverpool: 1960).

Sayers, R.S., *Gilletts in the London Money Market, 1867–1967* (Oxford: 1968).

Sayers, R.S., *The Bank of England, 1891–1944* (Cambridge: 1976).

Scammell, W.M., 'The Working of the Gold Standard', *Economic and Social Research*, 17 (1965).

Scammell, W.M., *The London Discount Market* (London: 1968).

Schäfer, D. and Fleming, S., 'Forex Probe Poised to Eclipse Libor Cases', *Financial Times*, 10 March 2014.

Schäfer, D. and Fleming, S., 'Scandal Puts City's Reputation on the Line', *Financial Times*, 6 March 2014.

Schäfer, D. and Strauss, D., 'Moves into Forex Etrading Speed Up', *Financial Times*, 4 March 2014.

Schäfer, D., 'Shrinking Margins and Higher Costs Drive Down Returns', *Financial Times*, 5 November 2014.

Schenk, C.R., 'The Origins of the Eurodollar Market in London: 1955–1963', *Explorations in Economic History*, 35 (1998).

Schenk, C.R., *Britain and the Sterling Area: From Devaluation to Convertibility in the 1950s* (London: 1994).

Schenk, C.R., *Hong Kong as an International Financial Centre: Emergence and Development, 1945–65* (London: 2001).

Schenk, C.R., *The Decline of Sterling: Managing the Retreat of an International Currency, 1945–1992* (Cambridge 2010).

Schiltz, M., *Accounting for the Fall of Silver: Hedging Currency Risk in Long-Distance Trade with Asia, 1870–1913* (Oxford: Oxford University Press, 2020).

Schmidt, H., *Foreign Banking Arbitration: Its Theory and Practice* (London: 1875).

Schneer, J., *London 1900: The Imperial Metropolis* (New Haven: 1999).

Scholtes, S., 'Electronic Battle Heats Up', *Financial Times*, 28 July 2006.

Schrimpf, A. and Sushko, V., 'FX Trade Execution, Complex and Highly Fragmented', *BIS Quarterly Review* (December 2019).

Schrimpf, A. and Sushko, V., 'Sizing Up Global Foreign Exchange Markets', *BIS Quarterly Review* (December 2019).

Schubert, A., *The Credit-Anstalt Crisis* (Cambridge: 1991).

Schubert, E.S., 'Arbitrage in the Foreign Exchange Markets of London and Amsterdam during the 18th Century', *Explorations in Economic History*, 26 (1989).

Schuster, F., 'Foreign Trade and the Money Market', *The Monthly Review*, xiv (January 1904).

Schwartz, A.J., 'Introduction', in M.D. Bordo and A.J. Schwartz (eds), *A Retrospective on the Classical Gold Standard, 1821–1931* (Chicago/London: 1984).

Scott, G.J., 'The Bill-Broker in the Bank Parlour', *JIB*, 42 (1921).

Senior, S. and Westwood, R., 'The External Balance Sheet of the United Kingdom: Implications for Financial Stability?', *Bank of England Quarterly Bulletin*, 40 (2000).

Seyd, E., *Bullion and Foreign Exchanges* (London: 1868).

Seyd, E., *The London Banking and Bankers' Clearing House System* (London: 1872).

Sharpe, A., 'Amsterdam Prepares to Fight Back', *Financial Times*, 16 June 1994.

Sharpe, A., 'Cash Haven Lures Investors', *Financial Times*, 26 May 1994.

Shaw, R., 'London as a Financial Centre'. Reprinted in R.C. Michie (ed.), *The Development of London as a Financial Centre* (London: 2000).

Shephard, D.K., *The Growth and Role of UK Financial Institutions, 1880–1962* (London: 1971).

Simonian, H., 'Banking Growth Bolsters Demand', *Financial Times*, 3 June 1987.

Simonian, H., 'Dealers Welcome Rise in Volatility', *Financial Times*, 15 July 1988.

Sinclair, P.J.N., 'Central Banks and Financial Stability', *Bank of England Quarterly Bulletin*, 40 (2000).

Singh, M., 'We Need New Financial Pipes', *Financial Times*, 3 June 2022.

Singleton, J., *Central Banking in the Twentieth Century* (Cambridge: 2011).

Skorecki, A., 'Bank of England Lights a Fuse', *Financial Times*, 30 November 2004.

Skorecki, A., 'Bold Vision Demands a Response', *Financial Times*, 14 December 2004.

Skorecki, A., 'Cantor Split Off Bucks the Trend', *Financial Times*, 18 August 2004.

Skorecki, A., 'Cantor Wrestles to Stay Treasury Heavyweight', *Financial Times*, 8 February 2005.

Skorecki, A., 'Forex System That Takes the Waiting Out of Wanting', *Financial Times*, 4 January 2002.

Skorecki, A., 'Icap Forms Bond Trading Alliance with MarketAxess', *Financial Times*, 22 March 2004.

Skorecki, A., 'Icap Says Phone Broking Rules Market', *Financial Times*, 4 June 2004.

Skorecki, A., 'Voice-Broked Bond Trading Holds Its Own', *Financial Times*, 19 March 2003.

Skorecki, A., 'Web Power Helps Smaller Customers', *Financial Times*, 27 May 2004.

Smith St Aubyn, 'Business Diary'.

Smith, B.M., *The Equity Culture: The Story of the Global Stock Market*, Farrar, Straus and Giroux (New York: 2003).

Smith, C., 'Money Market Funds Need Reform to Prevent Runs, US Regulators Say', *Financial Times*, 23 December 2020.

Smith, C., Szalay, E. and Martin, K., 'Dollar Blues: Why the Pandemic Is Testing Confidence in the US Currency', *Financial Times*, 1 August 2020.

Smith, C.F., 'The Early History of the London Stock Exchange', *American Economic Review*, 19 (1929).

Smith, H., 'Reverberations from Volatility in the Real Economy', *Financial Times*, 6 October 2009.

Sobel, M., 'The Clean-Up of the Non-Bank Sector Needs to Begin Now Financial System Is Failing Its First Real Stress Test after the 2008–09 Crisis', *Financial Times*, 20 April 2020.

Spalding, W.F., 'The Establishment and Growth of Foreign Branch Banks in London, and the Effect, Immediate and Ultimate, Upon the Banking and Commercial Development of This Country', *JIB*, 32 (1911).

Spalding, W.F., 'The Foreign Branch Banks in England, and Their Influence on the London Money Market', *Economic Journal*, 22 (1912).

Spalding, W.F., *Dictionary of the World's Currencies and Foreign Exchanges* (London: 1928).

Spalding, W.F., *Eastern Exchange Currency and Finance*, 4th ed. (London: 1924).

Spalding, W.F., *Foreign Exchange and Foreign Bills*, 4th ed. (London: 1921).

Spalding, W.F., *The London Money Market: A Practical Guide to What It Is, Where It Is, and the Operations Conducted in It* (London: Sir Isaac Pitman, 1930).

Spicer, E.E., *An Outline of the Money Market* (London: 1908).

Spikes, S. and Cohen, N., 'It's Still Good to Talk on the Cutting Edge', *Financial Times*, 10 May 2007.

Spikes, S. and Larsen, T.P., 'Inter-Dealer Broking Behind Rapid Growth', *Financial Times*, 19 December 2006.

Spikes, S., 'Icap Chief Caps a 20-Year Rise to the Stars', *Financial Times*, 22 April 2006.

Spikes, S., 'Icap Snaps Up EBS for £464m', *Financial Times*, 22 April 2006.

Spring-Rice, D., 'The Financial Machinery of the City of London', *JIB*, 50 (1929).

Stafford, P. and Blitz, R., 'Undersea Cables Boost Euro Trading', *Financial Times*, 6 July 2017.

Stafford, P. and Mackenzie, M., 'Interdealer Brokers Braced for Shake-Up', *Financial Times*, 22 November 2012.

Stafford, P. and Mundy, S., 'Icap Nets Exchange Licence in Deal for Plus Unit', *Financial Times*, 19 May 2012.

Stafford, P. and Szalay, E., 'London Pulls Away from New York in Forex and Swaps as It Shrugs Off Brexit', *Financial Times*, 17 September 2019.

Stafford, P., 'Amsterdam Chosen as Tradeweb's EU Base', *Financial Times*, 4 August 2017.

Stafford, P., 'BGC Signs Trio of High-Frequency Trading Firms to Boost European Equity Options', *Financial Times*, 25 July 2019.

Stafford, P., 'Brexit Brings Headache to Industry Weary of Regulation', *Financial Times*, 11 October 2016.

Stafford, P., 'Brexit Poses Threat to London's Role as Global Hub', *Financial Times*, 10 October 2017.

Stafford, P., 'CME Clinches Spencer's Nex in Deal Set to Shake Up $500bn Treasuries Market', *Financial Times*, 29 March 2018.

Stafford, P., 'CME Expects No Asset Sales after Nex Purchase', *Financial Times*, 3 April 2018.

Stafford, P., 'CME Eyes Pole Position in Treasury Trades with Audacious Bid for Nex', *Financial Times*, 28 March 2018.

Stafford, P., 'Colourful World of Interdealers Faces Deep Structural Changes', *Financial Times*, 3 June 2014.

Stafford, P., 'Departure of TP ICAP Chief Exposes Tensions at Top', *Financial Times*, 11 July 2018.

Stafford, P., 'Electronic Trading Pioneer Throws Down Gauntlet to Brokertec on Treasuries', *Financial Times*, 8 June 2018.

Stafford, P., 'Exchanges Seek Slice of $5tn Forex Pie', *Financial Times*, 7 August 2015.

Stafford, P., 'Fears Over 'Last Look' Spur Tighter FX Code', *Financial Times*, 20 December 2017.

Stafford, P., 'Fintech Alley Cat Gets the Cream with £670bn CME Deal', *Financial Times*, 31 March 2018.

Stafford, P., 'Future of the City: London's Markets Rivalry with EU Intensifies', *Financial Times*, 16 December 2020.

Stafford, P., 'High-Speed Electronic Trading Leaves Regulator Far Behind', *Financial Times*, 3 November 2010.

Stafford, P., 'ICAP Chief Prepares for Radical Change of Direction', *Financial Times*, 26 February 2016.

Stafford, P., 'ICAP's New Direction Reflects Changing Future of Derivatives', *Financial Times*, 6 October 2016.

Stafford, P., 'Mifid 2 Rules Tighten Wall Street's Grip on Europe', *Financial Times*, 27 June 2019.

Stafford, P., 'Personal Touch Critical as Banks Trim Brokers', *Financial Times*, 29 June 2017.

Stafford, P., 'Sense of Urgency Underpins Fresh Scrutiny of Markets', *Financial Times*, 16 September 2014.

Stafford, P., 'Settlement a Blow to Spencer', *Financial Times*, 26 September 2013.

Stafford, P., 'Singapore Exchange Plans to Tighten Grip as Asia's Largest Forex Trading Hub', *Financial Times*, 11 June 2019.

Stafford, P., 'Spencer Considers a Financial Future without Nex', *Financial Times*, 17 March 2018.

Stafford, P., 'Swiss Broker to Set Up London Repo Venue', *Financial Times*, 19 May 2015.

Stafford, P., 'TP Icap to Buy Trading Venue Liquidnet for up to $700m', *Financial Times*, 9 October 2020.

Stafford, P., 'US Eyes Prize If Swaps Shift from London', *Financial Times*, 20 October 2016.

Stafford, P., 'Voice Brokers Answer Call for Liquidity', *Financial Times*, 12 August 2016.

Stafford, P., 'Voice Brokers Fight to Survive Europe's Shake-Up', *Financial Times*, 10 October 2017.

Stafford, P., Massoudi, A. and Mackenzie, M., 'Nasdaq Sets Stage for HFT in Treasuries', *Financial Times*, 5 April 2013.

Steele, F.E., 'On Changes in the Bank Rate of Discount, First, Their Causes; and Secondly, Their Effects on the Money Market, on the Commerce of the Country, and on the Value of All Interest Bearing Securities', *JIB*, 12 (1891).

Stein, J.L., 'The Nature and Efficiency of the Foreign Exchange Market', *Princeton Studies in International Finance* (1962).

Stephens, P., 'Living with Turbulence', *Financial Times*, 3 June 1987.

Stern, S., *The United States in International Banking* (New York: 1951).

Stevens, G.R., *The Canada Permanent Story, 1855–1955* (Toronto: 1955).

Stewart Patterson, E.L., *Domestic and Foreign Exchange* (New York: 1917).

Stockdale, Sir Edmund, *The Bank of England in 1934* (Bank of England, 1967).

Stone, I., *The Global Export of Capital from Great Britain, 1865–1914: A Statistical Survey* (London: 1999).

Stones, R., 'Government–Finance Relations in Britain, 1964–7: A Tale of Three Cities', *Economy and Society*, 19 (1990).

Storbeck, O. and Stafford, P., 'Deutsche Börse in Talks to Acquire Refinitiv Foreign Exchange Assets', *Financial Times*, 12 April 2019.

Straker, F., 'The Daily Money Article', *JIB*, 25 (1904).

Strauss, D., 'Five Big Banks Extend Their Domination of Forex Trading', *Financial Times*, 9 May 2014.

Stuart, R., 'Measuring Stock Market Integration during the Gold Standard', *Cliometrica*, (2023).

Stulz, R.M., 'The Limits of Financial Globalization', *Journal of Finance*, 60 (2005).

Sturmey, S.G., *The Economic Development of Radio* (London: 1968).

Subacchi, P., 'The System That Became a Non-system: The End of Bretton Woods Fifty Years Later', *Journal of European Economic History*, 51 (2022).

Sunderland, D., *Managing the British Empire: The Crown Agents, 1833–1914* (London: Royal Historical Society, 2004).

Swann, C., 'Big Banks Play Game of Brinkmanship', *Financial Times*, 25 June 1999.

Swann, C. and Cameron, D., 'FXall Set to Intensify Battle in Online Currency Trading', *Financial Times*, 10 May 2001.

Swanson, W.W., 'London and New York as Financial Centres', *Journal of the Canadian Bankers Association*, 20 (1914–15).

Sweet-Escott, B., *Gallant Failure: The British Overseas Bank Ltd, 1919–1939* (1977) (RBS Archives).

Swiss Bank Corporation, *Fifty Years of Swiss Banking in London: 1898–1948* (London: 1948).

Swiss Bank Corporation, *Foreign Exchange and Money Market Operations* (1992).

Sykes, E., 'Some Effects of the War on the London Money Market', *JIB*, 36 (1914).

Sykes, E.W., 'The Growth of London as the Financial Centre of the World, and the Best Means of Maintaining That Position', *JIB*, 23 (1902).

Sylla, R., 'Comparing the UK and US Financial Systems, 1790–1830', in J. Attack and L. Neal (eds), *The Origin and Development of Financial Markets and Institutions: From the 17th Century to the Present* (Cambridge: CUP, 2009).

Szalay, E. and Croft, J., 'Five Banks Face Forex-Rigging Lawsuits in London', *Financial Times*, 30 July 2019.

Szalay, E. and Stafford, P., 'Citigroup Calls for Burden of Managing Risky Trades to Be Shared More Widely', *Financial Times*, 17 April 2019.

Szalay, E. and Stafford, P., 'HSBC and Wells Fargo to Settle Currency Trades With Blockchain', *Financial Times*, 13 December 2021.

Szalay, E. and Toplensky, R., 'Banks Look for Closure in EU Benchmark Probe', *Financial Times*, 11 May 2019.

Szalay, E., 'Asset Managers Scramble to Cut Banks Out of Forex Dealing', *Financial Times*, 18 April 2019.

Szalay, E., 'Banks Resist Demand to Shed More Daylight on Forex Charges', *Financial Times*, 16 May 2019.

Szalay, E., 'CBOE to Challenge CME and Refinitiv With New FX Platform', *Financial Times*, 25 June 2020.

Szalay, E., 'Dispute Brews Between EU and Currency Traders on Mifid Reform', *Financial Times*, 1 December 2020.

Szalay, E., 'Fears Over Forex Trading Going Bump in the Night', *Financial Times*, 6 March 2019.

Szalay, E., 'Foreign Exchange Data Wars Heat Up as Rivals Take on Big Two', *Financial Times*, 1 December 2020.

Szalay, E., 'India Seeks to Lure Rupee Trading Back Onshore', *Financial Times*, 22 January 2020.

Szalay, E., 'Jump in London Rupee Trades Rings Alarms', *Financial Times*, 18 September 2019.

Szalay, E., 'Languid Forex Trading Due a Wake-Up Call', *Financial Times*, 2 January 2020.

Szalay, E., 'London Charm Offensive Pays Off in Race for Renminbi', *Financial Times*, 9 February 2019.

Szalay, E., 'Offshore Currency Trade Poses Challenge for India's Central Bank', *Financial Times*, 6 March 2019.

Szalay, E., 'Peer-to-Peer Forex Services Aim to Bypass Wall St Banks', *Financial Times*, 16 October 2019.

Szalay, E., 'Risks of Failure in $6.6tn Forex Market at Record High', *Financial Times*, 24 July 2020.

Szalay, E., 'UK Watchdog Lends Teeth to Currency Trading Code', *Financial Times*, 28 June 2019.

Szalay, E., 'Ultra Low Interest Rates Spur Euro to Become World's New Carry Trade', *Financial Times*, 6 December 2019.

Szalay, E., 'Yen Traders Wrongfooted as Flash Crash Strikes during Asia's Witching Hour', *Financial Times*, 4 January 2019.

Tamaki, N., *Japanese Banking: A History 1859–1959* (Cambridge: 1995).

Taylor, C.W., 'The Case against the Nationalisation of the Banks', *JIB*, 56 (1935).

Teichova, A., Kurgan-Van Hentenryk, G. and Ziegler, D. (eds), *Banking, Trade and Industry: Europe, America and Asia from the 13th to the 20th Century* (Cambridge: 1997).

Thackstone, H.H., 'Work of the Foreign Branch of a Commercial Bank', in *Current Financial Problems and the City of London* (London: Institute of Bankers, 1949).

The Banking Almanac, *List of Foreign and Colonial Banks with Offices/Agents in London: 1860, 1880, 1890, 1900, 1913*.

City Research Project, *The Competitive Position of London's Financial Services* (London: 1995).

Editorial Board, 'Non-bank Lenders Will Bear Brunt of Credit Crisis: Financial Risk Has Been Pushed from Banks into the Shadows', *Financial Times*, 24 March 2020.

Editorial Board, 'Shadow Banks Must Come Out of the Shadows', *Financial Times*, 7 December 2021.

Editorial Board, 'Threats to the Dollar's Dominance are Overblown', *Financial Times*, 19 April 2023.

Institute of Bankers, *The Bank of England Today* (London: 1964).

Mitsui Bank: A History of the First 100 Years (Mitsui Bank, 1976).

New Palgrave Dictionary of Money and Finance (London: 1992).

Statist, 14 August 1886, 179–80.

Thirlwell, J., 'A Look at American Banking', *JIB* (103, 1982).

Thomas, D., 'US Overtakes EU as Biggest Financial Services Export Market for Britain', *Financial Times*, 8 December 2021.

Thomas, S.E., *Banking and Exchange* (London: Gregg Publishing, 1930).

Thomas, S.E., *The Principles and Arithmetic of Foreign Exchange* (London: 1925).

Thompson, J., 'QE Sows Seeds of Next Crisis, Funds Warn', *Financial Times*, 2 December 2019.

Tigge, St. L., *A History of the Canadian Bank of Commerce* (Toronto: 1934).

Tiner, D., *Banking and Economic Development: Brazil 1899–1930* (London: 2000).

Tomlinson, J., 'Attlee's Inheritance and the Financial System: Whatever Happened to the National Investment Board', *Financial History Review*, 1 (1994).

Toniolo, G., (ed.), *Central Banks' Independence in Historical Perspective* (Berlin: 1988).

Triffin, R., *Our International Monetary System: Yesterday, Today and Tomorrow* (New York: 1968).

Triffin, R., 'The Evolution of the International Monetary System: Historical Reappraisal and Future Perspectives', *Princeton Studies in International Finance* (1964).

Tritton, J.H., 'Bills of Exchange and their Functions', *JIB*, 23 (1902).

Tritton, J.H., 'The Short Loan Fund on the London Money Market', *JIB*, 23 (1902).

Truptil, R.J., *British Banks and the Money Market* (London: 1936).

Tucker, E., 'The Square Mile Stays Out in Front', *Financial Times*, 29 May 1992.

Tucker, P., 'Macro, Asset Price, and Financial System Uncertainties', *Bank of England Quarterly Bulletin*, 47 (2007).

Tucker, S., 'Rivals to HK and Singapore Emerge', *Financial Times*, 19 November 2007.

Tuke, A.W. and Gillman, R.J.H., *Barclays Bank Limited, 1926–1969: Some Recollections* (Barclays Bank, 1972).

Tullio, G. and Wotters, J., 'Was London the Conductor of the International Orchestra or Just the Triangle Player? An Empirical Analysis of Asymmetries in Interest Rate Behaviour during the Classical Gold Standard, 1896–1913', *Scottish Journal of Political Economy*, 43 (1996).

Turner, A., 'British Holdings of French War Bonds: An Aspect of Anglo-French Relations during the 1920s', *Financial History Review*, 3 (1996).

Turner, C., 'Money London', in C. Sims (ed.), *Living London* (London: 1902).

Turner, J.D., 'Introduction to the Symposium on Banking and Currency', *Economic History Review*, 75 (2022).

Twentieth Century Fund, *Stock Market Control* (New York: 1934).

Tyson, G., *100 Years of Banking in Asia and Africa* (London: 1963).

Van Antwerp, W.C., *The Stock Exchange from Within* (New York: 1913).

Van Duyn, A., 'Only the Best Will Survive', *Financial Times*, 28 March 2001.

Vander Weyer, D., 'The Threats and Opportunities Facing British Banks: A 10 Year View', *JIB*, 101 (1980).

Viner, J., *Canada's Balance of International Indebtedness, 1900–1913* (Cambridge: 1924).

Vismara, A., 'Mifid 2 Drags Down an Ecosystem Along With Europe's Banks', *Financial Times*, 15 May 2019.

Wadsworth, J., *Counter Defensive: The Story of a Bank in Battle* (London: 1946).

Wagstyl, S., 'Glint of Change in the Gold Market', *Financial Times*, 5 December 1986.

Waight, L., *The History and Mechanism of the Exchange Equalisation Account* (Cambridge: 1939).

Wake, J., *Kleinwort Benson: The History of Two Families in Banking* (Oxford: Oxford University Press, 1997).

Ward, D., 'A Description of the Foreign Exchange Market in London', in 'Reconstruction in Europe', *Manchester Guardian Commercial*, 20 April 1922.

Wardley, P., *Women, Mechanization, and Cost-Savings in Twentieth Century British Banks and Other Financial Institutions* (Helsinki: WEHC, 2006).

Warren, H., *The Story of the Bank of England* (London: 1903).

Weatherall, D., *David Ricardo: A Biography* (The Hague: 1976).

Webb, S., 'Dutch Win Back State Debt Trade', *Financial Times*, 16 May 1994.

Weismuller, A.A., 'London Consortium Banks', *JIB*, 95 (1974).

Wells, S., 'Financial Interlinkages in the United Kingdom's Interbank Market and the Risk of Contagion', *Bank of England Working Paper*, 230 (2004).

Wendt, P.F., *The Classification and Financial Experience of the Customers of a Typical New York Stock Exchange Firm from 1933 to 1938* (Maryville: 1941).

Westminster Bank, *The Financial Machinery of the Import and Export Trade* (London: 1925).

Wetherilt, A.V., 'Money Market Operations and Volatility in UK Money Market Rates', *Bank of England Quarterly Bulletin*, 42 (2002).

Wharmby, S., 'The Foreign Exchange and Over-the-Counter Derivatives Markets in the United Kingdom', *Bank of England Quarterly Bulletin*, 41 (2001).

Wheatley, J., 'São Paulo Adopts a More International Approach', *Financial Times*, 21 October 2009.

Whitaker, A.C., *Foreign Exchange* (New York: 1919).

White, H.D., *The French International Accounts, 1880–1913* (Cambridge: 1933).

Whitmore, F., *The Money Machine* (London: 1930).

Wigglesworth, R. and Rennison, J., 'New Credit Ecosystem Blossoms as Portfolio Trades Surge', *Financial Times*, 11 October 2018.

Wigglesworth, R., 'How to Save the Treasury Market', *Financial Times*, 13 September 2022.

Wigglesworth, R., 'IMF Warns of "Tip Of The Iceberg" Threat Over Volatility', *Financial Times*, 12 April 2019.

Wigglesworth, R., 'Markets: Volatile Times', *Financial Times*, 10 January 2019.

Wigglesworth, R., 'Mysterious $11bn Swiss Swapsies', *Financial Times*, 21 October 2022.

Wigglesworth, R., 'US Treasury Market's Brush with Disaster Must Never Be Repeated', *Financial Times*, 21 September 2020.

Wigglesworth, R., Ivanova. P. and Smith, C., 'Financial Warfare: Will There Be a Backlash against the Dollar?', *Financial Times*, 7 April 2022.

Wilcox, M.G., 'Capital in Banking: An Historical Survey', *JIB*, 100 (1979).

Wild, J., 'Central Banks Eye Digital Money', *Financial Times*, 2 November 2016.

Wilgress, L.D., 'The London Money Market', *Journal of the Canadian Bankers Association*, 20 (1912–13).

Wilkins, M., 'Cosmopolitan Finance in the 1920s: New York's Emergence as an International Financial Centre', in R. Sylla, R. Tilly and G. Tortella (eds), *The State, the Financial System, and Economic Modernization* (Cambridge: 1999).

Williams, D., 'London and the 1931 Financial Crisis', *Economic History Review*, 15 (1962–3).

Williams, D., 'The Evolution of the Sterling System', in C.R. Whittlesey and J.S.G. Wilson (eds), *Essays in Money and Banking* (Oxford: 1968).

Williams, J.H., *Argentine International Trade under Inconvertible Paper Money, 1880–1900* (Cambridge: 1920).

Williams, P., 'The Foreign Exchange and Over-the-Counter Derivatives Markets in the United Kingdom', *Bank of England Quarterly Bulletin*, 44 (2004).

Wilson, R., *Capital Imports and the Terms of Trade: Examined in the Light of 60 Years of Australian Borrowing* (Melbourne: 1931).

Wine, E., 'Sidelined Cash May Stay Out of Stocks', *Financial Times*, 4 January 2002.

Winton, J.R., *Lloyds Bank, 1918–1969* (Oxford: Oxford University Press, 1982).

Withers, H., *International Finance* (London: 1916).

Withers, H., *Money-Changing: An Introduction to Foreign Exchange* (London: 1913).

Withers, H., *The English Banking System* (Washington: 1910).

Withers, H., *War and Lombard Street* (London: 1915).

Wood, J.H., *A History of Central Banking in Great Britain and the United States* (Cambridge: Cambridge University Press, 2005).

Wood, R.J., *The Commercial Bank of Australia Ltd* (Melbourne: 1990).

Woodlock, T.F., *The Stock Exchange and the Money Market* (New York: 1908).

Woytinsky, W.S. and E.S., *World Commerce and Governments* (New York: 1955).

Wynne-Bennett, H.D., *Investment and Speculation* (London: 1924).

Yeager, L.B., *International Monetary Relations: Theory, History and Policy* (New York: 1966).

Zhaojin, J., *History of Modern Shanghai Banking: The Rise and Decline of China's Finance Capitalism* (New York: 2003).

Bank of England Archives:

Correspondence: Edward B. Meyer to Bank of England, 26 June 1930; R. Holland-Martin (Martins Bank) to K.O. Peppiat, Bank of England, 23 September 1931; F.C. Souch, Secretary of the London Foreign Exchange Brokers Association to A.W. Gurney, Committee of London Foreign Exchange Managers, 7 April 1936; Reply from A.W. Gurney, 9 April 1936; A.W. Gurney to J.K. Jones, 9 April 1936; B.G. Catterns, Bank of England, to Sir Richard Hopkins, Treasury, 8 July 1938. Letter issued by Honorary Secretary of the London Clearing Bankers, 20 September 1931.

Memoranda: 1 November 1926, 27 April 1928, 1 May 1928, 17 May 1928, 4 December 1928, 9 March 1929, 28 March 1930, 4 February 1931, 20 February 1931, 11 March 1931, 29 September 1931, 8 October 1931, 4 April 1932; Balance of Payments, 8 February 1934, 17 June 1935, 16 December 1935, 11 January 1937, 18 January 1937, 8 April 1937, 16 June 1937, 15 October 1937, 17 November 1937, 14 January 1938, 27 January 1939, 2 February 1939.

Memoranda on Foreign Exchange Market Profits, 1935–9.

Reports: Sterling Dollar Exchange, 18 July 1928; Setting Up a Foreign Exchange Department at the Bank of England, 4 December 1928; Foreign Exchanges, 10 December 1928; London Foreign Exchange Market, 7 August 1930; Names to be Accepted in Connection with Foreign Exchange Dealings, 3 November 1930; Summary of the Meetings of the Committee for Transactions in Foreign Exchange and Gold with Representatives from Continental Europe, 24 and 25 November 1930; Exchange Control During the War, 12 January 1932; The Development of the Foreign Exchange Market: Report by George Bolton, 8 July 1936; Organisation of the Foreign Exchange Market: Report by George Bolton, 29 September 1936; Direct Dealing: Report by George Bolton, 31 March 1937, 5 April 1937; Foreign Exchange and Gold: Market Organisation and Technique, Report by George Bolton, 6 April 1937; War Measures, 8 July 1937; UK Treasury-War Measures: Foreign Exchange and Gold, Sir F. Phillips, 24 June 1938; Exchange Policy, 14 October 1938; Exchange Policy and Tactics, 9 November 1938; Foreign Exchange Market Reports, 26 January 1939.

Committee of London Foreign Exchange Managers: 9 June 1936, 13 July 1936; Report, 29 September 1936, 18 October 1936, September 1936, 18 October 1936.

London Foreign Exchange Brokers Association: Report of Sub-committee, 3 December 1936.

Notes of Conversations: With Mr Fraenkel at the Anglo-International Bank, 30 May 1928, 15 August 1928, 20 August 1928, 1 September 1928, 13 November 1928, 28 November 1928; With Mr Ogg at the Anglo-International Bank, 8 January 1929; With Mr Sampson of M. W. Marshall & Co, 29 May 1929; With Ottawa Conducted by George Bolton, 14 November 1938, 16 November 1938.

Exchange Equalisation Account: Quarterly Reports 1936–9; Report on the Exchange Equalisation Account, 13 July 1937.

Papers of Harry Arthur Siepmann:

Report, 24 March 1932.

The Staffing of Exchange Management, 2 December 1937.

Foreign Exchange Market Organisation, 29 January 1937.

Material for Treasury Evidence, 3 March 1937.

EEA-Relations with Agents, 13 May 1938.

The Depreciation of Sterling, 22 November 1938.

Sterling/Dollar Turnover, 1936–9.

Correspondence: 2 February 1928 to Dr F. Mlynarski, Warsaw, 7 March 1928 to Dr Bosch, 24 October 1928 to Herr Direcktor Tabalovits, Budapest, 1 November 1928 to E. Weber, 8 November 1929 to Gairdner at BOB, 2 January 1931 to R. Auboin, 2 June 1931 to Paul van Zeeland, 11 June 1931 to R. Auboin at Bank for International Settlements, 6 October 1931 to Professor Clay, 20 October 1931 to Dr Fuchs, 26 October 1931 to Sir Frederick Leith-Ross, 5 November 1931 to Dr Fuchs, 26 August 1932 to J. Postmus, 19 December 1932 to Soames Branco, 10 March 1933 to H.C.F. Finlayson, 6 November 1933 to Soames Branco, 27 October 1936 to Allan Sproul, Vice President Federal Reserve, 31 March 1936 to Sproul, 17 April 1936 to F.F. Powell, 2 May 1936 to Sproul, 27 November 1936 to Lady Blackett, 9 January 1937 to Munakata, 13 August 1937 to C. Rogers, 29 July 1938 to O. Hobson, 23 December 1938 to Per Jacobson, 30 December 1939 to Soames Branco.

Cattern Correspondence: 19 March 1935 to S.A. Sydney-Turner, 29 April 1935 to Sir Frederick Phillips, 4 June 1935 to Sir Frederick Phillips, 11 June 1935 to Signor L. Capodanno.

Interviews: With Mr Speed, the Manager's Assistant, Foreign Branch Office, Westminster Bank, 17 May 1928, 7 August 1930; With Mr Frankau of the Anglo-International Bank, 30 May 1928; With Mr Sampson of W. Marshall & Co., 29 May 1929.

Forward Exchange: Views of Sir Henry Strakosch, 7 February 1924.

Approximate Amounts of Foreign Currency Changing Hands on the London Market Daily, 28 January 1928.

Sir George Bolton, *Memoirs*, 13 January 1977.

Index

For the benefit of digital users, indexed terms that span two pages (e.g., 52–53) may, on occasion, appear on only one of those pages.

'n.' after a paragraph number indicates the footnote number.

A

Addis, Sir Charles, 64–65
Aldington, Lord, 223–224
Ali, O., 263–264
Allen, H., 244
Amsterdam, 111–113, 170, 197, 252–253
Anderson, B.M., 20, 88–89
Anglo-International Bank, 153–154, 158–159, 182–184
Anthony, R., 276
arbitrage, 76–77
  1850–1914 London FX and, 76, 81–82, 88, 89–93
  1850–1914 LSE, 76–90, 120
  1919–1939: end of arbitrage, 120
  1919–1939 LSE, 122–127
  1920s, 126
  1945–1970 London FX, 213
  1970–1992 London FX, 235–236
  Anglo-Australian arbitrage, 82–83
  Austria, 126
  Bank of England, 124
  banks and, 84–86, 90, 91
  Belgium, 81–82
  Canada, 81–82
  definition, 77
  Deutsche Bank, 81–82
  European banks, 81–82
  foreign exchange market, 78, 88–91, 120
  German Jews and, 83–86, 120, 126–127
  Gold Standard and, 88–89
  government interventions, 124–127
  importance of, 87–89, 120
  interbank market and, 90
  joint account arbitrage, 84–85, 124
  London-Continental Europe arbitrage, 79
  London-New York arbitrage, 80–82, 87, 88, 90, 124–125
  London-Paris arbitrage, 78–79
  London's central position, 85–86
  money market and, 86–87
  New York arbitrage, 83–84, 125–126, 215
  reluctance to commit to, 84–85

  replacement of arbitrage after World War I, 126–127
  revival of, 122–124, 126–127
  as speciality, 83–84, 127
  as speculation, 124, 127
  staff, 81, 84
  successful arbitrage, 83–85, 127
  telegraph and, 78–89, 120, 125
  telephone and, 85–86, 125
  World War I: end of arbitrage, 90, 122–123, 126–127, 188–189
Argentina, 15–16, 22–26, 57–58, 131
  LSE and, 82–83
  US and, 103–104
Armstrong, F.E., 124–125
Astley and Pearce, 240–241
Atkin, J., 9–10, 51–52
Australia, 114–116
  British overseas banks, 56–57, 62–63, 131
  Commercial Bank of Australia, 131
  Melbourne Stock Exchange, 82–83
Austria
  1931 banking crisis, 115–116
  Austrian banks in City of London, 63–64
  Credit-Anstalt, 126
automatization, 255–256, 276
  1970–1992 London FX, 236–237
  1992–2007 London FX, 253–254
  2007–2022 London FX, 273–274
  algorithmic trading, 253–254
  liquidity and, 253–254
  see also electronic trading

B

Bagehot, W., 50
Baltic Exchange, 24–25, 73, 104–105, 156–157, 172–173
Bankers Magazine, 169
Banking Almanac, 41–42, 53
Bank of America, 251–252, 267–268, 270
Bank of England
  1919–1939 London FX and, 156–157, 163, 167–168, 171, 174–176, 187–188, 190–191

Bank of England (*Continued*)
  1919–1939 London FX, lack of official recognition by Bank of England, 156–157, 190–191
  1919–1939 London FX and Bank of England control, 177–185, 187–188, 210
  1939–1945 London FX and Bank of England control, 184–186, 210–213
  1945–1970 London FX and Bank of England control, 189, 212–217, 221–224
  1945 foreign exchange market, 154–155
  1992–2007 London FX, 258–259
  2007–2022 London FX, 273–274, 278–279
  2008 Global Financial Crisis, 278–279
  2022 liability-driven investment crisis, 272
  arbitrage, 124
  Big Five banks and, 178–179
  bill brokers and, 35–37, 179–180
  British overseas banking, 132–133
  City of London and, 197–200, 204–205, 256–258
  exchange controls, 184–185, 219
  exchange rates, 15–16, 186
  fixed exchange rates, 185, 215–216
  foreign banks in London and, 206–207
  foreign exchange brokers and, 179–180, 182–184, 210
  foreign exchange department, 163, 182
  Gold Standard and, 101, 162–163
  government bonds, 273
  government ownership of, 196–197, 212–213
  'hot money', 185–186
  interest rates, 114–115
  intervention and control by, 110–111, 122–123, 182–186, 196, 197–198, 201–203, 210–213
  as lender of last resort, 35–37, 109–110, 142–143, 176, 187–188, 200–201, 204–205, 207–208, 256–258, 279
  London discount market and, 11–12, 35–37, 109–111, 114, 118–120, 176, 178–180, 203, 204–205, 232–233, 240
  London money market and, 206–208, 256–258
  UK monetary policy, 256–258
  UK£ and, 182–184, 257–258
  US$ and, 256–257
  World War II, 196
Bank of France, 33–34, 115–116, 170
Bank of Japan, 273
banks/banking
  1850–1914: management of money, 48
  1850–1914 London FX, 11–12, 19–20, 51–54, 71–73, 91–93, 285–286
  1919–1939 London FX, 133, 141–152, 175–176, 179–180, 187–191, 210, 286
  1920s concentration in banking, 139, 142–143
  1945–1970, 203
  1945–1970 London FX, 215, 217–224
  1970–1992 London FX, 230–231, 234–236, 238–239, 287
  1992–2007, 247
  2008 Global Financial Crisis, 266–267
  2020 Covid-19 pandemic, 271–272
  arbitrage, 84–86, 90, 91
  bills of exchange, 34–40, 49–52, 208–209
  branch networks, 37–38, 41, 48–50, 53, 54–58, 69–70, 102, 188–189, 231
  City of London, 41–42, 190, 196–198, 203–204, 223–224, 229
  compartmentalization of banking, 247–248
  competition, 33, 65, 67–68, 149
  correspondent system, 41–42, 50, 53–54, 142–145, 204, 231
  counterparty risk/trust, 117, 126–127, 134, 139–145, 150–154
  foreign exchange market, 1–4, 6, 8–9, 14–15, 128–129, 133–142, 155–157, 209–210, 250–254, 274–275, 279–280, 283, 288–289
  foreign exchange market: two-tier structure, 276
  foreign exchange risks, 58–59, 64–65, 90, 128–131, 139, 147–148, 150–151, 210
  government interventions, 133, 196
  interest rates, 32, 48
  internalization of banking, 49–51, 204
  internalization of foreign exchange, 57–59, 61, 63–64, 66–67, 72–73, 211–212
  lend-and-hold banking, 37–40, 46–50, 111–113, 130, 133, 139, 227–228
  liabilities, 38–39, 48
  liquidity, 32–33, 35, 37–39, 48–50, 234–235
  London discount market and, 11–12, 35–37
  London money market and, 32–34, 37–39, 41, 42, 46–47, 49–50, 71–72, 109, 110
  LSE and, 74–76, 79, 81–82, 88
  monetization of savings by, 13–14
  money market and, 133
  originate-and-distribute banking, 35, 37–38, 49–50, 111–113, 129, 133, 227–228, 262, 266–267
  reserves, 33, 50
  resilient banks, 48–49, 139–143, 151–152, 272
  Royal Exchange biweekly meetings and, 10–11
  securities, 33
  telegraph and, 49–54, 57, 67–68
  UK banking system, 141–150, 201–202
  World War I, 142–143
  World War II, 196, 203
  see also global banking; interbank market; US banking system

banks, types of
  deposit banks, 51–52, 69–70, 139–140,
    205–207
  investment banks, 48–49, 201–202, 267–269
  joint stock banks, 19–20, 43, 45–46, 54–55,
    68–69, 110–111, 139–140, 149–150, 153–154,
    161, 164, 168
  retail banks, 37–38, 47–49, 53–54, 143–144
  universal banks, 48–49, 66–67, 139–140, 161
  see also Big Five British banks; British overseas
    banks; central banks; foreign banks;
    megabanks; merchant banks; shadow
    banking/non-banks
Barclays Bank, 117, 267–268
  Big Five British banks, 142–143
  DCO (Dominion, Colonial and
    Overseas), 132–133
  'foreign' branches, 53–54, 211–212
  foreign department, 211
  foreign exchange market, 144–148, 211–212,
    251–252
  Lehman Brothers and, 267–268, 270
Bareau, P., 192
Barings Bank, 48–49, 259
BATS, 279–280
Bauer, R.M., 82–83
Beattie, A., 255
Belgium, 81–82
Berlin, 117–118
  1950s, 197
  Berlin money market, 114–115
  foreign exchange market, 9–10, 19–20, 27–28
  World War I, 104–105
Big Five British banks, 142–144, 178, 181–184
  1919–1939 London FX, 145–149, 152–154,
    159, 160–161, 163, 165, 168–169, 173,
    178–179, 210
  1930s, 168–169
  Bank of England and, 178–179
  dealers employed by, 160–161, 165, 173–174
  foreign exchange brokers, 153–154
  foreign exchange market, 145–149, 152–153,
    159
  as most trusted financial institutions in the
    UK, 173
  see also Barclays Bank; Lloyds Bank; Midland
    Bank; National and Provincial Bank;
    Westminster Bank
bill brokers, 35–39, 109–110, 113, 118–119
  Bank of England and, 35–37, 179–180
  London FX and, 43–44, 47–48, 166
  LSE and, 35–37
bills of exchange, 34–37, 45, 49–50, 53, 176
  1850–1914 London FX, 46, 60–61
  1914 moratorium, 110–111
  banks/banking and, 34–40, 49–52, 208–209

before World War I, 35–40, 45, 46, 109–110
  British overseas banks, 60–61
  definition, 34–35, 45
  foreign bill of exchange, 43–44
  foreign exchange market and, 53, 56
  London money market and, 34–40, 109–110,
    204–205
  sterling bills, 35, 39–40, 43–46, 52, 58–59,
    69–70, 143–144, 200–201
  sterling bills as international currency, 35,
    39–40
  telegraphic transfers and, 40, 51–52, 60–61
  US, 52
  see also treasury bills
bimetallism, 27–28, 68–69
BIS (Bank for International
  Settlements), 279–282, 288–289
  2008 Global Financial Crisis, 266
  Basel rules, 262
  as clearing mechanism for international
    payments, 101–102
  as coordinating body for world's central
    banks, 1, 245, 273–274
BIS surveys, 1, 4, 250–251, 258, 273–274, 279
  1986 survey, 234–235
  1992 survey, 1, 4–5, 234–235
  2019 survey, 27–28, 273–274
  2022 survey, 1, 4–5, 273–274
Blitz, R., 264–265
Bloomberg, 248–249, 254–255
Bolsa (Bank of London and South
  America), 131–133, 145–146
Bolton, Sir George, 70–71, 101, 141, 172–173,
  175–176, 180, 181–186
  on counterparty risk, 161–163
  professional career of, 162–163
Bonn and Company, 24–25, 134–135
Bordo, M.D., 12–13
Brazil, 14–15, 25–26, 131
Bretton Woods System
  1945–1970 London FX and, 221–222
  collapse of, 6, 91–92, 192–196, 224–225,
    227–228
  exchange rates stability, 4, 6
  fixed exchange rates, 1–2, 6, 192–194, 209–210,
    215–216, 262
  foreign exchange market and, 192–193,
    209–210
  government intervention, 193–194, 224, 262
  managed currency, 91–92, 192–193, 224
  monetary system and, 193–194
  monetary trilemma, 3–4, 193–196
  replacement of, 195–196
Brexit, 264–265
  see also UK
British Commonwealth, 199, 213–214

British Empire, 22–24, 27–28, 31–32, 43, 64–65, 105, 196–197, 199, 203, 217–218
  imperial markets, 107–108
British Overseas Bank, 137–138, 182–184
British overseas banks, 41, 66–67, 132–133, 197–198, 203, 205–207, 213–214, 216–217, 221–224
  Anglo-Indian banks, 58–61, 128–129, 131–133
  Australia, 56–57, 62–63, 131
  Bank of England and, 132–133
  bills of exchange, 60–61
  British 'foreign' branches, 53–55
  countries with UK£ as currency, 56
  foreign exchange market, 56–63, 71–73, 128–129, 131, 213–214, 221–222
  Hamburg branches, 65
  interwar years, 131
  Latin America, 57–58, 62–63, 131, 132–133
  London money market and, 109
  New Zealand, 56–57, 62–63, 131
  overseas expansion of Britain's domestic banks, 132–133
  South Africa, 57, 62–63, 131
  telegraph and, 57–62
  US and, 67
Broderick, T., 279
brokers, 8–9, 74–75
  dealer/broker combined role, 155, 158–159
  dealer/broker distinction, 159, 165, 166
  dealer/broker relationship, 173
  Dollar Certificate of Deposit, 235–236
  London discount market, 11–12, 153
  LSE, 74–76, 83–84, 110, 172–173
  Royal Exchange biweekly meetings, 10–11
  telephone and, 70–71
  see also bill brokers; foreign exchange brokers; inter-dealer brokers
Brooks, H.K., 31–32, 52
Brown, W.A., 1–2, 19–20, 27–28, 66, 88–89, 119–120, 124–125, 139, 190–191
Brown Brothers, 68–69, 135–136
Brown Shipley, 135–136, 158
Brussels, 26–27, 170, 197
Burn, G., 199–200
Burrell, H.V., 54–55
Bush, J., 238–239

C

Canada, 25–26
  arbitrage, 81–82
  Bank of Montreal, 66, 69–70
  Canadian Bank of Commerce, 69–70, 138–139
  Canadian banks, 46–47, 69–70
  Canadian money market, 46–47
Canadian Financial Post, 82
Canadian $, 27–28, 46–47, 69–70, 155

Cane, A., 226, 237–238
Cantor Fitzgerald, 249–250
carry trade, 215–216, 253–254, 276–277, 282
Carson, M., 30–31
Cattern, B., 168
Catterns, B.G., 101–102, 184
CBOE (Chicago Board Oprions Exchange), 279–280
Cedel, 233–234
central banks, 1, 94, 288–289
  2007–2022, 270–273, 279, 283
  BIS as coordinating body for world's central banks, 1, 245, 273–274
  cooperation between, 182–184
  currency stability and, 192–193
  fixed exchange rates and, 192–195, 224
  Global Code of Conduct, 280–281
  intervention and controls, 101–102, 117, 126–127, 192–195, 202–203, 224–225, 244, 287
  liquidity and, 272–273
  megabanks and, 248, 262–263, 288–289
  money market and, 272
  need for bilateral foreign currency swap lines between, 279
  power of, 270–271
  quantitative easing programmes, 270–273, 281–283
  see also Bank of England; Federal Reserve Bank
Ceylon, 58–59
Charles Fulton and Company, 234–235
Chartered Bank, 61, 65
Chase Manhattan Bank, 238–239, 251–252
China, 60–61, 64–65, 157
Chiozza Money, L.G., 34–35
Chrystal, K.A., 1–2, 90, 235–236
Citibank, 67–68, 251–252, 270
  see also National City Bank of New York
Citigroup, 267–268, 270, 281–282
City of London
  1850–1914, 22
  1850–1914 London FX, 22, 52, 63–64, 71–73, 91
  1919–1939, 102
  1919–1939 London FX, 22–24, 91–92, 108, 149, 167–171, 187, 189–190
  1920s, 105–106, 108
  1930s, 106–108, 115–116
  1931 financial crisis, 106–108
  1945–1970, 192, 196, 203–208, 217–218
  1945–1970 London FX, 214–215, 219–220, 223–224
  1960s, 199–202, 218–219, 221, 223–224
  1970s, 218
  1970–1992, 228

1970–1992 London FX, 22–24, 229–231, 234–235, 237–238, 243, 287–288
1992–2007 London FX, 246, 251, 260–261
2007–2022 London FX, 263–265, 278–279
2008 Global Financial Crisis, 263–264
2020 Covid-19 pandemic, 265
Asian banks in, 65
Australian banks in, 115–116
Austrian banks in, 63–64
Bank of England and, 197–200, 204–205, 256–258
banks/banking, 41–42, 190, 196–198, 203–204, 223–224, 229
Brexit, 264–265
Chinese banks in, 64–65
corporations/corporate finance, 197–199, 231–232
as cosmopolitan centre, 24–27, 229–230
domestic orientation, 103, 105, 107–108, 196–197
economic integration and, 22–24
electronic trading, 246
EU regulations, 229
Eurodollar and Eurobond markets, 218–219
European banks in, 62–63, 128–129, 219
as financial centre (1850–1914), 19–20, 22–29, 32, 40, 65, 66–67, 102–103, 108, 285–286
as financial centre (1919–1939), 105–108, 168–169, 190
as financial centre (1945–1970), 196–200, 202–204, 214–215, 217–218, 223–224
as financial centre (1970–1992), 228–230
as financial centre (1992–2007), 246–247, 257–258, 260–261
as financial centre (2007–2022), 263–265
financial specialization, 25–26, 229–230
foreign banks in, 41–42, 45–47, 51–54, 62–67, 79, 91, 115–118, 128–129, 197–201, 204, 205–209, 216–219, 228–229, 236–237, 246–247, 257–258
German banks in, 62–64, 104–105, 128–130
global banking, 29, 66, 102, 205, 217–220, 232–233, 237
government intervention/control, 196–200, 202–203
as international clearing house, 22–24, 27–28, 31–32, 42, 43–44, 53, 66, 109, 114–115, 128, 129, 264–265
international financial system and, 43
international orientation, 24–27, 108
investment banking, 25–27
Japanese banks in, 62–63, 65, 204, 219
London discount market, 11–12, 204–205
London money market, 22–24, 32, 53–54, 102–103, 109, 121, 190, 197–198, 204–205
LSE, 121

megabanks, 232, 265
multi-currency transactions, 216–217, 222–223, 264–265
praise of, 35–37
replaced by New York, 192
resident population in, 22–24
staff population in, 22–25, 53–54, 63–64, 265
UK government and, 103–107, 114–115
UK£ as basis of British operations, 219
US branches in, 70, 199–202, 204, 208–209, 218, 219, 221, 231–232
US$ and, 199–200, 208–209, 218, 264–265
'Wimbledonization', 278–279
World War I, 63–64, 102–105, 108, 190
World War II, 117–118, 196–197, 203
see also London; London FX
City of London Directory, 71, 154–155
Clare, G., 11–12, 42
CLS Bank (Continuous Linked Settlement), 259, 276–278, 281–282
CME (Chicago Mercantile Exchange), 241, 268–269, 279–280
Cohn, M., 77
Cole, A.C., 35–37, 43
Cole, W.A., 75
Committee on Currency and Foreign Exchanges, 101–102
communications
    financial operations and communications revolution, 16–19, 22–24, 30, 285–286
    foreign exchange market and communications revolution, 18–19, 89, 90–91, 93, 94–95
    global communications revolution, 224–227, 237–238, 262–263
    London as centre of global communications, 16–17, 102–103, 229
    market integration and, 17–18
    telecommunications, 226–227, 229, 237–238
    see also electronic trading; telegraph; telephone
compartmentalization
    2008 Global Financial Crisis, 266
    of banking, 247–248
    end of, 244, 266–267, 287
    fixed exchange rates, 195–196
    interwar years, 117, 126, 133
    of national financial systems, 126, 133
    see also government interventions/controls
competition, 226
    1990s, 244
    banks, 33, 65, 67–68, 149
    inter-dealer brokers, 249–250
    UK, anti-competitive practices, 201–203
computers/computing, 224–225, 254–255, 262–263, 287–288
    1970–1992 London FX, 237–239, 241–243

computers/computing (*Continued*)
    inter-dealer brokers, 248–249
    see also electronic trading
Conant, C.A., 76
Cooper, J.R.H., 223–224
Cornwallis, K., 15–16
corporations/corporate finance, 41, 47–48, 120,
    204, 268–269, 279–280
    City of London, 197–199, 231–232
    megabanks, 247–248, 262–263
counterparty risk/trust
    1919–1939 London FX, 160–163, 165, 166,
        173, 175–176, 187–188, 210
    1945–1970 London FX, 219–220
    2007–2022 London FX, 276
    2008 Global Financial Crisis, 259
    2020, 281–282
    Bank of Credit and Commerce
        International, 259
    Bankhaus Herstatt, 237, 259
    banks, 117, 126–127, 134, 139–145, 150–154
    Barings Bank, 259
    Bolton, Sir George on, 161–163
    CLS Bank (Continuous Linked
        Settlement), 259, 276–278, 281–282
    Drexel Burnham Lambert, 259
    foreign exchange market, 258–259
    London money market, 109–110
    megabanks, 262–263, 276–277, 281–282,
        287–288
Covid-19 pandemic (2020), 265, 271–272,
    281–283, 287–288
Cox, C., 279
Crammond, E., 22–24
Credit Lyonnais, 89, 170
Credit Suisse (Schweizerischer
    Bankverein), 63–64, 251–252, 267–268
crises
    1866 Overend, Gurney & Company
        crisis, 141–142
    1920s US domestic financial crisis, 106–107
    1930s Great Depression, 97–100, 143, 151–152
    1931 Austrian banking crisis, 115–116
    1931 German banking crisis, 115–116
    1931 global monetary crisis, 133
    1938 Czechoslovakian crisis, 182–184
    1956 Suez Crisis, 215–216
    1957 UK monetary crisis, 199
    1970s monetary crisis, 227–228
    1974 Herstatt crisis, 259
    1982 international debt crisis, 227–228
    2022 UK liability-driven investment crisis, 272
    twenty-first century, 245
    liquidity crisis, 115–116, 227–228, 257–258,
        266–267, 271, 273

    see also Covid-19 pandemic; Global Financial
        Crisis (1929–1932); Global Financial Crisis
        (2008)
currencies, *see* Canadian $; euro; French franc;
    German mark; Indian rupee, Japanese yen;
    Swiss franc; UK£; US$; vehicle currency
currency price, 13–14
    foreign exchange market, 8–9
    silver as basis for, 14–15, 46–47, 57–60, 65
currency risks, 5–6, 47–48, 137–138, 232–233
    1850–1914 London FX, 14–15, 55–56
    1960s, 217–218
    foreign exchange market and, 4, 217–218, 228,
        262, 283, 287
    Indian rupee, 59–60
    interwar years, 188–189
    UK departure from Gold Standard, 106–107
    see also foreign exchange risks
currency volatility, 13–14, 68–69, 209–210
    World War I, 95–96, 102
    interwar years, 114–115, 130, 139, 194–195
    1970s, 228, 287
    1970–1992 London FX, 237
    2007–2022, 283
    see also exchange rates volatility
Czechoslovakian crisis (1938), 182–184

D
Darmstädter und National Bank, 116
dealers, 8–9
    1919–1939 London FX, 91–92, 153, 157–159,
        161, 165–169, 171, 173–174, 187, 190, 286
    1945–1970 London FX, 212–213, 221
    2007–2022 London FX, 282
    abilities required from exchange dealers, 168
    Big Five British banks, 160–161, 165, 173–174
    dealer/broker combined role, 155, 158–159
    dealer/broker distinction, 159, 165, 166
    dealer/broker relationship, 173
    foreign exchange market, 148–149, 151–152,
        154
    negative perceptions of, 171
    Paris, 170
    Royal Exchange biweekly meetings, 10–11
    see also jobbers
Dealers' Association, 173–174
Deutsch, H., 100–101
Deutsche Bank, 48–49, 99–100, 251–253,
    267–268
    arbitrage, 81–82
    London branch, 62–64, 81–82, 128–129, 137
Deutsche Börse, 279–280
Dickson, M., 246
direct dealing
    1919–1939 London FX, 153–154, 168,
        174–176, 179–180, 190

1970–1992 London FX, 240–243
2007–2022 London FX, 273–274
megabanks, 241–242, 248–249, 274–275
discount market, *see* London discount market
Dixon, F., 70–71, 159–161, 163
Dollar Certificate of Deposit, 200–201, 235–236
Dowling, S.W., 149–151, 166–167
Drummond Fraser, Sir D., 114
Duke, W.K., 151–152
Dunn Fischer and Company, 26–27

E
E&C Randolph, 84–85
Eames, F.L., 79–80
East India Company, 58–59
Easton, H.T., 13–14, 29–30, 32, 43–44, 144–145
EBS (Electronic Broking Services), 253–256, 279–280
Eckardt, H.M.P., 27–28
EEA (Exchange Equalisation Account), 133, 182–184, 186
E.F. Satterwhaite, 84–85
Eichengreen, B., 9–10, 101
Einzig, P., 9–10, 107–108, 221
electronic trading
    1970–1992 London FX, 236–237, 239, 243
    1992–2007 electronic revolution, 253
    1992–2007 London FX, 253–254, 258–261, 287–288
    2007–2022, 268–269, 276
    2007–2022 London FX, 273–274, 276
    advantages of, 245
    carry trade and, 253–254
    City of London, 246
    CME, 279–280
    electronic trading platforms, 248–250, 253–254, 258–259, 268–269, 273–274, 276, 279–282
    electronic revolution and global financial markets, 244, 253–254, 262–263, 287–288
    electronic revolution as two-edged weapon, 245
    financial centres, 246
    foreign exchange market, 250–251, 254–256, 276, 279–280
    fund managers, 245
    global fund managers, 245
    high cost of, 245
    interbank market, 254–255
    inter-dealer brokers, 248–250, 268–269
    LSE, 279–280
    megabanks, 245, 247–249, 254–255, 262–263, 268–269, 281–282
    multi-bank platforms, 254–255
    New York, 246

    telephone/electronic trading combined, 255–256
    SWIFT, 245
    see also automatization; Bloomberg; computers/computing; EBS; FXall; NEX; Reuters
Escher, F.E., 80
Escher, M., 27–28, 42, 104–105
EU (European Union), 199, 288–289
    EC (European Commission), 264–265
    fixed exchange rates, 228
    UK as EU member, 228–229
    see also Brexit
euro, 260–261, 264–265, 273, 276
    monetary unification, 228, 251
Eurobonds, 233–234
    Eurobond markets, 218–219, 223–224, 229, 233–234
    US$, 218, 233–234
Eurodollar market, 205, 207, 218–219, 223–224
    US$, 218
Euroclear, 233–234
European Central Bank, 273, 288–289
Eurozone, 260–261
Evitt, H.E., 143, 168
Exchange Brokers, 154–155
exchange rates
    Bank of England, 15–16, 186
    exchange-rate risk, 43–44, 129, 209–210
    flexible exchange rates as adjustment mechanism, 285–286
    fluctuation, 3–6, 14–17, 19, 71–72, 129, 209–210
    headline rate of exchange, 8–9
    monetary trilemma and, 3–4
    UK£/US$ exchange rate, 55–56, 68–70, 186
    see also Bretton Woods System; fixed exchange rates; Gold Standard
exchange rates controls, 126, 242–243
    1930s, 106–108
    1939–1945 London FX, 212–213
    1945–1970 London FX, 212–213
    1970s, 2–3, 228–229
    Bank of England, 184–185, 219
    Japan, 141
    UK government, 98–99, 106–107, 131, 196–197, 201–202, 228–231
    World War I, 98–99
    World War II, 203
    see also fixed exchange rates
exchange rates stability, 6–7, 193–194
    1850–1914 London FX, 19, 93
    1919–1939 London FX, 177
    adjustment mechanisms, 6–7, 12–13, 19, 120, 189, 194–195, 224, 227–228, 285–286
    before World War I, 94–95, 99–100, 120

exchange rates stability (*Continued*)
  Bretton Woods System, 4, 6
  foreign exchange market and, 4, 6–7, 19,
    94–95, 100–101, 120, 128–129, 189, 194–195,
    209–210, 285–286
  Gold Standard, 4–5, 12–16, 20–21, 92, 98–101,
    285–286
  government interventions and, 92–93
exchange rates volatility, 6
  1919–1939 London FX, 164, 189
  before World War I, 15–16
  foreign exchange market and, 4, 14–15, 285
  Gold Standard, 94
  interwar years, 94–96, 137–138, 164, 188–189
  post-pandemic world, 95–96
  wars and, 15–16
  World War I, 129
  see also currency volatility

F
Federal Reserve Bank, 114–115, 207–208,
    256–257, 262–264, 288–289
  2008 Global Financial Crisis, 267–268
  Covid-19 pandemic, 271–272
  CLS Bank and, 259
  global monetary system and, 273
  inflation and, 273
  as lender of last resort, 102, 111–113, 257–258,
    267–268, 272
  liquidity, 271–273, 279
  power of, 271, 273
  treasury debt, 273
financial centres
  electronic trading and, 246
  post 2007, 263
  see also City of London; New York; offshore
    financial centres
financial derivatives, 226–227, 242–243, 262,
    266–267
financial history, 94
Financial News, 157–158, 180
Financial Services Authority, 256–257
financial system
  City of London and, 43
  clustering of financial markets, 246
  financial operations and communications
    revolution, 16–19
  government interventions/controls, 194–195
  telegraph, impact on financial
    operations, 16–18, 22–24, 30, 52
  telephone, impact on financial
    operations, 17–18, 22–24, 30–31
  UK, 201–203, 263–264
  see also global financial system
Financial Times, 83–84, 272
fixed exchange rates, 186

1939–1945, 192–195
1945–1970 London FX, 189, 215–218, 221–222
1973, 3–4, 6
advantages of, 6–7, 285
Bank of England, 185, 215–216
Bretton Woods System, 1–2, 6, 192–194,
    209–210, 215–216, 262
central banks intervention and, 192–195, 224
challenges, 99–100
collapse/end of, 6, 192–193, 209–210, 224
currency stability, 192–193, 285
EU, 228
foreign exchange market and, 192–195
Gold Standard, 8–9, 12–13, 188–191, 194–195
government intervention and, 194–196
inflation and, 285
managed currencies, 91–92, 94, 156–157, 189,
    202–203, 217–218, 224, 287–289
  see also exchange rates controls
foreign banks
  1919–1939 London FX, 180–182
  1970–1992 London FX, 236–237
  1992–2007 London FX, 258, 260–261
  2007–2022 London FX, 279
  Bank of England and, 206–207
  in City of London, 41–42, 45–47, 51–54,
    62–67, 79, 91, 115–118, 128–129, 197–201,
    204, 205–209, 216–219, 228–229, 236–237,
    246–247, 257–258
  currency speculation, 62–63
  Eurodollar and Eurobond markets, 219
  foreign exchange market and, 45–46, 62–63,
    213–214, 221–222
  interbank market, 208–209, 236–237
  London Interbank Market, 208–209
  London money market, 62–63
  Midland Bank and, 41–42
  in New York, 246–247
  sterling bills and, 43–44
  US$ as currency, 208–209
foreign exchange brokers
  1919–1939 London FX, 91–92, 153–155,
    157–161, 163, 164–168, 170–172, 174, 187,
    190, 210, 286
  1945–1970 London FX, 212–213
  1970–1992 London FX, 234–237
  abilities required from broker, 166–167
  Bank of England and, 179–180, 182–184, 210
  before World War I, 70–71, 154–155
  Big Five British banks, 153–154
  brokerage charges, 158–159, 175–176, 179–180
  dealer/broker combined role, 155, 158–159
  dealer/broker distinction, 159, 165, 166
  demand for, 155
  interwar years, 126, 134–135, 149–150
  negative perceptions of, 172

Paris, 170
Foreign Exchange Brokers Association, 163, 169,
   173–175
Foreign Exchange Committee, 174–175, 178
Foreign Exchange Committee of Bankers, 169,
   178–179
Foreign Exchange and Investments Ltd, 137
foreign exchange market
   as adjustment mechanism, 6–7, 19, 88, 120,
      189, 224, 227–228, 273–274, 285–286,
      288–289
   arbitrage, 78, 88–91, 120
   banks and, 1–4, 6, 8–9, 14–15, 128–129,
      133–142, 155–157, 209–210, 250–254,
      274–275, 279–280, 283, 288–289
   bills of exchange and, 53, 56
   complexity of, 2–3, 8–9
   costs involved in, 138–139, 153–154, 220,
      255–256, 276
   currency price, 8–9
   currency risks, 4, 217–218, 228, 262, 283, 287
   as decentralized but interconnected, 2–3
   definition of, 8–9
   EU monetary unification, 251
   exchange rates stability and, 4, 6–7, 19, 94–95,
      100–101, 120, 128–129, 189, 194–195,
      209–210, 285–286
   exchange rates volatility, 4, 14–15, 285
   fixed exchange rates and, 192–195
   foreign banks, 45–46, 62–63, 213–214,
      221–222
   fragmentation of, 2–3
   function of, 2–3, 8–9
   global financial system and, 2–3, 228, 282–283,
      287–289
   as global market, 1, 192, 251–253, 260–263,
      273–274, 281–282
   global monetary system and, 4
   Gold Standard and, 12–15, 57–58, 94
   growth of, 1–3
   importance of, 2–4
   as interbank market, 168, 187–188
   liquidity, 251–252, 274–276
   market creation and evolution
      context, 285–286
   monetary trilemma and, 3–4, 193–194
   money as unit of account, store of value, and
      means of exchange, 2–3, 8–9, 274–275
   national foreign exchange markets, 14–15
   negative perceptions of, 4, 100–102, 156–157
   as OTC market, 1
   physical/institutional structure, lack of, 1,
      11–12, 73, 94, 164
   regulation/self-regulation, 1, 277–283, 286,
      288–289
   resilience, 276–277, 281–282

scholarly neglect of, 1–4, 94
scholarship on, 6–7
speculation, 4, 15–18, 100, 101–102, 152–153,
   156–157
staff, 53–54, 134, 135, 138–139, 149–150,
   153–154, 163, 166, 182–184, 210–211, 220,
   276
strategies, 8–9
supply and demand, 4, 8–9, 19, 94–95, 239–240
telegraph and, 5–6, 17–18, 31–32, 72–73, 139,
   144
telegraphic transfers, 52, 56, 60–61, 139
telephone and, 134–135, 139, 144, 253–255
transactions, 2–3
transnational nature, 1–3
transparency, lack of, 2–3
turnover, 1–4, 27–28, 209–210, 234–235,
   250–252, 273–274, 279–282, 287
volume and value of, 1–4
as world's largest financial market, 1, 250–251,
   273–275, 277–278, 282, 287
   see also London FX; New York foreign exchange
   market
foreign exchange market: periods
   late nineteenth and early twentieth
      centuries, 14–15
   before World War I, 4–6, 12–13, 19–20, 50–51,
      67–68
   interwar years, 1–2, 95–96, 100–101, 130–131,
      134–135, 151–153, 188–189, 286
   World War I, 95–96, 129
   1970s, 6–7, 195–196, 287–288
   2007–2022, 283
   2008 Global Financial Crisis, 276–279,
      281–283
   2020 Covid-19 pandemic, 281–283, 287–288
   2022 Russian invasion of Ukraine, 281–283,
      287–288
   see also London FX
foreign exchange risks, 58–59, 90, 128–131, 139,
   150–151, 210
   Barclays Bank, 147–148
   forward markets and, 60–62, 149, 150
   HSBC, 64–65
Foreign Exchange Securities Trust, 137
Forester, C.S., 186–187
forward markets, 16–19, 238–239, 251
   1919–1939 London FX, 134–136, 144–147,
      150–151, 155–156, 160, 167–168, 170, 176,
      189
   1920s, 51–52
   1945–1970 London FX, 213, 215–216
   1970–1992 London FX, 234–236
   2007–2022 London FX, 282

forward markets (*Continued*)
absence of active forward markets in foreign exchange, 29–30
before World War I, 1–3, 29–30, 45–46, 58–59, 71–72, 91–92
exchange risk and, 60–62, 149, 150
government intervention, 170
interwar years, 45
Fraenkel, Mr, 153–154
France, 14–15
Frankau, Mr, 158–159
Frankfurt, 79, 197, 199, 251, 252–253, 264–265, 288–289
Fraser, D., 114, 141–142
Fraser, L., 24–25, 134–135
Freeland, C., 246
French Empire, 27–28, 184–185
French franc, 14–15, 114–116, 156–157
fluctuations, 15–16
foreign exchange market and, 45–46
importance of, 27–28
fund managers, 276–277
Brexit, 265
electronic trading, 245
global fund managers, 245, 247–248, 262–263, 270–271, 283
megabanks and, 247–248, 262–263
see also shadow banking/non-banks
Furniss, E.S., 39, 41–42, 100, 143–144
Furse, C., 246–247
futures trading, 8–9, 22–24, 150, 237–238, 240–241
FXall, 255–256, 279–280

G
Gardin, J.E., 55–56
Garnham, P., 274–275
Gellender, E.E., 76
Geneva, 202–203
George, E., 244, 256–257, 278–279
German Jewish financiers
anti-Semitism, 126–127
arbitrage, 83–86, 120, 126–127
German mark, 14–15, 62–63, 145–146, 156–157, 213–214
fluctuations, 15–16
importance of, 27–28
upward revaluation, 194–195
Germany, 14–15
1931 banking crisis, 115–116
1931 Standstill Agreement, 117, 137, 141, 145–146
Bankhaus Herstatt, 237, 259
banks/banking, 139–140
Dresdner Bank, 62–63
Discontogellschaft, 62–63

European war: impact on financial system, 43
German banks in City of London, 62–64, 104–105, 128–130
government interventions, 117
World War I, consequences of, 104–105
Gieve, Sir John, 257–258
Gilletts, 37–38, 118–119
Glahe, F.R., 1–2
global banking, 258–259, 276
1919–1939, 128, 168
1970, 231
1990s, 248
2020, 272
City of London, 29, 66, 102, 205, 217–220, 232–233, 237
global banks, 224–225, 247–248
London discount market, 118–120
London money market, 39, 46–47
US banks, 231–232
US$, 231–232
wholesale banking and, 247–248
see also banks/banking; megabanks
Global Financial Crisis (1929–1932), 119–120, 137–138, 143, 151–152
City of London, 106–108
Global Financial Crisis (2008), 260–262
Bank of England, 278–279
banks/banking, 266–267
BIS, 266
causes of/those responsible for, 266–269, 271
City of London, 263–264
CLS Bank, 260–261
consequences of, 268–269
counterparty risk, 259
Federal Reserve Bank, 267–268
financial system refashioning and, 263–264
foreign exchange market, 276–279, 281–283
government interventions, 266–269
interbank market, 267–268
inter-dealer brokers, 268–269
Lehman Brothers collapse, 262–263
as liquidity crisis, 266–267
London FX, 279, 287–288
megabanks, 262–263, 266–269, 276–277, 279
post-GFC reform, 271–272
securities, 266–267
as self-inflicted banking crisis, 271
as solvency crisis, 266–267
US$, 267–268
global financial system
2020 Covid-19 pandemic, 271–272
competition, deregulation and technology, 226
electronic revolution and global financial markets, 244, 253–254, 262–263, 287–288
foreign exchange market as global market, 1, 192, 251–253, 260–263, 273–274, 281–282

foreign exchange market as permanent feature
of, 2–3, 228, 282–283, 287–289
instability, 272
interbank market, 227–228
megabanks, 247–248, 262–263
resilience, 262
risks, 227–228
US Treasury and, 273
see also Global Financial Crisis (1929–1932);
Global Financial Crisis (2008)
Global Foreign Exchange Committee, 279–280
Glyn Mills, 137–138
Goldman Sachs, 95–96, 251–252, 267–268, 270
Gold Standard
arbitrage and, 88–89
Bank of England and, 101, 162–163
collapse of, 182–184, 188–189
currencies on, 15–16, 27–28, 46–48
economic integration and, 20–21
exchange rates stability, 4–5, 12–16, 20–21, 92,
98–101, 285–286
exchange rates volatility, 94
fixed exchange rates, 8–9, 12–13, 188–191,
194–195
foreign exchange market and, 12–15, 57–58, 94
interwar years, 94, 98–100, 286
membership of, 14–15
monetary system under, 19–21, 193–194
monetary trilemma, 3–4, 193–194
return to, 101, 178–179, 187–188, 190–191,
286, 288–289
UK's departure from, 97–100, 102, 106–108,
114, 116, 118–120, 130, 131, 134, 151–153,
162, 169–171, 174–175, 177–178, 182–184,
189
UK's return to (1925), 99–100, 106–107,
114–115, 137–138, 150–155, 157–159, 165,
169–171, 177, 189
US and, 46–47, 68–69, 99–100, 106–107
World War II, 99–100
Goodacre, H., 276
Goschen, G.J., 34–35, 53
government interventions/controls
1930s response to depression, 97–98, 151–152,
287
1939–1945 London FX, 211–213
1945–1970 London FX, 189, 192, 212–218,
221, 223–224
2008 Global Financial Crisis, 266–269
banks/banking, 133, 196
barriers to international trade and
finance, 97–98, 133, 245
Bretton Woods System, 193–194, 224, 262
City of London, 196–200, 202–203
EEA (Exchange Equalisation Account), 133
exchange rates stability, 92–93

fixed exchange rates, 194–196
foreign exchange market, 285
forward markets and, 170
Germany, 117
interventionism, 117, 182–184
Japan, 141, 237–238
LSE, 121–123, 196–197
monetary stability and, 92, 94, 95–96, 101–102,
224
technological change and, 242–243
UK, 133, 201–203, 205, 266
UK, London discount market, 110–111,
196–197
US, 101, 218
World War II, 194–196, 203, 224, 288–289
see also Bank of England; central banks;
compartmentalization; exchange rates
controls; regulation and control
Graham, G., 258–259
Grant, J., 262–263
Green, N., 67
Greengrass, H.W., 114
Greenwood, W.J., 74–75, 123
Gregory, M., 264–265
Gregory, T.E., 46, 139, 164
Gurney, A.W., 134, 170–171, 174–175

H
Hamburg, 61, 64–65, 197
Harrod, R., 88–89
Haupt, O., 77
Hawker, C., 162–163
Hawkins, J., 244
Hawtrey, R.G., 100–101
hedge funds, 268–271, 273, 276–277
Covid-19 pandemic, 272
foreign exchange market, 251–252, 255–256,
275–276, 282
see also shadow banking/non-banks
Helbert Wagg, 134–135
Heseltine Powell & Co, 81
Hichens, R., 74–75
Higgins, L.R., 75
high-frequency traders, 268–272, 282
see also shadow banking/non-banks
Hobson, O., 181, 204–205
Holden, E., 33–34, 55–56
Hong Kong
foreign exchange market, 237–238, 243,
252–253, 273–275
offshore financial centre, 195–196, 202–203
Howell, M., 273
HSBC (Hong Kong and Shanghai Bank), 48–49,
251–252, 281–282

HSBC (Hong Kong and Shanghai Bank)
(*Continued*)
  Hamburg branch, 64–65
  London branch, 64–65, 128–130
  telegraphic transfers, 64–65
Huber, R., 238–239
Huebner, S.S., 88
Hughes, C., 246
Hughes, J., 250–251, 258–259, 277–278

I

ICAP (Intercapital), 249–250, 255–256, 268,
  279–280
  TP ICAP, 268–269
India
  British overseas banks (Anglo-Indian
    banks), 58–61, 128–129, 131–133
  Exchange banks, 61–62, 128–129, 131–132,
    145–146
  exchange problems with, 59–60
  government monetary policy, 61–62
  Imperial Bank of India, 131–132
  Mercantile Bank of India, 61–62
  National Bank of India, 132–133
  Presidency banks, 58–61, 131–132
Indian rupee, 27–28, 58–62, 114, 128–129,
  131–132
  currency risks, 59–60
inflation, 96, 219–220, 244
  Federal Reserve Bank and, 273
  fixed exchange rates and, 285
  post-World War I, 97, 100–101, 104–105
  twenty-first century, 273, 285
Inouye, J., 110
Institute of International Finance (New
  York), 118–119, 133
integration
  communications and market
    integration, 17–18
  economic integration before World War I, 92,
    94–95
  economic integration and City of
    London, 22–24
  economic integration and Gold
    Standard, 20–21
  fixed exchange rates and economic
    integration, 285
  global economic integration, 92, 244, 251–252,
    262
  integration of financial markets, 224–225
interbank market, 72–73, 170
  1945–1970 London FX, 219–222
  1950s–1960s, 208–209, 232–233
  1960s, 222–223
  1970s, 233, 236–237
  1970–1992 London FX, 236–237, 243

  1980s, 227–228, 236–237
  2007–2022 London FX, 279, 282
  2008 Global Financial Crisis, 267–268
  arbitrage and, 90
  dollar-based inter-bank market, 219
  electronic trading, 254–255
  foreign banks, 208–209, 236–237
  foreign exchange market and, 236–237, 243
  foreign exchange market as, 168, 187–188
  global financial system, 227–228
  interbank borrowing and lending, 118–119,
    188–189, 205–206, 232–234, 240, 270
  interbank money market, 224, 227–228, 243
  London Interbank Market, 208–209, 233
  megabanks and, 232, 248, 254–255, 267–268,
    270
  originate-and-distribute banking, 266–267
  UK, 246–247
Inter-bank Research Organisation, 230–231
inter-dealer brokers, 159, 239–240, 253–254
  1945–1970, 205–206, 232–233
  1960s, 232–233
  1970–1992 London FX, 234–237, 239–243,
    287–288
  1980s, 240–242
  1990s, 249–250
  1992–2007, 248–250, 255–256
  1992–2007 London FX, 258–261
  2007–2022 London FX, 273–274
  2008 Global Financial Crisis, 268–269
  competition, 249–250
  computers/computing, 248–249
  electronic trading, 248–250, 268–269
  Eurobond market, 233–234
  importance of, 268
  megabanks, 248–250, 255–256, 268
  mergers and acquisitions, 249–250
interest rates, 17–19, 287
  1920s, 155–156
  1930s, 204–205
  1970s–1980s, 228
  Bank of England, 114–115
  banks, 32, 48
  differential interest rates, 155–156, 182,
    226–227, 253–254
  Federal Reserve Bank, 114–115
  fluctuations in, 77–79, 221–222
  Gold Standard, 20–21, 98–99
  London money market, 37
  LSE, 74–75
International Monetary Fund, 192–193, 288–289
interwar years, 188
  1930s Great Depression, 97–100, 143, 151–152
  arbitrage, end of, 120
  British overseas banks, 131
  City of London, 102

compartmentalization, 117, 126, 133
currency risks, 188–189
currency volatility, 114–115, 130, 139, 194–195
exchange rates volatility, 101–102, 137–138, 164, 188–189, 286
foreign exchange brokers, 126, 134–135, 149–150
foreign exchange market, 1–2, 95–96, 100–101, 130–131, 134–135, 151–153, 188–189, 286
forward markets, 45
global banking, 128
Gold Standard, 94, 98–100, 286
London money market, 109
New York foreign exchange market, 50–51
NYSE, 123, 125–126
regulation and control, 157, 288–289
shattered stability, 96
World War I, consequences of, 96–97, 100–101
see also London FX: 1919–1939; World War I
Iqbal, A., 95–96
Ireland, 33–34, 37–38, 132–133
Isaacs, J., 246–247

J
Jackson, H., 37, 43
Japan, 14–15, 22–24
government controls, 141, 237–238
Japanese banks in City of London, 62–63, 65, 204, 219
Mitsui Bank, 130, 213
see also YSB
Japanese yen, 27–28, 65, 130, 213–214
Jevons, W.S., 53–54
jobbers, 18–19, 74–75, 110, 123, 172–173
see also dealers
Johannesburg as financial centre, 26–27
Jones, G., 249–250
Joseph, L., 158
Jourdan and Newton, 71, 154–155
Journal of the Institute of Bankers, 54–55
J.P. Morgan, 48–49, 68–69, 251–252, 267–268, 270
J.W. Seligman & Co, 68–69, 84

K
Kay, R., 162–163
Kent, P., 246–247
Keynes J.M., 9–10, 35–37, 61–62, 91–92, 100, 156–157
on managed currency, 156–157
on consequences of World War I, 96
Kindersley, R.M., 126
King, M., 257–258, 265
King, W.T.C., 40
Kirkaldy, A.W., 122
Kleinwort, Sir Cyril, 199

Kleinwort Sons & Company, 135, 220
Kniffin, W.H., 106
Krugman, P., 97
Kuwait, 195–196, 202–203

L
Lambert, R., 229
Landells, W., 82–83
Larsen, P.T., 246
Lascelles, D., 237–241
latency, 245, 254–255, 276–277
Latin America
British overseas banks, 57–58, 62–63, 131, 132–133
US and, 103–104
League of Nations, 27–28, 97–98
Lehman Brothers, 262–263, 267–268, 270
Leigh-Pemberton, R., 228–229
lender of last resort, 208–209
1992–2007 London FX and, 258–259
2007–2022 London FX and, 279
Bank of England, 35–37, 109–110, 142–143, 176, 187–188, 200–201, 204–205, 207–208, 256–258, 279
Federal Reserve Bank, 102, 111–113, 257–258, 267–268, 272
Financial Services Authority, 256–257
Leon Brothers, 124
Lever, E.H., 45, 100, 165
liquid markets, 19, 77, 279–280
liquidity
1970–1992 London FX, 238–242
2007–2022 London FX, 276, 279
2008 Global Financial Crisis as liquidity crisis, 266–267
automatization and, 253–254
banks, 32–33, 35, 37–39, 48–50, 234–235
central banks and, 272–273
Federal Reserve Bank, 271–273, 279
flexible exchange rates and currency market liquidity, 285
foreign exchange market, 251–252, 274–276
liquidity crisis, 115–116, 227–228, 257–258, 266–267, 271, 273
liquidity of international markets hosted by London, 246–247, 251, 252–253, 265, 276
London money market, 109
LSE, 74–75, 82–83, 88, 110, 121, 123
megabanks, 251–252, 266–267, 270–271, 273
post-GFC reform, 271
Lloyds Bank, 115–116, 131, 132–133, 144–146, 157–158
Big Five British banks, 142–143
foreign business, 53–54, 211

Lloyds Bank (*Continued*)
  foreign exchange market, 144–146, 211, 220
LME (London Metal Exchange), 18–19, 73,
    156–157, 172–173, 222–223
L. Messel & Co, 124
Loewenstein, A., 125
London
  as centre of global communications, 16–17,
    102–103, 229
  as financial centre, 9–10, 22–24, 29–30, 42,
    94–95, 102, 124–125
  London/New York rivalry as financial
    centres, 106–108, 114–115, 117–118, 190,
    197, 218, 246, 263–265
  see also City of London; London FX; UK
London discount market, 11–12, 42, 109–110
  1919–1939 London FX and, 176–179,
    181–182, 187–188
  1920s, 114–115, 177
  1930s, 116–120
  1945–1970, 196–197, 203, 204–207, 232–233
  alternatives to, 111–113, 205–206
  Bank of England and, 11–12, 35–37, 109–111,
    114, 118–120, 176, 178–180, 203, 204–205,
    232–233, 240
  bankruptcy, 110–111
  banks and, 11–12, 35–37
  brokers, 11–12, 153
  City of London, 11–12, 204–205
  end of, 117–119, 232–233
  global banking, 118–120
  London money market and, 119–120,
    201–202, 204–205
  LSE and, 35–37, 119–120
  as model for London FX, 176
  treasury bills, 111–115, 118–119, 200–201,
    204–205
  UK government's intervention, 110–111,
    196–197
  UK£ and, 119–120, 205–206
  UK monetary policy and, 118–119
  World War I, 111–113
London FX
  eighteenth century, 9
  nineteenth century, 9
  beginnings of, 4–7, 9–12
  see also City of London; London FX:
    1850–1914; London FX: 1919–1939; London
    FX: 1939–1945; London FX: 1945–1970;
    London FX: 1970–1992; London FX:
    1992–2007; London FX 2007–2022; London
    FX's dominance
London FX: 1850–1914 (before World War I), 8,
    91, 285–286
  arbitrage, 76, 81–82, 88, 89–93

banks, 11–12, 19–20, 51–54, 71–73, 91–93,
    285–286
bills of exchange and, 46, 60–61
City of London, 22, 52, 63–64, 71–73, 91
currency risks, 14–16
exchange rates stability and, 19, 93
FX absence (ignored), 8–9, 8–9 n.1, 9–11,
    19–21, 29–30, 164, 285–286
FX absence: arguments for, 4–6, 27–28, 189
FX absence as mystery, 8–9 n.1, 9–12, 21, 25,
    73–74
FX existence: arguments for, 11–12, 14–16,
    19–21, 27–29, 31–32, 45–46, 53–74, 90–95,
    128, 285–286
FX identification with Royal Exchange biweekly
    meeting, 10–12
FX invisibility, 11–12, 19, 45, 57, 71, 90–93, 187
integration of global economy, 92
internalization of FX, 57–59, 61
location, 4–5, 22–25, 29–30, 72–74, 91–92,
    285–286
London money market, 22–24, 32, 71–72, 109,
    285–286
LSE and, 74, 76, 81–82, 88–93, 285–286
Royal Exchange, 73, 91, 164
technology and, 11–12
telegraph and, 11–12, 72–73, 92
telegraphic transfers, 52, 61
UK£ as vehicle currency, 53–54, 71–74, 128
world's foreign exchange market, 31–32, 66
World War I and, 102, 285–286
London FX: 1919–1939 (interwar years), 4–5,
    9–10, 94, 188, 210, 286
  1920s, 5–6, 11–12, 27–28, 45, 71, 91–92
  1920s–1930s transformation, 164, 170, 189
  accounts/descriptions of London FX, 164–168
  Bank of England and, 156–157, 163, 167–168,
    171, 174–176, 187–188, 190–191
  Bank of England intervention, 177–185,
    187–188, 210
  banks, 133, 141–152, 175–176, 179–180,
    187–191, 210, 286
  Big Five British banks, 145–149, 152–154, 159,
    160–161, 163, 165, 168–169, 173, 178–179,
    210
  City of London, 22–24, 91–92, 108, 149,
    167–171, 187, 189–190
  counterparty risk/trust, 160–163, 165, 166,
    173, 175–176, 187–188, 210
  dealers, 91–92, 153, 157–159, 161, 165–169,
    171, 173–174, 187, 190, 286
  dealers/brokers relationship, 173
  decline/demise of, 167, 170–171, 174, 180
  direct dealing, 153–154, 168, 174–176,
    179–180, 190
  exchange rates stability, 177

exchange rates volatility, 164, 189

failure to gain acceptance, 170–173, 187–188, 190–191

foreign banks, 180–182

foreign exchange brokers, 91–92, 153–155, 157–161, 163, 164–168, 170–172, 174, 187, 190, 210, 286

foreign exchange as novelty, 91–92, 95–96, 164–165, 187

forward market, 134–136, 144–147, 150–151, 155–156, 160, 167–168, 170, 176, 189

global banking, 128, 168

Gold Standard and, 170–171

Gold Standard, UK's departure from, 102, 106–108, 130, 131, 134, 151–153, 159, 162, 169, 174, 176, 177–178, 187–188

increase in volume and variety of foreign exchange business, 158

internalization of FX, 210

location, 108, 167–168, 190–191, 286

London discount market and, 176–179, 181–182, 187–188

London money market and, 155–157

London's central position, 151–152, 170, 190–191

physical/institutional structure, lack of, 164–166, 168, 169, 171, 172–176, 187–188, 190–191

praise of, 169–170

regulation and control, 157, 288–289

speculation, 168–169, 171, 189, 286

spot market, 146–147, 150–151, 155–156, 160, 167–168, 170, 176, 186, 189

success, 169, 187–188

telegraph, 164, 190–191, 210

telegraphic transfers, 150–151, 164

telephone, 154, 157–159, 164, 165–166, 168, 187, 190–191, 210

turnover, 155, 159, 166, 168–169

World War I and, 91–93

see also interwar years; World War I

London FX: 1939–1945 (wartime), 210–211

1939 Defence (Finance) Regulations Act, 211–212

Bank of England control, 184–186, 210–213

Barclays Bank, 211–212

closure of London FX, 151–152, 156–157, 184–189, 192, 210, 287

exchange controls, 212–213

government interventions/controls, 211–213

Lloyds Bank, 211

Midland Bank, 211

telegraph, 211–212

telephone, 211–212

teleprinter, 211–212

see also World War II

London FX: 1945–1970 (post World War II), 4–6, 192, 224, 287

1947 Exchange Control Act, 211–212

1950s, 215–218, 223–224, 287

1951: reopening of FX, 189, 192, 210, 212–213

1957: controls on use of UK£ by non-UK residents, 215–218, 221

1958: UK£ convertibility, 216–218, 220, 221, 223–224

1960s, 216–218, 220–224

arbitrage, 213

Bank of England control, 189, 212–217, 221–224

banks, 215, 217–224

Barclays Bank, 211

Bretton Woods System, 221–222

City of London, 214–215, 219–220, 223–224

counterparty risk/trust, 219–220

dealers, 212–213, 221

Eurodollar and Eurobond markets, 223–224

exchange controls, 212–213

fixed exchange rates, 189, 215–218, 221–222

foreign exchange brokers, 212–213

forward dealing, 213, 215–216

government controls and restrictions, 189, 192, 212–218, 221, 223–224

interbank market, 219–222

Lloyds Bank, 220

London money market and, 215–216, 223–224

London's restored central position, 214–218, 220, 221, 223–224, 287

re-emergence of FX, 217

substitution of London FX by foreign exchange centres abroad, 213–214, 217–218, 220

US$, 215–217, 220, 221–224

weak FX, 213–216

see also World War II

London FX: 1970–1992, 226, 242, 287

1974 Bankhaus Herstatt collapse, 237

1980s, 234–235, 237, 240–241, 243

1992, 237

arbitrage, 235–236

automated dealing systems, 236–237

banks, 230–231, 234–236, 238–239, 287

City of London, 22–24, 229–231, 234–235, 237–238, 243, 287–288

computers/computing, 237–239, 241–243

currency volatility, 237

direct dealing, 240–243

Electronic Broking Services, 237–238

electronic trading, 236–237, 239, 243

Eurobond market, 233–234

fibre-optic cable, 237–238

foreign banks, 236–237

foreign exchange brokers, 234–237

London FX: 1970–1992, (*Continued*)
  foreign exchange market as global
    market, 238–239
  forward markets, 234–236
  global communications revolution, 226
  interbank market, 236–237, 243
  inter-dealer brokers, 234–237, 239–243,
    287–288
  liquidity, 238–242
  London's central position, 236–238, 287
  megabanks, 238–239, 241–243, 287–288
  Reuters, 237–240
  spot markets, 234–235
  telephone, 237–241, 243, 287–288
  turnover, 234–235, 237, 243
  US banks, 234–235, 237–238, 287
  US$, 229–230, 234–236, 243, 287–288
London FX: 1992–2007 (electronic Forex), 244,
    250–251, 260
  Bank of England, 258–259
  City of London, 246, 251, 260–261
  electronic trading, 253–254, 258–261, 287–288
  EU monetary unification, 251
  foreign banks, 258, 260–261
  institutional structure, lack of, 258–259
  inter-dealer brokers, 258–261
  lender of last resort, 258–259
  London's central position, 251–253, 256–257,
    260–261, 287–288
  megabanks, 258, 260–261, 266–267
  turnover, 251, 253–254, 258, 260–261
  US banks, 256–258
  US$, 256–258, 260–261
London FX 2007–2022, 273–276
  2008 Global Financial Crisis, 279, 287–288
  2013 collusion/market manipulation, 279–280,
    287–288
  2020 Covid-19 pandemic, 287–288
  2022 Russian invasion of Ukraine, 287–288
  Bank of England, 273–274, 278–279
  Brexit, 264–265
  City of London, 263–265, 278–279
  counterparty relationships, 276
  dealers, 282
  direct dealing, 273–274
  electronic trading, 273–274, 276
  foreign banks, 279
  hedge funds and high-frequency traders, 282
  interbank market, 279, 282
  inter-dealer brokers, 273–274
  lender of last resort, 279
  liquidity, 276, 279
  London's central position, 263–265, 273–274,
    282
  megabanks, 276, 279–280
  resilience, 279, 287–288

  turnover, 273–274, 276
  US$, 276, 279
  see also Global Financial Crisis (2008)
London FX's dominance, 27–28, 149, 190–191,
    251, 256–257, 278–279, 288–289
  1919–1939, 151–152, 170, 190–191
  1945–1970, 214–218, 220, 221, 223–224, 287
  1970–1992, 236–238, 287
  1992–2007, 251–253, 256–257, 260–261,
    287–288
  2007–2022, 263–265, 273–274, 282
  change, adaptation to, 25, 260–261
  embedded infrastructure, 263–265, 276,
    287–288
  English as language of international
    finance, 246, 263–264
  geography, 6–7, 229–230
  inertia, 6–7, 25, 252–253, 260–261
  legal and regulatory infrastructure, 229–230,
    246, 252–253, 260–261, 263–264
  liquidity of international markets hosted by
    London, 246–247, 251, 252–253, 265, 276
  London as most important trading
    location, 4–6, 21, 22–24, 45–46, 108,
    223–224, 246, 273–276, 282
  mystery of, 6–7, 21
  time zone advantage, 6–7, 228–231, 246,
    252–253, 263–264, 276
London money market
  1850–1914, 48, 109, 285–286
  1850–1914 London FX and, 22–24, 32, 71–72,
    109, 285–286
  1919–1939, 109
  1919–1939 London FX and, 155–157
  1920s, 105
  1945–1970 London FX and, 215–216, 223–224
  1950s, 197–198, 215–216
  1960s, 232–233
  Bank of England and, 206–208, 256–258
  banks/banking and, 32–34, 37–39, 41, 42,
    46–47, 49–50, 71–72, 109, 110
  bills of exchange, 34–40, 109–110, 204–205
  British overseas banks and, 109
  Canadian banks and, 69–70
  City of London, 22–24, 32, 53–54, 102–103,
    109, 121, 190, 197–198, 204–205
  counterparty risk/trust, 109–110
  foreign banks and, 62–63
  foreign exchange component, 45, 129
  Franco-German War and, 33–34
  global banking, 39, 46–47
  importance of, 46–47, 119–120, 188–189
  international orientation of, 39, 43–44, 240
  liquidity, 109
  London discount market and, 119–120,
    201–202, 204–205

LSE and, 74–75, 86, 88
multi-currency basis of, 215–216
originate-and-distribute banking and, 129
as precursor of foreign exchange market, 46
sterling/non-sterling activity division, 256–257
supply and demand, 33–34, 37–38, 129, 143–144
treasury bills, 114
turnover, 38–39
as undermined during interwar years, 129–130
World War I, 110, 129
London Post Office Directory, 71, 154–155
London Stock Exchange, *see* LSE
LSE (London Stock Exchange), 18–19, 75
1850–1914, 73, 91, 121, 123–124
1850–1914 arbitrage, 76–90, 120
1850–1914 London FX, 74, 76, 81–82, 88–93, 285–286
1919–1939, 123–124
1919–1939 arbitrage, 122–127
1920s, 122–123
1945–1970, 196–197
Argentine and, 82–83
Australia (Melbourne Stock Exchange) and, 82–83
banks and, 74–76, 79, 81–82, 88
bill brokers and, 35–37
British government debt (consols), 75, 78–79
brokers, 74–76, 83–84, 110, 172–173
capital market and, 74–75, 90–91
City of London, 121
electronic trading, 279–280
European stock exchanges and, 79
financial operations and communications revolution, 17–18, 30–31
Foreign Funds Market Committee, 78
function of, 74–75
government intervention, 121–123, 196–197
international networks, 83
jobbers, 74–75, 110, 123, 172–173
liquidity, 74–75, 82–83, 88, 110, 121, 123
London discount market and, 35–37, 119–120
London money market and, 74–75, 86, 88
London's central position, 30–31, 75, 79, 82–83, 85–86, 88, 121, 123–124
as multipurpose organization, 74–75
NYSE and, 79–81, 83
regulation, 157, 172–173
restrictions imposed by LSE itself, 90, 121, 122–124, 126–127
securities, 25–26, 30–31, 74, 75–77, 82, 86–88, 121, 122, 201–202
speculation, 75, 81, 82, 120
as structure model for London FX, 172–173
telegraph and, 78–79, 82–83, 121
telephone and, 30–31, 79, 121, 172–173

UK£, 76
World War I, 121–122
see also arbitrage
Luxembourg, 202–203, 233–234, 265

M

McCallum, J., 229–230
Mackenzie, M., 262–263, 268
Madden, J.T., 117–118
Manchester Guardian, 9–10, 156–157
Manchester and Liverpool District Bank, 137–138
Marsh, D., 252–253
Martins Bank, 54–55, 137–138
Matching, 279–280
mathematical modelling, 1–2, 11–12
Mather, L.C., 223–224
Meeker, J.E., 106–107, 122–123
megabanks, 224–225, 262, 266–267
1970–1992 London FX, 238–239, 241–243, 287–288
1990s, 244
1992–2007 foreign exchange market, 248–252, 254–256
1992–2007 London FX, 258, 260–261, 266–267
2007–2022 London FX, 276, 279–280
2008 Global Financial Crisis, 262–263, 266–269, 276–277, 279
2009–2022, 267–271, 274–275, 280–281
2013 collusion/market manipulation, 279–280
Brexit, 265
carry trade, 276–277
central banks and, 248, 262–263, 288–289
City of London, 232, 265
compartmentalization of banking and, 247–248
corporations/corporate finance and, 247–248, 262–263
counterparty risk/trust, 262–263, 276–277, 281–282, 287–288
direct dealing, 241–242, 248–249, 274–275
electronic trading, 245, 247–249, 254–255, 262–263, 268–269, 281–282
emergence of, 232
Eurobond market, 233–234
European banks, 251–252
fund managers and, 247–248, 262–263
global financial system and, 247–248, 262–263
importance of, 247–248
interbank market, 232, 248, 254–255, 267–268, 270
inter-dealer brokers, 248–250, 255–256, 268
latency issue, 254–255

megabanks (*Continued*)
  liquidity, 251–252, 266–267, 270–271, 273
  originate-and-distribute banking, 232, 248, 266–267, 270–271
  regulation and control, 245, 248, 262–263, 267–268, 279, 280–281
  resilience of, 248, 258, 262, 270–271
  SWIFT, 247–248, 270
  technology and staff, 239, 262–263
  UK banks, 232
  US banks, 232, 251–252, 267–268, 270–271, 281–282
  Western Europe banks, 232
  see also banks/banking; global banking
Meissner, C., 263–264
merchant banks, 47–48, 52, 137–140, 158
  Anglo-American merchant banks, 67–69, 84
  arbitrage and, 84–86
  British merchant banks, 4–5, 56, 91, 134, 161
  foreign exchange market, 67–69, 128–129, 134–138, 213–214, 220
  interwar years, 134–136
  telegraph and, 67–69
  telephone, 134–135
Merrill Lynch Bank, 251–252, 267–268, 270
Mexico, 57–58
Meyer, E.B., 158
Meyer, G., 264–265
Midland Bank, 33–34, 48–49, 132–133
  Big Five British banks, 142–143
  foreign banks and, 41–42, 204
  'foreign' branches, 53–54
  foreign department, 211
  foreign exchange market, 54–56, 144–148, 211
Miller, H.F.R., 46, 114, 148, 165
monetary history, 3–4, 9–10, 94
monetary policy, 94
  government intervention and monetary stability, 92, 94, 95–96, 101–102, 224
  independent monetary policies, 228
  India, 61–62
  monetary trilemma and, 3–4
  UK, 118–119, 202–203, 207–208, 224, 256–258
  US, 224
  see also exchange rates; fixed exchange rates; government interventions/controls
monetary system
  1931 global monetary crisis, 133
  1970s monetary crisis, 227–228
  Bretton Woods System and, 193–194
  Federal Reserve Bank and global monetary system, 273
  foreign exchange market and global monetary system, 4
  Golden Ages for global monetary system, 193–194
    Gold Standard and, 19–21, 193–194
    World War I, 21
monetary trilemma
  Bretton Woods System, 3–4, 193–196
  foreign exchange market, 3–4, 193–194
  Gold Standard, 3–4, 193–194
  solution to, 195–196, 262
  three objectives: fixed rate of exchange, free movement of capital, autonomous monetary policy, 3–4, 193–194
money market, 37
  arbitrage and, 86–87
  banking and, 133
  Berlin money market, 114–115
  Canadian money market, 46–47
  central banks and, 272
  compartmentalization of, 117
  interbank money market, 224, 227–228, 243
  New York money market, 37, 46–47, 103, 111–115, 117–118
  see also London money market
Montagnon, P., 227–228, 238–239
Montreal Gazette, 16–17
Morgan Stanley, 267–268, 270
Morgenstern, O., 20–21
Morton Bliss/Morton Rose, 84
multinational companies, 231, 247–248, 251–252, 282, 283
M.W. Marshall & Co, 173–174

N
Nadler, M., 117–118
Nathan and Rosselli, 84–85, 124
National City Bank of New York, 48–49, 55–56, 67–68, 144
  see also Citibank
National and Provincial Bank, 134, 142–143
Nelson, S.A., 81–82, 85
Neptune (planet), 11–12, 15–16, 19, 74, 90–93
New York
  1930s: undermined as financial centre, 106–107
  1950s, 197, 213–214
  after World War II, 27–28
  arbitrage, 83–84, 125–126, 215
  Brexit, 265
  electronic trading, 246
  foreign banks in, 246–247
  as leading financial centre in the world, 263–264
  London-New York arbitrage, 80–82, 87, 88, 90, 124–125
  London/New York rivalry as financial centres, 106–108, 114–115, 117–118, 190, 197, 218, 246, 263–265

as major financial centre, 26–28, 103–104, 108, 190, 197, 203, 228–229, 246

New York money market, 37, 46–47, 103, 111–115, 117–118

replacing London as major financial centre, 103–107, 111–113, 192, 203, 213–214

safe haven status, 117–118

time zone, 263–264

World War I, 102–105, 190

World War II, 117–118

see also US

New York foreign exchange market, 6–7, 31–32, 50–51

1850–1914, 9–10, 19–20, 27–28

1950s, 213–214, 218, 220

1970–1992, 229–230, 234–235, 237–238

1992–2007, 250–251

2007–2022, 273–275

EU monetary unification, 251

interwar years, 50–51

London/New York rivalry, 27–28, 108, 170

replacing London as major FX centre, 192, 213

turnover, 237, 251

US legislative intervention and, 214

World War II, 213–214

see also New York

New York Stock Exchange, see NYSE

New Zealand

Bank of New Zealand, 138–139, 145–146

British overseas banks, 56–57, 62–63, 131

NEX, 268–269, 279–280

Nicholson, N.A., 11–12

non-banks, see shadow banking/non-banks

Northern Ireland: Belfast Bank, 146

Nurse, R., 27–28

NYSE (New York Stock Exchange), 76–77, 79–80, 117–118

1929 Wall Street Crash, 125–126

branch offices in London, 125–126

interwar years, 123, 125–126

LSE and, 79–81, 83

telegraph, 125–126

O

O'Brien, R.S., 234–235

offshore financial centres, 195–198, 202–203, 214, 220, 226, 242–243

OTC markets (over-the-counter), 1, 245, 248–249, 268–269, 276–277, 279–280

2008 Global Financial Crisis, 268–269

O'Toole, B., 273

Overend, Gurney & Company: 1866 crisis, 141–142

P

Packshaw, R., 241–242

Paris

as financial centre, 26–27, 115–116, 197

foreign exchange market, 9–10, 19–20, 27–28, 170, 252–253

Paris money market, 114–115, 117–118

World War I, 104–105

Patterson, S., 31–32, 62–63, 104–105

Pearce, L.G., 212–213

P.E. Schweder & Co, 81

Phelps, C.W., 141

Phillips, H.W., 10–12, 114, 137–138, 144–145, 166

Phillips, Sir Frederick, 169

Plender, J., 272

Plender, Sir William, 63–64

Portugal, 14–15

Powell, E.T., 96

Pownall, G.W., 27–28

Pratt, S.S., 31–32, 80

Pressnell, L.S., 29–30

Pretzlik, C., 246

R

Raymond, Pynchon & Co, 81

Razak, E. 276

Refinitiv, 279–280

regulation and control, 157

1919–1939 London FX, 157, 288–289

Amsterdam stock market, 157

EU regulations, 229

foreign exchange market self-regulation, 1, 277–283, 286, 288–289

LSE, 157, 172–173

megabanks, 245, 248, 262–263, 267–268, 279, 280–281

post-GFC reform, 271

US banking, restrictive legislation, 67–68, 139–140, 199–200, 208–209, 218, 231–232, 267–268

see also government interventions/controls

Reuters, 237–238, 248–249, 253–256

1970–1992 London FX, 237–240

Dealing 2000–2 system, 239

Revelstoke, Lord, 30, 43

Richard Irwin & Co, 84–85

Roberts, R., 106–107

Robinson, Clark & Co, 82–83

Rothschilds, the, 10–11, 17–18, 48–49, 78, 91, 162–163

Rousseau, P.L., 1–2

Royal Exchange, 73

biweekly meetings, 4–5, 91, 164

FX identification with Royal Exchange biweekly meeting, 10–12

see also London

Royal Institute of International Affairs, 124

Rozenraad, C., 42

Russia, 14–15, 25–26
  2022 invasion of Ukraine, 281–283, 287–288
  default on international debts, 121–122,
    188–189

S
Salmon and Company, 76
Sampson, Mr, 173–174
Samuel Montagu & Co, 56, 91
Sangway, J., 100–101
Saul, S.B., 29–30
Schmidt, H., 77
Schuster, F., 34–35, 43
Schwartz, A.J., 12–13
Scotland
  Bank of Scotland, 138–139
  banks/banking, 37–38, 132–133
  Clydesdale Bank, 146
Scott, G.J., 113, 153
securities, 20–21
  2008 Global Financial Crisis, 266–267
  banks/banking, 33
  London market, 25–26
  LSE, 25–26, 30–31, 74, 75–77, 82, 86–88, 121,
    122, 201–202
  US, 106
  see also arbitrage
Senior, S., 257–258
Seyd, E., 10–11
shadow banking/non-banks, 270–272
  see also fund managers; hedge funds;
    high-frequency traders
Sichel & Co, 71, 154–155
Siepmann, H., 170–171, 177–179, 181, 182–185
silver as basis for currency price, 14–15, 46–47,
  57–60, 65
Simon, J., 182–184
Singapore: foreign exchange market, 6–7,
  237–238, 243, 252–253, 273–275
Singh, J., 276–277
S. Japhet & Co., 85–86
Skorecki, A., 252–253
Smith St. Aubyn, 35–37, 110–111, 116, 118–119,
  177
Sobel, M., 271
Société Générale (France), 48–49, 162–163, 170,
  267–268
  London branch, 63–64, 128–130
Société Générale de Belgique, 170
South Africa, 25–26, 57, 62–63, 131
Spalding, W.F., 35, 46, 62–65, 127, 150–151
speculation
  1919–1939 London FX, 168–169, 171, 189, 286
  arbitrage as, 124, 127
  foreign banks and currency speculation, 62–63

foreign exchange market, 4, 15–18, 100,
  101–102, 152–153, 156–157
  LSE, 75, 81, 82, 120
  telegraph's impact on, 17–18
Speed, Mr, 155, 173–174
Spencer, M., 249–250, 268–269
Spicer, E.E., 32, 34–35, 43–44
spot markets, 18–19, 51–52, 61–62, 150–151,
  155–156, 251
  before World War I, 58–59, 91–92, 147
  1919–1939, 45
  1919–1939 London FX, 146–147, 150–151,
    155–156, 160, 167–168, 170, 176, 186, 189
  1920s, 51–52
  1945–1970 London FX, 215–216
  1970–1992 London FX, 234–235
  2007–2022 London FX, 280–282
Spring-Rice, D., 150–151
S.P. Scaramanaga, 70–71, 160–161, 166
Stafford, P., 263–265, 268–269, 279–280
Stamm, J., 85–86
Standard Chartered, 281–282
Statist, 79, 181
Stein, J.L., 1–2
Stephens, P., 239
Storbeck, O., 279
Suez Crisis (1956), 215–216
supply and demand, 13–14, 96
  British overseas banks, 57
  foreign exchange market and, 4, 8–9, 19,
    94–95, 239–240
  Gold Standard and, 12–13
  lender of last resort and, 208–209
  London money market, 33–34, 37–38, 129,
    143–144
  supply/demand balance, 33–35, 37–38, 71–72,
    143–144, 208–209
Swanson, W.W., 22–24
Sweet-Escott, B., 156–157
SWIFT (Society for Worldwide Interbank
  Financial Telecommunications), 226–227,
  245, 247–248, 262–263, 270
Swiss franc, 170, 182–184, 213–215
Switzerland, 117–118
  offshore financial centres, 195–196
  see also Credit Suisse; UBS
Sykes, E., 33–34, 37
Sylla, R., 1–2
Szalay, E., 263–264, 276, 280–281

T
Taylor, C., 246–247
Taylor, C.W., 143
Taylor, W.H., 157–158
technology
  calculating machine, 11–12, 187

fibre-optic cable, 226–227, 237–238, 246
global financial system and, 226
teleprinter, 211–212
see also automatization; communications;
  computers/computing; electronic trading;
  telegraph; telephone
telegraph, 11–12, 30–31
  1850–1914 London FX, 11–12, 72–73, 92
  1919–1939 London FX, 164, 190–191, 210
  1939–1945 London FX, 211–212
  Anglo-American Telegraph Company, 30–31,
    81
  arbitrage, 78–89, 120, 125
  banks/banking, 49–54, 57, 67–68
  British overseas banks, 57–62
  foreign exchange market, 5–6, 17–18, 31–32,
    72–73, 139, 144
  impact on financial operations, 16–18, 22–24,
    30, 52
  London-Paris link, 16–17, 78–79, 90–91
  London-New York telegraphic link, 79, 81–82,
    90–91
  LSE, 78–79, 82–83, 121
  NYSE, 125–126
  replaced by telephone, 30–31, 79
  speculation, 17–18
telegraphic transfers, 40, 45, 57, 61–62, 64–65,
  150–151, 155
  1850–1914 London FX, 52, 61
  1919–1939 London FX, 150–151, 164
  bills of exchange and, 40, 51–52, 60–61
  foreign exchange market and, 52, 56, 60–61,
    139
  US, 52
telephone, 11–12
  1891 London-Paris telephone
    connection, 17–18, 79, 121
  1919–1939 London FX, 154, 157–159, 164,
    165–166, 168, 187, 190–191, 210
  1939–1945 London FX, 211–212
  1970–1992 London FX, 237–241, 243, 287–288
  arbitrage, 85–86, 125
  brokers, 70–71
  foreign exchange market, 134–135, 139, 144,
    253–255
  impact on financial operations, 17–18, 22–24,
    30–31
  LSE, 30–31, 79, 121, 172–173
  telephone/electronic trading
    combined, 255–256
  replaced by electronic trading, 254–255
  replacing the telegraph, 30–31, 79
terminal markets, 18–19
Thomas, S.E., 45, 149, 166
Thomson Reuters, 276–277, 279–280
Times, 164, 214–215, 221, 223–224

Tokyo
  money market, 103–104
  as financial centre, 199, 228–229
  foreign exchange market, 229–230, 234–235,
    237–238, 243, 250–253, 260–261, 273–275
  trading foreign exchange, *see* foreign exchange
    market
treasury bills, 204–205, 211–212, 235–236
  Bank of England, 118–119, 204–205
  disadvantages, 114
  London discount market, 111–115, 118–119,
    200–201, 204–205
  London money market, 114
  see also bills of exchange
Triffin, R., 3–4
trilemma, *see* monetary trilemma
Tripartite Monetary Agreement (1936), 182–184
Tritton, J.H., 38–39
Truptil, R.J., 107–108
Tucker, P., 258
Tullett, D., 240
Tullet Prebon, 249–250, 268–269
Tullett and Riley, 240–241
Turner, C., 22–24
Twentieth Century Fund, 101, 123

U

UBS (Union Bank of Switzerland/UBS Group
  AG), 251–252, 267–268
UK (United Kingdom)
  1920s structural deficit, 130
  1939 declaration of war with
    Germany, 101–102, 184–185
  anti-competitive practices, 201–203
  banking system, 141–150, 201–202
  British government debt, 18–19, 75, 78–79,
    111, 114, 178–179, 196–197
  as EU member, 228–229
  exchange rates controls, 98–99, 106–107, 131,
    196–197, 201–202, 228–231
  financial system, 201–203, 263–264
  foreign debts, 196
  Gold Standard, departure from, 97–100, 102,
    106–108, 114, 116, 118–120, 130, 131, 134,
    151–153, 162, 169–171, 174–175, 177–178,
    182–184, 189
  Gold Standard, return to (1925), 99–100,
    106–107, 114–115, 137–138, 150–155,
    157–159, 165, 169–171, 177, 189
  government intervention, 133, 201–203, 205,
    266
  interbank market, 246–247
  interwar years, 130
  as largest trading nation, 29

UK (United Kingdom) (*Continued*)
  monetary policy, 118–119, 202–203, 207–208,
    224, 256–258
  share of global foreign exchange market, 4–5
  World War I, 130
  World War II, 196–197
  see also Brexit; British Empire; City of London;
    London; London FX
UK£, 4–6
  1850–1914 London FX and UK£ as vehicle
    currency, 53–54, 71–74, 128
  1957 monetary crisis, 199
  Bank of England and, 182–184, 257–258
  controls on external use of, 205, 213–218, 221
  convertibility of, 216–221, 223–224
  decline/demise as global currency, 6–7, 27–28,
    115–116, 192, 205, 213–214, 218, 260–261
  devaluation of, 99–100, 115–116, 130,
    194–195, 207
  displaced by US$, 6, 147–148, 192, 195–196,
    199, 203, 213–217, 231–232, 235–236
  exchange rate management, 182–184
  gold standard as sterling standard, 27–28
  as international currency, 4–5, 8–10, 14–15,
    19–20, 27–30, 42, 43–44, 56–57, 66–67, 105,
    120, 190–191
  London discount market and, 119–120,
    205–206
  LSE and, 76
  as most important currency in the world before
    1914, 73–74
  as overvalued, 98–100
  stabilization of international value, 182
  sterling area, 106–108, 184–185, 195–197, 199,
    203, 205–206, 213–214, 217–218
  sterling-based discount market, 208–209, 219,
    233
  UK£/US$ exchange rate, 55–56, 68–70, 186
  UK£/US$ market, 73–74
  UK£/US$ rivalry, 130
  unspent sterling balances, 130
  as vehicle currency, 14–15, 29, 53–54, 64–65,
    70, 71–74, 108, 128–129, 170, 190
  World War I, 98–99, 129
  World War II, 186
UK Treasury, 122–124, 142–143, 182–186
USSR (Union of Soviet Socialist
    Republics), 145–146
US (United States), 14–15, 25–26
  1920s domestic financial crisis, 106–107
  British overseas banks and, 67
  capital market, 263–264
  European war: impact on financial system, 43
  financial centres, 67–68
  foreign exchange market (before World War
    I), 50–51, 67–68

foreign exchange market (interwar years), 141
foreign exchange market (post 2007), 277–278
Gold Standard, 46–47, 68–69, 99–100,
    106–107
government interventions, 101, 218
as largest economy in the world, 73–74, 102,
    197, 263–264
monetary policy, 224
Securities and Exchange
    Commission, 125–126, 262–263
see also New York; New York foreign exchange
    market; NYSE
US banking system, 72–73, 102
  1930s banking collapse, 106–107, 115–118
  1930s Glass–Steagall Act, 139–140, 199, 204,
    266, 267–268
  1933 Securities Act, 125–126
  1970–1992 London FX and US
    banks, 234–235, 237–238, 287
  1992–2007 London FX and US banks, 256–258
  City of London, US branches in, 70, 199–202,
    204, 208–209, 218, 219, 221, 231–232
  megabanks, 232, 251–252, 267–268, 270–271,
    281–282
  restrictive legislation, 67–68, 139–140,
    199–200, 208–209, 218, 231–232, 267–268
  weakness in UK/US banking connection, 70
US$
  1945–1970 London FX, 215–217, 220, 221–224
  1970–1992 London FX, 229–230, 234–236,
    243, 287–288
  1992–2007 London FX, 256–258, 260–261
  2007–2022 London FX, 276, 279
  2008 Global Financial Crisis, 267–268
  Bank of England and, 256–257
  British banks and, 256–257
  City of London and, 199–200, 208–209, 218,
    264–265
  controls on external use of, 218
  currency volatility, 68–69
  Dollar Certificate of Deposit, 200–201,
    235–236
  Eurobonds and Eurodollar market, 218,
    233–234
  fluctuations, 15–16
  foreign exchange market and, 45–46, 259
  interbank market, 219
  as international currency, 27–28, 106–107, 190,
    197, 199, 243, 263–264, 267–268, 271, 273
  as reserve currency, 199, 273
  UK£ displaced by US$, 6, 147–148, 192,
    195–196, 199, 203, 213–217, 231–232,
    235–236
  UK£/US$ exchange rate, 55–56, 68–70, 186
  UK£/US$ rivalry, 130
  US$-based network, 131

as vehicle currency, 70, 73–74, 102, 108, 130, 131, 257–258, 260–261
US money market, 195–196, 271, 273
US Treasury, 257–258, 268–269, 271, 273

V

Van Antwerp, W.C., 80, 84–85
Van Beek, Mr, 55–56
vehicle currency/assets, 8–9, 108
  advantages of, 53–54
  stocks and bonds could as vehicle assets, 74
  UK£, 14–15, 29, 53–54, 64–65, 70, 71–74, 108, 128–129, 170, 190
  US$, 70, 73–74, 102, 108, 130, 131, 257–258, 260–261
Vollemaere, J., 276

W

Wadsworth, J., 151–152, 210
Wallis, S.H., 45, 165
Wall Street Crash (1929), 97, 106–107, 117–118, 125–126
Wall Street Journal, 16–17, 50–51, 104–105, 111–113
Ward, D., 9–10, 27–28, 100, 156–157, 164
Warren, H. 18–19, 27–28, 32, 37
wars, 43
  1870 Franco-German War, 33–34, 97
  exchange rates volatility, 15–16
  financial system disruption and, 96
  see also World War I; World War II
Weber, A., 265
Wells, S., 246–247
Wells Fargo, 281–282
Western Union Telegraph Company, 67
Westminster Bank, 137–139, 155, 174
  Big Five British banks, 142–143
  foreign exchange market, 144–145
Westwood, R., 257–258
West Yorkshire Bank, 131
Whale, B., 133
Whitaker, A.C., 104–105
Whitaker, G., 252–253
Whitmore, F., 113, 167
Wigglesworth, R., 268–269, 273
Wilgress, L.D., 22–24
Wilkins, M., 25
World War I
  1850–1914 London FX, 102, 285–286
  1919–1939 London FX, 91–93
  anti-German hostility, 122–123

  arbitrage, end of, 90, 122–123, 126–127, 188–189
  banks/banking, 142–143
  City of London, 63–64, 102–105, 108, 190
  consequences of, 96–97, 100–102, 104–105, 108, 122, 129, 188–189
  currency volatility, 95–96, 102
  exchange rates controls, 98–99
  exchange rates volatility, 129
  foreign exchange market, 95–96, 129
  monetary system, 21
  London discount market, 111–113
  London money market, 110, 129
  LSE, 121–122
  New York, 102–105, 190
  Paris, 104–105
  UK, 130
  UK£, 98–99, 129
World War II
  Bank of England, 196
  banks/banking, 196, 203
  City of London, 117–118, 196–197, 203
  consequences of, 196
  exchange rates controls, 203
  Gold Standard, 99–100
  government interventions, 194–196, 203, 224, 288–289
  internalization of FX, 210
  London FX, closure of, 151–152, 156–157, 184–189, 192, 210, 287
  New York, 117–118
  New York foreign exchange market, 213–214
  UK, 101–102, 184–185, 196–197
  UK£, 186
  see also London FX: 1939–1945
Woytinsky, W.S., 97
Wynne-Bennett, H.D., 124–125

Y

Yassukovich, S.M., 223–224
YSB (Yokohama Specie Bank), 48–49, 65
  arbitrage, 215
  exchange controls and, 141
  London branch, 65, 128–130

Z

Zurich
  1950s, 197–198, 214
  as financial centre, 203
  foreign exchange market, 6, 170, 192, 197, 213–215, 218, 220, 252–253
  offshore financial centre, 202–203, 214